THE COLLECTED VERSE OF

# JOHN, LORD HERVEY (1696–1743)

John, Lord Hervey (1696–1743), the confidant of Queen Caroline and antagonist of Alexander Pope, was a government minister, a political pamphleteer and a poet. In his verse writings, collected together for the first time in this edition, he savagely attacks his opponents, including the King and his ministers, as well as Pope, but he also expresses his deepest personal feelings. Hervey was married, with eight children, and his verse conveys his affection for his wife and family members, but his strongest commitment was to his lover, Stephen Fox. Some of his verse is written directly to Fox, but he also explores intense emotional conflicts in Ovidian epistles (which include 'lesbian' poems), in a verse tragedy, *Agrippina*; and through his collaborative poetic relationship with Lady Mary Wortley Montagu. Although his verse was sometimes mocked by contemporaries, he was a fluent and flexible versifier and a master of poetic argument.

**Bill Overton** (1946–2012) was Professor of Literature at Loughborough University. Publicly defining himself as a 'generalist', he published on nineteenth-century European novels, on Shakespeare and (increasingly after 1995) on eighteenth-century poetry. This edition of John, Lord Hervey's verse is his final work.

**Elaine Hobby** is Professor of Seventeenth-Century Studies at Loughborough University. She has edited midwifery manuals, life-writings and religio-political pamphlets, and is currently working on an edition of the writings of Aphra Behn for Cambridge University Press. She was Bill Overton's colleague from 1988, and was also his wife.

**James McLaverty** is Emeritus Professor of Textual Criticism at Keele University. Much of his work has focused on Hervey's great antagonist, Alexander Pope, and he is the co-editor, with Paddy Bullard, of *Jonathan Swift and the Eighteenth-Century Book* (Cambridge, 2013). He currently serves as one of the General Editors of The Cambridge Edition of the Works of Jonathan Swift.

John Lord Hervey,
son to John Earl of Bristol.

FRONTISPIECE

Portrait of John, Lord Hervey, by Enoch Seeman. Private collection.

# THE COLLECTED VERSE OF
# JOHN, LORD HERVEY
# (1696–1743)

Edited by
BILL OVERTON
with Elaine Hobby and
James McLaverty

CAMBRIDGE
UNIVERSITY PRESS

**CAMBRIDGE**
**UNIVERSITY PRESS**

University Printing House, Cambridge CB2 8BS, United Kingdom

Cambridge University Press is part of the University of Cambridge.

It furthers the University's mission by disseminating knowledge in the pursuit of education, learning and research at the highest international levels of excellence.

www.cambridge.org
Information on this title: www.cambridge.org/9781107010178



First published 2016

Printed in the United Kingdom by Clays, St Ives plc

*A catalogue record for this publication is available from the British Library*

ISBN 978-1-107-01017-8 Hardback

# PREFACE

In 2006, when working on *The Eighteenth-Century British Verse Epistle*, Bill Overton decided that John, Lord Hervey, was a much better poet than had been recognised, and that his own next project would be to produce a scholarly edition of Hervey's verse. This book is the product of that recognition and resolution.

As 2012 dawned, with almost all of the necessary research completed and the editing under way, Bill learned that he had a terminal illness. In the months that followed, interwoven with that knowledge, was the delight and fascination of Hervey's verse. At the time of his death in September 2012, most of the poems had been edited to a fairly final state, but Bill had left till last the longest – 'Telemachus' and 'Agrippina'; those he had transcribed and begun to think about, but not edited.

The edition was completed by Jim McLaverty and Elaine Hobby, with the former editing 'Telemachus', 'Agrippina' and the 'Verse in Latin and in French', while the latter (with Jim McLaverty's guidance) rechecked all the transcriptions and produced the Lists of Emendations and Historical Collations. Jim McLaverty also wrote most of the introductory materials, drawing where possible on articles previously completed by Bill Overton.

Throughout, all three were supported by Linda Bree and her colleagues at Cambridge University Press, and by the wider community of eighteenth-century scholars. A little more detail of those involved can be found in the Acknowledgements.

# CONTENTS

* here indicates works of uncertain attribution

# ILLUSTRATIONS

# ACKNOWLEDGEMENTS

Thanks are due to many great libraries and repositories for allowing extensive access to their collections, many also providing further guidance by letter and email: Renu Barrett, Archives and Special Collections, McMaster University; Mike Bosson, Harrowby MSS Trust; June Can, Beinecke Rare Book and Manuscript Library, Yale University; Sarah Challenger, Library Assistant, Newport Reference Library; Lorraine Coughlan, John Rylands Library, University of Manchester; Julie Crocker, Assistant Archivist, Royal Archives; Diane Ducharme, Beinecke Rare Book and Manuscript Library, Yale University; Colin Harris, Bodleian Library; Kate Harris, Portland Collection, Longleat; Jeff Kattenhorn, British Library; Laurie Klein, Beinecke Rare Book and Manuscript Library, Yale University; Kathy Lafferty, Spencer Research Library, University of Kansas; Nottingham University Library Special Collections; Katie Vaughan, Suffolk Record Office, Bury St Edmunds; Emily Walhout, Houghton Library, Harvard University; Susan Odell Walker, The Lewis Walpole Library, Yale University; Sarah Wheale, Bodleian Library; Chloe Woodrow, the National Trust, Ickworth; Kate Yates, the National Trust, Ickworth.

Scholars who contributed freely to the project through sharing their expertise and providing research notes and guidance made this edition possible in a range of ways: Jennifer Batt and her colleagues in the Digital Miscellanies Index; Linda Bree, Commissioning Editor, Cambridge University Press; Audrey Carpenter; Elizabeth Einberg, Senior Research Fellow, Hogarth Project; Isobel Grundy, University of Alberta; Robert D. Hume, Pennsylvania State University; Jennifer Keith, University of North Carolina at Greensboro; Michael Londry, Independent Scholar; Rudolph Slobins, Harding Index, Magdalen College, University of Oxford; Stephen Taylor, University of Reading; James Woolley, Lafayette College, Pennsylvania.

The AHRC provided a much-needed semester's Research Leave to Bill Overton in 2012, and kindly allowed Elaine Hobby to spend the remnant of that grant to complete necessary archival work in 2014.

A team of generous scholars helped with the annotation of 'Telemachus' and 'Agrippina', reading the texts and making suggestions: Clare Brant, Isobel Grundy, Brean Hammond, Allan Ingram, Judith Milhous and Marcus Walsh. We are particularly grateful to Valerie Rumbold for the time she devoted to the edition, helping to identify allusions and suggesting emendations, and to Hermann Real for advising us on Daniel Casper von Lohenstein's *Agrippina*.

Roger Lonsdale, Adam Rounce, Richard Rouse and Stephen Bernard lent a sympathetic ear to editorial problems, often offering good advice, and it was through the agency of Stephen Bernard that we approached Llewelyn Morgan, who so promptly and generously translated Hervey's 'Ad Regem' for us. Wendy Perkins reviewed the translations of Hervey's verse and commented helpfully on Hervey's French. At Loughborough Gillian Spraggs and Arianna Maiorani helped with Latin and Italian puzzles, and many colleagues in the English and Drama Department provided encouragement and enthusiasm, even though this also deprived them of Bill Overton's presence, and relieved them of Elaine Hobby's (the last of these much helped by Loughborough University's generous granting of a full year's Study Leave).

The librarians at the British Library, Taylorian Institution and Bodleian Library offered valuable assistance. Special thanks are due to David Busby and his colleagues in the Bodleian Upper Reading Room for the time and energy they devoted to solving a variety of technical and scholarly problems.

The Overton family gave joy and encouragement throughout: George, Julie, Lily and Missy; Henry, Rachel, Jacob and Oliver; Susan, Keith, Gisela and perhaps most of all Grace, who never failed to ask, with real interest, when the book would be finished. Elaine Hobby's other nearest and dearest contributed more than they can guess or would admit to: Claire Bowditch, Lyndsay Croft, Frankie Debenham, Laurian Vega and, as always, Chris White. John Isherwood and Jill Cooke made it possible for Bill Overton to continue to think and write for much longer than anyone thought credible.

Thanks and also apologies are due to those kind individuals and institutions in addition to those named here who supported Bill Overton's research: this note has been constructed in part from his database, and there is no doubt that some of the debts most obvious to him were not recorded there; please accept the editors' gratitude.

# CHRONOLOGY

1696 born 15 October, Jermyn Street, London

1712 entered Westminster School, January; 'earliest surviving literary composition' written at Westminster, paraphrase of Horatian ode, dialogue with Lydia, Poem 58 (Halsband, p. 12; SRO 941/46/5)

1713 entered Clare College, Cambridge, 20 November

1714 'Ad Regem', 18-line Latin poem to commemorate accession of George I (Poem 100), printed in *Mœstissimæ ac Lætissimæ Academiæ Cantabrigiensis Carmina Funebria et Triumphalia*; father became Earl of Bristol

1715 graduated MA, leaving at Christmas

1716 left England in early June with tutor, Daniel Jouneau, first for Paris (where he met the Abbé Jean Terrasson among others, and from where he wrote to his father probably, Halsband suggests, via Charles Churchill, though Anne Oldfield delivered the letter), then to Hanover, where he met Lady Mary Wortley Montagu (though probably not for first time), and also Prince Frederick; returned January 1717, having not been allowed to visit Italy because of mother's anxiety

1718 friction between King and Prince of Wales led, in effect, to establishment of two courts; Lady Bristol became Lady of Bedchamber to Princess Caroline

1719 in mid-June, 'Hervey exploited his literary talent with a "ludicrous composition of his own" (his father writes) "supposed to be an amourous epistle from Clack to Squire on their separation"' (Halsband, p. 36; Clack[stone] being the 'gallant' of a woman servant at Ickworth, and their separation a satirical parallel to that of the Bristols; epistle was in prose, but 'By now Hervey had shown an alarming zest for writing verse', p. 37); first recorded meeting with Mary Lepell, 28 October 1719 (at Lady Grizel Baillie's)

1720 married Mary Lepell, 21 April; in autumn, Hervey cleared £20,000 from South Sea shares before Bubble burst; marriage announced 25 October, married life beginning in Bond Street; breach between King and Prince of Wales healed

1721 first child, George William, born 3 August

1722 Hervey tried to cheer his ailing brother up by passing on two ribald epitaphs about Duke of Bolton (SRO 941/47/2), and some verse by Montagu; when mother had to go into waiting in summer, 'he tried to cheer his disconsolate father by showing (in his father's opinion) "all the treasures of his compositions in verse and prose"' (Halsband, p. 47; *Letter-Books*, II, 220)

1723 first daughter, Lepell, born 15 April; poem 'The Statue speaks to my Lord' (Poem 48) improvised in summer (Halsband, p. 50; SRO 941/53/1); half-brother Carr died, 14 November, passing on courtesy title of Baron Hervey of Ickworth

1724 'doggerel verse' by Lady Mary in April 'contains the gossip that "Lady Hervey [is] with child, and her Husband is dying"' (Halsband, p. 52; *Montagu Letters*, II, 41); second son, Augustus John, born 19 May; further signs of breach between Lady Bristol and Herveys

1725 elected MP for Bury St Edmunds, 2 April; on advice of Cheyne, Hervey adopted vegetarian diet; bought lease of house in Great Burlington Street in October; satirical ballad on Mary Lepell by Pulteney and Chesterfield (*New Foundling Hospital for Wit*, 1784, VI, 224–8)

1726 wrote *Monimia to Philocles* (Poem 1), according to Halsband (p. 61), probably in summer at Bath, printed in Dublin; in the autumn friendship begun at Bath with Henry Fox, plus subsequent correspondence; wrote to Fox 3 December about seeing Mary Toft (who claimed to have given birth to rabbits)

1727 second daughter, Mary, born; met Stephen Fox, end of January; *An Answer to the Occasional Writer No. II*, Hervey's 'first identified political pamphlet' (Halsband, p. 66), published anonymously in February; took part for first time in parliamentary business, 14 March, and published *The Occasional Writer, No. IV. To His Imperial Majesty*; 14 June, Walpole informs Prince of Wales that his father has died and he is now King; Hervey supported Walpole on accession of George II, alone except for Charles Churchill, advising him in an anonymous letter given in *Some Materials* (Sedgwick, I, 32–3); 18 August re-elected MP for Bury; death of favourite sister Elizabeth affected him greatly; Montagu described Coronation (took place 11 October 1727) to him in letter (II, 85–7); disappointment over not being given a post

1728 moved Address of Thanks to royal speech on opening of Parliament, 27 January; seriously ill in March, with SF in close attendance, 'yet in mid-April he was seen riding with Mrs. Oldfield, the actress, in her coach' (Halsband, p. 76; Delany, *Autobiography* I, 160, 168, 171); 'some time before the summer', awarded pension of £1,000 (Halsband, p. 68); left England with Stephen Fox, 12 July (see Halsband, pp. 77–8, for possible motives), initially for the spa at Ostend, then, after six weeks, to Paris, finally leaving for Italy in October, arriving on 4 November in Turin, then by early December in Rome; left for Naples 29 December o.s.

1729 left Naples 9 April for Rome, Rome for Florence beginning of June; operation while in Florence, probably by Dr Antonio Cocchi, to remove protuberance under chin; in August left for Pisa, then Genoa and Turin on way back to England, departing from Lyons for Paris 11 October; saw Voltaire (whom he had first met in 1726) and showed him his letter from Italy (Poem 16); visited court at Versailles; arrived back in England 25 October; to Ickworth 2 November (his son Frederick born 'exactly nine months later' (Halsband, p. 87); left London 9 December to join SF at Bath

1730 February, *A Summary Account of the State of Dunkirk*, anonymously defending Walpole; 3 March, attended third performance of *Sophonisba*, for which he wrote an epilogue for Anne Oldfield (Poem 35), 'but another's epilogue was spoken, and by Mrs. Cibber' (Halsband, p. 103); end of April, appointed Vice-Chamberlain to King's household and so member of Privy Council; re-elected MP 16 May; 23 October Anne Oldfield died, Hervey acting as pall-bearer at funeral and as one of three executors; assigned lease of London house to SF 14 November; anonymous *Observations on the Writings of the Craftsman*, late November, followed by *Sequel of a Pamphlet Intitled Observations on the Writings of the Craftsman* and *Further Observations on the Writings of the Craftsman*, all before 17 December when he left London to join SF in country

1731 returned to London 2 January; 'Dedication' to William Yonge's *Sedition and Defamation Display'd*; 8 January had first (probable) epileptic seizure; Pulteney published *A Proper Reply to a Late Scurrilous Libel*, responding to Yonge's pamphlet on assumption it was all by Hervey (though also mentioning previous ones by Hervey); challenged Pulteney to duel fought 25 January; published further pamphlet, *A Letter to Caleb D'Anvers*; duel got much satirical coverage; possible composition of *Journalists Displayed* (Poem 26); joined SF in country after few weeks of summer at Ickworth, and took him to Houghton Hall for a week; to London in August; there writes (according to Halsband, p. 123) 'From Hampton-Court' (Poem 7); autumn, affair with Anne Vane led to jealousy of Prince of Wales when the Prince started affair with her, especially when he felt supplanted as Prince's adviser by Dodington

1732 *The Modish Couple*, a Restoration-type comedy that he and Prince 'sponsored and perhaps helped to write' (Halsband, p. 130), though Capt. Charles Boden/s was nominal author, opened 10 January but had to close after three nights; possible author of *The Public Virtue of Former Times, and the Present Age Compared*, mid-February; alienated Prince in April by trying to blackmail Anne Vane into repairing his relationship with him; son born to Anne Vane 5 June and claimed by Hervey, Prince and Lord Harrington; Hervey's legitimate son William had been born on 13 May; *Some Remarks on the Minute Philosopher*, response to Berkeley's *Alciphron*, published in autumn (copy later presented to Voltaire)

1733 read Voltaire's *Zaïre* and sent copy to Henry Fox; publication on 8 March of the attack on Pope *To the Imitator of the Satire of the Second Book of Horace* (Poem 22), after he had been increasingly angered in succession by Pope's epistles to *Burlington, Bathurst* and first *Imitation of Horace; Reply of a Member of Parliament to the Mayor of his Corporation* published March in defence of Walpole's Excise Bill; defended the Bill in debate 16 March (it was later quietly withdrawn); elevated to House of Lords as Baron Hervey 12 June; to Ickworth for brother Thomas's election in his place as MP for Bury 29 June; began compiling *Some Materials* (Halsband, p. 130), or in 1734 (Halsband, pp. 151–2, perhaps spurred on by Burnet), going back in broad outline to accession of George II in 1727 (first published, incompletely, 1848); formed friendship with Conyers Middleton; *Epistle from a Nobleman to a Doctor of Divinity* (Poem 18) published 10 November, probably not intended for publication, and leading to a lot of trouble including various lampoons; hoax robbery of Lady Hervey, SF and others on way to Goodwood, as joke against William Sherwin (late July?); Voltaire wrote September to ask his opinion of *Letters Concerning the English Nation* (see Halsband, pp. 159–60 for relations with Voltaire and Montesquieu); *A Letter to the Craftsman on the Game of Chess*, c. 22 September; 'To Stephen Poyntz' (Poem 17) published in *Daily Advertiser* 15 November (repr. *Gentleman's Magazine*, November 1733, 602)

1734 first speech in Lords, 17 January, to move Address of Thanks; Emily Caroline Nassau born end of January (described derogatively by Hervey); stage-managed marriage of Anne, Princess Royal, to William, Prince of Orange, 14 March; *The Conduct of the Opposition and the Tendency of Modern Patriotism*, 3 April; active in getting his friend Benjamin Hoadly appointed Bishop of Winchester, August; *Ancient and Modern Liberty Stated and Compared*, October; Lady Hervey suffered miscarriage 6 October

1735 *An Epistle to Dr Arbuthnot*, 2 January; revival of affair with Anne Vane ('based on love, jealousy, and politics', Halsband, p. 183), as result of which he ghost-wrote letters for her to stop the Prince, who wanted to get rid of her, from treating her unfairly (she was to die March 1736); illness in December; fitted with 'Egyptian pebble teeth' around then (Halsband, p. 188)

1736 eighth and last child, Caroline, born February; SF married to Elizabeth Strangways-Horner 15 March in secret because of her father's opposition; met Francesco Algarotti, bearing letter of introduction from Voltaire, end of March; *Quaker's Reply to the Country Parson's Plea*, 6 April; Prince of Wales's marriage, 27 April; wrote 'The Death of Lord Hervey' to amuse Queen Caroline (text in *Some Materials*; repr. by Moore, Appendix 1); wrote tribute to Algarotti's *Il Newtonianismo per le dame* (Poem 79) in letter of 16 August (published in enlarged edition with Lady Mary's tribute, 1739); Algarotti left England early September

1737 *A Letter to the Author of Common-Sense*, 26 April; 'An Examination of the Facts & Reasonings contain'd in a Pamphlet intitled a Letter from a Member of Parliament to his Friend in the Country' drafted (not published, but a few copies apparently printed with 1739 on title page) (Halsband, pp. 209–10); stayed with father at Ickworth, 5–30 June, because of latter's illness but probably also to avoid speaking on Scotch Bill to which he was opposed; birth of a daughter to Prince of Wales 31 July; Queen Caroline fell ill 9 November, died 20 November; funeral 14 December; wrote epitaphs in Latin and English (Poems 32, 107); ended memoirs 'abruptly' (Halsband, p. 231, adding: 'Sometimes his memoirs seem to be materials for the reign of Queen Caroline'); Halsband, p. 279: 'By 1737 Hervey had somehow become reconciled with Pulteney'

1738 arrival of King's mistress, 12 June; annual visit to Houghton, July; commissioned Hogarth's conversation piece including himself, Fox brothers, Winnington and Duke of Marlborough; began advising Middleton on MS of *Life of Cicero*, 27 August

1739 speeches in Lords supporting ministry on various measures including peace with Spain; promoted subscription of Middleton's *Life of Cicero*; return of Algarotti, March, only to sail for Russia with Lord Baltimore, 21 May; Lady Mary left for Italy, July; Algarotti back from Russia early October; war declared on Spain, 19 October; Parliament quiet, so spent time with Algarotti

1740 appointed Lord Privy Seal, 1 May, vacating apartment at St James's Palace, rented house in Grosvenor Street, moving there 9 June; Voltaire congratulated him on appointment; Algarotti left in haste for Berlin, 6 June, after summons from Frederick the Great, whose father had died; to Goodwood and Houghton for short visits in summer, Ickworth briefly in between (Halsband, pp. 261–2 on Hervey giving his daughters scientific education); further speeches for ministry in Lords in November and December

1741 Middleton's *History of the Life of Marcus Tullius Cicero* published 2 February, its fulsome Dedication provoking much satire; spoke against attempt to remove Walpole from office, 13 February; Lady Bristol died early May; SF created Lord Ilchester, largely thanks to Hervey's efforts, same month; to Bath, 2 September; serious illness on return to London, October

1742 Walpole resigned, 11 February, followed on 12 July by Hervey as Lord Privy Seal (only kept in office by King, out of respect for late Queen), after negotiations with King; defended Walpole (now Lord Orford) in Lords, 25 May; *A Letter to Mr. C—b—r, On his Letter to Mr. P*, 19 August; *The Difference between Verbal and Practical Virtue* (Poem 24), 24 August; expressed resentment of King in *The Patriots are Come* (Poem 27, first in manuscript, apparently first printed as *A New C—t Ballad*); friendship with SF ended as a result of his insistence that SF join opposition and latter's refusal (letter of 20 November; according to Halsband, pp. 292–3, Hervey had fallen out with Henry Fox not long before); *Miscellaneous Thoughts on the Present Posture both of our Foreign and Domestic Affairs*, 1 December, defence of Walpole ministry and attack on its successor

1743 *The Question Stated, with Regard to Our Army in Flanders*, 22 January; several further speeches in Lords till end of February; executor for Duchess of Buckingham, whose will left him her mansion in St James's Park; last letter to Lady Mary, 18 June; drew up own will 'A week later' (Halsband, p. 304); died at Ickworth, 5 August

# ABBREVIATIONS

BL British Library

Bodleian Bodleian Library, Oxford

*Chesterfield Bibliography* Sidney L. Gulick, *Chesterfield Bibliography to 1800*, 2nd edn (Charlottesville, VA: for the. Bibliographical Society of America by the University of Virginia, 1979; 1st edn 1935)

Chesterfield, *Wit and Wisdom* *The Wit and Wisdom of the Earl of Chesterfield*, ed. by W. Ernst-Browning (London: Richard Bentley and Son, 1875)

*Complete Peerage* *The Complete Peerage of England, Scotland, Ireland, Great Britain and the United Kingdom, Extant, Extinct or Dormant*, new edn, ed. by G. E. C[okayne], with Vicary Gibbs, H. A. Doubleday, Geoffrey H. White, Duncan Warrand and Lord Howard de Walden, 13 vols. in 14 (1910–59)

Croker, *Memoirs* John Wilson Croker, *Some Materials: Memoirs of the Reign of George II, from his Accession to the Death of Queen Caroline, by John, Lord Hervey*, 2 vols. (London: John Murray, 1848)

Delany, *Autobiography* *The Autobiography and Correspondence of Mary Granville, Mrs. Delany*, ed. by Lady Llanover [Augusta Waddington Hall], 6 vols. (London: Richard Bentley, 1861–2)

Dodsley Dodsley, Robert (comp.), *A Collection of Poems by Several Hands*, ed. by Michael F. Suarez, SJ, 6 vols. (London: Routledge/Thoemmes Press, 1997)

Dryden, *Poems* *The Poems of John Dryden*, ed. by Paul Hammond and David Hopkins, 5 vols. (London and New York: Longman, 1995–2005)

Dryden, *Works* *Plays: All for Love, Oedipus, Troilus and Cressida*, ed. by George R. Guffey, Maximillian E. Novak and Alan

Roper, vol. XIII (1984), in *The Works of John Dryden*, 20 vols. (Berkeley: University of California Press, 1956–2002)

*Essays & Poems* Lady Mary Wortley Montagu, *Essays and Poems and 'Simplicity', a Comedy*, ed. by Robert Halsband and Isobel Grundy, 2nd edn (Oxford: Clarendon Press, 1993; 1st edn 1977)

Foxon D. F. Foxon, *English Verse 1701–1750*, 2 vols. (Cambridge: Cambridge University Press, 1975)

Gage, *History and Antiquities* John Gage, *The History and Antiquities of Suffolk. Thingoe Hundred* (Bury St Edmunds: John Deck; London: Samuel Bentley, 1838)

Grundy Isobel Grundy, *Lady Mary Wortley Montagu* (Oxford: Oxford University Press, 1999)

Grundy, 'New Verse' Isobel Grundy, '"New" Verse by Lady Mary Wortley Montagu', *Bodleian Library Record*, 10 (1981), 237–49

Grundy, 'Verse of Lady Mary Wortley Montagu' Isobel Grundy, 'Verse of Lady Mary Wortley Montagu: A Critical Edition' (unpub. PhD thesis, Oxford University, 1971)

Halsband Robert Halsband, *Lord Hervey: Eighteenth-Century Courtier* (Oxford: Clarendon Press, 1973)

Halsband, *Life of Montagu* Robert Halsband, *The Life of Lady Mary Wortley Montagu* (Oxford: Oxford University Press, 1956)

Harrowby Harrowby Manuscripts Trust, Sandon Hall, Stafford

*Ickworth Parish Registers* *Ickworth Parish Registers. Baptisms, Marriages & Burials: 1566–1890*, ed. by S[ydenham] H[enry] A[ugustus] H[ervey] (Wells: Ernest Jackson, 1894)

Ilchester *Lord Hervey and his Friends: Based on Letters from Holland House, Melbury, and Ickworth*, ed. by the Earl of Ilchester (London: John Murray, 1950)

Ilchester and Langford-Brooke Earl of Ilchester and Elizabeth Langford-Brooke, *The Life of Sir Charles Hanbury-Williams: Poet, Wit and Diplomatist* (London: Thornton Butterworth, 1929)

JMA John Murray Archive, London

*Letter-Books* *Letter-Books of John Hervey, First Earl of Bristol, with Sir Thomas Hervey's Letters during Courtship and Poems during Widowhood, 1651–1750*, 3 vols. (Wells: Ernest Jackson, 1894)

Lindsay, *Index* Alexander Lindsay (comp.), *Index of English Literary Manuscripts* (London: Mansell, 1986–1997), III, *1700–1800*, Part 4: *Sterne to Young* (1997)

Loeb The Loeb Classical Library. The following editions (published at various times by London: Heinemann, and Cambridge, MA: Harvard University Press) have been used:

*Catullus, Tibullus, Pervigilium Veneris*, trans. by Francis Warre Cornish, J. P. Postgate and J. W. Mackail respectively, 2nd edn, rev. G. P. Goold (1988; repr. with corrections 1995)

Cicero, *Brutus*, trans. by G. L. Hendrickson (1939)

Cicero, *De Oratore*, trans. by E. W. Sutton and H. Rackham, 2 vols. (1942)

Cicero, *Post Reditum ad Quirites*, in *Orations, XI: Pro Archia, Post Reditum in Senatu, Post Reditum ad Quirites, De Domo Sua, De Haruspicum Responsis, Pro Plancio*, trans. by N. H. Watts (1923)

Dio Cassius, *Roman History*, trans. by Earnest Cary, 9 vols. (1925)

Horace, *Odes and Epodes*, trans. by C. E. Bennett (1914)

Horace, *Odes and Epodes*, ed. and trans. by Niall Rudd (2004)

Horace, *Satires, Epistles and Ars Poetica*, trans. by H. Rushton Fairclough (1916)

Livy, *The History of Rome, XI*, trans. by Evan T. Sage (1936)

Lucretius, *De Rerum Natura*, trans. by W. H. D. Rouse, ed. by Martin Ferguson Smith, 2nd edn rev. (1992)

Martial, *Epigrams*, ed. and trans. by D. R. Shackleton Bailey, 3 vols. (1993)

Ovid, *Fasti*, trans. by Sir James George Frazer, 2nd edn rev. G. P. Goold (1989)

Ovid, *Heroides and Amores*, 2nd edn, trans. by Grant Showerman, rev. G. P. Goold (1977)

Ovid, *Metamorphoses*, trans. by Frank Justus Miller, 2nd edn rev. G. P. Goold, 2 vols. (1984)

*Plutarch's Lives*, trans. by Bernadotte Perrin, 11 vols. (1914–26)

Seneca, *Epistles 66–72*, trans. by Richard M. Gummere (1920; repr. 2006)

Seneca, *Moral Essays*, trans. by John W. Basore, 3 vols. (1958). Vol. I contains 'De Clementia'

Seneca, [*Tragedies*], ed. and trans. by John G. Finch (2004)

Suetonius, [*Lives of the Caesars*], trans. by J. C. Rolfe, 2 vols. (1939)

Tacitus, [*Histories and Annals*], trans. by John Jackson, 5 vols. (1937)

Terence, *The Eunuch*, in *Terence: The Lady of Andros, The Self-Tormentor, The Eunuch*, trans. by John Sargeaunt (1918)

Terence, [*Plays*], I, trans. by John Barsby (2002)
Velleius Paterculus, *Compendium of Roman History*, trans. by Frederick W. Shipley (1924)
Virgil, *Eclogues, Georgics, Aeneid*, trans. by H. Rushton Fairclough, rev. edn, 2 vols. (1965)

*London Stage* — *The London Stage 1660–1800*, ed. by Arthur H. Scouten, Part 3: *1729–1747* (Carbondale: Southern Illinois University Press, 1961)

Milton, *Poetical Works* — *The Poetical Works of John Milton*, ed. by Helen Darbishire, 2 vols. (Oxford: Clarendon Press, 1952)

*Montagu Letters* — *Complete Letters of Lady Mary Wortley Montagu*, ed. by Robert Halsband, 3 vols. (Oxford: Clarendon Press, 1965–7)

Moore — Lucy Moore, *Amphibious Thing: The Life of Lord Hervey* (London: Viking, 2000)

*ODNB* — *Oxford Dictionary of National Biography* (online edition: www.oxforddnb.com)

*OED* — *Oxford English Dictionary Online* (online edition: www.oed.com)

Overton, 'Death and Futurity' — Bill Overton, 'Lord Hervey: Death and Futurity', in Mascha Hansen and Jürgen Klein (eds.), *Great Expectations: Futurity in the Long Eighteenth Century* (Frankfurt am Main: Peter Lang, 2012), pp. 141–60

Overton, 'Embedded Verse' — Bill Overton, 'Embedded Extempore Verse in the Intimate Letters of John, Lord Hervey (1696–1743)', *MLR*, 110 (2015), 379–98

Overton, 'Poetic Voice and Gender' — Bill Overton, 'Lord Hervey, Poetic Voice and Gender', *Review of English Studies*, 62 (2011), 594–617

Overton, *Verse Epistle* — Bill Overton, *The Eighteenth-Century British Verse Epistle* (Basingstoke: Palgrave Macmillan, 2007)

Percival — *Political Ballads Illustrating the Administration of Sir Robert Walpole*, ed. by Milton Percival (Oxford: Clarendon 1916) (available at https://archive.org/details/politicalballads00percrich)

Percival, *Diary* — *Diary of Viscount Percival, Afterwards First Earl of Egmont*, 3 vols. (London: HMSO, 1920–3)

Pope, *Correspondence* *The Correspondence of Alexander Pope*, ed. by George Sherburn, 5 vols. (Oxford: Clarendon Press, 1956)

Pope, *Prose* *The Prose Works of Alexander Pope*, II: *The Major Works, 1725–1744*, ed. by Rosemary Cowler (Oxford: Basil Blackwell for the Shakespeare Head Press, 1986)

Pope, *Twickenham* *The Twickenham Edition of the Poems of Alexander Pope*, ed. by John Butt *et al.*, 11 vols. in 12 (London: Methuen; New Haven: Yale University Press, 1939–69). The following volumes have been used:

I *Pastoral Poetry and An Essay on Criticism*, ed. by E. Audra and Aubrey Williams (1961)

II *The Rape of the Lock, and Other Poems*, ed. by Geoffrey Tillotson, 3rd edn (1962; 1st edn 1940)

III. ii *Epistles to several Persons (Moral Essays)*, ed. by F. W. Bateson, 2nd edn (1961; 1st edn 1951)

IV *Imitations of Horace*, ed. by John Butt, 2nd edn (1953; 1st edn 1939)

VI *Minor Poems*, ed. by Norman Ault and John Butt (1964)

VII–VIII *The Iliad of Homer*, ed. by Maynard Mack *et al.* (1967)

IX–X *The Odyssey*, ed. by Maynard Mack *et al.* (1967)

Sedgwick *Some Materials towards Memoirs of the Reign of King George II, by John, Lord Hervey*, ed. by Romney Sedgwick, 3 vols. (London: Eyre and Spottiswoode, 1931)

SF Stephen Fox

*Shakespeare Works* *William Shakespeare: The Complete Works*, ed. by Stanley Wells and Gary Taylor, 2nd edn (Oxford: Clarendon Press, 2005; 1st edn 1986)

SRO West Suffolk Record Office, Bury St Edmunds

Urstad Tone Sundt Urstad, *Sir Robert Walpole's Poets: The Use of Literature as Pro-Government Propaganda 1721–1724* (Newark: University of Delaware Press; London: Associated University Presses, 1999)

Urstad, 'Hanbury Williams' Tone Dagny Sundt Urstad, 'Works of Sir Charles Hanbury Williams', unpublished PhD thesis (University of Cambridge, 1987)

Walpole, *Correspondence* *The Yale Edition of Horace Walpole's Correspondence*, ed. by W[ilmarth] S[heldon] Lewis *et al.*, 48 vols. (New Haven: Yale University Press; Oxford: Oxford University Press, 1937–83)

Walpole, *Royal and Noble Authors* Horace Walpole, *A Catalogue of the Royal and Noble Authors of England, with Lists of their Works*, 2 vols. ([Twickenham]: Strawberry-Hill, 1758)

Walpole, *Works* (1798) *The Works of Horatio Walpole, Earl of Orford*, ed. by Mary Berry, 5 vols. (London: G. G. and J. Robinson, 1798)

# INTRODUCTION

This introduction was written by James McLaverty, drawing on Bill Overton's headnotes and incorporating material from his four essays on Hervey.[1] Those pioneering essays treat central aspects of Hervey's writing and initiate the task of re-evaluating his verse.

## *Hervey's life*

John Hervey, second Baron Hervey of Ickworth (1696–1743), was born into a family committed to Whig politics and literary culture. He pursued both interests, serving as a loyal supporter of the Walpole administration from 1729 until 1742 when it finally fell, and demonstrating his writing skills not only in some of the most cogent political pamphlets of the period but also in verse, in memoirs, in letters (especially to Stephen and Henry Fox and Lady Mary Wortley Montagu) and even in drama. His father, the Earl of Bristol, was a country Whig, critical of his son's support for Walpole and the court, but he remained on affectionate terms with him throughout his life. When Hervey's half-brother, Carr Hervey, died on 14 November 1723, Hervey became heir to the earldom, with the courtesy title Lord Hervey. He became MP for Bury St Edmunds on 2 April 1725, took oaths as Vice-Chamberlain of the royal household on 7 May 1730, and, when Walpole felt the need for support in the House of Lords, he was given a seat through his father's barony on 12 June 1733. On 1 May 1740 he was promoted to Lord Privy Seal, but Walpole left office in early 1742 and Hervey had to give up his post on 12 July of that year. There followed a period of political opposition during which he satirised the King and quarrelled with his closest friend, Stephen Fox. Hervey had suffered

1. 'Lord Hervey, Poetic Voice and Gender', *Review of English Studies*, 62 (2011), 594–617; 'Lord Hervey: Death and Futurity', in Mascha Hansen and Jürgen Klein (eds.), *Great Expectations: Futurity in the Long Eighteenth Century* (Frankfurt am Main: Peter Lang, 2012), pp. 141–60; 'Embedded Extempore Verse in the Intimate Letters of John, Lord Hervey (1696–1743)', *MLR*, 110 (2015), 379–98; 'John, Lord Hervey', in Jack Lynch and Gary Day (eds.), *The Encyclopedia of British Literature 1660–1789*, 3 vols. (Oxford: Wiley Blackwell, 2015), s.n.

from ill health, including some form of epilepsy, throughout his life, and he died on 5 August 1743, predeceasing his father.

Hervey's private life was complex. Although he married his wife, Mary Lepell, for love (21 April 1720), although they had eight children and although, as was not unusual at the time, he had several mistresses, the closest relationship of his life was with a man, Stephen Fox. That relationship probably extended to physical sex, which Hervey may also have enjoyed with other men, including Frederick, Prince of Wales.[2] The fact that Hervey enjoyed intimate relationships with men may bring to mind the famous remark attributed to Lady Mary Wortley Montagu, that the world consisted of 'men, women and Herveys', though it is important to know that, as Isobel Grundy observes, it 'may glance at other members of his family beside himself, and other eccentricities besides the sexual'.[3] In 1731 William Pulteney, a leader of the opposition Whigs, responding to a pamphlet attack he thought was by Hervey, described him as 'such a delicate Hermaphrodite, such a pretty, little, Master-Miss'. He went on to compare political corruption with a prevailing sexual 'Vice':

> It is well known that there must be *two Parties* in this Crime; the *Pathick* and the *Agent*; both equally guilty. I need not explain These any farther. The Proof of the Crime hath been generally made by the *Pathick*; but I believe that Evidence will not be obtained quite so easily in the Case of *Corruption*, when a Man enjoys every Moment the Fruits of his Guilt.[4]

The attack implicated Stephen Fox and cast Hervey in a passive but culpable role in political and sexual corruption. He responded by challenging Pulteney to a duel in which they both suffered minor injuries. The thrust of Pulteney's charges became notorious through Pope's caricature of Hervey as Sporus in his *Epistle to Dr Arbuthnot* (1735).[5] Pope's caricature has distorted most accounts of Hervey because, as Linda Zionkowski has argued, they 'have echoed Pope's assumptions about the effect of sexual

2. For an investigation of the relationship, see Hannah Smith and Stephen Taylor, 'Hephaestion and Alexander: Lord Hervey, Frederick, Prince of Wales, and the Royal Favourite in the 1730s', *English Historical Review*, 124, no. 507 (2009), 283–312 (289).

3. Grundy, p. 336, citing Walpole, *Correspondence*, XVII, 274, n. 31; Montagu, *Essays & Poems*, pp. 39, 41; and a letter dated 6 February 1725 from Claude Amyand to James Jurin.

4. *A Proper Reply to a Late Scurrilous Libel* (London, 1731), pp. 5, 11; quoted in part by Halsband, pp. 109–11. The pamphlet *A Proper Reply to a Late Scurrilous Libel* was reprinted with an introduction by H. T. Dickinson (New York: AMS Press, 1998).

5. *An Epistle to Dr. Arbuthnot*, lines 305–33, in Pope, *Twickenham*, IV, 117–20; Sporus was a youth Nero castrated and married.

"deviance" on a writer's moral and literary capacity'.[6] While Pope's satire has made it difficult to take Hervey seriously as a writer, a significant proportion of his writing has not been available for evaluation. Some has been long out of print, some survives only in manuscript and some is unattributed or has been ascribed to other writers.

The year 1729 marked a clear watershed in Hervey's life. It was then that he returned from Italy, where he had spent over a year with Stephen Fox to recover his health, committed himself to politics and began to devote much less time to imaginative writing, turning instead to political satire, pamphleteering, the record of court and political life and familiar correspondence. While some of his verse before 1729 is of a social and complimentary nature, it includes four 'Epistles in the Manner of Ovid', an imitation of one of Persius' satires, two Horatian odes to Stephen Fox, an elegy on his sister Elizabeth and probably a verse adaptation of the first three books of Fénelon's *Les Aventures de Télémaque*. These poems contain attacks on the code of aristocratic male promiscuity and on the double standard of sexual morality for men and women. The same viewpoint is reflected in other poems by Hervey from this period, including 'The Countess of — to Miss —', a lesbian amatory epistle, and an elegy for Lady Abergavenny, who died shortly after her husband cast her out and sued for divorce on grounds of adultery. Although some of these poems found their way into print, others, including 'The Countess of — to Miss —' (Poem 8) and at least one other lesbian love poem (Poem 9), exist until now only in manuscript.

After 1729 Hervey began to take himself less seriously as a writer, except for political, historical or satirical purposes. From this period date *Some Materials towards Memoirs of the Reign of King George II*, unpublished till long after his death; *To the Imitator of the First Satire of the Second Book of Horace* (Poem 22), the poem attacking Pope that he co-wrote with Lady Mary Wortley Montagu and that neither may have meant to be published; and other works written for entertainment that he certainly did not intend for print. The most important of the latter are *An Epistle from a Nobleman to a Doctor of Divinity* (Poem 18, 'To Dr Sherwin in Answer to a Latin Letter in Verse'), a humorous poem that contains a further attack on Pope, got into print and caused a furore; 'Agrippina' (Poem 66), a verse drama that parallels relationships within the royal family to those within that of the Emperor

6. *Men's Work: Gender, Class, and the Professionalization of Poetry, 1660–1784* (New York: Palgrave, 2001), p. 235.

Nero; 'To the Queen' (Poem 19), a long verse epistle that, in its witty account of various personages at court, works as a kind of humorous apologia; and a succession of epitaphs, including one in Latin on Queen Caroline (Poem 32) and one on himself (Poem 34). But his memoir, *Some Materials*, is his most significant contribution to posterity – a work that is still both an entertaining read and an important resource for historians. The memoirs end in 1737, when the Queen's death had a powerful effect on Hervey. He wrote little verse, except for important fragments embedded in letters to Montagu and to Francesco Algarotti, the charming Italian he and Montagu both courted, until after his dismissal from government in 1742. Then his writing career revived briefly, with two further political pamphlets, the bitter satirical epigram 'On Health' (Poem 46) and another poem attacking Pope, *The Difference between Verbal and Practical Virtue* (Poem 24).

## *The character of Hervey's verse*

Hervey wrote verse all his life. He came from a family where verse played an important role: his father and mother both wrote verse occasionally; his father was fond of quoting the verse of others in his letters; and Hervey's own verse was preserved at Ickworth, the family home.[7] Although Montagu said writing verse in court circles was almost as common as taking snuff (*Montagu Letters*, II, 24), Hervey's output was regarded as quite exceptional. Pope alludes dismissively to his prolific versifying at the start of their quarrel, when writing about attacks on his own verse:

> The Lines are weak, another's pleas'd to say,
> Lord *Fanny* spins a thousand such a Day.
>
> (*First Satire of the Second Book of Horace*; *Twickenham*, IV, 5, lines 5–6)

Not everyone thought Hervey's devotion to poetry was compatible with his role as an aristocrat and leading courtier. George II reportedly told him, 'You ought not to write verses; 'tis beneath your rank: leave such work to little Mr. Pope'.[8] But Hervey was not to be dissuaded: this collection ranges from verse written at school and university to material he was working on in the summer of 1743, the year of his death.

7. See Descriptions of Manuscript Sources (pp. 605–14).

8. *Memoirs of Viscountess Sundon*, ed. by A. T. Thomson, 2nd edn, 2 vols. (London: Henry Colburn, 1847), II, 224 (cited by Halsband, p. 144).

Hervey's verse is notable for the force of its poetic argument. He was an eminent pamphleteer, the most distinguished controversialist among Walpole's supporters, and his rhetorical skills also help shape his achievement as a poet. He writes in an impressive range of genres and styles, often with dazzling figurative skill and metrical sophistication, but always with a subdued palette of metaphor and simile. He is a witty writer, but his wit lies in command of figures rather than of tropes. His thought is laid out in complex patterns rather than in the extended metaphors and similes of a metaphysical poet. This tendency of his art can be observed operating on a large scale in his political and familial tragedy 'Agrippina', where the drama is constructed of internal debates, disputes with advisers, and scenes of persuasion in which questions of right rule and individual freedom are deliberated. In the play's most powerful scene, the ceremony in the Temple of Concord that ends Act IV, the action is disrupted by an eclipse that seems to rebuke Nero's hypocrisy, only for Seneca to counter this conclusion with an argument that distinguishes the uncommon from the unnatural.

Hervey's habit of mind is persistently analytical and antithetical. Although his writing displays an intimate understanding of all aspects of classical rhetoric, he is particularly attracted to what the rhetoricians called *confutatio*, the part of an oration that drew in and refuted an opponent's argument. In attacking Bolingbroke's interpretation of British history, for example, his own pamphlet *Ancient and Modern Liberty Stated and Compared* (1734) uses many of the same examples to present a progressive alternative to Bolingbroke's pessimism. One of the attractions of poetry for Hervey was that it provided him with the opportunity for freer play with contrary ideas in more intricate patterns of language, ranging over not only politics and literature but also the most intimate aspects of human experience. In poetry Hervey's fondness for antithesis, the juxtaposition of contraries in ways that sharpen differences between them, extended to figures that explored more complex contrasts. Chief among these was antimetabole or chiasmus, the ABBA pattern of words or phrases, usefully thought of as crossing or flipping, which wittily plays with possibilities of inversion, something that was of wider significance to Hervey.[9]

9. The best introduction to this topic is still Brian Vickers, *Classical Rhetoric in English Poetry*, rev. edn (Carbondale and Edwardsville: Southern Illinois University Press, 1989). See also Jennifer Richards, *Rhetoric* (London: Routledge, 2008), and Richard A. Lanham, *A*

These figures of speech were an appropriate expression of his political and personal situation. As Vice-Chamberlain, he was both a political operator and an entertainer. He formed an essential link between the government and the monarchy, representing one to the other and minimising opportunities for conflict, but he also entertained the Queen with gossip or cards. He was the ally of the Queen, sharing her desire that the King should imagine her ideas were his own, but his own relation to her in some ways resembled hers to the King. He made monarchy work while having reservations about the institution in general and George II in particular.[10] His poetry frequently criticises the emptiness and futility of court life, but he did not leave it of his own volition. His personal life was if anything a more complex attempt to sustain different identities. A married man with eight children, his most powerful emotional commitment was to Stephen Fox, with whom he shared a London house. Whether his relation with Fox, or with Frederick, Prince of Wales or Francesco Algarotti, was physical is probably less important to his poetry than that it took him beyond ordinary relations, turning a social insider into a potential outsider and translating a man with an assured place in the patriarchal order into something close to a conventional female role. The attacks on Hervey by Pulteney and Pope dramatise and ridicule these conflicting sides of his nature, but in much of his verse Hervey turns them to positive effect. Most strikingly, and not only in the poems modelled on Ovid's *Heroides*, but also in his longest works, 'Agrippina' and 'Telemachus', and in the poems connected with Lady Abergavenny, Lady Mary Wortley Montagu and the Countess of Stafford, he presents female desire, intellectual energy, eloquence and resistance to oppression. In other poems he plays with heterosexual/homosexual ambiguities or presses a libertine argument towards even more radical conclusions.[11] Perceptively, Pope encouraged his readers to connect Hervey's sexual personality and his writing in his denunciation in *To Arbuthnot*:

*Handlist of Rhetorical Terms*, 2nd edn (Berkeley: University of California Press, 1991), though definitions of terms differ.

10. Dislike of the King runs throughout *Some Materials*; for a representative judgement, see Sedgwick, III, 750–1. Although Hervey supported the Hanoverian royal house, his picture of monarchy in *Ancient and Modern Liberty Stated and Compared* (1734) is one of tyranny.

11. The ambiguities are to be found in Poems 5 (addressed to Stephen Fox or to a young lady), 10 ('Verses Sent to —'), and 11 ('Epistle to —'); the libertine arguments in Poems 7 ('To the Same') and 106 ('Chanson au Curé de —').

His Wit all see-saw between *that* and *this*,
Now high, now low, now Master up, now Miss,
And he himself one vile Antithesis.
(*Twickenham*, IV, 119, lines 323–5)

Pope makes Hervey's favourite rhetorical figure stand metaphor for the man, but that is not a representation from which Hervey would necessarily have dissented. It is his evaluation that would have been wholly different.

## *Epistles and odes*

Hervey's skill in developing the formal Ovidian epistle is most evident in what is probably the last example, written in the late 1720s. 'Roxana to Usbeck' (Poem 4) reworks the epistolary bombshell that ends Montesquieu's *Persian Letters* when Usbeck's favourite wife confronts him with the hatred, defiance and desire for freedom that have led her to take a lover in his absence, a lover who has been killed in the harem. Hervey immediately casts her defiance as a response to an orthodox morality.

Think not I write my innocence to prove,
To sue for pity, or awake thy love:
No mean defence expect, or abject pray'rs;
Thou know'st no mercy, and I know no tears:
I laugh at all thy vengeance has decreed,
Avow the fact, and glory in the deed. (lines 1–6)

The purpose of the opening paragraph is, characteristically, to set out the argument that is captured in the anaphora of line 4, 'Thou know'st no mercy, and I know no tears'; Usbeck's cruelty justifies Roxana's resistance. The vigour of the challenge to conventional morality is conveyed within careful patterning: the three elements of the first couplet present the expected response; the three elements of the third the alternative, with a complete counter evaluation as a climax. The passage shows Hervey's characteristic mastery of the couplet form, the rhyme words grammatically varied and the caesura's position flexible, with 'abject pray'rs' appearing as a short scornful addition to its line and the final line gaining force from isocolon.

The first paragraph of 'Roxana to Usbeck' is Hervey's addition to Montesquieu's letter and in the remainder of the poem he develops both Roxana's personal revulsion from her husband and the argument that supports her unfaithfulness. A good example is how he expands a sentence in the original that runs: 'Non! J'ai pu vivre dans la servitude, mais j'ai toujours été libre: j'ai reformé tes lois sur celles de la Nature, et mon esprit s'est toujours tenu dans l'indépendence.'[12] This becomes:

> No, Usbeck, no, my soul disdain'd those laws;
> And tho' I wanted pow'r t' assert my cause,
> My right I knew; and still those pleasures sought,
> Which Justice warranted, and Nature taught:
> On Custom's senseless precepts I refin'd,
> I weigh'd what heav'n, I knew what man design'd,
> And form'd by her own rules my free-born mind. (lines 57–63)

While the French has an epigrammatic concision, Hervey makes Roxana much more assertive. He adds words such as 'pow'r', 'right', 'Justice' and 'Custom's senseless precepts'; he runs on the opening couplet to produce a dramatic pause after 'My right I knew'; and, in a line that anticipates Mme de Merteuil in Laclos's *Les Liaisons dangereuses*, has Roxana declare that she has made her rules for herself.[13]

He also takes us, as Montesquieu does not, into the intimacies of relations between Roxana and Usbeck, presenting her feelings 'as thy slaves this wretched body led | To the detested pleasures of thy bed' (lines 83–4). The sense of separation from her own body and the neat oxymoron of 'detested pleasures' convey her state of alienation.[14] Deprived of her lover, Roxana's final means of self-assertion, the use of what power she has, is to kill herself, a motif that Hervey returns to elsewhere.

The formality of the Ovidian epistles contrasts with the ease of Hervey's verse letters to his wife and to Stephen Fox. The letter *To Lady Hervey from Italy* (Poem 16, 1729), a poem from which Voltaire extracted and published a critique of the Italian Church, uses its relaxed iambic tetrameters to be explicit about style:

12. Charles de Secondat, Baron de Montesquieu, *Œuvres complètes*, ed. by Roger Caillois, 2 vols. (Paris: Gallimard, 1949–51), I, 372.

13. '[M]es principes . . . sont le fruit de mes profondes réflexions; je les ai créés, et je puis dire que je suis mon ouvrage' (Choderlos de Laclos, *Les Liaisons dangereuses* in his *Œuvres complètes*, ed. by Laurent Versini (Paris: Gallimard, 1979), p. 170).

14. Biographers searching for an explanation of Hervey's final treatment of his wife (Halsband, p. 304; Moore, pp. 299–300) might find a clue in this poem, though the next poem to be discussed, 'Verse Letter to Lady Hervey from Italy', presents an affectionately positive impression of their relationship ('Since love and you inspire my Heart').

Tho by this Post (my Dear) I chose
To write in Verse, pray dont supose,
With tropes, and flights that I design
To raise my Style, and swell each Line.
Those fustian trappings of a Poet,
Are what I never wear, you know it. (lines 1–6)

The short phrase and double-syllable rhyme at the end of the paragraph clinch the sense of intimacy, though Hervey then playfully undercuts his claims with an extended simile on bards and strolling players to conclude the paragraph. This beginning anticipates the range of styles that the poem commands. A chatty, colloquial English is available for dealing with the discomforts of the journey. In Florence the beds are musty, the fare coarse, 'And Gnats extreamly busy there' (line 34); at Lerici the fleas and bugs make the gnats seem unimportant (lines 71–2); sailing the next day produces conditions that defeat polite vocabulary:

And now began, through all the Crew,
Each Head to turn, each Mouth to ——
(You know the Rhyme and 'tis more clean,
To lett you guess at what I mean.) (lines 86–9)

But Hervey's range extends from this colloquial intimacy, through the satire on Italian superstition, to an outburst of personification and apostrophe in response to Genoa ('Oh! Freedom! Benefactress fair!', line 130), contrasted with Milan, which is caught in a chiastic bind, followed by a vivid summarising metaphor:

Her Vintage press'd by foreign Hands;
A foreign Hand her Harvest spoils,
Vienna fatten's on her Toils. (lines 141–3)

The poem's closing reference to *Othello* catches the tone of literate intimacy that sustains it:

Yet dont imagine, that I think,
This casual Child of Pen and Ink,
Deserving to be sent so far,
But that ev'n Trifles light as Air,
(As from Othello I can prove,)
Cease to be such to those who love. (lines 220–5)

As the trifle in *Othello* is Desdemona's handkerchief, the reference lightly colours this letter as a reassurance.

Hervey's capacity for writing a different kind of poem again is demonstrated by his elegant and reflective imitation of one of Horace's most famous odes. The poem is sometimes called 'To A Young Lady who desired to know her Fortune' (Poem 5a), but when it appeared in the *Gentleman's Magazine* (June 1736) it was called 'Horace Ode XI. Lib. I. Imitated. The Advice. To S—n F—x Esq.' (Poem 5b), while in Dodsley's *Collection* (1755) it begins 'Forbear, my dear Stephen' (Poem 5c). Modelled on Horace's famous *carpe diem* ode, the success of the 'To a Young Lady' version of the poem depends on the combination of a light anapaestic metre with compact sententiae. Rhetorically the initial entrapment by an antimetabole or crossing over of ideas, 'Who anticipate Care their own Pleasure destroy, | And invite Disappointment who build upon Joy' (lines 3–4), is reinforced by polyptoton (repetition of the same word element), 'All Ills unforeseen we the easiest endure; | What avails to *foresee* unless *Foresight* could cure?' (lines 9–10), and the easy metaphor of wisdom literature, 'To day's all the Treasure poor Mortals can boast' (line 19). Hervey's metrical and rhetorical skills are ideally suited to this form of public writing.

However, when the *Gentleman's Magazine* version of the poem is considered, as its title invites us to, in the context of Hervey's relationship with Fox, it acquires a different emphasis, even though its text is close to that of 'To a Young Lady'. The poem belongs to the early years of their relationship (they met in 1727 and one of the manuscripts is dated 1728), when Hervey's health was a source of anxiety. What would have been in question for them at this time, therefore, would have been the nature of their relationship and its future. In this light, Hervey can be seen as addressing the issue of his health directly, narrowing the generality of Horace's poem:

> Perhaps, many years are allow'd me by Fate,
> Or next winter, perhaps, is the last of their date. (lines 5–6)

The happiness of the present is much more clearly identified with a personal relationship, even though the same couplet is used:

> Even now whilst I write, time steals on our youth,
> And a moment's cut off from thy friendship and truth!
> (lines 13–14)

Horace's advice is to 'strain the wine and cut back far-reaching hopes to within a small space',[15] but Hervey's and Fox's concern is whether you can

15. *vina liques, et spatio brevi spem longam reseces* (lines 6–7); the translation is the Loeb's.

'build upon joy' (line 4). The conclusion too is subtly different from Horace's *carpe diem*:

> Then seize the swift blessing, enjoy the dear *now*. (line 19)

The day is a special gift, something already precious to them.

The version in Dodsley's *Collection*, addressed to 'dear Stephen', should similarly be viewed as celebrating this particular relationship. Hervey changes two pronouns so that lines 3–4 read: 'Perhaps many years are allow'd us [instead of 'me'] by Fate, | Or next winter perhaps is the last of their [instead of 'my'] date'. This makes the appeal more urgent and more direct, because it invokes a shared relationship. One couplet in 'To a Young Lady' is missing from this third version: 'Then no more on Hereafter thy Wishes employ; | Who live to the Future the Present destroy'. The sentiment is appropriate for a poem to a young woman 'who desired to know her Fortune', as two of the manuscripts have it, but to an intimate friend in a mutually loving relationship it might have been heavy-handed. Finally, the third version changes the position of another couplet, bringing forward the lines that provide the penultimate couplet in the other versions, 'To-day's all the treasure poor mortals can boast, | For to-morrow's not gained, and yesterday's lost' (lines 15–16). It also substitutes for the verb 'come' the more expressive 'gained'. The effect is to emphasise what becomes the penultimate couplet and so end the poem more strongly:

> Even now whilst I write, time steals on our youth,
> And a moment's cut off from thy friendship and truth:
> Then seize the swift blessing, enjoy the dear now,
> And take, not expect, what hereafter'll bestow. (lines 17–20)

Hervey has so subtly shaped his verse that the same words can be read as teaching classical wisdom or as celebrating an unconventional relationship that is joyful but uncertain of its progress.

A similar enjoyment of ambiguities over gender can be found in another *carpe diem* poem, 'The Countess of — to Miss —' (Poem 8), that is also *une épître à clef*. In it an older woman – she admits to 'fifty Winters' (line 61) – courts a younger, inexperienced one. The older woman, Isobel Grundy has suggested, is Claude-Charlotte, Countess of Stafford (c. 1665–1739),[16] while the addressee, who is named only as Sophia, may have been Sophia Howe, whose desertion by Anthony Lowther is reflected in Hervey's

16. Grundy, pp. 337, 191–2, 203.

*Monimia to Philocles.*[17] The poem's chief aim seems to be to celebrate lesbian love. This is remarkable for a text by a male writer, especially at a time when, as Emma Donoghue has shown, ignorance and myths about erotic relationships between women were widespread; and when, as Ros Ballaster has put it, erotic acts between women in pornographic texts were 'represented as expression of sexual lust performed because sexual contact with men is denied them'.[18] The Countess's case is, as might be expected from Hervey, carefully constructed and argued. The poem begins with an eight-line introduction in which the Countess states her aim: to convince her addressee of her passion. This is followed by twelve lines in which she imagines, and is erotically excited by imagining, the impact of her avowal as her addressee reads it. Then follows the poem's main body in two sections of roughly equal length. In the first, the Countess argues that sex with another woman is safer because it is not threatened by pregnancy or scandal, and then rejects arguments from morality in a way that is characteristic of the sceptical, heterodox outlook that Hervey and Montagu shared. In the second, the Countess states her attractions. Here she supports her contention that her vigour and spirits are undiminished by acknowledging disarmingly that she has never been a beauty, and adding that she can offer instead 'A Wit sublime to distant Countrys known | An Ornament and Honour to my own' (lines 73–4). She goes on to compare herself to Sappho in looks, strength of desire and expressive ability, before rejecting Phaon-like rivals. The poem ends with a six-line coda in which she restates the strength and inalterability of her love, ending: 'And if a Being after Death there be, | No Heav'n I ask, but what I ask in thee'.

The poem is remarkable for the absence of satirical intent; the Countess is not mocked. If it were not for the title, much of the argument could come just as easily from a man as from a woman until line 22, when the Countess identifies 'Man, false Man' as the enemy who threatens her addressee with 'Undoing' (line 23). Other indications that the Countess is the agent of humour and not its object are when she refers to 'fat Fit—n' wallowing in

17. These identifications are discussed further in the headnote to the poem and in Overton, 'Poetic Voice and Gender', 607–8.

18. Emma Donoghue, *Passions Between Women: British Lesbian Culture 1668–1801* (London: Scarlet Press, 1993); Ros Ballaster, '"The Vices of Old Rome Revived": Representations of Female Same-sex Desire in Seventeenth and Eighteenth Century England', in Suzanne Raitt (ed.), *Volcanoes and Pearl Divers: Essays in Lesbian Feminist Studies* (London: Onlywomen Press, 1995), pp. 13–36 (21).

her arms (line 66), and the 'demi-man's' lack of erotic flammability (line 96); that her account of her own charms is frank and confident; and, most of all, that her arguments for lesbian love do not lack cogency.[19] Hervey uses the line-unit deftly and persuasively in examples such as 'An unprolifick, and a harmless Friend' (line 25), and 'Admitted to the Joy, exempted from the Pain' (line 34), the second of which provides the climax for one of the poem's two forceful triplets. The argument also has room for wit, as when the Countess declares that, if her appeal succeeds, 'Eve shall have sin'd, and Thou been curs'd in vain' (line 33).

But perhaps the poem's most interesting and potentially winning quality is its attitude to gender boundaries. It is, of course, inherently transgressive, not only as an expression of one woman's sexual attraction to another, but also because the power to make a sexual overture was conventionally limited to a man. Two short passages in particular stand out for the openness of their attitudes to gender. In the first of these, Hervey has the Countess refer to the myth of Vertumnus and Pomona, in which the former courted the latter in the guise of an old woman, stating: 'No vulgar Eye the latent Man descry'd, | A Woman's form the vig'rous Youth bely'd' (lines 41–2). The myth is not only highly appropriate to a poem in which a man writes as an older woman courting a younger one but also, in the line 'A Woman's form the vig'rous Youth bely'd', Hervey adapts it to give the female priority over the male, as if Vertumnus would not change back to a man afterwards. It is a vivid and witty appropriation. In the second passage, he has the Countess lay claim to a parallel kind of androgyny:

No Beauty Nature on my Cheek bestow'd,
Where Lillys never bloom'd, nor Roses glow'd:
But Female Softness to my Form deny'd,
With more than Man she has my Soul supply'd. (lines 69–72)

19. It is tempting to suggest that Hervey might have read Aphra Behn's 'To the fair *Clarinda*, who made Love to me, imagin'd more than Woman', which includes the lines:

In pity to our Sex sure thou wer't sent,
That we might Love, and yet be Innocent:
For sure no Crime with thee we can commit;
Or if we shou'd – thy Form excuses it.

(*The Works of Aphra Behn*, ed. by Janet Todd
(London: Pickering, 1992), I, 288: lines 12–15)

But evidence of an interest in Behn on Hervey's part is lacking, and his diction is quite different.

This has especially interesting implications, because the gender identity it adumbrates is the opposite of Hervey's. What is especially striking, however, is Hervey's ability to assume convincingly the voice not only of a woman, but also, in light of his own gender identity, a mannish one.[20]

## *Telemachus and Agrippina*

Both Hervey's three-book poem, 'Telemachus' (Poem 65), probably in its final form dating from the late 1720s, and his five-act tragedy, 'Agrippina' (Poem 66), written a decade later, can be seen as extensions of his imitations of Ovid's *Heroides.* They concern themselves with the plight of a central female figure, Calypso or Agrippina, whose emotional commitment to a young man, Telemachus or Nero, is not reciprocated; in each case he is infatuated by a younger woman, Eucharis or Poppæa. The representation of character in Ovid draws upon rhetorical exercises that appear to have had even more influence on Hervey. In *ethopoeiae* the student was required to make a speech appropriate to a particular character, presenting both emotion and argument; in *suosoriae* the student was to imitate a historical figure debating a course of action.[21] In 'Telemachus' the debate is sometimes internal (Calypso's uncertainty about whether to banish Telemachus) and sometimes it is dramatised (Telemachus and his advisor Mentor's disagreement about whether he should remain on the island). In 'Agrippina' the debates are more various – Agrippina, Nero and Poppæa debate with themselves and with their advisers – about good rule, good counsel, the relation of private and public life, the resistance to tyranny and the history and future of Rome. But the two works have some common themes.

Both 'Agrippina' and 'Telemachus' investigate the relation of women to power. Agrippina is an empress and Calypso a goddess but their exercise of power is constrained by their commitment to a young man, son or lover. In Tacitus (and in Daniel Casper von Lohenstein's mid-seventeenth-century German play, *Agrippina*) the parallel is closer because Agrippina attempts to seduce her son. In Hervey's play the decline of Agrippina's power is

20. There are two other poems that may be called 'lesbian': 'Verses Sent to —' and 'To Molly on Easter Eve'. They are discussed in Overton, 'Poetic Voice and Gender'.

21. See Ovid, *Heroides: Selected Epistles*, ed. by Peter E. Knox (Cambridge: Cambridge University Press, 1995), pp. 15–18, and *The Suosoriae of Seneca the Elder*, ed. by William A. Edward (Cambridge: Cambridge University Press, 1928).

balanced by the rise of Poppæa's, with Nero reduced to the role of their instrument; in 'Telemachus' Calypso's influence is counterbalanced by that of the goddess Minerva, disguised as an old man, Mentor, and Telemachus' power of decision is even more limited than Nero's. Both Telemachus and Nero (somewhat like Hervey himself) have an apparent choice between duty and love, but neither experiences the exercise of full freedom in making it. Although Hervey's translation of *Télémaque* largely avoids political debate, like 'Agrippina' it examines the nature of the regal temperament. Hervey shows in his rulers a potential for nobility and eloquence that can descend into passionate self-indulgence and vice. He is especially interested in the role of advisers to princes: their potential for debating issues; the restraining influence they can exercise; their capacity for encouraging vice; and their role in executing policy. In Fénelon's *Télémaque* and even more in Racine's plays, Hervey found models of how these themes could be debated through the exploration of character in highly charged situations.

'Agrippina' is the more impressive of the two works. If Hervey's verse is less exploratory than in some of his shorter pieces, he finds a style that is sinewy and rapid. In the play's central scene, in which Agrippina confronts Nero with her efforts on his behalf and his failures of prudence (III. 2. 298–321), there is a fine balance of abstraction and detail:

NERO Rumor for truth too Lightly you receive,
And Each exaggerated Tale beleive.
AGRIPPINA The *Milvian Bridge* and the *Flaminian Way*,
Your Haunts by Night for Acts that Shun the Day,
Can Witness that the Charge is not unjust;
Nor are the loose Associates whom you trust,
Careful to hide, but to divulge your shame;
Proud to enrol their Own with *Nero*'s Name.
In the Wild Havock of this Ruffian War
Nor Rank, Nor Sex, Nor Youth, Nor Age You spare;
From the Rude Touch of their Offensive hands,
The Noble Virgin unprotected Stands:
Nor can the wealthy Matron's num'rous Train,
Her Decent Steps from Violence maintain.
The hoary Senator, as vainly bears
The Double Sanction of his Robe and years:
And ensign'd Magistrates themselves endure
Those Wrongs their Office was design'd to cure:
Nor Safety those, Nor these Respect can Boast;

All order banish'd, all Distinction lost.
In Vain the Nightly Watch or City-Guard
Station'd, or Marching to protect each Ward,
And some mask'd Courtier wispers in their Ear
*Your aid is Treason, Cæsar revels there.*

Even though this is the scene in which Nero temporarily capitulates, he remains impressively articulate. At his first appearance in the play, in Act II, Scene 2, Nero is given fifteen lines from one of Hervey's own epistles (56–70), and here in III.2 in the confrontation with his mother his speech has a classical dignity, with an inverted word order placing the most important word, 'Rumor' at the head of the sentence and the inverted foot making the claim more emphatic. Agrippina's response is the more persuasive, however, for the straightforwardness of her syntax and her claim to direct knowledge of Rome. The synecdoche in which the thoroughfares of Rome represent her citizens is particularly powerful because of its sense of concreteness. Throughout the play Agrippina is dignified by her close knowledge of Rome and its history. She then follows an antithesis conveying the warped values of Nero's companions (they are not 'Careful to hide, but to divulge your shame') with a powerful anaphora borrowed from *To the Imitator* which sums up the recklessness of their conduct: 'Nor Rank, Nor Sex, Nor Youth, Nor Age You spare'. Agrippina, then, through her account of raucous petty violence, conjures up a damaged Roman society, with offence to the virgin, the matron, the senator and the magistrate. She concludes tellingly with the vignette of the whisper that the source of order in Rome is responsible for the offence against it. The passage owes much to Tacitus and Suetonius, but the balance between scene and significance is very much Hervey's own.

All Hervey's characters are fiercely articulate. Poppæa, Agrippina's chief antagonist, is from her first entrance remarkable for her intelligence, conveyed by figurative wit:

Beset with dangers, and allarm'd with Fears,
Why am I left a Prey to all these Cares?
Cares, Dangers, Fears, occasion'd all by You
And yet in all, by You abandon'd too:
Uncertain what to dread or what expect
Told of Your Love yet proving your Neglect;
Is it a Hard Request my Sorrows make,
Or to protect me Quite or quite forsake? (II.2.180–7)

Her speech deploys various parallels and oppositions to point to an underlying paradox: her protector is responsible for her danger; she is told of his love but her situation denies it. The final line shapes a dilemma she insists Nero resolve. In some ways, Poppæa's behaviour reflects her rhetoric: she threatens separation in order to achieve greater closeness; she leaves Nero in apparent defeat only to return with more power.

The final scene of 'Agrippina' explores Hervey's favoured issue of power and resistance. In Poem 4, 'Roxana to Usbeck', suicide offers Roxana a form of control over her life; it constitutes a form of self-assertion for the powerless, even though it leaves the actor passive. The issue is explored in Hervey's letters and in other poems.[22] In her tragedy, Agrippina fully acknowledges her defeat, and rejects Pallas' urgings to resist her son militarily and bring her country to civil war. She cannot kill herself but finds some consolation in the knowledge that someone else will do so, Hervey's triplet rising to a sense of achievement in that death:

> When all we know of being is Distress,
> Not being will at least our Greifs supress
> Nor should be call'd Misfortune, but Redress. (V.3.143–5)

In her final speech Agrippina persuades Anicetus to make her death serve her own ends by turning her into a symbol of the evil in which she is implicated:

> Since *Nero*'s Counsel have my Death decree'd,
> And by the Son the Mother's Doom'd to bleed;
> I ask you not this destin'd Life to spare,
> You know no Mercy, and I know no fear:
> But in your Crulty this Justice Show;
> Turn from my honest heart the impious Blow,
> And Plunge thy Sabre in the guilty Womb,
> That Gave this Monster to Afflicted *Rome*. (V.3.261–8)

Even a defeat such as this, Hervey urges, can be given value.

### *Satires*

Although his treatment of character is rarely shaped by satiric impulse – Nero is not satirised in 'Agrippina' and neither is the unnamed Countess in her poem – satire interested Hervey: it was an aspect of his role as a polemicist, but it was also a way of expressing a profound dissatisfaction with his society. His

22. For a full discussion, see Overton, 'Death and Futurity'.

early *Satire in the Manner of Persius* (Poem 20), though not published until 1739 (with revisions), is a carefully composed dialogue between Atticus and Eugenio expressing a bleak world view. The conflict between them is muted – Eugenio feels human injustice and deceitfulness acutely; Atticus has the same world picture but advocates a restrained responsiveness – and the debate ends, unusually for Hervey, with a recommendation of trust in divine power:

> His Rules are fix'd, and all his Ways are Just.

The writing is at its most vivid when it analyses the betrayals of young Eugenio, particularly by the hypocrite 'Who talks on any Secret but his own' (line 124), but the absence of illustration and metaphor weakens a poem that is fluently and cogently argued.

Hervey's most famous satire, his attack on Pope, *To the Imitator of the First Satire of the Second Book of Horace* (Poem 22), probably planned with Montagu but written by Hervey, has qualities quite contrary to those of the imitation of Persius. The glittering malice of the poem seems to obstruct its movement, as it comes to a series of devastating conclusions:

> Whilst none thy crabbed Numbers can endure,
> Hard as thy Heart, and as thy Birth obscure. (lines 16–17)
>
> [Pope's physical being is] A Sign-Post Likeness of the noble Race,
> That is at once Resemblance and Disgrace. (lines 25–6)
>
> [His satire] is an *Oyster-Knife* that hacks and hews;
> The Rage, but not the Talent of Abuse;
> And is in *Hate*, what *Love* is in the Stews. (lines 29–31)
>
> To thee 'tis Provocation to *exist*. (line 37)
>
> [It] shews the Uniformity of Fate,
> That one so *odious*, should be born to *hate*. (lines 50–1)
>
> No; like thy self-blown Praise thy Scandal flies,
> And as we're told of Wasps, it stings and dies. (lines 83–4)
>
> But as thou hat'st, be hated by Mankind;
> And with the Emblem of thy crooked Mind,
> Mark'd on thy Back, like *Cain*, by God's own Hand,
> Wander, like him, accursed through the Land. (lines 105–8)

The poem explores a series of tropes, rejoicing in the emblems that Pope and his work can be said to provide, and Hervey presents these resemblances with characteristic rhetorical skill. His starting point, the parallel texts of Pope's Horatian imitations, are a gift to his antithetical imagination. They are taken to symbolise not similarity but difference. Then, in the familiar criss-cross movement of line 17, metrical inadequacy represents both cruelty and low birth. Pope's physical being stands throughout the poem for alienation from mankind, an artistic and personal impotence. His satire is a prostitution to hatred, but the antagonism he shows to others is a response to their natural aversion from him. The final lines of the poem bring together the reciprocal animosity and the emblematic interpretation of Pope's hunchback into a final religious casting out. *To the Imitator* is a powerful poem (Hervey thought it was good enough to plan a second edition), but there is something reckless and unreflective about its cruelty. Significantly Pope used it to annotate his counterattack in *To Arbuthnot*, seeing in *To the Imitator* a sort of quarry of material that could be worked with nuance and subtlety into even greater poetry.

Recklessness of a different kind informs the major political satire of Hervey's final years, *The Patriots Are Come* (Poem 27). This poem further demonstrates Hervey's versatility: swinging along at a fast pace in anapaestic tetrameters (to the tune of 'Derry Down'), it tells the story of the forming of the ministry after Walpole's fall, with Carteret presenting his demands to the King. They included the dismissal of Hervey from his position as Lord Privy Seal, though that action is not discussed directly. The combination of a popular style with political daring is apparent from the first stanza:

> O England, attend, while thy fate I deplore,
> Rehearsing the schemes and the conduct of pow'r;
> And since only of those who have power I sing,
> I am sure none can think that I hint at the King. (lines 1–4)

Slyly the move to exonerate the writer from the charge of sedition constitutes the sedition itself. The overt stance is of support for the King, while the verse constantly ridicules him, pitying him as someone left with only the 'paraphernalia' (line 8) of kingship. Hervey finds a simile that presents him as a victim of bullying:

> And just like a top they all lash'd him about,
> Whilst he like a top with a murmuring noise
> Seem'd to grumble, but turn'd to these rude lashing boys.
> (lines 14–16).

The King's murmuring and grumbling is an ingenious development of an image essentially designed to show his powerlessness. And when he speaks it is with simple-minded selfishness: 'Let but me and my money, and Walmoden stay' (line 24). Carteret replies that the King can have his mistress but that Carteret, and the Prince of Wales, will have the money. The attacks on the members of the incoming ministry are less subtle than the attack on the King (Hervey perhaps loses some of his credit for enlightened treatment of gender by referring to Spencer Compton as the Countess of Wilmington), but his characterisation of the central situation is sufficiently vivid to make this a powerful political intervention.

## *Elegies*

Some of Hervey's best writing is in occasional pieces and among these the elegies stand out. The poems he wrote for his sister, Lady Elizabeth Mansel and, in anticipation, for his father and for himself are remarkable for the precision with which they establish their tributes, and his poem on Lady Abergavenny subtly explores conflicting responses to a notorious case of adultery, where feelings of compassion were at odds with general condemnation. The poem on Lady Elizabeth (Poem 28) takes advantage of Hervey's characteristically argumentative mode to stress its own sincerity through comparison with 'venal Poets':

> They sing the requiem with a quiet heart,
> Their incense, Flattery; their Affliction, Art. (lines 5–6)

For Hervey and his readers, Roman Catholic ceremonial would itself suggest show, and the close-knit juxtaposition ('their Affliction, Art') condenses the indifference evoked in the previous line. Hervey goes on to detail the development of his relation with his sister from a natural attachment to one shaped by reason and experience. Some of the writing about his feelings is simple and conventional, 'Nor shall thy image from this breast depart, | 'Till the last feeble pulse desert my heart' (lines 23–4), as is his sense of his sister's virtues, but the poem concludes with an unusual intellectual honesty by offering a consolation that is bracketed or open to challenge. Emotionally the conclusion offers a heavenly reward, expressed through emphatic preparatory parachesis:

> Whilst Praise, and Rapture all thy hours employ,
> Unmix'd, unchangeable, unending Joy. (lines 69–70)

But that ending is subject to a series of conditions being fulfilled: *if* there is new life after death and the dead retain their virtue, *if* after death is not the same as before life, *if* vice and virtue are not simply human notions, *if* God values us, *then* there will be joy. It is easy to read those conditions as deployed simply to generate a climax, but no reassurance is directly provided and it seems unlikely that Hervey was confident that the conditions were met. His religious views as laid out in *Some Remarks on the Minute Philosopher* (London, 1732) were those of a sceptic; and two of his poems (54 and 106) scoff at Christian doctrine. In this light the poem ends in a painful ambiguity.

Hervey's epitaph on his father (Poem 33) is built on a compelling paradox, that his grave contains

> The sacred Dust of one, so truely great,
> He never sunk to Offices of State. (lines 3–4)

On that basis the poem goes on to celebrate his independence of mind. The epitaph Hervey wrote for himself (Poem 34) is more equivocal. It concerns itself with a failure of reciprocal admiration less dramatic than Pope's but still something of a problem for the memorialiser. The poem begins surprisingly conversationally, the lines flicking between different aspects of independence:

> Few men he lik'd; and fewer still believ'd;
> Fewest of all he trusted, none deciev'd: (lines 1–2)

It then confesses that 'lik'd by many, he by few was lov'd' (line 6), before going on to declare Hervey, nevertheless, a loyal friend. It concludes:

> He had a truly warm and honest breast,
> Let his own writings speak the rest. (lines 11–12)

An aspiration this edition should help him to fulfil.

The poem on Lady Abergavenny (Poem 29) responds to a notorious scandal and court case. Lord Abergavenny was informed by his servants that his wife was committing adultery with one of his closest friends, Richard Lyddel. She was then sent home to her father, gave birth to a son eleven days later, and lived for only a further fifteen days. The poem's apparent aim is to present an impartial judgement, extending sympathy to her while condemning her actions, but its conclusion goes much further. The opening creates an appropriate distance and balance:

> Young, thoughtless, gay, unfortunately fair,
> Her pride to please and pleasure all her care;
> With too much kindness, and too little art,
> Prone to indulge the dictates of her heart . . . (lines 1–4)

The characterisation is that of Pope's Belinda in *The Rape of the Lock*, with the qualification that here there is genuine feeling: 'too much kindness' and 'the dictates of her heart'. These early judgements proved unproblematic, but the poem came in for severe criticism from the *Grub-street Journal* when it attempted to approve Lady Abergavenny's end and thereby find some consolation for the reader.[23] The lines are perplexing:

> Good nature still to soft compassion wrought,
> Shall weep her ruin, whilst it owns her fault;
> For if her conduct in some steps betray'd
> To virtue's rules too little reverence paid,
> Yet dying still she show'd so dear her fame,
> She could survive her guilt, though not her shame.
> Her honour dearer than her life she proved,
> But dearer than them both the man she lov'd. (lines 14–21)

The *Journal* objected that sin should be more important than reputation and that Lady Abergavenny's death did not restore her to her lover, who was still living. By 'guilt' I think Hervey simply means having been found guilty; his view is that her death was a response to her disgrace and ostracism; she could not live without honour and that he admires. The final line, however, twists away from this argument; it does not, as the *Journal* believes, try to complete it. Hervey simply declares that for Lady Abergavenny love was paramount, and in doing so he challenges the morality of the rest of the poem. There is a possible resonance with his own life, as not long before this poem he had begun to imperil his own honour through his love of Stephen Fox.

## *Embedded verse*

A significant part of Hervey's poetic achievement was his output of improvised verse, much of it embedded in letters. Hervey was proud of the ease with which he wrote verse, claiming for it an almost Wordsworthian immediacy of emotional expression. In a letter to Stephen Fox, excusing a letter that has not been preserved and that appears to have been wholly in verse, he claimed: 'tis, some Days, so much more natural to me to write in verse than prose, that I did it for my ease, and 'twas

23. *Grub-street Journal*, 19 (14 May 1730). The *Journal*'s version of the poem is reprinted as an appendix to this edition's text.

only want of time that hindered me putting it into a common Epistolary Form'.[24] A complementary reason is implicit in a remark eight years later to another intimate friend, Francesco Algarotti: 'as my thoughts, without any affectation, fall some Days so naturally into Rhyme, that I am forced to think twice to put them into Prose, and that I never constrain my Nature when I write or speak to you, forgive the Inconveniency of my Sincerity for the sake of that Affection which occasion's it'.[25] Hervey suggests here not only that he sometimes writes verse more easily than prose, but also that, for him, verse is the natural form for expressing affection. More generally, in the same way that shifts into verse in prose drama of the Restoration and earlier eighteenth century tend to suggest heightened emotion, he seems to have used verse in his letters to express feelings of particular force or complexity.

Much of Hervey's best extempore verse appears in the early stages of his relationship with Stephen Fox, especially from late 1729, when the two returned from their stay in Italy, to late 1731, after which they were able to live together for a while. Directness of emotional statement and endearment is given force by the balance and concision of the verse. Two representative examples occur near the end of a letter dated 2 October 1731, the initial couplets simply but effectively organised according to a series of antitheses, providing a clear structure and line of development.

> 'Tis You alone my Fears & Wishes make,
> From you my Thoughts their various Tincture take.
> With every Good, whilest you are present, blest,
> Of all, when you are absent, dispossesst.
> Each hour at best a Blank; not one enjoy'd;
> A tedious Waking, or a sleeping Void.
> And whilest the present I should strive to tast,
> I wish the Future or I weep the past.
>
> It is ridiculous to say one writes in a Hurry when one writes in Rhyme; but 'tis true; & you know I do not lye when I say I sometimes can write as fast in Verse as I can in prose. Adieu Dinner is on y$^{e}$ Table. Vendredi Viendra

24. SRO 941/47/4, p. 73 (9 January 1728); Ilchester, p. 26. The manuscript is in the hand of a scribe.

25. JMA, Letter 5, f. 4r; copy in SRO 941/47/4, p. 587 (30 October 1736); Ilchester, p. 254.

And sure I am I would not change that Hour
For all the while Ones Fate has in it's power. (Poems 75–6)

Hervey attaches his verse easily to a social reality that it nonetheless transcends.

The verse, even in the letters to Fox, varies in the ardour it expresses. One of the earlier items (Poem 67) cautions him about the dangers of a 'restless Mind', and one of the later reflects on those of an over-sensitive emotional state, remarking:

For few or can, or wish to bring Relief,
And every touch we feel augments our Grief. (Poem 78)

These are examples of Hervey's ability not only to express emotion in verse but to analyse it and to advise. After 1731, however, the fact that he and Fox were able to spend more time together resulted in fewer letters, and several years later the relationship cooled, especially after Fox's marriage in 1736.[26]

The second important recipient of Hervey's embedded extempore verse was Francesco Algarotti. Introduced to Hervey by a letter from Voltaire that he had brought with him, Algarotti (1712–64) had come to London in March 1736 while he was writing *Il Newtonianismo per le dame*.[27] Having entranced Montagu as well as Hervey by his intelligence, charm and good looks, he left London on 6 September. Hervey's first three letters to him were written while he was staying with Stephen Fox in the country before Algarotti's departure. The letter of 16 August 1736 is of particular interest because Algarotti used the six lines of verse that it contains as one of the commendatory poems prefacing the second edition of his book, and because corrections in the manuscript show that they were composed in the process of writing the letter:

When the gay Sun no more his Rays shall boast,
And human Eyes their Faculty have lost:
Then shall thy writings on those Subjects dye
Thy Wit and Learning in Oblivion lye,
England shall cease to boast her *Newton's* Head,
And Algarotti's Works no more be read. (Poem 79)

26. For details of the marriage, see Halsband, pp. 188–91.

27. Naples: Giambatista Pasquali, 1739, sig. A6$^r$. The book was translated by Elizabeth Carter in 1739 as *Sir Isaac Newton's Philosophy Explain'd for the Use of the Ladies* (London: for E. Cave, 1739), but the translation does not include any commendatory verses (for further details, see the headnote to Poem 57).

The wittily negative forecast of the poem powerfully aligns the fates of Algarotti and Newton himself. Not all the verse written to Algarotti is as serious as this. For example, this barbed gibe at Hervey's rival for Algarotti's affections, Lady Mary Wortley Montagu, occurs in a letter that also contains verse that compliments Algarotti:

> In black & white whilst Chloris' Mind you trace,
> With red and white whilst she adorns her Face;
> 'Tis true she trys by Nature and by Art,
> Each way to force a Passage to your Heart;
> But for her Vows compleat Success to find,
> To make her Lover pleas'd, as well as kind,
> She should be never mute, You always blind. (Poem 82)

The sharp, balanced final line brings together the criticism of Montagu for use of cosmetics with recognition of her wittiness and her skill with words.

It was Montagu who received most of Hervey's embedded verse in the last six years of his life. The ten examples, amounting to a total of 100 lines, show the greatest emotional complexity of all the extempore verse that he embedded in letters.[28] Perhaps the most powerful appears when he wrote to her as she was about to leave for Italy in a failed attempt to join Algarotti there. The letters of the period involve four passages of verse, one bidding her farewell, two complimenting her and the fourth wishing a second spring to one of her maturer admirers. All express a moving generosity of spirit, testifying to the strength of a friendship that had begun nearly twenty years earlier and that had survived all the tribulations of the emotional triangle involving Algarotti. Hervey's farewell is a good example:

> Since all the Pray'rs of weeping Friends were vain,
> To stay your hated Passage o'er the Main,
> Suffer at least our wishes to pursue
> That charming Object which eludes our View,
> And take from real Grief this fond Adieu.
> Where'er you dwell, where'er you bend your way,
> Or fix'd by Land, or roving o'er the Sea,
> Be yours each Pleasure (more you can not find,)
> Which Those regret whom you have left behind:

28. Poems 81, 86, 91–3, 95–9.

May all the Transports jealous Minds suggest
Are tasted in a happy Rival's Breast,
And all the Envious fancy we enjoy,
Gild ev'ry Scene, & ev'ry Sense employ;
May ev'ry Hour in gay Succession move,
Your Days all Luxury, your Nights all Love. (Poem 91)

The passage is carefully constructed, not only showing Hervey's characteristic fluency at writing verse, but also suggesting that the emotions expressed are deep and sincere. In the opening five lines, this comes largely from several adjectives: 'hated' is surprisingly violent in a valediction, but highly effective for conveying strength of feeling, while 'charming' pays tribute to the pleasures that Hervey and others close to Montagu are losing, and 'real' and 'fond' have much more robust meanings than they have now. The remaining ten lines change the point of view to Montagu herself, not only acknowledging why she is leaving but also endorsing her motives and wishing her success in realising them. In this there is not the least hint of reproach. Instead, Hervey both wishes Montagu the pleasures she gives to others and dissociates himself from envy. The chiasmus in 'Gild ev'ry Scene, & ev'ry Sense employ' is a telling example, but, considering his own strong feelings for Algarotti, the closing line is even more remarkable for what it wishes her: 'Your Days all Luxury, your Nights all Love'.

This discussion of Hervey's extempore verse raises the questions of how seriously he took it, and how seriously it is to be taken. On the one hand, his letter-books suggest that he meant the letters they contain to be published, presumably after his death, especially because he took the trouble to annotate and correct them in his own hand. On the other, he did not keep copies of any of his letters to Montagu or most of those to Algarotti, and even his letters to the Fox brothers are incompletely represented, those of his letters that survive in autograph form having been passed on to his family after his death. To some extent, his attitude to the extempore verse that he embedded in letters probably reflects his attitude to his verse in general, especially as an aristocrat who did not write for money and because it came to him so easily. But this does not mean it should not be taken seriously. The aim of this discussion is to provide a clear idea of the range of extempore verse that Hervey embedded in letters, of its expressiveness and of its value as poetry.

## *Conclusion*

Hervey's verse has value as the self-expression of a man who held a significant social and political position (a central figure at the Hanoverian court and a close ally of Walpole for many years), who was an influential government pamphleteer, and who has proved the pre-eminent memoirist of his period. It is also of interest as the output of Alexander Pope's most important opponent, someone who could offend and frighten him, play the haughty aristocrat to his hesitant gentleman/bourgeois, and yet provide source material for some of his greatest poetry. There is interest too in observing an early eighteenth-century aristocrat writing intimately for the court and for his various circles of friends. Hervey's verse would be much less valuable, however, if it was not so well adapted to expressing radical points of view, directly or obliquely challenging orthodoxies about sexual conduct, religious belief and relations between men and women. Most commentary on Hervey's poetry, from Hanbury Williams to Robert Halsband, is contemptuous,[29] but it is noteworthy that Pope was dismissive rather than critical of Hervey as a poet, and that Montagu and Algarotti both clearly admired him. Rhetorically and metrically accomplished, witty, vivid, memorable, Hervey is remarkable for his exploration of forms of experience neglected or unavailable to his contemporaries. Much of his best writing has been inaccessible to the reading public until now; the aim of this edition is finally to get him a sympathetic hearing.

29. See, for example, Halsband, p. 61 and p. 290.

# EPISTLES

# INTRODUCTION TO EPISTLES

In *The Eighteenth-Century British Verse Epistle* Bill Overton presents a comprehensive analysis of the wide range of epistolary verse in this period.[1] There is a constant interplay between the two elements in the term 'verse epistle'; sometimes one predominates, sometimes the other. Overton organises verse epistles round a central case, from which examples might diverge in various respects: 'The central case in the category of verse epistle may be defined as having the following properties: it is written communication; it is in a verse form accepted as epistolary; it is addressed from distance; its authorship is single and undifferentiated; and it has a single named addressee' (p. 21). A central distinction is between those epistles that are written in the person of the author (as Horatian epistles are) and those written as a character (as Ovid's *Heroides* are). The former range from personal letters actually written as verse to essays only remotely connected with their addressee. Overton distinguishes six basic types of verse epistle: the familiar; the humorous; the dramatic (including the Ovidian); the discursive (the essay-epistle); the satirical; and the complimentary. Some of Hervey's epistles fall straightforwardly into one of these categories, but some are mixed.

## *Epistles in the Manner of Ovid*

The four poems that comprise Hervey's 'Epistles in the Manner of Ovid' first appeared together in the four-volume edition of Dodsley's *Collection* published in 1755. No printed text or manuscript prior to that date so much as puts two of the poems together, let alone gives them a collective title, although three were published during 1746–7 in non-consecutive numbers of Dodsley's periodical *The Museum*.[2] Hervey refers to none of the

1. *The Eighteenth-Century British Verse Epistle* (Houndmills, Basingstoke: Palgrave Macmillan, 2007).

2. *The Museum; Or, the Literary and Historical Register*, 3 vols. (London: for R. Dodsley, 1746–7), I, 92–5 (no. 3, 26 April 1746); II, 14–19 (no. 14, 27 September 1746); III, 378–80 (no. 36, 1 August 1747). The poem not included is *Monimia to Philocles*.

poems in his surviving correspondence, though he quotes from one of them, and though his father quotes from another in a letter to him, in both cases without citing the source.[3] Nevertheless, the four clearly belong together, though they were not necessarily planned as a group. The fact that two, 'Flora to Pompey' and 'Arisbe to Marius Junior', are free imitations of poems by Fontenelle may indicate Hervey's starting point, especially if, as seems likely, 'The Adventures of Telemachus in the Island Ogygia' (Poem 65), his unfinished verse adaptation based on the first three books of Fénelon's *Les Aventures de Télémaque*, dates from around the same period. The greater daring and complexity of the other two poems in the series, *Monimia to Philocles* and 'Roxana to Usbeck', suggest that they were written later. *Monimia to Philocles* must have been written in whole or part by 6 September 1725, when Lord Bristol quoted from it, and seems unlikely to date from before 1724, when Sophia Howe ('Monimia') was replaced as a Maid of Honour.[4] 'Roxana to Usbeck' must have been written in whole or part by 27 September 1731, when Hervey quoted from it in a letter to Stephen Fox. Possibly it dates from 1729–31, when Hervey and his wife got to know Montesquieu, the writer of *Les Lettres Persanes*, the epistolary narrative that provided his source, though Hervey had certainly read the book before then.[5]

Both the heroic epistle and the imitation were well-established genres. The former goes back to Ovid's *Heroides*, verse letters to their lovers by rejected or deserted women.[6] In the British Renaissance, Michael Drayton introduced a key change by taking his heroines not from classical myth or epic, as, with a single exception, had Ovid, but from English history.[7] The Restoration further inflected the genre, not only by adapting it to satire and parody, but crucially by taking its subjects from contemporary life instead of from myth, literature or history. It was not, however, until the eighteenth century that this third and final transformation of the genre was turned to purposes beyond satire or parody. This gave its heroines the same serious attention as Ovid and Drayton had devoted to theirs, often using

3. See pp. 37 n. 2 and 11 below. 4. *British Journal*, 24 October 1724.

5. Robert Shackleton, *Montesquieu: A Critical Biography* (London: Oxford University Press, 1961), pp. 117–46. Hervey's earliest recorded reference to the book seems to have been in a letter to Stephen Fox dated 13 June [1727] (SRO 941/47/4, p. 57), though someone as cultivated as he would surely have read it soon after its publication.

6. The following very brief summary is based on the account of the heroic epistle in *Eighteenth-Century British Verse Epistle*, pp. 133–59.

7. The exception is Sappho, in *Heroides* XV, 'Sappho to Phaon'.

them as channels for social criticism or protest. The most striking example is probably Lady Mary Wortley Montagu's 'Epistle from Mrs. Y[onge] to her Husband'. Indeed, it seems to have been Montagu, who wrote two further poems of a similar kind, who first converted the genre to such an end.[8] Perhaps, too, it was Montagu's example that helped inspire Hervey's single poem of this type, *Monimia to Philocles*.

In Britain, the classical imitation also originated in the Renaissance. Dryden provided a good working definition when distinguishing between different kinds of translation in his Preface to *Ovid's Epistles* in 1680: 'The third way is that of imitation, where the translator (if now he has not lost that name) assumes the liberty not only to vary from the words and sense, but to forsake them both as he sees occasion; and taking only some general hints from the original, to run divisions on the ground-work as he pleases.'[9] This is the kind of poem Hervey produced in his other three Ovidian epistles. The two imitated from Fontenelle are themselves imitations in the looser sense that they are ventures in an established genre. 'Roxana to Usbeck', while also based on a modern rather than a classical text, goes further in transforming a prose rather than a verse epistle, and in adapting it to Ovidian conventions.

The order in which Dodsley printed the four epistles is not necessarily the order in which Hervey would have placed them if he intended them to stand together. It is probably also not the order in which they were composed. There seems no good reason, however, to arrange them differently in this edition. The two Fontenelle imitations provide the filling in a sandwich the two outer layers of which differ from each other: a heroic epistle updated to the present, and an Ovidian imitation of a non-Ovidian original.

## *Epistles to Stephen Fox*

Unlike 'Epistles in the Manner of Ovid', the three epistles addressed to Stephen Fox belong to the other tradition in the genre: not the heroic or

8. 'Epistle from Mrs. Y[onge] to her Husband'; 'Epistle from Arthur G[ra]y to Mrs M[urra]y', 'Miss Cooper to ——', in Lady Mary Wortley Montagu, *Essays and Poems, and Simplicity, a Comedy*, ed. by Robert Halsband and Isobel Grundy (Oxford: Clarendon Press, 1977, repr. 1993), pp. 230–2, 221–4, 227–30.

9. *The Poems of John Dryden*, ed. by Paul Hammond and David Hopkins, 5 vols. (London and New York: Longman, 1995–2005), I (ed. by Paul Hammond, 1995), 385.

Ovidian, but the Horatian. While the Ovidian type is characteristically a verse letter from a legendary or historical woman to the man who has deserted her, the Horatian subdivides into two variants: the familiar letter, and the verse essay addressed to a friend or patron. *The Eighteenth-Century British Verse Epistle* distinguishes between the two with the terms 'familiar' and 'discursive'.[10] Because, unlike heroic epistles, Horatian epistles are intended to resemble informal communications, their diction and versification are usually fairly plain. Their style tends to be less elevated, and their versification less elaborate, though these are matters of degree rather than radical difference. Among the three epistles to Fox, the second is an example of the familiar type, the third of the discursive. But the first poem in the series, which underwent several processes of revision, is not, properly speaking, an epistle at all; and neither is the second insofar as it follows the poem by Horace on which it is based. Both, as a variant title to one and an epigraph that occurs in some versions of the other make clear, are imitations not of epistles by Horace but of odes. However, not only do the three poems belong together, but the idea of the verse epistle that was current in the period was highly flexible.[11] It is significant, too, that all three are in continuous verse – couplets of iambic pentameter in two cases and anapaestic tetrameter in the other – unlike any of the stanzaic forms that are always used for Horatian odes. Biographically, the poems are of special interest because they come from the period in which the relationship between Hervey and Fox was at its most intense. This fact gains further importance in light of the probability that the earliest circulated versions of the first poem almost certainly pre-date that relationship and are addressed not to a man but a woman.

## *Other amatory verse*

Ovidian epistles constitute but one type of amatory verse that uses, or touches on, the letter form.[12] The culture of letter writing in the eighteenth century, with its powerful role in shaping the novel, influenced much verse that represented relations between lovers. The poems by Hervey in this section are love poems addressed to a particular person, although that person is not usually identified. In one case, 'Written as from Lady Mary

10. *Eighteenth-Century British Verse Epistle*, pp. 6–31, 66–97, 104–32, 133–59.
11. For discussion and examples, see *Eighteenth-Century British Verse Epistle*, Chapter 1.
12. The category is discussed in *Eighteenth-Century British Verse Epistle*, pp. 160–7.

Wortley to Monsieur Algarotti' (Poem 15), both sender and recipient are named in an epistle that is both familiar and dramatised. Two other poems, 'The Countess of — to Miss —' and 'To Molly on Easter Eve', belong to that set of poems (the persons being identifiable to Hervey's coterie) that offers present-day events in disguise.[13] These poems also allow Hervey to play with gender expectations, for they may both be addressed from woman to woman. Other poems in the group present an argument for love, often with a colouring of *carpe diem.*

### *Complimentary and satirical epistles*

Complimentary and satirical epistles can be seen as two sides of the same coin: the one takes advantage of the freedom and familiarity of the genre to praise, the other to blame.[14] One strand of complimentary epistle may be seen as developing from the commendatory verses that were sometimes prefixed to volumes, often praising the work of a colleague, but another strand praised a patron, or wished-for patron. Hervey's example of a complimentary epistle, 'To Mr Poyntz' (Poem 17) shows a development of the second type, in which personal friendship is associated with praise of a public figure. In the two satirical poems, 'To Dr Sherwin' (Poem 18) and 'To the Queen' (Poem 19), Hervey exploits the epistle form by using his relationships with two very different figures for both general and personal satire. The remaining poem 'Verse Letter to Lady Hervey' (Poem 16) mixes modes: its satirical critique of Italy is embedded in a comic and intimate narrative of a journey that nonetheless stimulates political reflection.

13. See the discussion in *Eighteenth-Century British Verse Epistle*, pp. 154–60.

14. This argument is to be found in expanded form in the chapter 'Satirical and Complimentary' in *The Eighteenth-Century British Verse Epistle*, pp. 168–96.

# EPISTLES IN THE MANNER OF OVID

# 1 Monimia to Philocles

***Main source.*** Harrowby MS 255, pp. 79–88, because of the high probability that Montagu transcribed it from a copy made available to her by Hervey.

***Complementary manuscript sources.*** Delany MS [1], item 23; BL Add. MS 28101, ff. 221v–223v; Yale, Osborn Collection c.392, pp. [1]–7 (first page misnumbered 3); Yale, Osborn Collection fc.51, pp. 146–54.

***Complementary print sources.*** *Monimia to Philocles* (Dublin: s.n., 1726); *Monimia to Philocles ... To which is added, Glotta a poem* (Dublin: by S. Powell for J. Thompson, 1728); *Gentleman's Magazine*, 15 (June 1745), 325–6; *London Magazine*, 22 (September 1753), 433–5; Dodsley, *Collection* (1755), IV, 82–9, collated with 1782 edn (IV, 86–93).

***Attribution.*** The poem is attributed implicitly to Hervey by his father, the Earl of Bristol, who quoted two lines from it in a letter dated 6 September 1725 (*Letter-Books*, II, 394). All but one of the manuscript copies are attributed, the exception being Osborn fc.51: Harrowby as by 'the same' (i.e. Hervey), Delany 'Lord Hervey' (at the end and in a different hand from that of the transcriber); BL Add. 28101 'L$^{d}$. ['Mr.' crossed out] Hervey'; and Osborn c.392 'Ld. Harvey'. The first printed copy to be attributed is that in the *London Magazine*.

***Context and date.*** The remark by Lord Bristol quoted above indicates that the poem, or at least a substantial part of it, had been written by September 1725. There is no other evidence to date it except for the chronology of the real-life events on which it is based. The figures represented by Monimia and Philocles were Sophia Howe and Anthony Lowther. Sophia was a Maid of Honour to Caroline, Princess of Wales, at the same time as Mary Lepell, who married Hervey in 1720. Anthony Lowther, who had been a Member of Parliament since 1714, was celebrated for his good looks. Sophia fell passionately in love with him and they had an affair. When he broke with her in 1720, the same year as her friend Mary Lepell's marriage, she protested so violently and publicly as to ruin her reputation and bring about her virtual banishment from society. Accounts of the affair were given by Henrietta Jannsen in a letter to Lady Denbigh, quoted by Lewis Melville [Lewis S. Benjamin] in *Maids of Honour* (London: Hutchinson, 1927), pp. 210–11, and by Mrs Delany, as reported by Mary Hamilton in Delany, *Autobiography*, VI, 163, with further information in Horace Walpole, *Correspondence*, XXXIV, 256–7; XL, 180. Her replacement as Maid of Honour in 1724 is reported in several newspapers, as are her illness and death on 4 April 1726 (*British Journal*, 24 October 1724; *Daily Journal*, 25 February 1726; *Daily Post*, 14 April 1726; *Chronological Diary* of *The Historical Register*, XI (London: by

R. Nutt, 1726), p. 15). Two variants in manuscript copies suggest that Lowther had begun an affair with another woman. Line 22 is rendered in most versions as '*Monimia*'s lost, and *Philocles* unkind', but Montagu's reading, the one adopted in this edition, is 'Belinda's False, and Philocles unkind', varied in the Delany manuscript to '*Amyntor*'s lost, and *Harriot* proves unkind'. Indeed, Mrs Delany, the owner of the latter, was to claim in 1783, when she told the story to a friend, that Lowther was already courting another woman whom he later married, though in fact he died unmarried on 27 November 1741 (*Autobiography*, VI, 163; *Gentleman's Magazine*, 11 (November 1741), 609; *Complete Peerage*, VIII (1932), 133, note d).

More intriguing is the question why the poem was first printed in Ireland, a fact that, as David Foxon notes, 'has not been explained' (I, 340). Citing information from Foxon himself, Halsband remarks: 'The publication (1726) may have been arranged by James Arbuckle, Irish essayist, who reprinted it in 1728 along with his own topographical poem *Glotta*' (p. 325). It may be relevant, however, that on 18 May 1726, about six weeks after Sophia Howe's death, Lowther was appointed one of the Commissioners of Revenue in Ireland, and that by 22 July he had arrived in Dublin to take up his post (*Chronological Diary* of *Historical Register*, XI (1726), 22, reported in *London Gazette*, 24 May 1726; *Daily Post*, 22 July 1726). As Hervey had himself become a Member of Parliament the year before, it is possible that some political rivalry was involved. Alternatively, a copy of the poem, which would have circulated in manuscript, could have been passed to the Dublin printer to cause political mischief, especially as the first edition and its successor, also published in Dublin, bear a subtitle making it clear that the poem refers to contemporary events. This reads:

> Being a Letter from an Unfortunate LADY, after Her Retirement from Court to one of the most remote and solitary Parts of *England*, to a young NOBLEMAN; who, after a long Courtship, had not only basely forsaken, but also treated Her in a most cruel and inhuman Manner.

The only other text of the poem to carry a subtitle is that in the *Gentleman's Magazine* nearly twenty years later. While this also makes it clear that the poem refers to contemporary events, it has no political implications: 'An Epistle from a lady in *France*, to Mr. L. a gentleman at *London*, who had debauch'd her'. Another puzzle is why the second Dublin edition is accompanied by reprints of Arbuckle's *Glotta: A Poem Humbly Inscribed to the Right Honourable the Marquess of Carnarvon*, first published in Glasgow by William Duncan in 1721 and, more incongruously still, of 'A Poem on the Taking Port St. Mary's', a lewd account of the rape of nuns by English soldiers at Puerta de Santa Maria opposite Cadiz in 1702, apparently first printed as *A Poem on the Taking St. Mary's* (London?: s.n., 1703?; Foxon P643), followed by at least four reprints, three of them in collections, before 1728. 'A Poem on the Taking Port St. Mary's' is not featured on the title page. Perhaps the aim was to fill out a publication that, from the poor quality of the printing and the small format (duodecimo, in contrast to the 1726 octavo), seems to have been aimed at the lower end of the market. The Dublin editions are also distinctive in featuring an epigraph. This draws attention not to contemporaries but to the poem's generic heritage in the Ovidian heroic epistle, fusing as it does two distiches that occur in different poems from the *Heroides*:

> Non mihi grata dies: noctes vigilantur amarae:
> Nec tener in misere pectore Somnus adest
> An potes, O Scopulis undaque ferocior illa,
> Si moriar, titulum mortis habere meæ.

The first distich is from *Heroides* XII, Medea to Jason, 169–70: 'I take no pleasure in the day; my nights are watches of bitterness, and gentle sleep is absent from my wretched soul' (Loeb, p. 155). The second is from *Heroides* XV, Sappho to Phaon, 189–90: 'Or, if I perish, O more savage than any cliff or wave, can you endure the name of causing my death?' (Loeb, p. 195). Appropriate though these are, the fact that they occur in no other copy suggests that they were not chosen by Hervey.

***Textual commentary.*** The fact that there are clear connections between some of the sources, manuscript and print, may cast light on the circulation and copying of handwritten texts and the processes by which the poem found its way into print. First, there can be little doubt that the 1728 Dublin edition was reprinted directly from its 1726 predecessor, making a few corrections to punctuation, and introducing three substantive variants: 'in' for 'no' (53), 'Prison' for 'Prism' (129) and 'immortal' for 'immoral' (147), all clearly printer's errors. As the third of these readings also occurs in both manuscripts in the Osborn Collection, but nowhere else, it seems to suggest a further connection. However, the likelihood of a direct link between the 1728 Dublin edition and the two Osborn manuscripts is much diminished by various substantive differences between the three texts, including one line (60) unique to the two Dublin editions, and by the fact that there are only ten other cases of agreement over substantive variations, all occurring in one or more other sources and two in only one of the Osborn manuscripts. There is rather stronger evidence for a link between the Dublin texts and that of the *Gentleman's Magazine*, for the three substantive variants that they share include two lines (122–3) that appear nowhere else. Again, though, connections are blurred, in this case because, in accordance with its normal editorial practices (see C. Lennart Carlson, *The First Magazine: A History of the Gentleman's Magazine* (Providence, RI: Brown University Press, 1938), pp. 229–30), the *Gentleman's* took considerable liberties with the text, so producing a relatively large number of unique variants. Similarities also appear both between the two texts in the Osborn Collection and between them and that in the *London Magazine*. Specifically, the three texts share a total of six substantive variants that occur nowhere else; a further seven shared only with the text in Dodsley's *Collection*, the most striking of which is the omission of lines 190–1; and 'Belinda's False' (22), which only appears elsewhere in the Harrowby manuscript. Several speculations are therefore possible.

For example, the Osborn manuscripts and the text in the *London Magazine* may stem from a common source, or one of the former may have provided the basis for the text in the *Magazine*, or vice versa. It seems likely, too, that the Dodsley text is indebted in some way to one or more of these precursors.

There is external as well as internal evidence for dating some of the manuscripts. The earliest seems to have been Mrs Delany's, for the collection in which it occurs has a heading that includes the phrase 'Transcrib'd in the year 1728'. That Mrs Delany had read the poem by 1728 is confirmed by her remark in a letter to her sister dated 9 October 1729: 'did you tell me that Ha Ha made the verses of Moninia [sic] to Lothario if you did you told a Lye for they were printed a great while ago and another author named for them but I don't know who' (Manuscript Letters of Mrs. Mary Delany, Newport Reference Library M416.6/012/DEL, Vol. 1; repr. in bowdlerized form in *Autobiography*, I, 217). 'Ha Ha' was probably Henry Hervey, one of Lord Hervey's younger brothers (for the fullest account of his life, see D[oris] A[lmon] Ponsonby, *Call a Dog Hervey* (London: Hutchinson, 1949), pp. 122–40), and it is likely that he provided the source for Mrs Delany's transcript (*Autobiography*, I, 179). The next of the manuscripts to be copied was almost certainly Montagu's, for its position in Harrowby 255 suggests that it was copied after 1730. The series of Hervey poems in Harrowby 255 begins on p. 72 with 'The Countess of — to Miss —', with 'Monimia to Philocles' occupying pp. 79–88; while two of the poems that occur before this, 'The Mistriss' and 'The Lover', occur on pp. 55–7 and 57–60 respectively and were, according to Isobel Grundy, copied after 1730 (Grundy, 'Verse of Lady Mary Wortley Montagu', pp. 442, 438). Probably the other three complementary source manuscripts date from about the middle of the century or later. BL Add. MS 28101 is the 'Family Miscellany' compiled by Ashley Cowper, Clerk of the Parliaments, according to Alexander Lindsay 'mid-century' (*Index*, p. 540). Evidence to date the two manuscripts in the Osborn Collection is lacking, but their much more sparing use of initial capitals, compared with the other three manuscripts, suggests that they were the last of the five to have been transcribed. The last to be printed of the published sources, that in Dodsley's *Collection*, appeared in 1755. In common with nearly all of the verse in the *Collection*, it remained little changed in later editions. Collation with the final edition of 1782 indicates a relatively small number of changes, all in accidentals except for the making singular of one plural noun ('Transports' becomes 'transport' in line 156).

Substantive variants have been adopted from the nine complementary sources where they agree in suggesting transcription errors on Montagu's part (see the List of Emendations). As Montagu seems to have transcribed verse into her albums for her own use, she tended to punctuate very lightly, and to paragraph and use initial capitals inconsistently. For instance, there is no punctuation at the end of many lines in her manuscript. Her copy is therefore not given authority in such matters; any changes required by the syntax of Hervey's often carefully balanced lines are editorial, and are detailed in the List of Emendations.

# Monimia to Philocles[1]

Since Language never can describe my Pain,
How can I hope to move[2] when I complain?
Yet such is Woman's Frenzy in Distress,
We love to plead, tho' hopeless of Redress.

Perhaps (affecting Ignorance) thou'lt say,
From whence these Lines? whose Message to convey?
Mock not my Grief with that feign'd cold demand,
Too well you know the wretched writer's Hand,
But if you force me to avow my Shame,
Behold them prefac'd with Monimia's Name.

Lost to the World, abandon'd and forlorn,
Expos'd to Infamy, Reproach, and Scorn,
To Mirth and Comfort lost, and all for you,
Yet lost perhaps to your Remembrance too,
How hard my Lot! What Refuge shall I try?
Weary of Life, and yet afraid to dye?
Of Hope, the Wretch's last resort, bereft,
By Freinds, by Kindred, by my Lover left.
Oh frail Dependance of confiding Fools,
On Lovers Oaths, or Freindship's sacred Rules:
How weak in modern Hearts! too late I find
Belinda's False, and Philocles unkind.[3]
To these Reflections, each slow-wearing Day,
And each revolving Night a constant Prey,
Think what I suffer – nor ungentle hear
What Madness dictates in my fond Despair.
Grudge not this short Relief (too fast it flys)
Nor chide that Weakness I my self despise.

1. *Monimia to Philocles*: the heroine of Otway's she-tragedy *The Orphan* (1680), Monimia is an epitome of suffering femininity; Philocles is perhaps named after the character of that name in Dryden's *Secret Love; or, The Maiden Queen* (1667), admitted by Dryden to be unheroic. In the Delany manuscript, he is called instead Lothario.

2. *move*: 'To rouse or excite feeling in (a person); to affect with emotion, esp. with tender feeling or compassion; to stir (the feelings, etc.)' (*OED*).

3. *unkind*: stronger sense than in present-day usage ('Lacking in kindness or kindly feeling; acting harshly or ungently to others', *OED*).

One moment sure may be at least her due,
Who sacrific'd her all of Life for you;
Without a Frown this Farewell then receive,
For 'tis the last my hapless Love shall give.
Nor this I would, if Reason could command,
But what Restriction reins a Lovers Hand?
Nor Prudence, Shame, nor Pride, nor Interest sways,
The Hand implicitly the Heart obeys.
Too well this Maxim has my conduct shewn,
Too well that Conduct to the World is known.

Oft have I wrote, and often to the Flame
Condemn'd this after-witness of my Shame;
Oft in my cooler recollected Thought,
Thy Beauties and my Fondness half forgot
(How short those Intervals of Reason's Aid!)
Thus to my self in Anguish have I said:
Thy vain Remonstrance foolish Maid! give o'er,
Who act the Wrong, can ne'er that Wrong deplore.

Then sanguine Hopes again delusive reign,
I form[4] thee melting, as I tell my Pain.
If not of Rock thy flinted[5] Heart was made
Nor Tygers nurs'd thee in the desart Shade,
Let me at least thy cold Compassion prove,
That slender sustenance to greedy Love!
Tho' no Return my warmer Wishes find
Be to the Wretch, tho' not the Mistriss kind,
Nor while I count my Melancholy State
Forget 'twas Love and thee that wrought my Fate.
Without Restraint, habituated to range
The Paths of Pleasure, can I bear the Change?
Doom'd from the World unwilling to retire

4. *form*: 'To frame in the mind, conceive (an idea, judgement, opinion, etc.). Formerly also, to imagine' (*OED*).

5. *flinted: OED* 2: 'Hard, cruel, unfeeling', still current in the 1720s though the latest example in *OED* is dated 1587; see e.g. Leonard Welsted, 'The Faultless Fair', in his *Epistles, Odes, &c. Written on Several Subjects. With a Translation of Longinus's Treatise on the Sublime* (London: for J. Walthoe and J. Peele, 1724), p. 184.

In bloom of Life, and warm with young desire,
In lieu of Roofs with regal Splendor gay,
Condemn'd in distant Wilds to drag the Day,
Where Beasts of Prey maintain their savage Court,
Or human Brutes (the worst of Brutes) resort:
Yes, yes, this Change I could unsighing see,
For none I mourn but what I found in thee;
There centers all my woes, thy Heart estrang'd,
I mourn my Lover, not my Fortune, chang'd.
Blest with thy Presence, I could all forget
Nor gilded Palaces in Huts regret.
But exil'd thence, superfluous is the rest,
Each place the same, my Hell is in my Breast;
To Pleasure dead, and living but to Pain,
My only Sense to suffer, and complain.

As all my Wrongs distressful I repeat,
Say, can thy Pulse with equal Cadence beat?
Canst thou know Peace? is Conscience mute within?
That upright Delegate for secret Sin!
Is Nature so extinguish'd in thy Heart
That not one spark remains to take my part?
Not one repentant Throb, one gratefull Sigh?
Thy Breast unruffled, and unwet thy Eye!
Thou cool Betrayer! temperate in Ill!
Thou nor Remorse, nor Thought humane canst feel;
Nature has form'd thee of the rougher kind,
And Education more debas'd thy Mind.
Born in an Age when Fraud and Guilt prevail,
When Justice sleeps, and Interest holds the Scale,
Thy loose Companions, a licentious Crew,
Most to each other, all to us untrue;
Whom Chance or Habit mix, but rarely Choice,
Not leagu'd in Freindship, but in social Vice,
Who indigent of Merit or of Shame,
Avow those Crimes which others blush to name;
By right or wrong disdaining to be mov'd,

Unprincipl'd, unloving, and unlov'd.[6]
The Fair who trust their prostituted Vows,
If not their Falsehood, still their Boasts expose,
Nor knows the wisest to elude the Harm,
Ev'n she whose Prudence spurns the tinsel Charm,
They know to slander, tho' they fail to warm.
They make her languish with fictitious Flame,
Affix some specious Scandal to her Name,
And, baffl'd by her Virtue, triumph o'er her Fame.
These are the Leaders of thy blinded Youth,
'Twas these Seducers laugh'd thee out of Truth,
Whose scurril Mirth all solemn Tyes prophane,
Or Friendship's Band, or Hymen's sacred Chain.[7]
Morality as Weakness they upbraid,
Nor even revere Religion's hallow'd Head;
Alike they spurn Divine and Human Laws,
And treat the Honest,[8] like the Christian Cause.
Curse on that Tongue whose vile pernicious Art
Delights the Ear but to corrupt the Heart;
That takes advantage of the chearfull Hour,
When weaken'd Virtue bends to Nature's Power;
And would the Goddess in thy Soul deface,
To substitute Dishonor in her Place.

With such you lose the Day, in false Delight,
In lewd Debauch you revel out the Night
(Oh fatal Commerce to Monimia's Peace);
Their Arguments convince, because they please.
While Sophistry for Reason you admit,
And wander dazzl'd by the Glare of Wit;
Wit that on Ill a specious Lustre throws,

6. *Unprincipl'd, unloving, and unlov'd*: compare Milton, *Paradise Lost*, 'Unrespited, unpitied, unrepriev'd' (II. 185), and 'Unshaken, unseduc'd, unterrifi'd' (V. 896), cited by Roger Lonsdale (ed.), *The Poems of Gray, Collins and Goldsmith* (London: Longmans, 1969), glossing a line in Goldsmith's *The Deserted Village* (p. 687).

7. *Hymen's sacred Chain*: marital obligation, Hymen being the god of marriage in Greek and Roman mythology.

8. *Honest*: 'Of things, conditions, actions, etc ... b. Free from disgrace or reproach; respectable, decent, seemly, befitting, becoming' (*OED*).

And in false Colours every Object shows;
That gilds the Wrong, depreciating the Right,
And hurts the Judgment, while it feasts the Sight.
So in a Prism[9] to the cheated Eye
Each pictur'd Trifle takes the Rainbow Dye;
With borrow'd Charms the shining Prospect glows,
And Truth revers'd the faithless Mirror shows;
Inverted Scenes in bright Confusion lye,
The Lawns impending o'er the nether Sky;
No Just, no real Images we meet,
But all the gaudy Vision is Deceit.

Oft I revolve in this distracted Mind
Each Word, each Look, that spoke my Charmer kind.
But oh how dear their Memory I pay,
What Pleasures past can present Cares allay?
Of all I love for ever dispossess'd,
Oh what avails to think I once was blest?
Hard Disposition of unequal Fate,
Mix'd are our Joys, and transient is their Date;
Nor can Reflection bring their Taste again,
Yet gives an after-sting to ev'ry Pain.
Thy fatal Letters (Oh immoral Youth!)
Those perjur'd Pledges of fictitious Truth,
Dear as they were, no second Joy afford,
My Cred'lous Heart once leap'd at ev'ry Word;
My glowing Bosom throb'd with thick-heav'd Sighs,
And floods of Rapture rush'd into my Eyes;
When now repeated (for thy Theft was vain,
Each treasur'd Syllable my Thoughts retain),[10]
Far other Passions rule, and different Care,
My Fears are Greif, my Transports are Dispair.

Why dost thou mock all Tyes of constant Love?
But half his Joys the faithless ever prove;

9. *Prism*: the simile is from discoveries by Sir Isaac Newton published in his *Opticks* (1704), though first developed in his student days at Cambridge in the mid-1660s (*ODNB*).

10. *thy Theft . . . my Thoughts retain*: this telling detail suggests that Hervey's account is based on close personal information, perhaps via his wife or one of her friends.

They only taste the Pleasures they receive,
When sure the noblest is in those we give.
Acceptance is the Heaven which Mortals know,
But 'tis the Joy of Angels to bestow.
Oh emulate (my Love) that Task Divine,
Be thou that Angel, and that Heaven be mine;
Yet, yet, relent, yet intercept my Fate –
Alas, I rave, and sue for new Deceit:
As soon the Dead shall from the Grave return,
As Love extinguish'd with new Ardour burn;
Oh that I dar'd to act a Roman Part!
And stab thy Image in this faithfull Heart,
Where rivetted to Life secure you reign
(A cruel Inmate) Author of my Pain;
But Coward like, irresolute I wait
Times tardy Aid, nor dare to rush on Fate;
Perhaps may linger on Life's latest Stage,
Survive thy Cruelties, and fall by Age.
No – Grief shall swell my Sails, and speed me o'er
(Dispair my Pilot) to that long'd for shore,
Where I can trust, and thou betray no more.

Might I but once again behold thy Charms,
Might I but breathe my last in those dear Arms,
On that lov'd Face but fix my closing Eye,
Permitted where I might not live to dye;
My soften'd Fate I would accuse no more,
But Fate has no such Happyness in store.
'Tis past, 'tis done; what gleam of Hope behind?
When I can ne'er be false, nor thou be kind;
Why then this Care? 'tis weak, 'tis vain, farewell!
At that last Word, what Agonies I feel!
I can no more – the Soul and Body part
With lighter Pains – when will they break my Heart?
I faint, I dye, remember I was true,
'Tis all I ask – Eternally Adieu.

# 2 Flora to Pompey

***Main source.*** Lilly Library, Delany MS [1], item 17 (not foliated or paginated), because it is closest to the date of composition and because Mrs Delany (then Mrs Pendarves) probably received it from Hervey's younger brother, Henry. For Mrs Delany's acquaintance with Henry Hervey, see p. 14 above.

***Complementary manuscript source.*** Portland Papers (University of Nottingham), Pw V 118/4 (p. 134 rev.). This consists only of the first ten lines of the poem among a series of other poems and a menu headed 'Easter Dinner 1732', written on the reverse pages of an account book for Viscount William Vane covering the period from 17 May 1722 to 2 May 1724. Two of the other items are complete copies of Hervey's 'Arisbe to Marius Junior' and 'Verses Address'd to the Imitator of the First Satire of the Second Book of Horace', the satire on Pope that he co-authored with Lady Mary Wortley Montagu. One of the other two, 'Amintor to Silvia from Holland' is by a writer as yet unidentified; the other, 'On a report that the D[uche]ss: Marlborough wou'd give 500 lb &c', is by Allan Ramsay (*The Works of Allan Ramsay*, ed. by Alexander Kinghorn and Alexander Law, 6 vols. Edinburgh and London: William Blackwood & Sons, [1945–74]), IV, 260), and was printed in *The Old Whig*, 16 September 1736, p. 2. The fragment from 'Flora to Pompey' fills the remainder of the page on which 'Amintor to Silvia from Holland' ends. Although it is not clear why the transcript is incomplete, it seems significant that the next page (p. 132 rev.) holds the menu 'Easter 1732', the reverse of which is blank, and that the following page has been cut out (and so was never numbered). This, and the fact that 'Verses Address'd to the Imitator' begins at the top of the next page (p. 131 rev.), suggests that space had been left for the rest of the copy until the empty leaf was removed.

***Complementary print sources.*** 'Flora to Pompey', in *The Museum*, 1 (1746), 92–5 (no. 3, 26 April); Dodsley, *Collection* (1755), IV, 90–4, collated with 1782 edition (IV, 94–8).

***Attribution.*** Dodsley 1755; all subsequent attributions seem to stem from this. Neither the Delany manuscript nor the Nottingham fragment is attributed.

***Context and date.*** As indicated in the headnote for 'Epistles in the Manner of Ovid' above, the poem almost certainly dates from the 1720s, at a time when Hervey seems to have been developing his verse-writing skills in part by adapting French originals. His lengthy but unfinished verse adaptation 'The Adventures of Telemachus in the Island of Ogygia' (Poem 65), based on the first three books of François de Salignac de La Mothe-Fénelon's *Les Aventures de Télémaque*, was probably also begun during this period. Like the next poem in the series, 'Arisbe to

Marius Junior', 'Flora to Pompey' adapts a heroic epistle by Bernard le Bovier de Fontenelle first published in 1688 with three companion pieces in his *Poésies Pastorales* (London: Paul & Isaak Vaillant, 1707; Paris: M[ichel] Guérout, 1688). Fontenelle wrote the four poems early in his career. They are prefaced by a note indicating that they are experiments in imitation of Ovid's *Heroides*, though with their subjects taken from history rather than legend ('Avertissement', p. 126). In the case of 'Flora à Pompée', Fontenelle's source, which he rendered suitably more dramatic, was Plutarch's 'Life of Pompey' (Loeb, V, 120–2). Making much freer with 'Flora à Pompée' than with 'Arisbe au jeune Marius', Hervey added further enhancements, particularly in developing the role of Pompey's friend Geminius. This may account for the fact that neither the manuscript nor the print sources for his poem acknowledge a debt to Fontenelle, as they do for 'Arisbe to Marius Junior'. In producing Ovidian imitations, Fontenelle honours the spirit of the originals, for, as Peter E. Knox puts it, the 'distinguishing feature of O[vid]'s *Heroides* is their inspiration from works of literature' (*Heroides: Select Epistles* (Cambridge: Cambridge University Press, 1995), p. 18). As 'Flora to Pompey' is modelled specifically on Fontenelle's poem as well as generally on Ovid's heroic epistles, Hervey adds a further intertextual layer. It is difficult to deny that his versions of Fontenelle work better than the originals. Part of the reason for this is that the heroic couplet that he adopted as the conventional equivalent in English of the Latin elegiac distich – a couplet in dactylic metre consisting of a hexameter followed by a pentameter – is much better suited for epistolary verse than Fontenelle's cross-rhymed quatrains. Although Fontenelle shows skill in varying the form of the quatrain for each of his four poems, and in some of his choices of rhyme-words, the stanza-breaks keep interrupting continuity. As a result, his experiments appear little more than academic exercises. Hervey's adaptations, especially 'Flora to Pompey' which expands the seventy-six lines of the original to 108, are much livelier. Examples are cited in the notes where his language and versification surpass Fontenelle's in expressing the passionate emotions that are fundamental to the genre. The literal translations accompanying the French are mine.

***Textual commentary.*** A few substantive variants have been adopted from one or more of the complementary sources. These comprise the title, which is absent from the two manuscripts; the insertion of '*Geminius*' where it is clearly required in the prefatory outline; the insertion of a word in line 99 which is otherwise a metrical stress short; and two changes of pronoun where the sense seems to require them. In a few cases, and as indicated in the historical collation, the punctuation in the text from Dodsley's *Museum*, which makes for greater readability than that of either manuscript, has been substituted where there are no consequences for the sense, but the paragraphing of the Delany manuscript has been preserved. The text of the first printing in Dodsley's *Collection* in 1755 differs only in accidentals from that of the final edition of 1782.

# Flora to Pompey

Pompey, *when he was very young, fell in Love with* Flora, *a* Roman *Curtizan, who was so very Beautifull that the* Romans *had her Painted to adorn the Temple of* Castor *and* Pollux. Geminius (Pompey's *Friend) afterwards fell in Love with her too; but she, prepossess'd in Favour of* Pompey, *would not listen to* Geminius. *Pompey, in compassion to his Friend, yeilded up his Mistress; which* Flora *took so much to Heart, that she fell dangerously Ill upon it; and in that Sickness is suppos'd to have written the following Letter to* Pompey.[1]

E'er Death these closing Eyes for ever shade,
That Death thy Cruelties have welcome made,
Receive, thou yet lov'd Man, this one Adieu!
This last farewell to Happiness and you;
My Bed floats with my Tears,[2] my Trembling Hand
Can scarce the letters form, or Pen command;
The dancing Paper swims before my Sight,
And scarce my self can read the words I write;
Think you behold me in this lost estate,[3]
And think your self the Author of my Fate:
How vast the change! your *Flora*'s now become
The gen'ral Pity, not the boast of Rome!
This Form, a Pattern to the Sculptor's Art,
This Face, the Idol once of *Pompey*'s Heart,
(Whose Pictur'd Beauties Rome thought fit to Place
The Sacred Temples of her Gods to Grace)
Are charming now no more: the Bloom is fled,
The Lillies languid, and the Roses Dead:[4]

1. The prose introduction translates the French fairly closely but expands it in a few places.

2. *My Bed . . . Tears*: compare Fontenelle, 'Je t'écris dans un lit tout baigné de mes pleurs' (*Poésies*, p. 130; 'I write to you in a bed completely bathed with my tears').

3. *estate*: 'State or condition in general, whether material or moral, bodily or mental' (*OED*).

4. *The Lillies . . . Dead*: a characteristic example of an effective line that has no precedent in Fontenelle.

Soon shall some Hand the Glorious Peice deface,
Where Graecian Pencills[5] tell what *Flora* was:
No longer my Resemblance they impart,
They lost their likeness, when I lost my Heart.

Oh that those Hours could take their turn again
When *Pompey*, lab'ring with a jealous Pain,
His *Flora* thus bespoke:[6] "Say my Dear Love,
"Shall all those Rivals unsuccessful prove?
"In vain for ever shall the Roman Youth,
"Envy my Happiness, and tempt thy truth?
"Shall neither Tears, nor Pray'rs thy Pity move?
"Ah! give not Pity, 'tis akin to Love.
"Would *Flora* were not Fair to such excess,
"That I might Fear, tho' not adore her, less!"

Fool that I was, I sought to cure that Grief,
Nor knew Indiff'rence follow'd the relief;
Experience taught the cruel Truth too late,
I never dreaded, 'till I found my Fate;
'Twas mine to ask, if *Pompey's* Self could hear
Unmov'd, his Rival's unsuccessfull Pray'r?
To make thee swear, He'd not thy Pity move,
Alas! such Pity is no Kin to Love!
'Twas thou thy self (ungrateful as thou art!)
Bade me unbend the rigour of my Heart,
You chid my Faith, reproach'd my being true
(Unnatu'ral thought) and labour'd to subdue
The constancy my Soul maintain'd for you;
To other Arms your Mistress you condemn'd
Too cool a Lover and too warm a Friend.[7]
How couldst thou thus my lavish Heart abuse,
To ask the only thing it could refuse?
Nor yet upbraid me, *Pompey*, what I say,
For 'tis my Merit that I can't obey.

5. *Graecian Pencills*: i.e. Greek painters.
6. *bespoke*: past tense of 'bespeak', 'To speak to (a person), to address' (*OED*).
7. *Too cool a Lover and too warm a Friend*: another effective addition, like line 18 in its use of the simple device, encouraged by the heroic couplet, of syntactical parallelism.

Yet this alledg'd against me as a fault,
Thy Rage fomented and my ruin wrought;
Just Gods! what tye, what conduct can prevail,
O'er fickle man, when truth like mine can fail!
Urge not to gloss thy crime the name of Friend,
We know how far those Sacred Laws extend;
Since other Heroes have not blush'd to prove,
How weak all Passions when oppos'd to Love;
Nor boast the Virtuous conflict in thy Heart,
When gen'rous Pity took *Geminius'* part,
'Tis all Heroick Fraud, and Roman Art.
Such flights of Honour might amuse the Crowd,
But by a Mistress, ne'er can be allow'd.
Keep for the Senate, and the grave debate,
That infamous Hypocrisy of State,
There words are Virtue, and your trade deceit.
No Riddle is thy change, nor hard t'explain,
*Flora* was fond,[8] and *Pompey* was a Man.
No longer then a specious Tale pretend,
Nor plead fictitious Merit to thy Friend:
By Nature false, you follow'd her decree,
Nor Gen'rous art to him, but base to me.[9]
You say you Melted at *Geminius'* Tears,
You say you felt his Agonizing Cares;
Gross Artifice! that this from him could move,
And not from *Flora*, whom you say you Love!
You could not bear to hear a Rival Sigh,
Yet bear, unmov'd, to see your Mistress Dye.
Inhumane Hypocrite! not thus can He
My wrongs, and my distress obdurate see!
He, who receiv'd, condemns the Gift you made,
And joins with me the giver to upbraid,
Forgetting He's oblig'd, and mourning I'm betray'd.

8. *fond*: 'Infatuated, foolish, silly. Since 16th c. the sense in literary use has been chiefly: Foolishly credulous or sanguine' (*OED*).

9. *By Nature . . . to me*: Compare Fontenelle: 'Tu n'es au fond qu'un Amant infidelle, | Et non un amy généreux' (*Poésies*, p. 132; 'You are fundamentally an unfaithful lover, and not a generous friend'). Hervey's lines are much more forceful.

He loves too well, that cruel gift to use,
Which *Pompey* lov'd too little to refuse;
Fain would he call my Vagrant Lord again,
But I the kind Ambassador restrain;
I scorn to let Another take my Part,
And to my Self will owe, or lose thy Heart.

Can nothing e'er rekindle Love in thee?
Can nothing e'er extinguish it in me?
That I could tear thee from this injur'd Breast!
And where you gave my Person give the rest!
At once to grant, and Punish thy request![10]
That I could place thy worthy Rival there!
No second insult need my Fondness Fear;
He views not *Flora* with her *Pompey's* Eyes,
He loves like me, he Doats, Despairs, and Dyes.
Come to my Arms thou Dear Deserving Youth,
Thou Prodigy of Man, thou Man with Truth![11]
For him,[12] I will redouble every Care,
To please, for him, these fading Charms repair,
To Crown thy Vows, and Sharpen thy despair.[13]

10. *Can nothing ... thy request*: Compare Fontenelle: 'Faut-il que de mon coeur, helas! rien ne t'efface? | Quel charme malheureux a sçû me prévenir? | Que je voudrois l'adorer en ta place | Pour te plaire, ou pour te punir?' (*Poésies*, p. 132; 'Must it be, alas, that nothing can efface you from my heart? What unhappy spell knew how to prevent me? How I wished to adore him in your place in order to please you or punish you'). Hervey's version dramatically begins a new verse paragraph, adds the question whether Pompey's love can be revived, and expands and sharpens her wish that she could love his friend as he had asked. The syllepsis 'At once to grant, and Punish thy request', given extra emphasis because it ends a triplet, is especially telling. The Delany manuscript has 'my request', clearly incorrect because it was Pompey who made the request, and because the French has *te punir* (punish you).

11. *Come to ... with Truth*: The fact that these two lines address Geminius may account for the apparent confusion in some editions of some of the pronouns that follow (see notes below). Because Hervey here expands Fontenelle's text, the latter provides no basis for comparison.

12. *him*: Delany has 'thee', here and in the line following; this cannot be correct because Flora refers to her wish to please Geminius, not Pompey.

13. *thy despair*: Delany has 'his despair', but this cannot be correct; it is Pompey, whom Flora is addressing, whose vows will be crowned if she gives herself to Geminius, and who she hopes will despair as a result. The laudatory terms in which she refers to Geminius exclude the possibility that she might wish him to despair.

Oh! 'tis illusion all, and Idle Rage![14]
No second Passion can this Heart engage;
And shortly *Pompey* shall thy *Flora* prove
Death may dissolve, but nothing change her Love.

14. *Rage*: 'Madness, insanity; a fit or attack of madness' (*OED*).

# 3 Arisbe to Marius Junior

***Main source.*** Portland Papers (University of Nottingham), Pw V 118/2 (pp. 138–41 rev.), chosen because it is almost certainly the earlier of the two manuscripts to have been transcribed. For details about the contents of Pw V 118, see the headnote for 'Flora to Pompey' above. 'Arisbe to Marius Junior' is the first of the poems to have been added to the volume when it had been reversed, after the accounts for 1722–4 were signed off as correct in June 1724. It is followed by 'Amintor to Silvia from Holland'.

***Complementary manuscript source.*** Bodley MS Montagu e. 13, ff. 105r–109r.

***Complementary print sources.*** 'Arisbe to Marius junior', in *The Museum; Or, the Literary and Historical Register*, 3 vols. (London: for R. Dodsley, 1746–7), II (1746), 14–19 (no. 14, 27 September); Dodsley, *Collection* (1755), IV, 95–101, collated with 1782 edition (IV, 99–108).

***Attribution.*** Dodsley 1755; all subsequent attributions seem to stem from this. Neither the Nottingham nor the Bodleian manuscript is attributed.

***Context and date.*** See the section on 'Epistles in the Manner of Ovid' in the headnote above, and 'Context and date' for Poem 2, 'Flora to Pompey'. 'Arisbe to Marius Junior' is based on a heroic epistle by Fontenelle first published in 1688 (*Poésies*, pp. 133–7), the source of which is in Plutarch's 'The Life of Marius' (Loeb, IX, 577–9). The name 'Arisbe', however, appears to be Fontenelle's addition, for Plutarch refers to her only as 'one of the concubines of the king' (p. 577). 'Arisbe to Marius Junior' has much in common with 'Flora to Pompey': it derives from Fontenelle (and Plutarch); it almost certainly dates from the 1720s; and it converts Fontenelle's cross-rhymed quatrains to heroic couplets. The main difference is that, while 'Arisbe to Marius Junior' is also a free imitation of the original rather than a translation, it does not depart from the French to nearly the same extent. Indeed, it has the same number of lines as the original until line 104, after which Hervey treats the French with greater freedom, not only by introducing new content but by compression, so that his version ends up eight lines shorter. As with 'Flora to Pompey', his adaptation is more vigorous and dramatic, partly as a result of his skill with the heroic couplet. Examples of how he improved on Fontenelle are given in the notes, where literal translations from the French are mine.

***Textual commentary.*** It has been necessary to adopt only five substantive variants from one or more of the complementary sources, and only a small number of accidental variants; these are indicated in the List of

Emendations. However, as the Welbeck manuscript lacks paragraph divisions, those from the Bodley manuscript have been provided. The single main difference between the manuscript and the printed sources is that, while the former set the poem out continuously, as is appropriate for its verse form of heroic couplets, the latter present it in numbered quatrains. Presumably this was a misguided attempt to match it to the form of Fontenelle's original. The poem is restored to continuous couplets in some later printings, such as that in *Bell's Classical Arrangement of Fugitive Poetry*, 16 vols. (London: John Bell, 1789–94), VII, 63–8. The text of the first printing in Dodsley's *Collection* in 1755 has two minor substantive variants, both noted, from that of the final edition of 1782, but otherwise differs only in accidentals.

## Arisbe to Marius Junior. From Fontenelle

*When Marius*[1] *was Expell'd from Rome by Sylla's*[2] *Faction, and retir'd into Africa, his Son (who accompany'd him) fell into the Hands of Hiempsal, King of Numidia, who kept him Prisoner. One of the Mistresses of that King fell in Love with Marius junior, and was so generous to contrive and give him his Liberty, tho' by that means She sacrificed her Love for ever. 'Twas after he had rejoin'd his Father, that She writ him the following Letter.*

Of all I valued, all I lov'd bereft,[3]
Say, has my Heart this little Comfort left?
That you the Mem'ry of my Truth retain,
And think with grateful Pity on my Pain?
Tho' but with Life my Sorrows can have End,
(For Death alone can join me to my Friend)

1. *Marius*: Gaius Marius (157–86 BCE), Roman military leader and statesman.

2. *Sylla*: Lucius Cornelius Sulla Felix (c. 138–78 BCE), usually known as Sulla, was a subordinate who became both a military and a political rival. According to Plutarch, Marius and his son fled Rome for North Africa after one of Sulla's victories in the civil conflicts of the period.

3. *Of all I valued, all I lov'd bereft*: Hervey's inversion of word order makes for a more arresting start than the French, which begins: 'Depuis que je me suis privée | De tout ce qui flattoit mes plus tendres desirs' ('Since I was deprived of you, of everything that delighted my most tender desires').

Yet think not I repent I set you free,[4]
I mourn your absence, not your Liberty.
Before my Marius left Numidia's Coast,
Each Day I saw him; scarce an hour was lost;
Now Months and Years must pass, nay Life shall prove
But one long Absence from the Man I Love.
Painful Reflection! Poyson to my Mind!
Was it but mortal too, it would be kind:
But mad with Grief I search the Palace round,
And in that Madness dream you're to be found.
Wouldst thou believe it? to those walls I fly
Where thou wert Captive held; there frantick Cry,
These Fetters sure my Vagrant's flight restrain'd;
Alas! these Fetters I my self unchain'd.

The live-long Day I mourn, I loath the light,
And wait impatient each returning Night:
What tho' the horrid Gloom augment my Grief?
'Tis grateful[5] still, for I wish no relief.
That Coz'ner Hope intrudes not on my Woe;
One only Interval my Sorrows know;
When Dreams, the kind reversers of my Pain,
Bring back my Charming Fugitive again.
Yet there's a Grief surpassing all the rest;
A jealous Demon whispers in my Breast
Marius was false: for Liberty alone,
The Show of Love the Hypocrite put on.
Then I reflect (ah! would I could forget!)
How much your Thoughts on War and Rome were set.
How little Passion did that Conduct prove!
Too Strong thy Reason, but too weak thy Love.
Thy Sword 'tis true a Father's Cause Demands,
But 'twas a Mistress gave it to thy Hands,

4. *Yet think not I repent I set you free, | I mourn your absence, not your Liberty*: 'Je ne me repens pas d'avoir brisé vos chaînes, | Je me plains de ne vous voir plus', *Fontenelle* ('I do not repent having broken your chains, I grieve for not seeing you any more').

5. *grateful*: 'Pleasing to the mind or the senses, agreeable, acceptable, welcome' (*OED*).

To Love and Duty just give each their Part
His be thy Arm, and mine be all thy Heart.

But what avail these Thoughts? fond Wretch! give o'er;
Marius, or false or true, is thine no more:
Since Fate has cast the Lot, and we must part,
Why should I wish to think I had his Heart?
Yes: let me cherish that remembrance still;
That Thought alone shall soften ev'ry Ill;
To tell my Soul, his Love, his Truth was such,
All was his due, nor have I done too much.
Deceitful Comfort! let me not perswade
My Credulous Heart its Fondness was repay'd:
It makes my Soul with double anguish mourn
Those Joys which never, never must return.
Perhaps ev'n you what most I wish oppose,
And in the Roman all the Lover lose:
I'm a Numidian, and your Soul Disdains
To bear th'inglorious Weight of Foreign Chains.
Can any Climate then so barb'rous prove,
To Stand Excluded from the Laws of Love?
His Empire's universal, unconfin'd,
His Proxy Beauty, and his Slaves Mankind.
Nor am I a Numidian but by Name,
For I can Int'rest[6] for my Love Disclaim:
My Virtue Shows what 'twas the Gods design'd,
By chance on Africk Clay, they stamp'd a Roman Mind.[7]
Not all the Heroes which your Rome can boast,
So much for Fame, as I for you have lost:
Yourself I lost: oh! grateful then Confess,
My Tryal greater, tho' my Glory less.

6. *Int'rest*: 'A business, cause, or principle, in which a number of persons are interested; the party interested in such a business or principle; a party having a common interest; a religious or political party, business connection, etc.' (*OED*); the meaning here is patriotic loyalty.

7. *My Virtue Shows what 'twas the Gods design'd, | By chance on Africk Clay, they stamp'd a Roman Mind*: 'La naissance n'est rien où la vertu decide, | Je suis Romaine par le cœur', *Fontenelle* ('Birth is nothing where virtue decides, I am Roman in my heart'). Hervey emphasises the line further with an extra foot.

Yes, partial Gods! Inflictors of my Care!
Be witness what I felt, what Grief, what Fear!
When full of Stifled Woes the Night He fled,
No sighs I dar'd to breathe, no Tear to shed.
Whilst men of Faith approv'd, a chosen Crew,
Firm to their Trust, and to their Mistress true,
With Care too punctual my Commands obey,
And in one Freight my Life and Thee convey.

The harder Task was mine; condemn'd to bear
With brow Serene, my Agonizing Care;
To mix in idle Talk, to force a Smile,
A King and jealous Lover to beguile.
Think in that dreadful Interval of Fate,
All I held dear, thy Safety in Debate,
Think what I suffer'd, whilst my Heart afraid,
Suggests a thousand Times that all's betray'd.
A thousand Times revolving in my Mind
The doubtful Chance, Oh! Love! said I, be kind:
Propitious to my Scheme, thy vot'ry aid,
And be my Fondness by Success repay'd.
Now bolder grown, with Sanguine Hopes elate,
My Fancy represents thy Smiling Fate.
The Guards deceiv'd, and ev'ry Danger o'er,
The winds already waft him from the Shore.

These pleasing Images anew impart
Life to my Eyes, and Gladness to my Heart;
Dispel the Gloomy Fears that cloud my Face,
And Charm the little Flutterer[8] to Peace.
But now the King, or tasteless to my Charms,
Or weary of an Absent Mistress' Arms,
His own Apartment seeks, and grateful Rest,
That courted stranger to the careful Breast.
Whilst I, by Hopes and Fears alternate sway'd,
Impatient ask the Slaves if I'm obey'd.
'Tis done they cry'd, and struck me with Despair;

8. *Flutterer*: i.e. her heart.

For what I long'd to know, I dy'd to hear.[9]
Fantastick Turn of a distracted Mind;
I blam'd the Gods for having been too kind;
Curs'd the Success they Granted to my Vows,
And this Assistant Hand that fill'd my Woes.

Such was my Frenzy in that Hour of Care,
And such th'Injustice of my blind Despair,
That even those ungrateful I upbraid,
Whose fatal Diligence my Will obey'd.
Scarce Marius did thyself escape my Rage;
(Most lov'd of Men!) when Fears of black presage
Describe thy Heart so fond of Liberty,
It never gave one parting Throb for Me.
At every Step you should have turn'd your Eye,
Dropt a regretful Tear, and heav'd a Sigh;
The Nature of the Grace[10] I show'd was such,
You not deserv'd it if it pleas'd too much.
A Lover would have linger'd as he fled,
And oft in Anguish to himself have said,
Farewell for ever! Ah! yet more he'd done,
A Lover never would have fled alone.
To force me from a hated Rival's Bed,
Why comes not Marius at an Army's Head?
Oh! did thy Heart but wish to see that Day,
'Twould all my past and future Woes o'er pay.
But vain are all those Hopes: preserve thy Breast
From Falsehood only, I forgive the Rest:
Too happy, if no envy'd Rival boast
Those Joys Arisbe for her Marius lost.

9. *'Tis done they cry'd, and struck me with Despair; | For what I long'd to know, I dy'd to hear*: 'Je brûlois de l'apprendre, & quand je l'eus recue | J'en pensay mourir de douleur', *Fontenelle* ('I burned to know, and when I had received the news I thought I would die of grief').

10. *Grace*: 'Favour, favourable or benignant regard or its manifestation' (*OED*).

# 4 Roxana to Usbeck

***Main source.*** 'Roxana to Philocles' in Dodsley, *Collection* (1755), IV, 102–6, because no manuscript has come to light and because the only text printed earlier, that in Dodsley's periodical *The Museum*, is incomplete.

***Complementary sources.*** 'Roxana to Philocles', in *The Museum*, III, 378–80 (no. 36, 1 August 1747), repr. in *The Chester Miscellany*, 1 September 1747 (*The Chester Miscellany . . . From January 1745, to May 1750* (Chester: by and for Eliz. Adams, 1750), pp. 244–6); Dodsley, *Collection* (1758), IV, 98–102, collated with 1782 edition (IV, 106–10).

***Attribution.*** Dodsley 1755; all subsequent attributions seem to stem from this. However, it is relevant that Hervey quoted lines 20–1 in a letter to Stephen Fox dated 27 September 1731 (SRO 941/47/4, p. 223).

***Context and date.*** See the headnote for 'Epistles in the Manner of Ovid' above. Although, like 'Flora to Pompey' and 'Arisbe to Marius Junior', the two previous poems in the series, 'Roxana to Usbeck' is a free imitation of a French original written in the form of a letter, its model was not a poem. As the subtitle indicates, it comes from Montesquieu's *Lettres Persanes*, first published in 1721. Montesquieu's book is a kind of philosophical novel based on the experiences of two Persians, Usbeck and Rica, who travel to Europe and enter French society. Its epistolary form enables a wide range of different points of view to be exchanged, especially on topics both in European and in Persian culture, but it also represents some of what takes place in the travellers' absence. The letter Hervey chose to rework, numbered 150 in the first edition, is one of those written from Persia. It is an epistolary bombshell that ends the book in which Roxana, Usbeck's favourite wife, confronts him with the hatred, defiance and desire for freedom that have led her to take a lover in his absence. The fact that Hervey quoted a couplet from the poem in a letter of September 1731 indicates that it must have been written at least in part by that date, and may imply an assumption on his behalf that Fox was already familiar with it. Since there is evidence that two of the epistles in the series were written in the 1720s, it is more than reasonable to suppose that 'Roxana to Usbeck' comes from the same period or soon after. As Robert Shackleton explains, Montesquieu was in England from November 1729 to May 1731 (*Montesquieu: A Critical Biography* (London: Oxford University Press, 1961), pp. 117–46). Hervey met him during his stay and they became friendly, though his wife got to know him better (Shackleton, pp. 120, 126, 142, 293). It is tempting to speculate that he may have written the poem during that period or, if he had already written it, that he showed it to him then. While not departing from the sense of the original,

Hervey brings out its implications forcefully. In the standard modern edition (*Lettres Persanes*, in *Montesquieu: Œuvres complètes*, ed. by Roger Caillois, 2 vols. (Paris: Gallimard, 1949), I, 372–3), Roxane has 312 words. Hervey expands these to 847, whereas Ozell's translation of 1722 has 353 (*Persian Letters. Translated by Mr. Ozell*, 2 vols. (London: for J. Tonson, 1722), II, 307–9), and the most recent has 335 (Montesquieu, *Persian Letters*, trans. Margaret Mauldon (Oxford: Oxford University Press, 2008), pp. 212–13). The extent of the freedom he allowed himself is consistent with the likelihood that the poem was the last of the series to be written. Some examples of how he expanded the French are provided in the notes.

***Textual commentary.*** The earliest complete printed source, Dodsley 1755, provides the basis for the text, on the ground that the later ones introduce, without any apparent authority, variants in the form of what seem to be either printer's errors or editorial changes. Had it been complete, the text in the 1747 *Museum* would have been adopted instead. Because the 1755 text repeats the error 'Philocles' for 'Usbeck' in the title of the *Museum* text, and because there are few substantive differences between them, it is likely that it was based on the same or a similar manuscript. The omission of lines 13–54 from the latter is, however, puzzling. As forty-two lines could conceivably make up a leaf written on both sides, one possible explanation is that such a leaf was omitted from the copy used by *The Museum*. This would imply that the preceding page, which would have contained the title, summary and first twelve lines, would have been a verso. If this was so, the high cost of paper at the period would make it more than likely that the recto would have contained other material, so suggesting that it was part of a larger manuscript. Another possible explanation is that the forty-two lines were, in effect, censored. The section contains the poem's most explicit celebration of unconstrained sexuality and free-thinking when Roxana refers to joys that are 'so refin'd, so exquisitely great, | That their excess compensated their date' (16–17), and rejects 'idle tales, which only fools believe' (37). Although her reference to 'dervises' (40) is a reminder that she is a Muslim, not a Christian, her protests against 'superstition' (38), and, in the same section, against the tyranny of marriage, could have been read as applying equally to English as to Persian culture. They would also have seemed the more shocking to many contemporaries as words attributed to a woman. The poem's outspokenness on such matters may, too, help explain why no manuscript copies appear to have survived, in contrast to the existence of manuscripts of other poems in the same series. As a result, there are few textual variants, and the 1755 text has been followed, except for a few changes in punctuation where required by the syntax; these are indicated in the List of Emendations.

## Roxana to Usbeck. From *Les Lettres Persannes*

Roxana, *one of* Usbeck's *wives, was found (whilst he was in* Europe) *in bed with her lover, whom she had privately let into the seraglio. The guardian eunuch, who discovered them, had the man murdered on the spot, and her close guarded till he received instructions from his master how to dispose of her. During that interval she swallowed poyson, and is supposed to write the following letter whilst she is dying.*

Think not I write my innocence to prove,
To sue for pity, or awake thy love:
No mean defence expect, or abject pray'rs;
Thou know'st no mercy, and I know no tears:
I laugh at all thy vengeance has decreed,
Avow the fact, and glory in the deed.[1]

Yes, tyrant! I deceiv'd thy spies and thee;
Pleas'd in oppression, and in bondage free:
The rigid agents of thy cruel laws
By gold I won to aid my juster cause:
With dextrous skill eluded all thy care,
And acted more than jealousy could fear:
To wanton bow'rs this prison-house I turn'd,
And bless'd that absence which you thought I mourn'd.
But short those joys allow'd by niggard Fate,
Yet so refin'd, so exquisitely great,
That their excess compensated their date.

I die: already in each burning vein
I feel the poys'nous draught, and bless the pain:

1. *Think not ... the deed*: there is no precedent for the poem's opening lines in the French, which begins 'Oui, je t'ai trompé' (*Lettres Persanes*, p. 372; 'Yes, I have deceived you' (*Persian Letters*, p. 212)), expanded by Hervey to 'Yes, tyrant! I deceiv'd thy spies and thee' (line 7).

For what is life unless its joys we prove?
And where is joy, depriv'd of what we love?[2]

Yet, ere I die, this justice I have paid
To my dear murder'd lover's injur'd shade:
Those sacrilegious instruments of power,
Who wrought that ruin these sad eyes deplore,
Already with their blood their crimes atone,
And for his life have sacrific'd their own.

Thee, tho' restraint and absence may defend
From my revenge, my curses still attend:
Despair like mine, barbarian! be thy part,
Remorse afflict, and sorrow sting thy heart.
Nor think this hate commencing in my breast,
Tho' prudence long its latent force suppress'd;
I knew those wrongs that I was forc'd to bear,
And curs'd those chains Injustice made me wear.[3]

For could'st thou hope Roxana to deceive
With idle tales, which only fools believe?
Poor abject souls in superstition bred,
In ign'rance train'd, by prejudice misled;
Whom hireling dervises[4] by proxy teach
From those whose false prerogative they preach.
Didst thou imagine me so weak of mind,
Because I murmur'd not, I ne'er repin'd,
But hugg'd my chain, and thought my jaylor kind?
That willingly those laws I e'er obey'd,
Which Pride invented, and Oppression made?
And whilst self-licens'd through the world you rove,
To quicken appetite by change in love;
Each passion sated, and each wish possess'd

2. *For what . . . we love?*: this is the couplet quoted by Hervey in his letter to Stephen Fox dated 27 September 1731 (SRO 941/47/4, p. 223). There is no precedent for it in the French.

3. *Thee, tho' . . . me wear*: There is no precedent for these eight lines in the French, which does not express hatred for Usbeck so directly.

4. *dervises*: 'dervis' and 'dervise' were the normal spellings at the period: 'A Muslim friar, who has taken vows of poverty and austere life' (*OED*).

That Lust can urge, or Fancy can suggest;
That I should mourn thy loss with fond regret,
Weep the misfortune, and the wrong forget?[5]

Could I believe that heav'n this beauty gave,
(Thy transient pleasure, and thy lasting slave;)
Indu'd with reason, only to fulfil
The harsh commands of thy capricious will?[6]
No, Usbeck, no, my soul disdain'd those laws;
And tho' I wanted pow'r t' assert my cause,
My right I knew; and still those pleasures sought,
Which Justice warranted, and Nature taught:
On Custom's senseless precepts I refin'd,
I weigh'd what heav'n, I knew what man design'd,
And form'd by her own rules my free-born mind.

Thus whilst this wretched body own'd thy pow'r,
Doom'd, unredress'd, its hardships to deplore;
My soul, subservient to herself alone,
And Reason independent on her throne,
Contemn'd thy dictates, and obey'd their own.[7]
Yet thus far to my conduct thanks are due,
At least I condescended to seem true;
Endeavour'd still my sentiments to hide,
Indulg'd thy vanity, and sooth'd thy pride.

5. *And whilst . . . forget?*: this attack on the double standard of sexual morality recalls those in *Monimia to Philocles* and in Lady Mary Wortley Montagu's 'Epistle from Mrs. Y[onge] to her Husband'.

6. *For could'st . . . capricious will?*: These twenty-one lines significantly expand the French, which reads: 'Comment as-tu pensé que je fusse assez crédule pour m'imaginer que je ne fusse dans le monde que pour adorer tes caprices? que, pendant que tu te permets tout, tu eusses le droit d'affliger tous mes désirs?' (*Lettres Persanes*, p. 372; 'How could you suppose me so credulous as to believe that the sole purpose for my existence was to adore your caprices? That while you permitted yourself everything, you had the right to frustrate every desire of mine?' (*Persian Letters*, p. 213)).

7. *No, Usbeck . . . obey'd their own*: compare Montesquieu's text, which these twelve lines expand significantly: 'Non! J'ai pu vivre dans la servitude, mais j'ai toujours été libre: j'ai reformé tes lois sur celles de la Nature, et mon esprit s'est toujours tenu dans l'indépendance' (*Lettres Persanes*, p. 372; 'No: I may have lived in servitude, but I have always been free: I have reformed your laws to conform to those of nature, and my spirit has always remained independent' (*Persian Letters*, p. 213)).

Tho' this submission to a tyrant paid,
Whom not my duty, but my fears obey'd,
If rightly weigh'd, would more deserve thy blame,
Who call it Virtue, but prophane her name:
For to the world I should have own'd that love,
Which all impartial judges must approve:
You urg'd a right to tyrannize my heart,
Which he solliciting, assail'd by art,
Whilst I, impatient of the name of slave,
To force refus'd, what I to merit gave.

Oft, as thy slaves this wretched body led
To the detested pleasures of thy bed;
In those soft moments, consecrate to joy,
Which extacy and transport should employ;
Clasp'd in your arms, you wonder'd still to find
So cold my kisses, so compos'd my mind:
But had thy cheated eyes discern'd aright,
You'd found aversion where you sought delight.
Not that my soul, incapable of love,
No charms could warm, no tenderness could move;
For him, whose love my ev'ry thought possess'd,
A fiercer passion fill'd this constant breast,
Than truth e'er felt, or falshood e'er profess'd.

This stile unusual to thy pride appears,
For truth's a stranger to the tyrant's ears;
But what have I to manage or to dread?
Nor threats alarm, nor insults hurt the dead:
No wrongs they feel, no miseries they find;
Cares are the legacies we leave behind:
In the calm grave no Usbecks we deplore,
No tyrant husband, no oppressive pow'r.
Alas! I faint – Death intercepts the rest:
The venom'd drug is busy in my breast:
Each nerve's unstrung: a mist obscures the day:
My senses, strength, and ev'n my hate decay:
Tho' rage a while the ebbing spirits stay'd,

'Tis past – they sink beneath the transient aid.
Take then, inhuman wretch! my last farewel; 110
Pain be thy portion here, hereafter, hell:
And when our prophet shall my fate decree,
Be any curse my punishment, but thee.[8]

8. *Take then ... but thee*: the last four lines constitute a further addition by Hervey. The French ends simply with the words 'je me meurs' ('I am dying') (*Lettres Persanes*, p. 373).

# EPISTLES TO STEPHEN FOX

# 5a To a Young Lady Who Desired to Know her Fortune
# 5b Horace Ode XI. Lib. I. Imitated. The Advice. To S—n F—x Esq.
# 5c An Imitation of the Eleventh Ode of the First Book of Horace

***Main sources.*** There are three versions of this poem, distinctive enough for each to be printed here.

5a. Lilly Library, Delany MS [1], item 36, chosen because it appears to be the earliest, and, like other items in the Delany manuscripts, is likely to have been passed on by Hervey's brother Henry.

5b. *Gentleman's Magazine*, 6, 351 (June 1736), chosen because this seems to be the earliest appearance of this version and it is closely similar to the text in *The Prompter*, printed in the same month. It may have reached the editor through Samuel Johnson, who, as Doris Almon Ponsonby explains, was a close friend of Hervey's brother Henry (*Call a Dog Hervey* (London: Hutchinson, 1949), pp. 110, 129, 137, 140). The fact that, unusually in the *Gentleman's*, the text contains two contractions, as noted below, may suggest close following of a manuscript, unless they resulted from the constraints of typesetting.

5c. Dodsley, *Collection* (1755), IV, 109. It is likely that the editor received a copy from Hervey's friend John Hoadly. In his edition of the *Collection*, Michael F. Suarez notes that Dodsley asked for more of Hervey's verse in a letter dated 26 October 1757 (I, 168). There are no complementary sources, manuscript or print, other than those cited for the associated Poems 5a and 5b, but there are many subsequent reprints of this version, including in the final, 1782, edition of Dodsley's *Collection*.

***Complementary manuscript sources.*** 5a. BL Add. MS 32463, f. 121r; Brotherton Lt q 20, f. 82r; Portland Papers (Longleat) Vol. XVIII, ff. 295r–296r; BL Harley MS 7318, f. 127v; Yale Osborn Shelves Poetry Box V/12.

5b. Yale Osborn Collection c.138, f. 29.

***Complementary print sources.*** 5a. *London Journal*, 19 June 1731, p. 3; *The Orrery Papers*, 2 vols., ed. by the Countess of Cork and Orrery (London: Duckworth, 1903), II, 321–2.

5b. *The Prompter*, no. 164, 1 June 1736; *A New Miscellany in Prose and Verse* (London: for T. Read, 1742), pp. 40–1; *The Museum*, I, 132 (no. 17, 8 November 1746); *The Masquerade* (London: for J. Bouquet, 1752), p. 225.

***Attribution.*** Brotherton Lt q 20, f. 82r (1732–c. 1741) 'by Ld Hervey'; Dodsley (1755). The similarities between the three poems, and the fact that the two earliest printed versions indicate that the addressee was Stephen Fox, clearly connect them with Hervey. The poem is claimed by Lord Orrery in *The Orrery Papers*, but there is no firm evidence supporting his authorship, and his copy reads much more like a refined version than an original poem.

***Context and date.*** The comparatively large number of manuscript and print sources suggests that the poem appealed to many readers of the period. It did so, however, in three distinct versions. As pointed out in the general headnote to Epistles above, these versions diverge from each other sufficiently to justify their presentation as different poems. A key difference is that, while 'To A Young Lady who desired to know her Fortune' is addressed to a young woman – in the case of one manuscript, Lady Hervey – the Horatian imitations are addressed to a male friend. A good hypothesis is that the version addressed to a young woman is the earliest. It must have been written by 1728, the date at the head of the Delany manuscripts. The version of the Horatian imitation addressed to Stephen Fox must have been completed by mid-1736, because it is to him that the *Prompter* and *Gentleman's Magazine* texts clearly refer under the partial cloak of the first and last letters of his name. However, this version of the poem is highly likely to date from several years earlier, the friendship between Hervey and Fox having become intimate in the summer of 1727. It is not impossible that the Fox version was written first, during the early months of the relationship between Hervey and Fox in 1727–8, with the more socially acceptable 5a 'To a Young Lady' being made available to readers first. At the latest, Hervey probably produced the poem to Fox around the same time as another of his Horatian imitations addressed to him, Poem 6, 'To Mr. Fox, Written at Florence 1729'.

The biographical and historical context for the 5a version of the poem is that of light verse intended as elite social entertainment. Such verse could be impromptu, or could be represented as such – one of the manuscripts calls the poem 'an extempore Answer', while another indicates that it was 'Written off hand'. Hervey seems to have written a number of such poems in the 1720s and, like other verse of the same kind, it was probably not intended for print publication. The generic context is that of the *carpe diem* tradition, especially in light of the fact that, while not explicitly identifying itself as a Horatian imitation, 'To A Young Lady who desired to know her Fortune' is clearly an adaptation of the very ode by Horace that uses the phrase by which the genre is known.

Generically, the 5b version of the poem, 'Horace Ode XI, Lib. I. Imitated', is what the title declares it to be, though it should not be assumed that the title of any of the versions of the poem is Hervey's. Among the titles of the sources for 'An Imitation', four designate it as such, but two do not. One is the single manuscript source, discussed below. The other is the *Prompter*, which introduces it thus: 'The following Lines are a very pretty Imitation of the 11th Ode of the 1st Book of Horace. I can't say, I have ever seen them in print; my Correspondent assures me they never were: on which Assurance, I venture, without any further Inquiry, to present them to my Readers.' The part of the general headnote above that discusses 'Epistles to Stephen Fox' provides further information about the Horatian imitation, and it is a striking paradox that it is not this version, but the 5a 'To a Young Lady' that is in one key respect closer to the Horatian model than the later ones, because only that one is addressed, like the Latin original, to a woman. By contrast, in all the sources but one, although the later versions are identified explicitly as imitating Horace's poem, they are addressed to a man. One way of understanding the change in the addressee's gender in these two later versions is discussed in Overton, 'Poetic Voice and Gender', pp. 615–16.

In 'Horace Ode XI, Lib. I. Imitated', Hervey expanded the eight lines of his Latin original to twenty (and to twenty-two, in all but one of the sources for 'To a Young Lady'). This, however, represents less lengthening than the numbers suggest, partly because Latin is a more concise language than English, and partly because it would be very difficult to follow the complex metre of Horace's poem line by line, even if Hervey had tried to translate it literally. Specifically, each line of the Latin consists of sixteen syllables made up from eight disyllabic feet, whereas each line of the English consists of eleven or twelve syllables made up from four feet, most of which contain three syllables. The anapaestic metre that Hervey chose for his imitation is appropriate because the faster pace produced by a preponderance of light stresses suits the theme of living in the moment as time is always slipping away. A contemporary verse translation by John Duncombe, provided in Appendix 1 for purposes of comparison, solves the problem of lines in Latin that would be unnaturally long in English by, in effect, spreading them across two. Writing in quatrains composed of alternating iambic tetrameter and trimeter, Duncombe follows the original closely and uses only twenty lines – or ten tetrameter-plus-trimeter units – to do so. Yet, skilful though it is, the short lines, the higher proportion of heavy stresses, and the continual breaks between quatrains – emphasised by the fact that each is numbered – lack the pace and fluency of Hervey's anapaestic tetrameter couplets. The liberties authorised by the genre of imitation, as opposed to translation, allowed Hervey not only to change the addressee's gender but to expand on the original in a way aimed at conveying its spirit rather than its literal sense. In this way, lines 7–10 and 13–14 in Hervey's poems, which have no direct precedent in the Latin, all emphasise the importance of living in the present – of being grateful for what one has, and of enjoying it to the full while it lasts. Such was the message he seems to have wanted to convey to Fox. It would have been especially poignant if the poem was written in the late 1720s when Hervey was continually subject to illness.

***Textual commentary.*** Among the sources for 'To A Young Lady who desired to know her Fortune', it may be significant that, if a composite text were produced on the basis of the most widely shared variants, most of the differences would be found in the Delany and Brotherton manuscripts. This is relevant to the questions of how, and to what extent, different manuscript versions circulated, and how far their intermediaries varied them. The text in the *London Journal* appears to derive from BL Add. MS 32463, with which it shares, uniquely, its title and a variant reading in line 11. There are few clear affinities between the other manuscripts, though it is worth noting that in line 8 three have a variant ('Exalt' for 'Exult', presumably a transcription error), that is repeated in three of the printed versions of 'An Imitation of the Eleventh Ode of the First Book of Horace'. As the Delany manuscript (like most of the others) is punctuated only lightly, that of the carefully punctuated BL Add. MS 32463 has sometimes been substituted; see the historical collation, which cites variants in estimated order of transcription or publication: Delany; BL Add. MS 32463; *London Journal*; Brotherton; *Orrery Papers*; Portland Papers (Longleat); BL Harley; Yale Osborn Shelves Poetry Box V.

The most significant differences between Poems 5a and 5b are the change in gender of the addressee, the explicit identification of the poem as a Horatian imitation, the omission of lines 15–16 and the variations in a number of pronouns. Among these changes, the omission of lines 15–16 takes the emphasis away from 'possession', implying sexual love, and the changes in pronouns, though these are not consistent in the various sources, tend to render the poem more personal. The versions in *The Masquerade* and the Osborn Collection contain the largest number of variants. While the former is an example of an attempt to improve on the original, especially in its exuberant closing couplet, the latter, which does not identify itself as a Horatian imitation, is of interest as an example of the kinds of change that occurred during the processes of manuscript transcription and circulation. It has, however, no claim to authority, because it comes from a commonplace book dated about 1787, around sixty years after the poem was first written. Other variants between the sources include considerable differences in punctuation, italicisation and use of initial capitals. As these do not significantly affect the sense, they are not noted.

Poem 5c resembles Poem 5b in the alteration to the gender of the addressee and its explicit identification as an Horatian imitation, but parts company from it in repositioning three couplets, omitting another and restoring a fifth from Poem 5a, 'To A Young Lady'. The lines that are repositioned are 7–8, 'Who anticipate care, their own pleasure destroy, | And invite disappointment who build upon joy', which occur as 3–4 in the two previous versions; 15–16, 'To-day's all the treasure poor mortals can boast, | For to-morrow's not gained, and yesterday's lost', which occur a couplet later in Poems 5a and 5b, as lines 19–20 and 17–18 respectively; and 17–18, 'Even now whilst I write, time steals on our youth, | And a moment's cut off from thy friendship and truth', which occur as lines 13–14 in Poem 5b, but as 17–18 in 5a. The lines omitted from 5c, 'Then no more on Hereafter thy Wishes employ; | Who live to the Future the Present destroy', occur as 13–14 in Poem 5a and 15–16 in Poem 5b; while the lines omitted from Poem 5b, 'From reflection and hope little comfort we find, | To possession alone let thy thoughts be confin'd', occur as lines 13–14 in Poem 5c and 15–16 in Poem 5a.

## 5a To A Young Lady who desired to know her Fortune

Forbear, my dear Nymph, with a fruitless Desire,
Into Truths which are better conceal'd to inquire.
Who anticipate Care their own Pleasure destroy,
And invite Disappointment who build upon Joy.
Perhaps many Years are allow'd me by Fate,
Or next Winter perhaps is the last of my Date;
Let Credulous Fools whom Astrologers Cheat
Exult, or dispond, as they vary deceit.
All Ills unforeseen we the easiest endure;
What avails to *foresee* unless *Foresight* could cure?
And from Ills by that Art how can *Wretches* be freed,
Since that Art must be false, or those Ills be decreed?
Then no more on Hereafter thy Wishes employ;
Who live to the Future the Present destroy.
From Reflection and Hope no Comfort we find,
To Possession alone let thy Thoughts be confined.
Even now whilst I'm writing time Steals on our Youth
And a Moment's cut off from thy Friendship and Truth;
To day's all the Treasure poor Mortals can boast,
For To Morrow's not come, and Yesterday's lost;
Then seize the swift Blessing, enjoy the dear Now;
And expect not what Fate will hereafter bestow.

## 5b Horace Ode XI. Lib. I. Imitated. *The* ADVICE. To S—N F—X Esq

Forbear, my dear *S–n*, with fruitless desire,
Into truths, which[1] are better conceal'd, to enquire;
Who anticipate care, their own pleasure destroy,
And invite disappointment, who build upon joy.
Perhaps, many years are allow'd me by fate,
Or next winter, perhaps, is the last of their date.
Let credulous fools, whom astrologers cheat,
*Exalt*, or *despond*, as they *vary* deceit.

1. *which*: although the *Gentleman's Magazine* rarely uses contractions, it prints 'which' as w$^{ch}$ (with the small ch appearing directly over the w); see headnote.

All ills unforeseen, we the easiest endure;
What avails to *foresee*, unless *foresight* could cure!
And from ills, *by their art*, how can wretches be freed,
When *that art* must be *false*, or *those ills* be *decreed?*
Even now whilst I write, time steals on our youth,
And a moment's cut off from thy friendship and truth!
Then no more on hereafter, thy wishes employ,
Who build on the *future*, the *present* destroy:
*To-day*'s all the treasure poor mortals can boast,
For *to-morrow*'s not *gain'd*, and *yesterday's lost.*
Then seize the[2] swift blessing, enjoy the dear *now*,
And *take*, not *expect*, what hereafter'll bestow.

## 5c An Imitation of the Eleventh Ode of the First Book of Horace[3]

Forbear, my dear Stephen,[4] with a fruitless desire
Into truths which are better conceal'd to enquire;
Perhaps many years are allow'd us by Fate,
Or next winter perhaps is the last of their date:
Let the credulous fools whom astrologers cheat,
Exult or despond, as they vary deceit;
Who anticipate care, their own pleasure destroy,
And invite disappointment who build upon joy;
All ills unforeseen we the easiest endure,
What avails to foresee, unless foresight could cure?
And from ills by their art how can wretches be freed,
When that art must be false, or those ills be decreed?
From reflection and hope little comfort we find,
To possession alone let thy thoughts be confin'd;
To-day's all the treasure poor mortals can boast,
For to-morrow's not gained, and yesterday's lost;
Even now whilst I write, time steals on our youth,

2. *the*: printed as 'y$^{e}$', unusually in the *Gentleman's Magazine*; see headnote.

3. Dodsley 1782 adds 'To Stephen Fox, Esq; afterwards Earl of Ilchester', probably in an effort to boost the aristocratic associations of the *Collection*.

4. *Stephen*: changed to 'Ste' in Dodsley 1782, using the familiar form of the name often used by Hervey.

And a moment's cut off from thy friendship and truth:
Then seize the swift blessing, enjoy the dear now,
And take, not expect, what hereafter'll bestow.

## Horace, Book I, Ode XI

Ask not, Leuconoë (we cannot know), what end the gods have set for me, for thee, nor make trial of the Babylonian tables! How much better to endure whatever comes, whether Jupiter allots us added winters or whether this is last, which now wears out the Tuscan Sea upon the barrier of the cliffs! Show wisdom! Busy thyself with household tasks; and since life is brief, cut short far-reaching hopes! Even while we speak, envious Time has sped. Reap the harvest of to-day, putting as little trust as may be in the morrow! (Horace, *Odes and Epodes*, trans. C. E. Bennett (Loeb, p. 33))

# 6 To Mr. Fox, Written at Florence 1729
# In Imitation of the 6th Ode of the 2nd Book of Horace

***Main source.*** Harrowby MS 81, ff. 66r–66v. Although a scribal copy, this appears to be the earliest of the surviving manuscripts, because below it is Montagu's draft of the lines she wrote in reply, beginning 'So sung the Poet in an Humble Strain'. As Halsband and Grundy indicate, Montagu wrote her response in October 1729 and sent it to Hervey in France, 'where, however, it missed him' (*Essays & Poems*, p. 256).

***Complementary manuscript sources.*** BL Harley MS 7318, ff. 130r–131r; Portland (Longleat) XIX, ff. 329r–331r; Brotherton Lt 119, ff. 99–101 (rectos only).

***Complementary print sources.*** *The Windsor Medley*, 'The third edition' (London: for A. Moore, 1731; ESTC T069084), pp. 3–5, collated with three other editions of the same year (ESTC N025099, T058887, N025098); *Gentleman's Magazine*, 7, 628 (October 1737); Dodsley, *Collection* (1748), III, 181–3, collated with later editions up to 1782 (III, 194–6).

***Attribution.*** Harrowby; *Windsor Medley*; *Gentleman's Magazine*; Brotherton; Dodsley 1748 (expanded in BL copy in hand of Horace Walpole).

***Context and date.*** Hervey left England with Stephen Fox on 12 July 1728 in an attempt to recover his health and spirits by visiting France and Italy. The poem's subtitle, 'Written in Florence 1729', indicates that it must have been written between July 1729, when he and Fox arrived in Florence, and August, when they left. Following further travel in Italy and France, and a short visit to Paris, the two arrived in London on 25 October (Halsband, pp. 77–8; 82; 84; 87). Fox looked after Hervey when he was seriously ill in the earlier part of the tour, but the roles were reversed when Fox became ill in December (Halsband, p. 80). After Fox's recovery, however, Hervey's condition again worsened. He describes it in 'An account of my own constitution and Illness, with some rules for the preservation of health; for the use of my children', paying tribute to the care Fox gave him: 'Mr. Fox never left me night or day; I saw nobody but him and servants; he went out with me whenever I was able to go out, read to me at home when I had not spirits to talk, and constantly lay in my room. I looked so dreadfully that he has sometimes come to my bedside and doubted if I was only sleeping or dead' (Sedgwick, III, 978). It is this care that the poem celebrates. Hervey treats his Horatian model with great freedom, completely changing the emphasis of the original. While Horace addresses a friend who is prepared to accompany him to Spain, presumably for military service, but devotes twenty of the poem's twenty-four lines to celebrating places where he would like to spend his old age (Tibur (Tivoli, near Rome), and Tarentum (Taranto in the heel of

Italy)), Hervey spends twenty-six of the fifty-four lines of his version thanking Fox in the warmest terms for the unconditional love he showed as a travelling companion and carer. In other words, Horace addresses a friend about a journey he might make (though perhaps he might not), but Hervey expresses his gratitude for one who has not only accompanied him on a long journey but has nursed him through severe illness and back to health. If Horace's projected journey was for military service, the motive for travel was also very different. Similarly, although the second half of Hervey's poem is closer to the rest of Horace's, its tone is much more personal and affectionate. Hervey also uses a quite different metre. Horace's poem consists of six stanzas in Sapphic metre, quatrains in which the first three lines consist of eleven syllables and the last of five. In his translation of the poem, provided in Appendix 1, John Duncombe opted for the simpler form of iambic tetrameter quatrains rhyming in couplets, as did Sir James Marriott in an imitation included in the same edition. While this conveys something of the lightness and grace of the original, Hervey's heroic couplets, the form of choice for serious verse in the period, are in keeping with the passionate sincerity of his tribute to his friend.

***Textual commentary.*** The Harrowby manuscript contains some unusually placed initial capitals, which have been adjusted and noted. The manuscript copy that seems the latest of the three, in Brotherton Lt 119, contains the largest number of variants, though some appear to be transcription errors. There are no obvious affinities between any of the manuscript or printed copies that might serve to connect them, other than some variants shared between the Harley and Portland manuscripts. As was its wont, the *Gentleman's Magazine* takes some textual liberties.

## To Mr. Fox. Written at Florence 1729
## In Imitation of the 6th Ode of the 2nd Book of Horace[1]

Thou dearest Youth! who taught me first to know
What Pleasures from a real Friendship flow;
Where neither Int'rest nor Deceit have Part,
But all the Warmth is native of the Heart:
Thou know'st to comfort, soothe, or entertain,
Joy of my Health, and Cordial to my Pain.
When Life seem'd failing on her latest Stage,
And fell Disease anticipated Age;
When wasting Sickness, and afflictive Pain,
By Æsculapius' Sons[2] oppos'd in vain,

1. The *Windsor Medley* and Dodsley copies provide the opening words of Horace's poem as an epigraph: *Septimi, Gades aditure mecum* ('Septimius, you would go with me to Cadiz').

2. *Æsculapius' Sons*: doctors, Æsculapius being the Greek and later Roman God of medicine.

Forc'd me reluctant, desperate, to explore
A warmer Sun, and seek a milder Shore;
Thy steady Love, with unexampled Truth,
Forsook each gay Companion of thy Youth;
Whate'er the Prosp'rous, or the Great employs,
Bus'ness, and Int'rest, and love's softer Joys;
The weary Steps of Misery to attend,
To share Distress, and make a Wretch thy Friend.
If o'er the Mountain's snowy Height we stray,
Where Carthage[3] first explor'd the venterous way;
Or thro' the tainted Air of Rome's parch'd Plains,
Where Want resides, and Superstition reigns;
Chearful, and unrepining, still you bear
Each dangerous Rigour of the various Year,
And kindly anxious for thy Friend alone,
Lament his Suff'rings, and forget thy own.
Oh! would kind Heaven, those tedious Suff'rings past,
Permit me Ickworth,[4] Rest, and Health at last,
In that lov'd Shade, my Youth's delightful Seat,
My early Pleasure, and my late Retreat,
Where lavish Nature's favourite Blessings flow,
And all the Seasons all their Sweets bestow;
There might I trifle, carelessly, away
The milder Evening of Life's clouded Day,
From Business, and the World's intrusion free,
With Books, with Love, with Beauty, and with Thee,
No farther Want, no Wish yet unpossess'd,
Could e'er disturb this unambitious Breast:
Let those who Fortune's shining Gifts implore,
Who sue for Glory, Splendour, Wealth, or Power,
View this unactive State with scornful Eyes
And Pleasures, they can never taste, despise;
Let them still court that Goddess' falser Joys,
Who, whilst she grants their Pray'r, their Peace destroys.

3. *Carthage*: alluding to Hannibal's crossing of the Alps.

4. *Ickworth*: the family home of Lord Bristol, where Hervey grew up, where his wife and family lived when not in London, and where he sometimes retreated.

I envy not the foremost of the Great,
Not Walpole's self directing Europe's Fate;
Still let him load Ambition's thorny Shrine,
Fame be his Portion, and Contentment mine.
But if the Gods, sinister, still deny
To live in Ickworth, let me there but die;
Thy Hand to close my Eyes, in Death's long Night,
Thy Image to attract their latest Sight;
Then to the Grave attend thy Poets Hearse,
And love his Memory, as you lov'd his Verse.

# 7 To the Same. From Hampton-Court, 1731

***Source.*** Dodsley, *Collection*, 2nd edn (1748), III, 183–90, in preference to what Michael F. Suarez calls 'the poorly edited, miserably produced' first edition of the same year (*Collection*, ed. by Suarez, I, 5). No manuscript seems to survive, though lines 119–23 appear in an eighteenth-century commonplace book with the attribution 'Ld. Hervey's Letter to Mr Fox' (Bodley MS Eng. misc. f. 79, p. 113).

***Complementary sources.*** Dodsley, *Collection*, 1st edn (1748), III, 183–9; (1782), III, 197–204.

***Attribution.*** Dodsley from 1748.

***Context and date.*** According to Robert Halsband, Hervey sent the poem to Stephen Fox after a crisis in their relationship caused by his unguarded confession of the strength of his feelings for Frederick, Prince of Wales, and by his absorption in court life (Halsband, p. 123). Although the crisis came to a head at the end of August, the phrase 'From Hampton-Court' in its title indicates that it could have been written at any time during the autumn when he was in residence there.

The year 1731 was one of the most fraught in Hervey's life. It began with the first of what seem to have been two epileptic seizures, followed by a duel with William Pulteney in which he was slightly wounded; his friendship with Frederick reached its most intimate phase in the summer; and he was increasingly caught up in and irked by his duties as a courtier – although, in attempting to mollify Fox, he may have exaggerated this. Near the end of the year, he not only had a further seizure, but, thanks to Frederick supplanting him in the affections of his mistress Anne Vane and replacing him with a rival confidant, George Bubb Dodington, his friendship with Frederick collapsed into bitterness and hatred. The poem's ostensible motive is the tension between his wish to be with Fox and the courtly obligations that so often kept the two apart. Its epigraph, however, suggests a subtext of a quite different kind. Taken from Seneca's Letter 70 to Lucilius, its message that 'no man is unhappy except by his own fault' is clearly relevant to the choice he had to make between his friendship with Fox and his career at court. But the context of Seneca's remark is an argument in favour of suicide, and it seems no coincidence that, at the time when Hervey would have been writing the poem, he was violently disturbed by the suicide of a Bath friend of his, Fanny Braddock. It was to Fox that, on 27 September 1731, Hervey wrote a long and emotionally intense letter in which he not only defended Braddock against her detractors, but also raised a number of speculative, free-thinking questions about religion and morality that parallel those in the poem (SRO 941/47/4, pp. 212–24; the letter, and Hervey's views on suicide, are discussed in Overton, 'Death and Futurity').

Probably only Fox could have understood this subtext – a striking example of how a literary epistle may carry a quite different meaning for its actual addressee than for any external reader. The large questions raised by the poem are libertine both in the sexual and the political sense. While they must have appealed to Fox, and probably also to others in the same network of free-thinking friends, many other readers of the period are likely to have found them shockingly heretical. It is probably for this reason that, in contrast to the other two poems to Fox, which seem to have circulated quite widely, no manuscript copies survive and that the poem was rarely reprinted.

***Textual commentary.*** Like Poem 5c, 'An Imitation of the Eleventh Ode of the First Book of Horace', the poem may have come to Dodsley from Hervey's friend John Hoadly. A few corrections have been adopted from the 1782 edition, as indicated in the historical collation.

## To the Same. From Hampton-Court,[1] 1731

*Bono loco res humanæ sunt, quod nemo,*
*nisi vitio suo, miser est.*[2] (Seneca in Epist.)

Whilst in the fortunes of the gay and great,
The glare of courts, and luxury of state:
All that the meaner covet and deplore,
The pomp of wealth, and insolence of pow'r:
Whilst in these various scenes of gilded life,
Of fraud, ambition, policy, and strife;
Where every word is dictated by art,
And ev'ry face the mask of ev'ry heart;
Whilst with such diff'rent objects[3] entertain'd,
In all that's really felt, and all that's feign'd,
I speculate on human joys and woes,
Till from my pen the verse spontaneous flows;
To whom these artless off'rings should I bring,
To whom these undigested numbers[4] sing,
But to a friend? – and to what friend but you,

1. *Hampton-Court*: One of the royal residences, where Hervey had rooms as Vice-Chamberlain to the King's household, to which he had been appointed in April 1730 (Halsband, pp. 96–7).

2. *Bono . . . est*: 'Humanity is well situated, because no man is unhappy except by his own fault' (Seneca, *Epistles 66–72*, 'Letter 70' (Loeb, pp. 64–5)).

3. *objects*: 'something placed before or presented to the eyes or other senses' (*OED*).

4. *numbers*: 'Metrical periods or feet; lines, verses' (*OED*).

Safe, just, sincere, indulgent, kind and true?
Disdain not then these trifles to attend,
Nor fear to blame, nor study to commend.
Say, where false notions erring I pursue,
And with the plausible confound the true;
Correct with all the freedom that I write;
And guide my darken'd reason with thy light.

Thee partial heav'n has bless'd, profusely kind,
With wit, with judgment, and a taste refin'd.
Thy fancy rich, and thy observance true,
The last still wakeful, and the first still new.
Rare blessings! and to few divided known,
But giv'n united to thyself alone.
Instruction are thy words, and lively truth,
The school of age, and the delight of youth.

When men their various discontents relate,
And tell how wretched this our mortal state;
That life is but diversify'd distress,
The lot of all, and hardly more or less;
That kings and villagers have each their share,
These pinch'd with mean, and those with splendid care;
That seeming pleasure is intrinsick woe,
And all call'd happiness, delusive show;
Food only for the snakes in envy's breast,
Who often grudges what is ne'er possess'd;
Say, for thou know'st the follies of mankind,
Can'st tell how obstinate, perverse, and blind;
Say, are we thus oppress'd by Nature's laws,
Or of our miseries, ourselves the cause?

Sure oft, unjustly, we impute to fate
A thousand evils which ourselves create;
Complain that life affords but little joy,
And yet that little foolishly destroy.
We check the pleasures that too soon subside,

And break the current of too weak a tide.
Like Atalanta,[5] golden trifles chace,
And baulk that swiftness which might win the race;
For life has joys adapted to each stage,
Love for our youth, ambition for our age.
But wilful man inverting her decrees,
When young would govern, and when old would please,
Covets the fruits his autumn shou'd bestow,
Nor tastes the fragrance whilst the blossoms blow.
Then far-fled joys in vain he would restore,
His appetite unanswer'd by his pow'r:
Round beauty's neck he twists his wither'd arms,
Receiv'd with loathing to her venal charms:
He rakes the ashes, when the fire is spent,
Nor gains fruition,[6] tho' he gains consent.
But can we say 'tis Providence's fault,
If thus untimely all her gifts are sought,
If summer-crops which must decay we keep,
And in the winter would the harvest reap?

When brutes, with what they are allow'd content,
Listen to Nature, and pursue her bent,
And still their pow'r with their ambition weigh'd,
Gain what they can, but never force a trade;
A thousand joys, her happy followers prove,
Health, plenty, rest, society, and love.
To us alone, in fatal ign'rance proud,
To deviate from her dictates 'tis allow'd:
That boasted gift our reason to believe,
Or let caprice, in reason's garb, deceive.
To us the noble privilege is giv'n
Of wise refining on the will of heav'n.
Our skill we trust, but lab'ring still to gain
More than we can, lose what we might obtain.

5. *Atalanta*: in Greek mythology, a huntress who agreed to marry any man who could outrun her but was defeated by a suitor who dropped golden apples in her path that she stopped to pick up.

6. *fruition*: sexual pleasure, commonly believed to be necessary for both partners if conception was to result from intercourse.

Will the wise elephant desert the wood,
To imitate the whale and range the flood?
Or will the mole her native earth forsake,
In wanton madness to explore the lake?
Yet man, whom still ideal profit[7] sways,
Than those less prudent, and more blind than these,
Will quit his home, and vent'rous brave the seas.
And when his rashness its desert[8] has found,
The fool surviving, weeps the fool that's drown'd.

Herds range the fields, the feather'd kind[9] the grove,
Chuse, woo, caress, and with promiscuous love,
As taste and nature prompt, adhere, or rove;
They meet with pleasure, and with ease they part,
For beasts are only coupled by the heart.
The body still accompanies the mind,
And when this wanders, that is unconfin'd:
The love that join'd the sated pair once fled,
They change their haunts, their pasture, and their bed.
No four-legg'd ideots drag, with mutual pain,
The nat'ral cement pass'd,[10] an artful chain:[11]
Th' effect of passion ceases with the cause,
Clogg'd with no after-weight of forms or laws:
To no dull rules of custom they submit,
Like us they cool, but when they cool, they quit.[12]

Nor find we in the wood, the sea, or plain,
One e'er elected o'er the rest to reign.
If any rule, 'tis force that gives the law,
What brutes are bound in voluntary awe?
Do they, like us, a pageant idol raise,

7. *ideal profit*: imaginary advantage.

8. *desert*: 'That which is deserved; a due reward or recompense, whether good or evil' (*OED*).

9. *feather'd kind*: birds.

10. *The nat'ral cement pass'd*: once the erotic bond has lapsed; in this period, the stress is on the first syllable of 'cement'.

11. *an artful chain*: the bond of marriage.

12. *Herds range the fields … when they cool, they quit*: with some minor changes, these fifteen lines are given to Nero in Poem 66 'Agrippina', II. 2. 56–70.

Swoln with false pride, and flatter'd by false praise?
Do they their equal, sometimes less, revere?
At once detest and serve, despise and fear?
To strength inferior, do they bend the knee?
With ears and eyes of others, hear and see?
Or ever vest[13] a mortal god with pow'r
To do those wrongs they afterwards deplore?
These institutions are of man alone,
Marriage and monarchy are both our own.
Publick oppression, and domestick strife,
Are ills which we ourselves annex'd to life,
God never made a husband, king, or wife.
Boast then, oh man! thy profitable gain,
To folly polish'd, civiliz'd to pain.

Here, would I launch into the various field
Of all the cares our prejudices yield;
What multiply'd examples might be told,
Of pains they give, and joys that they with-hold?
When to credulity tradition preaches,
And ign'rance practises what error teaches!

Wou'd any feather'd maiden of the wood,
Or scaly female of the peopled flood,
When lust or hunger call'd, its force resist?
In abstinence, or chastity persist?
And cry, 'If heav'n's intent was understood,
'These tastes were only giv'n to be withstood.'
Or wou'd they wisely both these gifts improve,
And eat when hungry, and when am'rous love?

Yet superstition in religion's name,
With future punishment and present shame,
Can fright weak woman from her lover's arms,
Who weeps with mutual pain her useless charms:
Whilst she, poor wretch! consum'd in secret fires,
With pow'r to seize, foregoes what she desires,

13. *vest*: 'To invest (a person) *with* some quality, esp. power, authority, etc' (*OED*).

Till beauty fades and inclination dies,
And the fair tree, the fruit ungather'd, dies.

But are these ills, the ills which heav'n design'd?
Are we unfortunate, or are we blind?
If in possession of our wishes curs'd,
Bath'd in untasted springs we dye with thirst;
If we make miseries, what were blessings meant,
And benefits convert to punishment?

When in the spring the wise industrious bees
Collect the various bloom from fragrant trees,
Extract the liquid sweet of ev'ry flow'r,
And cull the garden to enrich their store:
Should any pedant bee of all the hive,
From this or that perfume, the plund'rers drive,
And say, that he by inspiration knows,
The sacred, tempting, interdicted[14] rose,
By heav'n's command, tho' sweetest, useless grows:
Think you the fool would ever be obey'd,
And that the lye would grow into a trade?
Ev'n Turks would answer, no – and yet, we see
The vine,[15] that rose, and Mahomet, that bee.
To these, how many proofs I yet could add,
That man's superior sense is being mad?
That none, refining, their true int'rest view,
But for the substance, still the shade pursue.
That oft perverse, and prodigal of life,
(Our pow'r and will at everlasting strife)
We waste the present for the future hour,
And, miser-like, by hoarding, still are poor;
Or foolishly regretful of the past,
The good which yet remains neglect to taste.

Nor need I any foreign[16] proof to bring,
Myself an instance of the truths I sing.
Whilst in a court, repugnant to my taste,

14. *interdicted*: forbidden. 15. *The vine*: referring to Islamic prohibition of alcohol.
16. *foreign*: 'Proceeding from other persons or things' (*OED*).

From my lov'd friend these precious hours I waste,
Why do I vainly here thy absence mourn,
And not anticipate thy wish'd return?
Why stay my passage to those happy fields,
Where fate in thee my ev'ry pleasure yields?
Fortune allows the blessings I refuse,
And ev'n this moment, were my heart to chuse,
For thee I should forsake this joyless croud,
And not on paper think, but think aloud:
With thy lov'd converse fill the shorten'd day,
And glad my soul. – Yet here unpleas'd I stay,
And by mean, sanguine views of int'rest sway'd,
By airy[17] hopes, to real cares betray'd;
Lament a grievance which I might redress,
And wish that happiness I might possess.

17. *airy*: 'Like air in its (apparently) intangible or empty character' (*OED*).

# OTHER AMATORY VERSE

# 8 The Countess of — to Miss —

***Main source.*** BL Add. MS 78522, ff. 191r–194v, a very careful copy.

***Complementary sources.*** Harrowby MS 255, pp. 72–6; BL Add. MS 22629, ff. 195r–195v (fragment consisting of lines 65–102 except for lines 79–80, which are omitted).

***Attribution.*** 'By L. Hervey' in Harrowby ms; unattributed in other sources.

***Context and date.*** The fact that the poem refers to 'St— s wit' (line 91), an evident reference to Philip Dormer Stanhope (1694–1773), who did not become Earl of Chesterfield until his father's death in 1726, suggests that it was written in or more likely before that year. While information is lacking to determine the context with any degree of certainty, it seems likely that, as Isobel Grundy suggests, the nominal writer of the epistle is Claude-Charlotte, Countess of Stafford (Grundy, p. 337). After 1719 Lady Stafford (c. 1665–1739) spent most of her time in England, where she soon met Montagu (Grundy, pp. 191–2); Hervey presumably met her not long afterwards. On these grounds the poem cannot have been written before the early 1720s. Its subject could indeed lay claim to wit though not to beauty, as the Countess of the poem does, even quite plausibly to having been celebrated in verse by Charles Saint-Évremond (line 65). Hervey praises her wit and good company in letters to Stephen Fox as well as in his 'Memoirs' (SRO 941/47/4, p. 168; Sedgwick, II, 551). Although she would have been nearly sixty when the poem was probably written, the 'fifty Winters' to which she admits may suggest that she succeeded in deceiving those who knew her about her age, unless it is humorous colouring on Hervey's part. As with Lord Chesterfield, some of the figures who are part-named in the poem may also be identified and support a date in the earlier or mid-1720s. 'Lowth— rs beauty' (line 91) clearly refers to Anthony Lowther, the lover and betrayer of Sophia Howe; 'Dal— h' (line 93; 'Dal—th' in BL Add. MS 78522) probably means Lady Jane Douglas, Countess of Dalkeith (1701–29); and the 'demi-Man' whom the Countess claims she is capable of exciting to desire, signified in line 95 by 'H— gh', and by 'Harb—h' in BL Add. MS 22629, is almost certainly Bennet Sherard, first Earl of Harborough (1677–1732). A tentative identification is of 'fat Fit—n' (line 66; 'Dear F——' in BL Add. MS 22629), as Sir Alexander Fitton (1630?–98), who had followed James II to St Germains. A tempting possibility for the identity of the addressee, named as Sophia in line 86, is Sophia Howe, who would certainly have been better off in a lesbian relationship than the disastrous one she had with Anthony Lowther. This would correspond with the poem's likely date, and with the presence of the manuscript fragment of the poem among the papers of Lady

Suffolk, who had been Howe's friend and correspondent. If such an identification is valid, the woman uncharitably termed 'that Hag your Mother' (line 64) would be Ruperta Howe (1673–1740), the illegitimate daughter of Prince Rupert and the actress Margaret Hughes, whose husband was the diplomat Emanuel Scrope Howe (*c.* 1663–1709). Although Ruperta was younger than Lady Stafford, the scandal in which she was involved in 1706 as a result of correspondence with the Duchess of Marlborough might have provoked the word 'Hag' (see Stuart Handley, 'Howe, Emanuel Scrope (*c.* 1663–1709)', *ODNB*). The wider context of the poem's circulation is that of society gossip, suggested by the fact that, presumably as part of the game, not all of the names are the same in the three manuscripts. For discussion of the poem's gender implications, see Overton, 'Poetic Voice and Gender'.

***Textual commentary.*** BL Add. MS 78522 is a very careful copy, systematically punctuated. This has been collated with Harrowby MS 255, which is given priority in the case of substantive variants, and in its very limited use of exclamatives, because of the high probability that Montagu transcribed it from a copy made available to her by Hervey. Montagu's copy was for her private use, and as is typical of the volume it appears in, end-of-line punctuation is almost entirely absent, and there is no perceptible system used in the assigning of initial capitals to words. A copy of part of the poem appears in the Suffolk Papers, BL Add. MS 22629, prefaced by a comment in a different hand, 'Verses – some very indecent & all dull' (lines 65–102, though omitting 79–80, 'Nor glow'd her amorous Breast with fiercer Fire, | More prone to Love, more urg'd by strong Desire'). This volume also includes two letters from Sophia Howe to Lady Suffolk, both dated 1719 in pencil (ff. 4–7v). So as to reflect the conditions of manuscript circulation, which tended not only to permit but sometimes even encouraged variants, the text has not been normalised other than to expand contractions; the few editorial corrections, all affecting punctuation, are indicated in the List of Emendations.

## The Countess of — to Miss —

If after all I have already done,
My Passions force be yet to thee unknown;
If not the mute Confession of my Eyes,
If not assiduous Visits, frequent Sighs,
Have told thee (Charming Fair[1]) the tender Tale
And plaintive Terms are wanting to reveal
The meaning of my Soul, let this remove
All Doubt, all Ignorance, and know I love.

1. *Fair*: '2. One of the fair sex, a woman; *esp.* a beloved woman' (*OED*).

Perhaps thy Heart (too unexperienced Maid)
Starts at the bold Confession I have made.
Methinks I see at every Line you read
O'er your warm Cheek successive Blushes spread;
The Paper dances in thy dazel'd Eyes,
O'er all thy Frame the soft Confusion flys,
Heightn'ing thy Charms; how that dear Image fires
My Veins? what Heat! what Vigour it inspires!
Oh how I long to strain thee to my Breast
To comfort, and assure thee thus distress'd:
With my warm Lip to dry the modest Tear,
And in a Flood of Pleasure drown thy Fear.
But let no fears thy Peace of Mind annoy,
'Tis Man, false Man, who courts you to destroy
And brings Undoing blended with the Joy:
My fond Embrace no dire Effects attend,
An unprolifick,[2] and a harmless Friend.
Tho' all the Day we revel in Delight,
And Joys uninterrupted crown the Night,
No censuring Tale, no Scandal shall ensue,
My Sex a Sanction both for me and you:
Nor shall Reproach attaint[3] thy spotless Fame,[4]
Nor Signs repugnant to a Virgins Name.
Still shall thy Shape its taper Form retain,
Eve shall have sin'd, and Thou been curs'd in vain,
Admitted to the Joy, exempted from the Pain.[5]

Thrice happy Maid,[6] who thus secure shalt rove
Through all the pleasant Paths of dang'rous Love:

2. *unprolifick*: incapable of impregnating (*OED* 'prolific': 'Fertile, not barren; capable of generating or producing offspring; generative, reproductive').

3. *attaint*: 'To sully (lustre, purity, etc.)' (*OED*).

4. *Fame*: 'The character attributed to a person or thing by report or generally entertained; reputation' (*OED*).

5. *Eve . . . Pain*: 'Unto the woman [God] said, I will greatly multiply thy sorrow and thy conception; in sorrow thou shalt bring forth children; and thy desire shall be to thy husband, and he shall rule over thee' (Genesis 3: 17, Authorized Version).

6. *Thrice happy Maid*: i.e. the addressee would be trebly fortunate in enjoying sexual pleasure without the pains of social disgrace or pregnancy.

Safe from the lashing Prudes inveighing Tongue,
Uncensur'd by the Old, unenvy'd by the Young.
Vertumnus thus Pomona[7] once caress'd,
To her alone the Lover stood confess'd;
No vulgar[8] Eye the latent[9] Man descry'd,
A Woman's form the vig'rous Youth bely'd.
Such is the Safety of the Love I give,
The harmless Gift undaunted then receive:
Nor let thy Virtue furnish a Pretence;
Virtue's the tim'rous Child of Ignorance;
Which tho' the hireling Priests by Habit teach,
They still corrupt the Chastity they preach
And fright the Milk-Maid from the Clowns Embrace,
To sin with safety in a wholesome Place.[10]

Think not the silly few, who fear to take
The proffer'd Joy, abstain for Conscience sake:
They not abhor the Guilt, but fear the Shame,
And glose[11] their Cowardice with Virtues Name.
What Pity 'twere that Angel Form of thine,
Turn'd for Delight, cast in a Mold divine,
By Cant[12] betray'd, by Prejudice misled,
Should obstinately fly my proffer'd Bed,

7. *Vertumnus thus Pomona*: the myth is best known from Ovid's *Metamorphoses*, XIV, 623–97, 665–771 (Loeb, II, 344–50, 346–8). In it Vertumnus tries unsuccessfully to woo Pomona in various guises, but is unable to gain admittance to her presence and plead his love until disguising himself as an old woman. The parallel is appropriate to an older woman courting a younger one, especially as Hervey has the Countess omit any reference to Vertumnus only winning Pomona once he has resumed his shape as a young man.

8. *vulgar*: 'Of persons: Belonging to the ordinary or common class in the community; not distinguished or marked off from this in any way; plebeian' (*OED*).

9. *latent*: 'Hidden, concealed' (*OED*).

10. *hireling Priests … Place*: meaning that the clergy preach chastity not because they believe in it but because they are paid to do so and by habit, frightening the milkmaid so that she avoids the peasant who is courting her and has sex with clerics under the cover of their profession and its conveniences. The anti-clerical stance is characteristic of the free-thinking attitude Hervey shared with Montagu and Lady Stafford.

11. *glose*: 'To veil with specious comments; to palliate; to explain away, extenuate' (*OED*).

12. *Cant*: 'Affected or unreal use of religious or pietistic phraseology; language (or action) implying the pretended assumption of goodness or piety' (*OED*).

Still to my warm Pursuit refuse thy Charms
And keep 'em for a Husband's languid Arms!

My Blood (in vain by fifty Winters[13] chill'd)
Still mantles[14] in my Veins, with Spirits[15] fill'd;
My Limbs as active still, my Nerves as strong,
As when that Hag your Mother[16] had me young;
As when St Evremont[17] first sung my Charms
And fat Fit—n[18] wallow'd in my Arms.
Nor is it Time has plough'd this rugged Face,
Coarse as it is, 'tis what it allways was;
No Beauty Nature on my Cheek bestow'd,
There Lillys never bloom'd, nor Roses glow'd:
But Female Softness to my Form deny'd,
With more than Man She has my Soul supply'd:
A Wit sublime to distant Countrys known,
An Ornament and Honour to my own:
The Muses me, and me the Loves have crown'd,
Myrtle and Lawrel on my Temples bound:
Not Sapho's self[19] more sweetly touch'd the Lyre
When Sapho sung what Phœbus[20] did inspire:

13. *fifty Winters*: see headnote.

14. *mantles*: 'Of the blood, a blush, etc.: to suffuse the cheeks. Of the face or cheeks: to be suffused with glowing colour, to flush' (*OED*).

15. *Spirits*: 'One or other of certain subtle highly-refined substances or fluids (distinguished as *natural, animal*, and *vital*) formerly supposed to permeate the blood and chief organs of the body' (*OED*).

16. *that Hag your Mother*: see headnote.

17. *St Evremont*: Charles de Marguetel de Saint-Denis, sieur de Saint-Évremond (1613–1703), spent most of the latter part of his life in self-imposed exile in England, and was much admired for his wit and style.

18. fat Fit—n: possibly Sir Alexander Fitton (1630?–98), Lord Chancellor of Ireland, who followed James II into exile at St Germains.

19. *Sapho's self*: Sappho (c. 610–c. 580 BCE), born on the Greek island of Lesbos, was the greatest female poet of antiquity. According to traditions most famously given currency in 'Sappho to Phaon', a verse epistle credited to Ovid as part of his *Heroides* but not definitely by him, she had sexual relationships with women but fell in love with a man, Phaon, and committed suicide because he did not return it. See *Ovid, Heroides: Select Epistles*, ed. by Peter E. Knox (Cambridge: Cambridge University Press, 1995), pp. 13–14, 278–9; 'Introduction', *Sappho Through English Poetry*, ed. by Peter Jay and Caroline Lewis (London: Anvil Press, 1996), pp. 11–18.

20. *Phœbus*: Phoebus Apollo, in his role as god of poetry and music.

Nor glow'd her am'rous Breast with fiercer Fire,
More prone to Love, more urg'd by strong Desire.
How much in all our kindred Fates agree,
She for her Flora burn'd,[21] and I for thee.
And tho' no Beauty deck'd her sallow Face
Short like my-self, nor of superiour Grace,
Yet still her Vows a fair Reception find;
Oh! be Sophia like the Lesbian[22] kind;
Nor dread their Fate, to fond Regret betray'd,
Too soon the fickle Spoiler[23] left each Maid:
But thou no Change, no rival Phaon fear,
Thy-self my latest, and my dearest Care;
Not St— s wit, with Lowth— rs Beauty joyn'd,[24]
Should tempt the firmness of my constant Mind:
Not ev'n Dal— h[25] shall shake my stedfast Truth,
In all the winning Bloom and Fire of Youth.
What tho' her Charms even H— gh[26] might fire,

21. *Flora burn'd*: presumably one of the lovers imputed to Sappho, though the name does not occur in Ovid's poem; it may be a coded reference to a 1720s contemporary; *burn'd*: 'Of persons, of the heart, etc.: To be on fire (with desire, lust, passion, wrath)' (*OED*).

22. *Lesbian*: At this period the primary meaning was an inhabitant of Lesbos; the sense concerning sexual orientation does not occur till the late nineteenth century.

23. *fickle Spoiler*: Phaon, who, having left Lesbos, Sappho imagines betraying girls in Sicily (*Heroides* XV, 51–5).

24. Philip Dormer Stanhope (1694–1773), Earl of Chesterfield after his father's death in 1726, was celebrated for his wit; Anthony Lowther (c. 1694–1741), Sophia Howe's former lover, for his good looks. In BL Add. MS 78522, 'Rich—ds' appears in place of 'Lowth— rs', which seems more likely to refer to Sarah, Duchess of Richmond (1706–51) than to her husband, Charles Lennox, second Duke of Richmond (1701–50), if to either. 'G——r' appears instead in BL Add. MS 22629, which may refer to John Leveson-Gower, first Earl Gower (1694–1754). The variations in allusions to contemporaries illustrate one of the social functions served by manuscript verse of a scandalous nature.

25. *Dal— h*: probably Lady Jane Douglas, Countess of Dalkeith (1701–29); the pronoun 'her' (line 95) excludes reference to a man, and in context it is apt that a woman should prove more attractive than a series of men.

26. *H— gh*: almost certainly Bennet Sherard, Earl of Harborough. A *jeu d'esprit* sent by Lady Hervey to Henrietta Howard on 27 July 1729 in which typical pictorial subjects are attributed to various people well known in society includes: 'Virgin. By Lord Harborough' (BL Add. MS 22628, f. 26v). As John Wilson Croker remarks in his edition of Lady Suffolk's letters, 'The allusions to Lord Harborough's want of gallantry are frequent in the letters of the day' (*Letters to and from Henrietta, Countess of Suffolk, and her Second Husband, the Hon. George Berkeley*, 2 vols. (London: John Murray, 1824), I, 345).

And warm that demi-Man into Desire,
'Tis you alone I wish, in you I find
All the collected Beautys of your Kind:[27]
No Power on Earth shall alienate my Flame,[28]
Till Death dissolve this Transitory Frame;
And if a Being after Death there be,
No Heav'n I ask, but what I ask in thee.

27. *Kind*: 'A class (of human beings or animals) of the same sex; a sex (in collective sense)' (*OED*).

28. *Flame*: 'A burning feeling or passion, *esp.* of love' (*OED*).

# 9 To Molly on Easter Eve

***Main source.*** Harrowby MS 81, ff. 148r–v, chosen because, if it is in Maria Skerrett's hand, as Isobel Grundy indicates in her typewritten catalogue of the volume, it probably pre-dates the copy in Harrowby 255 in the hand of Lady Mary Wortley Montagu.

***Complementary manuscript source.*** Harrowby MS 255, pp. 77–8.

***Complementary print source.*** *Fog's Weekly Journal*, 7 November 1730 (much shorter, consisting only of eight lines).

***Attribution.*** Montagu (Harrowby 255; unattributed in Harrowby 81); *Fog's* refers to the writer as one of 'Our Modern Coxcombs'.

***Context and date.*** 'Molly', the poem's addressee, is Maria Skerrett, whom, according to Lady Louisa Stuart, Montagu met in 1720. Along with Claude-Charlotte, Countess of Stafford, she was one of Montagu's closest friends in the 1720s and 1730s. Pressed by Sir Robert Walpole to become his mistress, she had been won over by the autumn of 1724, despite advice against this from Montagu (Grundy, pp. 225, 191–2, 250; Montagu, *Essays & Poems*, pp. 55–6). As I have noted in 'Lord Hervey, Poetic Voice and Gender', Grundy remarks that the poem '*may* have been written as from Hervey's patron Walpole to Maria Skerrett', but does not consider whether it might have been addressed as if to Skerrett by Montagu herself (Overton, 'Poetic Voice and Gender', p. 611; Grundy, p. 337). In her catalogue to Harrowby 81, Grundy attributes just that speculation to Lois Kathleen Mahaffey, whose doctoral thesis does not mention 'To Molly on Easter Eve', but does imply that Montagu and Skerrett were lovers, that Pope found out and that the discovery helped provoke his satirical attacks on both of them (Lois Kathleen Mahaffey, 'Alexander Pope and his Sappho: Pope's Relationship with Lady Mary Wortley Montagu and its Influence on his Work' (unpublished PhD thesis, University of Texas, 1963), pp. 169–73, 186–9, 201–4, 220–4). However, as my article goes on to suggest, textual evidence indicates that the poem is written in a woman's voice, not a man's, and that, while the writer was Hervey, that voice is Montagu's. The distinction with which it begins, between 'Prudes' and 'well disciplin'd Girls in their white Sarsnet Hood' on the one hand, and the writer and addressee on the other, applies much more closely to two women than to a man addressing a woman. Equally significant, its mockery not just of prudery but of what it presents as religious superstition, in this case to do with Easter, is of a piece with Montagu's and Hervey's free-thinking; and its dismissal of 'the ignorant Crew, | Who their Pleasure neglect, and their Interest persue' does not match a Prime Minister who was very good at pursuing his interests, though by no means indifferent to pleasure. Although Grundy states that Montagu's own poems to Skerrett 'give no hint of an erotic relationship' and, on the basis of many years of research on Montagu, that 'her orientation towards men seems well established', this does not exclude the possibility that, as I have argued, it is 'a jeu d'esprit drawing humorously outrageous inferences from their closeness' (Grundy, pp. 269, 346; Overton, 'Poetic Voice and Gender', p. 612).

The poem seems unlikely to have been written before 1727, the year in which, according to Robert Halsband, Hervey and Montagu became close friends (Halsband, p. 30; Grundy, p. 336). As the two exchanged their verse, it probably responds to two poems by Montagu, 'The Lover: A Ballad', and 'The Mistriss', both of which are in the same metre of anapaestic tetrameter, although arranged in stanzas rather than, like Hervey's poem, continuously (*Essays & Poems*, pp. 234–6, 236–8). The further intertextual link indicated by the version in *Fog's Weekly Journal* with Horace's Ode XXVIII, Book III, may suggest a date closer to 1730, especially because Hervey was abroad between July 1728 and October 1729. Horace's poem is from a man to a woman. If, as the textual evidence suggests, Hervey's is from a woman to a woman, the change in the writer's gender complements the one he had already made, or was about to make, to the addressee's gender in his imitations of Ode XI, Book I (Poems 5b and 5c). They too are in the same metre, highly suitable for humorous verse in *carpe diem* mode. The writer of the article in *Fog's* that includes a different and much shorter version of the poem takes exception to its advocacy both of religious and of sexual infidelity. As Hervey was a member of the government and *Fog's* an opposition newspaper, it follows in the tracks of an attack earlier in the year on the poem on Lady Abergavenny (Poem 29), in this case probably by Hervey, published by another opposition newspaper, *The Grub-street Journal*. Both writers not only produce different versions of the poem they criticise, but also a poem of their own that, they claim, is both aesthetically and morally superior. The poem in *Fog's* quotes two lines from Montagu's 'Wednesday', which was not printed until 1747, but if, as Grundy suggests, *Fog's* '*may* have been making public some verse exchange between her and Hervey' (Grundy, p. 337), the motive was probably political animus. It is as conventional in metre, iambic pentameter couplets, as in sentiment. Although Horace's poem does not scorn religion, it proposes to celebrate the feast of Neptune in private rather than in public. Its tone is humorous, as in its invention of a consul called Bibulus to indicate the vintage of the wine they are to drink. Hervey's anapaestic tetrameter couplets, with their lively, buoyant rhythm, are pacier than Horace's quatrains composed alternately of lines of eight and twelve syllables, because the stanza divisions, and the shifts from shorter lines to longer, keep slowing the tempo down. John Duncombe's translation, provided in Appendix 1, follows the original not only by using quatrains but by lengthening the last line in each one from tetrameter to pentameter, yet its iambic metre is less effective than Hervey's anapaests at conveying a spirit nicely captured by its phrase 'frolic Airs'. Montagu and Skerrett no doubt appreciated the wit and brio of the adaptation.

***Textual commentary.*** There are few textual differences, none of them significant, between the two manuscripts. Neither copy is punctuated carefully; the copy supposedly in Maria Skerrett's hand throughout writes 'uss' for 'us', which has been emended. The facts that both have the same correction in line 5, and that two of the words that are overwritten appear in the version in *Fog's*, suggest that they were copied from the same original, and that it was that text, or one close to it, to which *Fog's* had access.

## To Molly[1] on Easter Eve

Whilst Prudes (who because they can't sin will be good),
And well disciplin'd Girls in their white Sarsnet[2] Hood,
Are preparing to tast of this spiritual Feast
Dispens'd by some Fool, or some Knave of a Priest,
Some Blockhead who credits the Nonsense he's saying,
Or some Hypocrite conscious what farces he's playing,
Let us, my dear Molly, improve the short Night,
And season each moment with mutual Delight;
Let us seize on[3] the Heaven allow'd here by Fate
And leave the Reversion[4] to those that can wait.
Let us first, tete-a-tete,[5] to your Dressing Room Fire
With Champain, and a snug little supper retire,
With singing and chat we'll prolong the Repast,
Not live by the Watchman, but live by our Taste,
And when we have laugh'd at the ignorant Crew,
Who their Pleasure neglect, and their Interest persue,
Who the Present with Views to the Future employ,
And compounding for Ease, never aim at a Joy!
When we've run over all Speculation supplys
In the Wretches we pity, and those we despise,
The unhappyly Great, or the fruitlessly Wise,

1. *Molly*: see headnote.

2. *Sarsnet*: sarsenet, 'A very fine and soft silk material made both plain and twilled, in various colours' (*OED*).

3. *seize on*: punning on 'season' in the previous line, and perhaps echoing Horace's famous phrase *carpe diem* ('seize the day') in Book I, Ode II.

4. *Reversion*: 'The right of succeeding to the possession of something, or of obtaining something at a future time' (*OED*).

5. *tete-a-tete*: 'Together without the presence of a third person; in private (of two persons); face to face' (*OED*; properly tête à tête).

Let us riot in Bliss, which they only can prove
Who think nothing in Life worth possessing but Love.
Let us crown ev'ry Wish, give a Loose to Desire,
And alternately quench and rekindle the Fire,
Till tir'd tho' unsated, I sink on thy Breast
And dream of my Heaven, where awake 'tis possess'd.

## Horace, Book III, Ode XXVIII

What better could I do on Neptune's festal day? Nimbly bring forth, O Lyde, the Caecuban stored away, and make assault on wisdom's stronghold! Thou seest the day is waning, and yet, as though the fleeting hours were standing still, thou delayest to bring from out the store-room a waiting jar that dates from Bibulus' consulship.

In responsive song we will sing, I of Neptune and the Nereids' sea-green tresses. Thou, in answer, on thy curving lyre shalt hymn Latona and the shafts of swift-moving Cynthia; and in final song her who holds Cnidos and the shining Cyclades, and visits Paphos with her team of swans. Night also shall be celebrated with a fitting lay. (Horace, *Odes and Epodes*, trans. C. E. Bennett (Loeb, p. 271))

# 10 Verses Sent to —

***Main source.*** Harrowby MS 81, ff. 141r–1v, chosen because its corrections are incorporated into the text in Montagu's hand in Harrowby MS 255, so suggesting it is the earlier of the two.

***Complementary manuscript source.*** Harrowby MS 255, pp. 88–9. No other manuscript sources have come to light.

***Complementary print source.*** 'A Song', in *The Museum*, III, 289–90 (no. 34, 4 July 1747).

***Attribution.*** Although it is unattributed in both manuscripts and in *The Museum*, the fact that, in Harrowby MS 255, the poem comes sixth in a series of eight poems attributed to Hervey suggests it is also his. The poem that comes after it, 'Epistle to —' (Poem 11), is also a love poem; the one before is 'Monimia to Philocles' (Poem 1). There are stylistic grounds, too, for attributing the poem to Hervey. These include the violence of some of the language, unusual in a poem even about disaffected love, as in the word 'destroy' in the first line, repeated in the first line of the second stanza, and 'wound' in line 4; the use of antithesis, as in the second line, 'Unpleas'd all Day, asleep all Night', and the opposition of 'wound' and 'delight' in the fourth; the extended political metaphor that begins with 'Tyrant's Part' in the fourth stanza and culminates only at the poem's climax at the end of the seventh; and the ellipsis in the final line – a striking compression rarely found in conventional love poems of the period, which tend to aim more at grace and elegance than at forcefulness.

***Context and date.*** If the poem is by Hervey, it is most likely to have been written before the early 1730s, after which most of his verse is humorous or satirical. Its most interesting feature is that, in the two manuscript versions, the gender of all three parties to whom it refers is female. It appears to have existed in two forms, one as in *The Museum* and in Harrowby MS 81 before the words indicating the gender of two of the parties were altered, the other as altered in Harrowby MS 81 in a hand that is difficult to identify but that may be Montagu's, and as transcribed in Harrowby MS 255. Conventional gender roles at the period strongly suggest that, on the evidence of the words in the third stanza referring to the writer's 'Beauty', the gender of the writer in both versions is female. (Another possibility is that Hervey is here, as the speaker of the poem, referring to his own much-heralded 'Beauty', and that the 'Youth' of the first version could be Stephen Fox, whom he addresses with that term in Poem 6.)

That of the addressee in the second version is changed from male to female by the alteration of 'Youth' to 'Nymph' in line 13; more intriguing still, that of the potential rival from male to female by the alteration of the pronouns in lines 24, 28 and 31. In both versions a woman reproaches her lover with lack of attention and threatens to substitute a rival. The changes connect the poem to two others by Hervey in Harrowby MS 255 that play with gender roles, 'The Countess of — to Miss —', and, if the argument to that effect in the headnote for 'To Molly on Easter Eve' is valid, the latter also. As I have suggested in 'Lord Hervey, Poetic Voice and Gender', Hervey may have followed Montagu's lead in writing verse that transposed conventional gender roles, as she had done most spectacularly in 'Epistle from Arthur G[ray] to Mrs M[urra]y' ('Poetic Voice and Gender', pp. 597–8). Whether the textual changes stem from a text authored by Hervey or whether Montagu put them in herself, they produce a most unconventional love poem for the period – in effect, a lesbian triangle – especially if written by a man.

***Textual commentary.*** The version in *The Museum* conforms closely to that in Harrowby MS 81 before it was altered; the version as altered could hardly have been printed at the period, if it was available to Dodsley at all. Most of the differences between the two versions are discussed above. Grundy's invaluable typed catalogue at the end of Harrowby MS 81, printed in a form giving first lines and folio numbers in Margaret M. Smith, *Index of English Literary Manuscripts*, Vol. 3, *1700–1800*, Part 2: *John Gay – Ambrose Philips* (London: Mansell, 1989), pp. 191–2, describes the version of the poem it contains as: 'untitled verses in Lord Hervey's hand. A copy by Lady Mary in H MS 255, [ff. 48–9 (now pp. 88–9)], is headed "Verses sent To —"'. Against this is written '*not* in Ld H's hand R. H. 1972'. The annotation, which is by Robert Halsband, is correct; the hand remains unidentified.

## Verses Sent to —

Whilst Time in Absence you destroy,
    Unpleas'd all Day, asleep all Night;
You waste those Hours you might employ,
    And wound that Heart you might delight.

2.

Perhaps my Quiet to destroy,
    Whilst thus I mourn, may please thy Pride:
But is my Pain thy only Joy?
    Say, hast thou not a wish beside?

3.

To this neglected Form, in vain,
The Gods its little Beauty gave,
If you the Conquest still disdain,
Or like the Triumph, not the Slave.

4.

But oh! misjudging Nymph![1] beware,
Nor wanton act a Tyrant's Part;
Tho' Empire[2] be thy only Care,
Who rule secure, must rule the Heart.

5.

Precarious is that Monarch's Pow'r,
Whose Slaves reluctantly obey:
For those who once his Right deplore,
Are quickly Rebels to his Sway.

6.

Then say some new Invader's Arms
Successfull by this means shou'd prove;
Who not engross'd by Glory's Charms,
May what she[3] conquers deign to love.

7.

If wisely this revolted Heart,
Impatient of its Wrongs and Pain,
Shall take the kind Usurper's Part,
Solicit hers,[4] and break thy Chain;

1. *Nymph*: replacing 'Youth' in the manuscript, and replaced by 'Youth' in the copy published in *The Museum*, 4 July 1747.

2. *Empire*: 'Paramount influence, absolute sway, supreme command or control' (*OED*).

3. *she*: corrected from 'he' in the manuscript, and changed to 'he' in the copy published in *The Museum*.

4. *hers*: corrected from 'his' in the manuscript, and changed to 'his' in the copy published in *The Museum*.

8.

Repentant then too late thou'lt grieve
The Change thy Folly wrought in me;
When Gratitude to her[5] shall give
That Heart the want of it[6] lost thee.

5. *her*: corrected from 'him' in the manuscript, and changed to 'he' in the copy published in *The Museum*.

6. *it*: the antecedent is 'Gratitude'.

# 11 Epistle to —

***Main source.*** Harrowby MS 255, pp. 90–3, chosen because of the strong probability that Montagu transcribed it from a copy made available to her by Hervey.

***Complementary manuscript source.*** None has come to light.

***Complementary print sources.*** *London Magazine*, 19 (February 1750), 89; Dodsley, *Collection* (from 1755).

***Attribution.*** Harrowby MS 255; *London Magazine*; Dodsley.

***Context and date.*** The poem shares a couplet (the second lines vary) with Poem 4 'Roxana to Usbeck' which is quoted in a letter to Stephen Fox dated 27 September 1731 (SRO 941/47/4, p. 223); it is reasonable to infer that the poem was written before or around that date. The lines occur in a section of the letter expressing Hervey's devotion (contractions have been expanded and 'whislt' corrected to 'whilst'):

> One Thing I am sure of that whilst I have you, I shall never be tempted to hang my-self and that if I was to lose you nothing but want of courage could hinder me; no consideration would tempt me to live tho' there might be some Abject Weakness that might make me fear to dye,
>
> For what is Life unless it's Joys we prove
> And where is Joy depriv'd of all we Love.
>
> You can not tell how often and how tenderly I think of You, never with indifference, never with out emotion; but with the Tears starting into my Eyes with Sorrow at our Seperation or blushing with pleasure at the Thoughts of our meeting.

'Epistle to —' appears to invite a heterosexual interpretation, and if in that aspect it had an actual, existing addressee rather than a nominal one – if, that is, it was more than a literary exercise – that addressee may have been Anne Vane (d. 1736), especially as Lucy Moore suggests the first phase of Hervey's affair with her began in late 1730 (Moore, pp. 94, 96); it ended in December 1731 when Hervey discovered that Vane had also become the mistress of Frederick, Prince of Wales (Halsband, p. 129). Although he is known to have had other mistresses, she is the one to whom his letters and memoirs pay most attention, and he was sufficiently attracted to her to re-establish their liaison three years later when Frederick, Prince of Wales, who had set her up as his mistress early in 1732, had begun to tire of her (Halsband, pp. 135, 182). Generically, the poem is a textbook example of a *carpe diem* poem in epistolary mode, and it is discussed as such in my *Eighteenth-Century*

*British Verse Epistle* (pp. 160–1). It has many connections with Poem 5, which is an imitation of Horace's famous *carpe diem* ode, including the possibility that it can be interpreted as addressed to a man, not a woman.

***Textual commentary.*** The two most significant differences between Montagu's transcript and the two printed versions are that the former includes paragraph divisions and the latter do not, and that there are substantive verbal variations between former and latter in lines 9, 13 and 22. There are few differences between the two printed versions and only one minor substantive variation (the/those, line 31), so suggesting either that the one in Dodsley's *Collection* was based on that in the *London Magazine*, or that both stem from the same manuscript. Montagu's punctuation, spelling and use of initial capitals are much less idiosyncratic here than in some of her manuscripts, but she has omitted punctuation needed for the sense at the end of lines 15, 19, 27, 29, 31, 35, 37, 39, 41, 43–5, 49, 76; this has been added editorially. The other few emendations to her copy are indicated in the List of Emendations.

## Epistle To —

What shall I say to fix thy wav'ring mind,
To chase thy doubts, and force thee to be kind?[1]
What weight of Argument can turn the Scale,
If Intercession from a Lover fail?
By what shall I conjure[2] thee to obey
This tender Summons, nor prolong thy Stay?

If unabated in thy constant breast
That Passion burns, that once thy vows profess'd:
If Absence has not chill'd thy present Flame,
Its Ardour and its Purity the same:
Indulge these Transports[3] and no more controll
The Dictates of thy fond consenting Soul:
By no vain Scruples be thy Purpose sway'd
And only Love implicitly obey'd;

1. *kind*: 'Of persons, their actions, etc.: Affectionate, loving, fond; on intimate terms. a kind girl: a mistress' (*OED*).

2. *conjure*: 'To entreat (a person) by something for which he has a strong regard; to appeal solemnly or earnestly to; to beseech, implore' (*OED*).

3. *Transports*: '3. The state of being "carried out of oneself", i.e. out of one's normal mental condition; vehement emotion (now usu. of a pleasurable kind); mental exaltation, rapture, ecstasy' (*OED*).

Let Inclination[4] this debate decide,
Nor be thy Prudence, but thy Heart thy Guide.
But real Prudence never can oppose
What Love suggests, and Gratitude avows:
The warm, dear Raptures, which thy Bosom move,
'Tis Virtue to indulge, 'tis Wisdom to improve.[5]
For think how few the Joys allow'd by Fate,
How mix'd their Cup, how short their longest Date:
How onward still the stream of Pleasure flows,
That no reflux the rapid Current knows;
Not even thy Charms can bribe the ruthless hand
Of rigid Time, to stay his ebbing sand.

Fair as thou art, that Beauty must decay;
The Night of Age succeeds the brightest Day;
That Cheek where Nature's sweetest Garden blows,
Her whitest Lilly, and her warmest Rose;
Those Eyes, the meaning Ministers of Love,
Who, what thy Lips can only utter, prove,
These must resign their Lustre, those their bloom,
And find with meaner Charms one common doom.
Pass but some few short Years, this Change must be;
Nor one less dreadfull, shallst thou mourn in me:
For tho' no Chance can alienate my Flame,
Whilst thine, to feed the Lamp, shall burn the same,
Yet shall the stream of Years abate that Fire,
And cold Esteem succeed to warm Desire:
Then on thy Breast unraptur'd shall I dwell,
Nor feel a Joy beyond what I can tell.
Or say, should Sickness antedate that Woe,
And Intercept what Time would else allow;
If Pain should pall my Taste to all thy Charms,
Or Death himself should tear me from thy Arms:
How would thou then regret with fruitless Truth,
The precious squander'd hours of Health and Youth?

4. *Inclination*: 'Liking, affection' (*OED*).
5. *improve*: 'To turn (a thing) to profit or good account, to employ to advantage; to make profitable use of, take advantage of, avail oneself of, utilize; to make use of, use, employ' (*OED*).

Come then my Love! nor trust the future Day,
Live while we can, be happy while we may:
For what is Life unless its Joys we prove?
And what is Happiness but mutual Love?[6]
Our Time is Wealth no frugal Hand can store,
All our possession is the present Hour,
And he who spares to use it, ever poor.
The golden Now is all that we can boast
And that (like Snow) at once is grasp'd and lost.
Haste, wing thy passage then, no more delay,
But to these Eyes their sole Delight convey.
Not thus I languish'd for thy Virgin Charms
When first surrender'd to these eager Arms,
When first admitted to that Heaven, thy Breast,
To mine I strain'd that charming Foe to rest.
How leaps my conscious Heart when I retrace[7]
The dear Idea[8] of that strict Embrace?
When on thy Bosom quite entranc'd I lay,
And lov'd unsated the short Night away:
While half reluctant you, and half resign'd,
Amidst fears, wishes, pain, and pleasure joyn'd;
Now holding off, now growing to my Breast,
By turns reprov'd me, and by turns caress'd;

Oh how Remembrance throbs in ev'ry vein!
I pant, I sicken for that Scene again:
My senses ake, I can no word command,
And the Pen totters in my trembling Hand.
Farewell, thou only Joy on Earth I know,
And all that Man can taste of Heaven below.

6. *For what … Love*: Hervey quoted this couplet in a letter to Stephen Fox dated 27 September 1731 (SRO 941/47/4, p. 223); presumably Fox had already read the poem and so would know the lines. A couplet even closer to the letter's is found in Poem 4 'Roxana to Usbeck': 'For what is life unless its joys we prove? | And where is joy, depriv'd of what we love?' (lines 20–1).

7. *retrace*: 'To trace again in thought or memory; to recall; to go over again, to recapitulate' (*OED*).

8. *Idea*: 'The mental image or notion of something previously seen or known, recalled by the memory' (*OED*).

# 12 An Epistle to a Lady

***Main source.*** Portland Papers (Longleat), XX (1727–64, Verse de Société, etc.), ff. 63r–64v, chosen because the same collection includes other verse by Hervey and for the evidence it provides of manuscript circulation.

***Complementary manuscript source.*** No other manuscript has come to light.

***Complementary print sources.*** *London Magazine*, 2 (September 1733), 472; Dodsley, *Collection* (from 1748); *Poems Written Occasionally by the Late John Winstanley ... with Many Others*, ed. by George Winstanley, 2 vols. (Dublin: by S. Powell, for the editor, 1751), II, 218–21. John Winstanley died in 1750; the previous volume had been published in 1742.

***Attribution.*** Although *Literature Online* identifies the poem as by Hervey, this is on the basis of what seems to have been the assumption that ascriptions of a series of poems to 'the Same' in Dodsley's *Collection* can also be extended to unattributed poems that follow them. Such an assumption is, of course, wholly unwarranted. In this case, the two unattributed poems following Hervey's 'To the Same. From Hampton-Court, 1731' are both ascribed to him, though the first, 'The Poet's Prayer', is certainly by William Dunkin (see Dodsley, I, 146–7), and authorship of the second, this 'Epistle to a Lady', is uncertain. The poem is one of the relatively few in Dodsley's *Collection* to which Suarez was unable to assign an author (Dodsley, VI, 413–14); and it is discussed as an example of an unattributed amatory epistle in my *Eighteenth-Century British Verse Epistle* (pp. 161–2), illustrating a possible approach when a personal context appears to be lacking. Neither the manuscript nor any of the three printed sources yields any evidence concerning attribution. For example, as Bryan Coleborne points out in his *ODNB* article on John Winstanley in reference to *Poems Written Occasionally*, 'Since both volumes refer to the poems in their extended titles as "interspers'd with many others, by several ingenious hands", Winstanley's authorship of individual poems remains uncertain.' All the same, the discussion in the following paragraph offers some evidence, in part stylistic and in part circumstantial, that the poem may be by Hervey.

***Context and date.*** The manuscript provides little evidence of date because, like the previous volume in the series, it is arranged alphabetically by first line. However, if the date range given in the title is accurate, the poem cannot have been written before 1727; and it cannot have been written after September 1733, when it was printed in the *London Magazine*. The stylistic evidence for its composition by Hervey is the forceful manner of its expression, especially in its handling of heroic couplets. It is characterised by the kinds of antithesis that make his prose as well as his verse so distinctive, and by the deftness of their construction. The poem begins arrestingly with the antithesis 'akes with anguish, pines with grief', and its brief opening verse paragraph ends with a part-chiasmus – 'sorrow friendship' followed by 'friendship modesty' – complicated by 'sorrow, cruelty' in the following line. Further terse examples of chiasmus follow, for instance 'lost the one, the other dy'd' (line 20), 'Nor she can' | 'nor I can' (line 22), and, most effectively of all, 'The joy's imagin'd, real the despair' (line 69), along with such dramatic antitheses as 'Condemn'd to suffer, but denied redress' (line 47), and 'torture constancy, or sadden love' (line 63). But the poem does not overdo such devices and puts others to strong use too, especially the unexpected run-on line, as in 'chides the waves that rolled | Himself ashore, but sunk his dearer gold' (lines 13–14); asyndeton – a series of words without connectives, as with the verbs 'alters, adds, defames' (line 36), and 'Insinuates, dissembles, lyes, betrays' (line 42); and cogent though sparing use of such enhancements to the heroic couplet favoured by Hervey as the alexandrine – ''Tis hard to feel the smart, and not lament the wound' (line 4), itself a further example of antithesis – and the triplet, of which there are two (lines 33–5, 70–2), the second of which gives the poem a plangent climax. If the poem is not Hervey's, it is difficult to think of another poet writing around 1730 who could have produced it.

The circumstantial evidence is slighter, but still worth considering. In part it rests on the assumption that the poem refers to a real-life drama. If this is valid, it is possible that, like Poem 11, 'Epistle to —', it came out of Hervey's relationship with Anne Vane. As remarked in the Headnote to that poem, the first phase of that affair took place from late 1730, but it ended when Hervey discovered that Vane was also the lover of Frederick, Prince of Wales. In the first flush of his anger, he wrote to Stephen Fox on 25 December: 'Lett their Folly fall on their own Head, & their Wickedness on their own Pate. they neither know nor suspect that I have detected them, nor ever shall: for the easyest, the most natural & the justest Revenge one can take upon People who imagine they impose upon one, is to let them fancy they do; & instead of being their Dupe, let them make themselves their own' (SRO 941/47/4, p. 329). He felt strongly enough about his betrayal to end the letter with twelve lines of embedded verse (Poem 78). All the same, his remarks have to be read in the context of a letter written to his male lover – a context made very clear by the comparison that precedes the verse: 'I would no more divulge my being vex'd than you would formerly have done your being clap'd.' If, therefore, 'Epistle to a Lady' was written to Anne Vane, it is possible that it constitutes an attempt to rescue himself from the affair with dignity, perhaps even to keep the liaison alive. It would have been written a little later than his letter to Fox, but before the Prince installed Vane formally as his mistress in late January 1732 by taking a house for her (Percival, *Diary*, I, 255).

Details of the episode would be clearer had not the part of Hervey's memoirs dealing with events between May 1730 and the late summer of 1732 been destroyed, presumably, as Romney Sedgwick argues, by Hervey's grandson Frederick William Hervey, 1st Marquess of Bristol, on account of its scandalous nature (Sedgwick, I, xi–xiv). Yet the text of the poem offers some possible clues.

First, it emphasises that the writer appears to have no choice but to accept the loss of his lover. The second line declares that both the addressee and 'heaven' 'deny relief'; and the poem's two extended metaphors, one involving shipwrecked treasure, the other a bereaved mother, seem to state that the loss is irrevocable. If the poem does refer to Hervey's affair with Vane, this emphasis can be understood the other way round, as an implicit appeal for her not to leave him. Such an interpretation would also explain why it refers to no third party, because that would give offence, and why, in the comparison 'As angels mingle, or as saints admire' (line 24), and such expressions as 'virtuous ardour' (line 26), it insists on the chastity both of the addressee and of the writer's motives in courting her. Flattery of this kind would have appealed to a woman who did her best to protect her reputation as a Maid of Honour when there were clear grounds for doubting it. At Bath just over a year before, in October 1730, Vane had, as Robert Halsband puts it, 'been so disturbed by reports from court that she was with child that she forced herself to go out in public frequently, against her health and inclination, to disprove the gossip' (Halsband, p. 128); and Viscount Percival reports that, when the Prince installed her, already several months pregnant, as his mistress, she wrote to the Queen 'to desire leave to go for some months to her grandfather's' (Percival, *Diary*, I, 218), evidently in an attempt to cover up a fact of which the Queen was already well informed. Vane's sensitivity over her reputation would help further explain why the poem blames no third party but what it styles, in a rhetorical sequence of thirteen lines, as 'Scandal, a busy fiend, in truth's disguise' (lines 33–45; 33). A further piece of possible evidence is that, as mentioned in the headnote to Poem 11, 'Epistle to —', Hervey was sufficiently attracted to his former mistress to renew his affair with her in mid-1734 after the Prince had effectively cast her off – a reconciliation he describes wittily in his memoirs (Sedgwick, II, 388–9). Although Hannah Smith and Stephen Taylor remark, in a notably well argued and carefully documented essay, 'Hephaestion and Alexander: Lord Hervey, Frederick, Prince of Wales, and the Royal Favourite in England in the 1730s', that there is no 'evidence that Hervey felt a strong emotional attachment to Anne Vane' (*English Historical Review*, 124, no. 507 (2009), 283–312 (300)), his return to her in 1734 is not necessarily to be explained only in political terms as motivated by animus against the Prince of Wales. Psycho-sexual as well as emotional motives may also have played a part. However, if the poem is by Hervey, and if it was addressed to Vane, it failed in what I am suggesting may have been an implicit effort to retain her as his mistress. Such a failure might account for what seems to have been a misguided attempt on Hervey's part in April 1732 to blackmail Vane into helping to restore him to favour with the Prince (Halsband, pp. 135–6). Yet, despite the bitterness and anger that produced this attempt, and that it produced in turn, even such powerful emotions did not prevent either her or him from renewing their affair two years later.

***Textual commentary.*** The manuscript is in a good clear hand, with few blots or crossings-out, but it uses initial capitals unevenly (e.g. the word 'friendship' lacks an initial capital in line 6 but has one in line 7), and sometimes punctuation is omitted, especially at the ends of lines. For these reasons, initial capitalisation and punctuation are more often taken from the carefully printed texts in the *London Magazine* and the second Dodsley edition – the first edition being unreliable because, as Michael F. Suarez has pointed out, it is poorly printed and contains many errors (Dodsley, pp. 5–9). Details of all such substitutions are given in the List of Emendations. Only one substantive reading is preferred from the printed texts over the manuscript – 'sweetener' for 'Sweetness' (line 17). As there are only a few variants in the 1782 edition of Dodsley, none substantive, these are not recorded.

## An Epistle to a Lady

When the heart akes with anguish, pines with grief,
And heaven and you alike deny relief;
When even the flatt'rer hope is no where found,
'Tis hard to feel the smart, and not lament the wound.
Permit me, then, to sigh one last adieu,
Nor scorn a sorrow friendship owes to you:
A friendship modesty might well return;
A sorrow, cruelty it self might mourn.

Think how the miser, pierc'd with inward pain,
Looks down with horror on the troubled main;[1]
Or wildly roams along the rocky coast,
T'explore his treasures in the tempest lost;
Hates his own safety, chides the waves that rolled
Himself ashore, but sunk his dearer gold.
Like him afflicted, pensive, and forlorn,
I look on life, and all its pomp with scorn.[2]
You was[3] the sweetener of each busy scene;

1. *main*: 'Short for main sea . . .; the open sea' (*OED*).

2. *I look . . . with scorn*: this outlook is characteristic of Hervey in the last twelve years of his life.

3. *You was*: this form of the verb 'to be' continued in use with a second person singular pronoun into the seventeenth and eighteenth centuries, but as early as Swift's time it was increasingly restricted to informal, non-literary uses such as in correspondence. See *Merriam-Webster's Dictionary of English Usage*, 2nd rev. edn (Springfield, MA: Merriam-Webster, 1995), p. 972, citing Barbara M. H. Strang, *A History of English* (London: Methuen, 1970), p. 140. Here it seems designed to promote a sense of intimacy as well as informality.

You gave the joy without, the pain within.
Pleasure and you were both so near ally'd,
That when I lost the one, the other dy'd;
Pain too has lavish'd all her killing store;
Nor she can add, nor I can suffer more.

In vain I view'd you with as chaste a fire,
As angels mingle, or as saints admire;
By reason prompted, passion had no part,
A virtuous ardour that refin'd the heart.
In vain I sought a friendship free from fault,
Where sex and beauty were alike forgot.
A friendship by the noblest union join'd,
The female softness, and the manly mind.
Courage to conquer evils, or endure;
Sweetness to sooth the pain, and smiles to cure.
Scandal, a busy fiend, in truth's disguise,
Like fame all cover'd o'er with ears and eyes,[4]
Learns the fond tale, and spreads it as she flies.
Nor spreads alone, but alters, adds, defames,
Affects to pity, tho' her duty blames.
Feigns not to credit all she sees or hears,
But hope the evil only in her fears.[5]
Pretends to weigh the fact in even scale,
And wish, at least, that justice may prevail.
Insinuates, dissembles, lyes, betrays,
Plays the whole hypocrite such various ways,
That innocence itself must suffer wrong,
And honour bleed, the prey of slander's tongue.

Such is my fate, so grievous my distress,
Condemn'd to suffer, but denied redress:
Too fond of joy, too sensible of pain,
To part with all that's dear, and not complain:[6]

4. *fame . . . ears and eyes*: traditional emblems of Fame in the Renaissance also equipped her with two trumpets.

5. *But hope the evil only in her fears*: i.e. she also pretends to hope that she has reason only to fear that the slander is true. This kind of elliptical expression is characteristic of Hervey.

6. *complain*: 'To give expression to sorrow; to make moan, lament' (*OED*).

Too delicate[7] to injure what I love,
Or ask the pity fame[8] will ne'er approve.
What more remains, then, but to drop my claim,
And by my conduct justify my flame?[9]
Burst the dear bands, that to my heart-strings join,
And sacrifice my peace, to purchase thine?

As the fond mother, who delirious eyes
Her dying babe, will scarce believe it dyes:
But strains it still with transport in her arms,
Dwells on its lips, and numbers o'er its charms;
Pleads that it slumbers, and expects, in vain,
To see the little cherub live again;
So my torn heart must all the sorrows move[10]
That torture constancy, or sadden love:
Yet fondly follow your dear image still,
Fancy I hear you speak, I see you smile:
Doat on a phantom, idolize the name,
And wish the shade[11] and substance were the same.

Alass! how fruitless is the idle pray'r!
The joy's imagin'd, real the despair.
Like Adam forc'd his Eden to forego,
I lose my only Paradice below,
And dread the prospect of succeeding woe.

7. *delicate*: 'Finely sensitive to what is becoming, proper, or modest, or to the feelings of others' (*OED*).

8. *fame*: 'The character attributed to a person or thing by report or generally entertained; reputation' (*OED*).

9. *flame*: 'A burning feeling or passion, *esp.* of love' (*OED*).

10. *move*: 'to find out, learn, or know by experience; to have experience of; to go through, undergo, suffer' (*OED*).

11. *shade*: 'An unsubstantial image of something real; an unreal appearance; something that has only a fleeting existence, or that has become reduced almost to nothing' (*OED*).

# 13 Mr Hammond to Miss Dashwood

***Main source.*** Brotherton Collection, University of Leeds, Lt 119, ff. 70r, 71r (rectos only).

***Complementary manuscript sources.*** BL Add. MS 57836, f. 113r; Yale Osborn Collection c.83/1, no. 114; c.130, pp. 81–3; c.175, p. 54.

***Complementary print sources.*** *An Elegy to a Young Lady, in the Manner of Ovid. By ––––––. With an Answer: By a Lady, Author of the Verses to the Imitator of Horace* (London: [Sam Aris] for J. Roberts, 1733); Dodsley, *Collection*, IV, 77–9 (1755), 80–2 (1782).

***Attribution.*** 'Wrote by Mr. H——d' in the Brotherton manuscript; '[James] Hammond' according to a manuscript note in an unidentified hand in the British Library copy of the Roberts edition, shelf mark 1346. m. 34; and Dodsley. These attributions are, however, questionable. As Isobel Grundy has pointed out, the poem did not appear in Dodsley's edition until 1755, so that Hammond's name was not publicly linked with the poem 'till 22 years after its publication, and thirteen after his death'. Moreover, she continues, 'Chesterfield, in printing his dead friend's other *Love Elegies*, 1743, makes no mention of this early publication, though a contemporary owner of Chesterfield's edition copied most of it at the end of Bod[leian Library] 2799 c. 21'; and the poem's style 'differs widely from the elegant classical and pastoral conceits (and quatrain stanzas) of Hammond's elegies i–xiv, of which Chesterfield wrote in his preface, "*Tibullus* seems to have been the Model, our author judiciously preferred to *Ovid*"' ('Verse of Lady Mary Wortley Montagu', p. 528; italics and Roman reversed). For example, the chiastic structure of lines 6, 8 and 40, and the antithetical structure of lines such as 9, 27 and 32, are much more characteristic of Hervey or Montagu than of Hammond. The primary motive for including the poem is to introduce the answer that follows, attributed by some, including Grundy, to Montagu and by others to Hervey. But the possibilities should not be excluded that this poem too was written by either Hervey or Montagu, or that it and its answer were produced in collaboration. Both were adept at writing amatory epistles in the voice of another, as other poems and accompanying discussion in this edition make clear; both were much interested in the problems posed for a woman of the period over how to choose a husband; and both poems demonstrate the skilful use of the heroic couplet that each writer commanded. The attribution in the British Library copy is also open to question, because it must have been added following the publication of Dodsley's widely circulated collection. The same point may also apply to that in the Brotherton Collection copy, though this seems to have been compiled at an earlier date, the date-span of its contents indicating the period 1740–51, and the compilation probably dating from before the marriage of its owner, Mary Capell, in 1758. The copy in BL Add. MS 57836 casts no light on dating, because the date-span of the collection ranges from about 1729 to about 1801, and the materials in it seem arranged in no particular order. More significant may be the fact that the poem and its answer were first published by James Roberts, a trade publisher who was, as Grundy points out in her article '*Verses Address'd to the Imitator of Horace*: A Skirmish between Pope and Some Persons of Rank and Fortune', 'Hervey's usual outlet for his anonymous writings in support of Walpole' (*Studies in Bibliography*, 30 (1977), 102). Roberts was the distributor of a vast range of material, but his association with the Montagu–Hervey circle is evidenced. For example, in 1732 he had published Hervey's *The Public Virtue of Former Times, and the Present Age Compared*, and *Some Remarks on the Minute Philosopher* (the latter not a pro-Walpole publication but a response to Berkeley's *Alciphron*), and in 1733 he was to publish not only the pamphlet under discussion here but also a more famous one associated with Hervey and Montagu, *To the Imitator of the First Satire of the Second Book of Horace*, plus two other works by Hervey, *Reply of a Member of Parliament to the Mayor of his Corporation*, and (though probably not with Hervey's consent) *An Epistle from a Nobleman to a Doctor of Divinity*. Montagu, Grundy indicates, had used Roberts as 'an agent in 1727 when advertising for her runaway son', and in 1737–8 she was to employ him again 'as distributor for her anonymous journal in support of Walpole, *The Nonsense of Common-Sense* ('*Verses Address'd to the Imitator of Horace*', 103). The evidence therefore points to authorship of the poem by Hervey or Montagu, or both, rather than by Hammond.

***Context and date.*** The poem must have been written not long before its publication in 1733, advertised in the *Daily Post, London Evening-Post, St. James's Evening Post* and *Weekly Miscellany* at various dates from 28 to 31 March. James Hammond (1710–42) was a political ally and acquaintance of Hervey's, but, according to James Sambrook, in 1733 he was 'drawn by Chesterfield into the opposition circle centred upon the prince of Wales', becoming 'equerry to the prince from 1733 (salary £300 p.a.) to his death' ('Hammond, James', *ODNB*). Although it is uncertain that Hammond received his salary before 1738 ('Household of Prince Frederick 1729–51', www.history.ac.uk/publications/office/fred), his place at Frederick's court was clear, and it is therefore unsurprising that, in a letter to Henry Fox dated 1 September 1734, Hervey indicated that the friendship was virtually over, for he could now communicate with Hammond only by letter. In response to a request from Fox about some verses Fox had sent him, he wrote: 'As to asking Mr Hammond's Opinion of them, it must be by Letter if I do, for he has never been near me these six Months; not that our Friendship dy'd any violent Death, it was a cronical Case; it began to languish in the Autumn, continued weak all Winter & is now in the very last Stage of a Consumption. I believe I may say of him as Anthony does of Dolabella, *He was once my Friend, but time & other views* *have bound him fast to Chesterfield* (BL Add. MS 51396, f. 134r; printed in Ilchester, p. 205). Details about Catherine Dashwood, the epistle's supposed addressee, are much more elusive. According to the anonymous writer of 'The Life of James Hammond', prefacing a volume of his *Poetical Works* first printed in 1781 in Edinburgh at the Apollo Press, she was Hervey's ward, but Hervey opposed the marriage. Without identifying his source, the writer states: 'It has been alleged for his Lordship, that the incompetence of Mr. Hammond's fortune, and also the lady's, would by no means authorise him to yield his consent: and from this motive he is said to have written the Answer to an Elegy of Mr. Hammond' (*Poetical Works*, p. viii). He goes on to suggest, however, that the real ground for refusal may have been 'Mr. Hammond's political principles, and his intimacy with the leaders of a party to which this nobleman was by no means a friend' (*Poetical Works*, pp. viii–ix). This seems plausible, but no further documentary evidence has come to light. For example, no reference to any Miss Dashwood seems to occur either in Hervey's papers or in those of his father. All the same, it may be significant that she died unmarried, ending her days in 1779, thirty-seven years after Hammond's death, as one of the Women of the Bedchamber to Queen Charlotte (Croker, *Memoirs*, I, xxxi), not, it should be noted, as a Lady of Bedchamber, a position sometimes mistakenly assigned to her (see for instance Halsband, *Life of Montagu*, p. 145).

Because no manuscript of either poem survives among either Montagu's papers or Hervey's, their occasion will almost certainly remain impossible to determine. It is significant, however, that in a bound volume in the care of the National Trust at Ickworth (18.B.4.8) a copy of the 1733 Roberts edition of the two poems was bound up with three other works partly or wholly attributable to Hervey: *To the Imitator of the Satire of the Second Book of Horace* (Poem 22), *An Epistle from a Nobleman to a Doctor of Divinity* (Poem 18) and *Epitaphium Reginae Carolinae. The Second Edition, Corrected. With an English Translation* (Poem 107). The first two were also published by Roberts in 1733. While it is not known who had the poems bound together, or when, this fact may suggest authorship of the second poem, and even perhaps also the first, by Hervey. It was he, not Hammond, who would be named as the writer of poems 'in the manner of Ovid', and this poem is properly defined as an epistle, a genre in which he was expert, rather than as an elegy. Furthermore, as Montagu seems to have kept copies of all her poems, it is also significant that neither of these survives in her collections, though it is possible that not all of her literary remains have survived. Because James Dallaway, the first editor of Montagu's works accepted by her family, claims that he printed as Montagu's those poems he found among her papers, because the claim was repeated by subsequent editors and others and because not all of these poems survive in Montagu's collections, Isobel Grundy suggests that a volume of her verse has not survived ('Verse of Lady Mary Wortley Montagu', pp. 212, 218, 506). There were seven such poems, as detailed by Grundy (p. 212, n. 3), plus a manuscript copy of *Verses to the Imitator of the Satire of the Second Book of*

*Horace*. However, this is a small number of poems to have comprised a volume. Other possibilities are that the two wrote either or both poems as a kind of spoiler to a developing romance, or even as a literary exercise that did not necessarily imply any reference to the two people who would become associated with them.

***Textual commentary.*** None of the sources has any claim to authority, because none bears evidence of any link with the author or authors. The presence of numerous variants also indicates that they cannot have had one or more common sources. The Brotherton manuscript has been chosen as the primary source for this edition because it presents good, clean copies of both poems. In contrast, the Roberts edition of the responding poem, 'Answer to the foregoing Lines', includes one clear error and much overly emphatic use of italics, while the Dodsley edition of both poems has to be ruled out because it was first printed over twenty years later and its provenance is unknown. BL Add. MS 57836 presents interesting problems because it contains the largest number of variants and is ten lines shorter, and it is not followed by the responding poem although its title, 'The First Elegy to Delia', indicates that it is part of a series. If it belonged to a series, it is possible that its companion pieces have been lost. It seems more likely, however, that the name 'Delia' in the title is evidence of an attempt to link it to Hammond's *Love Elegies. Written in the Year 1732* (London: G. Hawkins, 1743 [1742]), most of which are addressed to a woman so called, although it does not appear in the first edition and, when it does appear, is placed last or next to last in the series rather than first. The first edition of *Love Elegies* to contain the poem seems to have been that published in Edinburgh by W. Ruddiman in 1759, where its title is 'To Miss D—w—d. Elegy XVI. In the Manner of Ovid'. It similarly appears last or next to last in the series in editions of Hammond's *Poetical Works*, as in the first of these (Edinburgh: at the Apollo Press by the Martins, 1781), pp. 43–5, with reprints into the following century, the later of which added the best-known poems by Hervey. The most significant difference between the version in Add. MS 57836 and the others is that the former does not include lines 20–8, in which the poet claims that his addressee has succeeded in obtaining revenge on behalf of women for his previous misogyny. If the poem was an early draft, it is possible that these lines were added later. Alternatively, they could represent a deletion on second thoughts, especially as other differences also tend to soften its tone. The three versions in the Osborn Collection at Yale University date from much later in the century but are included for their historical interest as examples of album verse. The pair of poems in Osborn c.83/1 (nos. 113–14) are followed by a song of Dryden's subscribed 'Salisbury Journal Decem 4 86'; the two in Osborn c.130 are sandwiched between poems by Anna Letitia Barbauld and Hester Chapone respectively; and Osborn c.175 is an eight-line fragment entitled 'Emma or the Child of Sorrow' that has evidently been adapted for another purpose.

In editing the Brotherton manuscript, punctuation has been added from complementary texts where it is necessary to clarify the sense, as indicated in the List of Emendations. As the Brotherton manuscript is not paragraphed, variations in paragraphing are not noted.

## Mr. H—d to Miss D—d

Oh say, thou dear possesser of my breast,
Where is my boasted liberty and Rest,
Where the gay moments which I once have known,
Oh! where that heart I fondly thought my own?
From place to place I solitary roam,
Abroad uneasy, nor content at home.[1]
I scorn the Beauties common Eyes adore,
The more I view them, feel thy worth the more.
Unmoved I hear them speak, and see them fair,
And only think on thee, who art not there.
In vain would Books their former succour Lend,
Their Wit and Wisdom can't releive[2] their Friend;
Wit can't decieve the pain I now endure,
And Wisdom shews the Ills without the cure.
When from thy Face I waste the tedious day,
A thousand schemes I form, and things to say;
But when thy Presence gives the time I seek,
My Heart's so full, I wish, but cannot speak;
And could I speak with Eloquence and ease
Till now not studious of the art to please,
Could I at Woman who so oft exclaim,
Excuse, nor blush, thy Triumph and my Shame,
Abjure these maxims I so lately priz'd,
And Court that Sex I foolishly dispis'd?[3]
Own thou hast soften'd my obdurate mind,
And thou reveng'd the wrong of Womankind.

1. The chiastic structure of this line in all the versions but BL Add. MS 57836 is much more characteristic of Hervey or Montagu than of Hammond. See also lines 8 and 40, and the antithetical structure of lines such as 9, 27 and 32

2. *releive*: this is a characteristic Hervey spelling, as is 'decieve' in the next line, and 'beleive' in line 44, though not unique to him. But 'deceive' is spelt conventionally in line 43.

3. *dispis'd*: another characteristic Hervey spelling, repeated in line 37.

Lost were my words, and fruitless all my pain,
In vain to tell thee what I writ in vain;
My humble sighs shall only reach thy Ears,
And all my Eloquence shall be my Tears.
And now (for more I never must pretend.)
Deaf to the Lover, Listen to the Friend;
Thousands would fain thy little Heart ensnare,
For without danger none like thee are fair:
But wisely chuse who best deserves thy flame,
So shall the Choice it self become thy Fame;
And not dispise 'tho' void of winning Art,
The plain and honest Courtship of the Heart;
The skillfull Tongue in Love's persuasive Lore,
Tho' less it feels, will please and flatter more,
And meanly Learned in that guilty Trade,
Can long abuse a fond unthinking Maid.
And since their Lips so knowing to deceive,
Thy unexperienc'd youth might soon beleive,
And since their Tears in false submission dress'd,
Might thaw the icy Coldness of thy Breast,
Oh! shut thine Eyes to such deceitfull woe,
Caught by the Beauty of thy outward Show.
Like Me they do not love, whate'er they seem,
Like Me with passion founded on Esteem.

# 14 The Answer to Mr Hammond to Miss Dashwood

***Main source.*** Brotherton Collection, University of Leeds, Lt 119, ff. 72, 73, 74 (rectos only).

***Complementary manuscript sources.*** Yale Osborn Collection c.83/1, no. 114; Yale Osborn Collection c.130, pp. 83–6.

***Complementary print sources.*** *An Elegy to a Young Lady, in the Manner of Ovid. By – – – – – –. With an Answer: By a Lady, Author of the Verses to the Imitator of Horace* (London: [Sam Aris] for J. Roberts, 1733); Dodsley, *Collection*, IV, 79–82 (1755); IV, 83–5 (1782).

***Attribution.*** The poem is attributed to Hervey by the Brotherton manuscript, by Dodsley and by most other printed sources in the period, but to 'a Lady, Author of the Verses to the Imitator of Horace' in the Roberts edition. Against that ascription in the British Library copy of the Roberts edition, shelf mark 1346. m. 34, is the comment in an unidentified hand 'Lady Mary Wortley – but the poem is printed as Lord Hervey's'; and both Robert Halsband and Isobel Grundy attribute the poem to her, though Grundy concedes that Hervey 'could have had a hand in it' (Halsband, *Life of Montagu*, pp. 145–6; Grundy, 'Verse of Lady Mary Wortley Montagu', pp. 153–5, 528–31 (p. 531); Grundy, pp. 308–9). The ascription in the Roberts edition may perhaps be explained as a ploy to attract buyers, especially as an ascription to a nobleman, or to Hervey by name, would have been unlikely to do so. Two other facts are significant. First, the poem and its companion piece are very similar stylistically; second, as Isobel Grundy has shown, 'The Answer' is a point-by-point refutation of its predecessor ('Verse of Lady Mary Wortley Montagu', pp. 153–5). It is therefore possible that the two were written either by the same person or by two people in collaboration. Hervey is the more probable candidate in light of his political connections with Hammond. These are cast in relief by lines 19–28, which argue that by marrying Dashwood Hammond would blight his political career. Also relevant is the associated argument that Hammond's income was not sufficient to enable him to marry. Here dates are crucial. As James Sambrook points out in his *ODNB* article, in 1732 Hammond received 'a £200 gratuity from the civil list for carrying back to London the Act of Concurrence of the Dutch states general to the treaty of Vienna'. While this would have represented no convincing financial basis for matrimony, especially as his father, Anthony Hammond, was heavily in debt, his prospects improved in the following year, when the poem was printed, as he had an estate worth £400 per year bequeathed to him by a relative ('Hammond, Anthony', *ODNB*; 'Hammond, James', *ODNB*). In the same year, too, he may have begun to receive an annual salary of £220, raised to £300 in 1734, on becoming equerry to the Prince of Wales, although, as explained in the headnote to Poem 13, his warrant of salary seems to date only from 1738. If the poem was written before Hammond's income increased significantly, the argument against marriage on the ground that his income was inadequate would have been very strong. It would have been weaker if the poem was written after either or both increases, though both were at so moderate a level that, even combined, they might not have been deemed sufficient. If Hervey was Catherine Dashwood's guardian, such financial considerations strengthen the case for his authorship. So do the political factors. Furthermore, the reference to Hammond's political ambitions would have carried particular piquancy in light of his defection to the opposition, especially in light of what had by then become hatred on Hervey's part for the Prince of Wales.

***Context and date.*** See the headnote to Poem 13.

***Textual commentary.*** See the headnote to Poem 13. As in the case of that poem, the fact that some variants in the two printed copies agree but others differ indicates derivation from different manuscripts. Details of the two manuscripts in the Osborn Collection at Yale University are given in the headnote to Poem 13; neither is textually significant. The Roberts edition is over-paragraphed, but the Brotherton text has only one paragraph break, so two further breaks, at lines 27 and 54, have been added from the Dodsley. There is no punctuation at the end of lines 3, 9, 11, 19, 27, 29, 34; that supplied editorially mostly follows the Roberts edition.

## The Answer

Too well these Lines that fatal truth declare,
Which long I've known, yet now I blush to hear.
But say, what hopes thy fond ill fated Love?
What can it hope, tho' mutual it should prove?
This little Form[1] is fair in vain for you,
In vain for me thy honest heart is true;
For would'st thou fix dishonour on my name
And give me up to Penitence and shame;
Or gild[2] my honour with the name of Wife,
And make me a poor virtuous Wretch for Life?[3]

1. *little Form*: Grundy and Halsband note that 'Catherine Dashwood was known to her circle as "dear little Dash"', citing *The Autobiography and Correspondence of Mary Granville, Mrs. Delany*, I, 563 (*Essays & Poems*, p. 270).

2. *gild*: the Brotherton manuscript instead says 'yeild', which must be a transcription error, as it seems unlikely that marriage could be represented as a surrender of honour.

3. *For would'st . . . Wretch for Life*: Halsband and Grundy record Horace Walpole's note, written in a copy of Chesterfield's *Miscellaneous Works*, that Dashwood, finding that Hammond 'did not mean marriage, broke off all connection, though much in love with him'; but Grundy also reports Lady Corke's account, told in old age to John Wilson Croker,

Could'st thou submit to wear the marriage chain,
Too sure a Cure for all thy present pain?
No Saffron Robe for us the Godhead wears,
His Torch inverted[4] and his face in Tears.
Tho' every softer wish were amply crown'd,
Love soon would cease to smile when fortune frown'd;
Then would thy Soul my fond consent deplore,
And blame what it sollicited before.
Thine own exhausted, would reproach my truth,[5]
And say I had undone thy blinded Youth;
That I had damp'd Ambition's nobler Flame,
Eclips'd thy Talents, and obscur'd thy name;
To Madrigals and Odes thy Wit confin'd,
That might in Senates, or in Courts have shin'd;
Gloriously active in thy Country's Cause,
Asserting Freedom, and inacting Laws.

Or say at best, that negatively kind,
You inly mourn'd, or silently repin'd;
The jealous Demons in my own fond breast,
Would all these thoughts incessantly suggest,
And tell what sence must feel, tho' pity had suppress'd.
Yet added Grief my Apprehension fills,
If there can be addition to those Ills,
When they shall cry, whose harsh reproof I dread,
'Twas thy own fault, thy folly's on thy head.
Age knows not to allow for thoughtless youth,
Nor pities tenderness, nor honours truth;
Holds it Romantick to confess a Heart,
And says, those Virgins act a wiser part
Who Hospitals and Bedlams would explore,
To find the Rich, and only dread the Poor;
Who legal Prostitutes for interest sake,

that she 'had at first accepted, but afterwards rejected him, on – Lady Corke, and indeed all *Kitty's* contemporaries thought – *prudential reasons*' (Croker, *Memoirs*, I, xxx–xxxi; Grundy, 'Verse of Lady Mary Wortley Montagu', p. 531).

4. *Saffron Robe . . . Torch inverted*: Hymen, the god of marriage, was traditionally supposed to wear a saffron-coloured robe; inverting his torch would signify a thumbs-down.

5. *Thine own . . . my truth*: The elliptical construction is characteristic of Hervey.

Clodios and Timons[6] to their bosom take;
And if avenging Heaven permit increase,
People the World with folly and disease.
Those, Titles, deeds, and Rent-Rolls only Wed,
And the best bidder mounts their venal Bed;
And the grave Aunt and formal Sire approve,
This Nuptial Sale, this Auction of their Love.
But if regard to sense or worth is shewn,
That poor degenerate Child, her Friends disown,
Who dares to deviate, by a virtuous choice,
From her great Name's Hereditary vice.

These scenes my prudence Ushers to my mind
Of all the Storms and Quick Sands I must find,
If I embark upon this summer Sea
Where flattery smooths and pleasure Gilds the Way.
Had our ill fate ne'er blown thy dang'rous flame
Beyond the Limits of a friend's cold name,
I might upon that score thy *Heart* receive,
And with that guiltless name my own deceive;
That commerce[7] now in vain you recommend,
I dread the silent Lover in the Friend;
Of Ignorance I want the poor excuse,
And know I both must take or both refuse.

Hear then the safe, the firm resolve I take,
Ne'er to encourage one I must forsake.
Whilst other Maids a shameless path pursue,
Neither to honour, nor to interest true,
And proud to swell the triumph of their Eyes,
Exult in Love, from Lovers they dispise;
Their Maxims all revers'd I mean to prove,
And tho' I Like the Lover, quit the Love.

6. *Clodios and Timons*: Publius Clodius Pulcher, who lived at the time of Julius Caesar, was noted for licentiousness, avarice and ambition; Timon's story of lavish generosity succeeded by poverty and misanthropy was dramatised by Shakespeare in *Timon of Athens*, though the allusion may also refer to Pope's Timon, a type of wealth unaccompanied by taste, in his *Epistle to Burlington* (1731).

7. *commerce*: 'Intercourse in the affairs of life; dealings' (*OED*).

# 15 Written as from Lady Mary Wortley to Monsieur Algarotti

***Source.*** BL Egerton MS 23, ff. 239r–v.

***Complementary manuscript sources.*** None known.

***Complementary print sources.*** None known, but there is a transcript in Grundy, 'Verse of Lady Mary Wortley Montagu', pp. 698–700.

***Attribution.*** The only two possible authors are Hervey and Lady Mary Wortley Montagu, because only they knew the strength of Montagu's feelings for Algarotti. As Grundy points out, 'The title suggests Hervey impersonating Lady Mary, though its phrasing may be due to the Italian scribe's misunderstanding English usage.' Grundy adds, however: 'The balance of probability favours Hervey', and the various echoes of other poems by Hervey that she cites and that are noted below strengthen the probability ('Verse of Lady Mary Wortley Montagu', pp. 698, 698–700).

***Context and date.*** Francesco Algarotti arrived in London in late March 1736, bearing a letter of introduction to Hervey from Voltaire (Halsband, p. 192). Hervey introduced him to Montagu, of whom he may already have heard from the same luminary, 'who quoted her poetry about this time' (Grundy, p. 357). Both he and she found themselves strongly attracted to the charming young Italian. After a stay of several months, Algarotti left on 6 September (Grundy, p. 360). As the poem refers to his impending departure, it must have been written shortly before that date. More generally, the context for the poem includes rivalry for Algarotti's affection, illustrated by the fact that, although Algarotti spent his last evening in England with Montagu, he told Hervey that his supper companion had been the scientist Martin Folkes. The rivalry would continue as Hervey and Montagu conducted parallel correspondences with their friend, and when Algarotti revisited England in 1739 (Halsband, p. 247–8), until Montagu left England in July of that year in what would turn out to be the misguided hope of living with him in Italy (Grundy, pp. 388–95, 436–9). There are also two literary contexts. The first is that of the Ovidian epistle, a form in which both Hervey and Montagu were well practised. It is signalled most obviously by the epigraph from 'Sappho to Phaon', conventionally part of the *Heroides* though not accepted by all scholars as by Ovid (see *Ovid, Heroides: Select Epistles*, ed. by Peter E. Knox (Cambridge: Cambridge University Press, 1995; repr. 2000), pp. 36–7, 279). The association with Sappho is apt not only in light of the situation of an older woman pleading for the affections of a younger man, but because it invokes the

Greek poet's name in a way very different from that of Pope's satires, highlighting her skill and reputation as a poet. Another of Ovid's epistles is 'Dido to Aeneas'. This, too, though also with a nod to Virgil's *Aeneid*, the poem invokes when it links Algarotti's return to Italy with Aeneas' voyage to Rome, leaving Montagu behind in the role of Dido. A further possible twist to the poem's intertextuality is its apparent allusiveness to poems by Hervey that he may have shown or read to Algarotti and that Montagu certainly knew, because she transcribed two of them. It is especially significant not only that two of the poems echoed are from Hervey's 'Epistles in the Manner of Ovid', but that another is Poem 8, 'The Countess of — to Miss —'. The circumstance in the latter of an older woman addressing a younger one, and its argument that, in default of physical attractions, she can offer wit and charm, present an especially close parallel. This, too, is one of the ways in which Peter E. Knox's remark that 'the distinguishing feature of O[vid]'s *Heroides* is their inspiration from other works of literature' (*Ovid, Heroides*, p. 18) applies as much to this poem as to the whole tradition of the Ovidian heroic epistle.

***Textual commentary.*** As Grundy indicates in her edition, the manuscript was 'copied in an Italian hand, among Algarotti's papers' (p. 698). There are various transcription errors, such as 'forman' for 'formam' in the first line of the epigraph, and 'desing'd' for 'design'd' in the opening line. These have been corrected as indicated in the List of Emendations, but otherwise the manuscript's spelling, punctuation, use of initial capitals and italics have been preserved except where noted and for the expansion of contractions. As Grundy notes, the spelling 'recieve' (line 11), which is characteristic of Hervey, was 'perhaps copied by the scribe'.

## Written as from Lady Mary Wortley to Monsr. Algarotti[1]

Si mihi difficilis formam Natura negavit
Ingenio formæ damna rependo meae.

Ovid, Sapho to Phaon.[2]

Since common forms could never be design'd,
To check the free and cramp the noble mind,[3]

1. *as from ... Algarotti*: as Grundy remarks, 'The title suggests Hervey impersonating Lady Mary' ('Verse of Lady Mary Wortley Montagu', p. 698). Grundy's proposal that the Italian scribe may in this instance have misunderstood English usage seems unlikely, especially because, as she also indicates, Montagu's letters to Algarotti 'express her feelings more cautiously and obliquely'.

2. *epigraph*: 'If nature, malign to me, has denied the charm of beauty, weigh in the stead of beauty the genius that is mine' (Ovid, *Heroides* XV, Sappho to Phaon, 31–2 (Loeb, p. 183).

3. *Since ... noble mind*: Grundy compares the opening line of Hervey's *Monimia to Philocles*, 'Since Language never can describe my Pain', and lines 612–13 of Swift's *Cadenus and Vanessa*, 'That common forms were not design'd | Directors to a noble mind'. The first parallel is in keeping with the convention followed by many heroic epistles

And that the dumb Intelligence of Eyes,
My Prose, my Verse, my Languishings and Sighs,
In vain have hinted what I fain would prove,
Without a farther Preface Know – I Love.[4]
Perhaps, too delicat, thou mayst upbraid,
This frank Confession which my Pen has made,
But if I break my Sex's rigid Laws,
Pardon the Crime reflecting on the Cause:
Nor with contracted Brow recieve Severe
This Rhapsody of Wishes and despair:
The Venial Fault behold with partial Eyes,
Nor chide my Weakness, tho' you may despise.[5]
My forc'd Complaint indulgently attend,
For if unwelcome 'tis the last I'll send,
Nor this I would if Judgment could Command,
But oh! when Love and Nature prompt my Hand,
What Art, what Skill can Stop their rapid Course,
Or what Philosophy can tame their Force?[6]
Not ev'n thy Fav'rite *Newton*[7] this could do,
He could discover Nature, not subdue;
And might by his Philosophy as soon,
Hinder the Tide's obedience to the Moon,
Bid each attracted orb it's Sphere forsake,

in which the writer begins by justifying her letter. The second highlights the heterodox attitude to religion and morality that Hervey and Montagu shared, not at all an emphasis of Swift's poem.

4. *Know – I Love*: Grundy compares lines 7–8 of Poem 8, 'The Countess of — to Miss —', 'let this remove | All Doubt, all Ignorance, and know I love'.

5. *Nor chide . . . despise*: Grundy compares Montagu, 'Wednesday', line 66, 'A Man may pity, but he must despise', and 'Monimia to Philocles', line 28, 'Nor chide that Weakness I my self despise'.

6. *My forc'd . . . their Force*: Grundy compares these six lines to *Monimia to Philocles*, lines 31–6: 'Without a Frown this Farewell then receive, | For 'tis the last my hapless Love shall give. | Nor this I would, if Reason could command, | But what Restriction reins a Lovers Hand? | Nor Prudence, Shame, nor Pride, nor Interest sways, | The Hand implicitly the Heart obeys.'

7. *Newton*: Algarotti was still working on his *Il Newtonianismo per le dame* (1737; translated by Elizabeth Carter in 1739 as *Sir Isaac Newton's Philosophy Explain'd for the Use of the Ladies*). This was an important work of popularisation for Newton's theories, prefaced in the second edition by commendatory verses from both Montagu and Hervey. See Poem 57 and notes.

And vagrant Courses through this System take,
As free my Soul from Love's resistless Laws,
Or make another of that Love the Cause.

Oft to divert my headlong Passion's Course,
I've try'd by turns both Pride and Reason's Force,
But call'd alas! for ineffectual Aid,
When thus, unheard, those Monitors have say'd,
"Thy vain Pursuit unhappy Wretch forbear
"Nor you nor England is this Strangers Care
"The Bark unmoor'd, now waits to waft him oer
"He like Æneas Seeks the latian[8] Shore
"Whilst – you, like Dido, may his Flight deplore".[9]
But what avail Remonstrances of Art,
To Combate Nature in the Soresick Heart;
I found these Friends a useless Pow'r apply'd;
Be dumb, yee Phlegmatic, dull Churls, I cry'd
In vain you tell me he prepares to fly;
Must we not live because we once must dye?[10]

8. *latian*: Latin, or Italian. The same word appears in the Bodleian manuscript of Poem 55, 'Verse Dialogue between Hervey and Montagu', line 58; in this poem, which is also about Algarotti, Hervey wrote and then deleted 'Latians [replacement for 'Romans'] were always Masters of Mankind'.

9. *The Bark . . . Flight deplore*: Grundy compares Poem 3, 'Arisbe to Marius Junior', lines 91–2, 'The Guards deceiv'd, and ev'ry Danger o'er, | The winds already waft him from the Shore'.

10. *Must we not . . . dye*: the Epicurean attitude expressed in this line is characteristic of Hervey at the time. See Overton, 'Death and Futurity'.

# COMPLIMENTARY AND SATIRICAL EPISTLES

# 16 Verse Letter to Lady Hervey from Italy

***Main source.*** BL Add. MS 51345, ff. 18r–23r.

***Complementary manuscript source.*** SRO 941/47/4, p. 40, a fragment consisting of lines 42–56 in a letter to Lady Mary Wortley Montagu dated 12 October 1729 from Lyons.

***Complementary print sources.*** Voltaire, *Letters Concerning the English Nation* (London: for C. Davis and A. Lyon, 1733), pp. 195–6, a fragment also consisting of lines 42–56, but, for reasons to be considered below, rendered loosely in French despite the fact that he wrote most of the book in English. For a modern editor's comments, see Voltaire, *Letters Concerning the English Nation*, ed. by Nicholas Cronk (Oxford and New York: Oxford University Press, 1994), pp. ix, xx, xxv–xxvii, xxix–xxxi. A complete modernised text of the poem is given in Ilchester, pp. 35–6 (lines 1–28 and 216–29), and pp. 283–7 (the remainder).

***Context and date.*** The poem must have been written in early October 1729, because Hervey included lines 42–56 in his letter to Montagu dated the 12th of that month. It describes the first and most difficult leg of the journey he and Stephen Fox made back to England: from Florence, which they left in August, via Pisa, Leghorn, Lerici, Genoa, Turin and across the Alps by the Mont Cenis pass to Lyons. At the end of the next leg of the journey, in Paris, Hervey and Fox renewed their acquaintance with Voltaire, to whom Hervey evidently not only showed his poem but gave a copy. The lines describing Italy appealed to Voltaire's anti-clerical, libertarian convictions. When he rendered them in French in *Letters Concerning the English Nation*, he used the opportunity to give those convictions full rein. As Nicholas Cronk remarks, the translation 'is highly tendentious, and without the English for comparison, the reader is led to attribute the anti-clerical satire to Hervey rather than to his translator'. Cronk also points out that 'this is the only occasion on which Voltaire provides a translation without the original', and speculates whether he might 'have been playing a joke on Hervey'. It seems more likely, however, given that the book was aimed at a French as well as an English audience, that his motive was to co-opt Hervey, albeit without first obtaining his approval, as a fellow anti-cleric.

Two letters Voltaire wrote to Hervey, before and after publication of the book respectively, show some compunction about this. They were first discussed and edited by T. J. Barling, 'Voltaire's Correspondence with Lord Hervey: Three New Letters', *Studies on Voltaire and the Eighteenth Century*, 62 (1968), 13–27, and then, as part of *Les Œuvres Complètes de Voltaire* (vols. 85–35), by Theodore Besterman in *Correspondence and Related Documents*, 2nd edn, 51 vols (Geneva:

Institut et Musée Voltaire, 1968–77), II, 148–50, 387–9. The original manuscript of the three letters (the third is from Hervey to Voltaire) is in SRO 941/47/1 (an unbound, unfoliated manuscript consisting of five letters to Hervey: two from Voltaire; one in French from Prince d'Orange dated 6 February 1734; a scribal copy of two letters from the Prince of Wales to Hervey, undated). In Voltaire's first letter, dated conjecturally 15 January by the Electronic Enlightenment online database (http://www.e-enlightenment.com), Voltaire enclosed his translation of part of Hervey's poem, referring to it, as T. J. Barling puts it, 'rather apologetically'. Barling continues, 'There is at this stage no suggestion that the rendering will appear in any publication' ('Voltaire's Correspondence with Lord Hervey', p. 15). 'Rendering' is the right word, for Voltaire refers to it as 'a loose imitation' and attempts to excuse its inexactness on the ground that 'french poetry is not Strong enoug to Stik closely to your [verses, quoting the first four lines he adapted]' (*Correspondence and Related Documents*, II, 149; SRO 941/47/1). As the lines he enclosed differ in some respects from those printed in the following year, it is possible either that he revised them before publication or that, at least in some cases, his handwriting defeated the compositor or printer. By the time he wrote the second letter, dated 14 September 1733, Voltaire was aware that Hervey had read his book, which had been published in the previous month. As Barling points out, 'It would seem that Voltaire had not received from the Englishman any assurance concerning the liberties taken with the original poem' ('Voltaire's Correspondence with Lord Hervey', 15–16). Voltaire wrote, in what Barling rightly calls 'somewhat constrained terms': 'Mais que direz vous de la liberté que j'ay prise de mettre en vers français les vers charmants dont vous m'aviez dit une partie sur votre voiage d'Italie? et que direz vous de la liberté qu'on a prise de les imprimer?' ('But what will you say about the liberty I have taken of putting into French verse the charming lines part of which you spoke to me about your Italian journey? and what will you say of the liberty taken of having them printed?' (*Correspondence and Related Documents*, II, 388; SRO 941/47/1, p. 2; my translation).) The problem was his overt anti-clericalism – a position that Hervey to some extent shared but that, as a letter from him dated 23 June 1736 clearly shows, he did not consider it politic to display (*Correspondence and Related Documents*, II, 14 [dated 4 July n.s.]; SRO 941/47/6, p. 1 and p. 4; noted by Barling, p. 16). For purposes of comparison Voltaire's imitations of Hervey's lines are provided, with my literal translations, in Appendix 2. Like Hervey's, the lines are octosyllabic, but Voltaire's are *vers libres*, in the older sense of the term, in which the rhyme scheme varies. The printed version, but not the one Voltaire sent to Hervey, sets the poem out in quatrains (in the case of one stanza, a cinquain).

Other contexts for the poem are the nature of Hervey's relationships with his wife and with Stephen Fox, its content and its genre. Fox is here portrayed by Hervey as his 'Fidus Achates', or faithful friend, who makes his 'Welfare all his Care' but who is otherwise mentioned relatively little. Hervey pays greater deference to his wife, who would not have been able to join him on the journey, even if she had wanted to do so, because of her duties as Mistress of the Robes to the

Queen, quite apart from the demands of four small children (see D[oris] A[lmon] Ponsonby, *Call a Dog Hervey* (London: Hutchinson, 1949), p. 50; Ilchester, p. 31). Halsband notes that 'It was not considered odd that his wife should remain at home' (Halsband, p. 78). Early in the letter he declares: 'love and you inspire my Heart' (line 28), and describes thus his motive for returning over land: 'quite impatient to pursue | My way to England, and to you' (lines 59–60). Later, while staying with the Colmans in Turin, he claims: 'Whilst to your Love and Merit true, | My sole enquiry was of You' (lines 156–7), distinguishing his interests from those of Fox, which concerned politics; refers to the letter as 'What truth and Kindness are inditing' (line 219); and states that what would be trifles to others, such as his letter, 'Cease to be such to those who love' (line 225). Although such remarks, along with the sheer length and entertainment-value of the letter, may represent an attempt on his part to make up for his long absence and the closeness of his relationship with Fox, they do not support Lucy Moore's suggestion that the reference to Fox as his 'Fidus Achates' 'cannot have pleased her' (Moore, p. 59). Instead, she always referred to Fox with affection, and her correspondence with him is in the same key. It seems to have been some time later that Hervey's relationship with her cooled.

Appropriately in light of its aim of entertaining its addressee, and other readers, the content of the poem is quite various. It not only describes, amusingly, the vicissitudes undergone by the travellers on their journey, but also passes on political news, in which Mary Hervey always maintained an interest, and expresses criticism of Italian politics and society from a firmly Whig point of view, committed to certain religious and political freedoms. Its genre, as pointed out in the general headnote to this section, is that of the familiar epistle. For that kind of poem its iambic tetrameter couplets, with their occasional hypermetrical end-of-line light stresses and humorous double rhymes, are very well suited. The effect is very different from that of a poem on a similar subject first printed twenty-five years previously and certainly known by Hervey, Joseph Addison's 'Letter from Italy' (1704), and intentionally so (see *The Miscellaneous Works of Joseph Addison*, I, *Poems and Plays*, ed. by A. C. Guthkelch (London: G. Bell and Sons, 1914), 51–61).

***Textual commentary.*** The poem, which is untitled, is on three sheets, each folded once to produce a total of twelve pages. It is paginated from two to eleven in the bottom left hand corner of each page except the first. There is an inscription in a different hand pasted on to the previous page (f. 17r): 'Lord Hervey, and Lord Ilchester were in Italy together, when the enclosed was wrote by the former, to Lady Hervey, then in England.' The poem is almost certainly in Hervey's hand, and the manuscript appears to have been divided between two periods of transcription: an earlier one, when the beginnings of all the lines, and the entirety of some of them, were written out; and a later one, in which the latter part of the lines was added, two lines (60 and 154) omitted at the first writing being squeezed in between those before and after them, and a small number of emendations made.

The result is a manuscript in two shades of ink, in which the second part of most lines is in a rather tidier hand. Perhaps this is a copy made very quickly by Hervey of the fair copy sent to his wife; given its inclusion in a manuscript collection consisting largely of Hervey's letters to Stephen and Henry Fox, it seems likely that the copy was made for one of them, Hervey needing to write out only the first few words of many of the lines, being able to recall and fill in the remainder later. Some crossings-out in the second half of lines might suggest that Hervey at first misremembered words, and then corrected himself; a few changes made in the later, tidier writing to words in the first part of a line suggest some running revisions, too. (For instance, 'ev'ry', in the first half of line 123, has been substituted for 'all the'.) Another possible explanation for the state of the manuscript is that the text – or that tidier part of it that definitely seems to be in Hervey's own hand – is an early draft of the poem sent to his wife. Evidence supporting the latter possibility is that there are more corrections after line 86. For details, see the List of Emendations. The original letter appears not to have been preserved, all Hervey's letters to his wife evidently having been destroyed.

## Verse Letter to Lady Hervey from Italy

Tho by this Post (my Dear) I chose
To write in Verse, pray dont supose,
With tropes, and flights that I design
To raise my Style, and swell each Line.
Those fustian trappings of a Poet,
Are what I never wear, you know it.
Such Bards like stroling Players shine,
Who with black Gemms, and Tinsel fine,
Strut on some little country Stage,
And tho' prophaning Shakespear's Rage,[1]
Think they're the Oldfields[2] of the Age.
I hate the Pedantry of Schools,[3]
Nor write, nor speak, nor act by Rules:
No Invocation of a Muse,
By way of Preface I produce;

1. *Rage*: 'Poetic, prophetic, or musical enthusiasm or inspiration' (*OED*).

2. *Oldfields*: Anne Oldfield (1683–1730), a leading actress of the period and a family friend of the Herveys. Hervey was to serve as one of the pall-bearers at her funeral in the year after the poem was written and as one of the executors of her will (*ODNB*; Halsband, pp. 27–8, 103–4). Poem 31b is the epitaph he wrote for her.

3. *Pedantry of Schools*: this view is expressed humorously in Hervey's *Epistle from a Nobleman to a Doctor of Divinity* (Poem 18).

No Allegory dark will sing,
Nor unlike Similys will bring,
That lead astray the Reader's Brain,
And puzzle what they ought t'explain.
The little Scheme that I lay down,
Is barely[4] telling how we've gone,
From Arno's Banks,[5] to those of Rhone.[6]
If then my Numbers seem uncouth,
Think to attone they're fraught with truth:
And when I would say something kind,
Why should a Muse inspire my Mind,
Or Nature borrow ought[7] from Art?
Since love and you inspire my Heart.

Persuant then to my Design. —
From Florence, fam'd for Silks and Wine,
To Pisa first we bend our Course,
And vile the Inn, tho' I've found worse.
Our Beds were musty, coarse our fare,
And Gnats extreamly busy there:
A Gothick Church,[8] and leaning Tow'r,
Are all the Sights in Pisa's Store.
Thence to Leghorn,[9] so prosp'rous made
By Strangers, Industry, and Trade;
A Face of Bus'ness here you see,
As if they boasted Liberty,
And, like their Port, themselves were free.[10]
Throughout all Italy beside,

4. *barely*: 'Without literary or artistic effect; bald, meagre, unadorned' (*OED* 'bare').

5. *Arno's Banks*: Florence, where Hervey and Fox's journey started.

6. *those of Rhone*: Lyons, where the part of the journey described was to end.

7. *ought*: i.e. aught, 'Anything whatever' (*OED*).

8. *Gothick Church*: Santa Maria della Spina, in the centre of Pisa by the river Arno, built in 1230.

9. *Leghorn*: anglicised from the Italian *Livorno*, a port city by the Tyrrhenian Sea on the western coast.

10. *free*: a free port is one 'open to all traders, or which enjoys exemption from particular customs duties, regulations, etc.' (*OED*). Hervey plays on the sense of political freedom.

What does one find, but Want,[11] and Pride?[12]
Farces of superstitious Folly,
Decay, Distress, and Melancholy:
The Havock of despotick Pow'r,
A Country rich, it's owners[13] poor;
Unpeopled towns, and Lands untill'd,
Bodys uncloath'd, and Mouths unfill'd.
The Nobles miserably great,[14]
In painted Domes, and empty State,
Too proud to Work, too poor to eat.
No Arts the meaner Sort employ,
They nought improve, nor ought enjoy.
Each Clown[15] from Mis'ry grows a Saint,
He prays from Idleness, and fasts' from Want.[16]

Finding the fickle Wind averse,
The Vessels bad, the Wether worse,
And quite[17] impatient to pursue
My way to England, and to you.[18]
After consulting dearest Ste:[19]
To stay no longer both agree;
So back, by Land, o'er Pisa's Plain,
In thunder, Lightning, and in Rain,
(Just like the Witches in Macbeth,

11. *Want*: 'The state of lacking the necessaries of life; penury; destitution. Also, the condition of lacking food; famine; starvation' (*OED*).

12. *Pride*: 'Magnificence, splendour; pomp, ostentation, display' (*OED*).

13. *owners*: as Italy was mostly under either foreign or papal control, the word suggests that Hervey believed its true owners were the indigenous populace.

14. *great*: 'Distinguished in appearance; of lofty or imposing aspect' (*OED*).

15. *Clown*: 'A countryman, rustic, or peasant' (*OED*).

16. *Throughout all Italy . . . from Want*: these fifteen lines were transcribed by Hervey in his letter to Montagu from Lyons of 12 October 1729, and rendered very loosely in French by Voltaire (see headnote). The final one has an extra foot to mark the climax of the passage.

17. *quite*: 'As an intensifier: completely, fully, entirely; to the utmost extent or degree' (*OED*), rather than 'As a moderating adverb: to a certain or significant extent or degree; moderately, somewhat, rather; relatively, reasonably' (*OED*).

18. *My way . . . you*: this line is squeezed in between those before and after it; see headnote.

19. *Ste*: familiar form of Stephen Fox's first name, often used by Hervey in their correspondence.

Or good old Lear on the wide Heath:)
To Lerici[20] we take our Road:
But there we made no long abode.
We sup'd, and then to Bed we went
Not for our Rest, but Punishment:
For Fleas and Bugs kept such a Rout,
That Pisa's Gnats were nothing to't:
We scratch'd, and toss'd, and burn'd all Night;
And sleepless saw revolving Light;
Which at the earlyest Peep of Day,
Into the Chamber where we lay,
Found an unintercepted Way.
For Door or Window there was none,
To keep out either Wind or Sun:
We rose, imbark'd, and with fair Gale,
Clear Sky, and a smooth Sea sett Sail.

But soon as we had clear'd the Bay,
And gott a League or two to Sea;
The Wether chang'd, the Wind grew high,
The Sea grew rough, and dark the Sky.
And now began, through all the Crew,
Each Head to turn, each Mouth to ——
(You know the Rhyme and 'tis more clean,
To lett you guess at what I mean.)
But to revenge th' affront the Sea,
Pour'd such a Torrent back on me,
That from my Foot, up to my Head,
I had not one unwetted Thread.
My Cloaths were changing, when old John,[21]
Cry'd, 'Speak or else by G–d we're gone,
'Pray look, nay 'tis no laughing matter,
'Her very Sails are under Water;
'Make 'em my Lord gett nearer Shore,

20. *Lerici*: a coastal town in northern Italy, roughly halfway between Leghorn and Genoa.

21. *old John*: evidently an English servant who accompanied Hervey and Fox; not otherwise identified.

'Furl all the Sails and ply the Oar;
'Damn their Feluccas,[22] such a Boat,
'In such a Sea a'n't worth a Groat.'
I took his Counsel, and in short,
At Genoa gott safe in Port.
And as sick Drunkard, and clap'd Rake,[23]
Swear (whilst they're suff'ring) that they'l take
A Bottle and a Whore no more;
So Ste: and I, our fright not o'er,
And seeming still on Billows tosst,
Resolve no more to quitt the Coast;
But sleep on dry Land, in a Sure Inn,
And go to Lyons round by Turin.
As soon as each had fill'd his Belly,
With heart'ning Soup, and Vermicelli;[24]
Still giddy, jaded, and half dead
For want of Rest, we hast to Bed;
Nor wanted rocking, for we soon
Slept, and ne'er wak'd 'till next Day noon,
When Genoa three Days we'd been in,
To rest our Bones and wash our Linnen;
Tho much contented with our Lodging,
We grew impatient to be jogging.[25]
With Ortelans[26] the Consul[27] fed us,
And ev'ry Day to Sights he led us;
He did the Honours of the Town,
As well as all had been his own;
And of all Countrys I have cross'd,

22. *Feluccas*: 'small vessel[s] propelled by oars or lateen sails, or both, used, chiefly in the Mediterranean, for coasting voyages' (*OED*).

23. *clap'd Rake*: *clap'd*: infected with gonorrhoea; *Rake*: 'A fashionable or stylish man of dissolute or promiscuous habits' (*OED*).

24. *Vermicelli*: 'A kind of pasta made in the form of long, slender, hard threads' (*OED*).

25. *jogging*: 'to move on at a heavy or laboured pace, to trudge; hence, to move on, go on, be off' (*OED* 'jog').

26. *Ortelans*: 'A migratory bunting . . . formerly widely regarded as a delicacy' (*OED*) (properly 'ortolans').

27. *the Consul*: George Jackson, whom Hervey later tried to help advance in the consular service (Halsband, p. 84, citing Walpole, *Correspondence*, XVII, 186, 430).

A fairer City none can boast;
By Streets of Marble beauteous made,
By Situation apt for Trade.
Oh! Freedom! Benefactress fair!
How happy who thy Blessings share!
These barren Hills these rocky Shores,
Cheer'd by thy Smiles, produce such Stores,
That Plenty flows in ev'ry Place,
And Gladness sitts on ev'ry Face.
Whilst Milan's Sons oppress'd by Pow'r,[28]
Their Fate in Paradise deplore;
Ah! what avail her fertile Plains,
Her Olives, Vines, and swelling Grains?
A foreign Prince[29] her Wealth demands,
Her Vintage press'd by foreign Hands;
A foreign Hand her Harvest spoils,
Vienna[30] fatten's on her Toils.
Digression this[31] perhaps you call,
But since I'm in for't take it all.—

Our journey hence I need not tell,
Twas nothing bad, nor nothing well.

With Coleman and his pretty Wife[32]
(Who seem's to dread a Florence-Life)
Behold us then at Turin prating,
We questioning and they relating.
Factions and Parliaments and Court,
What News, what Scandal and what Sport?
Treatys and Commerce Peace, and War,[33]

28. *Milan's Sons . . . Pow'r*: one of the provisions of the Treaty of Utrecht (1713) was that the duchy of Milan had passed from Spanish to Austrian dominion.

29. *A foreign Prince*: Charles VI, Emperor of Austria 1711–40.

30. *Vienna*: capital of the Austrian Empire.

31. *Digression this*: the previous fourteen lines clearly express Hervey's Whig politics.

32. *Coleman . . . Wife*: Francis Colman (*bap.* 1691, *d.* 1733), envoy to the court of the Grand Duke of Tuscany, was the father of the dramatist George Colman the elder (*ODNB*). His wife Mary was one of the three sisters of Anna Maria Pulteney (*Complete Peerage*, II: 23), with whose husband, William, Hervey's relationship had not yet cooled.

33. Like line 60, this one is squeezed in between those above and below it; see headnote.

Seem'd my Friend Ste's peculiar Care
Whilst to your Love and Merit true,
My sole enquiry was of You.
This Joy was mine one Day alone,
For lo! to morrow Coleman's flown;
Twas right; his Embassy asks Hast,
For Florence says her Duke cant last;[34]
And if the English dont take Care,
Don Carlos[35] shall succeed him there,
Our Peace perhaps may turn to Warr;
The Face of things again may alter,
And Spain once more besiege Gibralter.[36]

We, one Day more, at Turin stay'd,
Whilst to her King[37] my Court I pay'd;
On whose unkingly, royal Head,
Pallas,[38] such partial Gifts has shed;
Him-self the weight of Rule sustain's
He's lov'd by those o'er whom he reigns,
And wears a Crown yet dont want[39] Brains.
By Method now I come at last,
To tell you how the Alps we pass'd:
A dreadful Journey; I remember,
Twas hardly worse ev'n last November:[40]

34. *Duke cant last*: 'Gian Castone, 7th and last of the Medici Grand-Dukes. He died in 1737' (Ilchester, p. 286, n. 2).

35. *Don Carlos*: 1716–88, second son of Philip V, King of Spain, for whom his ambitious mother, Elisabeth Farnese, second wife of Philip, was to secure the duchy of Parma in 1731; and who, having conquered the kingdoms of Naples and of Sicily, was to be crowned their king in 1735.

36. *Spain ... Gibralter*: Gibraltar was ceded to Britain under the Treaty of Utrecht, a provision that remains contentious.

37. *her King*: Victor Amadeus II (1666–1732), Duke of Savoy 1675–1730 and King of Sardinia 1718–32.

38. *Pallas*: Pallas Athene, Greek goddess of wisdom. Hervey pays tribute to Victor Amadeus's astuteness as ruler and diplomat. For further details of the latter's career, see Geoffrey Symcox, *Victor Amadeus II: Absolutism in the Savoyard State, 1675–1730* (Berkeley and Los Angeles: University of California Press, 1983).

39. *want*: 'Not to have; to be without, to lack' (*OED*).

40. *last November*: when Hervey and Fox had crossed the Alps on their outward journey, arriving in Turin by the fourth of that month (Halsband, p. 80).

Imagine, Child![41] our piteous Plight,
No Food by Day, no Rest by Night.
How wett, how comfortless, how cold,
We pass'd mount Sinis[42] can't be told:
Impervious to a Chaise;[43] we rode
In Chairs,[44] eight human Creatures Load:
Twelve Miles beneath our Weight they groan,
Five up, five plain way,[45] and two down.
To name each Village where we lay
Is needless sure, but ev'ry Day,
Before Aurora[46] oped the East,
To lett out Thetis' nightly Guest;[47]
We're haul'd out of our Beds to stray
O'er Rocks and Hills, a tedious Way,
Such Hills in fabled Fights we're told
The Gyants threw at Gods of old,[48]
Tho so enormous ev'ry one,
That each a Country seem's alone.
These in full Bulk conspicuous rise,
Those lose their Summits in the Skys;
Whilst this it's Form so odly shrouds,
It's Head's in Snow, it's Foot in Clouds;
The Whole, what Scenes romantick[49] crown!

41. *Child*: 'In contemptuous or affectionate address' (*OED*), here clearly the latter, though with more than a little condescension.

42. *mount Sinis*: mountain in the Alps overlooking a pass that provided the chief way across the Alps between France and Italy until the early nineteenth century when Napoleon built a road.

43. *Chaise*: 'A carriage for travelling, having a closed body and seated for one to three persons, the driver sitting on one of the horses' (*OED*).

44. *Chairs*: 'An enclosed chair or covered vehicle for one person, carried on poles by two men' (*OED*); evidently these chairs accommodated two passengers.

45. *plain way*: i.e. on the flat. 46. *Aurora*: Roman goddess of the dawn (Greek Eos).

47. *Thetis' nightly Guest*: Thetis, a sea-goddess, is presented as having as a nightly guest Apollo, Greek god of the sun.

48. *Such Hills . . . of old*: in classical mythology, the Giants, angered by the defeat of the Titans, fought a war against the Gods in which they hurled against Jupiter rocks so massive that they became mountains when they landed on earth, islands when they landed on water.

49. *romantick*: 'Characterized or marked by, or invested with, a sense of romance; arising from, suggestive of, or appealing to, an idealized, fantastic, or sentimental view of life or reality; atmospheric, evocative, glamorous' (*OED*).

A Grove in Air, a pendent Town.
Here Barrenness and Plenty joyn,[50]
For Snows surround the rip'ning Vine.
Cascades and Rivers, Flocks and Fields,
Each vary'd View promiscuous yields;
Sometimes, o'ertaken by the Night,
We climb by Cynthia's[51] doubtfull Light,
O'er Precipices, such a Height,
So steep their Sides, the Way so streight;
That if Achilles self[52] were there,
Achilles might confess a Fear.
But sick or well, where'er I move,
In ev'ry Hardship that I prove,
Fidus Achates[53] still is near,
And makes my Welfare all his Care.

But all our frights and dangers past,
To Lyons safe we came at last;
Witness my Hand; – for there I'm writing,
What truth and Kindness[54] are inditing.[55]
Yet dont imagine, that I think,
This casual Child of Pen and Ink,
Deserving to be sent so far,
But that ev'n Trifles light as Air,[56]

50. *joyn*: in contemporary pronunciation, the diphthong would have produced a perfect rhyme with 'Vine'.

51. *Cynthia*: 'A poetic name for the Moon personified as a goddess' (*OED*).

52. *Achilles self*: Greek hero of the Trojan War, the allusion possibly suggested by the mention of Thetis, his mother, in line 189 (Loeb, I, 542; II, 96, 100, 326).

53. *Fidus Achates*: 'Faithful Achates', referring to Stephen Fox; Achates being the companion of Aeneas in Virgil's *Aeneid*, the phrase means a true friend. It occurs in Books VI.158, VIII.521 and 586, and XII.384.

54. *Kindness*: the sense is probably closer to *OED* 1, 'Kinship; near relationship; natural affection arising from this', than to the modern sense.

55. *inditing*: 'To put into written words, write, pen (a letter, etc.); to inscribe, set down, or enter in writing. In later use, passing into 3, the "wording" being more thought of than the actual writing (*OED* 4)'; 3a 'To put into words, compose (a poem, tale, speech, etc.); to give a literary or rhetorical form to (words, an address); to express or describe in a literary composition'.

56. *Trifles light as Air*: alluding to *Othello* III. 3. 322–4, when Iago decides to use the handkerchief dropped by Desdemona as evidence of the infidelity he will allege against her, but obviously without sinister implication.

(As from Othello I can prove,)
Cease to be such to those who love;
I send it for this Cause alone;
And for the rest I freely own,
'Tis the poor Offspring of a Day,
Just to be read and thrown away.[57]

57. *thrown away*: the facts that Hervey took the trouble to make this transcript and to make some corrections to it suggest that the remark constitutes humorous self-deprecation and is not to be taken literally.

# 17 To Mr. Poyntz upon Returning Him Dr. Secker's Sermon on Education

***Main source.*** William Hervey's commonplace book, SRO 941/53/1, p. 122, copied after February 1751. This is chosen because it has several variant readings from the others that seem to improve on them, so suggesting the possibility that, like several other poems in the same collection, it was copied from a text written out or annotated by Hervey himself.

***Complementary sources.*** Bod. MS Rawl. poet. 152, ff. 218r–219r, and BL Add. MS 28101, f. 206r. The poem appears to have been printed first in *The London Evening-Post*, 13–15 November 1733, p. 2, and the *Gentleman's Magazine*, 3, 602 (November 1733). It was reprinted in *New Foundling Hospital for Wit*, IV (1771), 119–20, and its subsequent editions (1784: I, 240–1; 1786: I, 242–3).

***Attribution.*** All the above sources except Bod. MS Rawl. poet. 152 (none given).

***Context and date.*** Thomas Secker (1694–1768), who had been appointed a royal chaplain in 1732 and became rector of St James's, Piccadilly, in 1733, gave a sermon by invitation at Oxford on 8 July of the latter year, Act Sunday (Graduation Day or Commencement), on the subject of 'the advantages and duties of an academical education'. As was customary, the sermon was printed for the University. After holding the bishoprics of Bristol and of Oxford, he ended his career as Archbishop of Canterbury. Stephen Poyntz (c. 1685–1750) enjoyed a successful diplomatic career before his appointment in 1731 as governor and steward for the King's second surviving son, William Augustus, Duke of Cumberland (1721–65). Hervey thought well both of Secker and of Poyntz, describing the former and his fellow churchman Martin Benson as 'learned and ingenious men, of unexceptionable characters', and Poyntz as 'a man of learning, of sense, and of reputation' (Sedgwick, II, 405, 345). His poem belongs to a genre of complimentary verse accompanying a gift appropriate to the recipient. For all its urbane manner, it has a political agenda. Frederick, Prince of Wales, was in bad odour with the King and Queen, and the object of Hervey's particular animus. By ignoring Frederick's existence and celebrating his younger brother as a 'lov'd Marcellus' (line 17), the poem seeks to erase his right to the throne. Hervey was later to take a less enthusiastic view of the Duke, if, as seems likely, he wrote 'Adelphi' (Poem 45). A response appeared in the short-lived monthly *The Honey-Suckle* in 1734 (London: for Charles Corbett), pp. 120–1. Entitled 'To Mr. Poyntz, occasion'd by a late Poem from Lord H—y to Mr. Poyntz, with Dr. Secker's Sermon on Education', and attributed to a 'Mr. H. L.' who contributed other items to later editions, it commends both Hervey and Poyntz but emphasises the importance of a solid grounding for the young Duke in religion.

***Textual commentary.*** In the few cases where punctuation in the SRO text is lacking or is illogical, it is provided from the best consensus of the other sources; see List of Emendations. Initial capitals are retained, the SRO manuscript striking a balance between their heavy use in the earlier texts and their elimination for common nouns in the latest. The generally accepted spelling 'Poyntz' is preferred to SRO's 'Pointz'.

## To Mr. Poyntz upon returning him Dr. Secker's Sermon on Education

While Secker's rules in this discourse I view,
How quick each maxim turns my thoughts to you:
Who in each Art of Education skill'd,
Severe in precept, yet in manner mild,
Can form the Man, and yet not shock the child.
You by perswasion to instruction join'd,
Know without force to cultivate the mind:
And to rough tasks communicating ease,
Can to the taught, ev'n make the teacher please;
Whilst to a Court[1] adapting ev'ry Rule,
Without enervating the strictest school,
At once you strengthen and adorn the Heart,
With Spartan Virtue and Athenian art.[2]
Nor vain thy toil, nor fruitless are thy cares,
For see! thy royal charge, in ripening years,
The second hope of our Augustan age,[3]
Like lov'd Marcellus,[4] ev'ry heart engage:
But to his days Heav'n grant a longer date,
Nor to Marcellus' Virtues add his fate:
Long may he live, the glory of our Isle,

1. *to a Court*: Hervey makes clear the special requirements of a royal education.

2. *Spartan virtue and Athenian art*: connoting military discipline and philosophical wisdom respectively; see the related antithesis in line 25.

3. *Augustan age*: a stock comparison between Britain and the Rome of Augustus Caesar.

4. *Marcellus*: nephew of Augustus Caesar, apparently groomed as his successor until dying at the age of nineteen.

And 'both Minerva's'[5] on his fortunes smile:
Let this in Senates[6] her assistance yeild,
Let that direct, and guard him in the field:[7]
In peace or war, still useful to the state,
In council prudent, and in action great.
Then ev'ry Truth, throughout this theory shewn,
Shall from thy Practise in this youth be known:
And the World find, by one example taught,
How well on Poyntz's Conduct Secker wrote.

5. *both Minerva's*: i.e. both Minervas. Minerva was goddess both of war and of wisdom; the quotation marks point to Dryden's line 'He both *Minerva's* justly makes his own' ('To the Earl of Roscommon, on his Excellent Essay on Translated Verse', 72).

6. *Senates*: government. 7. *in the field*: in battle.

# 18 To Dr Sherwin in Answer to a Latin Letter in Verse

***Main source.*** BL Add. MS 51396, ff. 99r–102v, as an enclosure in a letter to Henry Fox, then in France, dated 20 October 1733 (ff. 97r–98r). The letter enclosing the poem, but not the poem itself, is reprinted in modernised form by Ilchester, pp. 178–9. The presence of line numbers, and of corrections apparently in Hervey's hand, suggest that it is a fair copy.

***Supplementary manuscript source.*** Hervey's annotated copy of the Roberts edition detailed below, which is held by the National Trust at Ickworth, shelfmark 18.B.4.8. No other manuscript source has come to light.

***Complementary print source.*** *An Epistle from a Nobleman to a Doctor of* Divinity*: In Answer to a* Latin *Letter in Verse. Written from* H——n-C—t, Aug. *28. 1733* (London: [Sam. Aris] for J. Roberts, 1733). This was reprinted several times in 1734 by various publishers as an addition to the satirical riposte *Tit for Tat.* Lines 121–61 were reprinted in the *Grub-street Journal*, 13 December 1733, as part of an attack on Hervey; and, on 3 January 1734, the same newspaper printed a parody of various lines from the poem entitled 'The Belle-Man of S. James's Verses for the year 1734. Prologue', reprinted two days later in *The Daily Journal.*

***Attribution.*** Authorial.

***Context and date.*** According to the Roberts edition, the poem dates from August 1733, when Hervey was with the court at Hampton Court, but the copy in the letter to Henry Fox is dated 20 September. In that letter, dated 20 October 1733, Hervey asks for Fox's opinion of the poem, saying it was 'written to Dr. Sherwin to entertain the Richmond-Caravan in their late Progress'. Letters dated 12 August and 11 October, printed by the Earl of March (Charles Henry Gordon Lennox) in *A Duke and his Friends: The Life and Letters of the Second Duke of Richmond*, 2 vols. (London: Hutchinson, 1911), I, 254, 279 indicate that Charles Lennox, second Duke, was in waiting at court on those dates, while another letter states that he would be at Greenwich on 18 September and at Shoreham on 22 September (I, 254). Hervey's date of 20 September, therefore, may suggest that the poem was written to amuse the Duke and his companions on their journey from London back to his country seat at Goodwood in Sussex, though Halsband suggests that the 'Progress' was 'from Goodwood to Hampton Court' (p. 162). William Sherwin was a Canon of Chichester who was a comic butt for the Duke and Duchess of Richmond and their friends. Earlier in the same year, the Duke had staged a mock highway robbery involving Sherwin, who had responded in ways they found predictably Falstaffian. The story is told by the Earl of March in *A Duke and his Friends* (I, 264–73) and by Halsband (pp. 158–9).

Hervey's poem was not intended for publication. He says in a letter to Stephen Fox dated 6 December 1733 that it was 'printed without [his] knowledge' (BL Add. MS 51345, f. 62r). As its title indicates, it was a response to a poem in Latin written to him by Sherwin. No copy of Sherwin's letter, manuscript or printed, seems to have survived. That it got into wider circulation is proved by the publication in 1735 of *Tit for Tat. Part II. By the Author of the First Part. To Which is Added, The Latin Letter from a Doctor of Divinity to a Noble Lord, Burlesqu'd* (London: for P. Monger). It seems that Sherwin felt sufficiently flattered by the poem he received in reply as to show it around, by which means it found its way into the press. Hervey was later to retaliate with a piece of invective entitled 'Dr Sherwin's Character design'd for his Epitaph' (Poem 23). However, the fact that the primary readership for the epistle was not its nominal addressee but, by Hervey's account, the Duke and his entourage, suggests that Sherwin was also in part its butt. In the event, it caused most offence not to Sherwin, who seems to have been incapable of appreciating irony, at least where his *amour-propre* was involved, but to Pope, for Hervey could not resist allowing himself an attack on the latter. Earlier in the year (on 8 March 1733) had appeared *To the Imitator of the First Satire of the Second Book of Horace* (Poem 22), the satire on Pope by Hervey in collaboration with Lady Mary Wortley Montagu. This and the further attack in the epistle addressed to Sherwin were to provoke further literary passages-at-arms between the three. When the *Daily Courant* of 20 November 1733 advertised *An Epistle from a Nobleman from Hampton-Court, to the Reverend Dr. Sherwin* and added to it 'The Reverend Dr. *Sherwin's Latin* Epistle to the *Lord Hervey*; and also, Verses on the said Dr. by the same Lord', the threat of publication of the satire on Sherwin (Poem 23) and the implication that the *Epistle to a Nobleman* was by Hervey led him to ask the Duke of Newcastle to intervene with the *Courant*. Two days later it published what Hervey himself identified as the false assurance that 'there was no such Poem wrote by the Lord Hervey, nor Latin Epistle sent to his Lordship by Dr. *Sherwin*' (Ilchester, p. 179). Consequently a retraction was issued on 10 December. Pope then pressed what he took to be an advantage by issuing an advertisement in *The Craftsman* of 29 December, saying that 'unless the said noble Lord shall this next Week in a Manner as *publick as the Injury*, deny the said Poem to be his, or contradict the Aspersions therein contain'd, there will with all Speed be published A MOST PROPER REPLY to the same'. Pope may have had in mind his *Letter to a Noble Lord*, which he had printed but decided not to make public, or three anonymously published pieces that may be his: *The Belle-man of St. James's his Verses for the Year 1733, A Most Proper Reply to the Nobleman's Epistle to a Professor of Divinity* and *Horace versus Fannius*; but for full retaliation he waited until 1734–5, when he published his devastating characterisation of Hervey as Sporus in *An Epistle to Dr. Arbuthnot*. Hervey was to re-enter the fray in 1742 with a prose pamphlet, *A Letter to Mr. C—b—r, On his Letter to Mr. P——.* and Poem 24, *The Difference between Verbal and Practical Virtue Exemplify'd* (see the headnote to Poem 22, *Verses Addressed to the Imitator* and Halsband, pp. 162–5, 175–8, 233–4, 288–91). What is relevant for present purposes is not the lengthy quarrel but the nature of Hervey's attack. Even though he does not seem to have intended the poem to be printed, it is significant that, when it was published, he was delighted to be told that it had enraged Pope. 'Pope is in a most violent fury, & J'en suis ravis', he told Stephen Fox in a letter dated 6 December 1733 (BL Add. MS 51345, f. 62r; Halsband, p. 162).

Unlike *To the Imitator*, the epistle to Sherwin does not satirise Pope's person. Robert Halsband is not quite correct, however, in stating that it 'is aimed only at his writings' (p. 162), for, as Linda Zionkowski argues, it also targets what Hervey saw as his transgression of codes applying to social rank (*Men's Work: Gender, Class, and the Professionalization of Poetry, 1660–1784* (New York and Basingstoke: Palgrave, 2001), pp. 108–11). This, for example, explains why it contains a gibe at the occupation of Pope's father before he retired, albeit as '*Hatter*' (line 145) rather than as linen-merchant. But none of the few who have written on the poem seems to have noticed that Pope is likely to have been annoyed at least as much by a part of the poem that does not mention him directly at all: lines 88–91, in which Hervey presents a definition of wit in an obvious attempt to outdo his enemy's in *An Essay on Criticism*:

> *True wit* is *Nature* to advantage dress'd,
> What oft was *Thought*, but ne'er so well *Exprest*,
> *Something*, whose truth convinc'd at sight we find,
> That gives us back the image of our mind.
> As shades more sweetly recommend the light,
> So modest plainness sets off sprightly wit.
> (*Twickenham*, I, 272–3, lines 297–302)

While Pope's definition of wit is vulnerable to Johnson's objection, in his 'Life of Cowley', that it 'depresses it below its natural dignity, and reduces it from strength of thought to happiness of language' (*Lives of the Most Eminent English Poets*, ed. by Roger Lonsdale, 4 vols. (Oxford: Clarendon Press, 2006), I, 200), Hervey's is not. This is because Hervey emphasises 'thought' rather than expression, just as he criticises Pope in lines 125–47 for borrowing his ideas from others and clothing them in his own language. 'True Wit is Reason in her gayest Strain,' he declares, 'That can at once inform, and entertain' (lines 88–9). Similarly, he goes on to state that what wit offers are 'lively Truths' that it invites its readers to 'explore' (line 90).

Hervey also has the candour to admit that his verse is open to the criticism of facility, remarking: 'And *Pope* with Justice of such Lines may say, | *Lord Fanny spins a thousand in a Day*' (lines 123–4), slightly misquoting line 6 of *The First Satire of the Second Book of Horace*, printed earlier in the same year by L. G. (Lawton Gilliver): 'Lord *Fanny* spins a thousand such a Day'. Pope repeated the soubriquet for Hervey, which he seems to have used first in *A Master Key to Popery* (1731), in later works (see Pope, *Prose*, p. 406). But Hervey follows this concession immediately with the charge that 'Such *Pope* himself might write, who ne'er could think' (line 125). Zionkowski convincingly explains the rebuke to his own facility in social-cultural terms, suggesting that the profession of writing was so incompatible with genteel social status that Hervey 'responded to potential criticism by treating verse as a form of mindless recreation' (*Men's Work*, p. 109). Yet the conflict went deeper than this. Above all, it accounts for the irony to which he subjects himself and other male members of the aristocracy in lines 7–49. Here he represents himself as typical of his rank in that he has forgotten most of the little he learned at school and has abused his elite social status by getting it to cover up for his lack of knowledge and understanding. In fact, despite his professions of ignorance, Hervey could not only read but write Latin, and, as the *Letters Between Lord Hervey and Dr. Middleton Concerning the Roman Senate*, published poshumously by W. Strahan and T. Cadell in 1778, were to show, he was an accomplished Latin scholar. That scholarship also informed Poem 66, the five-act play 'Agrippina' he was writing in the mid-1730s, which is certainly neither light nor trivial, though its composition would have been little known outside Hervey's immediate circle. As a result of the pose he adopts, however, the poem falls between two stools. It almost achieves a serious critique of the social order of which he was a member, and it delivers not only a definition of wit that is better than Pope's, but also a challenge to the intellectual authority of Pope's verse. Yet it is hamstrung both by the social prejudices that disfigure his attack on Pope and by nothing less than a refusal to take his own intellect and powers of composition with the seriousness they deserved. In this way it is pivotal in his career, falling chronologically between poems such as the 'Epistles in the Manner of Ovid' that show every sign of careful artistry, and the satirical squibs and other occasional verse that were largely to characterise its last ten years.

***Textual commentary.*** Because the manuscript appears to be a fair copy, because parts of it are in Hervey's hand, and because it presents no problems of readability, it is printed as it stands with the usual exceptions: that contractions are silently expanded, including the ampersands that are used throughout apart from at the beginnings of lines. Other changes are indicated in the List of Emendations, including the addition of italics to words not italicised in the manuscript (this is necessary because italics are marked in the manuscript only between lines 124 and 157, and so beyond those lines have been adopted from the printed edition).

## To Dr Sherwin in answer to a Latin Letter in Verse

Supliant Your Pardon first I must implore
(Dear Doctor!) that I've never wrote before:
But in the constant Bustle of a Court,
Betwixt our Forms,[1] our Busyness, and our Sport;
Tho you may think whole Days are unenjoy'd
Yet scarce one Moment passes unemploy'd.

In the next Place, when I declare how long
I've taken leave of *Greek* or *Latin* Song;[2]
That all I learn'd from *Doctor Freind*[3] at School,
From *Gradus*,[4] *Lexicon*, or Grammer-Rule;
Of Saphic, Lyric, or Iambic[5] Odes,
Or *Doctor King*'s[6] Machinary of Gods,
Has quite deserted this poor *John-Trot*[7] Head,
And left plain, native *English* in it's Stead:
I'm sure your courteous Rev'rence will forgive
The homely Way in which you now recieve
These hearty Thanks, from an illiterate Hand,
For Favours which I barely understand.

You know the Proverb says, That of a Cat,
The Creature's Skin is all that you can get;
So from no Head you ever can recieve
More Wit than such a Head has got to give:
Let for this Reason then, my Learned Friend,

1. *Forms*: 'A set method of outward behaviour or procedure in accordance with prescribed usage, etiquette, ritual, etc.' (*OED*).

2. *Song*: i.e. poetry.

3. *Doctor Freind*: Robert Freind (1666/7–1751) was headmaster of Westminster School from August 1711 until May 1733, a period that included Hervey's year and a half as a pupil there from January 1712 (*ODNB*; Halsband, pp. 11, 15).

4. *Gradus*: 'Short for *Gradus ad Parnassum* "a step to Parnassus", the Latin title of a dictionary of prosody until recently used in English public schools, intended as an aid in Latin versification' (*OED*).

5. *Saphic, Lyric, or Iambic*: sapphic and iambic are types of metre used in Latin verse, including by Horace in his odes; lyric is a kind of verse characterised by songlike qualities.

6. *Doctor King's*: William King (1663–1712) was the author of *An Historical Account of the Heathen Gods and Heroes; Necessary for the Understanding of the Ancient Poets* (1710), 'much used in schools' (*ODNB*).

7. *John-Trot*: 'a man of slow or uncultured intellect, a bumpkin, a clown' (*OED* 'John').

Gracious, accept the All I have to send.
Nor wonder that my Brain no more affords,
But recolect the Privilege of Lords;
And when you see me fairely write my Name,
For *England*'s *Sake* wish all could do the same.
Nay, I perhaps could not so much have done,
Had I been bred and born an eldest Son;
A Noble Father's Heir, spoild by his Mother,
Leaves Learning always to his Younger Brother;
Who at the Bar[8] must prate[9] to earn a Groat,[10]
Whilst all *our* Bus'ness is to dress[11] and vote.

The very Moment therefore I grew Great,[12]
A Lazy titled Heir to an Estate;
For fear my Education might bely,
By some mean Badge of Sense, my Quality,[13]
Which to good Blood, by old prescriptive Rules,
Gives Right hereditary to be Fools;
I streight began upon a quite new score,
Neglected all that I had learn'd before;
And not to seem a Novice in my State,
Or ign'rant what belong'd to being great,
With little judgment, and good store of Pride,
Still took upon me allways to decide:
In ev'ry Company was bold and loud,
Behav'd my-self as rudely as I could,
And ne'er discours'd of what I understood.

8. *Bar*: i.e. in a court of law.

9. *prate*: 'To talk or chatter; to speak foolishly, boastfully, or at great length, esp. to little purpose; to prattle' (*OED*).

10. *Groat*: 'Taken as the type of a very small sum' (*OED*).

11. *dress*: referring to the official garb a member of the House of Lords would have to wear in order to attend.

12. *grew Great*: Hervey's elder half-brother Carr died on 15 November 1723, with the result that Hervey acquired the courtesy title Baron Hervey of Ickworth and became the Earl of Bristol's heir (*ODNB*).

13. *Quality*: 'Nobility, high birth or rank, good social position' (*OED*).

Tis thus among *the Great*:[14] if any one,
By Chance has *wit*, so aukardly tis shown,
That 'tis a less Misfortune to have none:
For still he goes on this erroneous Rule,
That no body with *wit* can be a Fool.
Yet by Example, at his own Expence,
Proves one may have it without *common Sense*.
For, void of Prudence, and too vain of Parts,
How oft good Heads have plainer shown bad Hearts?
When in Obscurity perhaps the *Last*
Without the *First*, had fortunately past;
Thus whilst to Wit their sole Ambition tends,
(Whilst for one Joke they give up fifty friends)
Tho ne'er adapted to a manly Use,
But squander'd all on Trifles or Abuse
They think the world so blind as to admit,
All Understanding is compris'd in *Wit*.
That dang'rous Flow of a licentious Brain,
Which wanting Skill its ardour to restrain,
Converts to Ill, like Nourishment to pain.

Perhaps You'll say (to it's Excuse inclin'd)
If 'tis an Ill, 'tis of a pleasing Kind.
I grant it is; but still 'tis a Disease;
Are Calentures[15] not Ills because they please?
Or who will call the Gout or Stone[16] a Good,
Because engender'd by the richest Blood?[17]
Luxuriant Branches show a fertile Root,
But unrestrain'd would bear but little Fruit;
So Wit unprun'd, and wanting Judgment's Aid,

14. *the Great*: 'Eminent by reason of birth, rank, wealth, power, or position; of high social or official position; of eminent rank or place' (*OED*).

15. *Calentures*: 'A disease incident to sailors within the tropics, characterized by delirium in which the patient, it is said, fancies the sea to be green fields, and desires to leap into it' (*OED*).

16. *Stone*: 'hard morbid concretion in the body, esp. in the kidney or urinary bladder, or in the gallbladder' (*OED*), i.e. gallstone.

17. *engender'd by the richest Blood*: for a full discussion of theories of the gout, especially early-modern theories, see Roy Porter and G. S. Rousseau, *Gout: The Patrician Malady* (New Haven and London: Yale University Press, 1998).

Is the crude Fruit of a good useless Head.
Such Wits are nought but glit'ring Ignorance,
What *Monkeys* are to Men, they are to Sense;
Imperfect Mimicks, ludicrous, and mean,
Who often bite that Fool they entertain.
Their Tricks may please, their Quickness may surprise;
At first we wonder, but at Last despise;
The Wise avoid such Animals with Care
And he who laughs the loudest, laughs in Fear:
True Wit is Reason in her gayest Strain,
That can at once inform, and entertain:
Her lively Truths attentive we explore,
Pleas'd we commend, instructed we adore.[18]
But of this rare, this estimable kind,
In the great World, few Instances we find;
Tho aiming at it, dissolute, and loud,
And of the Faults they ought to blush for, proud,
How oft We hear some Witling[19] pert and dull,
By Fashion *Coxcomb*,[20] and by Nature *Fool*;
With hackney Maxims in dogmatic Strain
Scoffing *Religion* or the *Marriage-Chain*:
Then from his common-Place book he repeats
"That Lawyers all are Rogues, and Parsons Cheats,
"Physicians ignorant, and Courtiers Slaves,
"Great Kings but Actors, and great Statesmen Knaves:
"That Vice and Virtue's nothing but a Jest;
"And all Morality Deceit well dress'd;
"That Life it self is like a wrangling Game,
"Where some for Int'rest[21] play, and some for Fame;
"Whilst ev'ry Gamester at this Board we meet,

18. *True Wit ... we adore*: Hervey's definition of wit is implicitly not only a riposte to Pope's in *An Essay on Criticism*, lines 297–302, but also an attempt to outdo it. See headnote.

19. *Witling*: 'A petty wit; one who fancies himself a wit; a pretender to wit; one who utters light or feeble witticisms' (*OED*).

20. *Coxcomb*: 'a foolish, conceited, showy person, vain of his accomplishments, appearance, or dress; a fop' (*OED*).

21. *Int'rest*: 'That which is to or for the advantage of any one; good, benefit, profit, advantage' (*OED*).

"Must either be the Bubble,[22] or the Cheat".
And when this Catalogue he has run o'er,
And empty'd of whip'd Cream his frothy Store,
Thinks he's so wise, no *Solomon* knows more:
That the thin texture of his flimsey Brain,
Is fit the Weight on *Walpole's* to sustain:
In *Senates* to preside, to mold *the State*,
And fix, in *England*'s Service, *Europe*'s Fate.

Since such you'l find most Men of our Degree,
Excuse the Ignorance apears in Me;
Nor marvel whilst that Ign'rance I reherse,
That still I know enough to do't in Verse:
Guiltless of Thought, each Blockhead may compose
This nothing-meaning Verse, as fast as Prose:
And *Pope* with Justice of such Lines may say,
*Lord Fanny spins a thousand in a Day.*
Such *Pope* himself might write, who ne'er could think,
He who at *Crambo*[23] plays with pen and Ink;
And is call'd Poet, 'cause in Rhyme he wrote
What *Dacier*[24] construed, and what *Homer* thought:
But in Reality this Jingler's Claim,
Or to an Author's, or a Poet's Name,
No better is when you examine it,
Than each dull *Dictionary*'s Claim to Wit;
That gives you nothing at it's own Expence,
But a few modern Words for ancient Sense.
'Tis thus, whene'er *Pope* writes, he's forc'd to go
And *beg a little Sense*, as School-Boys do:
For All cannot invent, who can translate,[25]

22. *Bubble*: 'a dupe, a gull' (*OED*).

23. *Crambo*: 'A game in which one player gives a word or line of verse to which each of the others has to find a rhyme' (*OED*).

24. *Dacier*: Anne Le Fèvre Dacier (1647–1720) was famous for her classical scholarship, especially her translations of Homer's *Iliad* and *Odyssey* – epics later translated into English by Pope – into French.

25. *For All cannot invent, who can translate*: The quotation (though not marked as such in the manuscript) is from 'The Translator's Preface' to François Rabelais, *The Whole Works of F. Rabelais*, trans. by Sir Thomas Urquart, Peter Anthony Motteux and others. If Hervey

No more than those who cloath us can create.
When we see *Celia* shining in Brocade,
Who thinks tis *Hinchlif*[26] all that Beauty made?
And *Pope*, in his best Works, we only find
The gaudy *Hinchlif* of some beauteous Mind.
To bid his Genius work without that Aid,
Would be as much mistaking of his trade,
As 'twould to bid your *Hatter*[27] make a *Head*.
Since this Mechanic's,[28] like the other's Pains,
Are all for dressing other Peoples Brains.

But had he not (to his eternal Shame)
By trying to deserve a Satirist's Name,
Prov'd he can ne'er invent but to defame:
Had not his *Taste*[29] and *Riches*[30] lately shown,
When he would talk of Genius to the Town,
How ill he chuses, if he trusts his own:
Had he in Modern Language only wrote
Those Rules which *Horace* and which *Vida*[31] taught:
On *Garth*,[32] or *Boileau*'s model[33] built his Fame,

used the two-volume edition of 1708 (London: for James Woodward), the remark 'not many condescend to translate, but such as cannot invent' occurs in II, iv.

26. *Hinchlif*: implicitly a dressmaker; the goods of a Thomas Hinchliff, including 'rich Gold, Silver, and Silk Brocades' are listed for sale after the death of Thomas Hinchliff, mercer, in the *London Evening-Post* for 17 October 1741.

27. *Hatter*: in allusion to the occupation of Pope's father, though *ODNB* terms it 'linen merchant'.

28. *Mechanic*: 'A manual worker, an artisan' (*OED*).

29. *Taste*: the first edition of Pope's poem now known as *An Epistle to Richard Boyle, Earl of Burlington*, published in 1731, was variously subtitled in early editions *Of Taste* or *Of False Taste*.

30. *Riches*: early editions of Pope's poem now known as *An Epistle to Allen, Lord Bathurst* were entitled *Of the Use of Riches, an Epistle to the Right Honorable Allen, Lord Bathurst*.

31. *Horace and . . . Vida*: like Horace, Marcus Hieronymus Vida (c. 1480–1566) wrote an *Art of Poetry*, first published in Latin c. 1517, that was highly influential in the neo-classical period and that Pope praises in *An Essay on Criticism*, lines 704–8.

32. *Garth*: Samuel Garth (1660/1–1719) was a physician and poet who produced the influential mock-heroic poem *The Dispensary* (1699) and encouraged Pope to publish *The Rape of the Lock* (*ODNB*).

33. *Boileau's model*: Nicolas Boileau-Despréaux (1636–1711) was a French poet and critic whose work includes an *Art of Poetry* and a mock-heroic poem, *Le lutrin* (*The Lectern*), both first published in 1674, that influenced not only Garth but Pope and others.

Or sold *Broome*'s Labours,[34] printed with *Pope*'s Name;
Had he ne'er aim'd at any Work beside,
In Glory then he might have liv'd and dy'd:
And ever been, tho' not with Genius fir'd,
By *School-Boys* quoted and by *Girls* admir'd.[35]

So much for *Pope* — and were I not afray'd,
Tho I wrote more, that you no more would read;
I now would try to jumble into Rhyme,
Th' account you ask of how we pass our time:
But by the manner of your spending your's,
Guess; and you'll not be very wide of ours:
For *Courts* are only larger Familys,[36]
The Growth of each, few Truths, and many Lyes;
Like you we *lounge*,[37] and feast, and play, and chatter;
In private satirize, in Public flatter:
Few to each other, all to one Point true;
Which one I shant, nor need explain: Adieu.

34. *Broome's Labours*: William Broome (*bap.* 1689, *d.* 1745), who contributed eight of the twenty-four books in Pope's translation of Homer's *Odyssey*, along with notes to the whole poem, bitterly resented 'Pope's attempt to blur the details of the collaboration', in which Elijah Fenton also participated (*ODNB*).

35. This line is followed in the manuscript by four deleted ones: 'So much for Pope, nor this I would have say'd | Had not the Spider first his venom shed | For who begins can ne'er be a good Friend | Nor a wise Foe who thus attack'd will end'. The first of those two deleted lines are also marked on the Ickworth copy, with the second couplet replaced by four other lines: 'For the first Stone I ne'er unjustly cast | But who can blame the Hand that throw's the Last | And if one comon Foe a Wretch has made, | Of all Mankind – his Folly on his Head'. This proposed addition was also then deleted.

36. *For Courts . . . Familys*: Hervey was later to write: 'The intrigues of Courts and private families are still the same game, and played with the same cards' (Sedgwick, II, 623).

37. *lounge*: presumably italicised because considered to be slang.

# 19 To the Queen

***Main source.*** 'Some Materials towards Memoirs of the Reign of King George II', RA GEO/MAIN ff. 53672r–53676r, in the Royal Archives at Windsor Castle, because this is the text that represents Hervey's latest intentions.

***Complementary manuscript source.*** 'Manuscript of the Memoirs of the Reign of George II from 1727–1737', SRO 941/47/13–14 (14), ff. 115r–119r.

***Complementary print sources.*** None. The poem was first printed in bowdlerised form by John Wilson Croker in *Memoirs*, II, 148–58; and in a modernised text in Sedgwick, II, 576–84.

***Attribution.*** Authorial.

***Context and date.*** The poem was written to amuse the Queen in the summer of 1736. It is introduced as follows in *Some Materials*: 'the first of the two Pieces that I shall here transcribe was written upon the Queen's bidding him write no more; an Epigram in Martial which he had paraphrased & apply'd to Lord Burlington's House at Chiswick & his Lordship's Performances as an Architect, having got about, & made Lord & Lady Burlington, & their Friend his Grace of Grafton extreamly angry with him' (SRO 941/47/13, f. 114v; Windsor f. 53671v; Sedgwick, II, 574). The epigram is Poem 41; the second of the two pieces is Hervey's *jeu d'esprit* 'The Death of Lord Hervey; Or, a Morning at Court: A Drama', missing from the Windsor manuscript but printed from the SRO manuscript in Sedgwick, II, 585–96. Generically, 'To the Queen' is a familiar epistle in humorous vein, though at another level it is also an apologia. In the latter respect it prompts interesting comparison with Pope's *An Epistle to Dr Arbuthnot*, first printed about eighteen months previously, for, while offering an appearance of apology, it gives further grounds for offence to the very persons who would be most likely to feel offended by it – including of course, most notoriously, Hervey himself. The main difference between the two poems is that, while Pope's was written for publication, Hervey's had to be kept private, 'Veil'd,' as he put it, 'by [his] well-lock'd Bureau from the Light' (line 267). Hervey had to rely on his ability to amuse the Queen, as well as on his close friendship with her, to finesse humorous or satirical commentary on many of his fellow courtiers that would have proved embarrassing in the highest degree had it been published, especially as there is even an implicit reflection on the King (see line 126 and note). Pope's chief recourse, on the other hand, was his wit and his ability to amuse the reader outside the poem, as well as various evasive or otherwise self-exculpatory devices such as his account of his own life and experience as a poet. The other main difference consists in the relation between writer and addressee. Pope depends to some extent on the external reader's awareness of Arbuthnot's reputation as a good man, so helping to guarantee his own moral standing. Hervey, on the other hand, really is addressing the Queen, and the considerable evidence that his regard for her was deep and heartfelt leaves no reason to doubt the sincerity of the compliments he pays her.

***Textual commentary.*** Although the introductory matter and title of the poem in the SRO manuscript are in Hervey's hand, the body of neither copy of the poem is autograph. The facts that the SRO copy contains autograph corrections and insertions, and that the Windsor copy contains autograph notes, demonstrate that both were made before Hervey's death. This explains the apparent contradiction with Sedgwick's remark that a copy of the whole manuscript of *Some Materials* 'had been made in 1781 by General Hervey' (Sedgwick, I, xii). What is now the Windsor text of 'To the Queen', made many years previously, had evidently been inserted into that copy of *Some Materials*. The fact that all the Windsor annotations are in Hervey's hand, and the appearance that they are in the same ink, suggests that they were added at the same time, perhaps even on the same day. Evidence of dating for the Windsor manuscript is that a note to line 242 about John Potter must have been inserted in 1737 or later, as it was only in that year that he obtained the post to which it refers of Archbishop of Canterbury. Although the Windsor text has been chosen as the primary source on the ground that it represents Hervey's latest intentions, a few readings have been adopted from the SRO text where there is evidence of a transcription error. Similarly, italicisation follows that of the SRO text because that of the Windsor manuscript, which is rather more sparing, is also inconsistent by comparison. See the Historical Collation for details of the differences between the manuscripts. Side notes added by Hervey himself to the Windsor Castle copy are included here as footnotes, and identified by an asterisk next to the note-number, and the phrase 'autograph note, *Windsor*'.

## To the Queen

'Tis true, great Queen! I have your dread Commands,
No more with Ink to stain these Scribbling hands;
No more in *ducktisk*[1] Verse, or *teufflish*[2] Prose,
To *raccomode*[3] my Friends or Lash my Foes;

1. *ducktisk*: humorous misspelling of the German word *tüchtig*, 'proficient'.
2. *teufflish*: similar misspelling of *teuflisch*, 'devilish'; German was of course the Queen's first language.
3. *raccomode*: French *raccommoder*, 'to help out', French being the language normally spoken at court.

But how shall I this flippant Pen restrain?
Like Hellebore[4] so long 't has purg'd my Brain
I should go Mad, were I to Stop the Drain.
If then like *Midas'* Barber[5] I am curst,
And feel that I must either vent or burst,
Allow me still those Midwives Pen and Ink
(To you at least, let me on Paper think;)
Tis *a sharp Labour*,[6*] You may make it *safe*,
I shall be brought to Bed and you will laugh.
To you I'll tell each *Betty-Cotton* Tale,[7*]
And harmless Joke, whilst sourer Blockheads rail:
Let *Fog* and *Danvers*[8*] call each Courtier Slave,
Each Senator a mean corrupted Knave;
And all your Palace-Crew, from Prow to Helm,
*Huns-nas, Bernheuter, Reckel, Hecks*, and *Schelm*.[9*]
Let envious *Brudnal*[10*] her great Friends abuse,

4. *Hellebore*: 'Any of various medicinal plants valued chiefly for their strong purgative properties' (*OED*); in the Suffolk Record Office manuscript, Hervey wrote 'Hellebore' in place of 'Rhubarb', perhaps seeking a less domestic resonance.

5. *Midas' Barber*: there are various versions of the story, but Hervey's classical education and interests make it likely that he refers to Ovid's in *Metamorphoses*, XI. 146–93 (Loeb, II, 130–2) (in the most widely circulated eighteenth-century translation, *Ovid's Metamorphoses in Fifteen Books* (London: for Jacob Tonson, 1717), XI, 224–96). This tells how Apollo gave Midas ass's ears for preferring, as judge of a music contest, Pan's music to his own; and how Midas' barber, required to keep the secret under threat of execution if he revealed it, confided it to a hole in the ground, only for the reeds that sprang up there to reveal it indiscriminately with the help of the wind.

6. *a sharp Labour*: 'alluding to some cant language often used by the Queen upon a story Lord Hervey told her but too long to be recited' (autograph note, *Windsor*).

7. *Betty-Cotton Tale*: 'another cant word for secret' (autograph note, *Windsor*).

8. *Fog and Danvers*: 'two of the weekly Journalists that wrote against the Court' (autograph note, *Windsor*); 'Fog' refers to *Fog's Weekly Journal*, a newspaper edited by Nathaniel Mist from France where he had fled for security, '*Danvers*' to Caleb Danvers, the pseudonym of Nicholas Amhurst, joint owner and key contributor to *The Craftsman*; see Jeremy Black, *The English Press in the Eighteenth Century* (London: Croom Helm, 1987).

9. *Huns-nas, Bernheuter, Reckel, Hecks, and Schelm*: 'In German words for rogue, Rascal, Coward, Scoundrel and Villain' (autograph note, *Windsor*); Croker glosses as '*dog's nose, last-bones, yawner, cheat, rogue*' (*Memoirs*, II, 149).

10. *Brudnal*: 'Mrs Brudnal, one of the Q's Bed-Chamber women, a very ill-temper'd, ill natured, silly vicious Lyar' (autograph note, *Windsor*); Susannah Brudenell had been appointed as one of the Women of the Bedchamber by 1735 (www.history.ac.uk/publications/office/queencaroline#wom); Lucy Worsley explains that, 'Because the Ladies of the

And little *Titch*[11]* with lower Scandal Souse;[12]
'Tis no such Rancour Stimulates my Soul,
I only ask to call a Fool, A Fool:
No Vice to give, no Virtue to deny.
I would no more than Lady *Sundon*[13] lye:
And ne'er a present, or an absent Friend,
Or basely will give up, or cool defend;
Nor ev'n my Foes I would unhappy make,
To smile, is all the Liberty I'll take.

And freely thus whilst I unpack my Breast,
Where safer can the Cargo be address'd
Than to my gracious Queen; who angry, spares,
And whilst She chides my Faults, my Folly bears?
Whose Goodness ev'ry day and Hour I prove,
And look upon like Heaven, with Fear and Love;
Whose mercy still, when I offend, I trust,
Owning the Rules I swerve from to be Just:
Whose Sense I feel, whose Merit I discern,
And wish to Practice what I daily learn;
I wish my Conduct to your Maxims true,
Yet can't that Conduct I approve, pursue.[14]

Bedchamber had become too grand to do real work . . . the Women of the Bedchamber, while technically inferior, began to wield the greater influence' (*Courtiers: The Secret History of Kensington Palace* (London: Faber & Faber, 2010), p. 49).

11. *Titch*: 'Mrs. Titchburn, another of the Q's Women of the Bedchamber with a better head than the other, and the same disposition' (autograph note, *Windsor*); Charlotte Amelia Tichborne was appointed Woman of the Bedchamber to Princess Caroline in February 1715, and continued when Caroline became Queen (www.history.ac.uk/publications/office/caroline#wom).

12. *Souse*: 'To soak; to be or become soaked or drenched; to fall with a plunge; to go plunging or sinking in water, etc.' (*OED*), here used metaphorically.

13. *Lady Sundon*: Charlotte Clayton, later Lady Sundon (c. 1679–1742), was another of the Women of the Bedchamber, first appointed in October 1714 when Caroline was Princess of Wales; 'in June 1735 she became Lady Sundon, following her husband's elevation to the Irish peerage as Baron Sundon of Ardagh' (www.history.ac.uk/publica tions/office/caroline#wom; *ODNB*); Hervey had a high opinion of her, reflecting: 'I knew her intimately, and think she had a really warm, honest, noble, generous, benevolent, friendly heart' (Sedgwick, I, 67).

14. *Yet can't . . . pursue*: echoing Ovid's *video meliora proboque, | deteriora sequor* (*Metamorphoses*, VII, 20–1 (Loeb, I, 342)), translated by Nahum Tate as 'I see the Right,

With Gifts so rare, thee, partial Heav'n has bless'd,
Your Rank is less uncommon than the rest:
With ev'ry good of Nature or of Art,
Or for the Social, or the Royal Part:
Whatever dignifys, or softens state,
In private Amiable, in Publick great:
With all those Quality's that recommend,
The best Companion, or the kindest Friend:
When Serious, just, when gay for ever new,
Quick in Discernment, in Reflection true.
All that the *Greek* or *Roman* Sages thought,
What *Plato, Socrates*, or *Tully*[15] wrote,
*Philosophers* or *Moralists* have taught;
Drawn from the Head and Dictated by Art,
Was the Prophetic Picture of thy Heart;
By Precept they, You by Example teach,
And Practice ev'ry Virtue which they preach.
Whate'er the grave Historians Page has shown,
Whate'er Experience tells, to Thee is known,
The ancient and the modern World thy own:
Whilst Policy on Maxims unrefin'd,[16]
To gentle Sway,[17] and steady Conduct join'd,
The mildest Temper and the firmest Mind,
Told to the distant, by the nearer seen,
Compleat the Woman, and Adorn the Queen:
A Queen whom *most* proclaim and *none* disown,
An Ornament and Bulwark to her throne.

If then each morning with your Converse fir'd,
(These Talents ponder'd, and these Gifts admir'd,)

and I approve it too, | Condemn the Wrong, – and yet the Wrong pursue' (*Ovid's Metamorphoses* (Tonson), VII. 28–9).

15. *Tully*: anglicised form for the name of Marcus Tullius Cicero (106–43 BCE), Roman philosopher, statesman and orator.

16. *unrefin'd*: Croker comments: 'So in MS., but I do not understand it; *undefined* would make a kind of sense' (*Memoirs*, II, 150), but the sense of sayings that are not over-sophisticated seems clear enough.

17. *Sway*: 'Power of rule or command; sovereign power or authority; dominion, rule' (*OED*).

When all the trappings and Constraints of Pride,
For ease postponed, for Pleasure thrown aside;
Your words no longer dictated by Art,
Your mind unloaded and unlock'd your Heart;
When each Court Animal, from first to last,
Like those in *Eden*, in Review has pass'd,
And Each (I won't say Brute) receiv'd it's Name,
According to the Merits of its Claim,
Or mischievously wild, or dully tame:
Pursuant to the Sketch such Scenes afford,
If I their worth endeavour to record;
If from your Presence afterward retir'd,
When only pleas'd I fancy I'm inspired,
And recollecting in my pensive Walk,
Think I can write as I have heard you talk;
So well the Merit of Your Stile is known,
It can't seem strange, or strange to you alone,
When I would have *mine* please, I chuse your own.
May I not then great Queen! your Pardon claim?
Should any Priest his own Enthusiast blame?
Should those reproach the Stroke who give us Aim?
Or Cordials to a feeble Brain apply'd,
Should those who made us Drunk our Transports chide?
No more a canting Parson Satan paints
Who damns the Devils he made for not being Saints.

Oh! let me then describe without controul,
This Ideot *Pon*, or t'other Ideot *troll*,[18]
Some are so great to name them is offence;
But mayn't I mention Mrs. *Eighteen-Pence*?[19]*

18. *Pon . . . troll*: Hervey provides no explanatory notes, but it is possible that 'pon', which lacks an initial capital in the Suffolk Record Office manuscript, is a nickname for a courtier who had the mannerism of contracting the word 'upon' (as in "pon my honour'); Croker glosses 'troll', which has an initial capital neither in Windsor nor in SRO, as 'German for *trollop*' (*Memoirs*, II, 151), though the term already had its Scandinavian sense of 'gnome' (*OED*).

19. *Mrs. Eighteen-Pence*: unexplained, though in Windsor the name has a note-number indicating that Hervey intended to supply a gloss.

Or *Privy-Nasy*[20*] with his open Mouth,
His Eyes half Shut, and at each corner Froth?
When *grinning horrible a ghastly Smile,*[21]
I hear him snorting, belching all the while,
Tell you *that two and two he's sure makes four*
*That Fruit too ripe is flat, unripe is sour.*
Internally at least (that's not uncivil,)
Good Queen let me repeat – *Oh! dummer Teuffel!*[22*]
Much harder Measure at your hands he found,
My touch is but a Fillip,[23] Your's a Wound.

When *Cow-Tail*[24*] tot'ring, waddles through your Rooms,
And with his useless Velvet Budget[25] comes;
Mayn't I reflect upon his Riddle-Fate,
Obscure in Eminence, and mean in State?
An Exile made by an uncommon doom,
*From* foreign Country's *to* his Native Home:[26*]

20. *Privy-Nasy*: 'A Cant name given by the Princesses to Lord Wilmington President of the Council' (autograph note, *Windsor*); Spencer Compton, Earl of Wilmington (c. 1674–1743), described by Hervey as 'a plodding, heavy fellow, with a great application, but no talents', had been appointed to the post in 1730 (*ODNB*; Sedgwick, I, 24).

21. *grinning horrible a ghastly Smile*: adapting Milton's phrase about Death, 'Grinn'd horrible a ghastly smile' (*Paradise Lost*, II, 846).

22. *dummer Teuffel*: 'dull devil in German' (autograph note, *Windsor*).

23. *Fillip*: 'A movement made by bending the last joint of a finger against the thumb and suddenly releasing it (so as to propel some small object, or merely as a gesture); a smart stroke or tap given by this means' (*OED*).

24. *Cow-Tail*: 'Lord Harrington made Secretary of State and a Peer, no body knew why, and after he was so, continued there tho' dislik'd by the King, Queen, and Sir R[obert] W[alpole] only because they did not know whom to put in his place' (autograph note, *Windsor*); William Stanhope, Baron Harrington (1730) and later first Earl of Harrington (1683?–1756), had been appointed Secretary of State in 1730 (*ODNB*); Hervey recorded in *Some Materials*: 'his credit at Court ran very low, and little deference was ever paid to his sentiments either by the King or Queen but when they tallied with their own' (Sedgwick, II, 346).

25. *Budget*: 'A pouch, bag, wallet, usually of leather' (*OED*), in this case containing official papers.

26. *An Exile . . . Native Home*: 'After the treaty of Seville he was made a Peer and Sec[retary] of St[ate], and of course recall'd for Spain; where every thing then important to this nation went thro' his hands, and when he came back he did nothing and was trusted with nothing' (autograph note, *Windsor*), referring to Stanhope's recall from the Congress of Soissons after the treaty had been signed in 1730; he had previously served in Spain as ambassador-extraordinary and plenipotentiary (*ODNB*).

In vain with Titles and distinctions graced,
By favors hurt, by Dignity's debased,
And sunk upon the Steps that others rais'd.
This Statesman's Fortune (odd as it may Sound,)
In that of Your *old-China* may be found;
For first at an enormous Price you bought him,
Then never used him, and Layn-by forgot him.

In Verse, or Prose, when privately I play
With Characters like these seen ev'ry Day;
If for Admittance to Your Eyes I Plead
That some great Princes certainly could read,[27]
Tho' I confess, alas! they're long since dead,
If to this Honor when I lay my Claim,
Great Sov'reigns and great Authors I should name;
Say to *Augustus* polish'd *Horace*[28] wrote;
And *Trajan* deign'd to read what *Pliny* thought:[29]
Perhaps my works you'll promise to admit,
When I have *Pliny's* Sense, or *Horace* Wit:
But tho, great Queen! their Talents I may want,[30]
And only daub, when these great Masters Paint;
Yet for your Mirth the liv'liest you may keep,
*Le Behn*[31]* shall read the dullest whilst you sleep.
And sure in Sleep no dulness you need fear,

27. *Some . . . could read*: Croker notes: 'An allusion, I fear, to the King's scanty literature', i.e. literacy (*Memoirs*, II, 152).

28. *Horace*: Quintus Horatius Flaccus (65–8 BCE) earned the favour of the Emperor Augustus.

29. *Trajan . . . Pliny thought*: Marcus Ulpius Nerva Traianus Augustus (53–117 CE; Emperor of Rome 98–117); Gaius Plinius Caecilius Secundus (61–c. 112), better known as Pliny the Younger, corresponded with Trajan and wrote a panegyric on him. Hervey is contrasting the relations between politics and culture in ancient Rome and in contemporary Britain.

30. *want*: 'Not to have; to be without, to lack; to have too little of; to be destitute of, or deficient in' (*OED*).

31. *Le Behn*: 'An Underservant to the Queen who used *to read* her to sleep' (autograph note, *Windsor*).

Who ev'n Awake, can *Schutz*[32] and *Lifford*[33] bear.
Who ev'ry Sunday suffer stupid *Slone*[34*]
To preach on a *dry'd Fly*, and *Hamstead-Stone*,
To show such wonders as were never seen,
And give Accounts of what has never been.
Who ev'ry Wednesday hear *Montandre*[35*] prate,
Of Politicks and Maxims out of Date,
And with old Fringes furbeloe[36] the State.
As well that *Ever-Green his* wife[37] might boast
The long-fled Bloom of a last-Century-Toast:
The same poor, Antiquated Merits grace
The Politicians Head and Beauty's Face:

32. *Schutz*: Augustus Schutz (1690–1757) was Master of the Robes and Keeper of the Privy Purse for George II and referred to by Hervey as 'another Court-booby' in Poem 27, *The Patriots are Come; Or, a New Doctor for a Crazy Constitution* (London: for W. Webb, [1742]), p. 5; for an account of him and his family, see Falconer Madan, *The Madan Family and Maddens in Ireland and England* (Oxford: Oxford University Press, 1933), pp. 66–8.

33. *Lifford*: Frederick William de la Rochefoucauld, Earl of Lifford (1666–1749), and his sister Lady Charlotte de Roucy, Hervey calls 'two poor miserable Court drudges' (Sedgwick, I, 253), the former featuring in 'The Death of Lord Hervey' (Sedgwick, II, 585–6).

34. *Slone*: 'Sir Hans Slone, a Physitian by Profession, a very dull fellow, a great Naturalist, and a very careful expensive collector of what few people besides himself would give a shilling for' (autograph note, *Windsor*); Sloane (1660–1753), whose collection provided the foundation of the British Museum, had been created a baronet in 1716, became physician-in-ordinary to George II in 1727 and was elected President of the Royal Society in the same year (*ODNB*); the expressions in the next line, 'a *dry'd Fly*, and *Hamstead-Stone*', indicate the dim view Hervey took of his interests as a naturalist.

35. *Montandre*: 'An old french Gentleman, with no more of the vivacity of his country-men than their religion, who fancied, because he had read a great deal, that he knew a great deal; a great talker by which he instructed others, no better than by reading he had instructed himself' (autograph note, *Windsor*); Francis de la Rochefoucauld, Marquis de Montandre (1672–1739), was appointed Master General of the Ordnance 1728 and promoted General in 1735 (Sedgwick, III, 998; *The Nobilities of Europe*, 2 vols., ed. by Marquis de Ruvigny (London: Melville, 1909–10; repr. n.p.: Adamant Media, 2006), II, 329–30).

36. *furbeloe*: 'To ornament with a furbelow', i.e. 'A piece of stuff pleated and puckered on a gown or petticoat' (*OED*).

37. *Ever-Green his wife*: Mary Ann, *née* von Spanheim, whom he married in 1710, when she was twenty-seven, would have been fifty-three at the time of writing; she survived until 1773 (*Nobilities of Europe*, II, 330; T. A. Heathcote, *The British Field Marshals, 1763–1997* (Barnsley: Lee Cooper, 1999), p. 100).

Each in their dif'rent Style have equal Charms,
I'd ask his Counsell, as I'd court her Arms.

But what can you Oh Queen! from dullness dread,
Who can resist such Loads of verbal Lead?
Who if Stupidity did Poison bear,
Must die like *Hamlet*, poison'd at your Ear:
When after *Walpole*'s clear, Strong Sense, you deign
To let his Echo,[38*] in ennervate Strain,
Lisp all that Sense, in Nonsense o'er again.
By turns of *Asoph*,[39*] and of *Clermont*[40*] talk,
Of Army's Marches, and a well-turf'd Walk,
A falling Empire[41] and a Planted Oak.
Thrice Happy Genius! that can handle still
These dif'ring Topicks with an equal Skill
Yet some Alledg these Honors not his own,
*Kent*[42*] makes his Gardens his Dispatches *Stone*:[43*]
But this is all the Envy of a Court,

38. *his Echo*: 'the Duke of Newcastle, Sec[retary of State]' (autograph note, *Windsor*); Thomas Pelham-Holles, Duke of Newcastle upon Tyne (1693–1768), had been appointed Secretary of State in 1724 (*ODNB*).

39. *Asoph*: 'besieged this summer by the Russians, at war with the Turk's' (autograph note, *Windsor*), i.e. Azov, a fortress commanding access to the Sea of Azov taken by Russia in the spring of 1736.

40. *Clermont*: 'The D. of Newcastle's Villa' (autograph note, *Windsor*), i.e. Claremont, Newcastle's estate in Surrey, where he employed Sir John Vanbrugh as architect and William Kent as both architect and landscape-designer (*ODNB*, 'Vanbrugh, Sir John'; 'Kent, William').

41. *a falling Empire*: Croker suggests Turkey (*Memoirs*, II, 154), threatened by Russia at this period as subsequently.

42. *Kent*: 'A Man much in fashion as a Gardiner, an Architect, a Painter and about 50 other things, with a very bad taste and little understanding, but had had the good luck to make several people (who had no taste or understanding of their own) believe that they could borrow both of him, and had paid for their error by ruining their fortunes in making Gardens and building houses that no body could live in, and every one laugh'd at' (autograph note, *Windsor*). Kent, whom Hervey had ridiculed in the epigram that had occasioned this very poem and was to ridicule further in a longer epigram (Poems 41 and 42), had been working at Claremont since about 1730 (*ODNB*).

43. *Stone*: 'The D. of Newcastle's first commis' (autograph note, *Windsor*), i.e. Andrew Stone (1703–73), private secretary to the Duke of Newcastle and 'virtually indispensable' to him: 'he wrote his speeches, offered advice, mediated and negotiated on his behalf, and carried out political and diplomatic errands' (*ODNB*).

(Where worth resides Envy will still resort)
For *Stone* to aid *his Grace* no more is able,
Than *Backenswants*[44*] to manage *Pomfret*'s Stable.[45]

Whilst things like these each Hour I see and hear,
If this vain World was all your Servant's Care,
I own 'twere better silently to pass,
Nor heed the chatt'ring Ape, nor braying Ass:
But as I think 'tis better for my Soul,
I should not, what Heav'n seems to will, controul;
And as by the devoutest Lips 'tis said,
That God for nothing, Nothing ever made;
So when these Animals come cross my way,
I laugh with that Devotion others pray;[46]
Thinking I execute the Will of Heav'n,
For to what other end could they be given?
Name Any other I'll from this refrain;
But well consider'd, boldly I maintain,
Unridicul'd, their being would be vain.
As well we might in Spight of Nature try
To make fat Geese like Carrier-Pigeons fly;
Bid the slow Ass like the train'd Race-Horse run;
Or darkling Owls like Eagles face the Sun;
As make the human Owl, or Goose, or Ass;
For any Species, but – it's own to pass;
Or e'er attempt, by *any Rule of Court*,
To turn to Bus'ness what was meant for Sport.
As then, Court-Brutes, who nothing understand,
Should never lead a Queen – but by the Hand,[47]
You may direct, but ne'er consult a Fool;

44. *Backenswants*: 'A German groom who did order and manage every thing in the Q's Stables, whilst Lord Pomfret a great fool, was her master of the horse' (autograph note, *Windsor*).

45. *Pomfret's Stable*: Thomas Fermor, Earl Pomfret, had been appointed master of the horse to Queen Caroline in 1727 (*ODNB*, 'Fermor [*née* Jeffreys], Henrietta Louisa, countess of Pomfret'); Hervey's point regarding Stone and Backenswantz is that underlings did their masters' jobs for them.

46. *that Devotion others pray*: i.e. that devotion with which others pray.

47. *by the Hand*: Croker notes: 'The duty of the Chamberlains' (*Memoirs*, II, 155).

None set the Horse, to drive that ought to pull:
And thus at Council when I see his Grace,
(The term's so general, pray let him pass;)
Methinks I see Your Coach-Horse in *Drost's*[48*] Place.

But Art to falsify God's Coin is vain,
The Head he stamps with Fool, shall Fool remain;
For Varnish, Mill, or Clip it e'er so much,
Your Sterling Fools will answer to the Touch;
Or did the Touchstone not decide their Fate,
Like Gold you still may know them by the Weight.
Well as I can I Nature then pursue;
Through Microscopes or Prisms nothing view;
Nothing to paint or magnify I try,
Behold each object with my naked Eye;
Nor Strive to force the things that will recoil,
But strive myself to Things to reconcile,
I learn from *Walpole*, at *Newcastle* Smile.

Yet think not whilst these Methods I pursue,
And give each *Cæsar* what is *Cæsar's* due;[49]
That I their Int'rest, or their Peace would shake;
Rest without Molestation may they take,
Or in their Sleep; or what they call awake.
And if the Brain that never thinks, can Dream,
Of either Slumber, Pleasure be the Theme.
Nor with their Bus'ness would I interfere,
Let each great Courtier dignify his Sphere;
Let *Shaw*[50*] snuff Candles when at night you play:[51]

48. *Drost's*: 'The Queen's Coachman' (autograph note, *Windsor*); Croker notes: 'Henry Drost was first coachman to the King' (*Memoirs*, II, 155), though the holder of that office is given as 'Oakes, T.', succeeded in April 1735 by 'Johnston, T. (att. Master of the Horse)' in the 'List of Office-Holders in Modern Britain' available online from the Institute of Historical Research (www.british-history.ac.uk/report.aspx?compid=4392).

49. *give each Cæsar what is Cæsar's due*: 'And Jesus answering said unto them, Render to Caesar the things that are Caesar's, and to God the things that are God's' (Mark 12: 17).

50. *Shaw*: 'One of the Queen's pages of the back stairs' (autograph note, *Windsor*).

51. *play*: i.e. at cards, a favourite evening amusement of the Queen, as Hervey remarked in a letter dated 31 July 1733 summarising for Charlotte Clayton the routine of a typical day at court: 'at Night the King play's at Commerce and Back-Gammon; and the Queen at

And when you dress at Noon, your Chaplins pray:
Let all the *Cabinet* with ductile hand
Sign what they read, and never understand.
Let Dupes you rally thankfully receive it:
Let *Teed*[52]* Mill Chocolate and *Purcel*[53]* give it:
What others dictate let great Statesmen write
And we *Gold-Keys*[54] learn all to read at Sight.
Let *Willmington*[55] with grave, contracted Brow,
Red-Tape[56] and Wisdom at the Council show,
Sleep in the Senate, in the Circle bow.
Let *Harrington*[57] still strive, and *Ilay*[58]* swim,
This always with, and that against the Stream.
*Argyle*[59] abuse the Bishops, Bishops him[60]

Quadril (BL Add. MS 20104, f. 6v); quadrille was a fashionable card-game, the ancestor of modern whist.

52. *Teed*: 'The Queen's Chocolate Maker' (autograph note, *Windsor*); John Teed was appointed to the post in 1735 (E. J. Burford, *Royal St. James's: Being a Story of Kings, Clubmen and Courtesans* (London: Robert Hale, 1988), p. 31).

53. *Purcel*: 'The King's Laundress that was always about the Queen in a morning to bring her breakfast. A forward, pert silly woman' (autograph note, *Windsor*); Margaret Purcell also features in Hervey's play 'The Death of Lord Hervey' (Sedgwick, II, 585, 586, 587; for brief details of her work, see Joanna Marschner, 'Queen Caroline of Anspach and the European Princely Museum Tradition', in Clarissa Campbell Orr (ed.), *Queenship in Britain, 1660–1837: Royal Patronage, Court Culture, and Dynastic Politics* (Manchester: Manchester University Press, 2002), pp. 130–42 (136, 138, 139, 140).

54. *Gold-Keys*: members of important court posts such as the one Hervey occupied, Vice-Chamberlain, wore gold keys as emblems of their office.

55. *Willmington*: see note to line 100.

56. *Red-Tape:* 'Woven red or pink tape used to secure legal documents and official papers' (*OED*).

57. *Harrington*: see note to line 110.

58. *Ilay*: 'Lord Ilay, brother to the D[uke] of Argyle whom Sir R[obert] W[alpole] employ'd in the management of all Scotch Elections, and all Scotch affairs' (autograph note, *Windsor*); i.e. Archibald Campbell, later third Duke of Argyll (1682–1761), described by Hervey as 'a man of parts, quickness, knowledge, temper, dexterity, and judgment; a man of little truth, little honour, little principle, and no attachment but to his interest' (*ODNB*; Sedgwick, I, 296).

59. *Argyle*: John Campbell, second Duke of Argyll and later Duke of Greenwich (1680–1743), described by Hervey as 'haughty, passionate, and peremptory; gallant, and a good officer; with very good parts, and much more reading and knowledge than generally falls to the share of a man educated a soldier and born to so great a title and fortune' (*ODNB*; Sedgwick, I, 297).

60. *Argyle . . . him*: a reference to altercations over the Quakers Tithe Bill, concerning which Hervey reports the Queen as having told the Bishops of Salisbury and Chichester 'that the Duke of Argyll was not the most manageable man in the world, that his

'Till ev'n Abuse becomes a tedious Theme.[61]
Let *Hare*[62]* abjure the Heresys he wrote
And broil us all for being what he taught.
*Sherlock*[63]* the Church's crippled State deplore,
Give up her Doctrines, but still grasp her Pow'r.
*Gibson*[64]* cabal;[65] and honest *Potter*[66]* grunt;
*Grantham*[67]* set Chairs, and wiser *Grafton*[68]* hunt:
Let one th' extent of his Discourse to show,
Vary *comment le va?*[69] and *how you do?*
T'other his Journals eloquently tell,
Which Hound first *hit it off*, what Horse *did well.*
Let nauseous *Selkirk*[70]* shake his empty Head

Presbyterian education had given him a spleen to all episcopacy, and that old squabbles with the Bishop of London had, joined to that general prejudice, made him take this occasion to gratify both' (Sedgwick, II, 540).

61. lines 234–7: the rhyme scheme is humorously altered from couplets to alternating.

62. *Hare*: 'B[ishop] of Chichester' (autograph note, *Windsor*); i.e. Francis Hare (1671–1740), who 'was involved in polemical exchange throughout his adult life', including the 'ironic and antideistic *Difficulties and Discouragements which Attend the Study of the Scriptures* (1714) and involvement in the Bangorian controversy' (*ODNB*).

63. *Sherlock*: 'B[ishop] of Salisbury' (autograph note, *Windsor*); i.e. Thomas Sherlock (1677–1761) (*ODNB*).

64. *Gibson*: 'B[ishop] of London' (autograph note, *Windsor*); i.e. Gibson, Edmund (*bap.* 1669, *d.* 1748) (*ODNB*), whom Hervey criticised for his combination of 'art and temper' (Sedgwick, I, 91).

65. *cabal*: 'To combine (*together*) for some secret or private end' (*OED*).

66. *Potter*: 'B[ishop] of Oxford afterwards Archb[ishop] of Canterbury' (autograph note, *Windsor*); i.e. Potter, John (1673/4–1747), who became Archbishop of Canterbury in 1737, recommended by Hervey (*ODNB*).

67. *Grantham*: 'The Queen's Lord Chamberlain, an old stupid Dutchman, whose vocabulary did not consist of above twenty words and even those he did not understand the meaning of'; i.e. Henry de Nassau, first Earl of Grantham (c. 1672–1754) (*Complete Peerage*, VI, 81), whose speech is parodied by Hervey in his play 'The Death of Lord Hervey' (Sedgwick, II, 590–1, 596).

68. *Grafton*: 'The King's Lord Chamberlain, an English Edition of the Queen's, very little improv'd, whose only pleasure was hunting' (autograph note, *Windsor*); i.e. Charles FitzRoy, second Duke of Grafton (1683–1757), appointed Lord Chamberlain to George I in 1724 and continuing in that post for the rest of his life (*ODNB*).

69. *comment le va*: French for 'how goes it?'

70. *Selkirk*: 'An old paraletic Scotch Earl, the servile follower of Every King de facto and every minister in power' (autograph note, *Windsor*); i.e. Charles Douglas (*né* Hamilton), second Earl of Selkirk (1663–1739), Lord of the Bedchamber to Mary II and William III, 1689–94, to William III, 1694–1702, and to George I and II, 1714–39 (*Complete Peerage*, XI, 616–17).

Through six Courts more, when Six have wish'd him dead,
*Charlotte*[71*] and *Schutz*[72] like angry Monkeys chatter,
None guessing what's the Language or the Matter.
Let *Pembroke*[73*] still in Midwife's Bawdy tell ye
The Pregnant Fables of her barren Belly:
And Dame *Palladio*[74] insolent and bold,
Like her own Chairman, whistle, stamp, and Scold;
Her quiet still preserv'd, tho lost her Fame,
As free from ev'ry Punishment, as Shame.
Her worn-out *Huntsman* frequent may she hold,
Nor to her *Mason-Husband* be it told,
That She, with Capital *Corinthian* grac'd,
Has finish'd *his* in the *Ionic* Taste.[75]

71. *Charlotte*: 'Lady Charlotte de Roussie, a very harmless french protestant, of a very great family, pensioned by the English Court, and used to be Constantly of the Queen's private Quadrille parties' (autograph note, *Windsor*), i.e. Charlotte de Roucy, sister of the Earl of Lifford (see note to line 139), whose evenings at court Hervey describes in a letter dated 31 July 1733 to Charlotte Clayton: 'where poor Lady Charlot run's her usual nightly Gantlet; the Queen pulling her Hood, Mr. Schutz sputtering in her Face, and the Princess-Royal rapping her Knuckles all at a time' (BL Add. MS 20104, f. 6v).

72. *Schutz*: see note to line 139.

73. *Pembroke*: 'The Dowager Countess married to Sir J. Mordaunt' (autograph note, *Windsor*); i.e. the widow of Thomas Herbert, eighth Earl of Pembroke (1656/7–1733), whose third wife she had become in 1725 and who married the Hon. John Mordaunt in 1735 (*ODNB*); according to Croker, 'She had no children by either marriage, and her fancied pregnancies were a constant theme of ridicule amongst her acquaintance' (*Memoirs*, II, 157).

74. *Dame Palladio*: Dorothy Boyle, Countess of Burlington (1699–1758), so nicknamed by Hervey because of the Palladian architectural interests she shared with her husband – interests lampooned in the very epigram (Poem 41) that occasioned the present poem.

75. *Her quiet … Ionic taste*: these six lines contain a series of allusions to the affair between Lady Burlington and the Duke of Grafton (on whom see note to line 243): '*Huntsman*' refers to the latter's love of hunting, while '*Mason-Husband*' probably has a double reference. The primary allusion is to Burlington's architectural pursuits, which are further ridiculed in '*Corinthian*' and '*Ionic*', referring to two of the three orders of classical architecture, the former of which had ornate capitals and the latter spiral scroll-like capitals that were 'sometimes called *horns*' (Croker, *Memoirs*, II, 157), enabling a gibe at the Duke's cuckolding. A likely secondary allusion is to the Masonic craft, with which, Jane Clark has argued, 'Burlington's architecture was widely identified', so that Chiswick House was seen as 'a symbolic centre, based on so-called Royal Arch Freemasonry' (Pat Rogers, *Pope and the Destiny of the Stuarts: History, Politics, and Mythology in the Age of Queen Anne* (Oxford: Oxford University Press, 2005), p. 126, citing Jane Clark, '"Lord Burlington is Here"', in T.

I could enumerate a Hundred more,
But for your sake the tedious List give o'er;
And end this Rhyming Circle I have run,
Just with the same Petition I begun.
Freely my thoughts of Men and Things to write,
Veil'd by my well-lock'd Bureau from the Light;
Or like choice Pictures, hid from common View,
To draw the Curtain back to only you.

And when from all the irksome Cares that wait,
On Rank, or Power, on Eminence and State;
You wish to borrow one relaxing Hour,
To think of *Sweedish* Subsidy's[76*] no more;
Domestic Feuds, or *Europe's* ballanc'd Pow'r:
How long your Fleet near *Tagus*' Banks must wait,[77*]
Or *Montemar* maintain the *Tuscan* State:[78*]
When from these thoughts to trifles you unbend
And with superior Taste ev'n those attend,
Sure He who *can* amuse you is your Friend.
Or in that Title if too much he claim,

Barnard and J. Clark (eds.), *Burlington: Architecture, Art and Life* (London: Hambledon Press, 1995), pp. 251–320).

76. *Sweedish Subsidy's*: 'A treaty was then upon the Anvil with Sweden' (autograph note, *Windsor*); such a treaty would presumably have involved the War of the Polish Succession (1733–8), in which Britain took no part, but none resulted.

77. *How long ... wait*: 'The English fleet lay then before Lisbon' (autograph note, *Windsor*); Croker explains: 'A powerful fleet under Sir John Norris had been sent, in May, 1735, to the Tagus, to countenance and protect Portugal against Spain; and it did not return till April, 1737' (*Memoirs*, II, 158); according to Alan David Francis, the aim was to protect British trade and the Portuguese coast (*Portugal, 1715–1808: Joanine, Pombaline, and Rococo Portugal as Seen by British Diplomats and Traders* (London: Tamesis, 1985), p. 67).

78. *Montemar ... State*: 'The Duke of Montemar the Spanish General' (autograph note, *Windsor*); i.e. José Carrillo de Albornoz, first Duke of Montemar (1671–1747), was a Spanish nobleman and military leader whose conquest of Sicily, when his title was Duke of Bitonto, is recorded in Sedgwick, II, 319; Spain had a claim to the Grand Duchy of Tuscany under the terms of the Treaty of Vienna (1731), but on the death without an heir of the last Grand Duke, Gian Gastone de' Medici, it passed to the Austrian Francis I (Paul Strathern, *The Medici: Godfathers of the Renaissance* (London: Jonathan Cape, 2003; repr. Vintage, 2007), pp. 408–9).

A faithful Servant half deserves the Name;
And tho more useful none can be more true,
Than I my lov'd and honor'd Queen! to You;
Whose Pleasures all my thoughts and Hours employ,
Your Service all my Aim, your Favor all my Joy.

# SATIRES

# INTRODUCTION TO SATIRES

Ashley Marshall's study *The Practice of Satire in England, 1658–1770* has emphasised the great extent of satirical writing in this period, examining over 3,000 separate items.[1] Although satire is best considered as a general mode in which persons, or vices, or social failings are attacked or ridiculed (with satiric writing found in drama, prose fiction and essays), it has a special role in verse of the period. Some poems were called satires, marking a distinctive genre within the mode. They were frequently modelled on the satires of Horace, Persius or Juvenal, which they sometimes formally imitated, and one of their topics might be satire itself, its nature and rationale.[2] But other verse forms could be intensively satiric. A verse epistle, a relatively dignified if conversational form, might dedicate much of its attention to a critique of its society, while lampoons and ballads formed a ready outlet for invective, particularly of a political nature.

Hervey's output of satiric verse varies in the objects of its attack and in the forms it takes. He ridicules his literary opponent Alexander Pope (*To the Imitator* and *The Difference between Verbal and Practical Virtue*), a member of his social circle ('Dr Sherwin's Character'), the political opposition (Lord Bolingbroke, John Barber, *The Craftsman*) and the King (*The Patriots Are Come*). His style is not as conversational as Horace's and his debt to Horace is not, unlike Pope's, usually explicit, but two of his major verse satires engage with Horace. *To the Imitator of the First Satire of the Second Book of Horace* tells Pope (the poem lacks the intimacy of an epistle) that he fails to write as politely as Horace, but *The Difference between Verbal and Practical Virtue* includes Horace among those (Pope is the great example) who do not practise what they preach.

1. *The Practice of Satire in England, 1658–1770* (Baltimore: Johns Hopkins University Press, 2013), p. 14. A less wide-ranging but perceptive treatment of the topic is Dustin Griffin, *Satire: A Critical Reintroduction* (Lexington: University Press of Kentucky, 1994).

2. P. K. Elkin, *The Augustan Defence of Satire* (Oxford: Clarendon Press, 1973) explores this aspect of satiric practice. Hervey shares with Pope an interest in the history and morality of satire.

Both poems address the morality of satire, while stopping short of reflecting on their own practice. In one short poem that provides a particularly ingenious imitation of Horace, 'Lord Bolingbroke, to Ambition' (Poem 21), Hervey transforms the address to Venus of the first ode of book IV into Bolingbroke's address to Ambition, a prolonged act of self-betrayal. No poem is modelled directly on Juvenal, but Hervey did write an early *Satire in the Manner of Persius: In a Dialogue between Atticus and Eugenio* in which both the dialogue form (with one of the speakers in the role of instructor) and the air of disillusionment accurately evoke Persius. Its Christian-Stoic conclusion is unusual in Hervey's writing.

Hervey's political commitment expresses itself freely in the ballad (Poems 25–7), a popular rather than classical form that readily lends itself to satire. The desire for popular appeal is sometimes suggested by an indication of the music to which the words should be sung. The form facilitates a more relaxed and aggressive style, with the aim of establishing popular sentiment on a current topic.[3]

Some of Hervey's verse not included in this section is richly coloured by satire. One of his epistles, 'To Dr Sherwin in Answer to a Latin Letter in Verse' (Poem 18) contains a critique of aristocratic literacy and an attack on Pope's satires, though the poem draws attention back to its addressee. Several of the epigrams are sharply critical, of aristocracy, or aristocratic architecture, or the royal family, or contemporary politics (Poems 41–6). When Hervey is reflecting on his contemporaries, satire is rarely far away.

3. The popularity of the form is evident in *Poems on Affairs of State: Augustan Satirical Verse, 1660–1714*, ed. by George deF. Lord, 7 vols. (New Haven: Yale University Press, 1963–75), whose index refers to forty-seven instances of ballad tunes.

# 20 A Satire in the Manner of Persius: in a Dialogue between Atticus and Eugenio

***Main source.*** *A Satire in the Manner of Persius: in a Dialogue between Atticus and Eugenio. By a Person of Quality* (London: for J. Clarke and J. Robinson, 1739).

***Complementary manuscript sources.*** Delany MS [1], item 22, Lilly Library, Indiana University; BL Add. MS 28101, ff. 6r–8v; Portland Papers (Longleat), XX, ff. 86r–91v; SRO 947/53/1, pp. 194–202.

***Complementary print sources.*** *A Satyr in the Manner of Persius. In a Dialogue between the Poet and his Friend. By a Certain English Nobleman* (London [i.e. Dublin]: s.n., 1730); *Select Poems from Ireland* (London: for T. Warner, 1730), pp. 1–14; *The Norfolk Poetical Miscellany* (London: for the author, 1744), I, 147–60; Dodsley, *Collection* (1758), V, 147–55.

***Attribution.*** Delany MS [1], item 22 ('first Lord Hervey'); BL Add. MS 28101 ('By L[or]d Harvey'); William Hervey, SRO 47/53/1; Dodsley, *Collection* (1758). Although there are two other attributions, to Ashley Cowper in a manuscript note in the British Library copy of the *Norfolk Poetical Miscellany* and, according to David Foxon, to Lord Paget in a manuscript note to a copy of the 1739 edition now at the University of Texas at Austin (Foxon H161·5), Hervey's authorship is confirmed by the fact that he quoted a version of lines 58–60 from the poem in a letter to Henry Fox dated 10 January 1727 (SRO 947/47/4, p. 38; printed in Ilchester, p. 14). It is unlikely to be significant that the text in *Select Poems from Ireland* is followed by a poem probably by Hervey, Poem 53, 'Lord Harvey on the Dutchess of Richmond', because the collection attributes it to Chesterfield, though the point is worth noting.

***Context and date.*** The poem must have been written in its entirety or in part by 10 January 1727 when Hervey quoted from it in his letter to Fox. That he quoted from it may imply that he had already shown a complete version to his friend. Further evidence of the poem's date is that it mentions the physician John Freind, who died in July 1728; in one of the manuscripts, that at Longleat, and in the *Norfolk Poetical Miscellany*, Freind's name has been changed to that of Sir Edward Hulse. A dating before January 1727 would place the poem's composition in the mid-1720s, probably a little after that of *Monimia to Philocles*, a time when Hervey seems still to have been uncertain about his choice of career. It is an ambitious poem in its length and its choice of subject matter, which is how to come to terms with human corruption and evil. Hervey does not attempt to imitate a particular satire. Rather, the words 'in the manner of Persius' in his title would probably have suggested two features to a reader of the period: the use of dialogue form and a Stoic point of view. In his 'Discourse on the Original and Progress of Satire' Dryden had commended Persius for his Stoic philosophy, describing it as

> the most noble, most generous, most beneficial to human kind among all the sects who have given us the rules of ethics, thereby to form a severe virtue in the soul; to raise in us an undaunted courage against the assaults of Fortune; to esteem as nothing the things that are without us, because they are not in our power; not to value riches, beauty, honours, fame or health any farther than as conveniences, and so many helps to living as we ought, and doing good in our generation: in short, to be always happy, while we possess our minds with a good conscience, are free from the slavery of vices, and conform our actions and conversation to the rules of right reason.[1]

Such a philosophy, combined with a Christian confidence in a future state, is reflected in the poem. The dialogue form enabled Hervey to deliver a satirical tirade on vice and corruption, and to answer it with a mixture of Stoic and Christian teaching. Both speakers, Atticus and Eugenio (in the 1730 text and three of the manuscripts, Poet and Friend), see humankind as irredeemably wicked. The only difference is that Atticus/Poet is older, and so is able to advise his friend on how to manage the despair that such knowledge produces. For this reason, the dialogue form provides a platform on two different levels rather than two lecterns ranged in clear opposition. While that form provided a stage on which he could play the role both of angry young man and of experienced adviser, the genre enabled him to produce a satire with a moral message in harmony with Christian thinking. The deployment throughout of Galenic theories of health that associate youth with springtime and joy, and age with bitterness also produces a coherent medical resonance of the significance of 'Spleen', or melancholy. It might further be noted that the quality that places the poem relatively early in Hervey's career is its optimism. After the death of his beloved sister Elizabeth in September 1727 and what seems to have been a breakdown that followed it, his views became less consoling and much more sceptical. Although, in an essay on Benjamin Loveling's *The First Satire of Persius Imitated* (1740), Cynthia S. Dessen claims that Hervey 'assumes a philosophic Stoic persona to defend his allegiance to Walpole',[2] the poem provides little evidence of a political stance of any kind. It may, however, have been printed – not necessarily with Hervey's consent or knowledge – in an attempt to neutralise attacks on Walpole through its message that there is little that human beings can do in order to improve their condition, except to pursue virtue in private.

1. *The Poems of John Dryden*, ed. by Paul Hammond and David Hopkins, 5 vols. (Harlow: Pearson Longman, 1995–2005), III (2000), 400.

2. See Dessen, 'An Eighteenth-Century Imitation of Persius', *Texas Studies in Literature and Language*, 20 (1978), 433–56 (454, n. 19).

***Textual commentary.*** The 1739 edition was printed by John Wright (Pope's printer for the second half of his career) and sold by John Clarke, who had been apprenticed to Lawton Gilliver (Pope's bookseller from the *Dunciad Variorum* to the *Works* of 1735) and was his partner between 1736 and 1739.[3] There is no evidence, however, of Pope's involvement with this publication, and in 1739–40 Clarke, who had been working with Wright since 1729, employed him in printing two pieces with no Pope connection. The 1739 edition shows clear evidence of revision, and, as it is difficult to make a plausible case for Pope's benevolent revision of Hervey's poem at this date, it is assumed the revisions are Hervey's. They remove three couplets that are loosely expressed, and tighten expression elsewhere. That the revision is likely to be authorial may be suggested by the fact that Hervey's son William used it to copy into his commonplace book, dating it '1739'. This edition, therefore, is chosen as source text. Broadly speaking, all the other texts conform to what seems to have been the earliest text to have been produced, the Delany manuscript, which occurs in a collection with the heading 'Transcrib'd in the year 1728'. There are few obvious patterns to variants, except that the text in *Select Poems from Ireland* tends to follow that in the 1730 Dublin edition, and that the text in the *Norfolk Poetical Miscellany* is closely related to those in two of the manuscripts, Portland (Longleat) and BL Add. MS 28101. No emendations are necessary to the 1739 text used here, except to the lineation which becomes confused after line 41. Spelling, punctuation and initial capitalisation have all been left unaltered except on the very few occasions noted.[4]

## A Satire in the Manner of Persius: in a Dialogue between *Atticus* and *Eugenio*

ATTICUS. Why wears my pensive Friend that gloomy Brow?
Say, whence proceeds th'imaginary Woe?
What prosp'rous Villain hast thou met to Day?
Or, hath afflicted Virtue crost thy Way?
Is it some Crime unpunish'd you deplore,
Or Right subverted by injurious Power?
Be *This*, or *That*, the Cause, 'tis wisely done
To make the Sorrows of Mankind your own;

3. James McLaverty, *Pope's Printer, John Wright: A Preliminary Study* (Oxford: Oxford Bibliographical Society, 1977), no. 141, p. 26, and 'Lawton Gilliver: Pope's Bookseller', *Studies in Bibliography*, 32 (1979), 101–24 (121–2). McLaverty does not identify the poem as Hervey's.

4. *1730* is divided into twelve numbered sections of unequal length. If there is any logic behind the division, it defies analysis, as there is no clear thematic basis for it and in some cases it even conflicts with the syntax. The dividing-points are therefore not noted.

To see the Injur'd pleading, unredress'd,
The Proud exalted, and the Poor oppress'd,
Can hurt thy Health, and rob thee of thy Rest.
Your Cares are in a hopeful Way to cease,
If you must find Perfection to find Peace.
But reek[5] thy Malice, vent thy stifled Rage,
Inveigh against the Times, and lash the Age.
Perhaps just recent from the Court you come,
O'er Public Ills to ruminate at Home.
Say, which of all the Wretches, thou hast seen,
Hath thrown a Morsel to thy hungry Spleen?[6]
What worthless Member of that Medley-Throng;
Who basely acts, or tamely suffers Wrong?
He who to nothing but his Int'rest true,
Cajoles the Fool he's working to undo?
Or that more despicable tim'rous Slave,
Who knows himself abus'd, yet hugs the Knave?
Perhaps you mourn our Senate's sinking Fame,
That Shew of Freedom dwindled to a Name;
Where partial Judges deal their venal Laws,
And the best Bidder hath the justest Cause?
What then?
They have the Pow'r; and who shall dare to blame
The Legal Wrong that bears Astræa's Name![7]
Besides, such Thoughts should never stir the Rage
Of youthful Gall – Reflection comes with Age;
'Tis our decaying Life's Autumnal Fruit,
The bitter Produce of our latest Shoot,
When ev'ry Blossom of the Tree is dead,
Enjoyment wither'd, and our Wishes fled:
Thine still is in its Spring, on ev'ry Bough
Fair Plenty blooms, and youthful Odours blow;
Season of Joy, too early to be wise,

5. *reek*: 'To exhale, emit, or give out (smoke, fume, vapour, etc.)' (*OED*); a variant spelling of 'wreak' is also given.

6. *Spleen*: in Galenic medical theory, 'the seat of melancholy or morose feelings' (*OED*); also 'Violent ill-nature or ill-humour; irritable or peevish temper' (*OED*).

7. *Astræa's Name*: in Greek mythology, Astræa is the goddess of justice.

The Time to covet Pleasures, not despise;
Yours is an Age when Trifles ought to please,
Too soon for Reason to attack thy Ease:
Tho' soon the hour shall come, when thou shalt know
'Tis vain Fruition all, and empty Shew.
But late examine, late inspect Mankind,
If seeing pains, 'tis Prudence to be blind.
Let not their Vices yet imploy thy Thoughts,
Laugh at their Follies, e're thou weep their Faults.
And when, as sure thou must, at length you find
What Things Men are, resolve to arm your Mind.
Too nicely never their Demerits scan,
And of their Vertues make the most you can;
Silent avert the Mischief they intend,
And cross, but seem not to discern, their End.
If they prevail, submit, for Prudence lies
In suffering well – 'Tis equally unwise
To see the Injuries we won't resent,
And mourn the Evils which we can't prevent.[8]

EUGENIO. You Counsel well to bid me arm my Mind;
Would the Receipt[9] were easy as 'tis kind;
But hard it is for Misery to reach
That Fortitude Prosperity can teach:
Could I forbid what has been to have been,
Or lodge a Doubt on Truths my self have seen;
Could I divest Remembrance of her Store,
And say, Collect these Images no more;[10]
Could I dislodge Sensation from my Breast,
And charm her wakeful Faculties to rest;

8. *'Tis equally . . . can't prevent*: Hervey quoted what was either an earlier version or an imperfect recollection of these lines in a letter to Henry Fox dated 10 January 1727: 'tis equally unwise | To see the injurys we wont resent | or weep Misfortunes which we can't prevent' (SRO 941/47/4, p. 38).

9. *Receipt*: recipe or remedy, a clear example of the poem's coherent use of contemporary medical thinking in its exploration of states of mind and body.

10. *no more*: all the complementary sources except for SRO and Dodsley here insert an additional couplet: 'No more let past Events survive in you, | In Lights too faithful usher'd to my View'.

Could I my Nature and my Self subdue,
I might, the Method you prescribe, pursue.
But, if unfeign'd Afflictions we endure,
If Reason's our Disease, and not our Cure;
Then *seeming* Ease is all we can obtain,
As One, who long familiariz'd to Pain,
Still feels the Smart, but ceases to complain.
Tho' young in Life, yet long inur'd to Care;[11]
Thus I submissive ev'ry Evil bear.
If unexpected Ills alone, are hard,
Mine should be light, who am for all prepar'd.
No Disappointments can my Peace annoy,
Disuse hath wean'd me from all Hopes of Joy:
The vain Pursuit for ever I give o'er;
Repuls'd, I strive; betray'd, I trust no more.
Mankind I know, their Nature, and their Art;
Their Vice their Own, their Virtue but a Part.
Ill play'd so oft, that all the Cheat can tell;
And dang'rous only, where 'tis acted well.
In different Classes rang'd, a diff'rent Name
Attends their Practice, but the Heart's the same.[12]
Their Hate is Int'rest, Int'rest too their Love;
On the same Springs these diff'rent Engines move:
That sharpens Malice, and directs her Sting,
And hence the honey'd Streams of Flattery spring.
Long I suspected what at last I know;
I thought Men worthless, now I've prov'd 'em so:
Reluctant prov'd it by too sure a Rule,
I learn'd my Science in a painful School.
He buys ev'n Wisdom at too dear a Price,
Who pays by sad Experience to be wise.

11. *As One . . . to Care*: these lines are the most autobiographical in the poem in that they reflect the physical suffering Hervey had endured as a result of his weak constitution.

12. *the same*: all the complementary sources except for Dodsley here insert an additional couplet: 'This shows the Foe, that hides it in the Friend, | The road is various, but the same's the end', except that Add. 28101 has 'within' for 'it in'; and Add. 28101, Longleat and Norfolk have 'same' for 'same's'.

Why did I hope, by sanguine Views possess'd
That Vertue harbour'd in an Human Breast!
Why did I trust to Flattery's specious[13] Wile,
The April Sunshine of her transient Smile!
Why disbelieve the Lessons of the Wise,
That taught me young to pierce her thin Disguise!
I thought their Rancour, not their Prudence spoke;
That Age perverse in false Invectives broke.
I thought their Comments on this gaudy Scene
Th'effects of Phlegm, and dictated by Spleen:
That, jealous of the Joys themselves were past,
Their Envy try'd to pall their Children's Taste.
Like the deaf Adder to the Charmer's Tongue,
I gave no Credit to the Truths they sung;[14]
But happy in a visionary Scheme,
Still sought Companions worthy my Esteem.
The Tongue, the Heart's Interpreter, I deem'd;
And judged of what Men were by what they seem'd.
I thought each warm Professor[15] meant me fair,
Each supple Sycophant a Friend sincere.
The solemn Hypocrite, whose close Design
Mirth never interrupts, nor Love, nor Wine;
Who talks on any Secret but his own,
Collecting all, communicating none;
Who still attentive to what others say,
Observes to wound, and questions to betray:
Of him, as Guardian of my private Thought,
In Morning Counsels cool Resolves I sought.
To him still open, cautionless consign'd

13. *specious*: replaced by 'spacious' in 1730, the phonetic spelling being a good indication that that edition was set in Ireland.

14. *Like the deaf Adder . . . sung*: alluding to Psalm 58: 3–5, 'The wicked are estranged from the womb: they go astray as soon as they be born, speaking lies. Their poison is like the poison of a serpent: they are like the deaf adder that stoppeth her ear; Which will not hearken to the voice of charmers, charming never so wisely.'

15. *Professor*: 'A person who makes open declaration of his or her feelings or beliefs, or of allegiance to some principle; one who professes (sometimes opposed, implicitly or explicitly, to one who practices)' (*OED*).

The inmost Treasures of my secret Mind;
My Joys and Griefs delighted to impart
In sacred Confidence, unmix'd with Art,
That dang'rous Pleasure of the honest Heart.
Whene'er I purpos'd to unbend my Soul
In social Banquets, where the circling Bowl
To Gladness lifts all Sorrows but Despair,
And gives a transient Lethe[16] to our Care,
I chose the Men whose Talents entertain,
And season Converse with a lively Strain;
Who thoughtless still, by Hope, nor Fear perplex'd,
Enjoy the present Hour, and risque the next;
These not the Luxury of slothful Ease,
Soft downy Beds, nor balmy Slumbers please.
While wakeful Kings on purple Couches own
The secret Sorrows of their envy'd Crown,
And wait revolving Light with shorter Rest,
Than ev'n those Wretches by their Pow'r opprest;
This jocund Train, devoted to Delight,
In chearful Vigils still protract the Night;
Nor dread the Cares approaching with the Day,
Thro' each Vicissitude for ever gay.
With such I commun'd, pleas'd that I could find
Recess so grateful to the active Mind:
And while the Youths in sprightly Contest try
With hum'rous Tale, or apposite Reply,
Or am'rous Song, or inoffensive Jest,
(The Zest of Wit) to glad the lengthen'd Feast,
My Soul, said I, depend upon their Truth,
For Fraud inhabits not the Breast of Youth:
Indulge thy Genius here, be free, be safe,
Mirth is their Aim, they covet but to laugh:
Pure from Deceit, as ignorant of Care,
Their Friendships and their Joys are both sincere.
I judg'd their Nature, like their Humour, good,

16. *Lethe*: in Greek mythology, 'A river in Hades, the water of which produced, in those who drank it, forgetfulness of the past' (*OED*).

As if the Soul depended on the Blood;
And that the Seeds of Honesty must grow
Wherever Health resides, or Spirits flow.
I see my Error, but I see too late,
'Tis vain Inspection to look back on Fate.
What are the Men who most esteem'd we find,
But such whose Vices are the most refin'd?
Blind Preference! for Vice, like Poison, shows
The surest Death is in the subtlest Dose.
To such Reflections when I turn my Mind,
I loath my Being, and abhor Mankind.
What Joy for Truth, what Commerce for the Just,
If all our Safety's founded on Distrust?
If all our Wisdom is a mean[17] Deceit,
And he who prospers, but the ablest Cheat?

ATTICUS. O early Wise! how well hast thou defin'd
The Worth, the Joys, the Friendships of Mankind.

EUGENIO. Blest be the Pow'rs,[18] I know their abject State.

ATTICUS. Yet bear with this, I hope a better Fate.
Thrice happy they, who view with steddy Eyes
This shifting Scene; who, temp'rate, firm, and wise,
Can bear its Sorrows, and its Joys despise.
Who look on Disappointments, shocks and strife,
And all the consequential Ills of Life,
Not as Severities the Gods impose,
But easy Terms indulgent Heav'n allows
To Man, by short Probation to obtain
Immortal Recompence for transient Pain.
Th'intent of Heav'n thus rightly understood,
From ev'ry Evil we extract a Good.
This Truth Divine, implanted in the Heart,
Supports each drudging Mortal thro' his Part,

17. *mean*: given as 'main' in 1730 and *Select Poems*; probably another phonetic spelling error.

18. *the Pow'rs*: whether the earthly or heavenly powers is meant here is uncertain; though the former seems more likely, the latter might be appropriate for a modern imitation of a classical original.

Gives a delightful Prospect to the blind;
The Friendless thence a constant Succour find;
The Wretch by Fraud betray'd, by Pow'r opprest,
With this Restorative still sooths his Breast:
This suffering Vertue cheers, this Pain beguiles,
And decks Calamity her self in Smiles.
When *Mead* and *Freind*[19] have ransack'd ev'ry Rule
Taught in *Hippocrates*' and *Galen*'s School,[20]
To quiet Ills that mock the Leaches Art,[21]
Which Opiates fail to deaden in the Heart;
This Cordial still th' Incurable sustains,
He triumphs in the sharp instructive Pains;
Nor, like a *Roman* Heroe, falsely Great,
With impious Hand anticipates his Fate,
But waits resign'd the slow Approach of Death,
'Till that great Pow'r who gave, demands his Breath.
Such are thy solid Comforts, Love divine!
Such solid Comforts, O my Friend, be Thine.
On this firm Basis thy Foundation lay
Of Happiness, unsubject to decay.
On Man no more, that frail Support depend,
The kindest Patron, or the warmest Friend.
The warmest Friend may one Day prove untrue,
And Int'rest change the kindest Patron's View.
Hear not, my Friend, the fondness they profess,
Nor on the Tryal grieve to find it less.

19. *Mead and Freind*: Richard Mead (1673–1754), described by *ODNB* as 'physician and collector of books and art', was appointed physician to George II in 1727; he was a close friend of another highly successful physician who was famous at the period, John Freind (1675–1728), not to be confused with his brother, the headmaster of Westminster School, Robert Freind. The Longleat and Norfolk versions of the poem substitute 'Hulse' for 'Freind', perhaps because Freind died in 1728. Sir Edward Hulse (1682–1759) was also a very well-known physician.

20. *in Hippocrates' and Galen's School*: Hippocrates and Galen were the two most famous physicians and writers of medical treatises of antiquity, and many of their theories and practices were still taken seriously; according to *ODNB*, Freind 'argued that modern, Newtonian theory and practice had confirmed many of the observations of Hippocrates'.

21. *the Leaches Art*: medicine, a 'leach' or 'leech' being 'one who practises the healing art' (*OED*).

With Patience each capricious Change endure,
Careful to merit where Reward is sure;
To Providence implicitly[22] resign'd,
Let this grand Precept poize thy wav'ring Mind.
With partial Eyes we view our own weak Cause,
And rashly scan his[23] upright, equal Laws.
For undeserv'd he ne'er inflicts a Woe,
Nor is his Recompence unsure, tho' slow.
Unpunish'd none transgress, deceiv'd none trust,
His Rules are fix'd, and all his Ways are Just.

22. *implicitly*: 'with implicit faith, confidence, submission, etc.; unquestioningly' (*OED*).

23. *his*: most of the other sources have 'her' here, and use feminine pronouns in the lines that follow too. This seems to suggest a classical idea of Providence, the goddess Fortuna, while the masculine pronoun adopted in 1739 seems to imply a Christian one, or even the figure of God himself.

# PERSONAL

# 21 Lord Bolingbroke, to Ambition. In Imitation of Horace. Ode I, Lib. 4

***Main source.*** 'Lord Bolingbroke to Ambition, In Imitation of Horace to Venus. Ode 1st. Book 4th.', in Portland Papers (Nottingham University), Pw V 784.

***Complementary manuscript source.*** BL MS Harley 7318, ff. 22r–23r.

***Complementary print sources.*** 'Harry Gambol's Soliloquy. In Imitation of Horace. Ode I. Lib. 4', in *As Much as May Be Publish'd of a Letter from the Late B— of R-ch-r to Mr. —. To which Are Added, the Several Advertisements for which Mr. Wilkins Was Assaulted at the Crown Tavern in Smithfield* (London: for A. Moore, [1728]), pp. 25–7 (fictitious imprint); 'Ode to Ambition', in *The History of the House of Lorraine* (London: [for E. Curll], 1731); *The False Patriot's Confession, or B——k's Address to Ambition* (London: for R. Charlton, 1737).

***Attribution.*** Walpole, *Royal and Noble Authors*, II, 141; Foxon H157·2; Urstad, p. 177; all referring to the 1737 edition.

***Context and date.*** The poem is Hervey's first venture into political verse. It was probably designed to embarrass Bolingbroke as Walpole's new administration under George II took shape. Bolingbroke and his allies faced a daunting task because, as H. T. Dickinson puts it, 'The tories were still split along Jacobite and Hanoverian lines, and they were demoralized and disorganized after more than a decade in opposition. Some of the party's most able members had defected to the court or even joined the whigs and it now had fewer than 200 MPs in the Commons' ('St John, Henry, styled first Viscount Bolingbroke (1678–1751)', *ODNB*). Although Hervey had been first elected as a Member of Parliament in 1725, he took little active interest in politics until the accession of George II gave him hopes of preferment. In the new Parliament of 1728, he was chosen to move the Address of Thanks following the King's address – 'a clear sign of the Ministry's regard for him as well as of his own aspiration for office' (Halsband, p. 76). A ballad ridiculing Bolingbroke's aspirations would have done his own ambitions no harm. The poem must have been written at some point between the time when the formidable nature of the task facing Bolingbroke became clear, probably in the autumn of 1727, and the date of 12 February 1728 given at the end of the first of the other two items printed alongside it. It gave brief but impressive evidence of how effective a writer Hervey would prove to be on the Government's side. This is clear not only from its wit as a satire on Bolingbroke's ambition and lack of principle, but also from the fact that, unusually for verse of this kind, which was characteristically ephemeral, it was reprinted in 1731 and 1737. The reprinting in 1731, coupled as it was with a 'History of the House of Lorraine', seems to have been timed to coincide with the successful visit of Francis, Duke of Lorraine, who would become the next Holy Roman Emperor and whose opposition to Jacobite principles the pamphlet celebrates on page 20.

The further reprinting in 1737 is more difficult to explain, but the unsigned address 'To the Reader' that heads the poem offers some clues:

> Having lately seen a Folio Pamphlet of Mr. *Pope's*, called, *An Imitation of* HORACE, Book *IV.* Ode *I.* occasion'd my Design of committing to the Press, some Lines which have long lain by me, and when communicated to me, were call'd by the same Title; I think there is something very strong, humourous and just in them, and more *à-propòs* to the Present Time, than either what passes under the Name of Mr. *Pope*, or a late Pamphlet, call'd, *The Man of Honour*; and if they prove any Satisfaction to the Publick, I have my Ends, nor value I what the Criticks may say, whether 'tis properly call'd an *Imitation* or not; tho' some have taken Mr. *Pope* to pieces on that Account. The natural Intent of these sort of Works may easily be guess'd at; and if an agreeable Entertainment be concomitant, 'twill be the better both for the Reader and Author. (sig. A2r)

This preface suggests that the motive for reprinting the poem was in part commercial, because the fact to which it refers – that Pope had very recently published an imitation of the same ode by Horace – smacks of an attempt to cash in with a rival poem.[1] But any reference to Bolingbroke and ambition at this period, let alone any use of the word 'Patriot', can only suggest that the predominant motive was political. Although Bolingbroke had retired from politics in May 1735, when he left England to settle in France, republishing the poem in 1737 was probably intended to help discourage the opposition at a time when the quarrel that broke out between the King and Frederick, Prince of Wales, renewed their hopes. The other poem to which the preface refers, *The Man of Honour*, is an ironical attack on the Government.[2] Hervey's imitation of Horace's ode charges one of the opposition's figureheads with dishonour in a way that is considerably more stylish.

The reference to 'Harry Gambol' in the title of some sources for the poem clearly points the poem at Bolingbroke: 'Harry Gambol' was one of the satirical names given to him, in allusion to his first name and his reputation as a man of pleasure with a mercurial character. Bolingbroke's reputation as a libertine also helps explain the appropriateness of Horace's farewell to Venus as a model, though the poem exploits the parallel at a general level and does not follow the original in any detail. The 1728 version is unique in including an epigraph, which it takes from lines 3–4 of the original: *Non sum qualis eram bonæ* | *Sub*

1. *Horace his Ode to Venus. Lib. IV. Ode I. Imitated By Mr. Pope* (London: for J. Wright by J. Roberts, 1737). The poem is a careful, elegant imitation of the original that has no political resonances. For a modern edition, see Pope, *Twickenham*, IV, 147–53.
2. London: s.n., 1737.

*regno Cynaræ* ('I am not the man I was in the reign of Cinara the Good' (Loeb 2004, p. 219); Cinara was the name of one of Horace's lovers). This aptly alludes to Bolingbroke's loss of power and influence. The six-line stanza form chosen by Hervey, which repeats a pattern in which one shorter line follows two longer ones, loosely matches Horace's quatrains, though the latter's repeating pattern consists of one shorter line preceding one longer one. Although Hervey's stanza form is best known as the 'Song to David' stanza, in reference to the later poem by Christopher Smart that made it famous, it was a favourite for album verse in the period and, especially in the hands of Sir Charles Hanbury Williams, it would shortly become a favourite for verse squibs on politicians.

***Textual commentary.*** A manuscript source has been chosen for this edition for two reasons: first, the poem almost certainly circulated in manuscript before finding its way into print; second, because the title of the first printed version, with its reference to 'Harry Gambol', seems to have been adapted in order to match the two items printed with it, both of which refer to Bolingbroke by the same nickname. The Portland (Welbeck) manuscript has been preferred to that in Harley MS 7318 because, unlike the former, it contains no clear errors. No textual emendations have therefore been necessary, other than to expand contractions. Minor differences in punctuation between the sources have been ignored; none affects the sense.

## Lord Bolingbroke, to Ambition, In Imitation of Horace to Venus. Ode 1st. Book 4th.[3]

1

Oh! Cease, Ambition, to molest
The quiet of this cheated Breast,
With hopes of future Power,
My Pleasure should be to look back,
Thankfull I have once escap'd thy Wreck,
And to enjoy the Shore.

2

For I that Statesman am no more,
Who Urg'd by thee, and back'd by Power,

3. *Horace to Venus. Ode 1st. Book 4th*: a translation of Horace's ode is given at the end of the text. The ballad also appeared under the title 'Harry Gambol's Soliloquy'; see headnote.

When Anna[4] fill'd the Throne,
Made Europe tremble at my Name,
And shook even Brunswicks lawfull Claim,[5]
To this contested Crown.

3

But now my Power, and Credits gone,
My Arts contemn'd, my Falsehoods known,
Dismiss me from thy Shrine,
By Friends deserted, Scorn'd by Foes,
What can my sanguine hopes propose?
Thy Lawrels I resign.

4

Can I in Parliaments Preside?
Can I the Royal Councils guide?
Who'll trust this faithless heart?
Me Whigs and Tories both disown!
Let George, or James, then wear the Crown,
Despair is still my Part.

5

The Credulous hopes of Fame or Power,
Shall tempt my Prudence now no more,
From Dawley's homely Shade;[6]
Let those, with popular applause
Assert their King and Country's Laws,
Who neither yet betray'd.

4. *Anna*: Anne (1665–1714), Queen of Great Britain and Ireland 1702–14; the word 'fill'd' may be a mischievous allusion to her notorious corpulence.

5. *Brunswicks lawfull Claim*: George Augustus, Electoral Prince of Hanover or Brunswick-Lüneburg, who became George I.

6. *Dawley's homely Shade*: 'Bolingbroke settled at Dawley, near Uxbridge, Middlesex, where he initially gave the impression of retiring from the political scene, but he very soon sought to rally the tory opposition in parliament and to ally it with the discontented whigs led by William Pulteney' (*ODNB*).

6

This Course my reason bids me Steer;
But if by Cursed Chance I hear
  Of Walpole's hated Name,
Again Ambition Swells my Breast,
Envy and Rancour break my Rest,
  And Reason I disclaime.

7

Craftsmen[7] and Libels I devise,
And jumble Rhapsodies of Lyes,
  His merit to defame,
All Day his Ruin I pursue,
By Night sometimes I've wrote it too,
  But then alas I Dream.

## Horace, Book IV, Ode I

The contests long suspended thou, Venus, wouldst renew. Be merciful, I beg, I beg! I am not as I was under the sway of kindly Cinara. O cruel mother of sweet Cupids, strive no more to bend, when near fifty years are past, one now callous to thy soft commands! Hie thee rather to the place where the persuasive prayers of young men call. More suitably, borne by thy gleaming swans, shalt thou haste in joyous revelry to the house of Paulus Maximus, if thou dost seek to kindle a fitting heart. For noble is he and comely, an eloquent defender of anxious clients, a youth accomplished in a hundred arts; and he will bear the standard of thy service far and wide and when prevailing o'er the gifts of some lavish rival he shall laugh in triumph, beside the Alban lakes he'll set thy marble statue beneath a roof of citron wood. Abounding incense shalt thou there inhale, and shalt take delight in the mingled strains of lyre and Berecyntian flute; nor shall the pipe be lacking. There twice each day shall boys, with maidens tender, hymning thy majesty, beat the ground with snowy feet, in triple time after the Salian fashion.

Me nor lad nor maid can more delight, nor trustful hope of love returned, nor drinking bouts nor temples bound with blossoms new.

7. *Craftsmen*: alluding to the leading opposition newspaper, *The Craftsman*.

But why, O Ligurinus, why steals now and then adown my cheek a tear? Why halts my tongue, once eloquent, with unbecoming silence midst my speech? In visions of the night, I now hold thee fast, now follow thee in flight o'er the Campus Martius' sward, now midst the whirling waves, O thou hard of heart! (Horace, *Odes and Epodes*, trans. C. E. Bennett (Loeb, pp. 284–5))

# 22 To the Imitator of the First Satire of the Second Book of Horace

***Main source.*** A copy of *To the Imitator of the Satire of the Second Book of Horace* (London: [Sam Aris] for J. Roberts, 1733), annotated by Hervey and bound up as the second item in a collection of five held by the National Trust at Ickworth, shelf mark 18.B.4.8.

***Complementary manuscript sources.*** BL Add. MS 35335, ff. 53r–54v, a scribal copy annotated by Hervey in a volume of material collected by Horace Walpole; BL Add. MS 31152, 25r–26v, from the papers of Thomas Wentworth, first Earl of Strafford (1672–1739); Bodley MS Eng. misc. c.399, ff. 76r–77v, from the letters and papers of James West (1704?–72), catalogued by March 1743; Portland Papers (Longleat), PO XIX, ff. 149r–150v; Portland (Welbeck), held at the University of Nottingham, Pw V 118/6, pp. 128–31 rev.; SRO 941/53/1 'MS Book. W[illia]m. Hervey', pp. 37–40.

***Complementary print sources.*** *To the Imitator of the Satire of the Second Book of Horace* (London: [Sam Aris] for J. Roberts, 1733); *Verses Address'd to the Imitator of the First Satire of the Second Book of Horace. By a Lady* (London: for A. Dodd, 1733): 1st edn, Foxon V39 (Dodd A); 2nd edn, Foxon V41 (Dodd B), and '5th edn' (1735), Foxon V44 (Dodd C).

***Attribution.*** The poem is usually identified as a joint production by Montagu and Hervey, perhaps with some small assistance from William Wyndham. However, questions of attribution have been distorted by the cloud under which Hervey's reputation has laboured since Pope's attack on him in *An Epistle to Dr. Arbuthnot* – an attack provoked in no small measure by this poem – and by a general presumption that Montagu was the more able poet. The key facts are that the poem was ascribed 'to a Lady' in the Dodd editions, and that most contemporaries believed that it had been written wholly or in part by Montagu; but that, nevertheless, Montagu never laid claim to it nor appears to have kept a copy in her manuscripts, while Hervey both claimed it as his in whole or part and annotated, apparently for publication as a second edition, a copy not only of the Roberts edition but also of a scribal manuscript copy later collected by Horace Walpole. Such evidence favours Hervey as the main author rather than Montagu, though it has to be borne in mind that the atmosphere surrounding the poem on its first publication was so noxious that her denial of authorship should not necessarily be taken at face value, and that it is possible that not all of her manuscripts have survived. The best discussions of the matter are in two outstanding scholarly essays: Isobel Grundy, '*Verses Address'd to the Imitator of Horace*: A Skirmish Between Pope and Some

Persons of Rank and Fortune', *Studies in Bibliography*, 30 (1977), 96–119; and James McLaverty, '"Of which being publick the Publick judge": Pope and the Publication of *Verses Addres'd to the Imitator of Horace*', *Studies in Bibliography*, 51 (1998), 183–204. Grundy and McLaverty have commented further in *Lady Mary Wortley Montagu* and *Pope, Print, and Meaning* (Oxford: Oxford University Press, 2001) respectively. Grundy is more confident than McLaverty in attributing the greater share of composition to Montagu, and provides the fullest argument for the possible involvement of Wyndham. The latter case, however, rests on slender grounds: an ascription by Lord Oxford written into his copy of Dodd A more than a year after the poem was first published; the fact that, in line 81 of *The First Satire of the Second Book of Horace, Imitated* ('Slander or Poyson, dread from *Delia*'s Rage'), Pope had libelled Wyndham's newly married wife, Lady Deloraine; the attack in *To the Imitator* on Pope's inability to restrain himself from casting aspersions even on 'Youth and Beauty' (here represented by Lady Deloraine); and what seems retaliation by Pope in lines 376–7 of his *Epistle to Dr. Arbuthnot* ('To please a *Mistress*, one aspers'd his life; | He lash'd him not, but let her be his *Wife*'). However, the fact that Wyndham had grounds for taking offence by no means proves that he did so by contributing lines to the poem, especially because he did not marry Lady Deloraine until April 1734 and because he has no reputation as a poet. It is therefore difficult to give much if any credence to an ascription that is not confirmed by any other source. It should also be added that little thought appears to have been given to the process of collaboration, if indeed *To the Imitator* was a collaborative product. While Hervey and Montagu would later improvise a verse dialogue (Poem 55), there are no indications that different paragraphs of this poem might have been written by them in turns, let alone of how several lines by another writer, Wyndham, could have been added. As the poem must have been written between 15 February, when Pope's *First Satire of the Second Book of Horace, Imitated* was published, and 8 March, when the Roberts and Dodd editions of *Verses* first appeared, the writers would have had to work quickly, especially as the period was curtailed by two unsuccessful attempts on Montagu's part to get Pope to provide an undertaking not to insult her further. It is possible that one of the writers, if more than one was involved, produced a draft to which one or possibly two others added. In the absence of any documentary evidence, this may be the most plausible conjecture.

Grundy provides the fullest discussion of attribution on grounds of method, style and content. The poem's plan she allots to Hervey, remarking that Montagu's other poetic attacks are in dramatic form, 'whereas Hervey always chooses to argue directly in his own person, like an orator speaking for the prosecution' ('*Verses Address'd to the Imitator of Horace*', p. 114) – or, it may be added, like a speaker in Parliament. The opening paragraph she also ascribes to Hervey, on the evidence of its heavy use of antithesis and subordinate clauses; in contrast, she observes, 'in most of Lady Mary's poems the first main verb occurs in the first or second line' (p. 112). 'On the other hand,' she continues, 'the extended climactic image occupying the last paragraph has many parallels among [Montagu's] verse, while

Hervey usually prefers to end with a detached, pointed couplet'. Grundy also points out that the poem has 'little of the careless syntax and construction which was Lady Mary's. She seldom uses "thou" and "thee" with so few lapses into "you"'; and she finds further evidence of Hervey's style in the 'exactly judged' antitheses of lines 89–94 (93–100 in her edition). More telling still, as her notes and those below show, is the fact that the poem contains more echoes and pre-echoes of Hervey's verse than of Montagu's. Grundy also draws attention to echoes between the poem and another response to Pope's *Imitation*, Henry Fielding's 'An Epistle to Mr Lyttleton'. Fielding, who was Montagu's cousin, wrote in her defence, but he never printed the poem and it survives only in a fair copy kept by her (Grundy, 'New Verse', pp. 240–5; see Henry Fielding, *The Journal of a Voyage to Lisbon, Shamela, and Occasional Writings*, ed. by Martin C. Battestin, with Sheridan W. Baker, Jr, and Hugh Amory (Oxford: Clarendon Press, 2008), pp. 86–98. However, as the poem's editors indicate that it was probably composed in mid-March, after the two versions *To the Imitator* and *Verses Address'd to the Imitator* had been published, it appears that Fielding's poem echoes them rather than they him. By that point he could easily have had access to one or other version of the poem in print if not in manuscript.

Evidence on grounds of content also leans towards Hervey. As Grundy indicates, the poem's criticism of Pope's scholarship suggests the attitude of 'one who has enjoyed the classical education proper to a gentleman' ('*Verses Address'd to the Imitator of Horace*', pp. 112–13); while the references to physical courage and to corporal punishment in lines 58–70 'would read oddly coming from Lady Mary' (p. 113). On the other hand, Grundy finds the idea of Pope as inhuman 'more characteristic' of Montagu, yet observes that the idea 'of his verse as unintentionally innocuous is more like Hervey' (p. 114). A point she does not take into account is that Hervey was a highly successful writer of political pamphlets, judged by Horace Walpole as 'equal to any that ever were written' (*Royal and Noble Authors*, II, 137). *To the Imitator* shows comparable adversarial skill, as do Hervey's caustic comments on many of his contemporaries in his memoirs. While evidence from the method, style and content of a text must always be evaluated carefully, and can never be definitive, in the case of *To the Imitator* it tends to suggest that Hervey's contribution was the largest.

***Context and date.*** As noted above, Pope published *The First Satire of the Second Book of Horace Imitated* on 15 February 1733. The opening verse paragraph contains a gibe at Hervey: 'The Lines are weak, another's pleas'd to say, | Lord *Fanny* spins a thousand such a Day' (lines 5–6; Pope, *Twickenham*, IV, 95–127). Although not especially offensive – quoting the second line, Hervey was to plead guilty to the charge in lines 123–4 of Poem 18, *To Dr Sherwin in Answer to a Latin Letter in Verse* – Hervey may have been irritated by Pope's deviation from Horace in the poem he claimed to be imitating, for his charges are general and do not refer to any particular person. Real offence was given, however, by two lines that no informed reader could have failed to recognise as attacking Montagu: 'From furious *Sappho* scarce a milder Fate, | Pox'd by her Love, or libell'd by her Hate' (lines 83–4). Although in this instance Horace named names (Horace, *Satires*, I. ii. 47–9 (Loeb)), his poem provided no basis for the charges Pope aimed at Montagu, so again the insult was gratuitous. But the poem does not only respond to Pope's gibes at Hervey, Montagu and Lady Deloraine. Hervey, in particular, had already criticised Pope's attacks on public figures. In a letter to Henry Fox of 16 January 1733, less than two months before *To the Imitator of the First Satire of the Second Book of Horace* must have been written, he remarked: 'I know no other News but that Pope has put out another Satyr which he calls the *use of Riches* & dedicates to Ld. Bathurst; he is so abusive in it, and in so much plainer terms than in his Chandois-Performance of impertinent Memory, that it is very probable, some of those to whom he pretends to teach the proper use of Riches, may teach him the proper Use of Cudgels' (BL Add. MS 51396, ff. 79v–80r). In the phrase 'Chandois-Performance' Hervey referred to Pope's character Timon in *Burlington*, widely assumed to represent James Brydges, first Duke of Chandos, though Pope denied the charge. However, quoting a letter written to Stephen Fox on 21 December 1731, soon after the first publication of *Burlington*, James McLaverty emphasises that much more was at issue: 'With a poem so "impertinent", any lord could serve as its victim . . . The case against Pope was not that the picture of Timon's Villa misrepresented Cannons; it was that Pope's subordinate position forbade criticism' (*Pope, Print, and Meaning*, p. 145). In this light, *To the Imitator* constituted an attempt to put the imitator in his place. It failed in that aim, although it is generally accepted as the most successful of all the attacks on Pope (see McLaverty, *Pope, Print, and Meaning*, pp. 181–2, and David Fairer, *English Poetry of the Eighteenth Century 1700–1789* (London: Pearson Education, 2003), pp. 63–5).

There is, however, a further possible twist to the poem's publishing history. In '"Of which being publick the Publick judge"', James McLaverty argues that primary responsibility for having the poem printed should be allotted not to Hervey, Montagu or an unknown person who had access to a manuscript, but to Pope himself. McLaverty summarises his argument in *Pope, Print, and Meaning*: 'the most likely explanation is that one version (*Verses*) was published by Pope himself, forcing calumny shrouded by the court out into the public, while the other (*To the Imitator*) was published by Lord Hervey, acting for both authors, in response' (p. 178). He adds: 'the likeliest explanation for the double publication of the poem on 8 March is that Pope threatened Hervey with publication, which Pope then went ahead with, and that Hervey took "publish and be damned" one step further by also publishing himself' (pp. 180–1). The argument is reinforced by a lot of evidence that there is no space to represent here, and much of it is persuasive. Pope's manoeuvre would have been designed to help his reputation, especially at court, which had been damaged both by his satire and, crucially, by attacks such as those constituted by the poem. As McLaverty puts it, Pope's 'chief concern at the time was with the poem's manuscript publication, particularly at court, and the damage it might do to his standing there; he had already been under pressure to withdraw his criticism of Lady Mary in the imitation of the *First Satire* as a sign of his loyalty to the King and Queen. Print publication of the attack on the imitator let him off the hook and gave him the chance to reply' ('"Of which being publick the Publick judge"', p. 183). The poem, precisely because it was so hard-hitting, not only helped vindicate him but also provided grounds for him to retaliate in future.

***Textual commentary.*** Hervey's annotated copy of the Roberts edition has been chosen as the main source for this edition because, although evidently unfinished, it appears to represent his latest recorded intentions. The main differences from the Roberts edition are as follows: the title is corrected, 'first' being inserted before 'Satire'; a Preface is added; a title page, including an epigraph from Horace, is provided, followed by the words 'the second Edition corrected by the Author, with a Preface'. Hervey also struck through what was evidently a first attempt at a title page, in which the poem is entitled 'A Genuine Copy Of the Verses adress'd To the Imitator of the first Satire of the second Book of Horace. with a Preface to the Reader. Publish'd by the Author.' This also has the epigraph from Horace; two couplets are substituted for one in lines 9–12; lines 22–6 are repositioned from their original place following line 10; a couplet is added in lines 40–1 but the following two couplets are struck through; a further couplet is struck through following line 78; a couplet is substituted in lines 95–6; and three footnotes are added. There are also various smaller verbal changes. As Grundy points out, there are relatively few differences between the two rival printed editions. These are: Dodd A inserts 'Verses Address'd' before the title as it is in Roberts and ascribes the poem to 'a Lady'; and there are minor verbal changes in lines 7, 53, 85 and 92 ('view' for 'views', 'He' for 'He'd', 'do yet' for 'then yet', and 'prized' for 'prais'd' respectively; only the second and last of these variations occur in Hervey's annotated copy). There are also various differences in punctuation. In addition to these changes, Dodd B inserts the same couplet inserted by Hervey in lines 38–9; and substitutes 'to' for 'of' in line 30, '*Porcupine*' for '*Porcupines*' along with 'Back shoots' for 'Backs shoot' in lines 71–2, and 'puny' for 'little' in line 78; while Dodd C, evidently published because copies of the earlier editions had run out, adds two footnotes referring to Pope's *Epistle to Dr. Arbuthnot* and makes one small verbal change, from 'Whilst' to 'While' in line 75. There are no clear relations between any of the manuscripts and the two printed versions, except that William Hervey's copy is a virtual transcript of Dodd C. The copy was made some time after 11 February 1751, the day when he began to compile his commonplace book; evidently he was unaware of the copy of the Roberts edition in the Library at Ickworth that his father had annotated. Significantly, however, Grundy observes that both the printed versions 'may have stemmed from the same source, since both omit lines 38–9' (lines 40–1 in Hervey's annotated copy provided here); and that the error in the title of the Roberts edition 'may indicate lack of authorial supervision' ('Verse of Lady Mary Wortley Montagu', pp. 511, 514). Minor variations between the manuscripts and the printed texts indicate that, except in the case of William Hervey's copy, none of the former stems from any printed copy. Counting only verbal variations, a few of which, like the first in Portland Papers (Welbeck) may be transcription errors, BL Add. MS 31152 has the largest number of unique variants, ten; while Bodley MS Eng. c.399 has eight, Portland (Welbeck) six and Portland (Longleat) four. This evidence suggests that the poem circulated quite widely in manuscript before and after print publication. BL Add. MS 35335 is of further interest for its autograph corrections to a scribal copy. The fact that these corrections do not all correspond to the annotated copy at Ickworth used as the main source for this edition indicates that it was produced independently and probably at a different period. On the evidence of a letter to Henry Fox dated 12 January 1734, Grundy speculates that Hervey may have corrected both his attacks on Pope, *To Dr. Sherwin* and *To the Imitator*, at the same time ('Verse of Lady Mary Wortley Montagu', p. 507). She further suggests that his preface 'To the Reader' must have been written soon after the publication of the Roberts and Dodd editions. If this is true, it may also apply to BL Add. MS 35335. In the poem as presented here, two footnotes that Hervey provided for his new 'To the Reader' and some additional side notes on the poem are included among the footnotes, and identified by an asterisk next to the note-number and the phrase 'autograph note, *Ickworth*'; the footnote that initially appeared in the Roberts edition and is found in all sources also appears among the footnotes, identified by an asterisk next to the note-number and that phrase 'Hervey's note, *Roberts*'.

## To the Imitator of the First Satire of the Second Book of Horace

——————— Omnes
Vicini oderunt, noti, Pueri atque Puellæ.
Miraris? ——————— Hor:[1]

1. *Epigraph*: 'every one hates you, neighbours and acquaintances, boys and girls' (Horace, *Satires*, I. i. 84–6 (Satires, Epistles and Ars Poetica, Loeb, pp. 10–11). Neither Dodd A nor Roberts has an epigraph; one from Juvenal was added to Dodd B, but it appears in none of the manuscripts except SRO: *Si Natura negat, facit Indignatio versus* (*Satires*, I. 79, where the last word is *versum*: 'If nature fails, then indignation generates verse' (*Juvenal: The Satires*, trans. by Niall Rudd (Oxford: Oxford University Press, 1991), p. 5)). McLaverty comments: 'The line is self-deprecating. The implication – that the writer is not gifted enough to compose ordinarily – is modestly amusing in the mouth of Juvenal or Swift or Pope; but in the mouths of Lord Hervey and Lady Mary it comes uncomfortably close to the truth' ("'Of which being publick the Publick judge'", p. 192). This assumes, however, that the epigraph is attributable to Hervey or Montagu. The fact that Hervey used a different epigraph – from Horace, apt to a response to a Horatian imitation – suggests that he was not responsible for it; and, if McLaverty is correct in arguing that Pope published the poem for reasons of his own, it would have been part of the joke against Montagu, who, it appears, he first believed to be solely responsible for it.

*To the Reader*

So hasty and incorrect a Copy of these Verses was first sent into the World, and one so much more imperfect is since printed, that I can not help indulging my Vanity so far, since they are to appear in Publick, as to set them forth in their best Dress.

And whilst I endeavour to do poetical Justice to the Composition I must take the same Opportunity to do moral Justice to the Design, especially since the Generality of the World has been so malicious as to insinuate that there is any thing in this Performance that carrys a Reflexion on *the celebrated Mr. Pope*, for whom I have always had the greatest and justest Regard.

I am less surprised at the Ill-nature shown to me by this Insinuation, as it is so conformable to *That* practised towards Mr Pope him-self, when *the monstrous Injustice* of his censorious Readers endeavour'd to fix such names to Characters of his drawing, as I dare swear no more enter'd into *his* Head on *that* Occasion, than his did into *mine* upon *this*.

As I have follow'd Mr Pope's Example[2]* in this publick Profession of my Innocence, I hope I shall also have his good fortune in recieving Absolution; and that He and all Mankind must allow my Apology[3]* to be as good as his, tho not my Verses.

## To the Imitator of the First Satire of the Second Book of Horace

In two large Columns[4] on thy motly Page,
Where *Roman* Wit is strip'd with *English* Rage;
Where Ribaldry to Satire makes pretence,
And modern Scandal rolls with ancient Sense;[5]
Whilst on one Side we see how *Horace* thought,

2. *Mr Pope's Example*: '*See the Preface to the second Edition of Taste an Epistle.' (autograph note, *Ickworth*).

3. *my Apology*: '¤See the same.' (autograph note, *Ickworth*).

4. *two large Columns*: This description and the seven lines that follow refer to the layout of Pope's *First Satire of the Second Book of Horace* in which the source text was printed on the left-hand pages and the imitation on the right-hand.

5. *And modern Scandal rolls with ancient Sense*: Grundy in *Essays & Poems*, where this poem is printed on pp. 265–70, compares 'But a few modern Words for ancient Sense' in the printed version of Poem 18, *To Dr Sherwin in Answer to a Latin Letter in Verse*, line 134 (revised as 'Replete with Words and indigent of Sense' in the Ickworth copy).

And on the other how he never wrote:
Who can believe, who views the bad and good,
That the mean[6] Copyst better understood
*Horace* than *Homer*? or was less to seek
In *Latin Spirit* than in *verbal Greek*?
For *This* like *That* thou shouldst have ask'd *Broome's* Aid
Who writes that Verse for which great *P–pe* is pay'd.[7]

*Horace* can laugh, is delicate,[8] is clear:
You only coarsely rail, or darkly sneer:
His Style is elegant, his Diction pure;
Whilst none thy crabbed[9] Numbers can endure,
Hard as thy Heart, and as thy Birth obscure.[10]

If *He* has Thorns, they all on Roses grow:
Thine like rude Thistles, and mean Brambles show;
With this Exception, that tho' rank[11] the Soil,

6. *mean*: 'Of low social status; *spec.* not of the nobility or gentry' (*OED*); the gibe at Pope's social status, repeated in line 17, is characteristic of Hervey.

7. *Horace . . . is pay'd*: except in BL Add. MS 35335, which has the same substitution, these two couplets in Hervey's annotated copy replace one in all the complementary sources: 'That Spirit he pretends to imitate | Than heretofore that Greek he did translate'. Immediately after the substituted couplet, Add. 35335 adds a further couplet: 'Broome would have told thee and have told thee true | That whilst the Paths of Horace you pursue'. The poem was not the first rebuke to Pope for inferior scholarship to Broome's; Broome translated eight of the twenty-four books of *The Odyssey* and provided all of the notes, while Elijah Fenton translated a further four (Anna Chahoud, 'Broome, William', *ODNB*). See J. V. Guerinot, *Pamphlet Attacks on Alexander Pope 1711–1744: A Descriptive Bibliography* (London: Methuen, 1969), pp. 118–20, 128–9, 192. Hervey would repeat the charge in *To Dr Sherwin in Answer to a Latin Letter in Verse* (Poem 18, line 157).

8. *delicate*: 'Exquisitely fine in power of perception, feeling, appreciation, etc.; finely sensitive' (*OED*).

9. *crabbed*: 'Of writings, authors, etc.: Ruggedly or perversely intricate; difficult to unravel, construe, deal with, or make sense of' (*OED*); the senses 'Proceeding from or showing an ill-tempered or irritable disposition; angry; ill-natured' and 'crooked', used of the human body, are also relevant.

10. *Hard . . . obscure*: Dodd C adds 'See Mr. *Pope*'s Epistle to Dr. *Arbuthnot*, p. 19', referring to line 381 of that poem and its note on Pope's parentage. SRO has a note giving the same connection.

11. *rank*: 'extremely rich, heavy, or fertile; liable to produce rank vegetation' (*OED*), comparing sense 6, 'vigorous or luxuriant in growth. In later use usually in negative sense: growing too luxuriantly or rampantly; thick and coarse.' The sense 'grossly coarse or indecent; obscene' is also relevant.

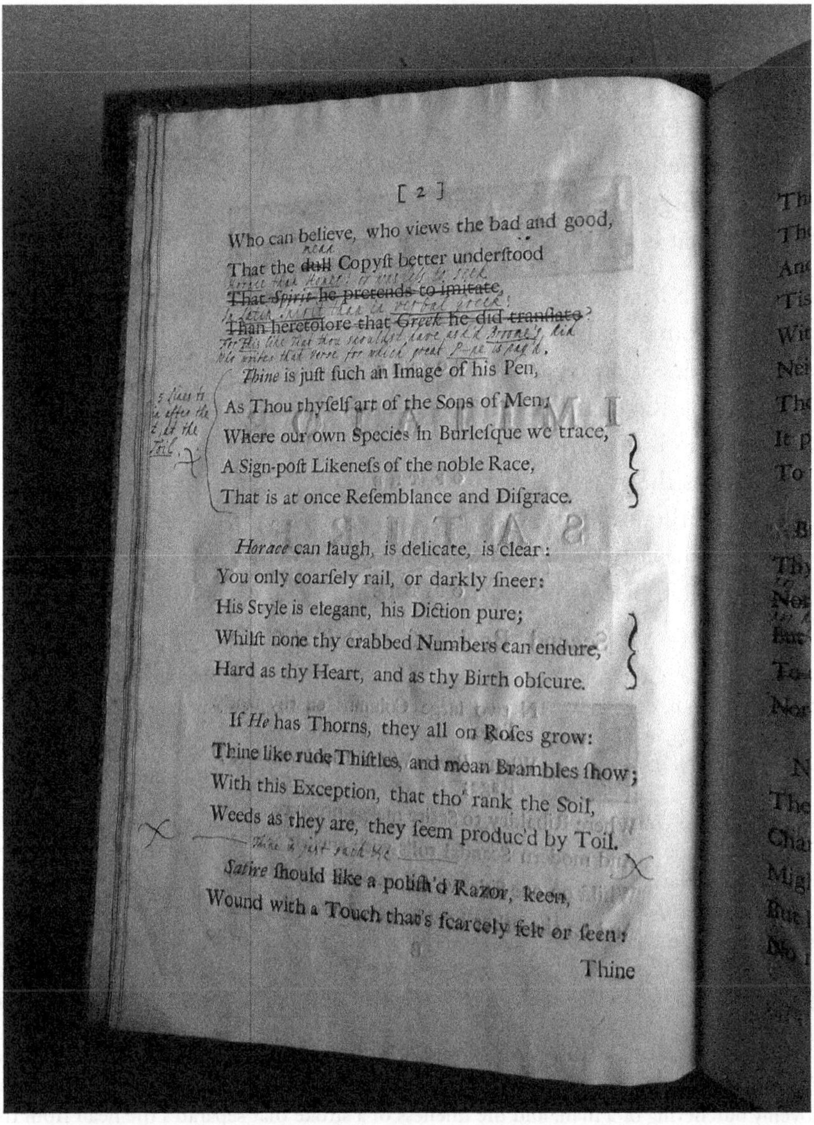


**Figure 1** Hervey's annotations on the Ickworth copy of *To the Imitator*, preparing a second edition.

Weeds as they are, they seem produc'd by Toil.
*Thine* is just such an Image of his Pen,
As Thou thyself art of the Sons of Men;
Where our own Species in Burlesque[12] we trace,
A Sign-Post Likeness of the noble Race,
That is at once Resemblance and Disgrace.[13]

*Satire* should like a polish'd Razor, keen,
Wound with a Touch that's scarcely felt or seen:
Thine is an *Oyster-Knife* that hacks and hews;
The Rage, but not the Talent of Abuse;[14]
And is in *Hate*, what *Love* is in the Stews.[15]
'Tis the gross *Lust* of Hate that still[16] annoys,[17]
Without Distinction, as gross Love enjoys;[18]
Neither to Folly, nor to Vice *confin'd*,
The Object of thy Spleen is *Human Kind*;

12. *Burlesque*: 'Grotesque imitation of what is, or is intended to be, dignified or pathetic, in action, speech, or manner; *concr.* an action or performance which casts ridicule on that which it imitates, or is itself ridiculous as an unsuccessful attempt at serious impressiveness; a mockery' (*OED*).

13. *Thine is … Disgrace*: these lines have been repositioned by Hervey from where they occur in all the complementary sources, where they follow their line 10 (line 12 here). Grundy in *Essays & Poems* compares a line from Fielding's 'Epistle to Mr Lyttleton', 'For thou art Surely not of human Race' (41), and four lines from Hervey's *The Difference between Verbal and Practical Virtue Exemplify'd* (Poem 24): 'It seems the Counterpart by Heav'n design'd | A Symbol and a Warning to Mankind: | As at some Door we find hung out a Sign, | Type of the Monster to be found within' (103–6). Abuse of Pope's physical appearance was well established; see Guerinot, *Pamphlet Attacks on Alexander Pope*, pp. xxix–xxx and passim.

14. *Satire should … of Abuse*: The lines recall Dryden's famous definition in his 'Discourse Concerning the Original and Progress of Satire': 'there is still a vast difference betwixt the slovenly butchering of a man, and the fineness of a stroke that separates the head from the body and leaves it standing in its place' (Dryden, *Poems*, III (2000), 423). By this standard, *To the Imitator* constitutes not satire but invective, as was almost certainly intended.

15. *Stews*: 'A brothel … In plural (chiefly *collect.*; sometimes, a quarter occupied by houses of ill-fame)' (*OED*).

16. *still*: 'Without change, interruption, or cessation; continually, constantly' (*OED*).

17. *annoys*: 'molest, injure, hurt, harm' (*OED*).

18. *'Tis the … Love enjoys*: Grundy in 'Verse of Lady Mary Wortley Montagu', where this poem is printed pp. 518–26, compares 'And such the Lust that breaks his nightly Dream' in *Difference between Verbal and Practical Virtue*, line 129.

It preys on all who yield, or who resist,
To thee 'tis Provocation to *exist.*

But if thou see'st[19]* a great and gen'rous Heart,
Thy Bow is doubly bent to force a Dart.[20]
No Dignity nor Innocence is spared,
Nor Age, nor Sex, nor Thrones, nor Graves revered.[21]

Not even Youth and Beauty can controul
The universal Rancour of thy Soul;
Charms that might soften Superstition's Rage,
Might humble Pride, or thaw the Ice of Age – – – –
But how should'st thou by Beauty's Force be mov'd,
No more for loving made, than to be lov'd.[22]
It was the Equity[23] of right'ous Heav'n,
That such a *Soul* to such a *Form* was giv'n;
And shews the Uniformity of Fate,
That one so *odious*, should be born to *hate.*

When God created Thee, one would believe,
He said the same, as *to the Snake* of *Eve:*[24]

19. *if thou see'st*: '*See TASTE, *an Epistle*' (Hervey's note, *Roberts*).

20. *But if . . . a Dart*: Grundy in 'Verse of Lady Mary Wortley Montagu' compares four lines from Fielding's 'Epistle to Mr Lyttleton': 'Say, against Chandois what thy Fury arm'd, | Was it what any other Breast had charm'd! . . . | Thy Darts when thrown at any noble Head, | Still fly where Honour, Virtue, Learning lead' (140–1, 144–5).

21. *No Dignity . . . Graves revered*: all the complementary sources, except for Hervey's other annotated copy, BL Add. MS 35335, follow this line with two couplets that he struck through: 'Nor only Justice vainly we demand, | But even Benefits can't rein thy Hand; | To this, or that, alike in vain we trust, | Nor find thee less ungrateful than unjust'. Hervey presumably deleted the lines on the grounds that they weakened the attack. Grundy in *Essays & Poems* compares a couplet in Poem 65, 'The Adventures of Telemachus in the Island Ogygia', probably written earlier: 'Horrid Confusion! Age nor Sex is spared; | Nor Royal Heads, nor ev'n their Gods rever'd' (1. 124–5).

22. *Not even . . . be lov'd*: These six lines are suggested by some commentators to have been contributed by William Wyndham.

23. *Equity*: 'The quality of being equal or fair; fairness, impartiality; even-handed dealing' (*OED*). The concept, which is invoked again in line 100, seems more characteristic of Hervey's thinking than of Montagu's.

24. *He said . . . of Eve*: in Dodd C and SRO the line is keyed to a footnote, 'See Mr. *Pope*'s letter ['Epistle' SRO] to Dr. *Arbuthnot*, p. 16'; this refers to line 319, 'Or at the ear of *Eve*, familiar Toad', to which Pope added the note, 'It is but justice to own that the Hint of *Eve* and the *Serpent* was taken from the Verses *on the Imitator of* Horace'.

*To Human Race Antipathy declare,*
*'Twixt them and thee be everlasting War.*
But, Oh! the Sequel of that Sentence dread,
And whilst you *bruise their Heel, beware your Head.*[25]

Nor think thy Weakness shall be thy Defence,
(The Female Scold's[26] Protection in Offence:)
Sure 'tis as fair to beat who cannot fight,
As 'tis to libel those who cannot write:
And if thou draw'st thy *Pen* to aid the Law,
Others a *Cudgel*, or a *Rod* may draw.[27]

If none with Vengeance yet thy Crimes pursue,
Or give thy manifold Affronts their due:
If Limbs unbroken, Skin without a Stain,
Unwhipt, unblanketed, unkick'd, unslain,
That wretched little Carcass you retain:
The Reason is, not, that the World wants Eyes,
But thou'rt so mean, they see, and they despise.
When fretful *Porcupines*,[28] with ranc'rous Will,
From mounted Backs shoot forth a harmless Quill;
Cool the Spectators stand, and all the while
Upon the *angry little Monster* smile:
Thus 'tis with thee – – – – Whilst impotently safe,

25. *When God . . . your Head*: see Genesis 3: 14–15:

> And the Lord God said unto the serpent, Because you have done this, you are cursed above all cattle, and above every beast of the field; upon your belly shall you go, and dust shall you eat all the days of your life: And I will put enmity between you and the woman, and between your seed and her seed; he shall bruise your head, and you shall bruise his heel.

26. *Scold*: 'a woman (rarely a man) addicted to abusive language' (*OED*).

27. *And if . . . may draw*: Hervey had remarked of Pope, several weeks before the poem was written, 'that it is very probable, some of those to whom he pretends to teach the proper use of Riches, may teach him the proper Use of Cudgels' (see headnote). Grundy in *Essays & Poems* compares a similar remark in a letter of 21 December 1731 to Stephen Fox: 'It is astonishing to me that he is not afraid this prophecy will be verified, which was told to him a year or two ago, "In black and white whilst satire you pursue, | "Take head the answer is not black and blue"' (SRO 941/47/4, p. 324). She also suggests that Montagu may have originated the couplet, since Horace Walpole 'recorded a similar remark as hers', citing Walpole, *Correspondence*, XIV, 243, n. 7.

28. *fretful Porcupines*: echoing 'Like quills upon the fretful porpentine' (*Hamlet*, I. 5. 20).

You strike unwounding, we unhurt can laugh.
*Who but must laugh* this Bully *when he sees?*
*A little Insect shiv'ring at a Breeze.*[29*]

Is this the *Thing* to keep Mankind in Awe?[30]
*To make those tremble who escape the Law?*[31]
Is this the *Ridicule* to live so long,
The *deathless Satire*, and *immortal Song?*[32]
No; like thy self-blown Praise thy Scandal flies,
And as we're told of Wasps, it stings and dies.[33]

If none then yet return th'intended Blow,
You all your Safety to your Dullness owe:[34*]
But whilst that Armour thy poor Corps defends,
'Twill make thy *Readers* few, as are thy *Friends*:
Those who thy *Nature* loath'd, yet lov'd thy *Art*;
Who lik'd thy *head*, and yet abhorr'd thy *Heart*;[35]
Chose thee to read, but never to converse;

29. 'See *Tast* an Epist.' (autograph note, *Ickworth*). The couplet 'Who but . . . Breeze' is adapted from Pope's *Epistle to Burlington*, lines 107–8, on Timon: 'Who but must laugh, the Master when he sees, | A puny insect, shiv'ring at a breeze!' All the complementary sources except BL Add. MS 35335 follow this with a couplet struck through by Hervey: 'One over-match'd by ev'ry Blast of Wind, | Insulting and provoking all Mankind'.

30. *Is this . . . Awe*: Grundy in 'Verse of Lady Mary Wortley Montagu' compares 'Is this the Muse that Laws and Pow'r defies!' in Fielding's 'Epistle to Mr Lyttleton' (line 104).

31. *To make . . . Law*: echoing Pope's 'Hear this, and tremble! you who 'scape the Laws' (*First Satire of the Second Book of Horace*, line 118, another line that has no precedent in the Latin); Grundy in *Essays & Poems* compares a couplet from Fielding's 'Epistle to Mr Lyttleton': 'Shew me the Man above the Laws accus'd, | The lawless Pow'r which Laws defend abus'd' (lines 148–9).

32. *Is this . . . immortal Song*: alluding to Pope's 'Satire's my Weapon . . . | Who-e'er offends, at some unlucky Time, | Slides into Verse, and hitches into Rhyme, | Sacred to Ridicule! his whole Life long, | And the sad Burthen of some merry Song' (*First Satire*, 69, 78–80). The lines occur just before those on Lady Deloraine and on Montagu.

33. *And . . . stings and dies*: this is not true of wasps or bumble bees, because their stings lack barbs and so can be withdrawn without self-injury, unlike those of honey bees, which cause not only the sting but part of the bee's body to be left behind.

34. *Safety to your Dullness owe*: '*See Taste and Riches two Epistles*' (autograph note, *Ickworth*). This refers to Pope's epistles to Burlington and to Bathurst, which used these words as key parts of their respective titles on first publication.

35. *Those who . . . thy Heart*: Grundy in *Essays & Poems* compares 'Whilst not one Man who likes his rhyming Art, | Allows him Genius, or defends his Heart' (*Difference between Verbal and Practical Virtue*, lines 138–9).

And scorn'd in *Prose*, him whom they prized in *Verse*:
Even they shall now their partial Error see,
Shall shun thy Writings, like thy Company:
Or thy late Works for Dormitives[36] shall keep,
And to thy *Taste* and *Riches* nightly sleep.[37]
Nor thou the Justice of the World disown,
When left forlorn an *Outcast*, and alone:
For tho' in Law, to murder be to kill,
In Equity[38] the Murder's in the Will.
Whilst then with Coward-Hand you stab a Name,
And try at least t' assassinate our Fame;[39]
Like the first bold Assassin's be thy Lot,
Ne'er be thy Guilt forgiven, or forgot:[40]
But as thou hat'st, be hated by Mankind;
And with the Emblem of thy crooked Mind,
Mark'd on thy Back, like *Cain*, by God's own Hand,
Wander, like him, accursed through the Land.[41]

36. *Dormitives*: 'A soporific medicine; a narcotic' (*OED*).

37. *Or thy . . . nightly sleep*: this couplet replaces one that Hervey crossed out: 'And to thy Books shall ope their Eyes no more, | Than to thy Person they would do their Door'.

38. *Equity*: 'the distinctive name of a system of law existing side by side with the common and statute law (together called "law" in a narrower sense), and superseding these, when they conflict with it' (*OED*).

39. *And try . . . Fame*: Grundy in *Essays & Poems* compares 'As he who durst assassinate thy Fame', a line from Fielding's 'Epistle to Mr Lyttleton' defending Montagu (33).

40. *Ne'er be . . . forgot*: Grundy in 'Verse of Lady Mary Wortley Montagu' compares 'Yet Sappho's Wrongs the Muse shall ne'ere forget' ('Epistle to Mr Lyttleton', line 162).

41. *Mark'd on . . . the Land*: see Genesis 4: 15: 'And the Lord said unto him, Therefore whosoever slayeth Cain, vengeance shall be taken on him sevenfold. And the Lord set a mark upon Cain, lest any finding him should kill him.'

# 23 Dr Sherwin's Character Design'd for his Epitaph

***Source.*** BL Add. MS 51396, ff. 110r–111v.

***Complementary manuscript sources.*** 'Parson F—d's Epitaph', BL Add. MS 51396, ff. 112r–113r.

***Complementary print sources.*** The poem has never been printed.

***Attribution.*** Authorial.

***Context and date.*** As mentioned in the headnote to Poem 18, 'To Dr Sherwin in Answer to a Latin Letter in Verse', William Sherwin was a Canon of Chichester who served as a comic butt for the Duke and Duchess of Richmond and their friends. Irritated by the fact that Sherwin had given his poem, even perhaps sold it, to a printer, Hervey wrote this coarse but lively satirical character portrait, not intending that Sherwin would ever see it. Unfortunately, as he explained in a letter to Henry Fox dated 11 February 1734, it too very nearly became public:

> What vexed me was the printer's having got a copy of Sherwin's 'Character', written by me, which they threatened to print. However I warded this blow, by turning the verses immediately into an 'Epitaph on Ford', and pretending they were written two years ago. This, by the Duke of Richmond's good management, passed on Sherwin; and he is now boasting of being abused with me by the *Craftsman* and says it is because he and I are known to be such useful and firm friends to the Government. (BL Add. MS 51396, f. 108v)

In light of Hervey's irritation, and his wish to provide further entertainment for the Duke and Duchess of Richmond and their friends, the poem is not to be taken literally, though no doubt there was some truth behind its humorous exaggerations. It is essentially a lampoon, to be judged on the basis of its abrasively witty caricature of a parson who valued flesh over spirit and personal interest over the well-being of his parishioners. This is also the emphasis of 'Parson F[or]d's Epitaph', which contains only a few changes designed to trick Sherwin into believing that the poem was not about him. The manuscript must have circulated quite widely, because in a letter to Conyers Middleton dated 15 November 1733 Hervey wrote: 'I am sorry to hear the Verses that you say were shown to you as written by me on Sherwin are got about; & beg you when you hear them spoken of, to say you have been told they were written for an Epitaph on Parson Ford two years ago' (SRO 941/47/4, p. 441). Middleton had already assured him that in Cambridge the poem had been applauded for its attack on 'an enemy to virtue and morality' (SRO 941/47/8, p. 2 of unpaginated letter).

***Textual commentary.*** The poem, enclosed in Hervey's letter to Henry Fox, is in the hand of Fox's brother Stephen. Hervey explains: 'Your brother whilst I have been writing my Letter has been copying this and thinks it so great a Merit that he insists on my telling it, as if you do not know his hand, or know his Lazyness so much better that the last might tempt you to doubt of the first' (f. 111v). Consistently with Hervey's humorous abuse of Stephen, the copy contains some misspellings and crossings-out and is only loosely punctuated, with most end-of-line stops absent. 'Parson F[or]d's Epitaph', which is in a different hand, is more carefully spelt and punctuated. It is not represented here as a separate poem because it is virtually the same one, the alterations from the original being relatively few. The corrections to both poems, including the numerous additions and changes to the punctuation, are recorded in the List of Emendations. Initial capitalisation has been left unaltered.

## Dr Sherwin's Character design'd for his Epitaph

In figure awkward, Nasty, Short, and Round
In Constitution more than morals sound;
For whilst he travel'd through Life's final stage,
The chearfullness of youth ran on to age.

As to his principles in publick Life,
As his pacific Genius[1] hated Strife,
The King de facto never wanted right,
For him he always talk'd, for none would fight.

Of Ministers his thoughts were much the same
Success determin'd him to praise or blame;
He lay'd no Failing at the prosp'rous door,
But still their merit measur'd by their Pow'r;
Whilst of their sense he judg'd by this short rule:
Who e'er is in, is wise, who out, a Fool.[2]

For his religion, what was bad, or good,
He ne'er considered, car'd, or understood;
Nor others with stale Priestly tales deceived,

1. *Genius*: 'Of persons: Characteristic disposition; inclination; bent, turn or temper of mind' (*OED*).

2. *As to . . . a Fool*: In these ten lines Hervey draws on the characteristics of the vicar of Bray, the subject of a song that dates from about 1720 and was popular in the period. Its chorus is: 'This is the law, I will maintain, Until my dying day, Sir, That whatsoever King may reign, Still I'll be the Vicar of Bray, Sir' (*OED* 'vicar').

But still as little taught as he beleiv'd;
By trade a Churchman, he receiv'd the pay,
And with his 'prentice left his flock to pray.[3]

For his morality 'twixt Man and Man
He was unhang'd:[4] 'Tis saying all I can:
For as Pandora's box[5] was fam'd of old
The seeds of ev'ry corp'ral ill to hold,
So in this precious caskett you might find
Th'accumulated ill of ev'ry Mind.
Of such an abject, ranc'rous, sordid[6] Soul
He ly'd, he cheated, he defam'd, he stole.
In short he practis'd every vice he could,
But oft bewailing his too virtuous Blood,
His vigour not obedient to his taste,
The Baudy[7] Wretch was impotently chast.

As far as Smiles and flatt'ry recommend,
He was to ev'ry man an equal friend:
As far as Slander Enmity can show
He was to ev'ry man an equal Foe.
His Memory a faithfull Record bore
Of evry titled Rogue, or Splendid whore,
Either in ancient or in modern times,
In the Historian's prose or Poet's Rhymes;
And if from his authority he swerv'd,
Twas only when his subject praise deserv'd.

3. *For his religion . . . pray*: the Anglican Church in the eighteenth century was notorious for abuses such as absentee parsons, the ''prentice' being a curate; benefices were often passed on through patronage, and the ministry was treated as little more than a source of income. See John Walsh, Colin Haydon and Stephen Taylor (eds.), *The Church of England c. 1689–c. 1833: From Toleration to Tractarianism* (Cambridge: Cambridge University Press, 2002).

4. *He was unhang'd*: proverbial.

5. *Pandora's box*: according to Greek myth, a container that was always to be kept shut, but that, when Pandora's curiosity led her to open it, released all kinds of evil into the world.

6. *sordid*: 'Of a coarse, gross, or inferior character or nature; befitting or appertaining to a mean person or thing; menial' (*OED*).

7. *Baudy*: an earlier spelling for 'bawdy', by the eighteenth century virtually obsolete.

The Great and Present, Sober he rever'd,
The Absent and the dead he never spar'd;
And when carousing, like some pamper'd Monk,
The holy Glutton, reverendly drunk,
Indulg'd in merriment, without control,
The Nat'ral Bent[8] of his injurious Soul;
All fared alike, and through the gen'ral Feast
He'd call around in some abusive Jest
The Coward, Knave, or Fool to ev'ry Guest;
But all alternate hurt, alternate laugh,
Offence so universal kept him safe;
Whilst by the Curse and Mercy of his fate
Condemn'd to ridicule, he's sav'd from Hate.

Thus liv'd this scurrilous, this worthless Priest,
At once despis'd, sought, slighted and caress'd.

8. *Bent*: 'Mental inclination or tendency; disposition; propensity, bias' (*OED*).

# 24 The Difference between Verbal and Practical Virtue Exemplify'd

***Source.*** *The Difference between Verbal and Practical Virtue Exemplify'd, In some Eminent Instances both Ancient and Modern. With a Prefatory Epistle from Mr. C—b—r to Mr. P.* (London: for J. Roberts, 1742).

***Complementary sources.*** None has come to light, manuscript or printed, though a facsimile of the pamphlet was reprinted along with one of the anonymous *Scribleriad* and an introduction by A. J. Sambrook as no. 125 in the Augustan Reprint Series (William Andrews Clark Memorial Library, University of California, 1967).

***Attribution.*** Horace Walpole, *Royal and Noble Authors*, II, 141; Foxon H156.

***Context and date.*** *The Difference between Verbal and Practical Virtue* is a companion piece to a prose pamphlet by Hervey, *A Letter to Mr. C—b—r. On his Letter to Mr. P—*. The two were published within a few days of each other, the prose attack being first advertised in the *London Evening-Post* for 19–21 August 1742 (issue 2306), the verse in the same newspaper for 12–14 August (issue 2303), though according to Foxon the latter's publication date was 24 August. As the title of his prose pamphlet indicates, Hervey was joining a controversy that Cibber had started, in his *Letter from Mr. Cibber, To Mr. Pope*, first advertised as published at the start of the month (*Champion, or Evening Advertiser*, 31 July; *London Evening-Post*, 3–5 August). In his letter Cibber claimed that, despite clashes with Pope in the past, he had shown forbearance for many years while Pope had not. He was therefore taking up the cudgels again. Hervey and Pope also had a history of reciprocal hostilities. The most notable of these on Hervey's part were *To the Imitator of the First Satire of the Second Book of Horace* (Poem 22) and (to use its published title) *An Epistle from a Nobleman to a Doctor of Divinity* (otherwise, *To Dr Sherwin*, Poem 18), on Pope's passage on Sporus in *An Epistle to Dr. Arbuthnot* in 1735, to which Hervey had not responded (see Poem 18 and its headnote). When Hervey returned to the fray several years later, it was in the enforced leisure of his dismissal from office as Lord Privy Seal and his effectual withdrawal from court. A further context is his interest in classical literature and history, shown for instance by the advice he had given the Cambridge scholar Conyers Middleton on his *History of the Life of Cicero* and by the correspondence between the two later published as *Letters between Lord Hervey and Dr. Middleton Concerning the Roman Senate* (London: for W. Strahan and T. Cadell, 1778). Perhaps because of the strength of that interest, the poem is markedly more effective in its first part, when it deals with classical writers, than in its second, where its attack on Pope stays largely at the level of stale generalities except where it descends to physical abuse. It should be borne in mind, however, that the first half of the poem, especially the long section dealing with Horace, is also an integral part of the satire on Pope. As A. J. Sambrook remarks, 'the attack on Horace is well conceived for Hervey's purpose and calculated to damage Pope who was in so many eyes, including his own, the modern heir of that ancient poet' (*Scribleriad*, p. i). Especially in his *Imitations of Horace*, Pope had defined himself in Horatian terms as the poet of honest retirement. Hervey seeks to undermine that image by drawing attention to the less attractive parts of Horace's history. He even goes so far as to insinuate, through his emphasis on what he presents as Horace's choice of might over right in capitulating to Octavian and accepting patronage from him as the Emperor Augustus, that the values of political independence boasted by Pope in his alliance with the so-called Patriot Opposition were empty.[1] More generally, the poem reflects the hard-headed, even cynical, attitudes that Hervey had developed during his time at court and that he expresses so often in his memoirs. While its focus is on the discord between the professed values and the actual behaviour of several Roman writers on the one hand and those he attributes to Pope on the other, it registers a more general unillusionment.

***Textual commentary.*** Although the prefatory letter is presented as 'from Mr. *C—b—r* to Mr. *P.*', it seems likely that it was written either in collaboration with Cibber or by Hervey alone. The latter seems more probable, for although, as Robert Halsband has pointed out (p. 289), Hervey and Cibber would have known each other personally from the time they had spent at court, Hervey mentions in his *Letter to Mr. C—b—r* that at the time of writing he is at some distance from London (p. 26). For the same reason, it is unlikely that Cibber collaborated on the poem. Indeed, the remark in the preface that he has 'had some Help' with it seems a joke at the expense of the reader who cannot penetrate the haze of humorous obfuscation surrounding the pamphlet's authorship. There being no other source, the Roberts text is used for this edition. It has not required emendation. The poem in Roberts's version includes footnotes labelled alphabetically and keyed at the left-hand edge of the line. These have been presented as numerical footnotes here, but with an asterisk added to the number to emphasise the fact that the note is Hervey's, and the phrase 'Hervey's note' opening its content; when needed, additional commentary is provided after the word 'Translation' or 'Comment', as appropriate.

1. For a discussion of similar critiques of Horace, see Howard D. Weinbrot, *Augustus Caesar in 'Augustan' England: The Decline of a Classical Norm* (Princeton, NJ: Princeton University Press, 1978), chapter 4 'Let Horace Blush, and Virgil Too', pp. 120–49.

# The Difference between Verbal and Practical Virtue Exemplify'd, In some Eminent Instances both Ancient and Modern

Dicendi Virtus, nisi ei, qui dicit, ea, de quibus dicit, percepta sint, extare non potest. Cic.[2]

Sic ulciscar genera singula, quemadmodum à quibus sum provocatus.

Cic. *post Redit. ad Quir.*[3]

*Mr. C—b—r to Mr. P.*

Have at you again, Sir.[4] I gave you fair Warning that I would have the last Word; and by —— (I will not swear in Print) you shall find me no Lyar. I own, I am greatly elate on the Laurels the Town has bestow'd upon me for my Victory over you in my Prose Combat; and, encouraged by that Triumph, I now resolve to fight you on your own Dunghil of Poetry, and with your own jingling Weapons of Rhyme and Metre. I confess I have had some Help; but what then? since the greatest Princes are rather proud than asham'd of Allies and Auxiliaries when they make War in the Field, why should I decline such Assistance when I make War in the Press? And since you thought most unrighteously and unjustly to fall upon me and crush me, only because you imagin'd your Self strong and Me weak, as *France* fell upon the Queen of *Hungary*;[5] if I like her (*si parva licet componere magnis*)[6] by first striking a bold and desperate Stroke myself with a little Success, have encouraged such a Friend to me, as *England*

2. *Dicendi* ... *non potest*: 'For excellence in speaking cannot be made manifest unless the speaker fully comprehends the matter he speaks about' (Cicero, *De Oratore*, I. xi. 48–9 (Loeb, pp. 36–7)); the Loeb text reads *Dicendi enim virtus, nisi ei, qui dicit, ea, de quibus dicit, percepta sint, exstare non potest*.

3. *Sic ulciscar* ... *ad Quir*: 'This being so, the requital I shall exact for their several crimes shall be accommodated to the provocation I have received from each class' (Cicero, *Post Reditum ad Quirites*, ix. 21 (Loeb, pp. 126–7)); the Loeb text reads *sic ulciscar facinora singula, quem ad modum a quibusque sum provocatus*.

4. *Have* ... *Sir*: referring to *Letter from Mr. Cibber*, published a few weeks before.

5. *France* ... *Hungary*: referring to hostilities begun by France among other countries against Maria Theresa of Austria shortly after her accession in 1740 as ruler of the Habsburg dominions.

6. *si parva* ... *magnis*: 'if we may compare small things with great' (Virgil, *Georgics*, IV. 176 (*Eclogues*, Loeb, pp. 208–9)).

has been to her, to espouse my Cause, and turn all the Weight of the War upon you, till you wish you had never begun it; with what reasonable and equitable Pleasure may I not pursue my Blow till I make you repent, by laying you on your Back, the ungrateful Returns you have made me for saving you from Destruction when you laid yourself on your Belly.[7] I am, Sir, not your humble, but your devoted Servant; for I will follow you as long as I live; and as *Terence* says in the *Eunuch, Ego pol te pro istis dictis et factis, scelus, ulciscar, ut ne impune in nos illus eris.*[8]

What awkard Judgments must they make of Men,
Who think their Hearts are pictur'd by their Pen;
That *this* observes the Rules which *that* approves,
And what one praises, that the other loves.
Few Authors tread the Paths they recommend,
Or when they shew the Road, pursue the End:
Few give Examples, whilst they give Advice,
Or tho' they scourge the vicious, shun the Vice;
But lash the Times as Swimmers do the Tide,
And kick and cuff the Stream on which they ride.

His tuneful Lyre when polish'd *Horace* strung,
And all the Sweets of calm Retirement sung,[9]*
In Practice still his courtly Conduct show'd
His Joy was Luxury, and Power his God;
With great *Mæcenas*[10] meanly proud to dine,[11]*

7. *saving . . . Belly*: an allusion to the most scandalous charge in Cibber's letter, in which he had told a story of going with Pope to a brothel and surprising him on top of a prostitute.

8. *Ego . . . eris*: 'I'll punish you, rascal, for what you've done and said, that you mayn't get off for nothing after befooling us' (Terence, *The Eunuch*, 5. 941–2 (Loeb, pp. 332–3)).

9. *Hervey's note*: 'Beatus ille qui procul negotiis, &c. Epod. 2. Cum magnis vixisse invita satebitur usque invidia. *Sat. 1. Lib. 2.*' *Translation*: 'Happy the man who, far from business concerns' (Horace, Epode II. 1 (*Odes and Epodes*, Loeb, ed. by Niall Rudd, pp. 272–3)); and 'Envy, in spite of herself, will ever admit that I have lived with the great' (Horace, *Satires*, I. ii. 76–7 (*Satires, Epistles and Ars Poetica*, Loeb, pp. 132–3)).

10. *Mæcenas*: Gaius Cilnius Maecenas (70–8 BCE) was a wealthy Roman, important for his advice to Augustus before and after he became Emperor and as a generous patron.

11. *Hervey's note*: 'Nunc quia Mæcenas tibi sum convictor. *Sat. 6. Lib. 1.*
—Tu pulses omne quod obstat
Ad Mæcenatem memori si mente recurras.
Hoc juvat, & melli est; ne mentiar. *Sat. 6. Lib. 2.*'

And fond to load *Augustus* flatter'd Shrine;[12*]
And whilst he rail'd at *Menas* ill-got Sway,[13*]
His numerous Train[14*] that choak'd the *Appian* Way,[15]
His Talents still to Perfidy apply'd,
Three Times a Friend and Foe to either Side.
*Horace* forgot, or hop'd his Readers would,
His Safety on the same Foundation stood.[16*]
That he who once had own'd his Country's Cause,
Now kiss'd the Feet that trampled on her Laws:
That till the Havock of *Philippi*'s Field,
Where Right to Force, by Fate was taught to yield,
He follow'd *Brutus*, and then hail'd the Sword,

*Translation*: 'now, because I consort with you, Maecenas' (Horace, *Satires*, I. vi. 47 (*Satires, Epistles and Ars Poetica*, Loeb, pp. 80–1)); 'You would jostle everything in your way, should you be posting back to Maecenas, thinking only of him. That gives great pleasure and is like honey, I'll not deny' (Horace, *Satires*, II. vi. 30–2 (Loeb, *Satires, Epistles and Ars Poetica*, pp. 212–13)).

12. *Hervey's note*: 'All his Works are full of Examples of Flattery to *Augustus*.' *Comment*: Hervey's charge is that Horace flattered Augustus in return for patronage.

13. *Hervey's note*: 'Epod. 4. *Mænas* was a Freedman of *Pompey* the younger; and he deserted from him to *Augustus*, then back from *Augustus* to *Pompey*, and then from *Pompey* to *Augustus* again. This is in all the Histories. *Appian. Dion*.' *Comment*: Horace's Epode 4 was thought to refer to Menodorus or Menas, a pirate who originally joined the forces of the younger Pompeius Sextus but repeatedly changed sides; Appian of Alexandria (c. 95–165 CE) and Lucius Cassius Dio Cocceianus, known in English as Cassius Dio, Dio Cassius or Dio, but in earlier times as Dion (c. 150–235 CE), were the best-known historians writing about Horace's Rome.

14. *Hervey's note*: 'Et Appiam mannis terit. *Epod. 4*.' *Translation*: 'wears down the Appian Way with his ponies' (Horace, IV. 14 (*Odes and Epodes*, ed. by Niall Rudd, Loeb, pp. 280–1)).

15. *the Appian Way*: named after Appius Claudius Caecus, who completed the first part of it in 312 BCE, the Appian Way was one of the earliest and strategically most important roads of ancient Rome, connecting the capital with Brundisium (Brindisi) in the south-east.

16. *Hervey's note*:

'O sæpe mecum tempus in ultimum
Deducte, Bruto militiæ Duce.——
Tecum Philippos & celerem fugam
Sensi, relictâ non bene parmulâ
Cum fracta virtus, & minaces
Turpe solum tetigere mento. Hor. *Ode. 7. B. 2*.'

*Translation:* 'My friend, so often carried with me into moments of the utmost peril when Brutus was in charge of operations . . . With you beside me I experienced Philippi and its headlong rout, leaving my little shield behind without much credit, when valour was broken and threatening warriors ignominiously bit the dust' (Horace, *Odes*, II. vii. 1–2, 9–12 (*Horace: Odes and Epodes*, pp. 108–11)).

Which gave Mankind, whom *Brutus* freed, a Lord:
Nor to the Guilt of a Deserter's Name,
Like *Menas* great (tho' with dishonest Fame)
Added the Glory, tho' he shar'd the Shame.[17]
For whilst with Fleets and Armies *Menas* warr'd,
Courage his Leader, Policy his Guard,
Poor *Horace* only follow'd with a Verse
That Fate the Freedman balanc'd, to rehearse;[18]
Singing the Victor for whom *Menas* fought,
And following Triumph which the other brought.

Thus graver *Seneca*,[19] in canting Strains,[20]*

17. *His Talents ... the Shame*: these thirteen lines sum up and comment further upon Horace's service in the army of Brutus and Cassius, defeated by Octavian at Philippi in 42 BCE.

18. *For whilst ... to rehearse*: the contrast is between the military leader Menas who went to war with fleets and armies, led by bravery and strategy, and Horace with his sole weapon of poetry; 'Fate the Freedman' may glance at the fact Horace's father was for part of his life a slave, while asserting that destiny is the only truly free agent.

19. *graver Seneca*: Lucius Annaeus Seneca (c. 4 BCE–65 CE) was a Roman Stoic philosopher, statesman and dramatist, notable for the seriousness of his outlook.

20. *Hervey's note:*

> In his Seneca reus factus est multorum scelerum, sed præsertim quod cum Agrippinâ rem haberet, nec enim in hâc re solum, sed in plerisque aliis contra facere visus est quam Philosophabatur. Quum enim Tyrannidem improbaret, Tyranni præceptor erat: quumque insultaret iis qui cum principibus versarentur, ipse à Palatio non discedebat. Assentatores detestabatur, quum ipse Reginas coleret & libertos, ac Laudationes quorundam componeret. Reprehendebat divites is, cujus facultates erant ter millies sestertium: quique luxum aliorum damnabat quingentes tripodas habuit de ligno cedrino, pedibus eburneis, similes & pares inter se, in quibus cœnabat. Ex quibus omnibus ea quæ sunt his consentanea, quæque ipse libidinose fecit, facile intelligi possunt. Nuptias enim cum nobilissimâ atque illustrissimâ fœminâ contraxit. Delectabatur exoletis, idque Neronem facere docuerat etsi antea tanta fuerat in morum severitate ut ab eo peteret, ne se oscularetur, neve una secum cœnandi causa discumberet. Vid. Dion. Excerpta per Xiphilinum, Lib. 61.

*Translation from Cassius Dio:*

> Seneca now found himself under accusation, one of the charges against him being that he was intimate with Agrippina. It had not been enough for him, it seems, to commit adultery with Julia, nor had he become wiser as a result of his banishment, but he must establish improper relations with Agrippina, in spite of the kind of woman she was and the kind of son she had. Nor was this the only instance in which his conduct was seen to be diametrically opposed to the teachings of his philosophy. For while denouncing tyranny, he was making

Talk'd of fair Virtue's Charms and Vice's Stains,
And said the happy were the chaste and poor;
Whilst plunder'd Provinces supply'd his Store,
And *Rome*'s Imperial Mistress[21] was his Whore.
But tho' he rail'd at Flattery's dangerous Smile,
A *Claudius*, and a *Nero*,[22] all the while,
With every Vice that reigns in Youth or Age,
The Gilding of his venal Pen engage,
And fill the slavish Fable of each Page.

See *Sallust*[23] too, whose Energy divine
Lashes a vicious Age in ev'ry Line:
With Horror painting the flagitious Times,
The profligate, profuse, rapacious Crimes,
That reign'd in the degenerate Sons of *Rome*,
And made them first deserve, then caus'd their Doom;

himself the teacher of a tyrant; while inveighing against the associates of the powerful, he did not hold aloof from the palace itself; and though he had nothing good to say of flatterers, he himself had constantly fawned upon Messalina and the freedmen of Claudius, to such an extent, in fact, as actually to send them from the island of his exile a book containing their praises – a book that he afterwards suppressed out of shame. Though finding fault with the rich, he himself acquired a fortune of 300,000,000 sesterces; and though he censured the extravagances of others, he had five hundred tables of citrus wood with legs of ivory, all identically alike, and he served banquets on them. In stating thus much I have also made clear what naturally went with it – the licentiousness in which he indulged at the very time that he contracted a most brilliant marriage, and the delight that he took in boys past their prime, a practice which he also taught Nero to follow. And yet earlier he had been of such austere habits that he had asked his pupil to excuse him from kissing him or eating at the same table with him. For the latter request he had a fairly good excuse, namely, that he wished to carry on his philosophical studies at leisure without being interrupted by the young man's dinners. (Cassius Dio, *Roman History*, LXI (Loeb VIII, 55–9))

21. *Rome's Imperial Mistress*: Seneca was convicted of adultery with Julia Livilla (18–41/42 CE), the youngest child of Germanicus and Agrippina the Elder and the youngest sister of the Emperor Caligula, and exiled to Corsica. He was also accused by Publius Sullius Rufus of having an affair with the Empress Julia Agrippina (15–59 CE), her sister.

22. *A Claudius, and a Nero*: Tiberius Claudius Nero Germanicus (10 BCE–54 CE) was Emperor of Rome from 41 CE until his death, and was succeeded by Nero Claudius Caesar (37–68 CE).

23. *Sallust*: Gaius Sallustius Crispus (86–c. 35 BCE) was a Roman historian and politician who extracted great wealth from his governorship of Africa.

With all the Merit of his virtuous Pen,
Leagu'd with the worst of these corrupted Men;
The Day in Riot and Excess to waste,
The Night in Taverns and in Brothels past:
And when the *Censors*,[24] by their high Controll,[25*]
Struck him, indignant, from the *Senate*'s Roll,
From Justice he appeal'd to *Cæsar*'s Sword,
And by Law exil'd, was by Force restor'd.[26*]
What follow'd let *Numidia*'s Sons[27] declare,[28*]
Harrass'd in Peace with Ills surpassing War;
Each Purse by Peculate and Rapine drain'd,

24. *the Censors*: In 50 BCE, the censor Appius Claudius Pulcher removed Sallust from the Senate for gross immorality, though the real reason may have been political; it was probably through Caesar's influence that he was reinstated in the following year; the Censors were officials in ancient Rome who were responsible for public morality and some aspects of government finance, and for carrying out the census of citizens.

25. *Hervey's note*: 'Collegæ tamen, multos Nobilium, atque inter eos Crispum etiam Sallustium, eum, qui historiam conscripsit, Senatu ejicienti non repugnavit. Dion. *Lib. 40*.' *Translation*: '[Lucius Piso] however did not resist Claudius when he drove from the senate all the freedmen and numbers even of the exclusive nobility, among them Sallustius Crispus, who wrote the history' (Cassius Dio, *Roman History*, XL (Loeb, III), 503–4)).

26. *Hervey's note*: 'Ab his Sallustius (qui ut Senatoriam dignitatem recupararet tum Prætor factus erat) propemodum occisus. Dion. *Lib. 42*.' *Translation*: 'These nearly killed Sallust, who had been appointed praetor in order to recover his senatorial rank' (Cassius Dio, *Roman History*, XLII (Loeb, IV, p. 197)).

27. *Numidia's Sons*: the inhabitants of Numidia, plundered by Sallust while he was imperial governor; a similar charge is made with '*Africk* Slaves' in line 66.

28. *Hervey's note*:

> Numidas quoque in suam potestatem Cæsar accepit, iisque Sallustium præfecit. Sallustius & pecuniæ captæ & compilatæ provinciæ accusatus, summam infamiam reportavit, quod quum ejusmodi libros composuisset, in quibus multis acerbisque verbis eos, qui ex provinciis quæstum facerent, notasset, nequaquam suis scriptis in agendo stetisset. Itaque etsi à Cæsare absolutus fuit, tamen suis ipsius verbis proprium crimen abunde quasi in tabulâ propositum divulgavit. Dion. *L. 43*.

*Translation from Cassius Dio*:

> taking over the Numidians, he reduced them to the status of subjects, and delivered them to Sallust, nominally to rule, but really to harry and plunder. At all events this officer took many bribes and confiscated much property, so that he was not only accused but incurred the deepest disgrace, inasmuch as after writing such treatises as he had, and making many bitter remarks about those who fleeced others, he did not practice what he preached. Therefore, even if he was completely exonerated by Caesar, yet in his history, as upon a tablet, the man himself has chiselled his own condemnation all too well. (Cassius Dio, *Roman History*, XLLII (Loeb, IV, p. 225))

Each House by Murder and Adult'ries stain'd:
Till *Africk* Slaves, gall'd by the Chains of *Rome*,
Wish'd their own Tyrants as a milder Doom.

If then we turn our Eyes from Words to Fact,
Comparing how Men write, with how they act,
How many Authors of this Contrast kind
In ev'ry Age, and ev'ry Clime we find.
Thus scribbling *P*— who *Peter*[29] never spares,
Feeds on extortious Interest from young Heirs:[30]
And whilst he made Old *S—lkerk*'s Bows[31] his Sport,
Dawb'd[32] minor Courtiers, of a minor Court.
If *Sallust, Horace, Seneca*, and *He*
Thus in their Morals then so well agree;
By what Ingredient is the Difference known?
The Difference only in their Wit is shown,
For all their Cant and Falshood is his own.
He rails at Lies, and yet for half a Crown,
Coins and disperses Lies thro' all the Town:
Of his own Crimes the Innocent accuses,
And those who clubb'd to make him eat, abuses.
But whilst such Features in his Works we trace,
And Gifts like these his happy Genius grace;

29. *Peter*: Peter Walter (1664?–1746), a moneylender satirised frequently by Pope in his later work, and usually under his first name: see *First Satire of the Second Book of Horace*, lines 3, 40, 89; *Second Satire of Dr. Donne*, lines 74, 80; *Epilogue to the Satires. Dialogue I*, lines 10, 121–2; *Epilogue to the Satires. Dialogue II*, 57–8; and also Howard Erskine-Hill's account in the second part of his *The Social Milieu of Alexander Pope: Lives, Examples, and the Poetic Response* (New Haven: Yale University Press, 1975).

30. *extortious ... Heirs*: Pope had annuities from the estate of the young Duke of Buckingham (1716–35), but the Duke's mother declined further arrangements before his majority (Pope, *Correspondence*, II, 525, on November 1728); Hervey was her executor.

31. *Old S—lkerk's Bows*: Charles Douglas (*né* Hamilton), second Earl of Selkirk (1663–1739), who had been Lord of the Bedchamber to Mary II and William III, 1689–94, to William III, 1694–1702, and to George I and II, 1714–39 (*Complete Peerage*, XI, 616–17), is cited as a master of court etiquette in Hervey's manuscript play 'The Death of Lord Hervey; Or, a Morning at Court' (Sedgwick, II, 593). He is satirised by Pope in *Epilogue to the Satires. Dialogue I*, lines 89–108, and *Dialogue II*, line 61, though Hervey's opinion of him was scarcely more favourable (see Poem 19, 'To the Queen', line 248, and note).

32. *Dawb'd*: 'court[ed] with flattery' (*OED*).

Let none his haggard Face, or Mountain Back,
The Object of mistaken Satire make;
Faults which the best of Men, by Nature curs'd,
May chance to share in common with the worst.
In Vengeance for his Insults on Mankind,
Let those who blame, some truer Blemish find,
And lash that worse Deformity, his Mind.
Like prudent Foes attack some weaker Part,
And make the War upon his Head or Heart.
Prove his late Works dishonest as they're dull;
That try'd by Moral or Poetic Rule,
The Verdict must be either Knave or Fool.
Whilst his false *English*, and false Facts combin'd,[33*]
Betray the double Darkness of his Mind;
That Mind so suited to its vile Abode,[34*]
The Temple so adapted to the God,
It seems the Counterpart by Heav'n design'd
A Symbol and a Warning to Mankind:
As at some Door we find hung out a Sign,
Type[35] of the Monster to be found within.[36]
From his own Words this Scoundrel let 'em prove
Unjust in Hate, incapable of Love;
For all the Taste he ever has of Joy,
Is like some yelping Mungril to annoy
And teaze that Passenger he can't destroy.
To cast a Shadow o'er the spotless Fame,
Or dye the Cheek of Innocence with Shame;

33. *Hervey's note*: 'See at least a hundred and fifty Places in his late Works.'

34. *Hervey's note*: 'In quo deformitas corporis cum turpitudine certabat ingenii; adeo ut animus eius dignissimo domicilio inclusus videretur. Vel. Pat. *L. 2. B. 69*.' *Translation*: 'whose deformity of body was rivalled to such an extent by the baseness of his character, that his spirit seemed to be housed in an abode that was thoroughly worthy of it' (Velleius Paterculus, *Compendium of Roman History*, II. lxix. 4 (Loeb, pp. 198–9)).

35. *Type*: 'That by which something is symbolized or figured; anything having a symbolical signification; a symbol, emblem' (*OED*).

36. *It seems . . . within*: as Isobel Grundy notes ('Verse of Lady Mary Wortley Montagu', p. 519), a similar charge appears in Poem 22, *To the Imitator of the First Satire of the Second Book of Horace*, lines 22–6: '*Thine* is just such an Image of his Pen, | As Thou thyself art of the Sons of Men; | Where our own Species in Burlesque we trace, | A Sign-Post Likeness of the noble Race, | That is at once Resemblance and Disgrace'.

To swell the Breast of Modesty with Care,
Or force from Beauty's Eye a secret Tear;
And, not by Decency or Honour sway'd,
Libel the Living, and asperse the Dead:
Prone where he ne'er receiv'd to give Offence,
But most averse to Merit and to Sense;
Base to his Foe, but baser to his Friend,
Lying to blame, and sneering to commend:
Defaming those whom all but he must love,
And praising those whom none but he approve.
Then let him boast that honourable Crime,
Of making those who fear not God, fear him;[37]
When the great Honour of the Boast is such
That Hornets and Mad Dogs may boast as much.
Such is th'Injustice of his daily Theme,
And such the Lust that breaks his nightly Dream;[38]
That vestal Fire of undecaying Hate,
Which Time's cold Tide itself can ne'er abate,
But like *Domitian*, with a murd'rous Will,
Rather than nothing, Flies he likes to kill.[39]
And in his Closet stabs some obscure Name,
Brought by this Hangman first to Light and Shame.[40*]
Such now his Works to all the World are known,
Who undeceiv'd, their former Error own;
Whilst not one Man who likes his rhyming Art,
Allows him Genius, or defends his Heart:[41]

37. *Of making . . . him*: alluding to Pope's declaration 'Yes, I am proud; I must be proud to see | Men not afraid of God, afraid of me' (*Epilogue to the Satires. Dialogue II*, lines 208–9).

38. *And such . . . Dream*: Grundy ('Verse of Lady Mary Wortley Montagu', p. 520) notes the similar idea in Poem 22, *To the Imitator*, lines 32–3: ''Tis the gross *Lust* of Hate that still annoys, | Without Distinction, as gross Love enjoys'.

39. *But like Domitian . . . kill*: Titus Flavius Caesar Domitianus Augustus (51–96 CE), Emperor of Rome (81–96 CE), of whom Suetonius records: 'At the beginning of his reign he used to spend hours in seclusion every day, doing nothing but catch flies and stab them with a keenly-sharpened stylus' (Suetonius, *Lives*, II. 325).

40. *Hervey's note*: 'See the Dunciad.'

41. *Whilst not . . . his Heart*: Grundy ('Verse of Lady Mary Wortley Montagu', p. 525) notes the similarity in thought and expression with Poem 22, *To the Imitator*, lines 89–90: 'Those who thy *Nature* loath'd, yet lov'd thy *Art*; | Who lik'd thy *head*, and yet abhorr'd thy *Heart*.'

But thus from Triumph snatch'd, and giv'n to Shame
Lash'd *into* Penitence, and *out* of Fame.
Since all Mankind these certain Truths allow,
And speak so freely what so well they know;
No wonder doom'd such Treatment to receive,
That he *can* feel, and that he *can't* forgive.
Were I dispos'd to curse the Man I hate,
Such would I wish his miserable Fate.
Thus striving to inflict, to meet Disgrace,
And wasted to the Ghost of what he was;
And like all Ghosts which Men of Sense despise,
Only the Dread of Folly's coward Eyes.
Thus would I have him despicably live,
Himself, his Friends, and Credit to survive,
Into Contempt from Reputation hurl'd,
His own Detractor thro' a scoffing World.[42]

42. *Thus would . . . scoffing World*: Hervey put an earlier version of these lines into a letter to Francesco Algarotti dated 30 October 1736: 'Were I to curse my Foe I'd have him live, | Him-self, his Friends, and Credit to survive: | Into Contempt from Reputation hurl'd, | His own Defamer to the scoffing World'. He added: 'But I forget my-self and instead of giving you a good Opinion of other People's Verses, I am giving you a bad one of my own', perhaps suggesting that the lines had already been written (John Murray Archive, Letter 5, f. 3v; copy in SRO, 941/47/4, p. 587).

# POLITICAL

# 25 The Barber Turn'd Packer. To the Tune of *Packington's Pound*

***Source.*** *The Barber Turn'd* Packer. *A New Ballad. To the Tune of* Packington's *Pound* (London: for A. Moore, 1730). The imprint is fictitious. No other contemporary sources, print or manuscript, are known, but the full text is given in Percival, pp. 29–30.

***Attribution.*** Percival, pp. lii–liii; Urstad, pp. 115, 266, n. 58. The case for Hervey's authorship is strong. Percival asks the relevant question 'Who but Lord Hervey could have done it?', pointing out that 'Wits were not plentiful on the side of the Ministry' (p. lii). He also draws attention to what he rightly calls 'a striking similarity between one stanza of the ballad and a passage in a pamphlet entitled *Observations on the Writings of the Craftsman*', written by Hervey and first published at the end of October 1730 (London: for J. Roberts; advertised as 'just published' in *Daily Journal*, 31 October 1730). The nub of his argument is that, although imputing Jacobitism to the opposition was nothing new, the terms in which the imputation is couched in ballad and pamphlet are very similar. Both allege that, the tactic of flattering the King and abusing his best friends having failed, the writers of *The Craftsman* resolved 'openly to attack even that sacred person, which hitherto they had only dared obliquely to touch, and collaterally to glance at' (*Observations*, p. 18), or, as the ballad more pithily puts it, to act on the recognition that 'he shaves the best, who *cuts close* to the *Crown*' (line 25).

***Context and date.*** The ballad must have been composed between 3 December 1729, when the trial to which it refers took place, and 8 January 1730, when, according to the *Monthly Chronicle*, it was published (Percival, pp. 26, 29; Foxon B65). Because it refers to 'the Year twenty-nine' (line 58), a date in the second half of December 1729 is most likely. As Percival states, the trial was of 'Richard Francklin, publisher of *The Craftsman*, for publishing a libel', and he quotes the offending passage (p. 25). The charge was brought by the Government in an attempt to frustrate the damaging campaign against its foreign policy and alleged domestic corruption run by the newspaper and its opposition backers. It failed, and nine days later, in celebration of the verdict of innocent, a ballad by William Pulteney appeared entitled 'The Honest Jury; Or, Caleb Triumphant'. 'The Barber Turn'd Packer' is a pro-Government response alleging that John Barber, 'the sheriff who had direction of the panel' (Percival, p. 29), had packed the jury with members who could be relied upon to find Francklin innocent. According to Percival, Barber 'was a noted Jacobite, and had been intimate with Bolingbroke and his clique as long ago as the late years of Queen Anne. These facts lent colour, if not truth, to the losers' allegations' (p. 29). Pulteney had been a friend and political ally of Hervey's, but the two had grown apart. If, as seems likely, it was Hervey who wrote the poem, he was showing that he could match, even surpass, his former comrade in political and literary wit. In contrast to Pulteney's ballad, which is a lively, hearty, rollicking performance that became 'one of the best-known political ballads of the century' (Percival, p. 26), *The Barber Turn'd Packer* works more at the level of clever political word-play. It is full of apt puns, starting with its title, and, as the emphasis on the first syllable of 'Packington' in line 9 makes clear, including the tune to which it is set.

***Textual commentary.*** As the text is printed clearly, and as there is no other source, no emendations have been necessary.

## The Barber Turn'd *Packer*.[1] A New Ballad. To the TUNE of *Packington*'s Pound.[2]

I.

No Writer of Scandal doth *Caleb*[3] excell,
Nor his Printer[4] in *packing* that Scandal up well,
Tho' hard of two *Packers* to say which is best,
Yet one's a clean *Shaver*[5] it must be confest;
He truly can crack
He scorns to *pack*
A Jury, to lay *Caleb* flat on his Back;
His Jury, like him, are so loyal and sound,
They'll go to no Tune but of *Pack*-ington's Pound.

1. *Barber Turn'd Packer*: John Barber (*bap.* 1675, *d.* 1741), was a printer who made 'an apparent profit of £30,000' in South Sea speculation that enabled him to retire from his profession and 'focus his energies on civic politics' (*ODNB*). A 'Packer' is one who packs a jury to obtain a favourable verdict.

2. *Packington's Pound*: an Elizabethan tune that was very popular from the seventeenth until at least the middle of the eighteenth century and that had featured the year before as Air 43, 'Thus gamesters united', in John Gay's *The Beggar's Opera.*

3. *Caleb*: Caleb D'Anvers, pseudonym for Nicholas Amherst, who ran the leading opposition newspaper *The Craftsman.*

4. *his Printer*: Richard Francklin, printer of *The Craftsman* and plaintiff in the trial.

5. *Shaver*: the first of the many puns in the ballad, an obvious reference to Barber's surname, and also an allusion to the slang meanings, 'One who pillages or plunders; an extortioner', or 'Fellow, chap, joker' (*OED*).

II.

When the Tryal came on, this *Shaver* addrest
Brother Printer, whose Ears[6] would allow him no Rest;
Quoth he,[7] Tho' 'twere Treason, you're safe, I assure ye,
King GEORGE makes the Judges, but who makes the Jury?
    Away with your Dumps,
    I, and honest Friend *Numps*,[8]
Will stand by the *Jacobite* Cause to the Stumps,
Nor for being its Friend, think yourself an Offender;
For I am not hang'd, who kiss'd Hand of *Pretender.*[9]

III.

When you flatter'd King GEORGE, yet abus'd his best Friends,
You saw by Experience you ne'er got your Ends.
Now you so out-do us, Affairs must go swimming,
Small Gain's to be gotten, dear *Caleb*, by *trimming.*[10]
    No Barber's Renown
    Is to shave Beard of Downe,
But he shaves the best, who *cuts close* to the *Crown*;[11]

6. *Ears*: reference to one of the possible punishments that Francklin might have received if found guilty, the cutting off or mutilation of one or both ears.

7. *Quoth he*: the words introduce the Jacobite prophecy that the writer puts into Barber's mouth and that occupies the rest of the poem up to its final stanza, using the same technique as the famous anti-Jacobite ballad 'Lillibullero' a generation before of ridiculing the enemy through their own words.

8. *Numps*: Percival notes: 'Humphrey Parsons (familiarly called "Numps") was brewer, alderman, M.P., and (after this date) twice Lord Mayor. He was a Jacobite' (p. 29). He was born in about 1676 and died in 1741 (*ODNB*).

9. *Pretender*: Percival notes: 'Barber had recently returned from Italy, where he had had an interview with the Pretender' (p. 29). 'In 1722 he was implicated in the Atterbury plot (an attempt to restore James Stuart to the throne) following Barber's departure in April for Rome bearing £50,000 in bills of exchange. Never formally accused or punished for this, he was nevertheless unable to return to England until August 1724' (*ODNB*).

10. *trimming*: 'To modify one's attitude in order to stand well with opposite parties; to move cautiously, or "balance" between two alternative interests, positions, opinions, etc.; also, to accommodate oneself to the mood of the times' (*OED*).

11. *cuts close to the Crown*: one of the poem's more mischievous puns.

And *Jemmy*[12] shall own, without any Bravado,
No *Jacobite* serves him like one Renegado.[13]

IV.

If *Lilly-Burlero* help'd turn out the Sire,[14]
Who knows but a Ballad may help in the 'Squire;[15]
And all he has lost (by *Whigg*-Judges undone)
By Twelve of *Our Peers*[16] again may be won.
Then a loyal new Catch[17]
Brother Printer shall fetch,
Alive with both Ears, from the Hands of *Jack Ketch*.[18]
Nor shall these Twelve Peers be byass'd by Pelf,[19]
They're *Jemmy*'s without it, as much as myself.

V.

Now Caleb's good Friends, a politick Crew,
Are all thorough Statesmen and Patriots true;
As plain all may read in the fine Things he writes,

12. *Jemmy*: James Stuart, the Pretender.

13. *Renegado*: Henry St John, 1st Viscount Bolingbroke (1678–1751), who had fled to France in 1715 on account of his known Jacobite sympathies and who did not return until ten years later (*ODNB*).

14. *If Lilly-Burlero . . . Sire*: referring to a political ballad to the tune of 'Lillibullero' that satirised Jacobite supporters and helped oust James II (father, 'the Sire', to James Stuart).

15. *the 'Squire*: either James Stuart or William Pulteney, in the latter case as successor to Walpole.

16. *Our Peers*: 'The point is that "our peers", the jurymen, were very "low" people' (Percival, p. 30). Chapter 29 of Magna Carta states: 'No Freeman shall be taken or imprisoned, or be disseised of his Freehold, or Liberties, or free Customs, or be outlawed, or exiled, or any other wise destroyed; nor will We not pass upon him, nor condemn him, but by lawful judgment of his Peers, or by the Law of the Land' (www.legislation.gov.uk/aep/Edw1cc1929/25/9/section/XXIX); in this sense, the word means 'equal' (*OED*).

17. *Catch*: 'Originally, a short composition for three or more voices, which sing the same melody, the second singer beginning the first line as the first goes on to the second line, and so with each successive singer' (*OED*).

18. *Jack Ketch*: the hangman (*OED ketch*).

19. *Pelf*: 'Chiefly *depreciative*. Money, riches (esp. viewed as a corrupting influence); lucre' (*OED*). In other words, the jurymen cannot be bribed; as the next line states, they can be relied upon as loyal Jacobites.

When the 'Squire or the Doctor[20] so learned indites.[21]
Who then without Fees
His Brain he doth squeeze,
To prove that the Moon it is made of green Cheese.
Those wholesome Prescriptions he writes not for Rhino,[22]
But waits his Reward from *Jure Divino*.[23]

VI.

Then *D'Anvers* shall rhime, and the Doctor shall pun,
And *W—e* shall tumble, as sure as a Gun.
Our *Pedlars* in Wit, with new Pannicks shall seize him,
And *Hawkers* of Ballads, by Millions, shall teaze him;
Our Punns he shall meet
In every Street.
The Knight[24] he shall truckle,[25] and *Caleb* be great;
Then *Numps* shall give Strong Beer, and I will give Wine-O,
To christen this Jury a Jury *de Vino*.[26]

VII.

Thus spoke Master *Packer*, and speak thus he may;
But God bless King GEORGE for ever, I say.
Tho' *Duncan*[27] so dumb says *D'Anvers* shall shine,
And conquer his Foes in the Year twenty-nine;

20. *the 'Squire or the Doctor*: 'It seems likely that the Squire is Pulteney, and that the Doctor is Dr. Arbuthnot, who sent an occasional "prescription" to *The Craftsman*. He was a Jacobite in sympathies' (Percival, p. 30).

21. *indites*: 'To put into words, compose (a poem, tale, speech, etc.)' (*OED*).

22. *Rhino*: slang for money (*OED*).

23. *Jure Divino*: by divine right, an allusion to the concept of the supposed divine right of kings maintained by Jacobites; the phrase becomes a kind of refrain at the end of each of the last three stanzas as the poem reaches its climax.

24. *the Knight*: Sir Robert Walpole.

25. *truckle*: 'To submit from an unworthy motive; to yield meanly or obsequiously; to act with servility' (*OED*).

26. *de Vino*: from wine, showing that the writer can match opposition ballads in punning.

27. *Duncan*: Duncan Campbell (c. 1680–1730), soothsayer (*ODNB*), whose gift for 'true *Second-Sight*' had been invoked by Pulteney's ballad (reprinted in Percival, pp. 27–8 [28]).

'Tis nought but a Joke
By Brasen-head[28] spoke,
To keep up the Heart of disconsolate Folk;
For Caleb may wait Years twice twenty-nine-O,
Before he comes in with his *Jure Divino.*

28. *Brasen-head*: not referring to any particular person, but to someone 'Hardened in effrontery; shameless' (*OED*).

# 26 The Journalists Displayed, A New Ballad. To the Old Tune of *Lillebullero*

***Main source.*** *The Journalists Displayed, A New Ballad. To the Old Tune of Lilleburlero* (London: by Peter Wiseacre in the Old Bailey, 1731). The imprint is fictitious.

***Complementary manuscript sources.*** BL Add. MS 51441, ff. 58r–58v; Brotherton Lt 24, ff. 37r–v from back.

***Complementary print sources.*** *The Journalists Displayed. A New Ballad. To the Old Tune of, Lullebullero* (London: for J. Johnson, 1731); *Daily Courant*, 5 February 1731; *London Journal*, 6 February 1731; *Read's Weekly Journal*, 6 February 1731; *Echo or Edinburgh Weekly Journal*, 3 March, 1731. Reprinted by Percival, pp. 48–9, and Urstad, pp. 214–15.

***Attribution.*** Attributed to 'Phil Lloyd' in BL Add. MS 51441; to Hervey on stylistic grounds by Percival, p. lii.

***Context and date.*** Although the ballad does not seem to originate from a particular event, its publication in early February 1731 is carefully targeted at the repetitious nature of much of the criticism of the Government in the main opposition newspaper, *The Craftsman*. As Percival remarks, 'Every reader of *The Craftsman* will appreciate the keenness, even if he would not grant the truth, of this satire on the narrow circle of interest and the mere factiousness of opposition displayed in that journal' (p. 48). Urstad similarly cites the ballad as an instance of the pro-Government claim 'that the language employed in opposition propaganda had become standardized to the point of being practically meaningless' (p. 214). The attribution in BL Add. MS 51441 to Philip Lloyd, who would become Equerry to the King later in the same year (*Gentleman's Magazine*, 1 (December 1731), 541), cannot be discounted, especially as it appears to be in the hand of Horace Walpole. Yet Percival makes a fair case for Hervey's authorship, pointing to a line such as 'To frighten the Mob, all Inventions they try' (25) as suggesting a court point of view. While this would not exclude Lloyd, he is not, unlike Hervey, otherwise known as a writer of pro-Government propaganda, and Percival is right to single the ballad out for its wit and rhetorical effectiveness. The inventiveness of nonce-words in the refrains is especially clever; and the cynical suggestion that the so-called patriots can be bought off by 'Places' is characteristic of Hervey's perspective.

***Textual commentary.*** Though poorly printed, the 'Wiseacre' text has been chosen because, unlike all the other printings but in accordance with the two manuscripts, it sets the poem out correctly in stanzas of eight rather than six lines. Probably the six-line format was employed in order to save space, especially important in a newspaper, but it does not fit the verse form of anapaestic tetrameter as it elongates two of the lines to eight feet. Where the 'Wiseacre' version is clearly incorrect or misleading, punctuation from one of the other printed sources has been adopted and, as in most of the printings, the refrain lines have been italicised. See the List of Emendations for details.

## The Journalists Displayed, A New Ballad.
## To the Old Tune of *Lillebullero.*

I.

Dear Friend, have you heard the fantastical Chimes,
*Ribbledum, Scribbledum, Fribbledum, Flash*;
As rung[1] by the *Journalists*, all of our Times?
*Satyrum, Traytorum, Treasondom, Trash*;
Popery, Slavery, Bribery, Knavery,
Irruptions, Corruptions, and Some-body's Fall;
Pensions and Places, Removes[2] and Disgraces,
And something and nothing, the Devil and all.

II.

These Sparks[3] they eternally harp on a String,
*Ribbledum, Scribbledum, Fribbledum, Flash*;
And this is the Song they on *Saturdays*[4] sing,
*Satyrum, Traytorum, Treasondum, Trash*;
Popery, Slavery, Bribery, Knavery,

1. *rung*: the Wiseacre text has 'sung'. 'Rung' is preferable because it is more consistent with 'Chimes' and appears in a majority of the texts.

2. *Places, Removes*: offices allocated by the Government or through Government influence, and removals from office.

3. *Sparks*: 'A young man of an elegant or foppish character; one who affects smartness or display in dress and manners. Chiefly in more or less depreciatory use' (*OED*).

4. *on Saturdays: The Craftsman* was published on Saturdays.

Irruptions, Corruptions, and Some-body's Fall;
Pensions and Places, Removes and Disgraces,
And something and nothing, the Devil and all.

III.

In poreing you need not your Spirits to pall,
*Ribbledum, Scribbledum, Fribbledum, Flash*;
For when you've read One of them, then you've read All,
*Satyrum, Traytorum, Treasondum, Trash*;
Popery, Slavery, Bribery, Knavery,
Irruptions, Corruptions, and Some-body's Fall;
Pensions and Places, Removes and Disgraces,
And something and nothing, the Devil and all.

IV.

To frighten the Mob, all Inventions they try,
*Ribbledum, Scribbledum, Fribbledum, Flash*;
But Money's their Aim, tho' their Country's the Cry,
*Satyrum, Traytorum, Treasondum, Trash*;
Popery, Slavery, Bribery, Knavery,
Irruptions, Corruptions, and Some-body's Fall;
Pensions and Places, Removes and Disgraces,
And something and nothing, the Devil and all.

V.

That the Joke is a stale one, we very well know,
*Ribbledum, Scribbledum, Fribbledum, Flash*;
'Twas just the same, Ages and Ages ago,
*Satyrum, Traytorum, Treasondum, Trash*;
Popery, Slavery, Bribery, Knavery,
Irruptions, Corruptions, and Some-body's Fall;
Pensions and Places, Removes and Disgraces,
And something and nothing, the Devil and all.

VI.

I'll tell you the Way, these Complainants to quell,
*Ribbledum, Scribbledum, Fribbledum, Flash*;

Give all of them Places, and all will be well,
*Satyrum, Traytorum, Treasondum, Trash*;
'Twill be no more Slavery, Bribery, Knavery,
Irruption, Corruption, and Some-body's Fall;
But stand up for Royalty! punish Disloyalty!
Stock it[5] and Pocket the Devil and all.

5. *Stock it*: either 'to set in the stocks; to punish by confining the feet (occas. the hands) in stocks' (*OED*), or 'To root up, pull up by the roots (trees, stumps, weeds, etc.); to extirpate by digging or grubbing; to fell (a tree) by digging round and cutting its roots with a mattock or similar instrument' (*OED*).

# 27 The Patriots Are Come; Or, a New Doctor for a Crazy Constitution. A New Ballad. To the Tune of *Derry Down*

***Main source.*** Transcript by Horace Walpole in *Horace Walpole, A Collection of Letters from Horace Walpole, youngest son of Sr Robert Walpole Earl of Orford to Horace Mann resident at Florence, 1741–1786*, The Lewis Walpole Library, Yale University, I, letter 53 (16 October 1742); printed (with small emendations) in Walpole, *Correspondence*, XVIII, 80–4.

***Complementary manuscript source.*** Bodley MS Eng. misc. b. 48, f. 2.

***Complementary print sources.*** *The Patriots Are Come; Or, a New Doctor for a Crazy Constitution. A New Ballad. To the Tune of Derry Down* (London: for W. Webb, 1742); *A New C—t Ballad* (Dublin [London?]: by James Stone, 1742); 'The Patriots are Come; Or, a Doctor for a Crazy Constitution. A New Ballad. To the Tune of, Derry Down', in *The New Ministry. Containing a Collection of All the Satyrical Poems, Songs, &c. Since the Beginning of 1742* (London: for W. Webb, 1742), pp. 20–5; *The S—te M—r's Are Come: Or a New Doctor for a Crazy Constitution. A New Ballad to the Tune of Derry Down* ([London?]: s.n., 1742); 'The Patriots are Come; Or, a Doctor for a Crazy Constitution. A New Ballad. To the Tune of, Derry Down', in *The Foundling Hospital for Wit*, I (London: for G. Lion, 1743), 20–4.

***Attribution.*** Horace Walpole, letter to Sir Horace Mann, 16 October 1742, in Walpole, *Correspondence*, XVIII, 80, n. 5; *The Grenville Papers: Being the Correspondence of Richard Grenville Earl Temple, K.G., and the Right Hon: George Grenville, Their Friends and Contemporaries*, ed. by W. J. Smith, 4 vols. (London: John Murray, 1852–3), I (1852), 16–17.

***Context and date.*** The poem comments bitterly on the new Government formed by John Carteret after Walpole's fall from power in February 1742 and Hervey's dismissal as Lord Privy Seal in July of the same year. It must have been written before 16 October 1742, the date of the letter from Walpole to Mann that contains Walpole's transcript. Walpole says 'it has not been printed' (*Correspondence*, XVIII, 84), but it soon found its way into press, the *Daily Advertiser* announcing publication 'this day' in its issue dated 22 October (The Bodleian copy of *The S—te M—r's Are Come*, Bodley Firth b. 22, f. 38r, has, written underneath the broadsheet in pencil, 'Oct. 1742'.) Although it portrays Carteret as virtually dictating the composition of the new ministry to the King, its satirical target is less an overweening Secretary of State than the King himself, whose behaviour has made such a state of affairs possible. Hervey's ire had a personal as well as a patriotic motivation, because he had not only been forced out of office but also humiliated by being offered no compensating appointment but only a pension for life of £3,000 that he had refused because it smacked of a pay-off. His private letters to his father, the Earl of Bristol, that he included in *Some Materials* and that contain accounts of his dealings with the King, including transcripts of letters, tell the full story from his point of view (Sedgwick, III, 942–59). Robert Halsband gives a more nuanced account in his biography (pp. 284–96). The poem, with its scathing portraits of the new ministry and a king who can be kept quiet so long as he has troops to review, is a good example of Hervey's ability to write satirical broadsides. In it he by no means attempted to disguise what Walpole called 'the niceness of his style' (*Correspondence*, XVIII, 80). Rather, he adopted a different style altogether. The poem's use of dialogue, and its rumbustious anapaestic tetrameter couplets, stem from a tradition of popular ballads that, for all his courtly refinement, he was equally able to exploit.

***Textual commentary.*** Because Walpole's transcript is clean and, for the most part, grammatical, it is given just as it stands, including occasional use of initial capitalisation, though apostrophes have been added where Walpole omitted them (see List of Emendations). His text has the further advantage of printing in full names and other terms that might cause offence, whereas all the printed texts, and the manuscript in the Bodleian Library, are much more guarded. These resort to dashes for various expressions that might invite a charge of libel, in most cases framing them by first and last letters to facilitate identification without providing it directly. Most of the printed sources provide the refrain 'Derry Down &c.' between the stanzas; this is omitted in Walpole's transcript and in *A New C—t Ballad*, and it is given after the first stanza only in the Bodley manuscript. The stanzas are not numbered in Webb's 1742 edition, in the edition titled *The S—te M—r's Are Come*, nor in *The Foundling Hospital for Wit*.

## The Patriots[1] are Come; Or, a New Doctor for a Crazy[2] Constitution

1.

O England, attend, while thy fate I deplore,
Rehearsing the schemes and the conduct of pow'r;

1. *Patriots*: the opposition had represented themselves as such since the 1730s.
2. *Crazy*: punning on *OED* sense 2, 'Having the bodily health or constitution impaired; indisposed, ailing; diseased, sickly; broken down, frail, infirm'.

And since only of those who have power I sing,
I am sure none can think that I hint at the King.

2.

From the time his Son made him old Robin depose,
All the pow'r of a King he was well-known to lose;
But of all but the name and the badges bereft,
Like old Women, his paraphernalia[3] are left.

3.

To tell how he shook in St James's[4] for fear,
When first these new Ministers bullied him there,
Makes my blood boil with rage, to think what a thing
They have made of a Man we obey as a King.

4.

Whom they pleas'd they put in, whom they pleas'd they put out,
And just like a top they all lash'd him about,
Whilst he like a top with a murmuring noise
Seem'd to grumble, but turn'd to these rude lashing boys.

5.

At last Cart'ret[5] arriving, spoke thus to his grief,
"If you'll make me your Doctor, I'll bring you relief;
"You see to your closet familiar I come,
"And seem like my Wife in the circle – at home."

6.

Quoth the King, "my good Lord, perhaps you've been told,
"That I used to abuse you a little of old;

3. *paraphernalia*: 'Articles of personal property, esp. clothing and ornaments, which (exceptionally at common law) did not automatically transfer from the property of the wife to the husband by virtue of the marriage' (*OED*).

4. *St James's*: the senior royal palace.

5. *Cart'ret*: John Carteret (1690–1763), from 1744 second Earl Granville, became Secretary of State in February 1742 after being in the forefront of the attacks on Walpole (*ODNB*).

"But now bring whom you will, and eke turn away,
"Let but me and my money, and Walmoden[6] stay."

7.

"For you and Walmoden, I freely consent,
"But as for your money, I must have it spent;
"I have promis'd, your Son (nay, no frowns) shall have some,
"Nor think 'tis for nothing we Patriots are come.

8.

"But, howe'er-little King, since I find you so good,
"Thus stooping below your high courage and blood,
"Put yourself in my hands, and I'll do what I can
"To make you look yet like a King and a Man.

9.

"At your Admiralty and your Treasury-board
"To save one single man you sha'n't say a word,
"For by God all your rubbish from both you shall shoot,
"Walpole's cyphers and Gasherry's vassals[7] to boot.

10.

"And to guard Prince's ears as all Statesmen take care,
"So, as long yours are[8] – not one man shall come near;
"For of all your court-crew we'll leave only those
"Who we know never dare to say boh! to a goose.

6. *Walmoden*: 'Lady Yarmouth' (Horace Walpole's note), Amalie Sophie Marianne von Wallmoden (1704–65), the King's mistress, created Countess of Yarmouth 1740 (*ODNB*).

7. *Gasherry's vassals*: 'Sir Charles Wager's nephew and Secretary to the Admiralty' (Horace Walpole's note); Francis Gashry (1702–62), who was not Wager's nephew though he married the widow of Charles Bolton, who was, served as Wager's secretary during his term as first lord of the Admiralty from June 1733 to March 1742, 'combining that post from 1738 with that of assistant secretary to the Admiralty board' (*ODNB*).

8. *as long yours are*: an insult, since asses' ears are proverbially long.

11.
"So your friend booby Grafton[9] I'll e'en let you keep,
"Awake he can't hurt and is still half-asleep;
"Nor ever was dang'rous but to womankind,
"And his body's as impotent now as his mind.

12.
"There's another court-booby, at once hot and dull,
"Your pious pimp Schutz,[10] a mean Hanover tool;
"For your card-play at night he too shall remain,
"With *virtuous* and *sober* and *wise* Deloraine.[11]

13.
"And for all your court-nobles who can't write or read,
"As of such titled cyphers all courts stand in need,
"Who, like parliament-Swiss,[12] vote and fight for their pay,
"They're as good as a new set to cry yea and nay.

9. *Grafton*: Charles FitzRoy, second Duke of Grafton (1683–1757), on whom Hervey remarks in *Some Materials*:

> His Grace's maxim was never to give a direct answer either to the most material or most indifferent question; so that the natural cloud of his understanding, thickened by the artificial cloud of his mistaken Court policy, made his meaning always as unintelligible as his conversation was unentertaining' (Sedgwick I, 266). Hervey epitomised these qualities in the speeches he gave Grafton in his play 'The Death of Lord Hervey' (Sedgwick, II, 595–6).

10. *Schutz*: Augustus Schutz (1690–1757) was Master of the Robes and Keeper of the Privy Purse; for details of his biography, see Falconer Madan, *The Madan Family and Maddens in Ireland and England* (Oxford: Oxford University Press, 1933), pp. 66–8.

11. *Deloraine*: 'Css dowager of Deloraine, Governess to the young Princesses' (Horace Walpole's note); Mary Scott, *née* Howard; other married name Wyndham Countess of Deloraine (*bap.* 1703, *d.* 1744), was governess to two of the King's daughters and had been one of his sexual conquests (*ODNB*); the epithets bestowed on her by Hervey, in Carteret's voice, are all, of course, ironic.

12. *parliament-Swiss*: a reference to the fact that Swiss soldiers served as bodyguards, ceremonial guards and palace guards at foreign European courts from the late fifteenth century, and more generally as mercenaries; they are best known today from their role as pontifical guards at the Vatican in Rome.

14.

"Tho' Newcastle's[13] as false, as he's silly, I know,
"By betraying old Robin[14] to me long ago,
"As well as all those who employ'd him before,
"Yet I leave him in place, but I leave him no pow'r.

15.

"For granting his heart is as black as his hat,
"With no more truth in this, than there's sense beneath that;
"Yet as he's a coward, he'll shake when I frown:
"You call'd him a rascal, I'll use him like one.

16.

"And since his Estate at Elections he'll spend,[15]
"And beggar himself, without making a friend;
"So whilst the extravagant fool has a souse,[16]
"As his brains I can't fear, so his fortune I'll use.[17]

17.

"And as miser Hardwicke[18] with all courts will draw,
"He too may remain, but shall stick to his law;

13. *Newcastle*: Thomas Pelham-Holles, Duke of Newcastle upon Tyne and first Duke of Newcastle under Lyme (1693–1768); Hervey gives an instance of his silliness in Sedgwick, III, 842–3, and, in the same work, reproduces a letter he sent to the King on 6 July 1742 in which he claimed that Newcastle was one of those men 'whose whole life has been one continued series of treachery and betraying since they first came into the political world' (Sedgwick, III, 953).

14. *old Robin*: Robert Walpole, first Earl of Orford (1676–1745); Carteret had been Walpole's rival for power since the 1720s, but the allusion here to Walpole being betrayed to him by Newcastle is difficult to explain; Newcastle continued as Secretary of State for the Southern Department, a post he had held since 1724, until 1748.

15. *And since . . . spend*: 'In the 1734 election he spent nearly £20,000' (Walpole, *Correspondence*, XVIII, 82, n. 10, citing Basil Williams, *Carteret and Newcastle* (Cambridge: Cambridge University Press, 1943), pp. 35–6).

16. *souse*: 'A French coin and money of account, equal to the twentieth part of a livre; a sol or sou' (*OED*).

17. *use*: 'To dupe, cheat, trick; to swindle or defraud *of* or *out of*' (*OED*).

18. *Hardwicke*: Philip Yorke, first Earl of Hardwicke (1690–1764), who had been Lord Chancellor since 1737 (*ODNB*); as Hervey generally gives a good opinion of

"For of foreign affairs when he talks like a fool,
"I'll laugh in his face, and will cry, go to school!

18.

"The Countess of Wilmington,[19] excellent nurse,
"I'll trust with the treasury, not with it's purse;
"For nothing by her, I've resolv'd shall be done,
"She shall sit at that board, as you sit on the throne.

19.

"Perhaps now you expect that I should begin
"To tell you the men I design to bring in;
"But we're not yet determin'd on all their demands;
"– and you'll know soon enough, when they come to kiss hands.

20.

"All that weathercock Pultney[20] shall ask, we must grant,
"For to make him a great noble nothing, I want;
"And to cheat such a Man, demands all my arts,
"For tho' he's a fool, he's a fool with great parts.

21.

"And as popular Clodius,[21] the Pultney of Rome,
"From a noble, for pow'r did Plebeian become,

him in *Some Materials*, the contempt for his lack of understanding of foreign affairs probably reflects more on the imagined speaker, Carteret, than on himself.

19. *Countess of Wilmington*: a derogatory reference to Spencer Compton, Earl of Wilmington (c. 1674–1743), described by A. A. Hanham as 'no more than a ministerial figurehead presiding over a group of ministers among whom Lord Carteret, due to his influence with the king, was the real controlling force' (*ODNB*).

20. *Pultney*: William Pulteney, Earl of Bath (1684–1764), at first Hervey's friend but then his bitter enemy, reflected in the duel the two fought in 1731; he was vilified as a sell-out when he accepted promotion to the Lords in July 1742.

21. *Clodius*: Publius Clodius Pulcher (c. 93–52 BCE) was a Roman politician notorious for his populist tactics; Hervey alludes to his renunciation of patrician rank in order to become a tribune of the plebeians, a position not open to patricians (*Oxford Encyclopedia of Ancient Greece and Rome*, ed. by Michael Gagarin (Oxford: Oxford University Press, 2010)) – a move that contrasts ironically with Pulteney's unpopular elevation to the peerage.

"So this Clodius to be a Patrician shall choose,
"Till what One got by changing, the Other shall loose.

22.

"Thus flatter'd, and courted, and gaz'd at by all,
"Like Phaeton,[22] rais'd for a day, he shall fall,
"Put the world in a flame, and show he did strive
"To get reins in his hand, tho' 'tis plain he can't drive.

23.

"For your foreign affairs, howe'er they turn out,
"At least I'll take care you shall make a great rout:
"Then cock your great hat, strut, bounce and look bluff,
"For tho' kick'd and cuff'd here, you shall there kick and cuff.

24.

"That Walpole did nothing they all us'd to say,
"So I'll do enough, but I'll make the Dogs pay;
"Great fleets I'll provide and great armies engage,
"Whate'er debts we make, or whate'er wars we wage."

25.

With cordials like these the Monarch's new guest
Reviv'd his sunk spirits and gladden'd his breast;
Till in raptures he cried, "My dear Lord, you shall do
Whatever you will, give me troops to review."

26.

But oh! my dear England, since this is thy state,
Who is there that loves thee but weeps at thy fate?
Since in changing thy Masters, thou art just like old Rome,
Whilst Faction, Oppression, and Slav'ry's thy doom!

22. *Phaeton*: according to Greek myth, as retold by Ovid in *Metamorphoses*, II. 1–400 (Loeb, I, 60–88), Phaeton, son of the sun-god Phoebus, obtained his father's promise to drive the sun's chariot for a day but failed to control it and was killed by a thunderbolt from Zeus.

27.

For tho' you have made that rogue Walpole retire,
You are out of the frying-pan into the fire!
But since to the Protestant Line[23] I'm a friend,
I tremble to think where these changes may end!

23. *Protestant Line*: the Protestant succession, secured by the Act of Settlement passed in 1701 to settle succession to the British throne on the Electress Sophia of Hanover and her Protestant heirs.

# ELEGIES, EPITAPHS AND AN EPILOGUE

# INTRODUCTION TO ELEGIES, EPITAPHS AND AN EPILOGUE

Elegies were originally poems composed in elegiac metre (a hexameter followed by a pentameter), and the term sometimes retains that general sense in English (in Donne's elegies, for example), but it has become associated, as it was in Greek and Latin literature, with poems of mourning. The elegy has a complex history, including the pastoral elegy, whose most famous English representative is Milton's *Lycidas*, but characteristically it laments the death of a known person, praises him or her, and seeks to provide consolation.[1] Hervey's elegy for his sister follows a conventional pattern, with reservations; the elegy for Lady Abergavenny struggles to reconcile conventional expectations with her fate.

An epitaph, shorter than an elegy and designed for a gravestone or monument, need not be in verse. Traditionally it creates an economical record, including the name of the person and some account of family and social role; it may also offer a prayer, consolation or wisdom.[2] Especially in the case of the Queen, where Hervey attempts to shape posterity's verdict, but to some degree in all his epitaphs, Hervey's evaluations attempt to connect personal and public qualities.

The epilogue, a speech that followed the conclusion of the action of a play in the early-modern theatre, permitted a change in the relation between stage and spectator. Usually spoken by one of the company's chief actors, it created an atmosphere of intimacy between performer and spectator and invited applause.[3] Sometimes there was a contrast between

1. See Eric Smith, *By Mourning Tongues: Studies in English Elegy* (Woodbridge: Boydell, 1977) and Donald C. Mell, *A Poetics of Augustan Elegy: Studies of Poems by Dryden, Pope, Prior, Swift, Gray, and Johnson* (Amsterdam: Rodopi, 1974). See also *The New Princeton Encyclopedia of Poetry and Poetics*, ed. by Alex Preminger *et al.* (Princeton, NJ: Princeton University Press, 1993), under elegiac distich, elegiac stanza and elegy.

2. See Joshua Scodel, *The English Poetic Epitaph: Commemoration and Conflict from Jonson to Wordsworth* (Ithaca, NY: Cornell University Press, 1991).

3. See Brian W. Schneider, *The Framing Text in Early Modern Drama: 'Whining' Prologues and 'Armed' Epilogues* (Farnham: Ashgate, 2011); Schneider's examination is of texts before 1660, but much of his material on the audience is useful for the eighteenth century.

the tone of the play and that of the epilogue, which might be designed to dissipate dramatic tension (rather as there is a contrast between this epilogue and Hervey's preceding elegies and epitaphs). In the early eighteenth century it was not uncommon for the epilogue to be written by a friend or supporter of the author; the epilogue to Addison's *Cato* (1713), for example, was by Samuel Garth, while the prologue was supplied by Pope. In proposing to follow Thomson's tragedy *Sophonisba* with a bawdy, energetic epilogue spoken by his friend Anne Oldfield, Hervey refuses that play's bleakness, suggesting a quite different connection of private and public concerns as the famous actress retires from the stage.

# ELEGIES

# 28 Verses to the Memory of my Dearest Sister the Lady Elizabeth Mansel

***Main source.*** Suffolk Record Office 941/53/1, pp. 214, 216, 218: a transcript made by Hervey's son William in his commonplace book some time after February 1751.

***Complementary manuscript source.*** 'Verses to the Memory of my dearest Sister Lady Barbara May; by Lord Hervey', Yale Osborn Shelves Poetry Box V/10.

***Complementary print sources.*** None known.

***Attribution.*** William Hervey; Yale Poetry Box V/10.

***Context and date.*** Hervey suffered two bereavements in 1727 the effect of which was so crushing as to place his own life in danger. The first loss was that of his sister Barbara, who died on 25 July at the age of eighteen; the second and more devastating was that of another sister, Elizabeth, who had long suffered ill-health and who died at the age of twenty-nine on 3 September (John Hervey, first Earl of Bristol, *The Diary*, ed. by S. H. A. H[ervey] (Wells: Ernest Jackson, 1894), pp. 49, 78, 27). Because some lines from the poem also appear in Hervey's epitaph for Elizabeth (Poem 30), there is no doubt that it mourns her death rather than that of Barbara, although the Yale manuscript assigns it to the younger sister. While the discrepancy is puzzling, it may perhaps be explained by an additional couplet in the Yale version that mentions 'dear Maria'. As Hervey had no sister named Maria, and as his wife Mary and the daughter named after her long outlived him, it is possible that the reference is to a bereavement suffered by the person who transcribed the poem. If that is the case, it is also possible that the transcriber assigned the poem to the wrong sister. It was probably written not long after Elizabeth Mansel's death, because lines 17–18 appear in a letter to Lady Mary Wortley Montagu from Hervey dated 7 November. No information is available about the date or provenance of the Yale transcript, but for the most part it agrees closely with William Hervey's. The fact that it is written in a diminutive hand may suggest it was made by a woman. But, in whatever way the two versions might be connected, there is no doubting the impact of the bereavement on the poet. Nearly a month after his sister's death, his father began a letter to him with the words: 'The melancholly dispairing strain your two last letters run in made me as uncapable of administering as I found you of receiving any comfort from mine', before delivering a homily on the necessity of submission to God's will (*Letter-Books*, III, 24); and, four years later, Hervey remarked: 'She had so many great, good, and useful, as well as agreeable, qualities, so nice a discernment, so just a judgment, so much sincerity, principle, and honour, that I lost in her not only an amiable companion but an affectionate friend and an able counsellor, and was so unaffectedly touched with this loss, that her death had like to have been the cause of my own' (Sedgwick, III, 971–2).

He went on to explain that his constitution was so 'shattered' that it was to recover from the bereavement that he went abroad (Sedgwick, III, 974). The qualities to which Hervey paid tribute in prose are cast into much sharper relief by the poem. Yet what is most remarkable about his elegy is the heterodox nature of the questions it poses in lines 47–56 concerning death and what lies afterwards. Although, on the face of it, the poem expresses no doubt that there is an afterlife and that his sister is in heaven, no fewer than six conditional clauses introduce these prospects, suggesting the very uncertainty they seek to deny. In doing so they echo the poem's sceptical epigraph that, however duteously they live, everyone is doomed to die. The closing affirmation is therefore all the more hard-won. Perhaps the most moving of all Hervey's poems, it is also one of the most effective elegies of its period. (For fuller discussion, see Overton, 'Death and Futurity'.)

***Textual commentary.*** William Hervey's transcript requires little emendation, but a few spelling errors and inadequacies in punctuation have been corrected by reference to the Yale version, as noted in the List of Emendations. His use of initial capitals has been left unchanged. There are relatively few differences between the two texts, the only ones that stand out being that in the title and the additional couplet in the Yale manuscript discussed above.

## Verses to the Memory of my dearest Sister the Lady Elizabeth Mansel

Vive pius, moriere pius, cole sacra, colentem
Mors gravis a templis in cava busta trahet.
(Ovid. El. 9. L. 3[1])

Whilst venal Poets consecrate to Fame
A Worthless title, or an empty name,
And on the Sculptur'd monument reherse
Fictitious merit in a partial verse,
They sing the requiem with a quiet heart,
Their incense, Flattery; their Affliction, Art.

From other Springs my tears and numbers flow,
Truth in the praise, and Nature in the woe;
Disdain not then, thou dear lamented shade,[2]
This little tribute by my friendship paid;

1. 'Live the duteous life — you will die; be faithful in your worship — in the very act of worship heavy death will drag you from the temple to the hollow tomb' (Ovid, *Amores*, III. ix. 37–8 (Loeb, pp. 488–9)). Hervey's own translation of these lines, headed as extempore, appears as Poem 60.

2. *shade*: 'The visible but impalpable form of a dead person, a ghost' (*OED*).

Friendship, suggested first by Nature's voice,
'Till Reason and Experience made it choice:
Thy truth my joy, thy judgment was my guide;
And that such worth could love me was my pride.

Oh! early lost, torn like reluctant fruit,
By some rude hand, fast cleaving to the shoot;
Just in the noon of life, those Golden days,
When the mind ripens, e'er the form decays:[3]
No more that form these longing eyes shall chear,
No more that mind delight my listn'ning ear;
Yet in Remembrance still those joys survive,
There still thy sweet society shall live;
Nor shall thy image from this breast depart,
'Till the last feeble pulse desert my heart:[4]
And whilst that hand, which hurried thee on fate,
Shall stretch my life's uncomfortable date;
Still as the year renews that hated day,
When Death untimely made thy Youth his prey,
These wretched eyes shall float thy Sacred tomb,
And annual tears commemorate thy doom.

Nor shall the Muse her voice neglect to raise,
Just to thy merit, careful of thy Praise,
Tho' Harmony refuse to grace her Song,
Nor Eloquence drop Manna on her tongue;
Yet on thy tomb, whose consecrated trust,
Shall be to shelter thine from common dust,

3. *Just in ... form decays*: in a letter from Bath dated 7 November (1727) to Lady Mary Wortley Montagu, Hervey wrote: 'I ever did and believe I ever shall like Women best

Just in the Noon of Life those golden Days
When the Mind ripen's e'er the Form decay's

and think them much more insipid Creatures (for above five Minutes at most) before the one is come, than after the other is gone' (SRO 941/47/2, p. 64). A different version of the lines appears in Hervey's epitaph on his sister (Poem 30).

4. *desert my heart*: the Yale manuscript follows this with an additional couplet, 'The last faint Thought that lingers in my Mind | Shall bear thy name, with dear Maria's join'd'. See discussion in headnote above.

With these plain truths she shall inscribe thy name,
A faithful record of thy deathless fame.

With Knowledge modest, and with wit sincere,
With merit humble, and with virtue fair:
Upright in all the Social Walks of life,
The friend, the daughter, Sister and the Wife:[5]
So just the disposition of her Soul,
Nature left Reason nothing to controul;
Firm, pious, patient, affable of mind,
Happy in life, and yet in Death resign'd.
But if departed Souls new beings find,
And merit ever dwelt in humankind,
If the dark moment subsequent to death,
Be not the same with what precedes our breath,
If 'tis not prejudice, and notion[6] all,
When vice or virtue, this or that, we call;
If He, who only knows what things[7] we are,
Deems such imperfect beings worth his care,
And that the purest of our sully'd kind,
Can claim reward, or ev'n his mercy find:
Already art thou summon'd to his throne,
His glory manifest, his Heav'n thy own:
Officious[8] Angels, fond of their new Guest,
So like themselves, conduct thee to his breast;
Thy mind enlarg'd to entertain[9] delight,
And thy Eye strengthen'd to endure his light;
To thee each world, created by his Grace
To dignify th'infinity of Space;

5. *the Wife*: Elizabeth Hervey had married Bussy Mansel on 7 May 1724 (Bristol, *Diary*, III, 74).

6. *notion*: 'Imagination, fancy' (*OED*).

7. *things*: 'In later use only in contempt or reproach, usu. suggesting unworthiness to be called a person' (*OED*).

8. *Officious*: 'Doing or ready to do kind offices; eager to serve, help, or please; attentive, obliging, kind' (*OED*).

9. *entertain*: 'to keep, hold, or maintain in the mind with favour; to harbour; to cherish; in weaker sense, to experience (a sentiment)' (*OED*).

And those deep truths, illustrated,[10] are shown,
To the fond search of darken'd Man unknown;
To thee, distinguish'd, foremost of the bless'd,
The Universal Vision stands confess'd;
Whilst Praise, and Rapture all thy hours employ,
Unmix'd, unchangeable, unending Joy.

10. *illustrated*: 'To throw the light of intelligence upon; to make clear, elucidate, clear up, explain' (*OED*).

# 29 On the Late Lady Abergavenny

***Main source.*** Manuscript in Charles Hanbury Williams Collection, Yale University, Vol. 84, f. 5r (no permanent call number, but currently Phillips 84–11402).

***Complementary manuscript sources.*** BL Add. MS 32463, f. 116r; BL MS Harley 7318, f. 128r; Portland Papers (Longleat), XX, f. 116r; ***adaptation*** Bodley Rawl. poet. 207, p. 157.

***Complementary print sources.*** *Universal Spectator*, 18 April 1730; *Grub-street Journal*, 4 May 1730; *Poetical Magazine* (London: by Dryden Leach for J. Coote, 1764), 5 (May 1764), 204; *Additions to the Works of Alexander Pope*, 2 vols. (London: for H. Baldwin, T. Longman and others, 1776), I, 155–6; Sir Charles Hanbury Williams, *The Works, of the Right Honourable Sir Chas. Hanbury Williams*, 3 vols. (London: Edward Jeffery and Son, 1822), I, 122–23; ***adaptation*** *Grub-street Journal*, 16 April 1730, repr. in *Faithful Memoirs of the Grubstreet Society* (London: for the Grubstreet Society, 1732), p. 6; *The Warbling Muses, or Treasure of Lyric Poetry*, ed. by Benjamin Wakefield (London: for G. Woodfall, 1749), 88–9.

***Attribution.*** 'By Lord Harvey', Charles Hanbury Williams Collection; 'by Charles, Duke of Dorset', *Works of Sir Charles Hanbury Williams*. The attribution to Hervey is from a small group of fourteen poems 'bound up with a "Book of Expenses of Lord Coningesby"', and it appears to have been Coningsby who produced the copy, because the poem before the one on Lady Abergavenny has underneath it a pencilled note reading 'This and the following poems were copied I think by Lord Coningsby' (Urstad, 'Hanbury Williams', p. 250; further details in private email from Susan Walker, Horace Walpole Archive, Yale University, 28 September 2011). Which Coningsby this was is, however, a puzzle. It cannot have been Thomas, first Earl of Coningsby, because he died on 30 April 1729, over six months before the poem was written. The only other possible candidate is Coningsby's grandson Richard, although he died in December of the same year, in the month during which the poem must have been written, after which the title passed to 'his daughter Margaret, on whose death in 1761 the title became extinct' (*ODNB*). Further possible documentary evidence for Hervey's authorship is that the collection of verse containing the poem attributed to him also includes 'To my Lord Harvey by Mr Litt—n', a verse epistle not printed until 1744 but dated 1730 (in *The Norfolk Poetical Miscellany*, 2 vols. (London: for the author [Ashley Cowper], 1744), II, 46–9). The attribution to the Duke of Dorset carries little weight because it comes from an edition that is notoriously unreliable, especially on such matters (see Urstad, 'Hanbury Williams', pp. 1, 41–8, 253 n. 3); because it dates from nearly a century after the poem was written; and because Dorset is not noted as a poet. Letters from Hervey to Stephen Fox, Lady Mary Wortley Montagu and his mother, on the other hand, demonstrate the great interest he took in the affair: having been discovered with a lover by servants (set to spy on her by her husband), Lady Abergavenny had been turned out of the house by her husband only a few days after the birth of her child. Hervey's letters on the subject to Montagu – her part of the correspondence does not survive – not only show that both were sympathetic to Lady Abergavenny, though critical of her folly, but suggest that both wrote poems on the subject. Hervey gives the story a humorous turn in the first letter in the series, which is to Fox and is dated 13 November, very soon after the news broke, but ends by writing: 'Joking apart 'tis a terrible Story and I would have her whip'd & her Serv[an]ts hang'd' (SRO 941/47/4, p. 90). This is in the style of one worldly aristocratic male to another, irritated by the exposure of a fellow member of the elite as a cuckold. Writing to Montagu and to his mother a month later, however, and, crucially, after Lady Abergavenny's death, Hervey's tone is more compassionate. When he told the story to his mother on 16 December, he ended: 'The fright, the Sorrow, and Despair hasten'd on her Labour, the Agitation of her Mind threw her into Fitts on her Lying in and all these things together kill'd her' (SRO 941/47/2, p. 237). Two days before, in a letter to Montagu, he had referred to Lady Abergavenny as 'this poor Creature', and had given his opinion, contrary to the orthodox one, that there was no reason to be glad of her death (SRO 941/47/2, pp. 46–7); and on 21 December he expresses the wish that Lady Abergavenny could have taken advice from Montagu herself: 'the greatest misfortune of her Life was not meeting with so able a Friend, whose Counsels might have turned her mourning into Joy, her Misfortunes into Advantages, and her Dishonour into Glory' (SRO 941/47/2, p. 49). Although such a remark can only have been made at least in part with tongue in cheek, the note it strikes is anything but censorious. Both letters also contain suggestions that Montagu, and Hervey himself, had written poems on the subject. One such attribution, to Montagu, is a poem to which he refers as an 'Epitaph' (SRO 941/47/2, p. 51, dated 21 December), while the other is *An Epistle from Calista to Altamont*, which is certainly not by Montagu but by Charles Beckingham (SRO 941/47/2, p. 26, dated 29 December). A hint that Hervey may also have written on the subject appears in the latter, when he speaks of having his 'Vanity flatter'd' at the favourable reception that several of his poems, circulated without attribution, had met with (SRO 941/47/2, pp. 25–6).

Stylistically, there are clear grounds for assigning the poem to Hervey. It begins dramatically, with a series of striking epithets; it relies greatly on techniques of organisation familiar elsewhere from his verse such as parallel and antithetical clauses and, especially, clauses the main verb of which is long delayed; and it makes deft use of the triplet (in lines 7–9) and alexandrine (line 11). Although all these techniques are the stock in trade of Augustan verse, few deploy them in so concentrated a form as Hervey. The viewpoint expressed is also recognisably his, and it is consistent with the attitudes expressed in his letters of December 1729, those written after Lady Abergavenny's death. In particular, it is a worldly, aristocratic outlook that pays more deference to 'honour' than to 'virtue's rules', but more still to love, even though outside the bounds of marriage. The poem in the form attributed to him, with its twist at the end, celebrates truth in love. This is to suggest that, in a social milieu in which many marriages were arranged, some on entirely cynical grounds, love may be sought elsewhere; that, when it is detected, a price has to be paid; but that the proper response should include compassion as well as reproof, though even the latter is directed more at the folly of having been detected than at the fault itself.

***Context and date.*** Katharine Tatton, daughter of Lt.-Gen. William Tatton, had first married Edward Neville, 13th Lord Abergavenny on 6 May 1724; he died of smallpox on 9 October 1724. She then married his cousin, William Neville, 14th Lord Abergavenny on 20 May 1725. Lady Abergavenny died on 4 December 1729, a little less than a month following her ejection by her husband from the family home after his servants had caught her in the act of adultery with his friend Richard Lyddel. She had given birth to a child less than a fortnight earlier. These events provoked not only a great deal of gossip, reflected in correspondence of the time, but also several poems. Both the amount of gossip and of other forms of response increased after Lord Abergavenny's suit for criminal conversation against his wife's lover, Richard Lyddel, produced a judgement in his favour to the tune of £10,000. These included several more poems, bringing the total to have survived on the subject to nine: *A Poem, Sacred to the Memory of the Honourable the Lady Aber —ny* (London: by A. Campbell, 1729); *An Epistle from Calista to Altamont* (London: for A. Moore, 1729); 'The *Elegy*', in *The Whole Life of the Lady Aber——ny* (London: for R. Jones, [1729?]); 'Verses upon the Lady A' (no known printing; two manuscript copies); 'An Elegy on Lady Aber—a—ny' (six manuscript copies, but apparently not printed till 1760 in *Public Ledger*, 12 July); 'On Lady Abergavenny' (apparently first printed in *Universal Spectator*, 18 April 1730); *A Pastoral Elegy on the Death of the Lady Hilaretta. In a Dialogue between Two Lords* (London: for A. More, [1730?]); *An Epistle from Altamont to Lorenzo* (London: by T. Read, 1739); and the adapatation of 'On Lady Abergavenny' that appeared in the *Grub-street Journal*, 4 May 1730.

Among these, the poem attributed to Hervey is of special interest because of a campaign against it, and the attitudes it represents, on the part of the *Grub-street Journal*. First, in a brief article published in the issue for 16 April 1730, a week after an attack on *An Epistle from Calista to Altamont*, the newspaper not only indicted 'Poem on Lady A y' on very similar grounds, but rewrote it with a quite different emphasis. Retitling it 'The Character of the Late A—y', and reducing the twenty-one lines of the original to sixteen, it points up the superficiality of Lady Abergavenny's life as a society beauty, the extent of her downfall, and the gravity of her crime. As an example of this last and most important alteration, where the original reads: 'For if her Conduct in some Steps betray'd | To Virtue's rules too little reverence paid', the revision has: 'And say, that when by lawless love betray'd | From the bright path of innocence she stray'd'. The unmistakable aim is to bring the poem into line with orthodox morality. More was to follow in the issue of the *Grub-street Journal* dated 4 May. Explaining for the first time that the version printed on 16 April was an adaptation, the editor devoted nearly a complete page of the issue to his response. This begins with an introduction deploring the publication of verse on what it terms 'the most heinous crimes, and dismal misfortunes, in a very ludicrous manner', and stating the paper's aims 'to promote the cause of learning and virtue, and to expose the patrons and propagators of nonsense, vice, and immorality'. Then comes a copy of the original poem, with nearly a column of commentary on the lines that the paper found most offensive, and finally a 52-line poem, the first part of which is based on the initial revision. The new poem is the sole didactic one to have survived on the subject. It not only portrays the contrast between Lady Abergavenny's privileged life and the misery of her downfall, but also attacks Lyddel for his betrayal of love and friendship, going so far as to declare: 'For crimes like these is any mulct too high? | For less the Criminal deserves to die'. Prominent in the response from the *Grub-street Journal* is the conviction that adultery was widely accepted and tolerated among the aristocracy and gentry, and that it was not a subject that should be treated lightly.

***Textual commentary.*** The present text is based on the manuscript in the Charles Hanbury Williams Collection. There are relatively few significant textual differences between the copies of this poem, but the most striking is the extra couplet in the Portland (Longleat) manuscript that attacks the hypocrisy of those who condemn Lady Abergavenny despite being guilty of the same crime. On the basis of shared variants, the closest connections are between the copies in BL Add. MS 32463, the *Universal Spectator* and the *Grub-street Journal* of 4 May 1730, and between those in *Additions to the Works of Alexander Pope* and the *Works* of Sir Charles Hanbury Williams. In these cases, either the later copies must have been made from the earlier, or all the copies must stem from some common source that has not come to light. Few textual changes have been necessary to the copy in the Horace Walpole Archive, except that its light punctuation has been supplemented from other texts, and that its haphazard use of initial capitals has been eliminated, as indicated in the List of Emendations. Because the version of the poem in the *Grub-street Journal* of 16 April 1730 is an adaptation that makes considerable changes, and because those in Bodley Rawl. poet. 207, *Memoirs of the Grubstreet Society* and *The Warbling Muses* are taken from it, its text, with a note of variants, is given separately after Hervey's poem.

## Poem on Lady A      y by Lord Harvey

Young, thoughtless, gay, unfortunately fair,
Her pride to please and pleasure all her care;
With too much kindness, and too little art,

Prone to indulge the dictates of her heart;
Flatter'd by all, solicited, admired,
By woman envied, and by man desir'd,
At once from full prosperity she's torn,
By friends deserted, of defence forlorn,
Exposed to talkers, insults, want and scorn;
By every idle tongue her story told,
The novel[1] of the young, the lecture of the old.
But let the scoffer or the prude relate
With rigour or despight her hapless fate,
Good nature still to soft compassion wrought,
Shall weep her ruin, whilst it owns her fault;
For if her conduct in some steps betray'd
To virtue's rules too little reverence paid,
Yet dying still she show'd so dear her fame,
She could survive her guilt, though not her shame.
Her honour dearer than her life she proved,
But dearer than them both the man she lov'd.

The adaptation in *Grub-street Journal*, 16 April 1730, also found in Bodley Rawl. poet. 207, *Faithful Memoirs of the Grubstreet Society* and *The Warbling Muses* (see headnote above).

## The Character of the late Lady A——y[2]

Young, thoughtless, gay, unfortunately fair;
Her pride to please, and dressing[3] all her care;
With too much kindness, and too little art,
Prone to indulge the dictates of her heart;
Flatter'd, caress'd, sollicited, admir'd;
By women[4] envied, and by men desir'd;
At once from ease, from wealth, from honour torn,
She fell expos'd to pain, to want, to scorn.

1. *novel*: piece of news (*OED*).

2. *The Character … A——y*: this *Grub-street Journal* title was varied to 'On Lady Abergavenny' in the Bodleian manuscript; to 'The Character of the Lady A—Y' in *Faithful Memoirs*; and to 'Song CCIX' in *The Warbling Muses*.

3. *dressing*: replaced by 'Pleasure' in *The Warbling Muses*.

4. *women*: 'Woman' in *The Warbling Muses*.

But when her sad disast'rous tale is told
To the gay Young, as lecture, by the Old;[5]
Let both to kind compassion mov'd bemoan
Her sudden ruin, while[6] her fault they own:
And say, that when[7] by lawless love betray'd,
From the bright path[8] of innocence she stray'd.
She could not long, depress'd with guilt and shame,[9]
Survive the death of virtue and of fame.[10]

5. *by the Old*: 'from the Old' in *The Warbling Muses.*
6. *while*: 'whilst' in *The Warbling Muses.*
7. *that when*: replaced by 'when' in *The Warbling Muses.*
8. *path*: 'Path' in *The Warbling Muses.*
9. *with guilt and shame*: 'by Guilt and Shame' in *The Warbling Muses.*
10. *fame*: the poem ends without a full-stop in the *Grub-street Journal*, an error removed in *Faithful Memoirs* and the Bodley manuscript.

# EPITAPHS

# 30 Epitaph on Lady Elizabeth Mansel

***Main source.*** *A Concise Description of Bury St. Edmund's: And its Environs* (London: Longman, 1827 [1825–7]), pp. 203–4.

***Complementary manuscript sources.*** SRO 941/53/1, p. 218; Special Collections, John Rylands University Library, University of Manchester, GB 133 Eng MS 737, f. 65r; Yale fc.51, p. 223; Yale c.83/2, no. 402; BL Add. MS 46916, f. 9.

***Complementary print sources.*** Edward Topham, *The Life of the Late John Elwes, Esquire* (London: by John Jarvis for James Ridgway, 1790), p. 109; John Gage, *The History and Antiquities of Suffolk. Thingoe Hundred* (London: by Samuel Bentley, 1838), pp. 317–18; *Ickworth Parish Registers. Baptisms, Marriages and Burials: 1566–1890*, ed. by S[ydenham] H[enry] A[ugustus] H[ervey] (Wells: Ernest Jackson, 1894), pp. 73–4.

***Attribution.*** William Hervey, SRO 941/53/1, p. 218; Yale fc.51, p. 223; Gage, *History and Antiquities*, p. 317.

***Context and date.*** Elizabeth Mansel, Hervey's favourite sister, died on 3 September 1727, and the epitaph must have been written soon afterwards. For full details, see the notes to his elegy, Poem 28, 'Verses to the Memory of my Dearest Sister the Lady Elizabeth Mansel'. The epitaph is in effect a condensed version of the elegy. It begins with the same epigraph from Ovid, and lines 3–10 and 12–13 virtually repeat lines 39–46 and 17–18 of the elegy.

***Textual commentary.*** The only authoritative source for the text is the tombstone itself, but unfortunately this is no longer accessible as visits are not permitted to its location in Ickworth Church. An early nineteenth-century transcript has therefore been chosen as the best available alternative. It agrees in every substantive respect with the transcript made by Hervey's son William at some point after February 1751, and it has been preferred to the one in *Ickworth Parish Registers* because the latter presents a modernised text. The only textual changes that have proved necessary are to punctuation to clarify syntax, as indicated in the List of Emendations; initial capitalisation has been left unaltered. All of the copies except three later ones that do not pretend to be transcripts agree in every respect except in accidentals. Yale c.83/2, no. 402 appears to be a direct copy of the printed version in *The Life of the Late John Elwes.* It is included as an example of the manuscript circulation of epitaphs, which was widespread in this period and continued into the nineteenth century, as with the version in the British Library, Add. MS 46916, f. 9, which has the largest number of variants. The epitaph is not to be confused with one of twenty lines printed as Hervey's in the *European*

*Magazine*, 32 (July–August 1797), p. 412, with the first line 'Reader attend! and if thine eye let fall', and last line 'You've liv'd in Paradise, she lives in Heaven'. Although this is stated as 'Now first published', it appears without attribution as 'On the Death of Lady *Betty Mansel*' in *A Choice Collection of Poetry, by the Most Ingenious Men of the Age*, ed. by Joseph Yarrow, 2 vols. (York: by A. Staples, 1738), I, 90–1, and as 'Sacred to the Memory of Lady *Elizabeth Mansel*' in *Major Pack's Poetical Remains* (London: for E. Curll, 1738), pp. 18–19. The only resemblance between the two poems is that line 6 of Hervey's epitaph (also line 42 of his elegy) seems echoed in 'The daughter, friend, the sister, and the wife' (line 14; 'The Daughter, Sister, Mistress, and the Wife' in the version attributed to Pack). The actual author of this other poem is likely to have been Hervey's younger brother Henry.

## Epitaph on Lady Elizabeth Mansel

*Vive pius; moriere pius; cole sacra, colentem*
*Mors gravis a Templis in cava Busta trahet.*[1]

Beneath the covering of this little stone
Lye the poor shrunk, yet dear, Remains of one,
With merit humble, and with Virtue fair,
With knowledge modest, and with wit Sincere;
Upright in all the social Paths of life,
The Friend, the Daughter, Sister, and the Wife:
So just the disposition of her Soul,
Nature left Reason nothing to control;
Firm, Pious, Patient, Affable of Mind,
Happy in Life, and yet in Death resign'd:
Just in the zenith of those golden days,
When the mind ripens e'er the form decays;
The hand of Fate untimely cut her thread,
And left the World to weep that Virtue fled,
Its Pride when living, and its Grief when dead.

1. *Vive ... trahet*: This is the same as for the elegy: Ovid, *Amores*, III. ix. 37–8 (Loeb, p. 488). It is represented inaccurately in Topham and omitted from most other copies, though Topham and Yale c.83/2 include Hervey's translation; see the lists of historical collations for Poem 28 and Poem 60. Gage and *Ickworth Parish Registers* include the prose lines at the top of the tombstone: 'Here lyeth interred the Lady Elizabeth wife of the Hon[oura]ble Bussy Mansel, and daughter of John Earl of Bristol, who died the 3rd of Sept[ember] 1727'.

# 31a Epitaph on John, Duke of Marlborough
# 31b Epitaph on Anne Oldfield

***Main sources.*** There are two versions of this poem, distinctive enough for each to be printed here.

31a. Epitaph on Marlborough, *The Works of the Right Honourable Lady Mary Wortley Montagu*, ed. by James Dallaway, 5 vols. (London: for Richard Phillips, 1803), V, 156.

31b. Epitaph on Anne Oldfield, *Gentleman's Magazine*, 1 (January 1731), 23.

***Complementary manuscript source.*** For Oldfield, Folger Shakespeare Library, W.b.11 (8).

***Complementary print sources.*** For Oldfield, *London Evening-Post*, 19 January 1731, p. 2; *Whitehall Evening-Post*, 19 January 1731; [Edmund Curll?], *Faithful Memoirs of the Life, Amours and Performances, of that Justly Celebrated, and Most Eminent Actress of her Time, Mrs. Anne Oldfield* (London: n.p., 1731), Appendix, p. 21; *A Choice Collection of Poetry, by the Most Ingenious Men of the Age*, ed. by Joseph Yarrow, 2 vols. (York: by A. Staples, 1738), I, 21.

***Attribution.*** The only known attribution of either epitaph to Hervey is by Horace Walpole in 'A Catalogue of the Royal and Noble Authors of England, with Lists of their Works', in the form 'Lines under the mezzotinto of Mrs. Oldfield' (Walpole, *Works*, I, 452). This refers to a portrait by John Simon after Jonathan Richardson, underneath which the lines were placed. Chaloner Smith, in *British Mezzotinto Portraits; Being A Descriptive Catalogue of these Engravings from the Introduction of the Art to the Early Part of the Present Century*, 4 parts (London: Henry Sotheran, 1878–84), quotes the epitaph (III (1884), 1106). However, the question of attribution is greatly complicated by the fact that the epitaph also appears, with slightly different wording, as the final four lines of the epitaph on the Duke of Marlborough attributed to Lady Mary Wortley Montagu. The source for this attribution is James Dallaway's edition of Montagu's works. In his prefatory Advertisement, Dallaway states: 'no letter, essay, or poem, will find a place in the present edition, the original manuscript of which is not at this time extant, in the possession of her grand-son' (*The Works of the Right Honourable Lady Mary Wortley Montagu*, I, iii–iv). Yet, as Isobel Grundy makes clear, unlike the great majority of verse in the Montagu canon, no manuscript has been traced of this poem and six others, no reference has been found to a missing volume that might contain them, and no other printing of the poem prior to that in Dallaway's edition is known ('Verse of Lady Mary Wortley Montagu', p. 212). What is highly likely is that, because the Duke of Marlborough died in 1722, and Anne Oldfield in 1730, the epitaph on the former would have been written before that on the latter. The epitaph on Oldfield would therefore have been adapted from its predecessor. As

Horace Walpole's attributions are, in general, considered reliable (see Urstad, 'Hanbury Williams', pp. 52–6, 64–77), the possibility exists that Hervey wrote the epitaph on Marlborough and that either he or another person adapted its last four lines to produce one on Oldfield. While Grundy is right to point out that Montagu was a friend of the Duchess of Marlborough and of two of his daughters (*Essays & Poems*, p. 224), the connections between the Duchess and the Hervey family were even stronger. She had used her influence to secure a peerage for Hervey's father in 1703, and he had demonstrated his support for the Duke after the latter's dismissal from all his offices by holding two dinners in consecutive weeks in 1712 at which he was a leading guest, the first with the Hanoverian envoy, Count Bohmer, and other prominent Whig lords, the second with another important envoy, Prince Eugene of Savoy (Halsband, pp. 8, 9). Friendship between the two families continued after Marlborough's return to England on the accession of George I and, although the Duchess and Hervey were later to fall out, there is no doubt that he would have been more than willing to demonstrate it by writing an epitaph for her husband in 1722. It is also relevant that, while Montagu is known to have written only one other epitaph, the ironic one on John Hughs and Sarah Drew that she produced in response to a sentimental effusion from Pope, it is a genre that, as the present section of this edition and his Latin epitaph for Queen Caroline show, Hervey made his own. The style of 'John Duke of Marlborough' is, too, more characteristic of him than of Montagu. Although both had a predilection for the devices of balance and antithesis that pack the poem, especially its closing four lines, the suspended main verb or key epithet is a hallmark of Hervey's style and it has a powerful impact both in line 6, at the end of the first clause, and in the two past participles that provide the poem's climax.

A further matter to be considered is the adaptation of the closing four lines of 'John Duke of Marlborough' to an epitaph on Anne Oldfield. Joanne Lafler, in *The Celebrated Mrs Oldfield* (Carbondale and Edwardsville: Southern Illinois Press, 1989), gives an account of Oldfield's position as the mistress of Charles Churchill, the illegitimate nephew of the Duke, and hence a member of the Marlborough circle (pp. 123–4). As Grundy suggests, if the Marlborough epitaph circulated in manuscript, as it almost certainly did, 'it was readily available for plagiary' ('Verse of Lady Mary Wortley Montagu', p. 419). On the other hand, the Hervey family were also friends of the actress, and Hervey served not only as an executor of her will but as a pall-bearer at her funeral (Halsband, pp. 27–8, 76, 103–4), and wrote an epilogue for James Thomson's play *Sophonisba* that she was to have spoken (Poem 35). Odd though it may seem to adapt part of so personal a poem as an epitaph to another subject, the last four lines are more appropriate to Oldfield than to Marlborough, and Hervey had also, around this time, changed the addressee of his imitation of Horace's Ode XI in Book I from a woman to a man (see variants to Poem 5 and accompanying notes). There is, therefore, a plausible case for regarding both poems as his. If, as seems highly likely, the epitaph on Marlborough circulated in manuscript, it could easily have found its way into the papers edited by Dallaway, but it is significant that Montagu is not recorded as having claimed it.

Finally, it is worth noting that another, and quite different, poem probably by Hervey appears on the same page of the *Gentleman's Magazine* as the epitaph. This is 'Written Impromptu to a Lady, Stung by a Bee' (Poem 49). It, and the epitaph, could have reached the editor of the magazine through Hervey's brother Henry.

***Context and date.*** John Churchill, first Duke of Marlborough (1650–1722), was the most celebrated of British military commanders. He achieved famous victories over the French at Blenheim (1704), Ramillies (1706) and Malplaquet (1709). He died on 16 June 1722 and was buried on 9 August. Recent assessments of his career are available in John B. Hattendorf, Augustus J. Veenendaal Jr and Rolof van Hövel tot Westerflier (eds.), *Marlborough: Soldier and Diplomat* (Rotterdam: Karwansaray, 2012); Hattendorf is also the author of the impressive entry in *ODNB*. Anne Oldfield (1683–1730) was one of the most famous actresses of her period. She died on 23 October 1730, and her funeral, followed by burial in Westminster Abbey, was a major public event. The poem must have been adapted from the epitaph on Marlborough shortly afterwards, given that it was printed in the following January.

***Textual commentary.*** The sole source for the epitaph on Marlborough is that in Dallaway's edition (*Works*, V, 156). There are two substantive variants between it and the epitaph on Oldfield, as noted. The only emendation to the text in Dallaway is to the position of a semi-colon, as recorded in the List of Emendations. As the various sources for Oldfield's epitaph differ only in accidentals, there are no substantive variants to record. The manuscript in the Folger Shakespeare Library appears to have been copied from the *Gentleman's Magazine*, because it is preceded and followed by exactly the same alternative epitaphs as are printed there.

## 31a John Duke of Marlborough

When the proud Frenchman's strong rapacious hand
Spread over Europe ruin and command,
Our sinking temples and expiring law
With trembling dread the rolling tempest saw,
Destin'd a province to insulting Gaul;
This Genius rose, and stopp'd the ponderous fall.
His temperate valour form'd no giddy scheme,
No victory rais'd him to a rage of fame;
The happy temper of his even mind
No danger e'er could shock, or conquest blind.
Fashion'd alike, by Nature and by Art,
To please, engage, and interest, ev'ry heart.

In public life by all who saw approv'd,
In private hours by all who knew him lov'd.

## 31b Epitaph on Anne Oldfield

Fashion'd alike by nature and by art,
To please, engage, and int'rest ev'ry heart:
In publick life, by all who saw, approv'd;
In private life, by all who knew her lov'd.

# 32 Epitaph on the Queen

***Source.*** *Gentleman's Magazine*, 7 (December 1737), 759.

***Complementary sources.*** None has come to light.

***Attribution.*** *Gentleman's Magazine*.

***Context and date.*** Queen Caroline died on 20 November 1737 after an excruciating illness. Hervey, who had become her intimate companion during his years at court, was nearby. He records the process of the final stages of her illness and her death in painful detail in *Some Materials* (Sedgwick, III, 877–915). The Queen's death affected him both personally and politically. Not only had he come to love her as a friend, but she was his main source of influence at court, and so it is with her death that his memoirs effectively end. In a letter from St James's to Conyers Middleton dated 4 February 1738, Hervey tells how the King hinted that he might write an epitaph on the Queen by remarking that she deserved an epitaph very different from one on Cardinal Mazarin applied to her satirically in a newspaper of the day (SRO 941/47/7, pp. 135–6; printed in part in Ilchester, pp. 276–7). He responded with one in Latin that was later printed, first on its own and then with an English translation: *Epitaphium Reginae Carolinae* (Poem 107). Hervey's brother, who had by then taken the name Henry Aston Hervey, wrote a verse translation that survives in manuscript in the Bodleian Library, MS. Add. A. 190. In a letter to his cousin and friend Charlotte Digby a month later, Hervey referred not only to the Latin epitaph, a copy of which he had sent her without telling her he had written it, but also to one in English (SRO 941/47/4, pp. 627–31 (4 March 1738); printed in Ilchester, pp. 279–81). As Lord Ilchester infers in his edition of a selection of Hervey's letters, it is this epitaph, presumably, that appeared in the *Gentleman's Magazine*. However, quoting the same letter to Mrs Digby as Lord Ilchester, Robert Halsband refers to the epitaph in the *Gentleman's* as a parody, evidently unable to believe that what now seems a mawkish and excessive display of feeling could have been intended seriously (p. 228). But Halsband offers no evidence for such a view, and the fact that the title represents the poem as extempore gives warrant for the volume of feeling exhibited. In his letter to Mrs Digby, Hervey remarked that, though he found the Latin poem difficult to write, the English one came easily: 'for truth furnish'd the thoughts, and my Heart felt too much for Words not to flow from me on that Occasion as naturally and plentyfully as my Tears' (SRO 941/47/4, p. 627; Ilchester, p. 279). Given, too, that Hervey's brother Henry had close contacts with the *Gentleman's* that would have provided an easy conduit for the poem, and in the absence of any poem that the *Gentleman's* epitaph might be seen as parodying, Halsband's view has to be rejected.

***Textual commentary.*** No emendations have been required to the *Gentleman's* text.

## Written *extempore* by Lord *H* ——, on the melancholy News of her Majesty's Death

While ev'ry heart bemoans the widow'd Lands,
And GEORGE, in sympathy, our tears demands;
Virtue and learning mourn their patron[1] lost,
The pride of *Anspach*,[2] *Britain*'s joy and boast:
Accept, great shade,[3] nor lower lays[4] refuse,
The greatest off'rings of a private muse;
Since *Britain*'s crimes[5] call loud for Heaven's wrath,
Crimes, strange! that claim a CAROLINA's death:
While higher strains the lofty theme engage,
And matchless worth e'en warms poetick rage;
Let my low flight her monument inform,
Which thus shall speak to ages yet unborn:–
Here lies inclos'd, – tremble, ye great and high! –
As much of human greatness as could die:

1. *their patron*: Caroline could certainly claim to have been a patron of learning. According to Stephen Taylor in his *ODNB* article on her, not only 'Leibniz and John Perceval, first earl of Egmont, were impressed by her learning and intelligence', but 'she acted as patron and intermediary in the correspondence between Leibniz and Samuel Clarke about Newtonian doctrines and the nature of free will', and 'consciously projected an image of herself as a promoter of enlightened ideas', placing 'busts of Boyle, Locke, Newton, Clarke, and Wollaston … in the hermitage she erected at Richmond'.

2. *Anspach*: the Queen's title in her own right was Princess Caroline of Brandenburg-Ansbach.

3. *shade*: 'The visible but impalpable form of a dead person, a ghost' (*OED*).

4. *lays*: songs.

5. *Britain's crimes*: Hervey may be referring here to an attack on the ministry in *A Poem Sacred to the Memory of … Daniel Pulteney … By the Author of the Duel* (1731). *The Duel* had praised William Pulteney at Hervey's expense. *A Poem Sacred to the Memory* praised Daniel's opposition to the court party, the 'servile Train' who 'Were pleas'd with Infamy, and proud of Shame', concluding with a hope that heaven might 'in spite of *Britain*'s Crimes, | A *Patriot Pulteney*, spare to latest *Times*'. The phrase also appears in Edward Young's 'The Sailor's Prayer': 'If Britain's Crimes support not Britain's foes' (line 3) published as part of his *Sea-Piece* in 1755.

Yet think not, mournful reader, aught amiss.
She's gone to heav'nly joys and endless bliss;
She's gone from care and pain[6] to peace above,
From GEORGE, that's first below, to him that's first above.

6. *care and pain*: these words, which refer to the appalling suffering the Queen underwent in the last stages of her illness, are much more plausibly read as the response of an eye-witness than as part of a parody.

# 33 Lord Hervey's Epitaph upon the Earl of Bristol

***Main source.*** BL Add. MS 5822, ff. 95v–96v. This is one of the manuscript volumes produced by the antiquary William Cole (1714–82).

***Complementary manuscript sources.*** None has come to light.

***Complementary print source.*** John Gage, *The History and Antiquities of Suffolk. Thingoe Hundred* (London: by Samuel Bentley, 1838), pp. 296–7, a modernised text of the BL manuscript.

***Attribution.*** Dr Philip Williams, Public Orator of the University of Cambridge and President (Senior Fellow) of St John's College, who transcribed the manuscript copied by Cole.

***Context and date.*** The poem was almost certainly written after Hervey's dismissal as Lord Privy Seal on 12 July 1742, because it was then that, after several fallow years following the Queen's death, the final phase of his writing career began. His mother had died in May of the year before, and his father had already attained the venerable age of seventy-seven, though as it happened he was to outlive Hervey, who died only a year later in August 1743. On the basis of its content, too, the poem is likely to have been written late in Hervey's career, for it reflects the bitterness about public life that had by then engulfed him. It is not known how the poem reached Dr Williams, but a possible intermediary might have been Conyers Middleton, Hervey's friend and correspondent at Cambridge, who was also a close friend of William Cole. In the event Hervey's epitaph was not inscribed on the Earl's tombstone, for which indeed it would probably have been too long. His relationship with the Earl had always been a close and a loving one, even though they had their political differences, and it is best regarded in two lights: as a statement of Whig principles concerning the proper relation between peer and country, and as a son's tribute to a father for whom he bore great respect and affection. The latter are amply attested by the graceful and moving closing triplet.

***Textual commentary.*** There is no reason for emending Cole's transcript, except for removing the innumerable underlinings for which he had a confirmed predilection. It is no exaggeration to say that they extend to almost every phrase in the poem.

## Lord Hervey's Epitaph upon the Earl of Bristol[1]

Here lies intomb'd, if upright, pious, just,
Are Qualities can consecrate mere Dust,

1. Title: this cannot be authorial, so it must have come from Williams or Cole.

The sacred Dust of one, so truely great,
He never sunk[2] to Offices of State.

Those Talents, which enabled him to fill
The highest Posts, depriv'd him of the Will.

Honours he saw by Merit seldom worn,
And Staffs[3] and Bags[4] by Kn—s and Blo—ds[5] born;
And rightly thought their Value was destroy'd,
When in such worthless Company enjoy'd.
And with this just Contempt for usual Fame,
And real Dignity, his proper Aim,
He first ennobled his own antient Name.[6]
The only Favour which the Crown could give,
He thought worth asking, or wou'd e'er receive.

The Name of Servant was too near to Slave;
So all his Service[7] he to England gave:
A loyal Subject therefore; but no more;

2. *sunk*: the first of the poem's several paradoxes reflecting the low esteem in which Hervey had come to hold public office.

3. *Staffs*: a staff is 'A rod or wand, of wood or ivory, borne as an ensign of office or authority; *spec.* as the badge of certain chief officers of the Crown' (*OED*).

4. *Bags*: reference to another emblem of office, such as the purse Hervey sports proudly as Lord Privy Seal in his portrait from the studio of Jean-Baptiste van Loo, painted a year or so before. The portrait may be seen in the National Portrait Gallery, and an image is easily accessible from the Gallery's website.

5. *Kn—s and Blo—ds*: Knaves and Blockheads.

6. *He first ... antient name*: the Hervey family had been long established as important landowners, but, according to the *ODNB* article on the Earl by Philip Carter, 'An earlier Hervey barony had become extinct on the death of William, Baron Hervey of Kidbrooke, in June 1642'. The reference here is to the elder John Hervey's accession to the House of Lords as a result of having been created Baron Hervey of Ickworth in the county of Suffolk in 1703. As 'an eager supporter of the revolution of 1688 and the Act of Settlement', he gained his peerage in recognition of his strong support for the Whigs, and especially through the influence of the Duke and Duchess of Marlborough, who were also instrumental in his being created Earl of Bristol shortly after the accession of George I in 1714 (*ODNB*). Gage quotes from the Duchess's memoir her remark: 'As for *titles of honour*, I never was concerned in making any peer but one, and that was my lord Hervey, the present Earl of Bristol' (*History and Antiquities*, p. 296; *An Account of the Conduct of the Dowager Duchess of Marlborough, from her First Coming to Court, to the Year 1710* (London: by James Bettenham, for George Hawkins, 1742), p. 297). The reference is to his first title.

7. *Service*: in context, this means above all support for the 1688 Revolution, the Act of Settlement and the Hanoverian succession.

He serv'd no Prince's Will,[8] but legal Power.
This, with a due Respect, he still obey'd;
To that no Court, no servile Flatt'ry paid.
The public Welfare, and the People's Cause,
His Country's Freedom, and her sacred Laws
Were the great Objects ever in his View,
Were the great Points he labour'd to pursue.

Yet glad, when Parliaments allow'd Retreat,
To seek the Shade of his paternal Seat:
Whose nat'ral Beauty by his Art improv'd
With half enthusiastic[9] Warmth he lov'd.

In rural Pastimes, and in letter'd Ease,[10]
Here he was ever pleas'd, and try'd to please.
To all around beneficent and kind;
Studious to give the Ease he wish'd to find:
Nor this from Ostentation, Rule, or Art;
But from an open, gen'rous, feeling Heart;
With all those Qualities, that recommend
The Master, Parent, Husband and the Friend.[11]

And in Life's sober Evening, tho' he told
Nestorian[12] Years, his Mind grew never old:

8. *He served no Prince's Will*: the Earl had demonstrated this by supporting the Prince of Wales against his father when the two fell out in 1717, after which his wife became one of the Ladies of the Bedchamber to Princess Caroline; in context, 'Prince' here means 'King'. As Carter remarks, in the 1720s the Earl 'was an opponent of the Walpole government, and in March 1733 spoke in favour of a reduced standing army' (*ODNB*), both of which stances were contrary to those of his son.

9. *enthusiastic*: 'Of feelings, convictions, etc.: That is of the nature of, that amounts to, *enthusiasm n. 3* ("Rapturous intensity of feeling in favour of a person, principle, cause, etc."); intensely ardent, rapturous' (*OED*).

10. *letter'd Ease*: literary pursuits; as Carter notes, the Earl was 'an accomplished author and scholar, examples of whose verse and interests in learning may be seen in his *Letter-Books*'.

11. *The Master, Parent, Husband and the Friend*: the line recalls one in Hervey's elegy and epitaph for his sister Elizabeth, 'The Friend, the Daughter, Sister, and the Wife' (Poem 30, line 6), although, reflecting the emphases of patriarchal culture, the order of the epithets is different.

12. *Nestorian*: 'Of, characteristic of, or relating to Nestor; resembling Nestor in longevity or wisdom', Nestor being a character in Greek mythology who, having been one of the

As clear, as penetrating, quick and gay
As at the Noontide of his youthful Day.

His Observations just, his Judgement true;
While Knowledge made his Converse ever new:
Those Proteus Gifts[13] so thro'ly he possest
Of suiting his Discourse to every Guest:
Each in their different Stile he entertain'd,
Still Cæsar-like[14] he saw, he spoke, he gain'd.

His Manner thus, and Principles approv'd,
He liv'd and dy'd esteem'd, and lik'd and lov'd.

But whilst, with what Fidelity I can,
I draw this Picture of the real Man,
Oh! let not late Posterity believe,
That one fictitious Praise these Numbers[15] give,
Or that, transmitted by a Son he lov'd,
That Son asserts more than the Father prov'd.
He only seeks, perhaps with too much Pride,
His Motive Gratitude, and Truth his Guide,
The Being, which to him his Father gave,
To give that Father's Worth beyond the Grave,
And Part of what shou'd never dye, to save.

Argonauts, took an advisory role in the Trojan Wars, being too old to fight, and later entertained Telemachus while he was searching for news of his father Ulysses.

13. *Proteus Gifts*: Proteus was a sea-god in Greek mythology who had the ability to change shape; to have his gifts is therefore to be a kind of Renaissance man, multi-talented.

14. *Caesar-like*: the reference is to Caesar's famous boast *Veni, vidi, vici* ('I came, I saw, I conquered'), according to Plutarch and Suetonius written by Julius Caesar in 47 BCE as a comment on his short war with Pharnaces II of Pontus in the city of Zela.

15. *Numbers*: 'Metrical periods or feet; lines, verses' (*OED*).

# 34 Lord Hervey's Epitaph on Himself

***Source.*** SRO 941/53/1, p. 210.

***Other sources.*** None is known. The epitaph was first printed in Halsband, pp. 306–7.

***Attribution.*** Lord Bristol, Hervey's father; William Hervey, his son.

***Context and date.*** According to Robert Halsband, Hervey wrote the epitaph in 1742 'while on a visit to Ickworth, and had given it to his father, who endorsed it: "Long o very long may it be before it will be engrav'd"' (Halsband, p. 306). William Hervey's transcript contains a longer version of this remark, written above the epitaph: 'My most dear & valuable son Ld. Hy's Epitaph written by himself in 1742. Long, o very long may it be before it will be engrav'd. (this written in Ld. B's hand-writing)'. The more general context is Hervey's dismissal from office in the same year, which may have given his fears about his mortality, never far from his mind, extra point. The epitaph was not actually used on his tomb, which instead, after a prose summary of his life and title, descent, offices and the date of his death, has a Latin epitaph provided by Conyers Middleton:

Huic versatile ingenium, sic pariter
ad omnia fuit,
Ut natum ad id unum diceres
Quodcunque ageret.

(Gage, *History and Antiquities*, p. 318;
*Ickworth Parish Registers*, p. 75)

The epitaph is not by Middleton, but is rather a remark by the Roman historian Livy on the elder Cato: 'his comprehensive genius was so adapted to everything alike that you would say that whatever he was doing was the one thing for which he was born' (Livy, *The History of Rome, XI (Books 38–39)*, chapter 40 (Loeb, pp. 348–9)). Bill Overton's colleague Gillian Spraggs, who identified this source, points out that it represents a graceful tribute from an author that Middleton and Hervey had studied very closely while conducting their learned correspondence on the Roman senate. A further self-memorialising is pointed to by Halsband (p. 307). Horace Walpole records a humorous self-appraisal from Hervey that is in keeping with the epitaph he wrote for himself. Walpole wrote in a letter to John Chute dated 6 February 1759 that 'the late Lord Hervey said, his arms should be *a cat,* scratchant, with this motto, *for my friends where they itch, for my enemies where they are sore*' (Walpole, *Correspondence*, XXXV, 109).

***Textual commentary.*** No emendations are required to William Hervey's transcript.

## Lord Hervey's Epitaph on Himself

Few men he lik'd; and fewer still believ'd;
Fewest of all he trusted, none deciev'd:
But as[1] from temper, principle or pride,
To gain whom he dislik'd, he never try'd,
And this the pride of others disapprov'd,
So lik'd by many, he by few was lov'd.[2]
To those he lov'd a real friend he brought,
And in that character without a fault.
What his opinions, Parts or conduct were,
This monument pretends not to declare;
He had a truly warm and honest breast,
Let his own writings speak the rest.[3]

1. *as*: 'Introducing an adverbial clause of respect: so far as, in the degree, manner, or case in which' (*OED*).

2. *he by few was lov'd*: Hervey's acid comments on many of his contemporaries in *Some Materials* show that he did not suffer a fool gladly.

3. The line is a foot short, leaving more to be said.

# EPILOGUE

# 35 Epilogue Design'd for *Sophonisba*

***Main source.*** *A Collection of Poems in Four Volumes. By Several Hands.* 4 vols. (London: Robert Dodsley, 1755, ESTC T115892), IV, 107–8.

***Complementary manuscript sources.*** None known.

***Complementary print sources.*** *Select Collection of Modern Poems* (Edinburgh: sold by A. Donaldson, 1759), pp. 56–7; *A Collection and Selection of English Prologues and Epilogues* (London: for Fielding and Walker, 1779), IV, 49–50.

***Attribution.*** Included in a group of poems in the *Collection*, the first of which is '*By the late Lord HERVEY*' and this '*By the Same*'.

***Context and date.*** James Thomson's *Sophonisba* was first performed at the Theatre Royal, Drury Lane on 28 February 1730 and ran for ten nights. James Sambrook provides an account of both the play and its reception in *James Thomson 1700–1748: A Life* (Oxford: Clarendon Press, 1991), pp. 81–95. It was a major social success, with the Prince of Wales attending a performance and Thomson's being introduced to Queen Caroline in order to present her with a copy of the printed play. Hervey saw the play on 3 March (Ilchester, p. 49).

Anne Oldfield, who played the part of Sophonisba to acclaim, was the mistress of Charles Churchill, the illegitimate nephew of the Duke of Marlborough, and through him became a friend of Hervey's parents and of Hervey himself (see Joanne Lafler, *The Celebrated Mrs Oldfield* (Carbondale and Edwardsville: Southern Illinois Press, 1989), pp. 123–4). When she died later that year, on 23 October 1730, Hervey was a pall-bearer at her funeral and one of her executors (Halsband, pp. 103–4). Hervey's epilogue was not the one printed with the play (which is identified as 'By a Friend'), and in any case the epilogue was spoken not by Anne Oldfield but by Jane Cibber, who was not in the play; in what Sambrook suggests was a reciprocal arrangement, Oldfield delivered the epilogue to the contemporary *Timoleon* (*James Thomson*, p. 90). Sambrook makes the suggestion that Hervey resented the rejection of his epilogue, but it is possible that it was written specifically for Oldfield's benefit night, announced in the *Daily Post* (6 March 1730) as a performance of *Sophonisba* on 19 March. Perhaps on that occasion Oldfield was to deliver the epilogue herself. Hervey had no known connection with Thomson at this time (he was later to disparage his poetry to Algarotti (Halsband, pp. 246–7)) or with the managers of Drury Lane, so the epilogue, even though it is concerned with the play rather than the actor, is most plausibly interpreted as a favour for her. However, as it turned out, the last performance of *Sophonisba* was that of 17 March, and Oldfield's benefit was instead a performance of Rowe's *The Fair Penitent*, though tickets for *Sophonisba* were accepted that night. The most likely explanation, therefore, for the epilogue's non-use and its destined speaker is that it was prepared as a gesture of friendship for a benefit whose nature was later changed.

In the play, Sophonisba, the daughter of Hasdrubal, leader of the Carthaginians, is motivated by love of country. She had been loved by Masinissa, defeated early in his life by Syphax, King of Masaesylia, but she married Syphax in an alliance against Rome. At the start of the play Syphax has been defeated by Masinissa, who is now fighting for Rome under the leadership of Scipio. Sophonisba fears for Carthage and for her own humiliation, taken captive to Rome. Masinissa, now her conqueror, still loves her, and she marries him (the previous marriage, Thomson insists, being annulled by their captivity) after he has vowed to obtain her release from Roman bondage. But Scipio refuses to assent to that release and Masinissa sends Sophonisba poison as her only possible release. She drinks it and dies.

The emotional pivot of the drama is the decision to marry at the end of Act III, Scene 3. Masinissa and Sophonisba have quarrelled because of Masinissa's jealousy of Syphax and their radically differing evaluations of Rome and its civilisation, but Masinissa's love overwhelms his anger.

MASINISSA. Since *Rome* and slavery drive thee to the brink;
Let this immediate night exchange our vows,
Secure my bliss, our future fortunes blend,
Set thee, the queen of beauty, on my throne,
And make it doubly mine. — *A wretched gift*
To what my love could give!
SOPHONISBA. What? marry thee?
This night?
MASINISSA. Thou dear one! yes, this very night . . .
I know thy purpose; it would plead for *Syphax*.
He shall have all, thou dearest! shall have all,
Crowns, trifles, kingdoms, all again, but thee,
But thee, thou more than all!
SOPHONISBA *(Aside)* Bear witness heaven!
This is alone for *Carthage*.

(*The Tragedy of Sophonisba* (London, 1730, ESTC T230316), pp. 40–1)

Thomson intended to heighten the problematic nature of the marriage by including a Nuptial Song celebrating sexual love; in the printed edition it is relegated to an appendix. In the play the action resumes the following day and Syphax comes to rebuke Sophonisba for her betrayal.

The comic nature of both Hervey's epilogue and the one printed with the play conflicts with the gravity of the tragedy and Thomson's political idealism; Thomson himself disliked such clashes of tone between play and epilogue (Sambrook, *James Thomson*, p. 85). Hervey's epilogue reinterprets Thomson's careful intertwining of the personal and political as a tale of the triumph of sexual desire and offers advice on the wisdom of withholding sexual favours. The contrastingly grave ending, however, accommodates this verse to Hervey's compassion for socially ostracised women such as Lady Abergavenny (Poem 29) and the heroines of his Ovidian epistles (Poems 1–4).

***Textual commentary.*** The text from Dodsley's *Collection* is presented unamended, except in the correction of 'charm' to 'charms' at the end of line 23, as clearly required by the rhyme. The Epilogue also appeared in *Select Collection of Modern Poems* (Edinburgh: sold by A. Donaldson, 1759), pp. 56–7, and in *A Collection and Selection of English Prologues and Epilogues* (London: for Fielding and Walker, 1779, IV, 49–50), the latter of which is reprinted by Pierre Danchin in *Prologues and EPILOGUES of the Eighteenth Century*, 8 vols. (Nancy: Presses Universitaires de Nancy, 1993), III, 343–44. The later copies vary from Dodsley in only two matters of substance (and in both cases, follow changes in the six-volume 1758 edition of Dodsley): 'charm' is corrected to 'charms' (l. 23), and 'But did she take the way to whet that sword' becomes, with opposite meaning, but the same bawdy innuendo, 'But did not take that way to whet the sword' (l. 21).

## EPILOGUE design'd for SOPHONISBA, And to have been spoken by Mrs. OLDFIELD By the Same.

Before you sign poor Sophonisba's doom,
In her behalf petitioner I come;
Not but our author knows, whate'er I say,
That I could find objections to his play.
This double marriage for her country's good,
I told him never would be understood,
And that ye all would say, 'twas flesh and blood.[1]
Had Carthage only been in madam's head,
Her champion never had been in her – bed:
For could the ideot think a husband's name
Would make him quit his interest, friends and fame;

1. *'twas flesh and blood*: that Sophonisba was motivated by sexual desire.

That he would risque a kingdom for a wife,
And act dependent in a place for life?
Yet when stern Cato[2] shall condemn the fair,
Whilst publick good she thunder'd in your ear,
If private interest had a *little* share.
You know, she acted not against the laws
Of those old-fashioned times; that in her cause
Old Syphax could no longer make a stand,
And Massinissa woo'd her sword in hand.[3]
But did she take the way to whet that sword?
Heroes fight coldly when wives give the word.
She should have kept him keen, employ'd her charms
Not as a bribe, but to reward his arms;
Have told him when Rome yielded she would yield,
And sent him fresh, not yawning, to the field.
She talk'd it well to rouse him to the fight,
But like Penelope, when out of sight,
All she had done by day, undid by night.[4]
Is this your wily Carthaginian kind?
No English woman had been half so kind.
What from a husband's hand could she expect
But ratsbane,[5] or that common fate, neglect?
Perhaps some languishing soft fair may say,
Poyson's so shocking – but consider pray,
She fear'd the Roman, he the marriage chain;
All other means to free them both were vain.
Let none then Massinissa's conduct blame,
He first his love consulted, then his fame.

2. *Cato*: a reference to the stern and unambiguous morality of the hero of Addison's *Cato* (London: for Jacob Tonson, 1713).

3. *make a stand . . . sword in hand*: phallic reinterpretation of Masinissa's military victory over Syphax.

4. *All she had done by day, undid by night*: In the *Odyssey*, Odysseus' loyal wife Penelope undertakes to answer her suitors when she has finished weaving a burial shroud, but she undoes the day's work at night. The epilogue argues that if sexual favours are granted in advance, a desired task will remain unaccomplished.

5. *ratsbane*: poison, specifically arsenic.

And if the fair one with too little art,
Whilst seemingly she play'd a patriot-part,
Was secretly the dupe of her own heart;
Forgive a fault she strove so well to hide,
Nor be compassion to her fate deny'd,
Who liv'd unhappily, and greatly dy'd.

# EPIGRAMS AND A RIDDLE

# INTRODUCTION TO EPIGRAMS AND A RIDDLE

Epigrams are short witty poems, concise and memorable. In the English tradition they are often a couplet or a quatrain; frequently satirical, though not necessarily so. As Coleridge has it in his poem 'Epigram':

> What is an Epigram? A dwarfish whole,
> Its body brevity, and wit its soul.[1]

In Greek culture epigrams were originally inscriptions, hence the need for concision. They came into English through the Greek Anthology and also through the writings of Martial and Catullus.[2] In the seventeenth century Ben Jonson and Herrick are the most notable practitioners, and the epigram is particularly associated with royalist and court circles.[3] Hervey's fondness for the epigrammatic seems to begin with the amatory aspects of court life and to progress to political matters.

Hervey writes some short, classic epigrams (notably Poem 39 but also 41 and 43), but in other poems he develops his argument beyond traditional length, while retaining the same qualities of wit and pithiness. These poems offer a definition, or provide a summing up, in epigrammatic fashion.

1. 'Epigram on Epigrams, from Wernicke' (Poem 305), Coleridge, *Poetical Works*, I, part 2, ed. by J. C. C. Mays, Bollingen Series LXXV (Princeton, NJ: Princeton University Press, 2001), p. 728.

2. See William Fitzgerald, *Martial: The World of the Epigram* (Chicago: University of Chicago Press, 2007), especially the first chapter.

3. See Ann Baynes Coiro, *Robert Herrick's Hesperides and the Epigram Book Tradition* (Baltimore, MD: Johns Hopkins University Press, 1988), especially part 2; G. Rostrevor Hamilton, *English Verse Epigram* (London: British Council and National Book League, 1965).

# 36 Mr *Harvey's* Answer to a Lady, Who Ask'd Him, *What Is Love?*

***Main source.*** BL MS Stowe 972 f. 4v(b)–5r.

***Complementary manuscript source.*** Brotherton Lt 12, p. 26.

***Complementary print sources.*** *Gentleman's Magazine*, 1 (July 1731), 305; *A Complete Collection of Old and New English and Scotch Songs*, 4 vols. (London: by T. Boreman, 1736), IV, 184; *The Universal Spectator and Weekly Journal*, 26 March 1737; *The Warbling Muses* (London: for G. Woodfall, 1749), p. 185; *Poems Written Occasionally by the late John Winstanley, . . . with Many Others*, ed. by George Winstanley, 2 vols. (Dublin: S. Powell for the editor, 1751), II, 266–7; *A Collection of Poems, from the Best Authors*, ed. by James Elphinston (London: by James Bettenham, 1764), p. 172; *A Select Collection of English Songs*, 3 vols. (London: for J. Johnson, 1783), I, 90–1; *The Poetical Farrago*, 2 vols. (London: by G. Stafford for J. Deighton, 1794), I, 54–5.

***Attribution.*** The sole attribution is that in the title to the Stowe manuscript, which is given as the title to the poem here. If this is correct, and if the poem is by Hervey, it must date from before 14 November 1723, for on the death that day of his elder half-brother Carr, the courtesy title Baron Hervey of Ickworth descended to him. It is possible that the poem dates from this time, as Hervey was writing social and other verse at the period. Alternatively, the poem could have been written later by Hervey's brother Henry, who was also an accomplished writer of light verse. Whether or not Lord Hervey wrote the poem – and the Stowe attribution strongly suggests that either he or his brother did so – it is included here because it complements two other poems on the same subject that are ascribed to him: Poem 37, 'To a Lady Who Ask'd, *What Is Love?*', and Poem 38, 'The Answer to a Receipt to Cure Love'. It could have reached the *Gentleman's Magazine* through Henry Hervey, although if it did so it might have been expected to have been attributed to him.

***Context and date.*** For discussion of the date, see the paragraph above. The social context of the poem is the manuscript circulation of light verse. Poems on the topic of love seem to have attracted special interest, as the other poems attributed to Hervey show, and as their later print circulation in the form of songs throughout the century attests further. For an example of another poem on the same topic that also dates from the mid-1720s, see Henry Baker, 'Love', in *Original Poems, Serious and Humorous* (London: for the author, 1725), pp. 74–5.

***Textual commentary.*** The Stowe text requires only a few minor emendations to punctuation, as indicated in the List of Emendations. Textual variants indicate that most of the printed copies seem to have taken their lead from the *Gentleman's Magazine*. The resemblances in the 1736 *Complete Collection, Winstanley*, the 1764 *Collection of Poems*, the 1783 *Select Collection* and the 1794 *Poetical Farrago* are especially noticeable.

## Mr *Harvey's* answer to a Lady, who ask'd Him *What is Love?*

I.

Love's no irregular Desire,
No sudden Start of raging Pain;
That in a Moment grows a Fire,
And in a Moment cools again.

II.

Not found in the sad Sonneteer,
Who sings of Darts, Despair, and Chains;
And, by whose dismal Verse 'tis clear,
He wants not only Heart, but Brains.[1]

III.

Nor is it centred in the Beau;
Who sighs by Rule, in Order dies;
Whose all consists in outward Show,
And Want of Wit, by Dress supplies.

IV.

No! Love is Something so divine,
Description would but make it less;
'Tis what I know, but can't define;
'Tis what I feel, but can't express.

1. *And, by . . . but Brains*: the pithiness of these two lines, unusual in a lyric poem, are especially characteristic of Hervey. His brother's verse is more conventional.

# 37 To a Lady Who Ask'd, *What Is Love?*

***Main source.*** BL MS Stowe 972, f. 12v(b).

***Complementary manuscript sources.*** Brotherton Lt q 20, f. 34v; BL Add. MS 75381, p. 82.

***Complementary print sources.*** *Gentleman's Magazine*, 2 (July 1732), 870; *The Craftsman*, 1 July 1732 (repr. in 'Caleb D'Anvers', *The Craftsman*, 14 vols. (London: for R. Francklin, 1731–7), ix (1732), 162–3); *The Scarborough Miscellany: for the Year 1734* (London: by J. Wilford, 1734), p. 54; *The Warbling Muses* (London: for G. Woodfall, 1749), pp. 187–8; 'H. C.', *Miscellanea Nova et Curiosa* (Dublin: by S. Powell, 1749), p. 341; 'Nestor Druid', *The Lady's Curiosity, or, Weekly Apollo* (London: by C. Sympson, 1752), p. 11; *The Bouquet: A Selection of Poems from the most Celebrated Authors* (London: by E. Hodson for J. Deighton, 1792). As a further example of continued circulation, the poem appears without attribution as the epigraph to Chapter V of the anonymous *Three Weeks in the Downs, Or Conjugal Fidelity Rewarded* (London: by John Bennett; Plymouth: by W. Bennett, 1829).

***Attribution.*** Brotherton ('To one who ask'd what Love is by L[or]d Hervey'); the only other attribution in any of the sources is to 'Mr. Greenaway' in the *Scarborough Miscellany*.

***Context and date.*** The poem appears to date from the early 1730s when it was first printed, and it may be related to two other poems on a similar subject attributed to Hervey: Poem 38 'The Answer to a Receipt to Cure Love', and Poem 36, 'Mr *Harvey's* Answer to a Lady, Who Ask'd Him, *What Is Love?*', which appears in the same Stowe manuscript and in a further Brotherton manuscript – although, in the latter case, the title 'Mr.' raises questions of attribution discussed in the headnote to that poem. Both poems may have reached the *Gentleman's Magazine* through Hervey's brother Henry. What is striking about them is their open-mindedness and their avoidance of libertine attitudes. These qualities are highlighted by comparison with Lord Lansdowne's epigram 'Definition of Love', which reflects the views of an earlier generation:

> Love is begot by fancy, bred
> By Ignorance, by Expectation fed,
> Destroy'd by Knowledge, and at best,
> Lost in the moment 'tis possess'd. (*The Genuine Works in Verse and Prose, of the Right Honourable George Granville, Lord Lansdowne*, 2 vols. (London: for J. Tonson, and L. Gilliver, 1732) I, 129)

***Textual commentary.*** As the poem must have circulated in manuscript before being printed, a manuscript source is preferable. The British Library dating of late eighteenth century rules out BL Add. MS 75381 as the main source. Of the other two manuscript copies, BL MS Stowe 972, f. 12v(b) seems, on the basis of the poems that surround it, to have been transcribed a little earlier than Brotherton Lt q 20. It is also a cleaner text, so that no emendations are required. There are relatively few textual variants across all copies.

## To a Lady who ask'd, *What is Love*?

'Tis somewhat that exists within,
By Pedants construed into Sin:
A Subtle particle of Fire
Which Heaven did with our Souls inspire;
Of such a mix'd, and doubtful Kind,
It pleases, while it racks the Mind:
In Lightning thro' our Eyes it breaks;
In Blushes glows upon our Cheeks;
Pants in the Breast, dilates the Heart,
And spreads its power thro' Every Part.
We feel it throb at every Kiss,
Yet know not why, nor what it is.

# 38 The Answer to a Receipt to Cure Love

***Main source.*** BL Add. MS 47127, f. 172r.

***Complementary manuscript sources.*** None has come to light.

***Complementary print sources.*** 'John Single', *The Batchelor's Recantation* (London: printed and sold by A. Dodd, 1731), pp. 11–12; *The Ulster Miscellany* ([Dublin?]: s.n., 1753), pp. 319–20; *The Ladies Complete Pocket-Book, for the Year of our Lord 1760* (London: for John Newbery, 1760), p. 16.

***Attribution.*** BL Add. MS 47127, f. 172r. The poem is indexed in the manuscript as 'Ld. Harvey . . . . . His Verses in answer to the receipt to cure Love' (f. 178v).

***Context and date.*** The poem responds to a widely circulated prose piece entitled 'A Receipt to cure / Love. 1726', the text of which is given in the manuscript as follows:

> Take eight Ounces of Consideration, and half the Quantity of Indifference, ten Grains of Ingratitude, Six Scruples of Patience, One Small Sprig of Rue, two good Handfulls of Employment, four Months Absence: Mix with it the constant Conversation of a Rival. To this you may add as much Discretion as Nature has allotted you; then boil altogether without Intermission till a third Part be consum'd, cooling it with a few Slights. Then spread it on the Thoughts of your Mistresses Imperfections, and apply the Plaister luke-warm to your Heart, Be sure not to take it off till it comes off itself, and if this proves not Successful your Case is very desperate.

What appears to be an earlier version of the recipe occurs in *Wits Secretary: or, the Lovers Magazine, an Accurate and Most Compleat Academy of Wit and Mirth* (London: for Daniel Pratt, [1720?]), p. 132; a much cruder attempt turns up in *Delights for Young Men and Maids* ([London]: by J. Cluer, [1725?]), n.p., reprinted in 1754 by William and Cluer Dicey, again presumably in London. The version in the British Library manuscript and the poem's three print instances is more subtle, and as will be easily seen, the poem refutes it point by point, emphasised in *The Batchelor's Recantation* and *The Ulster Miscellany* by italics. It comes from a period in the later 1720s when Hervey appears to have been attending more to verse, including light social verse such as this poem, than to other pursuits, especially politics; and it should be read in the context of Poems 36 and 37, which put forward similar ideas above love. It did not, however, achieve the circulation either of those two poems or of the recipe itself, which continued to occur in print and manuscript forms well into the nineteenth century.

***Textual commentary.*** The British Library manuscript requires only a few changes to spelling and punctuation, as indicated in the List of Emendations. The original use of initial capitals has been retained.

## The Answer
## by L$^d$ Harvey

O kind Physician, thy Receipt[1] will prove
Of little Service to thy Friend in Love.
Whene'er Consideration I apply,
New Beauties in the Charmer I descry.
To all Perfections she has just Pretence,
And thaws my Soul from cold Indifference.
Ingratitude's a Guilt she does not know,
She thanks the Heavens for Blessings they bestow.
She other Obligations never knew,
For all the Earth affords is but her due.
Speak Patience to the Wretch upon the Wheel
He knows no Torments like the Pangs I feel.
No Rue apply'd can e'er my Pains remove,
There is no Cure, alas! in Herbs for Love.[2]
Employment has my Peace of Mind destroy'd
For it's on her my Thoughts are all imploy'd.
To little Passions Absence gives a Cure,
To great Ones adds and makes 'em to endure:
So Wind puts out the Candle's glimmering Light,
But makes the Raging Furnace blaze more bright.
Each place produces Rivals to my View,
She but appears and She creates them new.
In vain, like me for Favours they implore,
And I'm a Slave with many Thousands more.
But Sure, where Numbers in Opinion meet

1. *Receipt*: remedy.

2. *There is no Cure . . . Love*: The line is italicised in the *Bachelor's Recantation* and accompanied by the footnote *Hei mihi quod nullis Amor est medicabilis herbis Ov.* The Latin sentence appears to conflate two from Ovid, *me miseram, quod amor non est medicabilis herbis* ('Alas, wretched me, that love may not be healed by herbs', *Heroides*, V. 149 (Loeb, pp. 68–9)), and *ei mihi, quod nullis amor est sanabilis herbis* ('Alas, that love is curable by no herbs', *Metamorphoses*, I. 523 (Loeb, pp. 38–9)).

To act as they do is to be discreet.
For Imperfections wou'd you Search the Fair
Find Spots in Ermines, tinge the Ambient Air.
Teach Me the Art to be no more her Slave,
And write thy Skill upon the restless Wave.
All these you must perform, ere you can find,
Fault in her Person, blemish in her Mind.

# 39 Extempore Epigram on Voltaire

***Source.*** Holograph letter from Mary Pendarves, later Delany, to her sister Charlotte, 29 February 1728, Newport Reference Library, q M416.6/012/DEL.

***Complementary manuscript sources.*** None.

***Complementary print sources.*** None; printed in Lady Llanover, *The Autobiography and Correspondence of Mary Granville, Mrs Delany*, 6 vols. (London: Richard Bentley, 1861–2), I (1861), 160.

***Attribution.*** Mary Pendarves, later Delany.

***Context and date.*** The epigram is introduced as follows: 'Mr Voltaires Henriade is not yet come out tis writ in French which for your Sake I am sorry for. You may remember in his crittisisms on Milton of a Passage he takes Notice of and finds great fault with in the Allegory of Sin & Death upon which My Lord Hervey (who by the by has been dying) said, of Voltaire who has not the reputation of being the best Man in the World'. It is followed by the remark 'he spoke it extempory' before the letter turns to another subject. The epigram reflects Hervey's view of what Voltaire had said about Milton rather than that of the man himself, whom Hervey knew and liked. Voltaire had been in England since 1726, and, as Halsband points out, Hervey had helped him find subscribers for a new edition of *Henriade*, 'published in March 1728, with Lord Bristol, Lady Hervey, and Hervey listed as buying copies' (p. 85). Voltaire composed a poem to Lady Hervey, later printed in Dodsley's *Collection* (1782 edn, IV, 238), and praised Hervey without naming him in his *Letters Concerning the English Nation*, in which he included his translation of some lines from Hervey's verse epistle to Lady Hervey about his journey from Florence to Lyons (see Poem 16 and headnote).

***Textual commentary.*** The epigram is provided just as Pendarves wrote it. It is untitled.

So much confusion so wicked and so thin
He seems at once a Chaos, Death, and Sin.

# 40 A Receipt to Make an Epigram

***Main source.*** BL Add. MS 70454, f. 63v.

***Complementary manuscript sources.*** Yale Osborn Collection c.229/2, ff. 7v–8r; Yale Osborn Collection c.152, p. 37.

***Complementary print sources.*** *Gentleman's Magazine*, 1 (November 1731), 495; *Grub-street Journal*, 25 November 1731, repr. in *Faithful Memoirs of the Grubstreet Society* (London: for the Grubstreet Society, 1732), p. 139; *The Weekly Amusement: or, The Universal Magazine* (15 March 1734; London: for J. and T. Dormer, 1735), II, 477; *Read's Weekly Journal*, 11 December 1736; *Joe Miller's Jests: or, the Wits Vade-Mecum* (London: for T. Read, 1743), p. 141, and many reprints; 'Ferdinando Foot', *The Nut-Cracker* (London: for J. Newbery, 1751), pp. 8–9; *The Sports of the Muses*, 2 vols. (London: by M. Cooper, 1752), II, 192. The epigram continued to be reprinted in numerous jest-books and the like till the end of the century and beyond.

***Attribution.*** 'By a Noble Lord', *Read's Weekly Journal*; 'the Right Hon. the late Lord Hervey', *Joe Miller's Jests*; 'the late Lord Hervey', *Nut-Cracker*; 'Lord Hervey', *Sports of the Muses*; 'by the Right hon[oura]ble Philip Earle of Chesterfield', Yale c.229/2; 'said to be wrote by Lord Chesterfield', Yale c.152; *Lord Chesterfield's Witticisms* (London: for Richard Snagg, [1773; repr. 1775?]), pp. 116–17. The fact that the larger number of eighteenth-century attributions – not all in texts recorded here – is to Hervey is not necessarily relevant, as the copies in many of the later jest-books seem to stem directly or indirectly from *Joe Miller's Jests*. More significant is that the poem does not appear in Chesterfield's *Miscellaneous Works* of 1777 (2 vols., London: for Edward and Charles Dilly), and that it is not claimed for Chesterfield either by Ernst-Browning, the editor of Chesterfield, *Wit and Wisdom*, the collection generally accepted as the most reliable, or by Sidney L. Gulick in his *Chesterfield Bibliography*. For two reasons it is difficult to know how much weight to attach to the attribution to Chesterfield in Yale c.292/2. First, although the poem occurs at the start of the collection, items do not appear to have been transcribed in chronological order and, where they are given dates, these range from 1705 to 1772. Second, the version given is shorter than the one in the British Library copy, as it does not contain lines 12–13 of the latter. This is in keeping with the later printings, starting with that of 1743 in *Joe Miller's Jests*. The other Yale manuscript, c.152, has the couplet that appears in the British Library copy but from its handwriting appears to date from later in the century. Although Walpole's attributions are generally reliable, that to Hervey in his *Works* of 1798 should probably be discounted, as the reference cited is the attribution in *The*

*Sports of the Muses* (I, 452). Nevertheless, Hervey seems the most likely author on stylistic grounds. Especially characteristic is the grammatical compression of line 4, a witty example of the very trait recommended. The triplet-cum-alexandrine of lines 9–11, though a common device in the period, is also deployed aptly and in Hervey's manner.

***Context and date.*** The epigram probably dates from the late 1720s or shortly before its first printings in November 1731. Its initial social context would have been the manuscript circulation of light verse; later, it descends into the stock in trade of jest-books.

***Textual commentary.*** The British Library copy has been chosen as the main source because it is probably the earliest. It comes from the collection of Edward Harley, Lord Oxford (1689–1741), more specifically from a volume entitled 'Miscellanies' described in the British Library catalogue as 'epigrams and poetry in the handwriting of Lord Oxford and Adrian Drift'. Punctuation has been supplied where it is lacking (see List of Emendations), but spelling and initial capitalisation have been left unchanged. Although the epigram was much reprinted, only a few general details have been gathered from items dated after the early 1750s, as the chances are that they simply reprint earlier copies. Substantive variants, while relatively few, may, however, help in the work of dating the manuscripts or of attribution.

## A Receipt[1] to make an Epigram

A pleasing subject first with Care provide,
Your matter must by Nature be Supply'd;
Nervous[2] your Diction, be your Measure[3] long;
Nor fear your Verse too Stiff if Sense be Strong;
In proper places proper Numbers Use,
And now the quicker, now the Slower choose,
Too Soon the Dactyle the performance Ends;[4]
But the Slow Spondee coming Thoughts Suspends.[5]

1. *Receipt*: 'A statement of the ingredients and procedure required for making a dish or an item of food or drink; = recipe n. 2. Also in extended use' (*OED*).

2. *Nervous*: 'Of argument, prose, poetry, literary style, etc.: vigorous, powerful, forcible; free from insipidity and diffuseness' (*OED*).

3. *Measure*: 'Rhythm in poetry as defined by syllabic quantity or stress' (*OED*); i.e. word-choice has to be compelling in proportion to line length.

4. *Too Soon the Dactyle . . . Ends*: as a dactyl consists of a heavier stress followed by two lighter ones, it has the effect of trailing off, especially at a line-ending.

5. *Slow Spondee coming Thoughts Suspends*: this is because a spondee, which consists of two heavier stresses, invites a pause.

Your last Attention on the Sting[6] bestow,
To that your good or ill Success you owe;
For there not Wit alone must Shine, but humour flow.[7]
If you'd receive Applause, or furnish Joy,
Your all-collected Strength on that Employ;
These Rules observ'd, your Epigram's compleated,
And Sure to please, altho' ten times repeated.

6. *Sting*: 'the "point" of an epigram or sarcasm' (*OED*).

7. *For there . . . flow*: the line is long, adding further emphasis to the triplet; at least two printings from the 1770s omit the first two words, reducing the alexandrine to a pentameter.

# 41 Note on Chiswick

***Main source.*** Manuscript at Chatsworth House, in the form of a letter addressed to the Countess of Burlington at Bath also containing the companion piece, Poem 42, 'Inscrib'd to Mr Kent'.

***Complementary manuscript sources.*** Portland (Welbeck) Pw V 693; Portland (Welbeck) Pw2 V 192; BL Add. MS 8127, f. 71r.

***Complementary print sources.*** *Gentleman's Magazine*, 6 (September 1736), 548; *A Collection of Select Epigrams* (London for C. Hitch and L. Hawes, and W. and J. Flackton, 1757), p. 37; *New Foundling Hospital for Wit*, IV (London: for J. Almon, 1771), 121; *New Foundling Hospital for Wit*, 6 vols. (London: for J. Debrett, 1784), I, 242; Samuel Ireland, *Picturesque Views on the River Thames*, 2 vols. (London: by T. and J. Egerton, 1792), II, 131. The poem is printed without attribution by Michael I. Wilson as part of Appendix III in *William Kent: Architect, Designer, Painter, Gardener, 1685–1748* (London and Boston: Routledge & Kegan Paul, 1984).

***Attribution.*** Authorial; see Sedgwick, II, 574. Most other sources, including all the complementary sources, ascribe the poem to Hervey, though the manuscript sources do not. There are no grounds for the occasional attribution to Chesterfield.

***Context and date.*** As Hervey puts it in *Some Materials*, the poem caused the Queen to tell him to stop writing, 'an Epigram in Martial which he had paraphrased and apply'd to Ld Burlington's House at Chiswick and his Lordship's Performances as an Architect, having got about, and made Ld and Lady Burlington, and their Friend his Grace of Grafton extreamly angry with him' (SRO 941/47/14, f. 114v). This episode took place in the summer of 1736, and the model by Martial, which appears above the Welbeck copy Pw2 V 192, consists of the last two lines of Epigram 50 in Book XII: *atria longa patent sed nec cenantibus usquam* | *Nec somno locus est. quam bene non habitas!* ('halls stretch at length. But there's nowhere a place to dine or sleep. How well you are – not lodged!', Loeb, III, 130–1). Burlington had constructed his villa at Chiswick with the help of William Kent several years previously. There is some unfairness in Hervey's critique, as becomes clear once the nature of the project is appreciated. Crucially, the villa was part of a linked group of buildings, with the result that, as Pamela Denman Kingsbury points out in her *ODNB* essay on Burlington, 'Erected in close proximity to an existing Jacobean house, the villa at Chiswick was designed without the amenities of a residence, which the earlier house provided.' All the same, the epigram, with its wittily chiastic second couplet, clearly hit home.

***Textual commentary.*** The Chatsworth manuscript has been chosen as the main source because, sent as it was directly to the Countess of Burlington, it may well have been the copy that caused the furore. The two manuscripts in the Portland (Welbeck) collection provide evidence of circulation, while the fact that the epigram reached the *Gentleman's Magazine* as early as September 1736 shows how wide this was. The British Library manuscript was probably copied from the *Gentleman's*, as its title and attribution to Hervey are in almost exactly the same form: 'Verses on the E— of B—, & His House at C—k. By the Author of the Noblemans Epistle to Dr Sherwyn'. As the Chatsworth manuscript is poorly spelt and badly punctuated, it has been corrected by reference to the complementary sources.

## Note on Chiswick

Posses'd of one great Hall for State,
Without one room to sleep, or eat,
How well you build let flattery tell,
And all Mankind how ill you dwell.

# 42 Inscribed to Mr. Kent

***Main source.*** Manuscript at Chatsworth House, in the form of a letter addressed to the Countess of Burlington at Bath also containing the companion piece, Poem 41, 'Note on Chiswick'.

***Complementary manuscript sources.*** Portland Papers (Welbeck) Pw V 693; Portland Papers (Welbeck) Pw2 V 192; BL Add. MS 8127, f. 71r.

***Complementary print sources.*** *Gentleman's Magazine*, 6 (September 1736), 548; *New Foundling Hospital for Wit*, IV (London: for J. Almon, 1771), 121–2; *New Foundling Hospital for Wit*, 6 vols. (London: for J. Debrett, 1784), I, 242–3. Like its companion piece, the poem is printed without attribution by Michael I. Wilson as part of Appendix III in *William Kent: Architect, Designer, Painter, Gardener*.

***Attribution.*** Hervey does not mention the poem in *Some Materials*, but the *Gentleman's Magazine* ascribes the poem to him and there are no other attributions.

***Context and date.*** The poem must have been written soon, even immediately, after its companion piece because it appears in the same manuscripts and because it was printed with it in the *Gentleman's Magazine* as early as September 1736. As a witty expansion of the original epigram, it must have given additional offence. William Kent, to whom the Chatsworth manuscript is ironically dedicated, carried out many of Burlington's designs. John Harris refers to 'the difficulty of disentangling Kent's work from Burlington's' in his *ODNB* essay on him.

***Textual commentary.*** See the headnote to Poem 41. The Chatsworth manuscript has again been chosen as the main source, and its erratic spelling and punctuation have required correction by reference to the complementary sources. Initial capitalisation has been retained.

## Inscribed to Mr Kent

Rare Architect, in whose exotick School,
Our English Connoisseurs may learn by rule
To spoil their Houses and to play the fool,
To all mankind (could we on paper live)
What charming Dwellings might thy Genius give!
And though when executed still we find
Thy plans have nothing to its use design'd,
Though to space, light, convenience you declare

Irreconcileable, perpetual war,
With Halls where groping Moles should only feed,
And Librarys where Lynxes' eyes can't read;
With Doors to common purposes such foes
Some never open, others never close;
Windows inverting what they were of old,
Nor form'd to let in Light nor keep out cold;
Chimneys in Cupboards, of full means possest
To fire the house, tho' not to warm the Guest;
Stairs which no Mortal can go up or down,
And leaden Sculls each Emblem-dome to crown;
Though such in every shape, in every part,
We find thy Unaccommodating art,
Yet who shall say thy works are not Divine,
When all must own there is no House of thine
In which (amongst the many have been try'd)
The Devil would or Mortal can reside.

# 43 Response to Compliment from John Whaley

***Source.*** BL Add. MS 71125, f. 10v. Printed in Walpole, *Correspondence*, XL, 22.

***Attribution.*** Horace Walpole.

***Context and date.*** The epigram is written on the verso of a letter from John Whaley to Horace Walpole dated 19 September 1736. Whaley writes: 'I have so often with pleasure heard you speak in praise of the author of the epigram you sent me and particularly in relation to his learning and correspondence about the Roman senate, that I have long entertained the same opinion of him which you do, as you will see from the under Lines, which perhaps you will not esteem Poetry, because they are so Plain and true.

To Lord Harvey, on his discourse on the Rom[an] Sen[ate]:

How Roman Senates once were fill'd
    From thy Judicious Pen we know;
That Virtue calls up Britains Peers
    Your self to future times will show.

Hervey's response is on the verso of the letter in Walpole's hand. It is accompanied by the note: 'On my Reading Ld Hervey the Epigram in this Letter He compos'd this Answer Extempore.' The discourse to which Whaley and the epigram refer is Hervey's correspondence with the Cambridge scholar Conyers Middleton about the Roman senate. Hervey evidently showed copies to friends, and eventually it was published, as he no doubt intended it should be, though this did not take place until 1779 (*Letters Between Lord Hervey and Dr. Middleton Concerning the Roman Senate*).

***Textual commentary.*** There is no reason to emend the original manuscript. Initial capitalisation is preserved.

## Response to Compliment from John Whaley

I read your Compliment, but there I see
Not what I am, but what I ought to be;
*Thus* Trajan's Character when Pliny raiz'd,[1]
'Twere better so to Praise, than to be prais'd.

1. *Trajan's Character when Pliny raiz'd*: Hervey refers to letters sent by Pliny the Younger (61–c. 112 CE) to the Emperor Trajan during his mission to Bithynia near the end of his life. The deference expressed by a government official addressing an emperor invites Hervey's suggestion that it represents a figure who exists in the realm of aspiration rather than of fact.

# 44 Norfolk House

***Main source.*** BL Add. MS 51441, f. 56r.

***Complementary manuscript sources.*** BL Add. MS 28095, f. 72r; Bodley MS Firth c. 16, p. 307; Newport Reference Library M411 012 WIL, [f. 1r]; Harvard University Library Houghton MS Eng 834, folder 71; Yale Osborn Collection c.154, pp. 9, 11; Yale Osborn Shelves Poetry Box V/12.

***Complementary print source.*** *Court Whispers: or, a Magazine of Wit* (London: for W. Webb, 1743), pp. 8–9. The text in the copy at the Houghton Library of Harvard University is struck through with a very large X.

***Attribution.*** Bodley MS Firth c. 16, 'By Ld Harvey'; Yale Poetry Box V/12, 'By the same' [as previous poem, 'By Lord Hervey']. Whether the poem is by Hervey is another matter. In favour of the attribution is the fact that it expresses a hatred for the Prince of Wales and a contempt for his brother William Augustus, Duke of Cumberland, that Hervey certainly felt. It could also be said to reflect the embitterment that engulfed him in 1738 after the death of Queen Caroline in November of the previous year. Stylistically, however, it lacks such Hervey hallmarks as balance and antithesis, and, although he had in his armoury a cruder style such as he used in his political ballads, it has none of the elegance that usually distinguishes his epigrams. A plausible alternative candidate is Sir Charles Hanbury Williams. His biographers, the Earl of Ilchester and Mrs Langford-Brooke, ascribe it and its companion piece, Poem 45, 'Adelphi' to him (pp. 122–3), though dating the two poems to 1743 and on no stronger grounds than that they occur along with two other poems on a folio tipped in at the end of a manuscript containing transcripts of thirteen poems by him. Tony Dagny Urstad, whose unpublished doctoral thesis, 'The Works of Sir Charles Hanbury Williams', represents the fullest attempt to determine the Hanbury Williams canon, rejects the ascription, remarking: 'The attributions are incorrect and illustrate with what lack of circumspection additions to his oeuvre have frequently been made' (Cambridge University, 1987, p. 28). The remark cannot, however, be accepted as definitive. It is based on the existence of alternative attributions to Hervey and, in the case of 'Adelphi', to Lord Orrery, and on the fact that no attribution to Hanbury Williams survives. All that can be added is that on stylistic grounds the two poems seem more likely to have been written by Hanbury Williams than by Hervey.

***Context and date.*** The poem is dated '1738' in the Bodley Firth manuscript. It responds to what was in effect an attempt to set up a rival court on the part of Frederick, Prince of Wales, who had moved there in the previous year after his marriage in 1736 to Princess Augusta of Saxe-Gotha. The house, at 31 St James's Square, had originally been built in 1722 for the Duke of Norfolk. The Prince and Princess lived there for the next several years until, with a growing family, they moved to Leicester House in 1743 (*ODNB*).

***Textual commentary.*** The copy in BL Add. MS 51441 has been chosen as the main source text because it is part of the Holland House papers and so is likely to come from a source close to Hervey. Appearing among the same unbound collection, though not on the same sheet as happens in several other manuscripts, is the related epigram, Poem 45, 'Adelphi', which has a different title in some manuscripts. The version in the Newport Reference Library folio is not only followed by 'Adelphi', but is preceded by an untitled response. More logically, the same response follows it in BL Add. MS 51441. This has the title 'To the Author of the Verses on Norfolk House' and runs:

Malicious Bard! suppose His Highness Lyes
In no Man Lying can be less a Vice
For How can Truth expect Him for Her Friend
Whom Truth for no one Virtue will commend?

As with the response, the copy of the poem used as the main source in this edition is completely unpunctuated, and so punctuation has been added according to the syntax. Spelling and initial capitalisation have been left unaltered.

## Norfolk House

To Norfolk House Lords, Knights and Squires repair
To view that matchless thing Great Britain's Heir.
It fawns and grins and prattles to the Crew,
And whispers mighty Threats against Sir Blue;[1]
Then struts and nods and gives itself Applause,
As if it meant to act by Truth and Laws.
But Men of Sense the Idol Calf despise,
And know that ev'ry Word it speaks it lyes.
Avert Ye Gods our Country's future Smart,
Bad is its Head, but ten times worse its Heart.

1. *Sir Blue*: Sir Robert Walpole, alluding to the ribbon of his Order of the Garter.

# 45 Adelphi

***Main source.*** BL Add. MS 51441, f. 95r.

***Complementary manuscript sources.*** BL Add. MS 28095, f. 72r; BL Add. MS 63648, f. 123r; BL Add. MS 21544, f. 152v; Bodley MS Firth c. 16, p. 306; Bodley Firth b. 22, f. 34v; Newport Reference Library M411 012 WIL, [f. 1r]; Harvard University Library Houghton MS Eng 834, folder 71; Yale Osborn Collection c.154, p. 9; Yale Osborn Collection fc.58, p. 132; Yale Osborn Shelves Poetry Box V/12.

***Complementary print source.*** *Court Whispers: or, a Magazine of Wit* (London: for W. Webb, 1743), p. 9. As with 'Norfolk House', the text in the copy at the Houghton Library of Harvard University is struck through with a large X. Although the online Folger Shakespeare Library *Union First Line Index of English Verse* suggests otherwise, Bodley Firth b. 22, f. 34v is a manuscript – a slip pasted into a collection consisting partly of printed and partly of manuscript items, which is, as a whole, catalogued by the Bodleian Library as a printed book.

***Attribution.*** Yale Poetry Box V/12, 'By Lord Hervey'; Bodley MS Firth c. 16, 'By L[or]d Orrery'. There are no other attributions. For reservations about the attribution to Hervey, see the headnote to Poem 44, 'Norfolk House'. Attribution to John Boyle, fifth Earl of Cork and fifth Earl of Orrery (1707–62) is, however, awkward. Although, as a Tory and a Jacobite, he was a member of the opposition, it seems unlikely that he would have expressed contempt for Frederick, Prince of Wales, around whom the so-called Patriot Opposition coalesced. The best that can be said is that the two poems belong together, as they have the same length, express complementary views and occur together not only in several manuscripts but also in the single printed source located; that they were therefore probably written by the same person; and that that person could have been Hervey, although, especially on stylistic grounds, Sir Charles Hanbury Williams is a possible alternative candidate.

***Context and date.*** Like 'Norfolk House', the poem appears to date from 1738 and looks forward pessimistically to a time when either Frederick, Prince of Wales, or his brother William Augustus, Duke of Cumberland, would be on the throne. Neither eventuality would, of course, occur. Because George II was to prove long-lived, the kingdom was to be inherited in 1760 by his grandson, born at Norfolk House in the same year in which the two poems were apparently written. For a possible later dating of the poem, see line 6, and note.

***Textual commentary.*** For the reasons for choosing the text in BL Add. MS 51441 as the main source, see the headnote to Poem 44, 'Norfolk House'. Like that text, that of 'Adelphi' in the same collection of manuscripts requires punctuation, which has been added, but spelling and initial capitalisation have been left unaltered.

## Adelphi[1]

Two hopeful Sons are sprung from George's Loyns,
And one in Folly, one in Dullness Shines.
From Freddy's Lips the Royal Nonsense flows,
And Fools and Ladies catch it as it goes.
More solid Will in Beef and Pudding deep
Makes Love and governs Navys in His Sleep.[2]
But Oh! when by inexorable Fate
Our Monarch rots with Caroline the Great,
Say, Britons, Say which then shall be your Head,
The prattling Monkey or the Lump of Lead?[3]

1. *Adelphi*: The title, meaning 'The Brothers', is that of a play by Terence often performed as a school exercise, for instance at Westminster School which William Augustus, later Duke of Cumberland, had attended. Underneath the title, Yale Poetry Box has 'P. of W. and D. of C'. This suggests that the copy was made by, or for, someone without immediate knowledge, and so has implications for dating and circulation.

2. *Makes Love . . . Sleep*: Cumberland was notorious for the number of his mistresses, and he took a strong interest in the navy before beginning his career as a soldier (*ODNB*). This line may suggest a later date for the poem than 1738, when he was still only seventeen and these traits were not yet established.

3. Underneath the poem, Yale fc.58 has, in a different hand, 'Duke of Cumberland and Prince Frederick'. Like the initials at the top of the copy in Yale Poetry Box V/12, this may suggest that the copy was made by, or for, someone without immediate knowledge, and so has implications for dating and circulation.

# 46 On Health

***Main source.*** Cancelled page in Dodsley, *Collection*, IV (1755), 113, repr. by Suarez in Dodsley, I, 167.

***Complementary manuscript sources.*** SRO 941/53/1, p. 203; BL Add. MS 59439, f. 25r; Bodley MS Firth b. 4, f. 50r.

***Complementary print sources.*** *London Evening-Post*, 24 January 1745; *London Magazine*, 14 (February 1745), 99; *Scots Magazine*, 7 (February 1745), 75; *Universal Magazine*, 7 (October 1750), 184; *London Magazine*, 19 (November 1750), 515; *A Collection of Select Epigrams*, ed. by John Hackett (London: for C. Hitch and L. Hawes; Canterbury: for W. and J. Flackton, 1757), pp. 42–3; *Colley Cibber's Jests* (Newcastle: for W. Charnley, 1761), pp. 90–1; *New Foundling Hospital for Wit*, III (London: s.n., 1769), 84–5; *Humours of the Times* (London: s.n., 1771), pp. 350–1; *New Foundling Hospital for Wit*, 6 vols. (London: for J. Debrett, 1784), I, 240–1.

***Attribution.*** William Hervey; all printed sources.

***Context and date.*** Hervey had always been subject to the ill-health that he describes so vividly in the account of his 'constitution and illness, with some rules for the preservation of health' that he compiled for the use of his children in 1731 (Sedgwick, III, 961–87). Nevertheless, the poem's references to the political situation at home and abroad make it clear that it was composed in the last year, probably the last months, of his life. Although he told Lady Mary Wortley Montagu in a letter dated 20 December 1742 that his health was 'Mended to a Miracle', in a letter dated 4 April of the following year he spoke to her of being 'confined these three weeks by a Fever' (SRO 941/47/2, pp. 135, 137). Most likely, then, the poem dates from between April and June or July of 1743, his condition having deteriorated considerably in the several weeks before his death on 5 August (Halsband, p. 304). The political references are explained briefly in the notes below. They concern Britain's relationship with Hanover but especially questions concerning the War of the Austrian Succession. This had begun in 1740 but, despite a peace treaty between Prussia and Austria, signed at Breslau on 11 June 1742 that ended the First Silesian War, continued until 1748, well after Hervey's death five years before.

***Textual commentary.*** In his edition of Dodsley's *Collection*, Michael F. Suarez tells how the first impression of the 1755 edition of Volume IV had to be withdrawn hastily from circulation. This was apparently because the Hervey family or their representatives had got wind of the poem's imminent publication, and objected on the grounds of potential damage to Hervey's posthumous reputation and embarrassment to his relatives and others on account of its 'inflammatory political content' (Dodsley, I, 166). A different poem, not by Hervey, had consequently been substituted. However, Dodsley seems not to have been able to round up and destroy all the copies that had been printed, and Suarez reprints the poem from one of the survivors, in the library of Worcester College, Oxford. This text of the poem, which probably reached Dodsley from Hervey's friend John Hoadly, has been chosen as the main source because it is superior to the only other text that has any potential claim to authority, that in William Hervey's commonplace book (SRO 941/53/1). The drawback of William Hervey's text is that it has two variants, in lines 15 and 21, that are difficult to defend. In light of the concern over the poem's publication in 1755, it is surprising that it had already achieved wide circulation through newspapers, and that it appears in books published in 1757 and 1761 respectively. But it is always difficult to suppress publication especially of a short item, and whoever did so in the case of Dodsley's *Collection* was not only in a position to do so but was especially concerned that the poem might have been published in a form that was not likely to prove ephemeral. There are relatively few variants between the different versions, though it is interesting to note that the newspaper texts play safe by not printing the proper name 'Hanover' or the word 'fools' in full. No alterations have been necessary to the copy as printed by Suarez from the Worcester College cancellandum.

## On Health

Tho' life itself's not worth a thought,
Yet, whilst I live could health be bought;
Whate'er brib'd senators[1] receive,
Or back again in taxes give;
Whatever force or fraud obtains,
What Prussia from Silesia gains,[2]
Or Hanover from England drains;[3]
Whate'er the Austrian wars have cost,

1. *brib'd senators*: political support could be obtained through the exercise of various forms of patronage. Walpole had been especially skilful in his use of the patronage system, earning a reputation for corruption that is now thought to have been exaggerated, especially because the opposition continued to exploit it after they succeeded him.

2. *What Prussia . . . gains*: as a result of the First Silesian War, part of the War of the Austrian Succession, Austria lost Silesia to Prussia.

3. *Or Hanover . . . drains*: the relation between Britain and Hanover, of which George II was Elector, proved controversial throughout his reign, especially because of the amount of time he preferred to spend there; and Britain paid for Hanoverian mercenaries, a subsidy that was increased during the War of the Austrian Succession in which they took part.

Or Hungary's queen[4] disburs'd or lost;
What France has paid[5] to shake her crown,
Or we, like fools, to keep it on;[6]
All that the Indies e'er supply'd
To beggar'd Spain, to feed the pride
Of that Italian fury-dame,[7]
Who keeps all Europe in a flame,
For her two brats,[8] those princely things,
Whom God made fools and she'd make kings:
In short, to sum up all, whate'er
Or Pride, or Avarice makes its care,
Did I possess it, I'd resign,
To make this richer treasure mine.

4. *Hungary's queen*: Maria Theresa (1717–80), who succeeded her father in 1740, though she could not succeed him as Holy Roman Emperor because women were debarred from that position.

5. *What France has paid*: France was one of the countries to take arms against Maria Theresa in the War of the Austrian Succession.

6. *Or we . . . on*: Britain supported Maria Theresa in the War of the Austrian Succession.

7. *that Italian fury-dame*: Elisabeth Farnese (1692–1766), Queen Consort of Spain, who influenced Spanish foreign policy heavily.

8. *her two brats*: Don Carlos (1716–88), who became King of Naples and Sicily in 1735 and, in 1759, King of Spain; and Philip (1720–65), who was to become Duke of Parma in 1748.

# 47 Riddle

***Source.*** Bodley MS. Eng. misc. b. 169, f. 59v, printed by Isobel Grundy in Grundy, 'New Verse', p. 239, and by Halsband and Grundy in *Essays & Poems*, p. 382.

***Attribution.*** Lady Mary Wortley Montagu.

***Context and date.*** As Grundy has shown, the riddle, along with one on the same subject by Montagu, appears to have been written at the same time as a verse dialogue that the two friends improvised at a meeting either on 21 or on 25 September 1736 ('New Verse', p. 245). For the dialogue, see Poem 55.

***Textual commentary.*** The texts are given as in the manuscript, except for the expansion of contractions and, in the case of Hervey's riddle, the insertion of a letter and a word that were omitted, presumably because, as Grundy remarks, it seems to 'have been written down hastily' ('New Verse', p. 239).

## Riddle

The Stuff which we find on beer when tis new[1]
And what all the World say when they say what's not true.[2]

Montagu provided her own riddle for the second part of her name:

What Bridgman oft shews as the best of his Works
And what would make tremble the fiercest of Turks.

As Grundy explains, 'the answer is clearly "Montagu", from "mounts" raised by Charles Bridgman (*d.* 1738), landscape gardener, and from "ague"' ('New Verse', p. 240).

1. *The Stuff . . . new*: the first line is easily decoded as 'wort'.
2. *what's not true*: equally clearly, the answer is 'lie', so producing 'Wortley'.

# OCCASIONAL VERSE – SOCIAL, HUMOROUS AND COMPLIMENTARY

# INTRODUCTION TO OCCASIONAL VERSE – SOCIAL, HUMOROUS AND COMPLIMENTARY

Much of Hervey's verse is occasional in the broad sense: an epistle springs from a journey undertaken or a gift received, a satire from a recent publication or a political event, an elegy or an epitaph from a current loss. A common name for a book of poems in the early eighteenth century was 'Poems on Several Occasions', a title (modest, unlike 'Works') that permitted a collection to be made with relaxed boundaries. The poems in this section of the edition are, however, occasional in a special sense because they respond to particular social events or observations.[1] They have something in common with French *vers de société*, light verse in aristocratic and court circles that constituted a celebration of a way of life. A leading, though satirical, poet in this mode in France was Jean-Baptiste Rousseau (1671–1741), one of whose poems was translated by Hervey (Poem 64). A contemporary English poet who excelled at humorous amatory verse was Matthew Prior (1664–1721), and his *Poems on Several Occasions* ran through thirty-eight editions in the eighteenth century.[2]

Although all the poems in this section are occasional, they play with different degrees of particularity and social intimacy. Their tone is also various, ranging from sentimental, in the eighteenth-century sense, to satirical. Three of them belong to the tradition of light amatory verse (Poems 49, 50 and 51). They may respond to real or imagined social exchanges, their aim being to declare love. The comparison of the Duchess of Richmond with Venus (Poem 53) and the poem planned for a statue in the Earl of Cadogan's garden (Poem 48), on the other hand, use identifiable events and places as the basis for extravagant and witty

1. Some of the most helpful recent reflections on occasional verse are to be found in the first chapter of Marian Zwerling Sugano's *The Poetics of the Occasion: Mallarmé and the Poetry of Circumstance* (Stanford, CA: Stanford University Press, 1992).

2. The first was in 1709. The total of editions is from ESTC and the meaning of 'edition' in this context is uncertain, but there were unquestionably many printings.

developments of such writing. The other poems in this section evidently arise out of friendship. The satirical and irreligious address to the Redlynch parson, Samuel Hill (Poem 54), shows powers of aggression similar to those demonstrated in the pretended answer of the Prince of Wales to the Queen's enquiry about the health of his wife and child (Poem 56). Both poems are frank, unbuttoned and trusting. Two other poems show writing itself as a form of intimacy: in Poem 55 Hervey and Montagu write together on the most personal of subjects, taking it in turns to express a point of view; in Poem 57 Hervey writes poignantly and philosophically in his friend Algarotti's book. Poem 52 is one of Hervey's simplest and most direct, a celebration of his return to his family, in which, with a characteristic twist and reservation, he celebrates their happiness as well as his own.

# 48 Written on the Gilded Statue in Lord Cadogan's Garden 1723

***Source.*** SRO 941/53/1, p. 208. There are no other sources. The poem seems first to have been printed in the *Annual Register*, 46 (1804), 932.

***Attribution.*** William Hervey.

***Context and date.*** In a letter to John Gay dated 3 July 1723, Mrs Howard (later Countess of Suffolk) remarks that Hervey and his wife were to join a party at Lord Cadogan's at Caversham in Berkshire to spend the rest of the summer (*Letters to and from Henrietta, Countess of Suffolk*, 2 vols. (London: John Murray, 1824), I, 107). The poem must have been written to amuse the hosts and guests during this visit. Although it is a good example of light social verse at the period, it goes beyond its genre in presenting a sharp critique of mercenary marriages. As William, Earl Cadogan (1671/2–1726), was married and nearing the end of his life, he would not have been in a position to take advantage of the statue's advice.

***Textual commentary.*** The text is given as it stands in William Hervey's transcript, but with one emendation required by the sense: the insertion of 'do' after the first word of line 15. There is also a case for inserting 'and' between 'Desert' and 'cold' in line 10; indeed the *Annual Register* text, which also inserts 'do' in line 15, makes this change. The line can, however, be left as it stands if it is read as trochaic, a metrical switch that would provide an effective climax to the sentence that it ends.

## Written on the Gilded Statue in Lord Cadogan's Garden 1723.
## The Statue speaks to my Lord.

In Vain to Celia's heart you sue,
By me instructed learn to woo:
In me her emblem you may find,
A beauteous form without a mind;
A prospect fair of Venal[1] Charms,
Doom'd to the Highest bidder's arms:

1. *Venal*: 'Exposed or offered for sale, that may be bought, as an ordinary article of merchandise'; or 'Capable of being acquired by purchase, instead of being conferred on grounds of merit or regarded as above bargaining for' (*OED*).

Tho' you had Beauty, Wit and Youth,
Tho' you had tenderness with Truth,
Nor this nor that her soul could move,
Blind to Desert, cold to Love.
Careless of Censure, deaf to Fame,
Unsway'd by Principle or shame;
So much our Qualities agree,
'Twill do for her that did for me;
Guild her but well, you may with ease
Carry her naked where you please.

# 49 Written Impromptu to a Lady Stung by a Bee

***Main source.*** Lilly Library, Delany MS [1], item 9.

***Complementary manuscript sources.*** Bodley MS Eng. poet. e. 40, f. 48r; SRO, 941/53/1, p. 208; Yale William Smith Papers Folder 74/19, p. 1.

***Complementary print sources.*** *Windsor Medley* (London: for A. Moore [fictitious], 1731), p. 8, and two other editions of the same year; *The Choice: Being a Collection of Two Hundred and Fifty Celebrated Songs*, 2 vols. (London: for W. Bickerton, T. Astley, R. Willock and J. Watson, 1733), II, 60; *A Complete Collection of Old and New English and Scotch Songs*, 2 vols. (London: by T. Boreman, 1735), II, 172, and same page of four-volume 1736 edn; *A Collection of Epigrams*, 2 vols. (London: for J. Walthoe, 1735), II, unpaginated, sig. H3r; *A Choice Collection of Poetry*, ed. by Joseph Yarrow, 2 vols. (York: by A. Staples, 1738), II, 49. The poem continued to be reprinted frequently either as a song or as an epigram throughout the century.

***Attribution.*** William Hervey; Yale Smith Papers attributes to 'late L[or]d Chesterfield', *Windsor Medley* to 'Mr. H.' The attribution to Chesterfield carries little weight, as many minor pieces were ascribed to him that he did not write. It is not surprising, therefore, that the poem does not appear in Chesterfield's two-volume *Miscellaneous Works* of 1777 (London: for Edward and Charles Dilly), and that it is not claimed for Chesterfield either by Ernst-Browning, the editor of Chesterfield, *Wit and Wisdom*, the collection generally accepted as the most reliable, or by Sidney L. Gulick in his *Chesterfield Bibliography*. 'Mr. H.' is unlikely to refer to Hervey, as he had held his courtesy title since 1723. It is possible that it refers to his brother Henry, or even to Thomas Hervey, though surviving verse by the two lacks finesse.

***Context and date.*** As the Delany manuscript is headed 'Transcrib'd in the year 1728', the poem must have been written not long before that date. It could have reached Mrs Pendarves, as she was then, through Hervey's brother Henry, although it appears that the transcriber did not know the author's identity. It is a standard example of the kind of complimentary verse that goes back to Edmund Waller in the previous century, distinguished, however, by the fact that, according to the Delany and SRO manuscripts, it was produced extempore.

***Textual commentary.*** The Delany text has been left unaltered, including use of initial capitalisation, except for the insertion of an apostrophe in 'Delia's'. There are no significant differences between the complementary sources, though two – the Bodley and Yale transcripts – give evidence of their dates; the SRO text is known to have been transcribed after 1751 when William Hervey began writing his commonplace book.

## Written Impromptu to a Lady Stung by a Bee

To heal the Wound a Bee had made
    Upon my Delia's Face,
His Honey on her Cheek She lade
    And bid me Kiss the Place;
Pleas'd I obey'd, and from the Wound
    Imbib'd both Sweet and Smart,
His Honey on my lips I found,
    The Sting Within my Heart.

# 50 Written on a Lady's Fan Who Had her Lover's Picture Painted on It

***Source.*** SRO 941/53/1, p. 208.

***Complementary sources.*** None has come to light.

***Attribution.*** William Hervey ('by the Same').

***Context and date.*** The poem probably dates from the earlier 1720s, as it has generic, thematic and stylistic affinities with Poem 49, 'Written Impromptu to a Lady Stung by a Bee'. Most likely Poem 51, 'Written at the Bottom of a Note from Lady . . . to Ld . . ..', dates from the same time. The genre is a Restoration tradition of light amatory verse that Waller especially had popularised. There was a vogue for fan poems in the period, six of which are reprinted in Bill Overton, (ed.), *A Letter to My Love: Love Poems by Women First Published in the Barbados Gazette, 1731–1737* (Newark, NJ: University of Delaware Press; London: Associated University Presses, 2001, pp. 51–2, 127–30). Brief though it is, the poem is distinctive in the way it hints at Platonic thinking about the relation between original and copy, and at the possibility that the lover may have fewer virtues than the poet.

***Textual commentary.*** No textual emendations have been necessary.

## Written on a Lady's Fan who had her Lover's picture painted on it

What[1] diff'rent Vertues have possess'd
    The form[2] by which you're charm'd,
The Copy serves to cool that Breast
    Th'Original has warm'd.

1. *What*: Whatever. 2. *form*: the first word to suggest a hint at Platonic thinking.

# 51 Written at the Bottom of a Note from Lady . . . to Ld . . . .

***Source.*** SRO 941/53/1, p. 210.

***Complementary sources.*** None has come to light.

***Attribution.*** William Hervey ('by the Same').

***Context and date.*** See the headnote to Poem 50, 'Written on a Lady's Fan', with which this poem, and Poem 49, 'Written Impromptu to a Lady Stung by a Bee', have affinities. That would place the poem in the 1720s. What is unusual about this example is that it suggests impromptu composition during a social gathering. The poet has intercepted a note from a lady to someone else, and uses the occasion, presumably after having been asked to return it, in order to pay surreptitious court to her. Its use of a pentameter to provide closure and emphasis to its tetrameter couplets is unusual and skilful.

***Textual commentary.*** No textual emendations to any aspect of the poem have been required.

## Written at the bottom of a note from Lady . . . to Ld . . . .

This message thro' a meaner hand,
Would small attention sure command;
But Silvia's wit, with charming ease,
Can teach e'en trifles how to please:
'Twas such an instance of his art,
That Lucky Angel did impart,
Who from the mass of common clay,
Where once, Sweet maid, thy beauties lay,
Could charms create unmov'd before,
And give the world my Silvia to adore.

# 52 On Ickworth Park in Suffolk

***Source.*** William Hervey's commonplace book, SRO 941/53/1, pp. 210, 212, copied after February 1751. This is carefully written. Like several other poems in the same collection, it was probably transcribed from a text written out or annotated by Hervey himself.

***Complementary sources.*** No other copy has come to light; the poem has never been printed.

***Attribution.*** William Hervey ('by the Same').

***Context and date.*** The poem can be dated more precisely than most of Hervey's verse. Its content indicates that it must have been written very soon after his return to the family home at Ickworth from his stay in France and Italy with Stephen Fox. After arriving in London on 25 October 1729, he set off for Ickworth on 2 November to be reunited with his parents and family (Halsband, pp. 85, 87). Lady Hervey and their children had spent most of the period of his absence there, Lady Hervey being a favourite of Lord Bristol, and Ickworth being the residence much preferred by the Earl. The family estate appealed to Hervey for much the same reasons as to his father, although he would soon be attracted back to the challenges of the political scene in London and the pleasures of his relationship with Fox. The poem was probably written in large part to convey to his family a sense of his happiness in having returned to them, and it is in this sense that it constitutes social verse rather than simply a conventional period exercise in praise of rural retirement. Its last seven lines, in particular, appeal to its readers as members of an intimate circle whose joy at his return makes up an important part of his pleasure in being reunited with them. In this and other respects it compares interestingly with Poem 6, 'To Mr. Fox, Written at Florence 1729', a more intimate poem in that it addresses the closest of his friends, one who had saved his life by nursing him during life-threatening illness. 'To Mr. Fox', written before the two travellers began their return journey to England, pays tribute to its addressee in the more contemplative form of iambic pentameter couplets, while the tetrameters of 'On Ickworth Park in Suffolk' give it a lighter, more lyrical texture appropriate to its pastoral mode. Although the latter poem invokes the stock pastoral trope of a contrast between nature and art, its first part, up to line 19, also succeeds in articulating the much less conventional experience of the mixture of new and familiar impressions that the returning traveller has to process, and in celebrating the peace and tranquillity of home and countryside that make this possible. The second part then manages the difficult task of thanking those he had left behind for their pleasure at his return, hinting delicately, especially in the phrase 'tho' not true', at the mixed emotions they must have felt on account of his long absence.

***Textual commentary.*** The carefulness of William Hervey's copy is such that no textual emendations are necessary. Spelling, punctuation and initial capitalisation have all been left unaltered.

## On Ickworth Park in Suffolk

Oh Ickworth! Fav'rite far above
The Shade of any other Grove,
How pleas'd thy beauties I review,[1]
So pleas'd I hardly think it true,
Whilst in my scarce unburden'd mind,
The jumbled images I find,
Of all where I have lately been,
Of all call'd fine, I've lately seen,
Where Grecian schools and Roman art
Have tried by Labour to impart
Those beauties Nature scatters here,
Or Nature's errors to repair:
But what true pleasure then we taste,
When wand'ring, foreign hurrys past,
From forms,[2] constraint, and care releas'd,
And by domestic habits eas'd,
Our thoughts recall'd are all unbent,
Nor longer how to please intent,
Find in the being pleas'd, content.
This and this only e'er repays,
Our irksome, worldly busy days:
Thus lately were my hours employ'd,
Thus now in leisure they're enjoy'd:
But to complete what is possess'd,
In this relax'd, contented breast,

1. *review*: the word probably carries the sense of 'see again' as well as 'survey'.
2. *forms*: 'A set method of outward behaviour or procedure in accordance with prescribed usage, etiquette, ritual, etc.; a ceremony or formality. (Often *slightingly*, as implying the absence of intrinsic meaning or reality.)' (*OED*).

Let the lov'd dwellers in this place,
With smiles their friend's arrival grace,
And tho' not true, make me believe,
Part of the Joy which I receive
This fugitive's return can give.

# 53 Lord Harvey on the Dutchess of Richmond

***Main source.*** Portland (Welbeck) Pw V 270.

***Complementary manuscript sources.*** Harrowby MS 255, pp. 78–9; BL MS Harley 7318, f. 108v; BL Add. MS 32463, p. 230; BL Add. MS 37683, f. 28v; BL Add. MS 47128, f. 42v; Chester Record Office DCC/16/101; Brotherton Lt 12, p. 45; Brotherton Lt 35, p. 57; Yale Osborn Collection c.53, pp. 53–4; Yale Osborn Collection c.233, p. 81; Yale Osborn Collection c.188, p. 91.

***Complementary print sources.*** *London Journal*, 31 January 1730; *Universal Spectator*, 11 July 1730; *Select Poems from Ireland* (London: for T. Warner, 1730), pp. 15–16; *A Collection of Epigrams*, 2nd edn, 2 vols. (London: for J. Walthoe, 1733), II, CCCXXIII; *Gentleman's Magazine*, 8 (December 1738), 653; *The Norfolk Poetical Miscellany*, 2 vols. [ed. by Ashley Cowper] (London: for the author, sold by J. Stagg, 1744), I, 171–2. There are numerous reprints after 1750, especially in collections of epigrams, but also in such well-known sources as *The Poetical Calendar*, ed. by Francis Fawkes and William Woty, 2nd edn, 12 vols. (London: by Dryden Leach for J. Coote, 1763), III, 111, *New Foundling Hospital for Wit* (1769 edn), p. 114, mistitled 'On the Duchess of Rutland'), and Pearch's *A Collection of Poems*, 4 vols. (London: for G. Pearch, sold by Joseph Johnson, 1775), II, 293–4.

***Attribution.*** The poem is attributed to Hervey in Portland (Welbeck) Pw V 270, BL Harley MS 7318 and Harrowby MS 255 (with 'by the E[arl] of Chesterfield' struck out), but to Chesterfield in nearly all other sources that contain an attribution, exceptions including *Additions to the Works of Alexander Pope*, and Horace Walpole's final edition of his *Catalogue of Royal and Noble Authors* (2 vols. (London: for H. Baldwin and others, 1776), I, 149–50; Walpole, *Works*, I, 452). It is presumably on the grounds of multiple attributions to Chesterfield, and unawareness of those to Hervey, that the poem is included by Ernst-Browning in Chesterfield, *Wit and Wisdom*, which represents his verse conservatively, and by Sidney L. Gulick in his *Chesterfield Bibliography* (p. 215). But the manuscript attributions carry weight, especially in light of the correction by Lady Mary Wortley Montagu to her transcript and a note in Robert Halsband's handwriting to the Portland (Welbeck) manuscript: 'it is in L[or]d Hervey's style, and I see no reason to doubt the attribution'. Another important point to bear in mind is the frequency with which poems not necessarily by Chesterfield were, because of his reputation as a wit, ascribed to him. On this Hervey commented tartly in his memoirs that, when an epigram Chesterfield probably in fact had written was attributed to him, 'he received the insinuation with the same sort of avowing denial that he generally put on when verses were ascribed to him which he had not written, or mistresses that he had not lain with' (Sedgwick, III, 651). Another factor to consider is the poem's date. If, as seems likely, it was written in 1729–30, this was while Chesterfield had to spend most of his time at the Hague, where he was ambassador between 1727 and 1732 (*ODNB*). Stylistically, too, the poem has a much stronger claim to be Hervey's than Chesterfield's. It has the brio and inventiveness that distinguish Hervey's best social and complimentary verse, whereas Chesterfield's output, which is slender, consists mainly of brief epigrams and mocks or teases rather than celebrates its subjects.

***Context and date.*** The poem is dated '1729' in BL Add. MS 32463 and '1730' in BL Add. MS 47128, but it must have been written before the end of January 1730 when it was printed in the *London Journal*. Hervey had returned from Italy with Stephen Fox in late October 1729, and it is clear from a comment in a letter to Lady Mary Wortley Montagu dated 29 December that he wrote various poems during the winter that circulated without attribution in manuscript: 'When I began to read, I grew more and more vain, and of course more and more happy; and but to do my-self justice, (after opening to you the weakness of my Heart) I can not help adding, that any Body must have a very good or a very bad Head, not to feel a little elate on hearing their Works were travelling about London and taken by every Body that read them for the Productions of Lady Mary's and L[or]d Chesterfield's' (SRO 941/47/2, pp. 25–6). It is likely that the poem was among those that circulated, although the comment already quoted from Hervey's memoirs on attributions to Chesterfield indicates that these would later produce rather less euphoria. Hervey's friendship with the Duke and Duchess of Richmond was well established before 1729. The Duchess was the daughter of the Earl of Cadogan for whom Hervey had written Poem 48, 'Written on the Gilded Statue in Lord Cadogan's Garden 1723'; and it was in the Duke's yacht, and in the company of the Duke and Duchess, that Hervey and Stephen Fox travelled to Ostend for a stay at the spa there before beginning their journey through France to Italy (Halsband, pp. 78–9). After returning from Italy, Hervey often enjoyed the Duke and Duchess's company at their Goodwood house-parties. William Pulteney, who gave the supper that provided the poem's occasion, was a mutual friend, though his relationship with Hervey had already begun to cool for political reasons, and would break down completely in February 1731 when the two fought a duel (Halsband, pp. 87, 107–16).

***Textual commentary.*** The manuscript chosen as the main source is a clear, grammatical copy that agrees in every respect, including the title, with another early manuscript, BL MS Harley 7318. It requires only two emendations, the insertion of possessive apostrophes in lines 2 and 10. All other features, including spelling and initial capitalisation, are left unaltered. From the number of times it occurs in manuscript and print forms, it proved highly attractive as an example of lively, witty social verse. Not surprisingly, variants are frequent, in part because the anapaestic tetrameter couplets that help provide its energy and brio readily allow for metrical substitutions.

## Lord Harvey on the Dutchess of Richmond[1]

What do Scholars and Bards and Astrologers wise
Mean by stuffing one's head with Nonsense and Lyes?
By telling one, Venus must always appear
In a Car or a Shell or a twinkling Star,[2]
Drawn by Sparrows or Swans or Dolphins or Doves,
And attended in form by the Graces and Loves;
That Ambrosia and Nectar is all she will tast,
And her Passport to Hearts, a Belt round her Waist?[3]
Without all this bustle I saw the bright Dame;
To Supper last night to Pulteney's[4] she came;
In a good warm Sedan, no fine open Car,
Two Chairmen for Doves and a Flambeau her Star,
No Nectar she drank, no Ambrosia she eat,
Her Cup was plain Claret, a Chicken her Meat;
Nor wanted the Cestus[5] her Bosom to grace,
For Richmond that night had lent her her Face.

1. Sarah, Duchess of Richmond (1706–51), 'the eldest daughter and coheir of William Cadogan, first Earl Cadogan', had married the Duke in 1719 though the two did not live together until 1722 (*ODNB*).

2. *Venus ... twinkling Star*: compare Poem 65, Telemachus, Book II, lines 80–102.

3. *By telling ... her Waist*: the poem refers to traditional representations of the triumph of Venus, especially from fifteenth- or early sixteenth-century Italian painting (see *The Oxford Guide to Classical Mythology in the Arts, 1300–1990s*, ed. by Jane Davidson Reid, with Chris Rohmann, 2 vols. (Oxford: Oxford University Press, 1993), under 'Aphrodite').

4. *Pulteney's*: William Pulteney (1684–1764), later Earl of Bath, was at the time a close friend not only of the Richmonds but also of the Herveys.

5. *Cestus*: a belt or girdle worn by Venus (*OED*).

# 54 Reveillez vous

***Source.*** BL Add. MS 51441, f. 23r.

***Complementary sources.*** None, manuscript or printed, has come to light.

***Attribution.*** BL Add. MS 51441 ('By L[or]d Hervey to Parson Hill').

***Context and date.*** The poem is addressed to the Reverend Samuel Hill, the clergyman at Redlynch, the Fox brothers' country estate in Somerset, and subsequently canon at Wells. Ilchester describes him as 'the great sporting parson constantly mentioned in a MS "Memoires de la Chasse" of the Fox family . . ., and their willing butt. He died in January 1753, "much regretted by all who knew him"' (p. 78, n. 4). He is mentioned in two letters by Hervey in 1731 to Frederick, Prince of Wales, describing life at Redlynch (printed in Ilchester, pp. 109–11). The poem was probably written in the early 1730s. It may even have been one of the 'fadaises' that Hervey, writing from London, remarked that he was sending to Henry Fox with the recommendation: 'You may make Hill sing them; and then light his pipe with them' (letter dated 23 January 1733; BL Add. MS 51396, f. 82*r; printed in Ilchester, p. 155). An idea of the kind of relationship Hill enjoyed with his patrons and friends may be gained from Sir Charles Hanbury Williams's epitaph:

> Death and the gout a victory have gain'd,
> And poor Sam Hill's interred beneath this stone,
> A greater pluralist was ne'er ordained,
> A man more singular was never known.
>
> (Ilchester and Langford-Brooke, p. 134)

Hervey's poem would have been intended to amuse male companions, probably at a drinking party or a similar entertainment. There is, however, an edge to it in that it gives expression to the sceptical beliefs that he certainly held, and it should be compared with Poem 106 'Chanson au Curé de —', which may also have been written to Hill. The title, 'Reveillez vous' ('Wake up'), is a parody of the call to spiritual enlightenment that Hill should have been spreading among his parishioners. It mockingly invites him instead to indulge himself even more in epicurean masculine pleasures.

***Textual commentary.*** The poem is printed as it stands in the manuscript, except that end-of-line punctuation has been added where the syntax requires it, the verb-form of the title has been corrected to 'Reveillez' from 'Reveilles', and an errant apostrophe has been removed from 'reversions'; see List of Emendations. Spelling and use of initial capitals are left unaltered.

## Reveillez vous

Dear Hill who minds your Bible Story,
All think it Priestcraft Ly's and Art;
'Tis full as stale as Whigg and Tory,
For Kings and Christ none care a Fart.[1]

From Mother Eve and her Creation
Down to the Whore of Babylon,
From Genesis to Revelation,
There's not one Truth, Hill, no, not one.[2]

And since reversions[3] are uncertain
And nothing sure but what We see,
Ne'er think of Heav'n behind a Curtain,
But laugh and drink and whore with me.

1. *All think ... a Fart*: Hervey is describing, in Mandevillian fashion, the way people actually behave whatever politics or religion they profess.

2. *There's not one Truth, Hill, no, not one*: the emphatic insistence of the line is evidence that the poem's intention is not merely humorous but reflects Hervey's actual position.

3. *reversions*: 'The right of succeeding to the possession of something, or of obtaining something at a future time; the action or process of transferring something in this way. Also: a thing or possession which a person expects to obtain' (*OED*); in this sense, life after death.

# 55 Verse Dialogue between Hervey and Montagu

***Main source.*** Harrowby MS 81, ff. 216r–217v.

***Complementary manuscript sources.*** SRO 941/47/2, pp. 69–71; Bodley MS Eng. misc. b. 169, f. 61r–61v.

***Complementary print sources.*** The dialogue was first printed by Robert Halsband and Isobel Grundy in *Essays & Poems*. Isobel Grundy provides a detailed account of the Bodleian Library manuscript in 'New Verse', pp. 244–9.

***Attribution.*** All the manuscripts are holographs.

***Context and date.*** It is possible to date the poem even more precisely than Poem 52, 'On Ickworth Park in Suffolk'. Its immediate context is the aftermath of Francesco Algarotti's departure from England and Montagu's recognition that she had fallen in love with him. Hervey was her confidant in the matter, and they discussed her position both in letters and in conversation. Isobel Grundy explains how a conversation either on Tuesday 21 or on Saturday 25 September 1736 produced the poem. 'At one of these meetings their "dispute whether Absence ended Love" took a literary turn. Lady Mary wrote down an epigram, "extempore", about the violence of her love. She drew a line across the sheet of paper after three couplets.' Lord Hervey then took the sheet of paper, turned it over, and began a reply with a couplet based on one of Cleopatra's in Dryden's *All for Love* that he had used in his own tragedy 'Agrippina' (Poem 66, II. 2, lines 114–15). They then exchanged couplets and quatrains, turning the paper over again to continue the debate under Lady Mary's epigram. In this way 'the paper going back and forth, they wove a philosophical dialogue about . . . love, and its possible cure' (Grundy, pp. 361–2). This is a description of the manuscript in Bodley MS Eng. misc. b. 169, which contains part of the poem (lines 44–73). At the same meeting or a subsequent one (that is, on the Tuesday or the Saturday), they must have gone on to complete the dialogue as we now have it by providing the opening section. Montagu retained the manuscript now in the Bodleian (it was probably extracted from the rest of her papers by Lady Louisa Stuart), but she did not have the whole poem as they had by then composed it. She, therefore, asked Hervey to send her the missing initial part (lines 1–43). Prefacing his reply with a gender-bending comparison, he responded, in a letter headed 'Kensington. Monday Morning' but otherwise undated: 'I take my-self to have been to You in this whole affair, in the Situation of *gentle Kate* to Harry Piercy. As for the first part of the Dialogue I have it not here but will write it out as well as I can from my Memory' (SRO 941/47/2, pp. 69–70). He scribbled over the words 'and so far you do trust this' after 'Piercy'.

The part he reconstructed from memory in that letter consists of lines 5–43, and the Monday in question may well have been that after the Tuesday or Saturday on which the dialogue had been written – or, perhaps, both the Tuesday and the Saturday, if it had been interrupted and taken up again. His rendering in that letter corresponds closely to the complete version of the dialogue found in Harrowby MS 81, which might either have been a copy made by them both for Hervey's retention when the poem was first composed extempore, or a subsequent development of it when they were together again.

***Textual commentary.*** The fair copy in Harrowby MS 81 is chosen as the main source for this edition, as for Halsband's and Grundy's. Adjustments to the poem are detailed in the List of Emendations, and include some end-of-line punctuation missing in the Harrowby copy but present in the complementary manuscripts. Details of these and of substantive variants, and of deleted words or passages in the manuscripts are provided in the Historical Collation.

## Verse Dialogue between Hervey and Montagu

L. H.[1] What is this Secret you'd so fain impart?
Open your own, rely upon my Heart:[2]
L. M. I wish to tell, but I would have you guess,
And think at least that it would pain me less
L. H. The Preface to your Question is refined,
And should I *guess* when I should *read* your Mind;
You'd fear some other might your Secret find.
L. M. My Secret can be guess'd, by only you
You see my trust – but see my Folly too.
L. H. You might be wise, and yet that Folly chuse;
Ask then, nor fear your Suit I shall refuse,
Or that your Trust I ever can abuse.[3]

1. These speech-prefixes, 'L. H.' for Lord Hervey, and 'L. M.' for Lady Mary, are present in the Suffolk Record Office copy, but not in the other manuscripts. For the parts of the dialogue absent from the SRO copy, the speech-prefixes are added editorially.

2. In the space after this couplet in the Harrowby manuscript, a line and four words have been struck out: 'A painfull secret should be guess'd not told | I wish to tell'. This is evidence of revision during the process of providing an introduction to Montagu's initial reflection, which appears here as line 44, and opens the Bodley partial manuscript.

3. Halsband and Grundy's note, citing a letter in the John Murray Archive in London, is relevant: 'Hervey kept LM's trust: in describing their meeting to Algarotti, he added, "elle m'a dit des choses, que comme elle m'a fait promettre avant que de les dire je ne les redirois point, je ne veux pas vous les communiquer"' ('she told me

I own you're rather form'd by Heav'n to grant,
But Heav'n can only know what 'tis we want;
Mortals tho e'er so willing all to give,
Must for a welcome Gift, some Hint recieve.
You may perhaps this wary Silence blame,
But won't you chide me more if I should name?

L. M. My Question short, but long will be the Pain,
I ask to one that can too well explain,
My Heart demands, you answer from the Brain.

L. H. Tis true I answer only from the Brain;
Fearing my Answer should be thought too plain,
For since you wish to know yet fear to read,
Cautious the winding Precipice I tread:
I combate Nature have recourse to Art,
And rack my Head that I may spare your Heart;
Like Rivers turn'd my Numbers useless grow,
Say shall they in their nat'ral Channel flow?

L. M. He laughs at Scars who never felt a Wound
(This Truth long since the Gentle Romeo found)[4]
The time may come to feel th' exstatic smart,
You may see Eyes and you may feel a Heart.[5]

L. H. A little longer yet your Pain endure,
Nature who made the Wound, will give the Cure;
For as the Characters in Sand we trace,
If unrenew'd (tho e'er so deep) will pass;
So all Impressions which our Passions make,
By Absence smooth'd, an even Surface take;[6]

things that I do not wish to communicate to you, as she had me promise before telling them to me that I should not at all repeat them').

4. *He laughs . . . Romeo found: Romeo and Juliet* II.2.1 ('He jests at scars . . .').

5. *You may . . . a Heart*: as Halsband and Grundy note, Montagu here quotes from her 'Answer to a Love Letter in Verse', line 34 (*Essays & Poems*, p. 245).

6. *For as . . . Surface take*: As Isobel Grundy remarks, the simile is borrowed from a poem by Montagu herself, 'Epistle [to Lord Bathurst]', lines 61–4 (Grundy, p. 362; *Essays & Poems*, p. 243). The fact that Hervey immediately follows a self-quotation by Montagu with an allusion to another poem by her is a good illustration of the dialogue's verbal fencing and its intimacy.

Thus Heav'n at once both covetuous and kind,
Has constituted ev'ry human Mind,
For as we lose the Merit to be true,
In recompense we lose the Mis'ry too.

L. M. A little Love[7] deserves not passions name
A Taper's light is hardly call'd a Flame
A Transient Wind extinguishes the Fire
And a short Absence cools a small desire
But when the Heat on the whole Vitals preys
Even Tempests but encrease the powerfull Blaze.[8]

L. H. As Poysons other Poysons will remove,
So Love may be expel'd by other Love.
This Doctrine Cleopatra held was true;
Won't Cleopatra's Med'cines do for You?[9]

L. M. Go bid the thirsty, overlabour'd swains
Seek Grecian Vines on Caledonian plains
With equal Hope you sooth my restless mind
(To this cold Climate cursedly confin'd)
To meet a second Lovely of the Kind

L. H. These Thoughts are not from Nature but a Book,
Into our Conduct, not our Writings look;
There Man and Woman equally you'll see,
Form'd by Receipts[10] you've heard explain'd by me,
I tell you what they are, You what they ought to be.

7. At this point, at the bottom of the page, SRO breaks off with 'You have the rest'. Hervey knew this because Montagu had originated the epigram from which the dialogue began.

8. *A little Love . . . powerfull Blaze*: Halsband and Grundy note: 'In the Bodleian MS, L[ady] M[ary] wrote these six lines as if to stand alone, heading them: "Epigram written extempore in a dispute whether Absence ended Love." Despite a line drawn below the epigram, she and Hervey pursued the dialogue on the verso of the sheet.' The two then built the rest of the dialogue around the epigram, which therefore provided its starting point and kernel.

9. *As Poysons . . . for You*: alluding to Dryden, *All for Love*, IV.1.136–7, 'And Love may be expell'd by other Love, | As Poysons are by Poysons' (Dryden, *Works*, XIII: Plays, 76). Halsband and Grundy note: 'When L[ady] M[ary]'s infatuation ended (1741), she received the same advice from Hervey', citing *Montagu Letters*, II, 240–1. The couplet also appears in Poem 66, 'Agrippina', II. 2. 114–15.

10. *Receipts*: recipes.

L. M. Sway'd by no moral, or affected Rules
(By Knaves invented and observ'd by Fools)
Judge of my Future Actions by my past
And call my Conduct, Nicety of Taste
L. H. In vain you talk of what you love and hate,
For when you're hungry, and have Food you'll eat.
L. M. Hunger's the Motive of the unbred Clown
To whose coarse Palate, all rank meat goes down
But Hunger never rais'd the Pain I feel
Which only one can give, and only One could heal.
L. H. I'm tired of all this fine poetic stuff;
Now call for Supper, we have writ enough.[11]

11. *I'm tired ... writ enough*: This final couplet, which appears only in the Harrowby copy, where it is in Hervey's hand and has been heavily scribbled over by Montagu, is here reinstated. As Halsband and Grundy note, 'The suppressed couplet at the end seems proof of genuine extemporaneity' (*Essays & Poems*, p. 286).

# 56 The Griff to the Queen

***Main source.*** SRO 941/47/13–14 (14), f. 320r.

***Complementary manuscript source.*** Royal Archives, Windsor: RA GEO/MAIN/53088–53977 (53871r).

***Complementary print sources.*** None; the poem was first printed in Croker, *Memoirs*, II, 424; and was reprinted in Sedgwick, III, 804.

***Attribution.*** The SRO text is in Hervey's hand and has been tipped into the manuscript.

***Context and date.*** The poem was written on or very soon after 20 August 1737 during a time of increased tension between the King and Queen and Frederick, Prince of Wales, following the birth of the latter's first legitimate offspring, his daughter Augusta. Hervey introduces it in the manuscript 'Some Materials' with the following words:

> When Lord North was sent from the P[rince] to enquire after her Health, Lord H[ervey] say'd he was sure he could dictate a much sincerer Message from your P[rince] on this Occasion than Lord North had deliver'd, upon which the Q[ueen] and the P[rinces]s Caroline begging him to do it, he went with the P[rinces]s Caroline into the next Room, and there wrote the following Letter to the Q[ueen] in the name of the *Griff* which was a Nick-name the K[ing] had long ago given the P[rince]. This is the original Paper. (SRO 941/47/13–14 (14), f. 319v, 321r)

This text replaces what Hervey originally wrote but then crossed through, as follows:

> he was sure he could dictate a much sincerer Message from your P[rince] on this Occasion than he believed Lord North would deliver, upon which the Q[ueen] and the P[rinces]s Caroline beg'd he would put it in writing, and send it in by her to divert the Q[ueen]. Accordingly she call'd for a Pen and Ink, and made him sit down that Moment to do it. He did so and this was the original Letter.
>
> The Griff to the Queen. (The *Griff* was a Nick-name given by the K[ing] to the P[rince]). (f. 321r)

The revision represents a clarification of the original text, and so is evidence of Hervey's wish to have his memoirs published, probably after his death. His poem is a clever piece of dramatic impersonation, showing off his skills as a mimic. Its stumbling anapaestic tetrameter couplets provide an appropriate form for a clumsy missive from a man whom both he and the Queen regarded as a booby. It also demonstrates Hervey's ability to compose verse extempore, the SRO manuscript being the original text.

***Textual commentary.*** There are no substantive variants in the Windsor copy. Punctuation has been added where the syntax requires it, and in two cases errant apostrophes have been removed (from 'your's' and 'bid's' in lines 12 and 13 respectively); see List of Emendations. Spelling and initial capitals have been left unaltered.

## The Griff to the Queen

From my-self and my Cub,[1] and eke[2] from my Wife
I send my Lord North, notwithstanding our Strife,
To your Majesty's Residence call'd Hampton Court,
*Pour savoir au vrai comment on se porte.*[3]
For 'tis rumour'd in town – I hope 'tis not true –
Your Foot is too big for your Slipper or Shoe.[4]
If I had the placing your Gout I am sure,
Your Majesty's Toe less pain should endure.[5]
For whilst I have so many curs'd Things in my Head
And some *Stick in my Stomach*[6] (as in Proverbs[7] 'tis said),
No just or good Reason, your good Son can see
Why, when mine are so plagued, yours, from Plagues should be free.
Much more I've to say but Respect bids be brief.
And so I remain your Undutyfull Griff.

1. *Cub*: a disparaging reference to the Prince's newborn daughter.

2. *eke*: deliberate archaism for 'also' used with humorous intent.

3. *Pour savoir au vrai comment on se porte*: 'To know the truth about how things are going'; French was the language normally spoken at court. Frederick had used it for the letters to the King and Queen dated 20 August that occasioned the poem, but these words are in a much less formal idiom.

4. *Your Foot ... Shoe*: a reference to the swelling caused by the gout from which the Queen was suffering.

5. *If I ... should endure*: as Croker puts it, 'the intended points of these uncouth and ill-natured lines is the supposed wish of the Prince that the gout could be removed from the Queen's foot to the more mortal regions of the *head* or *stomach*' (*Memoirs*, II, 424, n. 6).

6. *Stick in my Stomach:* 'said of something that makes a lasting (esp. painful) impression on the mind' (*OED*).

7. *Proverbs*: it is in fact a vernacular rather than a biblical expression.

# 57 Written in Algarotti's Book on Sir Isaac Newton's Philosophy of Light and Colours

***Source.*** SRO 941/53/1, pp. 202–3.

***Complementary manuscript sources.*** None has come to light.

***Complementary print sources.*** The poem seems never to have been printed previously.

***Attribution.*** William Hervey in the source, his commonplace book ('by Lord Hervey. 1742').

***Context and date.*** Francesco Algarotti, intimate friend of Hervey and Montagu, had published *Il Newtonianismo per le dame*, a series of dialogues explaining Newton's *Optics*, in Milan in 1737. Modelled, as Isobel Grundy points out, on Fontenelle's *Pluralité des mondes* (Grundy, p. 356), it was intended to popularise Newton's ideas, especially for a relatively uncultivated female readership. The book was quickly translated into English by Elizabeth Carter in two volumes as *Sir Isaac Newton's Philosophy Explain'd for the Use of Ladies* (London: for E. Cave, 1739), and a second Italian edition appeared in 1739 (Napoli: s.n.), prefaced by commendatory verses from Montagu and Hervey, Hervey's poem being taken from a letter to Algarotti dated 16 August 1736 (Poem 79). The present poem, written near the end of Hervey's life, reflects his scepticism about systems of all kinds, religious, scientific or philosophical. Its anapaestic tetrameter couplets help convey a sense of world-weary humour.

***Textual commentary.*** William Hervey's copy being clear and mostly grammatical, it requires very few changes. The only emendations made are the deletion of an unnecessary apostrophe in line 6 (where the second 'its' reads 'it's') and the insertion of a full stop at the end of line 7. Otherwise punctuation is left unaltered, as are spelling and initial capitals except in the title.

## Written in Algarotti's Book on Sir Isaac Newton's Philosophy of Light and Colours

On all Systems I look as I look upon Days,[1]
Some bright, clear, and fine and deserving our Praise;
Whilst some are so cloudy, so dark and so dull,

1. *On all . . . Days*: the comparison is well chosen, given that the book in which the poem is written is about the natural philosophy of light.

Who delights in such weather I think is a fool:
But let System or Day be ever so bright,
This must part with its credit, and that with its light,
One exploded will end, and t'other in Night.
And thus such respect to great Newton I pay,
As I do to our yet unextinguish'd *Today*;
Nor doubt but hereafter some Genius will rise,
The *tomorrow* in fine Philosophical skys;
Whilst the honors which now Newton's principles[2] boast,
In the herd of all Yesterday-Systems are lost,
His Colours and light sunk in Midnight you'll find,
His Attraction[3] decay'd, and his Optics struck blind;
And the phrase in Derision perhaps soon apply'd,
When People shall call it his Lunatic Tide:[4]
Thus the World in these things I firmly believe,
Shall truth, and some permanent Tenet recieve,
When such in Philosophy's sky shall prevail,
As Joshua show'd in Jehosaphet's vale,[5]
But till then each new Rule this Rule shall fulfill,
That Systems and days shall together stand still.[6]

2. *principles*: substituted for the word 'philosophy', which is blotted over.

3. *Attraction*: a reference to another famous scientific theory of Newton, his laws of attraction and repulsion.

4. *his Lunatic Tide*: referring to Newton's explanation of the lunar tides, the first scientifically convincing one, in his *Philosophiæ Naturalis Principia Mathematica*, which was first published in 1687 (*ODNB*).

5. *As Joshua . . . Jehosaphet's vale*: Joshua was the great Israelite military leader, assistant to Moses, at whose request the sun and moon stood still in the heavens (Joshua 10: 12–14), while the valley of Jehosaphat is the valley of decision, usually associated with the Day of Judgement (David Lyle Jeffrey (gen. ed.), *A Dictionary of Biblical Tradition in English Literature* (Grand Rapids, MI: Eerdmans; Leominster: Gracewing, 1992)); the reference is therefore to the Day of Judgement, when time will end.

6. *That Systems . . . stand still*: in other words, systems will be as transient as days.

# SHORTER TRANSLATIONS, PARAPHRASES AND IMITATIONS

# INTRODUCTION TO SHORTER TRANSLATIONS, PARAPHRASES AND IMITATIONS

Much of Hervey's verse has classical or French antecedents. Some of his epistles are modelled on Ovid's *Heroides*; his satires often have Horace or Persius in mind; Horace's odes clearly formed a starting point for some of his poems addressed to Stephen Fox; his longest, three-book, poem derives from Fénelon's *Télémaque*; and his tragedy 'Agrippina' is heavily influenced by Racine. In his Preface to *Ovid's Epistles* (1680) Dryden famously distinguished between three types of translation: 'metaphrase' ('or turning an author word by word, and line by line, from one language into another'), 'paraphrase' ('or translation with latitude, where the author is kept in view by the translator, so as never to be lost, but his words are not so strictly followed as his sense, and that too is admitted to be amplified, but not altered') and 'imitation' ('where the translator (if he has not lost that name) assumes the liberty not only to vary from the words and sense, but to forsake them both as he sees occasion; and taking only some general hints from the original, to run division on the ground-work as he pleases').[1] In this sense Hervey's 'Telemachus' is a distant imitation of Fénelon and the poems to Stephen Fox much closer imitations of Horace. The verse reserved for this section is closer still to its originals.

While some of Hervey's translations seem required of him, others clearly stem from personal enthusiasms. Poem 58 is an academic exercise, a formal paraphrase. Two of the other paraphrases (Poems 59 and 63) occur in letters to Lady Bristol, where, Hervey suggests, a translation of material in a foreign language might be polite and expected, though in the case of French in Poem 59 the implication might be that ignorance of the language is itself less than polite. The lines are quoted and then a translation, designed to capture the meaning closely, is provided. The same politeness towards someone without a traditional classical education may

1. Preface to *Ovid's Epistles*, in Dryden, *Poems*, I (1649–81), 384–5. An exceptionally valuable lecture on the topic by David Hopkins, 'John Dryden: Translator and Theorist of Translation' is currently available on the web: www.ucl.ac.uk/translation-studies/translation-in-history/documents/Hopkins_Dryden_pdf

lie in the translation of the line from Ovid's 'Sappho to Phaon' in the letter to the Prince of Wales (Poem 62), though in this case the original is attractively elaborated in what amounts to an imitation. 'Sappho to Phaon' is also quoted and translated in a letter to Montagu (Poem 61), though in a characteristic inversion, the praise applied to Montagu's letter writing comes from admiration not of Sappho's poetry but of Phaon's beauty. The remaining two poems seem even more personally motivated. Poem 60 paraphrases from one of Ovid's elegies the lines Hervey uses as the epigraph to his elegy on his sister, Lady Elizabeth Mansel (Poem 28). By contrast, Poem 64, a skilled and close translation of one of Jean-Baptiste Rousseau's epigrams, has fun with biblical narrative and with the relation of husbands and wives.

# 58 A Dialogue between Horace and Lydia: Horace, Book III, Ode 9 paraphrased

***Source.*** SRO 941/46/5.

***Complementary sources.*** There are none.

***Attribution.*** John, Lord Bristol, Hervey's father. The copy is endorsed: '9th Ode of the 3d B. of Horace paraphras'd by my dear Son Jack. 1713. Lord Bristol.'

***Context and date.*** As Halsband remarks, the poem is Hervey's 'earliest surviving literary composition', written at Westminster School shortly before he matriculated at Clare College, Cambridge, on 20 November 1713 (Halsband, pp. 12, 16). The word 'paraphrased' in the title is important, signifying as it does the aim not to offer a translation, but rather, as Dryden put it in his preface to *Ovid's Epistles*, a 'translation with latitude, where the author is kept in view by the translator, so as never to be lost, but his words are not so strictly followed as his sense, and that too is admitted to be amplified, but not altered' (Dryden, *Poems*, I, 384–5). For this reason, Hervey is able to lengthen the twenty-four lines of the original Latin to forty-four, and is under no obligation to attempt an approximation to the complex Latin metre, preferring standard iambic pentameter couplets with the garnish of two triplets and two alexandrines (lines 26 and 44). For purposes of comparison, C. E. Bennett's Loeb translation is provided at the end of this section. The choice of poem is an interesting one for two reasons. First, the ode is not among Horace's best known. Perhaps, therefore, it was set as a school assignment. Second, it is a dialogue. In his later work Hervey showed an ability to write in voices other than his own, and it is apt that his first known literary composition provided an opportunity for an exercise in just such a form.

***Textual commentary.*** Because it is a juvenile composition and the sense is never in doubt, the poem is printed here as it stands in the manuscript, with the original spelling, punctuation and use of initial capitals left unaltered. One ampersand in the title has, however, been expanded, the spelling error of 'paraphased' for 'paraphrase' been corrected, and no attempt is made to imitate Hervey's careful ornamentation of what was evidently a presentation piece for his father.

## The 9th: Ode of Horace, Book the 3d: paraphrased, being a Dialogue between Horace and Lydia.

Donec gratus nam tibi &ca:

HOR: Whilst happy Horace, Lydia's Heart, possess'd,
And reign'd without a Rival in your Breast;
Whilst no encroaching Youth more wellcome strove
T'enjoy thy Beautys, and engross thy Love
Nor round thy snowy Neck his Arm's did twine
Reaping that Bliss which once was wholly mine,
Victorious Caesar, of the world possess'd
Ne'er knew such happyness, was ne'er so bless'd
As Horace, in his Lydia's Arms caress'd

LYD: 'Till to his Lydia, Horace prov'd untrue,
And to anothers Arms (Inconstant) flew;
'Till Cloe's Eyes, my wand'ring Lover, gain'd,
And o'er his faithless Heart triumphant reign'd
No other hope, or fear, fond Lydia knew;
Her ev'ry wish was satisfy'd in you.
Nor was the celebrated Lydia's Name,
Inferior to our Mother Rehea's[1] Fame.

HOR: At Cloe's Alter now my vows I pay
And at her feet, my heart an offering lay
Where Cloe rules, tis freedom to obey
What Charms (ye Gods) to her fair Form belong?
What Heavenly Musick flows from her Sweet Tongue.
Even her Charming Lute, less rapture brings
'Tho' She her-self inspires the trembling strings
Oh! would kind Heav'n for her's, accept of mine
To save my Cloe's life, I would my own resign

1. *our Mother Rehea's*: Hervey uses the variant name Rhea for the Ilia of the original Latin, referring to the mythical mother of the twins Romulus and Remus, who founded the city of Rome.

LYD: With love of me the beauteous Calais burn's
A mutual Love, my gratefull Heart returns
To prove his flame, the tend'rest Oaths he Swore,
To prove how much the Charmer I adore,
Death's Sharpest Pains I twice would gladly bear,
Would Heaven in return, my Calais spare

HOR: What if my former Passion I renew,
And fan afresh the Smother'd Flame for you
If Cloe's Charms I throw neglected by?
And to my Lydia's Breast, again transported fly.

LYD: 'Tho' he was fairer than the Morning Star,
And could with Turtles constancy compare;
And you were falser than delusive Dream's,
Or painted Gardens in the Crystal Streams;
And rougher far than a tempestuous Storm
When boist'rous Winds, the boiling Deep, deform
Yet from his Arms without regrett I'd fly
With The I'de chuse to live, with The I'de chuse to dye

## Horace, Book III, Ode IX

'While I was dear to thee and no more favoured youth flung his arms about thy dazzling neck, I lived in greater bliss than Persia's king.'

'While thou wast enamoured of no other more than me, and Lydia ranked not after Chloë, in joy of my great fame I, Lydia, lived more glorious than Roman Ilia.'

'Me Thracian Chloë now doth sway, skilled in sweet measures and mistress of the lyre; for her I will not fear to die, if the Fates but spare my darling and suffer her to live.'

'Me Calais, son of Thurian Ornytus, kindles with mutual flame; for him right willingly I twice will die, if the Fates but spare the lad and suffer him to live.'

'What if the old love come back again and join those now estranged beneath her compelling yoke; if fair-haired Chloë be put aside and the door thrown open to rejected Lydia?'

'Though he is fairer than the stars, and thou less stable than the tossing cork and stormier than the wanton Adriatic, with thee I fain would live, with thee I'd gladly die.' (Horace, *Odes and Epodes*, trans. C. E. Bennett (Loeb, p. 213))

# 59 These empty Titles (Translation of Racine, *Britannicus*, I. 1. 89–90)

***Source.*** SRO 941/47/2, p. 241.

***Complementary sources.*** There is no other known copy, manuscript or printed.

***Attribution.*** The couplet is in a letter in Hervey's hand; he indicates his authorship.

***Context and date.*** The couplet occurs in a letter to Hervey's mother, Lady Bristol, dated 26 December [1727], in which he first repeats to her some medical advice for his sister Ann that his mother has asked him to obtain from Dr Cheyne. He next turns to the question of London gossip and political news, and Sir Spencer Compton's elevation to the peerage. Of this event, and quoting the same couplet from Racine's *Britannicus*, I. 1. 89–90 that he alludes to for his mother here, Hervey was to write in *Some Materials*:

> But as Sir Spencer Compton had conceived too strong hopes of being Sir Robert [Walpole]'s superior ever to serve in the House of Commons quietly under him, and that it might be dangerous, consequently, to suffer him in the chair of a new Parliament, Sir Robert advised the making him a peer. Accordingly he was created Baron of Wilmington; and on this occasion, I think, he might have said, like Agrippina, the mother of Nero, in Racine's *Britannicus*,
>
> "Tous ces présens, hélas! irritent mon dépit,
> Je vois mes honneurs croître, et tomber mon crédit."
>
> It was just his case. But he did not seem to feel the ridicule or the contemptibleness of his situation. (Sedgwick, I, 39)

According to the article on Compton in *ODNB*, it was on 8 January 1728 that Compton was created a peer, so Hervey was very well-informed to have had such early notice of his promotion. The close relationship between letter and memoir is interesting evidence of how Hervey drew on his earlier personal correspondence in writing parts of *Some Materials*; while the reference to Agrippina indicates that his interest in her story, which was to lead to him writing a full-length play about it several years later (Poem 66), was of long standing. Agrippina's remark may be translated literally as follows: 'All these gifts, Albine, excite my resentment, for while my honours accumulate my stock is falling'. She makes it early in the play when Nero is putting on a false show of respect to his mother. The closing reference to Mrs Howard – the letters in her name after its initial have been deleted in the manuscript – concerns her attempt to reach an accommodation with her abusive husband after her position as mistress to the Prince of Wales changed for the better when the latter became George II in June 1727. Although her husband made the negotiations as difficult as he could, he was finally 'bought off by an annuity of £1200, paid by Mrs Howard but largely provided by the new king', the document effecting her separation from her husband being signed on 29 February 1728 (*ODNB*).

***Textual commentary.*** As the sense is clear, the couplet is given as it stands in the manuscript, without alteration of any kind.

### Verse in its letter context

I know very little News that your Lady$^{sp}$ will not see in the Prints; S$^{r}$ Sp[encer] Compton's being made L$^{d}$ Willmington I conclude is already mention'd there: there are two Verses in Racine so apropos to these new Honours confer'd upon him, that I cant help mentioning them tho' in French: they are say'd by Agripina, in Britannicus to her Confidente Albine.

> Tous ces presens Albine irritent mon Depit,
> Je vois mes Honneurs croitre, et tomber mon Credit.

My Lord Bristol will explain these Verses much better than I can, but as I dont think it quite civil to write part of my Letter in a Language, untranslated, w$^{ch}$ your Lady$^{sp}$ does not understand, I will to save my-self from the imputation of that impolitesse give your Lady$^{sp}$ the best Version I can make of them

> These empty Titles more my Anger raise
> For whilst my Honours grow my Pow'r decay's.

There has been Hopes of an Accomodation between Mrs Howard & her Husband but I heard yesterday the Negociation was quite broke off again.

# 60 Tho' thy whole life should pass without a stain (Translation of some lines in Ovid, *Amores*, Book III, Elegy 9, Extempore)

***Source.*** SRO 941/53/1, p. 202.

***Complementary sources.*** There is no other known copy, manuscript or printed, though Hervey used the same distich from Ovid as the epigraph for Poem 28, 'Verses to the Memory of my Dearest Sister the Lady Elizabeth Mansel'.

***Attribution.*** William Hervey, in his commonplace book where the lines are transcribed.

***Context and date.*** There is no clear evidence as to context or date, though it seems likely that Hervey produced his translation at or around the time of writing his elegy for his sister. For further details, see the headnote to Poem 28. In William Hervey's transcript, the reference to the title of the poem is keyed to the original Latin, squeezed in below it before the next poem: *Vive pius, moriere pius, cole sacra, colentem | Mors gravis a templis in cava busta trahet.* The Loeb translation of a variant text is: 'Live the duteous life – you will die; be faithful in your worship – in the very act of worship heavy death will drag you from the temple to the hollow tomb' (Ovid, *Amores*, III. ix. 37–8 (Loeb, p. 489)).

***Textual commentary.*** As the sense is clear, the translation is presented as it stands in the manuscript, with no alteration to spelling, punctuation or use of initial capitals.

## Translation of some lines in Ovid, Elegia 9. Liber 3, Extempore by Lord Hervey

Tho' thy whole life should pass without a stain,
With piety alike in health or pain,
To Heav'n resign'd; Still Death shall be thy doom,
And snatch thee from the altar to the Tomb.

# 61 If equal Charms (Translation of Ovid, *Heroides XV: Sappho Phaoni*, lines 39–40)

***Main source.*** SRO 941/47/2, p. 45.

***Complementary sources.*** There is no other known copy, manuscript or printed.

***Attribution.*** The letter in which the couplet occurs is in Hervey's hand, and the couplet is clearly his improvisation.

***Context and date.*** The couplet occurs in a letter from Hervey to Lady Mary Wortley Montagu dated 14 December 1729, telling her that should she wish to write to him, she should address her letter to Stephen Fox's house, Redlynch. The verse lines are used to cap a compliment he pays to her about her letters, which he judges far superior to his own.

The compliment paid, Hervey continues his letter on quite different subjects, including that of ongoing gossip about the death of Lady Abergavenny (see Poem 29 and headnote). His source for the couplet is Ovid, Sappho to Phaon: *si, nisi quae facie poterit te digna videri, | nulla futura tua est, nulla futura tua est* ('If none shall be yours unless deemed worthy of you for her beauty's sake, then none shall be yours at all'; Ovid, *Heroides*, XV. 39–40 (Loeb, pp. 182–3)).

***Textual commentary.*** As the sense is clear, the translation is presented as it stands in the manuscript, with no alteration to spelling, punctuation or use of initial capitals.

## Verse in its letter context

'Tis smal encouragement to your Lady[sp] to enter into this Commerce,[1] to acknowledg the Ballance of Gain must always be against you; but I may very justly say to you on Letters what Sapho does to Phaon on Beauty;

> If equal Charms alone can favour find  
> Phaon alone to Phaon can be kind.

1. *this Commerce*: this correspondence by letter.

# 62 No more my Eyes thy Beauty charms (Imitation of Ovid, *Heroides XV: Sappho Phaoni*, lines 18–20)

***Main source.*** Letter of 6 November 1731 to Frederick, Prince of Wales, from Redlynch. SRO 941/47/4, pp. 266–71, p. 270; it is in the hand of an amanuensis; some of the letter, including these lines, is printed by Ilchester, pp. 107–9.

***Complementary manuscript sources.*** None known.

***Complementary print sources.*** None known.

***Attribution.*** Hervey's lines are a free translation of lines 18–20 of 'Sappho Phaoni', number 15 of Ovid's *Heroides.* No other source of the translation has been identified.

***Context and date.*** This an intimate letter between Hervey and the Prince of Wales, just before the end of their friendship. It contains an account of life at Redlynch, including the lines beginning 'Quant al Padrone' (Poem 105), and concludes with 'For if in Richmond-Morning-Walk' (Poem 77), which begins on a new page. In this section of the letter, Hervey enquires about the Prince's amours, ostensibly an older man taking an interest in a younger man's adventures. But by referring to the lines (by Ovid or his imitator) in which Sappho turns from the women she has loved to a man (Phaon the ferryman), it is not impossible that he is suggesting that he has himself supplanted women in Frederick's affections. By calling himself Hephaestion, sometimes regarded as Alexander's lover, he strengthens this possibility. After these lines he says he hesitates to send the letter, especially without covenanting that it is for the Prince's eyes alone.

***Textual commentary.*** Some of the letter and the verse are taken without alteration from the Suffolk Record Office manuscript.

## Verse in its letter context

I have Sent your Royal Highness a picture of our life in Black and white. I should be glad to see one of Kew. Is there any thing new added by way of Appendix? or do Vielleries[1] reign in such undisordered unchangeable Vicissitude, y[t] by looking at my Watch I may know whether Your Royal Highness is Walking, playing, dressing, *raccommoding*,[2] eating, or

1. *Vielleries*: properly vieilleries, old things, old customs.
2. *raccommoding*: mending (garments or relationships).

sleeping? if it would not be too bold for Hephestion[3] to pry into y$^e$ Sanctum Sanctorum[4] of your Employments, I would ask whether Roxana or Statira[5] is at present in Favour? Is la Moscula[6] Still flattered, by y$^e$ Hackney piper of *Dudley's & Trevor's*?[7] or do You say like Ovid. Non occulis grata est Atthys ut ante meis.[8]

No more my Eyes thy Beauty charms
No more my Heart thy Beauty warms
No more I languish for thy Arms.

Upon reading over this Galimatias[9] I feel some Doubts arising whether I ought to send It or no, especially w$^{th}$out covenanting y$^t$ It shall be expos'd to no[10] Eyes but Your Own. [The letter then moves into Poem 77 'For if in Richmond-Morning-Walk'.]

3. *Hephestion*: male intimate of Alexander the Great; pet name for Hervey while his friendship with Frederick lasted. See Hannah Smith and Stephen Taylor, 'Hephaestion and Alexander: Lord Hervey, Frederick, Prince of Wales, and the Royal Favourite in the 1730s', *English Historical Review*, 124, no. 507 (2009), 283–312.

4. *Sanctum Sanctorum*: holy of holies.

5. *Roxana or Statira*: Alexander's first two wives, as in Nathaniel Lee's often-performed *The Rival Queens* (1677).

6. *la Moscula*: Mary, Countess of Deloraine (*bap.* 1703, *d.* 1744).

7. *Still flatterd, by y$^e$ Hackney piper of Dudley's & Trevor's:* Hervey asks, Is Lady Deloraine still flattered by comparison with those broken-down prostitutes, the Lady Dudleys and Lady Trevors of the court? A *hackney piper* is a broken-winded horse, and *hackney* can mean a prostitute. Lady Dudley is referred to by the Queen as that woman who 'has lain with half the town as well as Fretz [the Prince]', while Lady Trevor is described as exceptionally ugly and pious, and peculiarly unlikely to commit adultery (Sedgwick, II, 615; I, 86–7).

8. *Non oculis . . . meis*: 'my eyes joy not in Atthis as once they did'. The poem continues 'nor in the hundred other maids I loved here to my reproach; unworthy one, the love that belonged to many maids you alone possess' (Ovid, *Heroides*, XV. 18–20 (Loeb, p. 183)).

9. *Galimatias*: 'Confused language, meaningless talk, nonsense' (*OED*).

10. *no*: emended from 'now', a clear scribal error uncorrected by Hervey.

# 63 This little House (Imitation of Catullus I, XXIV, 'Ad Furium')

***Source.*** SRO 941/47/2, p. 260.

***Complementary sources.*** There is no other known copy, manuscript or printed.

***Attribution.*** The letter in which the lines occur is in Hervey's hand, and the context makes clear that they are by him.

***Context and date.*** The letter, dated 27 November 1736, is to Lady Bristol, his mother. Hervey is advising her about her and her husband's health, and the unsuitability of Ickworth House as a winter dwelling. He writes:

> That I may follow the Example of other able Physicians I must beg leave to send my Prescriptions to my Lord Bristol in Latin, and ask your Ladyship's Pardon for so doing
>
> Furi, villula vestra non ad Austri
> Flatus opposita est, nec ad Favoni,
> nec saevi Boreæ, aut Apeliotæ;
> Verum ad millia quindecim, et ducentos,
> O ventum horribilem atqu pestilentem. (Catullus E, 21)

The poem quoted is an ode by Catullus now numbered 26, translated literally as follows:

> Furius, your farm has not been put up against the blasts of Auster nor Favonius nor fierce Boreas or Apheliotes, but against a mortgage of a cool fifteen thousand two hundred. What a horrid dangerous draught! (*Catullus, Tibullus, Pervigilium Veneris* (Loeb, pp. 31–3))

In his translation that follows, Hervey considerably distorts the meaning of the original, highlighting the draught and making no mention of the mortgage. Lord Bristol, to whom the letter was obviously meant to be shown, may have enjoyed this mischievous appropriation. He had intended to build a house suitable for a nobleman's country estate, but the original mansion had become dilapidated and so in 1702, as Halsband puts it, 'Instead of repairing or rebuilding it Hervey decided to occupy a farmhouse about half a mile away, and he began to enlarge and improve this modest dwelling' (p. 7). Although in the following year he consulted Sir John Vanbrugh about building a house more befitting his position, nothing came of this and the family continued to live at Ickworth House despite its small scale and other inconveniences. As Michael De-la-Noy explains, it was not until nearly the end of the century that Lord Hervey's son Frederick, then fourth Earl of Bristol, began the grandiose building in Italian style that is now Ickworth, although even this was not completed, at least for occupation, until 1829 by Frederick William, fifth Earl and first Marquess of Bristol (*The House of Hervey: A History of Tainted Talent* (London: Constable, 2001), pp. 124–5, 173).

***Textual commentary.*** As the sense is clear, the translation is presented as it stands in the manuscript, with no alteration to spelling, punctuation or use of initial capitals. The letter ends with the last line of the verses.

## Verse in its letter context

This Madam in plain English, is to prescribe London to Lord Bristol & to tell him that Ickworth House is not a proper Winter Habitation for the sick. nor have I borrow'd my Learning, like my other medecinal Brothers of the College from Galen, Hippocrates or Celsus, but from Catullus, & for your Ladysp's benefit (who not understanding the Original may bear the Copy) I send the following Translation

This little House which some plain Ickworth call,
And others, more jocosely, Paper-Hall,
By North or South Wind, or by East, or West,
No one can say is more or less distress'd;
For through each Door, each Window, and each Wall,
Good Ickworth hospitably takes them all;
And did the Compass furnish fifty more,
Your Bed would be no Shelter from their Pow'r.—
Since then this Cave of Æolus you find,
Nor sick, nor Winter Dwelling was design'd;
My wholsome Counsell is – to London come;
Catullus would have say'd, pray come to Rome.

# 64 Epigram from Rousseau (Translation of 'Epigrame contre les Femmes')

***Main source.*** SRO 941/53/1, p. 206.

***Complementary manuscript source.*** Harrowby MS 255, f. 30v.

***Attribution.*** William Hervey ('by Ld. Hy.'). The poem is unattributed in the Harrowby manuscript.

***Context and date.*** Nothing has come to light about the context and date of this poem. However, although it could have been written at almost any period of Hervey's life, the increasing scepticism of his outlook in his latter years makes it more likely to be a later than an earlier composition. The poem is a free translation of Jean-Baptiste Rousseau's 'Epigrame contre les Femmes':

Pour triomfer de l'humaine Nature,
Le Vieux Serpent cauteleux & madré
Tenta la Femme, & la Femme parjure
Fit parjurer l'homme inconsidéré.
Mais que nous a Moïse figuré
Par ce récit? Le sens en est palpable;
De tout tems l'Homme à la Femme est livré,
Et de tout tems la Femme l'est au Diable.[1]

A literal translation of the French is: 'In order to triumph over humankind, the old Serpent, cunning and duplicitous, tempted Woman, and Woman, forsworn, brought unthinking Man to forswear himself. But what did Moses tell us by this story? Its meaning is easily grasped: For all time Man is given over to Woman, and for all time Woman to the Devil'. The main change Hervey's poem makes to the original is to convert it into a satire on marriage rather than on women as such. This is facilitated by the ambiguity of *femme* in French, which means either 'woman' or 'wife' according to the context.

***Textual commentary.*** No emendations are necessary to the text, which is given as it stands in the manuscript; spelling, punctuation and use of initial capitals are all unaltered.

1. *Les Œuvres du Sieur Rousseau*, 3 vols. (Rotterdam: Fritsch et Böhm, 1712), I, 294.

## Epigram from Rousseau

When the Monarch of Hell took it first in his mind,
To attack this new World, and destroy Humankind,
Eve was dupe to the Serpent, and Adam to Eve,
So Moses recites, so Good Christians beleive.
But the Satire is plain of the waggish relation,
That thus the World's ruled in each age and each Nation;
Forgive me, Ye Fair, if the comment's uncivil,
Each Man by his Wife, and each Wife by the Devil.

# TELEMACHUS AND AGRIPPINA

# 65 The Adventures of Telemachus in the Island of Ogygia

***Source.*** Suffolk Record Office, SRO 941/47/17, catalogued as '"The Adventures of Telemachus in the Island Ogygia, taken from the French of Fenelon: in three Books." [in Herveys hand] *undated*.' From some evidence of eyeskip, this manuscript appears to be a fair copy of an existing draft or drafts, though Book I has pages where all the material is deleted and where new material is being prepared, initially on the pages opposite, but after that on new leaves added for the purpose.

***Complementary manuscript sources.*** None known.

***Complementary print sources.*** None.

***Attribution.*** The manuscript, with its evidence of composition, is in Hervey's hand.

***Context and date.*** Hervey's poem is a selective translation and elaboration of the first six books of François de Salignac de La Mothe-Fénelon's *Les Aventures de Télémaque, fils d'Ulysse*. Fénelon (1651–1715) was tutor to Louis XIV's grandson, the duc de Bourgogne, from 1689, and also Archbishop of Cambrai from 1695. The *Télémaque* was written at least in part as an introduction to the classical world, with lessons in kingship, for his pupil. It was first published in April 1699 in Paris in a version considerably shorter than the surviving authorial manuscripts, followed by an English translation. That same year there was a complete edition issued in Paris, with a full version in English published the following year. There is an account of the textual history of *Télémaque* in the second volume of Jacques Le Brun's Pléiade edition, Fénelon, *Œuvres* (Paris: Gallimard, 1997), pp. 1262–4, which also has a textual apparatus.

In 1717 an edition conforming to one of the revised manuscripts was published in Paris by Fénelon's great-nephew and sold by Flaurentin Delaulne. This edition was reproduced in London by Jacob Tonson in 1719 (*Les Avantures de Telemaque fils D'Ulysse* (London: for J. Tonson and J. Watts, 1719)). Although it was in twenty-four books, modern editions accept the earlier manuscript division into eighteen, and that is the division that will be used in references in this edition. There is a convenient modern edition in the series Cambridge Texts in the History of Political Thought, with the truncated title *Telemachus, Son of Ulysses*, ed. and trans. by Patrick Riley (Cambridge: Cambridge University Press, 1994). The first six books take place on Calypso's island, Ogygia, where Telemachus, son of Ulysses, and his guide Mentor (Minerva in disguise) have been cast ashore. Fénelon intertwines two strands of narration: first, the account of Telemachus' entertainment on the island and of his relationships with Calypso (a divinity), Eucharis (one of her attendants) and Mentor; and second, Telemachus' report of his adventures in Sicily, Egypt, Tyre, Cyprus and Crete. Hervey's major decision is to ignore Telemachus' narration and concentrate on the relationships on the island.

In focusing on the personal relationships on Ogygia, Hervey followed the line also taken by John Hughes in his opera *Calypso and Telemachus*, first performed and published in 1712, with a second edition in 1717. But Hughes creates in the god Proteus a rival for Eucharis' affections (and an opportunity for theatrical effects) and there is no evidence of any influence on Hervey's poem. At several points the poem echoes Pope – his translation of the *Iliad* (1715–20), *The Rape of the Lock* (revised version 1714) and also *Eloisa to Abelard* (1717) – but it must be remembered that Pope and Hervey drew on common classical sources. One line, 'And all Arabia breath's in smoaky sweets' (II. 119), is so close to Pope's 'And all *Arabia* breathes from yonder Box' (*The Rape of the Lock*, I. 134; Pope, *Twickenham*, II, 156) that Hervey's poem must post-date the publication of the revised *Rape* in March 1714. It is not impossible that Hervey's interest in *Les Aventures* was piqued by the publication of Tonson's edition in 1719, and quotations from the French will be from that text, but it seems likely that the poem in its present form was completed later than that. Two of Hervey's other poems, 'Flora to Pompey' and 'Arisbe to Marius Junior', are free imitations of French originals, poems by Fontenelle, and all three poems may date from a period of experiment with French literature in the 1720s. The publication of Pope's translation of the *Odyssey* in 1725–6 might have stimulated Hervey to work on his own imitation of Fénelon's continuation of Homer's epic. The appearance of lines from the final draft of the poem in a letter to Stephen Fox of 28 December 1727 adds some support to this hypothesis. The arrival in England of Prince Frederick in December 1728 would then have given further impetus to the translation of a work originally written for the petit dauphin, with the emphasis being placed on amatory rather than political education. But the date of composition of this work remains a matter of conjecture.

There were three English verse translations of Fénelon's *Les Aventures* published in the first half of the century, all entitled *The Adventures of Telemachus*: the first, of 'Book I' (present Books 1–3) only, was published by John Morphew in 1712 (Foxon A69); the second, of the first two books (present 1–2) only, published by James Roberts in 1729 (Foxon A68); and the third, by Francis Manning, of Book I (present 1), printed by John Watts and published by Roberts in 1738 (Foxon M83). The 1729 translation is dedicated to the Prince of Wales.

***Textual commentary.*** In his descriptions of Ogygia and in portraying Calypso's grief, Fénelon is influenced by Book V of the *Odyssey*, containing Mercury's visit to Calypso's cave, and Calypso's response to Jove's command; in Homer she helps Ulysses to build his ship, and in Fénelon she helps Mentor build his. There is also some influence from the episode of Dido and Aeneas in the *Aeneid* books IV (also V), but parallels are rarely close.

The first six books of modern editions of *Les Aventures de Télémaque* may be conveniently divided into sections. This summary represents extensively those used by Hervey and very briefly those he ignores.

**Book 1**

1.1. Calypso is desolate at the departure of Ulysses from Ogygia.
1.2. She meets Telemachus and Mentor who have been shipwrecked.
1.3. They are welcomed and taken to Calypso's grotto.
1.4. Mentor warns Telemachus that Calypso is more dangerous to him than the rocks that shipwrecked him.
1.5. At a feast the nymphs sing of Troy; Calypso leads Telemachus to believe that Ulysses, having mistakenly left her, has perished at sea. Telemachus says that grief at his father's death prevents him from responding to Calypso's invitation to stay with her.
1.6. Telemachus tells of his travels, chiefly to Sicily.
1.7. During the narration Calypso looks at Mentor and worries about him.

**Book 2**

2.1. Telemachus continues his story, in which he visits Egypt.

**Book 3**

3.1. Telemachus continues his story, in which he visits Tyre.

**Book 4**

4.1. Calypso interrupts Telemachus, saying it is time to sleep.
4.2. Left alone in their chamber, Mentor tells Telemachus he has made his story too attractive to Calypso, but that he cannot avoid continuing it.
4.3. The following morning Calypso asks Telemachus to continue his story, sometimes admiring Telemachus and sometimes watching Mentor watching her.
4.4. Telemachus continues his story, which begins, as he approaches Cyprus, with Venus and Cupid's appearing to him but being banished by Minerva. Cyprus is condemned for its effeminacy, and Venus' temple criticised for its dissoluteness.

**Book 5**

5.1. Telemachus continues his story, in which he visits Crete. When they sail from Crete, they are shipwrecked on Calypso's island by Neptune at the behest of Venus, who resents their condemnation of Cyprus.

**Book 6**

6.1. Calypso and her nymphs are deeply impressed by Telemachus and his story, though Calypso is anxious about Mentor and tries to discover from Telemachus and Mentor himself, whether he is a disguised god.

6.2. Days pass. Venus, still seeking revenge, appears to Calypso and leaves Cupid with her. Cupid is embraced by Calypso, by her nymph, Eucharis, and by Telemachus.

6.3. Mentor and Telemachus debate the nature of the island and its nymphs, and whether Telemachus should stay or obey the call of virtue and return to Ithaca.

6.4. Mentor, aiming to deliver Telemachus from the island, and noting that Calypso loves Telemachus but that Telemachus and Eucharis are in love, decides to make Calypso jealous.

6.5. Telemachus chooses to go hunting with Eucharis. Before a second hunt, Calypso denounces and curses Telemachus. Eucharis dresses for the hunt like Diana.

6.6. After giving expression to her internal conflict, Calypso tells Mentor where he can find trees and tools to build a ship.

6.7. At the end of the hunt, the hunters arrive at the place where Mentor has already built his ship. Fearing he is going to lose Mentor, Telemachus confesses his feelings for Eucharis. Calypso denounces Telemachus, wishes for his departure and destruction by Neptune, but still has inner desires for him to stay.

6.8. Telemachus asks Mentor for his help, and Mentor explains Cupid's activity. Telemachus says he wishes to leave with Mentor but he still hankers after Eucharis.

6.9. Cupid speaks to Calypso and gets her agreement that the nymphs will burn the ship.

6.10. As the ship burns, Mentor sees another ship at anchor in the bay and pushes Telemachus into the sea. As they swim to the ship, Telemachus reflects that Cupid is more to be dreaded than shipwrecks.

Hervey's principal decision was not to translate Telemachus' own story, which serves as an introduction to the ancient world and allows Fénelon to consider issues of kingship, particularly the dangers of absolute power and of evil or intimidated counsellors. Of the six books, Hervey makes no use of 2, 3 and 4, only a little of 5, and he develops only the first part of 1. He concentrates instead on the internal conflicts of the characters. Calypso is torn between her desire to keep Telemachus with her and her fierce resentment of his rejection of her. Telemachus is torn between his sense of duty to his mother, father and native land, and the sensuous and refined pleasures of the island, focused in the person of Eucharis. The struggle is more extraordinary in the context of Fénelon's complete narrative, where the temptations of Ogygia contrast with Telemachus' heroic success in resolving political difficulties in his narrative.

Fénelon writes in prose, but his writing is often imaginative and descriptive. He is particularly concerned to convey the beauty of Calypso's island so that the reader can appreciate it as a temptation to Telemachus. Hervey often bases his descriptions on Fénelon's, but he elaborates on the details of the natural scene, entertainments and personal beauty. He also develops the psychological aspects of personal relations in the narrative, exploring the internal conflicts of both Calypso and Telemachus. In that respect, Hervey's poem has more in common with his four poems in the manner of Ovid than it does with Fénelon's epic narrative.

Although this manuscript, in its neatly divided three books, was designed as a fair copy, there are heavy revisions of the early pages and corrections throughout. There are also marginal notes that might have been designed to prompt later revision. Some, not in Hervey's hand, identify passages as relating to 'Ick', presumably Ickworth, and 'P', just possibly the Prince of Wales. One non-authorial comment reflects interestingly on Hervey's versification. A note 'wants a foot' appears next to the final line of Mentor's couplet

> In Feavers, thus, delirious Wretches boast
> Their Health, and Madmen, Reason lost. (III. 463–4)

But the line is about loss and confusion, and the sound may have been intended to echo the sense. Similarly the closing alexandrine in a couplet about the harper allows Hervey the space to imitate the effects he gives an account of:

> His Plaints they count in mournfull Strains, and flow;
> Whilst sudden Rests, short Stops, his broken Accents Show.
> (I. 410–11)

Other alexandrines are to be found at I. 378, 449; II. 111, 125, 182, 210, 331, 343; and III. 287. Some of them close triplets or paragraphs; all seem designed for dramatic effect.

An account of alterations in the manuscript is to be found in the 'Account of the Manuscript of The Adventures of Telemachus in the Island of Ogygia' (pp. 713–734). In line with edition policy, contractions have been expanded. Capital letters, which have sometimes been omitted in the process of revision, have been supplied at the beginning of lines. Single quotations marks are applied consistently to speech, but Hervey's practice is followed in using double quotation marks for special cases of internal monologue. Underlines, whose significance is unclear, are not reproduced but are recorded in the account of the manuscript.

The chief reference works consulted are *The Oxford Classical Dictionary*, fourth edn, ed. by Simon Hornblower, Antony Spawforth and Esther Eidinow (Oxford: Oxford University Press, 2012) and *The Oxford Guide to Classical Mythology in the Arts, 1300–1990s*, ed. by Jane Davidson Reid, with Chris Rohmann, 2 vols. (Oxford: Oxford University Press, 1993). References to Ovid and Virgil are to the Loeb editions.

## The Adventures of Telemachus in the Island Ogygia taken from the French of Fenelon: in three Books

### BOOK the First

Calypso now in vain all Arts essay'd,
To close those wounds Ulisses Flight had made;[1]
What Hope of Cure, what respight can she find:
His Image still engross'd her tortur'd Mind,
She sees him absent, loves him tho unkind:
The Goddess wishes she could mortal prove,
How tastless Life depriv'd of what we Love.[2]
No more the mountains eccho to her Song,
The only Ear She sought to charm is gone,
By her no more the Chace or Dance is led,
The dear Companion of those joys is fled.
Her Nymphs with fruitless Pity see her Grief,
Deplore the Cause nor offer at releif.
To the close wood, and covert walk, unseen,
Oft She retires: where never-fading Green,[3]
With cheerfull carpett spreads the flowry Plains,
And Spring in all her Pride perpetual reigns.
In vain the Myrtles bloom, the Roses blow,[4]
And all the Seasons all their Charms bestow.
This fragrant Field, this ever-verdant Grove,
This once dear Mansion of her prosp'rous Love,[5]

1. In Book V of the *Odyssey*, Calypso is commanded by the gods to enable Ulysses to leave Ogygia and pursue his journey home.

2. *How tastless Life depriv'd of what we Love*: the line echoes 'And where is joy, depriv'd of what we love' (Poem 4, 'Roxana to Usbeck', line 21), quoted in a letter to Stephen Fox of 27 September 1731.

3. *never-fading Green*: cf. 'With Flow'rs adorn'd, and never-fading Green', a line from Rowe's *Tamerlane* anthologised in Edward Bysshe's *The Art of English Poetry*, 2nd edn (London, 1705), p. 84.

4. *the Myrtles bloom, the Roses blow*: the flowers of Venus (Virgil, *Eclogues*, VII. 62 (Loeb, p. 53); Ovid, *Fasti*, IV. 869–70 (Loeb, p. 252)).

5. *To the close wood . . . Mansion of her prosp'rous Love*: an early example of Hervey's adding specificity. The eight lines (14–21) translate 'Elle se promenoit souvent seule sur les gasons fleuris, dont un printems éternel bordoit son Ile' ('She often walked alone on the flowery lawns, with which an eternal spring bordered her island') (*Les Avantures* (Tonson), p. 1).

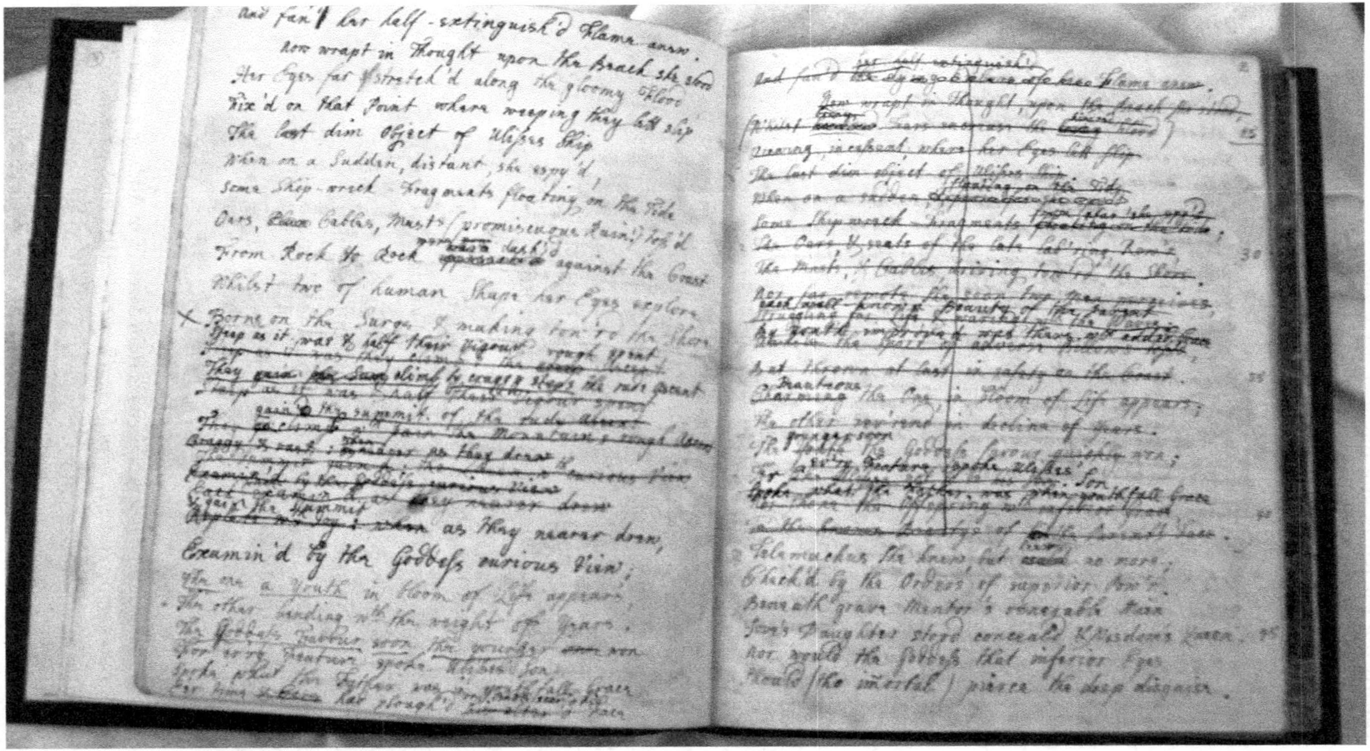

**Figure 2** Page in autograph manuscript of 'Telemachus', showing revisions of book 1 lines 23–49 in various stages.

Return the Pleasures she has lost, to View
And fan her half-extinguish'd Flame anew.

Now wrapt in Thought upon the Beach she stood,
Her Eyes far stretch'd along the gloomy Flood
Fix'd on that Point where weeping they lett slip
The last dim Object of Ulisses Ship.
When on a Sudden, distant, she espy'd,
Some Ship-wreck Fragments floating on the Tide;
Oars, Cables, Masts (promiscuous Ruin!)[6] toss'd
From Rock to Rock were dash'd against the Coast.
Whilst two of human Shape her Eyes explore
Borne on the Surge and making tow'rd the Shore.
Steep as it was and half their Vigour spent
They climb by craggy steps the rude Ascent
And gain the Summit: as they nearer drew,
Examin'd by the Goddess' curious View,
The one a Youth in bloom of Life appears,
The other bending with the weight of Years.
The Goddess' Favour soon the younger won,
For ev'ry Feature spoke Ulisses' Son;
Spoke what the Father was in youthfull Grace
E'er time had plough'd or Battle scar'd his Face.
Telemachus She knew, but knew no more;
Check'd by the Orders of superior Pow'r.
Beneath grave Mentor's venerable Mien
Jove's Daughter stood conceal'd and Wisdom's Queen.[7]
Nor would the Goddess that inferior Eyes
Should (tho immortal) pierce the deep disguise.[8]
Meantime the Queen advancing on the Plain
With counterfeited Anger thus began.
'Whence are you? say; and by what right you dare

6. *promiscuous Ruin*: cf. 'And one promiscuous Ruin cover all' in Addison's translation of a passage from Lucan in his *Remarks upon Several Parts of Italy* (1705), p. 384.

7. *Jove's Daughter ... Wisdom's Queen*: Minerva. Hervey follows Fénelon in using Roman names for the gods.

8. *Nor would the Goddess that inferior Eyes ... pierce the deep disguise*: Minerva does not allow Calypso, though she is immortal, to recognise her.

'To sett your impious Feet unbidden here?
'Come yee contemptuous of a Goddess' Pow'r
'With rash intrusion on this hallow'd Shore,
'Or Sin yee thus by ignorance mis-led?
'Whate'er the Cause, our ready Vengeance dread,
'Nor hope by Pray'rs our Pardon to obtain
'For Pray'rs or deprecating Tears are vain;
'Tho press'd by Storms, no Pilot makes this Bay
'But holds aloof and seeks a safer Sea.
'If not our Quick-sands and our Rocks he fears
'He know's our Edicts and our Laws reveres;
'Or daring to molest these peacefull Plains
'His Doom is Death or never-ending Chains;
'His Friends, his Parents and his native skys
'No more permitted to his weeping Eyes.'[9]
Desembling thus with Menaces she strove
To check the Dictates of commencing Love
That in her Eyes (where Nature know's no Art)
Spoke undisguis'd the Language of her Heart.[10]
'Goddess rever'd' (the Prince submiss reply'd)
'Tho' Wrath divine be hard for Man t' abide,
'Yet who can tim'rous urge a weak Defence
'Whose Cause is just, whose Plea is Innocence?
'Had I transgressive of your dread Command,
'With Voluntary Crime approach'd this Land,
'Well might I then the heavy Vengeance dread,
'By Heav'n inflicted on the impious Head,
'But conscious of no Guilt I know no Fear:
'By Fate compell'd I sought a Refuge here.
'Self-Preservation, Nature's eldest Law,

9. *Come yee . . . weeping Eyes*: these fourteen lines (54–67) are a late insertion in the MS and represent a significant expansion of the text; they elaborate sentiments expressed by Calypso after the evening feast (*Les Avantures* (Tonson) I. 8).

10. *the Language of her Heart*: Pope uses the phrase prominently in poems that probably post-date Hervey's: 'No Language, but the Language of the Heart' (*To Arbuthnot*, line 399); 'But still I love the language of his Heart' (*First Epistle of the Second Book of Horace*, line 78), Pope, *Twickenham*, IV, 126, 201. The phrase is found in Thomas à Kempis, *Imitatio Christi*, and other religious writing.

'Still prompting to preserve the Breath we draw,
'This means of Safety from the deathfull Tide
'Bad me to sieze: the Gods were on my Side;
'And hear'd my Pray'rs, for still we pray to gain
'Reprieve for Life, tho lengthen'd but to Pain.[11]
'No mad Defiance of your sacred Pow'r,
'Nor wild Ambition wrought me to explore
'These Seas, so distant from my natal Shore:
'In foreign Climes, with pious Zeal, I roam[12]
'To seek a Father, or to learn his Doom.'
'Who is that Father?' (interrupt's the Queen.)

'The best of Fathers and the best of Men.
'A King he was; Ulisses call'd; a Name
'Not unrecorded in the Rolls of Fame:
'When Greece was leagu'd, and half the World in Arms,[13]
'Vindictive[14] of bright Helen's ravish'd Charms;
'Ulisses' Counsels was their Fav'rite Guide,
'On him as on a God the Host rely'd.
'On each emergency, his ready Thought,
'Great Agamemnon, King of Kings besought.
'Not Nestor's Voice, the Chief so much reveres,
'Tho long Experience of three hundred Years
'Ripen'd the Wisdom of his hoary Hairs.
'Huge Ajax' Strength, Achilles' matchless Force,[15]
'By his Direction steer'd their wastfull Course;

11. *lengthen'd but to Pain*: Monimia talks of 'living but to Pain' in Poem 1 *Monimia to Philocles*, line 73.

12. *Goddess rever'd ... I roam*: these twenty lines (72–91), again a late expansion in the manuscript, elaborate Telemachus' reply to Calypso's extended complaint.

13. Hervey now summarises the action of the *Iliad*, celebrating Ulysses' stratagem of the wooden horse and giving customary accounts of the major figures. This account, down to line 129, is Hervey's addition, mostly made in his final revision of the poem, and draws on the epic vocabulary of Pope (*Twickenham*, VII–X).

14. *Vindictive*: avenging or retributive, a word that occurs once in Pope's *Iliad* (1715–20) and five times in his *Odyssey* (1725–6).

15. *hoary Hairs ... Huge Ajax' Strength, Achilles' matchless Force*: 'hoary hairs' occurs twice in Pope's *Iliad* (VI. 576; IX. 552; Pope, *Twickenham*, VII, 355, 460) and 'hoary' is common in the *Iliad* (thirty-four) and the *Odyssey* (seventeen); 'matchless force' appears twice in the *Iliad* (I. 384; XXI. 699; Pope, *Twickenham*, VII, 106; VIII, 450) and 'matchless' is common in the *Iliad* (forty), less so in the *Odyssey* (eight).

'Without it vain: nor able to destroy
'The sacred Walls of Heav'n-defended Troy:[16]
'For ten Years wasted in successless strife,
'For Restitution of the Spartan Wife:
'When Seas of Blood and Mountains of the Slain,[17]
'Had dy'd the Shore and heap'd the Field in vain:
'Their Fleets attack'd, and destitute of Aid,
'Their Chiefs desponding, and their Troops dismay'd.
'This wond'rous Man, with Skill divine indued,
'(What gives not Heav'n to one: so brave and good?)
'A Scheme concerts, by Thirst of Glory fired,
'(Or rather by Minerva's self inspir'd,)
'To work by Stratagem the City's Fall
'And fraudfull enter her devoted Wall.[18]
'The Plott succeed's: her Pallaces they raze;
'Her Structures tumble, and her Temples blaze:
'Horrid Confusion! Age nor Sex is spared;
'Nor Royal Heads, nor ev'n their Gods rever'd:[19]
'Amid the Tumult of these dire Allarms,
'Whilst Conquest, darkling, wait's the Grecian Arms,
'Ulisses' Brow, the Wreaths of Triumph crown,
'The Glory of the War was all his own.
'But what avail him all his Honours now?
'(Short are the Blessings which on Earth we know)
'Whilst all the Chiefs, who bear a Kingly Name,
'(His Brave Associates in the Field of Fame)
'From Toils releas'd, and ev'ry Danger past,
'Sweet Quiet, and domestick Comforts tast:

16. *Heav'n-defended Troy*: a recurring phrase in Pope's *Iliad* (II. 172; IX. 38 and 541; XVI. 863; Pope, *Twickenham*, VII, 136, 433, 460; VIII, 277).

17. *Mountains of the Slain*: cf. Nicholas Rowe, *Lucan's Pharsalia* (London: for Jacob Tonson, 1718), X. 795, p. 443, and Pope's *Iliad*, II. 50; Pope, *Twickenham*, VII, 129. The phrase or its like is common (e.g. in Addison's *The Campaign* (1704), line 353, p. 17), and appears in 'Telemachus' from its first draft.

18. *devoted Wall*: the phrase occurs three times in book II of Pope's *Iliad* (lines 17, 39 and 89; Pope, *Twickenham*, VII, 129–30).

19. *Age nor Sex . . . rever'd*: cf. 'No Dignity nor Innocence is spared, | Nor Age, nor Sex, nor Thrones, nor Graves revered' (Poem 22, *To the Imitator*, lines 40–1). Isobel Grundy first drew attention to the parallel.

'He, erring, sail's o'er Neptunes stormy Reign;
'And seeks his native Ithaca in vain.
'That unforgiving God with stedfast Hate,[20]
'Bar's his Return, and urges him on Fate.
'In vain his Son, his People, and his Wife,
'Make Vows to Jove, for Jove neglect's his Life.
'Yee upright Gods! if Virtue be your Care,
'Ulisses' Friends ought never to Despair.
'But Fears still busy in the Wretch's Breast,
'A Story dreadfull to my Soul suggest.
'They cry, already has he breath'd his last
'Choak'd by the Waves: against some Rock is cast
'The mangled Body, while the hapless Ghost,
'Wander's unbury'd on the Stygian Coast.[21]
'Pardon these Tears; the Privilege of Grief;
'Nor, if 'tis thine to give, refuse relief:
'If 'tis allow'd thee (Fair divine!) to read
'What Fate unalterable has decreed,
'Say has it destin'd, mercyfull, to save
'Or has it doom'd him to the peacefull Grave?'
So spake the pious Prince, nor knew to move
Her Pity only, for he warm'd to Love;
Such flowing Eloquence! such manly Grace
Such ripen'd Wisdom, with a blooming Face,
Amaze'd the Goddess, and resistless dart
Love's keenest Arrows through her kindling Heart.
With silent Rapture and devouring Look
She gaz'd enamour'd then benignant, spoke.

'Much of Thy Father's Fate sweet Youth I know,
'Too long the tale to be recounted now:

20. *That unforgiving God with stedfast Hate*: cf. 'Mixt with obdurate pride and stedfast hate', *Paradise Lost*, I. 58 (Milton, *Poetical Works*, I. 7). As the *Odyssey* explains, Neptune was punishing Ulysses for the blinding of Polyphemus, his son.

21. *Wander's unbury'd on the Stygian Coast*: in book IV of Pope's *Odyssey*, Menelaus is concerned for Odysseus, 'Whether he wanders on some friendless coast | Or glides in *Stygian* gloom a pensive ghost' (lines 141–2; Pope, *Twickenham*, IX, 127); in his *Iliad* Priam has similar concerns for his sons: 'All pale they wander on the *Stygian* coast' (Pope's *Iliad*, XXII. 71; Pope, *Twickenham*, VIII, 455). The unburied could not cross the river Styx.

'Tis time to change these Robes, which still retain
'The noxious Vapour of the soaking Main:
'Hence to my Grotto, there repose awhile,
'Recruit your Spirits,[22] and forget your Toil:
'Nor fear to find a Tyrant on these Plains,
'Alas I pity, nay I share your Pains;
'For Nature has not form'd my Heart of Steel,
'A savage Stamp, incapable to feel
'For others woes;[23] but fill'd my gen'rous Mind
'With Thoughts more suited to my tender kind:
'All Comfort then Calipso can afford,
'Doubt not to prove, affianced in my Word:[24]
'What Joys Ogygia yield's are freely thine,
'Nor Heav'n can add to those, if thou art mine:
'Thee will I tend with more than Mother's Love,
'And more than Mortal Joy thy Soul shall prove.
'How vast my Boon! how easy is thy Part!
'I ask no tribute but a gratefull Heart:
'Be that, that one Demand but fully pay'd
'I'll show'r down Blessings on thy favour'd Head.
'No Wish thy Soul shall furnish unpossess'd;
'No Passion urge unsated in thy Breast:[25]
'Successive Raptures shall incessant flow;
'But learn (Wise Youth!) thy Happyness to know,[26]
'For Joys are Joys, but as we think them so.
'If Heav'n has curs'd thee with a restless Mind,
'Perverse Defect so frequent in Mankind,

22. *Recruit your Spirits*: refresh, re-invigorate your spirits (*OED*). The ten lines that follow this one were added to the poem in Hervey's final revision.

23. *For Nature . . . others woes*: cf. 'Lo these were they, whose souls the Furies steel'd, | And curs'd with hearts unknowing how to yield . . . So perish all, whose breast ne'er learn'd to glow | For others' good, or melt at others' woe' (Pope, 'Elegy to the Memory of an Unfortunate Lady', lines 41–6; Pope, *Twickenham*, II, 366).

24. *affianced in my Word*: assured by my pledge or promise (*OED*).

25. *No Wish . . . unpossess'd . . . unsated in thy Breast*: cf. 'All then is full, possessing, and possest, | No craving Void left aking in the breast' (Pope, 'Eloisa to Abelard', lines 93–4; Pope, *Twickenham*, II, 327).

26. *But learn (Wise Youth!) thy Happyness to know*: this line and the seven following form, with minor variation, Poem 67 'But learn wise Youth', contained in a letter to Stephen Fox of 28 December 1727; the lines were added to 'Telemachus' in Hervey's final revision.

'If sweet Contentment mix not with thy Fate,
'That want alone will marr the happyest State;
'In vain the fav'rite Gifts of Jove you boast,
'Without that Blessing all the rest are lost.'[27]

So spoke the Fair, and homeward o'er the Plain
Conduct's the Prince, and joyn's her Virgin-Train.
(Who far from her, in social service, wait;
Such is the joyless Solitude of State.)
As some tall Oak the Forest's lofty Pride,
With Head majestick tops the Plants beside;
So mid her Nimphs she walks, with nobler Mien,
That told at once the Goddess, and the Queen.
A Purple Robe she wore with gracefull Pride;
Her Hair behind was negligently ty'd:
The Spring was rifled to adorn her Brow,
A light Cymar[28] o'erspread her Limbs below;
Whilst busy Winds oblige the curious Eye,
And half permit the View, and half deny.
A silken Garden by her Needle traced
Bloom'd on the Zone[29] that round her slender Wast
In ample Folds, collected from the Plain
The spotted Beautys of an Ermin Train.
Respect and Love at once her Eyes inspire,
For temp'ring Sweetness soften's ev'ry Fire:
With Grace divine, celestial Charms display'd,
Thus proudly as she step's the painted Glade,
The Royal Stranger, new to Beauty's Pow'r,
Indulg'd a Transport never felt before.
Wishes and soft Inquietudes arose,
And warmth unusual in his Bosome glows;
His Eyes, his Thoughts, o'er ev'ry Beauty rove,
With all the little previous Cares to Love,

27. *Alas I pity . . . Without that Blessing all the rest are lost*: both the earlier expression of pity and the offer of blessings in these twenty-six lines are Hervey's addition.

28. *Cymar*: 'a robe or loose light garment for women; esp. an under garment, a chemise' (*OED*).

29. *Zone*: girdle or belt (*OED*).

E'er yet the Conquest, testify'd by smart,
In it's full Vigour, rages in the Heart.[30]

With downward Looks, nor pleas'd the hoary Seer,
Lag'd far behind, and pensive clos'd the Rear;
He see's the Evils of the future Hour,
And joyless to the present, gain's the Bow'r.

What Heav'nly Visions here (confus'd Delight!)
Open at once solliciting the Sight?
Where'er the Stranger turn's his ravish'd Eyes,
New Beautys offer and new wonders rise,[31]
The Pomp of Nature, pure from Art or Toyl;
For ev'ry Charm spontaneous deck's the Soil:
No painted Domes here venerable rise,
Nor marble Columns climbing on the Skys
Nor polish'd Gems, nor burnish'd Metals shine,
(The far-sought Product of the Indian Mine).
Deep in a hollow Rock, each Nymph, apart,
And unindebted to the Sculptor's Art,
In private boasts her own sequester'd Bow'r,
By Shells and Pebles rudely crusted o'er;
For Tapistry a Vine; around each Stone
The Tendrils curl'd, the purple Burdens shone.
Pavilion'd in a larger Grot, the Queen
(Full in the center of the Sylvan Scene)
Her own sweet Mansion chose; from Phoebus' Pow'r,
A Citron-Grove defends the shelter'd Bow'r:
Such Perfumes scatter'd from it's Golden Head,
Arabian Gums less gratefull Odours shed;
Fair Fruits and Blossoms, clust'ring ev'ry Bough,
At once the Autumn and the Spring bestow,
For ever ripen, and for ever blow.
Nor noise within this sweet abode was heard,

30. *With Grace divine ... in the Heart*: these ten lines were added by Hervey in his final revision.

31. *Where'er ... his ravish'd Eyes ... new wonders rise*: cf. 'Where-e'er you tread, the blushing Flow'rs shall rise, | And all things flourish where you turn your Eyes' (Pope, 'Pastorals: Summer', lines 75–6; Pope, *Twickenham*, I, 77–8).

Save the soft Call of some enamour'd Bird;
Or murm'ring Zephir bearing on his Wing
The fragrant Plunder of perpetual Spring;
Or trickling Current of incessant Rills
That diverse wander down the Rocky Hills
And wide expanded o'er the Plains below
In silver Lakes, or mazy Rivers flow.
Warm from the Chase here oft the Goddess sought
Or limpid Bath, or cool refreshing Draught.
Alder, and Oak, high over-arching, made
With leafy Canopys, a gratefull Shade;
And on the Bank beneath promiscuous grows
The Woodbine, Jasmin, Violet, and Rose.
On airy Eminence the Grotto stood
Within the Prospect of the Ocean Flood.
A various Scene! for now along the Shore
The Billows tumble and the Surges roar
And streight a Calm succeeds, the Waves subside
And Dolphins dance upon the curling Tide.[32]
Beneath warm influence from meridian Skys
In curling Eminence the vines arise
Prop'd by the Palm and Elm; the generous Load
Avow'd the Bounty of the purple God.[33]
Pomegranate, Figg, and Olive Trees around,
Promiscuous Plenty the fair Prospect crown'd.
These native Beautys graciously the Queen
By turns display'd; nor fail'd to mix between,
Soft Word, and look, of amorous import,
To crown the Welcome to her Sylvan Court.
'Here break we off' (she say'd) 'Retire awhile,
'For Nature asks refreshment after Toyl.
'Where yonder Woodbine climbs that Myrtle Bow'r
'Impervious to the Sun's Meridian Pow'r:

32. At this point nine lines partially revised by Hervey, with some rhymes unsupplied, have been omitted from this text. They are to be found in the 'Account of the Manuscript of The Adventures of Telemachus in the Island Ogygia' listing the alterations to the manuscript.

33. *purple God*: Bacchus.

'My Damsel-Train with joint officious[34] Care,
'The healing Bath, or fragrant Oils prepare,
'The Spirits that, and these the Nerves repair.
'To crown the Goblet with the richest Juice
'Our mantling Vine's autumnal Gifts produce;
'To spoil the Garden of her fairest Fruit,
'Delicious Plant, cool Herb, and sav'ry Root,
'Be that my task; to soften thy delay
'And cheat the Progress of the ling'ring Day.
'For time, when absent from the Man we love,
'Employ'd for him, less slothfull seem's to move;
'But loiter not, ah! speed thy wish'd return,
'Each moment I shall count, each Moment mourn.[35]
'When next we meet I shall a Tale impart
'Will all thy Doubts resolve and ease thy Heart;
'For if a tender Mistress and a Friend
'Can banish Sorrow, thine is at an End,'
She say'd: and streight the weary Guests were led,
To seek refreshment on a vi'let bed.
By Nymphs expert their Grotto was prepar'd,
Nor Cost, nor Labour for their wellcome spar'd:
Of Cedar-wood a fragrant Fire they made,
The new Apparell round the fire was lay'd.
With secrett joy the Younger Stranger sees
Such Robes as would the vainest Fancy please.
With glossey Wool the labour'd Tunicks shine,
Not Snow so white, the Spider's nett so fine:
Of Tyrian dye[36] the silken Vestments were,
Emboss'd and rich with many a golden Star.
When Mentor thus, still watchfull to destroy
The earlyest Blossoms of ill founded Joy.
'Is it for You these trifles to admire?
'You who can boast Ulisses for your Sire?

34. *officious*: doing good offices.

35. *Where yonder Woodbine . . . each Moment mourn*: Hervey adds the description and the explicit statement of Calypso's feeling (lines 298–306); the twenty-one lines of Calypso's speech replace five lines in Hervey's first surviving draft.

36. *Tyrian dye*: royal or imperial purple.

'Think on the deathless Lawrells which he won,
'And lett the Father animate the Son.
'Adorn your Mind: and lett the Woemen grace
'The transient Beautys of a blooming Face.
'To Him, and him alone, is Glory due,
'Who can his Passions and himself subdue:
'Who Hardships can endure, and ease decline.
'This meritt is, and be this meritt thine,'
He say'd: Telemachus, with down-cast Eyes
And blushing, thus with modesty replys.
'Fear not that e'er forgetfull of my Name
'I should for Luxury abandon Fame.
'Rather may Jove demand my forfeit Breath
'And save my Honour tho he give me Death.
'It never shall be say'd, or say'd with Truth,
'Ulisses' offspring, prodigal of Youth,
'Effeminate declining War's Allarms,
'Spent a vain Life in Pleasure's lazy Charms.
'Yet gratefull still, for ever lett me own
'The gen'rous usage of this fair Unknown.'
'Oh! Shun her rather' (Mentor quick reply'd.)
'More dang'rous than the Rocks that lurking hide
'Their fatal Heads, beneath the faithless Tide.
'Dread all her Arts, dread her atractive Wiles;
'Dread ev'n her Bounty, her deceitfull Smiles.
'The Foe to Virtue is a short liv'd Joy,
'Of luscious Moments that will quickly cloy;
'Doubtfull it's Bliss, but certain to destroy.
'Trust not too far, nor credulous beleive,
'Beauteous She is but Beauty will deceive.
'Youth ever Sanguine, eager to obtain,
'Pursue's all joy and apprehend's no Pain:
'Bold, credulous, a Prey to ev'ry Snare,
'Prone lightly to confide, precautionless to dare.
'Of false Calypso's flatt'ry then beware,
'Nor court your Ruin with a list'ning Ear:
'Like Oyl smooth-gliding to your open Heart,
'Her Words a Joy, but pois'nous joy impart.

'An ambush'd mischief in each favour dread,
'(By specious falshood often we're betray'd)
'And call my counsells timely to your Aid.'

This say'd, they hasten to Calipso's Bow'r,
Who wait's impatient for th' appointed Hour.
Her Maids array'd in white, officious came;
(The spotless Emblem of their Virgin-Fame)
With modest Duty, and with dextrous Haste,
They brought a plain, yet exquisite Repast.
Birds by their Netts, Deer by their Arrows kill'd,
In tastfull Plenty, various Dishes fill'd.
While gen'rous Draughts, as Heav'nly Nectar sweet,
And Fountains clear, dilute the sav'ry Meat:
From Golden Jarrs they flow in purple Show'rs,
To golden Vases, wrought with golden Flow'rs.
Whatever Fruits are promis'd by the Spring,
Or Autumn yields, the Nymphs in basketts bring:
Whilst others (during the Repast) melodious sing.
They sung the Gods and Gyants joyn'd in Fight;[37]
Rash Semele's request and fun'ral Night;
The Birth of Bacchus; old Sylenus Care
To educate the Boy.[38] They sung the Fair,
Who with Hippomenes successless run,
Swifter of Foot, by Stratagem undone.[39]
And last of all they sung the Fate of Troy:
Ulisses' Praises all their Throats employ;
They praise his Conduct, and his Courage praise,
And to Herculean Fame his Labours raise.
With artfull Hand fair Euch'ris[40] touch'd the Lute;

37. *Gods and Gyants joyn'd in Fight*: the battle is summarised in Ovid, *Metamorphoses*, I. i. 151–62 (Loeb, I, 12).

38. *Semele's... Bacchus... Sylenus... educate the Boy*: see Ovid, *Metamorphoses*, I. iii. 253–315 (Loeb, I, 142–6).

39. *the Fair... by Stratagem undone*: Atalanta distracted from the race by Hippomenes' golden apples; see Ovid, *Metamorphoses*, II. x. 560–680 (Loeb, II, 104–12).

40. *Euch'ris*: in Fénelon it is Leucothoé (*Les Avantures* (Tonson), I. 7); Hervey is preparing for the relationship with Telemachus. The name is from the same root as eucharist (thanksgiving) but no allusion seems intended.

Her Lofty Strains the lofty subject sute.
Exalted Notes the ecchoing Grotto fill,
And o'er the rest distinct, proclaim her Skill.

Ulisses Son, for virtuous Duty fam'd,
No sooner heard his hapless Father nam'd,
But filial Love a filial Sorrow claim'd:
In vain to smother the distress he try's,
The ready Tears stood glitt'ring in his Eyes:
At length o'erflowing trickled down his Face,
And added Lustre to it's native Grace.
The Queen beheld the pious Youth distress'd,
And universal Sorrow damps the Feast.
But soon a Signal to her Nymphs She threw,
Who change the Theme and straight commence anew.
The Centaurs and the Lapithae they sing,[41]
Where drunken feuds a mutual Slaughter bring.
The Pow'r of Musick they reherse and show;
Like Orpheus-self[42] describing Orpheus' Woe:
The varying Tale, their varying Motion sutes;
Soft plays the Harper, and rough dance the Brutes.[43]
His Plaints they count in mournfull Strains, and flow;
Whilst sudden Rests, short Stops, his broken Accents Show.
In hollow Murmurs and hoarse Sounds they tell,
His vent'rous journey to the gates of Hell:
When he's to move th' inexorable King,
Rough Bases cease; pathetick Trebles sing:
Softly they sing, accompany'd by Lutes,
And softly eccho'd by complaining Flutes.
Then all in consort chaunt his granted Pray'r,

41. *Centaurs and the Lapithae they sing*: see Ovid, *Metamorphoses*, II. xii. 210–536 (Loeb, II, 194–218).

42. *Like Orpheus-self . . . Woods and Caves reply'd*: the next fifty-seven lines, present from the first surviving draft of Hervey's poem, develop out of a short reference to the Orpheus story ('& la descente d'Orphée aux Enfers pour en retirer Euridice' [and Orpheus' descent into hell to bring back Euridice], *Les Avantures* (Tonson), I. 8). The story is told by Ovid, *Metamorphoses*, II. x. 1–105 and xi. 1–84 (Loeb, II, 64–70 and 120–6).

43. *The varying Tale, their varying Motion sutes . . . rough dance the Brutes*: in these and the following lines, the emphasis on the suiting of sound to sense parallels that in Dryden's 'Alexander's Feast' and other hymns to St Cecilia.

His repossession of the willing Fair.
But when he came to turn his Eyes behind,
In hopes th' uncertain Follower to find;
The Song stop'd short: in slurring Notes they tell
The fleeting Shade gliding again to Hell.
Nor ending here their solemn movements, show
How ten successive Moons, his banefull Woe,
Forc'd him in lonely Coverts to complain
Of fruitless-promis'd Joy, and endless Pain.
So Philomela in the poplar Grove,[44]
With tunefull Sorrow, and maternal Love,
Mourn's her lost Young; defenceless born away,
By some inhuman Clown,[45] a callow Prey:
All Night th' unhappy Innocent remains,
Perch'd on a Bough, and warbling there complain's:
While to each Plaint, and each melodious Cry,
The Hills, the Valleys, Woods, and Rocks reply.
From Morn to Night, from Night to morn She mourn's;
In absent Flames the hapless Husband burn's.
His Griefs keep pace with the slow-wasting Night,
Cheerless he sees the Sun's revolving Light.
By whose bright Beams in vain the Globe's reveal'd,
A worthless Toy, Euridice conceal'd.
His potent Sorrow, with melodious Force,
Inverted Nature from her ancient Course.
To listen to his Harp, tall, stubborn Trees,
(In vain obstructed by the adverse Breeze)
Incline their Heads: upon their Branches stand
The feather'd Nation, an attentive Band;
Charm'd by the magick of his wond'rous Song,
They leave unheeded in the Nest their famish'd Young.
In vain the Sea expects the ebbing Flood;
Rivers forgott to flow, and listn'ning stood.

44. *So Philomela in the poplar Grove*: Hervey adapts Philomena's grief in *Odyssey,* book XIX, where she is responsible for the death of her son, to the nightingale's sorrow at the theft of her chicks.

45. *Clown*: a countryman, rustic or peasant, with the implication rude and uncouth (*OED*).

The rabid Wolves neglect the passing Prey,
And harmless at his Feet in rapture lay.
But ten long Months elaps'd in fruitless Grief,
The time approach'd for Death to bring relief.
The Thracian Dames,[46] with more than brutal Rage,
(For He could wrath of fiercest Brutes assuage:)
Thirst for his Blood, nor thirst they long in vain;
But freed his Soul at once from Life and Pain.
Whilst He, regardless of the Pains of Death;
In the last Murmurs of departing Breath;
'Dear, Dear Euridice' incessant cry'd;
'Euridice' the Woods and Caves reply'd.

Here ceas'd the Nymphs, when to the Youth apart,
The Goddess thus reveal's her love-sick Heart.

'Enough my Conduct has my kindness shown,
'Nor thou ungratefull to my Care disown,
'Tho dear the Father, dearer is the Son.
'Well might the justice of insulted Pow'r,
'Exact the forfeit of thy Life this Hour;
'Since thou hast dar'd to violate this Strand,[47]
'Sacred to me, an interdicted Land.
'This tho' the Queen and Goddess ill receive,
'The Lover and the Woman must forgive.
'In vain your Shipwreck for defence you move,
'Weak that defence to any judg but Love.
'The same advantages your Father knew,
'(For Love and Beauty are the Hero's due),
'But all my favours tastless he enjoy'd,
'For all his Thoughts Penelopy employ'd;
'Vainly employ'd; for never shall he view,
'What he, ungratefull, left me to pursue.
'Resolv'd to fly, he meditates his Flight;
'And like a lurking Robber fled by Night.
'The Coast of Italy he first explores,

46. *Thracian Dames*: the maenads, women inspired to ritual frenzy by Bacchus.
47. *this Strand*: the land bordering a sea.

'There man's his Ship and seeks his native Shores.
'But scarce the shore was vanish'd from his Eye,
'When gath'ring Clouds foretell a tempest nigh,
'Whilst distant Thunders grumble in the Sky.
'And now the black'ning Storms obscure the Day;
'In glitt'ring Sheets the forky Light'nings play.
'With shelving force descends the smoaky Rain,
'And mix'd with hail, beats on the turgid Main:
'The boist'rous Winds excite the wat'ry War,
'And jarring frustrate the poor Seaman's Care:
'In vain the Master crys, "Haste, furl the Sails";
'His Orders perish in the louder Gales.
'But all, by former Storms instructed, know
'The usual means to ward the coming Blow.
'Some stop the leaky Sides; some waves oercast;
'Some furl the flutt'ring Canvas round the Mast.
'They toil, they sweat, but all their Labor's vain,
'For uncontroul'd the tempest mock's their Pain.
'Some of the Sails, burst by the furious Blasts,
'Curl in the Air and bend the stubborn Masts;
'Whilst others, loaded with the soaking Showrs,
'Crack the Sail-Yards and drop: in vain the Row'rs,
'In all the agonizing Fears of Death,
'Tug at their Post, and spend their latest Breath
'In fruitless Pray'rs, for Miracles to save
'Their destin'd Bodys from the liquid Grave.
'In vain they try to steer a safer Course
'By the weak Rudder's unavailing Force:
'Too well the skillfull Pilot knew his Fate,
'And at the Idle Helm desponding sate.
'The Planks uncalk'd now gape on ev'ry Side,
'Their yawning Mouths admitt the rushing Tide.
'The Ship is unresisting whirl'd around,
'Now born aloft, and now She's dash'd aground.
'The Sailors give their fruitless Labour o'er,
'And their inevitable Fate deplore:

'With Eyes and Hands uplift, they send their Pray'rs
'To Heav'n for Aid, but Heav'n relentless hear's
'Their piercing Crys, and views unmov'd their Tears.
'Ulisses only with a Hero's Mind,
'Undaunted, his devoted Life resign'd.
'His End nor mean, nor proud, but truly great;
'He neither fear's, nor scorn's, but yields to Fate.
'When now a Billow bursts above their Heads,
'And all around it's watry Ruin spread's:
'The Ship and crew it bury's in the Deep,
'And seal's their Eyes in fast eternal Sleep.[48]
'Behold the Fate th' ungratefull Wretch must prove,
'Who proudly dares to slight my proffer'd Love;
'Nor Love alone, imortal Life to give
'With Love I offer'd, would he here but live.
'But he no joy from Ithaca could know,
'And deem'd immortal Life, immortal Woe.
'Compute the gains of his obdurate Mind,
'You see the Blessings which he left behind,
'And hear the Ruin which he went to find.
'Then by the Ills a headstrong Frenzy brought
'Upon the Father, lett the Son be taught.
'All thought of him is vain; your Hope as vain,
'To sway the Sceptre of his vacant Reign;
'The lawless Sutors to your Mother's Bed,
'That instant which you land, have doom'd you dead.
'No longer then your anxious mind employ
'On Hope delusive, Visionary Joy:
'Give your unprofitable Sorrows o'er,
'And yield to her who might subdue by Pow'r.
'To her who can immortal Bliss impart,
'And gives her Crown as freely as her Heart.'

48. *But scarce the shore . . . fast eternal Sleep*: these forty-six lines are Hervey's response to 'je fus vengée par la tempête. Son vaisseau après avoir été lontems le jouet des vents, fut enseveli dans les ondes' ('I was revenged by the tempest. His vessel, after having been the plaything of the winds for a long time, was buried beneath the waves' (*Les Avantures* (Tonson), I. 8)). Hervey is influenced by the storm in Pope's *Odyssey* (V. 375–424; Pope, *Twickenham*, IX, 190–2) but his account is more practical in focus.

Dissembling thus the Queen with Art reveal'd
Ulisses' danger, but his scape conceal'd.
(Tho' Gifts divine the Sea-born Goddess crown,
The female still presides, to falshood prone.)
The Hero long by ruthless Neptune toss'd,
Late found a Harbour on Pheacia's Coast;
Where good Alcinous Hospitable reign's,
The rich Possessor of Hiperia's Plains:
Thence well-rigg'd Vessels, at the King's Command,
Transport the Wandrer to his native Land.[49]
This Truth the Goddess carefully suppress'd
For well (if known) the Consequence she guess'd.
Deep lyes that Secrett smother'd in her Breast,
'Mong the few things that Love permitts to rest.
Bane to her Wishes, should it e'er be known,
The latest refuge of her Hope is gone.

At first the Prince the well-lay'd Tale believed,
And ev'ry Word as sacred truth reciev'd:
But now Suspicion call'd him to his guard,
And half disclos'd her Artifice appear'd.
Her words he ponder'd, and he guess'd their End;
And weigh'd the prudent warnings of his Friend.
He paus'd awhile, well heeding what he say'd;
Then wary thus a doubtfull answer made.

'If Griefs like mine could sudden Comfort find,
'Sure I should cease to mourn when you are kind:
'But oh! reflect with how severe a Hand
'The Gods chastise, and what their frowns demand.
'Think what Misfortunes I am doom'd to bear,
'And marvel at my patience, not my Care.
'I've lost a Father and I've lost a Crown
'Much as a Prince I mourn, more as a Son.

49. *Where good Alcinous ... to his native Land*: Fénelon notes the omission but Hervey supplies the detail.

'Time may perhaps the rage of Grief allay,
'(That only Lord our Passions will obey.)
'Then time afford, to soften that distress;
'Which yet nor Love nor Beauty can redress,
'You best can tell (for you his Virtues knew)
'How just these Tears, how much the Hero's due.'
He ended here; and wiped with manly Grace
The decent Sorrow from his dewy Face.
The Goddess pitying hear'd, and sought to cheer
With many a soothing Art his pious Care.

'In all thy Griefs' (She say'd) 'I take a Part.
'Oh! may I ever Share what moves thy Heart!
'Ev'n false Ulisses for thy sake I mourn:
'Tho' vain alas! for never from their Urn
'Can the cold Ashes into Life return.
'Pain is the Lott of Earth; then take thy Share,
'Tis Heav'n's to punish, and 'tis Man's to bear.
'But dawning Comfort wait's the future Hour,
'Tis big with joy, and thou shalt weep no more.
'What yet remains is thine; the past forgett:
'Reflexion for decrepit Age is fitt.
'Here sitt thee down; behold what Scenes invite,
'Each Object pregnant with some new delight.
'Amuse thy Woes, and to my ravish'd Ear
'In full th' Adventures of thy Life declare;
'Relate the Dangers which thy Youth has past;
'Relate them all, but dwell upon the Last:
'When happy Chance, or partial Jove's Command
'Decree'd thy Wreck to bless Calypso's Land.'

'I fear to tire'; (the modest Youth reply'd)
'Vain are thy Fears' (the Queen impatient cry'd.)
She press'd; and he reluctanctly comply'd.

Close by his Side th' enamour'd Goddess sate;
Nor lost a Word her Charmer did repeat.
With silent rapture on his Speech She hung;

And drank the gratefull Poyson of his Tongue.[50]
Whene'er the Tale on his Misfortunes ran,
Her heaving Bosome seem'd to share his Pain:
But when it vary'd and his safety told,
Her Eyes the transports of her Heart unfold.
The sudden joy unable to command,
She seiz'd in Rapture, and She press'd his Hand.[51]

Her Nymphs upon the Bank were placed around,
With Beauty like th' Iadalian Sisters[52] crown'd.
Their Bow's unbent upon their Sides were place'd,
Their slender Backs the dartfull Quiver graced;
With Eyes intent, and motionless to hear,
Fix'd on the sweet Historian all appear:
Nor fail'd to charm, the rare united Grace
Of hoary Wisdom, and a blooming Face.
With modest Eloquence, and decent Shame,
He told his Story to the eager Dame,
Whilst ev'ry Word add's fuel to her Flame.
The Blush ill-hid, and frequent Sigh confess'd
The inward Tumult of her raging Breast.
Nor Pride nor reason could its Force restrain,
Weak the restriction, impotent the Chain.
As Silent thus, (of publick Gloss afraid)
Unwillingly the Fair her Love betray'd;
She saw with Shame, with Anger and surprise,
Her ev'ry Motion watch'd by Mentor's Eyes.
Observant of each stolen Glance he stood,
Sagacious, penetrating, just and good.
He sees the Dangers which demand his Care;
Telemachus was Young, Calypso fair.

50. *th' enamour'd Goddess sate . . . And drank the gratefull Poyson of his Tongue*: cf. 'Still on that breast enamour'd let me lie, | Still drink delicious poison from thy eye' (Pope, 'Eloisa to Abelard', lines 121–2; Pope, *Twickenham*, II, 329). Isobel Grundy notes that Montagu wrote 'mine' next to the second line (private communication).

51. *Close by his Side . . . She press'd his Hand*: Calypso's powerful emotional response to the story is supplied by Hervey.

52. *th' Iadalian Sisters*: worshippers of Venus in Idalium.

Th' impending Ill he meditates to move,
And with the weight of Wisdom byass Love.

The Goddess anxious often view's him o'er,
Thinks him divine, and dread's superior Pow'r.
But there no Certainty her thoughts could trace,
And Love still draw's them to another Place.

The Prince his Tale had ended, and the Sun
Adown the Skys his Ev'ning Course had run;
And now attended by her starry Train,
The Silver Queen arising o'er the Plain,
Faintly forbids the Horrors of the Night,
And cheer's it's gloomy Face with doubtfull Light.
The drooping Flow'rs, with heavy Dew opprest,
Fold their soft Leaves and bow their Heads to rest
On Branches perch'd, the party-feather'd Throng
Chaunt their sweet Vespers in a sleepy Song.[53]
Promiscuous Herds lye dormant on the Plains,
And solemn Silence uninvaded reigns;
No Zephirs[54] murmur through the quiet Wood,
Nor curl the surface of the even Flood.[55]
When thus Calypso to the Youth addrest
Her courteous Speech. – 'Tis now the Hour of Rest;
'Retire my Love; and may restoring Sleep,
'Through ev'ry weary'd Limb balsamick creep!
'And when thy heavy Eye-lids gentle close,
'To meet the tranquil joy of soft repose,
'May Mimick Morpheus' counterfeiting Art,
'A gratefull Image to each thought impart!
'May no rude Dream encroach upon thy Rest,
'Or make thee groan by fancy'd Ills opprest!

53. *The drooping Flow'rs, with heavy Dew opprest ... sleepy Song*: cf. 'Observe the weary Birds, e're Night be done, | How they wou'd fain call up the tardy Sun, | With Feathers hung with Dew, . . . | The drooping Flow'rs hang their Heads, | And languish down into their Beds'. 'Orinda to Lucasia', in Katherine Philips, *Poems* (London: for Jacob Tonson, 1710), p. 191.

54. *Zephirs*: zephyrs, gentle breezes.

55. *Adown the Skys his Ev'ning Course had run ... the even Flood*: Hervey adds this evocation of night (lines 658–70).

'Lett pleasing Visions only fill thy Head,
'And lightly hover round thy peacefull Bed!
'May you with Pleasure dream of Love and me,[56]
'But if the Theme uneasy chance to be,
'(Which Heav'n avert) lett waking sett thee free.
'So if in Dreams I can not pleasing seem,
'Wake, and be pleas'd to find it but a Dream.'[57]

She spoke; and from her Eyes a tender Look,
Of amorous import, irradiate broke:
He bow'd respectfull, and with cold demean,
Unanswering heard the disappointed Queen.
Confus'd, incens'd, afflicted, she retired,
Mourn'd as a Lover and as Woman fired.
The Nymphs the Strangers to their Grotto led,
A common Grotto, but a sep'rate Bed:
On fragrant Greens their Lodging was prepar'd,
With Roses mix'd, in easy order rear'd.
A Lyon's Skin adorn'd the Prince's Bed;
A Bear's rough Hide on Mentor's Couch was spread:
Close in a Corner of the Grotto play'd
A bubling Fount: Sleep own'd its murmurring Aid,
And wrapt their Senses in his gratefull Shade.
In vain the Goddess sought her wonted rest,
The Tyrant Love expelle'd it from her Breast;
That busy God (who never knew controll)
Rang'd ev'ry Corner of her wakefull Soul;
One Posture and another then She trys,
But Sleep tho courted still avoids her Eyes:
Their Lids she often clos'd, but clos'd in vain,
By gushing Tears as often forced again.
The Father's falshood rankle's in her Mind,
And now the Conduct of a Son less kind;

56. *dream of Love and me*: in Fénelon Calypso makes no such direct avowal of feeling, merely saying she will be eager for the continuation of the story (*Les Avantures* (Tonson), IV. 65–6).

57. *But if the Theme ... but a Dream*: echoing Puck's farewell at the end of *A Midsummer Night's Dream*, and perhaps generally evoking Titania's fairies' role in that play.

Yet more than all the Coldness of his Heart,
She fear's his Friend, preventive to her Art.
Her ev'ry Care revolves; she feels again,
In sharp remembrance, all her former Pain;
Thus wrap'd in Woe, protracting Night She lay,
And sleepless saw the Dawn of op'ning Day.[58]

The End of the first Book.

## The Adventures of Telemachus In the Island Ogygia, from Fenelon Book the Second

Scarce had Aurora, rosy finger'd Maid!
The golden Portals of the Day display'd;[59]
Nor yet the Sun had chac'd the Dusk of Heav'n,
Nor yet the Stars were from their Empire driv'n:
When from her Couch th' uneasy Goddess rose,[60]
And ceas'd to court the fugitive repose.
To weep, unseen to breath unhear'd her pain,
She sought the distant solitary Plain;
Whilst morning Zephirs, from the neighb'ring Grove,
Eccho her Sighs, and fan her glowing Love:
The conjugal Companions of the Wood,
That in each Spray in warbling Couples stood,
Sad She beheld; for Envy fill'd her Breast,
Whilst ev'ry Fair her billing Mate caress'd.
By Words in vain to ease her Soul She try'd,
For utt'rance still the choaking Care deny'd,
Abortive on her Tongue each Accent dy'd.
Her Eyes were fix'd and dry with stupid Grief

58. *sleepless saw the Dawn of op'ning Day*: Calypso's sleepless night is Hervey's addition.

59. *Aurora … golden Portals of the Day display'd*: these lines come from Calypso's anticipation the night before (*Les Avantures* (Tonson), IV. 65); they possibly reflect Virgil's concern with the dawn in relation to Dido's suffering in the *Aeneid*, IV. 6, 129, 584 (Loeb, pp. 396, 404, 434).

60. *When from her Couch th' uneasy Goddess rose*: this and the next seventy-four lines, exploring Calypso's feeling and culminating in her appeal to Venus, are Hervey's addition. In *Les Aventures* the initiative for her appearance in Ogygia is Venus' own (*Les Avantures* (Tonson), VII. 123–5; modern book 6).

(Sad State of Woe! when Tears can bring relief:)
At length both Tears and Words their Prison broke,
And weeping thus the plaintive Lover spoke.

'Why Yee just Gods! of all your Works was Man
'The most ungratefull made? When you began
'A being like your-selves, of Form divine,
'Why did you deviate from the first design?
'Why in the Composition shuffle in
'This base ingredient, this alloy of Sin?[61]
'All Other Things their Benefactors own,
'And some return of gratitude is shown.
'When cooling Rains on Earth's sc'orch'd Bosome pour,
'Does She not pay for ev'ry drop a Flow'r?
'The Sap which from the Earth the Trees receive,
'Again the Trees in Leaves to shade her give:
'And gratefull Flow'rs their fragrancys bestow,
'To scent those Winds that caused their Buds to blow.
'By Man alone no kind returns are made,
'Favours to him are ever unrepay'd:
'Base to his Friend, but baser to the Fair,[62]
'For She who meritts ne'er employ's his Care.
'Why was my Heart this maxim doom'd to prove
'By two Examples of disas'trous Love?
'Ulisses first neglectfull of my Charms,
'Despis'd his Conquest, and forsook my Arms.
'And next Telemachus (ungratefull Youth!)
'With Coldness meets my Vows, with Art my Truth:
'Contemn's the Favours by my Bounty shown,

61. *This base ingredient, this alloy of Sin*: for ingratitude as a major sin, see Robert South in his sermon on the text 'And the Children of Israel remember'd not the Lord their God' in *Thirty Six Sermons and Discourses* (Dublin: Pat. Dugan and Jos. Leatly, 1720), pp. 140–52); Swift makes it a capital crime (*Gulliver's Travels*, ed. by David Womersley (Cambridge: Cambridge University Press), p. 87, part I, chap. vi). Hervey touches on the topic in Poem 38 'The Answer to the Receipt to Cure Love', 'Ingratitude's a Guilt she does not know, | She thanks the Heavens for Blessings they bestow' (lines 7–8).

62. *Base to his Friend, but baser to the Fair*: cf. 'Base to his friend, to his own interest blind' (Pope, *Odyssey*, VIII. 244; Pope, *Twickenham*, IX, 275), part of Odysseus' declaration on mutual obligation.

'Eludes my Wish, and spurn's my proffer'd Crown.
'Yet (gratefull torment of this raging Heart!)
'I can not, must not, will not lett thee part:
'Could I my Life I might my Love foregoe,
'But Death can never terminate my Woe.
'If Immortality disolv'd could be,
'Those Racks would doe it which I feel for Thee.'

She could no more, unequal to her Care;
Prone on the V'ilet carpet sunk the Fair:
The Stream of Life deserts each outward Part
And leaves the pallid Cheek to guard the Heart.
Her closing Eyes forgott their office quite,
Nor view'd the Sun's nor gave the World their Light.
Thus for awhile eclips'd the Goddess lay;
But as the rosy Harbinger of Day,
Throws off the Sable Mantle of the Night,
And cheer's the Sky with sweet revolving Light,
So Life restor'd uncurtain'd those fair Eyes,
So Warmth and Lustre to each Charm supplys:
Again the crimson Streams adorn'd her Face,
Danced through each Vein, and light up ev'ry Grace.
Then thus, with Hands uplift for Venus' Aid,
Half rais'd upon her Arm Calypso pray'd.

'If e'er thy Pity (gracious Queen of Love!)
'A Wretch could claim, or Misery could move;
'Compassionate behold my lost estate,
'Avenge my Wrongs, arest impending Fate.
'Thee Honour calls, Me soft desires employ:
'Be thine the triumph, and be mine the Joy:
'Subdue this Youth who disavows thy Pow'r,
'And Hecatombs shall float thy Shrine with Gore:
'My-self a Temple to thy Name will raise,
'Where sacred flames shall unextinguish'd blaze.'

Scarce had these Accents birth, when from above,
On fleecy Clouds, came down the Queen of Love;
Guided by Doves white as unsully'd Snow,

Her Chariot paus'd in Air, descending slow.[63]
The pompous[64] Load a golden Axle bear's
And rich with burnish'd Gold the Beam appear's:
The solid Wheels were orb'd with beaten Gold,
On silver Spokes the golden Orbits rowl'd.
The matchless Beautys of each nice turn'd Part,
Confess'd the master-piece of Vulcan's Art.[65]
The polish'd Sides with milk-white Iv'ry Shine,
(The Model, and the Architect divine:)
Here the sharp Chissel all it's force bestows,
And help'd by Colours, the nice Carving shows
How Venus from the genial Ocean rose.[66]
Fast fall the trickling Drops adown her Hair,
The amber-freight of gentle-playing Air.
Upon a Shell the Goddess seem's to Stand,
And docile Swans obey her whiter Hand.
Naked She shines confess'd in all those Charms,
Which won the Son of Juno[67] to her Arms.
With conscious, native Pride She seems to smile,
And Zephir wafts her to the Cyprian Isle.

Oppos'd to this Cithera's Domes arise,[68]
Aloft they tow'r, and seem to pierce the Skys.
Pillasters strong the pond'rous Roof uphold,

63. *Her Chariot paus'd in Air, descending slow*: this and the next eighty-four lines, describing Venus' descent, her chariot and her temples, are Hervey's elaboration of her simple descent in modern book 6. He is able to draw on Fénelon's account of her temples in Cyprus (*Les Avantures* (Tonson), IV. 73–5). The description of the chariot drawn by doves may owe something to the fresco (or its engravings) by Raphael and his assistants in the Villa Farnesina, Rome.

64. *pompous*: magnificent, splendid.

65. *Vulcan's Art*: Vulcan was the son of Jupiter and Juno and the husband of Venus; identified with the Greek Hephaestus, he is the divine master craftsman.

66. *How Venus from the genial Ocean rose*: the description accords with Sandro Botticelli's *Birth of Venus* in the Uffizi, Florence.

67. *Son of Juno*: Mars, the god of war.

68. *Cithera's Domes arise*: Cythera, a Greek island, the birthplace of Venus. The following five lines echo Pandemonium in Milton's *Paradise Lost*: 'Built like a Temple, where Pilasters round | Were set, and Doric pillars overlaid | With Gold'n Architrave; nor did there want | Cornice or Freeze, with bossy Sculptures grav'n, | The Roof was fretted Gold' (I. 713–17; Milton, *Poetical Works*, I, 23).

The Columns marble, and the Bases gold.
On numerous Steps with veiny Agate fraught,
(With plated Brass the shining Edges wrought:)
The Priests, in white array'd, the Temple gain,
And there with crimson Streams the Floor destain,
There Victims of unspotted white alone are slain.
Their Brows a Fillet rich,[69] their crooked Horns,
A fragrant Wreath of gayest Flow'rs adorn's.
Minstrells and Fifes attend them to their Doom
And pleas'd they dance into the pompous Tomb.
Perpetuall Fires upon the Altars blaze,
And sides of fretted Gold each Shrine display's:
A gratefull Scent the Goddess constant greet's,
And all Arabia breath's in smoaky sweets.[70]
On the Top point of all the Temple rear'd,
Her Image stands conspicuous and rever'd.
The Temple fragrant Myrtle Groves surround,
A thousand Cupids strew the flow'ry Ground.
The Cyclops' dext'rous Art the Figures own,
And Mulcifer's presiding Skill in all is shown.[71]

Behind each Figure to the Life express'd
The Gods in Banquet, an ambrosial Feast.
The Sire of Gods sitts high with decent Pride
Rever'd; his Sister-Consort by his Side.
Black plenteous Curls hang awfull from his Head,
Which o'er Olympus gratefull odours shed:
He quaff's repeated draughts that glad the Soul,
And fav'rite Ganymede presents the Bowl.[72]
To all the rest a Cup with Nectar crown'd,

69. *Fillet rich*: finely decorated headband.

70. *And . . . sweets*: 'And all *Arabia* breathes from yonder Box' (Pope, *The Rape of the Lock*, I, 134; Pope, *Twickenham*, II, 156).

71. *The Cyclops' dext'rous Art . . . And Mulcifer's presiding Skill . . . is shown*: in Hesiod's *Theogony* the Cyclopes are divine craftsmen who forge weapons for the gods; Mulcifer (or Mulciber) is another name for Vulcan.

72. *Sire of Gods . . . Sister-Consort . . . Ganymede presents the Bowl*: Jupiter and Juno preside; Ganymede, a Trojan youth, was carried off to Olympus by Jupiter.

The Heaven'ly Skinker[73] neatly dealt around.
For Melody the Muses all conspire,
And lawrell'd Phoebus touch'd the golden Lire.
Obedient to his Touch, the tunefull Strings
Delight the Gods, when as he play's, he sing's.

Thus the fair Prospect of th' Olympian Hill,
On Venus' Car, proclaim'd her Husband's Skill:
The Top was open, and the Sides around
With studded Gems in glitt'ring rows were crown'd:
Saphirs and yellow Jaspers blend their Rays,
Rubies and Em'rolds yield a mingled Blaze,
And borrow Charms; for in each Mirror-Stone,
A Venus sparkled, and the Graces shone.
The Paphian Queen[74] on cloudy Amber sate,
And at her Back the naked Graces wait:
Dext'rous, they frustrate the too busy Wind,
New turn the Curls, and loosen'd Braids rebind.

Gay Youthfull Bloom, and soft enchanting Grace,
Beauty it-self was seated in her Face:
Not with more Charms was the bright Goddess seen,
When she contended on th' Idalian Green;[75]
When Jove's fair Daughter, and the Queen of Heav'n,
The Pref'rance mourn'd to her so justly giv'n.[76]
The silken Reins were twisted round her Arm,
A thousand little Loves around her swarm:
The rosy Son sitt's at the Mother's Feet;[77]
With Cunning Look, at once both false, and sweet:
Around his Neck his gilded Quiver ty'd,
His fatal Bow hang's ready at his Side.

73. *Skinker*: one who serves drinks, here Ganymede.

74. *Paphian Queen*: Venus; Paphos was a city in Cyprus.

75. *Idalian Green*: Idalium in Cyprus was consecrated to Venus.

76. *Jove's fair Daugher, and the Queen of Heav'n, The Pref'rance mourn'd to her so justly giv'n*: Paris, asked to choose between Minerva, Juno and Venus, chose Venus. The judgement of Paris is the subject of a masque by Congreve (1701), a poem by Prior (1706) and numerous paintings.

77. *Son sitt's at the Mother's Feet*: Cupid.

And now the Chariot cleaves the airy Road,
And flow'ry Banks receive the heav'nly Load.
Venus alight's, advancing on the Green,
And thus accost's Ogygia's mournfull Queen.

'Look up, thou fair distress'd! thy Vows are heard,
'The sweet relief by Venus self prepar'd:
'Cythera's smoaking Altars I neglect,
'And aiding your's Olympus' joy's reject.
'Barely the Father fled, (unhappy Fair!)
'But be the Son our own peculiar Care:
'What though the Youth ev'n now his flight prepares:
'(A Man in falshood tho a Boy in Years;)
'What though his Mentor aid the close design;
'How vain is Wisdom's Force oppos'd to mine!
'Love's on thy side; see Love him-self is come
'To seal the Youth's irrevocable doom.
'Nor come we solely to assert thy Cause,
'We seek a Rebell who disclaim's our Laws:
'Revenge we seek, Revenge for injur'd Pow'r, disdain'd,
'Our Shrines neglected, and our Rites prophan'd.
'At Cyprus once he mock'd the homage shown
'By other Hearts, and dared to keep his own.
'Strike then my Son, strike with thy keenest Dart,
'Lett him who shun's thy Pleasure feel thy smart.
'As Bacchus once unknown in Naxos stay'd,
'So here shall Love: disguis'd, in ambush lay'd,
'Telemachus's Bane, Calypso's Aid.
'Then cease thy Cares; see smiling Comfort wait,
'With gratefull Hand, to smooth the Frowns of Fate.
'Blessings in Crouds attend thy future Days,
'And Heaven's King shall claim but second Praise.
'Tho' Life immortal be the Gift of Jove,
'The nobler Gift is Happyness in Love.'

She spoke, and reascending in her Car,
To Paphos bent, shot the rejoining Air.
Ambrosia as She flew distill'd around,
And scatter'd Perfumes glad the sacred Ground.

And now She lands where thousand Altars smoke,
And thousand bleeding Hearts her Aid invoke.

But Love, remaining in Calypso's Arms,
With added Fire her glowing Bosome warm's:
Around her Wast he curl'd (insidious Boy!)
So Flames embrace that Fuel they destroy.
The panting Goddess felt the pois'nous Dart
Pierce to her Soul, and ev'n transfix her Heart;
And for awhile to check th' unruly joy,
To Eucharis, her fav'rite Nymph, she gave the Boy.
Fatal the Gift, and fatal the Relief,
A present Ease but source of future Grief.
Too soon the God subdued her ready Heart,
An easy Prize to his unerring Art;
Youth, Health, and Woman ill resist the Dart.
This rais'd a Rival to Calypso's Love,
A Rival too that must triumphant prove:
For who so guarded to behold those charms,
Unlonging for the sweet Possessor's Arms?
The lovely'st Maid upon Ogygia's Plain,
Envy and Pride of all Calypso's Train:
Not half so noble stately Pines appear,
The Rose so blooming or the Pink so fair.
Her Limbs, her Shape, so gracefull to behold,
Of Heav'n She seem's, nor cast in mortal Mold:
Where She contends, ev'n Goddesses must yield,
And to superior Beauty quit the Field.
This haughty, yet contemn'd Calipso proves,
Since charm'd Telemachus her Rival loves:[78]
Fondly he loves, nor can conceal the Flame,
Each action speak's it with becoming Shame.
Sweet is the Morn of Love, serene and clear,
But fast succeeds the Noon's inclement Air,
With scorching jealousy, Distrust, and Care:
Deceit ensues, and all her train of Lyes,

78. *charm'd Telemachus her Rival loves*: in Fénelon, Telemachus' enchantment is directly attributed to an embrace of Cupid (*Les Avantures* (Tonson), VII. 125).

With Which the faithless veil the faithfull Eyes:
Then the black Night of frequent sharp Debate,
Half Reconcilements, and recurring Hate.
Not thus Telemachus, unpractis'd Youth,
Deal's in the Trade of Love, but loves with truth:
New to the Warmth, and guiltless of the Art,
He can nor conquer, nor disguise his Heart.

At first the thing was whisper'd by the Few,[79]
Who strong Conclusions from small motives drew:
The busy She, who ever-medling pry's,
And all things sees with magnifying Eyes:
But now from ev'ry common Mouth 'tis heard,
The Goddess slighted, and the Nymph prefer'd.
So little Caution in his Conduct's shown,
That ev'n to Mentor thus he made it known.

'Behold, my Friend, and Guide, this wondrous Place,
'It's artless Charms and Art-surpassing Grace;
'Behold how partial Jove's indulgent Hand,
'Profuse of Bliss, distinguishes the Land:
'Nor marvel, since my Fate allotts this Coast,
'No more I weep my native Country lost:
'Wellcome the Change! and bless'd the Soil I've found!
'Happy Event of all my Labours crown'd!
'How soft the Clime! the fertile Plains how fine!
'The Residance, and Habitants divine.
'Unlike the Cyprian Dames these Nymphs appear,
'Free with Discretion, and with Virtue fair:
'Careless they charm, contemn their Sex's Art,
'And not sollicit, but command the Heart.
'When chast Diana seek's the sportfull Plain,
'Not ev'n Diana boast's so fair a Train.
'But oh! if icy Age has left thy Heart
'Unfrozen still in any warmer Part;
'Behold that Angel Form, where you shall find

79. *At first the thing was whisper'd by the Few*: the gossip in this paragraph is Hervey's addition.

'Lucina's Virtue,[80] Venus' Beauty join'd;
'Behold, and after (if thou canst) reprove
'The Man whom Eucharis has taught to love;'

He spoke; and wish'd he could recall the Name,[81]
Abash'd he stood, o'erwhelm'd with conscious Shame:
In vain to stifle his Distress he try'd,
That Care but doubled what it sought to hide.
Trembling he stood; He knew a Storm was nigh,
And wish'd to hear, yet dreaded the Reply.

'Ill-fated Youth!' (the Sage began) 'Thou'rt lost:
'What Star malignant forc'd thee on this Coast?
'Sure thy good Angel slumber'd in that Hour,
'And o'er thy Fate rul'd some sinister Pow'r.
'The sanguine Hopes my Age had form'd are flown,
'And all my Labours at one Cast o'erthrown;
'False were those Hopes, false that prophetick Joy,
'That saw a future Hero in the Boy;
'I form'd thee dreadfull in the Field of Fight,
'Where deathless Glory and Renown invite:
'I form'd thee active in thy Country's Cause,
'Fond of her Right, tenacious of her Laws;
'Nor fear'd to see Telemachus's Name,
'Enroll'd the foremost in the Lists of Fame.
'Now what avail my Schemes; these silver Hairs
'White with the weight of never-ceasing Cares?
'I taught thee Virtue early to pursue,
'I taught thee Youth and nature to subdue;
'To curb the Will, with Reason to controul
'Passion, that fiend pernicious to the Soul.
'But all in vain, (tho' well the work began,
'And the wise Child anticipated Man)

80. *Lucina's Virtue*: probably a reference to Diana Lucina; Diana and Juno, the Lucinae, were both goddesses of light and childbirth. Hervey may also have in mind the virtuous Lucina raped in Fletcher's play *Valentinian* (1610–14), which was adapted by Rochester as *Lucina's Rape* (1684).

81. *wish'd he could recall the Name*: Fénelon's Telemachus does not utter the name.

'For Cupid, in the form of that fair Boy,[82]
'Whose fatal sports your leisure Hours employ,
'With specious, fraudulent, and pois'nous Art,
'Has all subverted, and seduced thy Heart:
'Here, on thy Ruin obstinately bent,
'The Lurcher[83] came, by angry Venus sent;
'With Vengeance fraught, for Pow'r despis'd they come,
'Nor canst thou but by Flight elude thy doom:
'Against thy-self is arm'd thy rebel Heart,
'An inward Foe, it takes th' Assailant's Part:
'And like a sensual Villain lend's it's Aid,
'By base and interested Views betray'd.
'Small were the Dangers of the Cyprian Land,
'Compar'd to these, which all thy Strength demand.
'If Vice be gross; 'tis Folly is her Prize;
'Horrid her Form to Wisdom's decent Eyes.
'And the loose Prostitute can only fire
'Our indignation, not instill desire.
'But when the Fair, by Modesty confin'd,
'Delight the Sense, and gain upon the Mind;
'When Beauty with prudential precepts warms,
'Wisdom is pleas'd, and Reason own's her Charms.
'Beware my Prince, for here the Danger lyes,
'Impostors oft' our cozen'd Hearts surprise,
'And fairest Looks the blackest Souls disguise.
'Then all our Days in Sloth inert we waste,
'To Glory lost, abandon'd to our Tast.
'Such is the Fate for thee, dear Youth! prepar'd,
'But timely be the faithfull Mentor hear'd:
'Your Crown, your Happyness, your Fame's at stake,
'Calipso and more dang'rous Eucharis forsake.
'Fly from the real Ill, the seeming joy,
'That smiles to wound, and courts you to destroy.

82. *For Cupid, in the form of that fair Boy*: although much of this exchange between Telemachus and Mentor comes from the passage after the encounter with Cupid, this explanation, and some of the moral instruction, is taken from the conversation after the hunt, just before they prepare to leave Ogygia (*Les Avantures* (Tonson), VII. 139).

83. *Lurcher*: swindler, rogue.

'Oh! yet reflect, (for soon 'twill prove too late,)
'When cooler Reason shall regain her Seat,
'When the short transports of thy Soul are dead
'And all the dazling mist of Passion fled;
'What then shall be thy Lott? – then shall thy Fault,
'In its true Form stand naked to thy Thought;
'Then fell Remorse, that ineffectual Care,
'Shall gnaw thy Soul, administring Despair;
'In vain repentance shall thy Life be spent,
'And sharp remembrance of thy Crime, it's Punishment.'

Thus Age and Wisdome spoke, but spoke in vain;
As stable Rocks repulse the beating Main;
So stood Telemachus to all unmov'd,
Firm to his purpose, true to her he lov'd.
'Whither' (he say'd) 'Or Wherefore should I goe?
'Ulisses wander's in the Shades below;
'And sure Penelopy (who long has mourn'd
'A vagrant Son and Husband unreturn'd)
'Forc'd by her Sire, to some new Lord is ty'd
'In second Nuptials, an unwilling Bride.
'Wouldst thou to Ithaca I urge my Flight,
'To meet the Horrours of that grating Sight?
'My Father's Bed by a leud Alien stain'd,
'And all her vow'd Fidelity prophan'd?
'Or grant my Fears too quick this Ill presage,
''Tis just at least to fear her Lovers' Rage:
'Me as a Check the lawless Crew behold,
'And hunt my Life, my Head the Price of Gold.
'The Son's excluded from the Father's Court,
'And Death suborn'd attend's in ev'ry Port.'

''Tis ever thus' (reply'd the Sage again)
'When Reason abdicates her equal Reign,
'And Appetite and Passion rule the Man.
'To gloss the Wrong false Arguments we find,
'And see the Right affecting to be blind:
'With subtil Reasonings fain we would deceive
'Our-selves, and Sophistry for Proof recieve:

'But Truth will still be Truth in spight of Art,
'Nor can the Head impose upon the Heart.
'Not all our Witt or Rhetorick can ease
'The Stings of Conscience, or Remorse appease;
'That Judge severe, unbyas'd, deal's his Laws,
'And naked sees the rotten, varnish'd Cause.
'Nor him shalt thou escape (perverse of Will!)
'Forc'd to discern and late detest the Ill.

'What Heav'n, all-gracious, has allready done
'In foreign Countrys, to restore thy own
'Hast thou forgott? What more than Mortal Pow'r
'Preserv'd thee on Sicilia's hostile Shore?
'Who in Egyptian Prisons, (helpless Boy!)
'Struck off thy Chains and turn'd thy Tears to Joy?
'When Atropos prepar'd to clip thy Thread,[84]
'Tyre's ruthless King insatiate for thy Head,[85]
'What Hand divine, invisible, withstood,
'And from the thirsty Tyrant sav'd thy Blood?
'So oft' preserv'd by Heav'n's peculiar Care,
'If yet you doubt the Fate the Gods prepare,
''Tis willfull Ignorance, and feign'd Despair.
'With impious Hand you push their Gifts away,
'And combate all their Bounty by thy Stay:
'But stay alone, whilst I far off deplore
'My fruitless Labours on a safer Shore.
'Degen'rate Off spring of a God-like Sire!
'Whom neither Precepts nor Example fire;
'Inglorious drag thy Days, doat on a Face,
'And shameless, what thy Father spurn'd, embrace.'

He spoke with Warmth; nor urg'd unheeded Truth;
Th' indignant Language rous'd the gen'rous Youth:
Glory and Love with equal Force controul,
In civil War they rend his wav'ring Soul;

84. *Atropos prepar'd to clip thy Thread*: Atropos was one of the three Moirai or Fates and determined the point of death.

85. *Tyre's ruthless King insatiate for thy Head*: Pygmalion in book 3 of modern editions of *Les Aventures*.

Both Passions strive, reluctant to obey,
And rule alternate with conflicting Sway.

'Is Immortality a Gift' (He cry'd)
'Of such light Moment, to be thrown aside
'And cheaply scorn'd?' – to this the Sage reply'd.

'All Gifts alike must Prudence disapprove
'That combate Virtue, or the Will of Jove.
''Tis Virtue call's thee to thy native Land,
'The Gods, thy Int'rest and thy Fame Command:
''Tis Virtue bids thee seek thy aged Sire,
'And check the Sallys of unchast Desire.
'Whilst Love, that Tyrant of a feeble Heart,
'And only Love prohibits thy Depart.
'Was it for this that Jove preserv'd thy Life,
'In Storms, in Prisons, and the Field of Strife;
'To waste in wanton Ease ignoble Days,
'And sing soft Sonnets to a Woman's Praise;
'Living to Shame, but dead to great Renown,
'What tho immortal Youth thy Years should crown?
'Boast not the Gift: it but augments the Wrong,
'He who survives his Virtue live's too long.'

Thus spoke the Friend his Counsells and his Fears:
The contrite Prince reply's with Sighs and Tears:
Replys which speak the Anguish of his Heart,
Encreas'd and not allay'd by Mentor's Art:
So Waters, cast on unextinguish'd fire,
New Fury to the raging flames inspire.
Nor what to hope he knew, nor what to fear,
A Prey each moment to some diff'rent Care:
Sometimes he wish'd, that in his own dispight,
His Friend would force him to the prudent Flight:
But oft'ner wish'd he would alone depart,
And what he could not conquer, cease to thwart.
Thus (like a Lake that's plough'd by jarring Winds:)
By varying Passions torn no rest he finds:
Pensive by Day he haunts the lonely Grove,

His Nights are such as wait on hapless Love.
By frequent Tears his Eyes grew fiery red,
And from his Cheek the gay Vermillion fled;
The glossy Plenty of his Curling Hair
Neglected hung; his Face no longer fair,
Became the meagre emblem of Despair.
Lost is the noble Aspect late he bore,
His Looks dejected speak the Prince no more.
No Likeness of his former self you trace,
Shorn of his Charms, the Ghost of what he was.
So some gay Flow'r that in the Morning blow's,[86]
And through the Field it's Fragrancys bestow's;
If overwarm'd by Noon's too piercing Rays,
(It's Colours fading) sicken's and decay's:
No more the gaudy Object feast's our Eyes,
No more diffuses Sweets in odorous Sighs,
It droops, it fades, it wither's and it dyes.

The pitying Mentor only mourn'd the Youth,
Whose rare offence was Tenderness and Truth;
He found how vain by Argument to prove
The dang'rous Errors of this fatal Love;
What then remains? – be Stratagem apply'd;
'Tis just when Reason fail's that Art be try'd.
He ponder'd long, and whilst the Scheme he lay'd,
The past, the present, and the Future weigh'd:
The good and bad Effects that might attend;
(A cool Spectator, and a carefull Friend).
Then thus resolves with Skill divine endued:
'Be Love' (say'd He) 'By Love him-self subdued;
'What neither Pray'rs nor Reason could effect
'Shall jealous Woman, whetted by Neglect.'

86. *So some gay Flow'r that in the Morning blow's*: this and the following six lines adapt Catullus, Poem LXII, 'As a flower springs up secretly in a fenced garden, unknown to the cattle, torn up by no plough, which the winds caress, the sun strengthens, the shower draws forth, many boys, many girls, desire it; when the same flower fades, nipped by a sharp nail, no boys, no girls desire it' (Loeb, p. 89). Air VI in *The Beggar's Opera* (London: for John Watts, 1728) is based on the same poem.

He sought the Queen, and finding thus addrest,
To fan the jealous Fury in her Breast.

'Hail! beauteous Goddess! whose prevailing Charms
'Can sooth the Hero from War's lov'd allarms;
'Can make Ulisses Son his Birth forgett,
'And for the Huntsman's Bow, the Warrior's quitt:
'The Sword and Shield his Arms no longer grace,
'The Horn and Arrow have usurp'd their Place;
'No Wonder thus, Adonis-like, he loves
'To lead the Chace, and through the Forest roves,
'Since fair Calypso's Venus of the Groves.'

'Ah! Mentor, no,' (the Goddess quick reply'd.)
'My Pow'r alas! the scornfull Youth defy'd.
'That Heart, that steely Heart, that woundless stood,
'Impregnable, when I unhappy woo'd,
'Soften'd, like Wax beneath the Taper's Flame,
'When Eucharis the fair Invader came.
'For Eucharis he haunt's the Plains and Groves,
'And not the Hunting but the Huntress love's.
'The Chace no Pleasure in her absence yields,
'Tedious the Sport, and dreary are the Fields.
'For her, impatient, he prevents[87] the Morn;
'And winds the early Summons of the Horn;
'Pursues her all the Day from Place to Place,
'Link'd to her Side, and gloating on her Face.
'Nor glows the Lover in unfruitfull Fires,
'But equal Love and equal warmth inspires;
'This from Report I learn'd of faithfull Spys,
'(For Jealousy beholds with Argus-Eyes;)[88]
'Nor unremark'd the cunning Pair have stray'd
'Sequester'd, to the distant, lonely Glade;
'Or to the closer Covert of the Grove,

87. *prevents*: anticipates (*OED*).

88. *Argus-Eyes*: Argus, the son of Jupiter and Niobe, had many eyes (detailed accounts differ). The jealous Juno set him to guard Io.

'An apt recess to veil their secret Love.[89]
'What Scenes Suspicion usher's to my Mind,
'When both were willing, and occasion kind!
'By Her the Youth, the Nymph by Him ador'd,
'Ravish'd with Joys they ne'er before explor'd.
'Oh! tis Destraction, Mentor! to my Rest!
'A thousand Daggers less would tear my Breast;
'But why with idle Tears doe I deplore
'The daring Insult, Vengeance in my Pow'r?
'Lett them this anguish and these Tortures share,
'Be Disappointment their's, and their's Despair,
'And all that Hell which they have planted here.'[90]

With that She smote her Breast in frantick Woe,
Her snowy Bosome redden'd with the Blow.
But now the Prince approaching with the Maid,
She call'd returning Reason to her Aid;
And recollected, in a milder Tone,
Her envious Orders thus the Queen made known.

'When all to morrow for the Hunt prepare,
'Our selves will in the Silvan Pleasures share:
'And teach the savage to our Darts to yield,
'Or trace with faithfull Hound the tainted Field.'

She say'd no more; but sought, with painfull Pride,
In calm Deceit her inward Rage to hide:
Too hard the Task; her Resolution fail'd,
Her Prudence yielded, and her Wrath prevail'd.
In loud revilings thus at once She broke,
Her Eyes with Fury lighten'd as She spoke.

'Was it for this (rash Boy!) you sought this Shore,
'To slight my Passion, and insult my Pow'r?
'Abandon'd by the Gods, I lent thee Aid,

89. *An apt recess to veil their secret Love*: the relation of Dido and Aeneas is consummated in a cave during the hunt (*Aeneid*, IV. 165–6 (Loeb, p. 406)).

90. *Ah! Mentor . . . that Hell which they have planted here*: the outburst of passion in this speech contrasts with Calypso's relatively restrained response in Fénelon, contrasting heroic exploits to enslavement by pleasure (*Les Avantures* (Tonson), VII. 129–30).

'And thus, ungratefull! is my Bounty pay'd:
'Neptune in vain thy hated Life pursued,
'I intercepted Death and rob'd the flood;
'But take the God his rescued Prey again,
'Dash thee on Rocks, or plunge thee in the Main;
'I give thee back to Fate: Yee Pow'rs above!
'And You below, avenge my injur'd Love:
'And as the Son's the Father's Crimes exceed,
'A double Portion of your Thunder speed!
'Perfidious Monster! never mayst thou see,
'That native Clime in vain prefer'd to me;
'Or to imbitter all thy Woes the more,
'Mayst thou behold but never touch the Shore:
'Descend to Styx a miserable Shade,
'Thy Eyes unclos'd, and fun'ral Rites unpay'd.[91]
'Oh! would the Fury of the Waves once more,
'Pale, Lifeless, cold, direct thee to this Shore;
'How would my Eyes indulge in cruel Joy,
'When Vultures should that fatal Form destroy.
'She too should see it, that detested Maid,
'Whom thy Soul loves, and curse her useless Aid:
'Whilst I, reproachfull, sharpen her Despair,
'Insult her Woes, and agravate her Care.'

She say'd and madly to her Grotto flew:
In Silence wrapt, the consternated Crew
Remain'd submiss: yet pleas'd the Nymph perceiv'd,
Calipso's Threats and Pray'rs alike receiv'd:
Nor this nor that the least impression make,
No varying Arts the stable Lover shake.
As some strong Ship at Anchor in the Bay,
Defy's the Storm and rides the roaring Sea;
So stands the Prince in all Attacks unmov'd,

91. *Styx a miserable Shade, | Thy Eyes unclos'd, and fun'ral Rites unpay'd*: cf. 'What can atone (oh ever-injur'd shade!) | Thy fate unpity'd, and thy rites unpaid?' (Pope, 'Elegy to the Memory of an Unfortunate Lady', lines 47–8; Pope, *Twickenham*, II, 366). The Styx was the river bounding the underworld.

And unreceeding holds to her he lov'd.

End of the 2d Book.

## The Adventures of Telemachus in the Island of Ogygia; Book the 3d

Supreme on Heav'n's fix'd Throne, the King of Fate,
By golden Clouds enshrin'd (celestial State!)
With all the lesser Gods assembled sate.
Minerva's Contests with the Cyprian Boy[92]
Claim their attention, their debates employ:
This they commend, and that they disapprove,
To Pallas some and some adhere to Love.
Whilst Jove unmixing saw the great Debate,
And left decision to the Hand of Fate.

Meantime Calypso, with revengefull Flame,
Impatient burning 'till the Morrow came,
Endured with Pain the Remnant of the Day;
The Night came on, all Night she sleepless lay;
Each Corner of her Couch the Fair explor'd,
No Corner of her Couch could Sleep afford.[93]
And now, the Shades dispers'd, the golden Sun
His Course diurnal through the Skys begun:
The swift immortal Coursers scour away,
And from their flaming Nostrils snort the Day:
When beauteous Eucharis to hunt prepar'd,
And like Diana clad, as fair appear'd.
Fearfull the Lover should forsake her Arms,
The anxious Maid collected all her Charms:

92. *Minerva's Contests with the Cyprian Boy*: Hervey begins his third book midway through book VII of Tonson's version (*Les Avantures*, p. 132), the debate on Olympus making a convenient break. Jove presides, while Minerva (Pallas Athena) and Cupid (the boy from Cyprus) contest the outcome.

93. *No Corner of her Couch could Sleep afford*: Hervey invents another sleepless night for Calypso to complement that at the end of book I. He may have in mind Dido's final troubled night in *Aeneid*, IV. 522–53 (Loeb, pp. 430–2).

Her own fair Hand a vary'd Garland wove,
Of Rose, and Myrtle the sweet Shrub of Love:
Her Iv'ry Brow the flow'ry Chaplett crown'd,
The flow'ry Chaplett with her Hair She bound.
The azure Mantle like a cloudless Night,
With gold bespotted glitter'd Starry bright:
The ample Folds a golden Clasp repress'd;[94]
A broider'd Zone confin'd her swelling Breast.
Her nimble Feet rich Purple Sandals brace,
Their whiteness peeping through the checker'd Lace.
No Pains She spar'd; nor wanted heav'nly Aid,[95]
For Love and Venus deck'd their fav'rite Maid:
Bent to subdue Telemachus's Heart,
They grace the Mortal with immortal Art;
Divine Cosmeticks on her Head they pour,
Brought by the Goddess from her Cyprian Store:
These ev'ry Charm, and ev'ry Grace contain,
That feed the Mistress Pride, or Lover's Pain;
Attractive sweetness, Elegance of Air,
And all the nameless Beautys of the Fair:
The dimpled Smile, the dazzling Bloom they give,
And hence their Fire the meaning Eyes recieve.

Now ceas'd the Labours of the toilet-Care,[96]
And Beauty so compleat adorn'd the Fair,
That envious Venus thought the Palm too sure;
Conquest she wish'd, but wish'd it less secure.

Surpris'd, Calipso, from afar, beheld
The Angel-Rival as She sought the Field:

94. *With gold bespotted . . . a golden Clasp repress'd*: Virgil emphasises gold in Dido's attire for hunting in *Aeneid*, IV. 133–9 (Loeb, p. 404).

95. *nor wanted heav'nly Aid*: the passage of twelve lines beginning here echoes Belinda's toilet, assisted by the Sylphs, at the end of the first canto of *Rape of the Lock*. Fénelon says only, 'Eucharis . . . usoit de mille artifices pour le retenir dans ses liens . . . pour la seconde chasse . . . elle étoit vêtue comme Diane' ('Eucharis used a thousand artifices to keep him bound to her . . . for the second hunt . . . she was dressed like Diana') (*Les Avantures* (Tonson), VII. 32).

96. *Now ceas'd the Labours of the toilet-Care*: cf. 'And the long Labours of the *Toilette* cease' (Pope, *Rape of the Lock*, III. 24; Pope, *Twickenham*, II, 171).

And turning to a Mirror-Fountain near,
Sigh'd to her-self, and own'd the Nymph more fair.
Then to her Bow'r asham'd, incens'd, She ran,
Vex'd to the Soul, and private thus began.

'Vain are my Schemes, and frustrate then my Care,
'Or to molest or part this envy'd Pair;
'Can I the Queen submit, debas'd, to prove
'I'm but the second Beauty of the Grove?
'Must I convince the Prince with Justice, He
'Prefer's the fairer Eucharis to Me?
'Heart-piercing Thought! – then what remaining Means,
'To dash their Joy, or mitigate my Pains?
'Be Mentor found, and be my last Command,
'To force the Traytor to his native Land:
'Alas! I rave; nor ever could endure,
'The painfull Safety of that dreaded Cure.
'If it be Fate, that he desert this Shore;
'(The Thought is Madness!) e'er that cursed Hour,
'In Mercy crush me with thy Thunder Jove,
'Nor Heav'n I ask, tis Heav'n enough to prove
'Rest from the Torments of despairing Love.

'What Course oh! Venus! shall thy Victim take?
'Twas You who urg'd me on, and now forsake.
'How treach'rous was thy Gift, thy Pois'nous Boy?
'Source of my Sorrow, Bane of all my Joy.
'In malice still delight's the cruel God,
'Who rules his Subjects with an Iron-Rod;
'Who still electing Wretches in his Train,
'Scarce sees one happy Slave in all his Reign;
'But counts his Triumphs by his Vot'rys' Cares,
'Fond of their Woes, exulting in their Tears.

'Happy that Wretch who call's his Life his own,
'And lay's at Will the painfull Burden down:[97]

97. *And lay's at Will the painfull Burden down*: for an analysis of this important theme in Hervey's writing, see Overton, 'Death and Futurity'. The sentiment is present at this point in Fénelon.

'I, curs'd with God-head, am condemn'd to bear
'The deathless Agonys of long Despair.
'Yet Vengeance still is mine;[98] nor will I lose
'That only ease permitted to my Woes;
'Dye then, base youth! and lett thy Blood attone
'The joynt Offences of the Sire and Son.
'But whither would my Rage? – no Fault is thine,
'Suppose thy Love a Fault, 'tis only mine;
'I to thy Breast convey'd the fatal Flame,
'Averse to Vice, and guiltless here you came;
'Virtue's strict Rules did all thy Actions grace,
'And Innocence sat smiling in thy Face;
''Twas I that charming Innocence betray'd,
'And call'd a vile Seducer to my Aid;
'Curs'd be his Aid, and curs'd my own design,
'I kept thee here; would I had kept thee mine!
'In vain I wish; impossible to be,
'Allready art thou gone and dead to Me:
'Be gone to Eucha'ris too, depart, depart;
'And leave the Body 'though you take the Heart.
'Be then this only wise, my last, Decree;
''Tis but this Struggle and Calypso's free.'

She say'd, nor taking Leisure to repent,
Haste in her Steps, to Mentor furious went:
Him, all his Cares revolving in his Breast,
Pensive She found, and thus with warmth addresst.

'Say, is it thus, inactive, and unjust,
'You execute your vast, Important Trust?
'Was it to Mentor, or Calypso's Care,
'Penelope consign'd Ulisses' Heir?
'Unhappy Prince! thy slothfull Guardian sleep's;
'Whilst constant Vigills thy Destroyer keep's:
'Ev'n now the vanquish'd Youth is forc'd to yield,
'And at this Crisis Mentor quitt's the Field.

98. *Vengeance still is mine*: cf., by contrast, 'Vengeance is mine; I will repay, saith the Lord' (Romans 12: 19).

'But haste, assist, avert th'impending Blow;
'Oppose thy Art, and snatch him from the Foe.

'In the remoter Part of yonder Glade,
'Behold that aged Forest's lofty Head!
'Tall, well-grown Poplars there arise so high,
'Their Tops seem little to the cheated Eye.
'Ulisses there that fatal Vessel made,
'Which from these widdow'd Arms th' Ingrate convey'd.
'Close by it's Limmits in a Cave you'll find,
'Cordage and Oars, and Sails to catch the Wind;
'Hatchetts, and ev'ry needfull Tool, with Nails,
'To carve the wood-work and to dress the Sails;
'Anchor's are there, or sturdy Ropes to moor
'The finish'd Vessel to the neigh'bring Shore.
'But to your Task; pause not to make reply
'Here what I will is Fate; obey or dye.'

She ceas'd: and wav'ring in unfirm Resolves,
Oft in her Mind this hated Choice revolves;
With Him whom more than Life she loves to part,
Or keep him harbour'd in a Rival's Heart.

Mentor exulting sought th' appointed Place,
Nor lost a moment in his eager Pace.
He gain'd the Grove, the Cave he search'd around,
The Trees he fell'd, the wanted Tackling found.
Expert he wrought, for e'er the dusk of Night,
The Ship was rig'd, and ready for their Flight.
Small time Minerva, Queen of Arts requires,
Perfection follows on the Maid's desires.

Meantime, uninterrupted at the Chace,
(How sweet the Raptures of a stoll'n Embrace!)
The am'rous Youth his willing Nymph enjoy'd,
And richest Love the tender Hours employ'd:[99]
This fear'd Calypso, and with jealous Care,

99. *Meantime … richest Love the tender Hours employ'd*: Hervey allows the lovers pleasures not granted by Fénelon and omits Eucharis' criticism of Mentor (*Les Avantures* (Tonson), VII. 134–5).

Hast's to divert the joys she wish'd to share:
Disorder'd to the Chace, with Spleen, she flys,
And mark'd their Commerce with vindictive Eyes:
Each word, each Motion, the sharp Spy perciev'd,
Not the mute Language of their Looks deciev'd.
In vain with swiftness to elude her Sight,
They quitt the Crew, and urge a devious Flight;
To Brake or Mead where-e'er they bend their way,
As eager Faulcons press the flying Prey;
So close, Calypso, or to Brake, or Mead,
Dogg's at each Turn, or follows where they lead.
Anxious for Mentor's Progress, still the Dame
Endeavour's there to force the hunted Game:
From far she hear's the Ax, and at each Stroke,
The Queen repentant like the Timber shook.

Now his Meridian past, the Pow'r of Day,
O'er all the Isle obliquely Dart's his Ray;[100]
With ruddy Light allready glows the West,
And ev'ry Shaddow lengthen's tow'rd the East:
When the weak Stag no longer could withstand
The close pursuit of the Dianian Band;
Straining, half-breathless, with a fainter Bound,
He toil's along, and lag's upon the Ground:
His Strength decay'd, he knew to trust his Life,
To Bay were vain, and shun'd th' unequal Strife.
His Hope was now a Sanctuary to prove,
In the known Covert of the neighb'ring Grove:
When from the Prince's Arm a deathfull Dart,
Unerring flew and quiver'd in his Heart.[101]

100. *Now his Meridian past, the Pow'r of Day . . . obliquely Dart's his Ray*: cf. 'Mean while declining from the Noon of Day, | The Sun obliquely shoots his burning Ray' (Pope, *Rape of the Lock*, III. 19–20; Pope, *Twickenham*, II, 170).

101. *Now his Meridian past . . . quiver'd in his Heart*: Hervey adds the evocation of the evening and the dying stag. In the *Aeneid*, Prince Ascanius kills Sylvia's pet stag (VII. 483–99 (Loeb, II, 34–6)); Hervey is even more sympathetic to the animal than Virgil is.

By this the Hunters to the Wood were brought,
Where all the Day the god-like Mentor wrought.
But he, his Task perform'd, had left the Shore,
And sought refreshment in the distant Bow'r;
Perhaps the healing Bath, or cordial Bowl,
Crown'd with the Juice that lifts the fainting Soul.
The Ship compleatly built Calypso view'd;
Straight all her Limbs a clammy Fear bedew'd;
With crimson Blush her Cheeks no longer glow,
And Tears, the ease of Grief, forgett to flow;
Darkness like Death o'erspread's her swimming Eyes,
Nor Breath remain'd but what supply'd her Sighs.
A livid Paleness did her Looks invade,
A thousand Symptoms inward Grief betray'd:
Her tott'ring Knees refuse to bear their Weight,
And sunk upon the flow'ry Turf she sate:
Straight to support her ran each frighted Maid,
Amid the rest her Rival offer'd Aid;
The proffer'd Aid, resenting she deny'd,
And dash'd with Rage th unwellcome Hand aside.
These Transports fear'd the Prince (their cause unknown)
But fear'd for Euch'ris Danger, not his own.
On what Design the fatal Ship was there,
Impatience prompted, and he long'd to hear:
Awhile the curious Question he suppress'd,
Then thus the scarce recover'd Queen address'd.

'For whom's the Vessel moor'd to yonder Ground?
'The Owner who? and to what Country bound?'

At first the Goddess, puzzled to reply,
Knew not or what to own, or what deny;
At length (resolv'd to cloak the Truth) she say'd,

'For Mentor, and by my Command 'twas made,
'Mentor remov'd, Telemachus is free,
'Unenvy'd mayst thou live and reign with me;
'He jealous watch'd thee with too strict an Eye,
'A seeming Guardian but a latent Spy.'

'Mentor forsake me!' (quick the Youth reply'd)
'Forbid it Heav'n;' (he wept and weeping sigh'd)
'Depriv'd of him, ah! what remain's for me?
'All I have left my Eucharis is Thee.'

From a full Heart unweigh'd this Answer broke,
Him-self too late condemn'd the Words he'd spoke.
Kindles at this anew Calypso's Rage,
Her Eyes gleam dreadfull, and her Frowns presage
Impending Ill: as when a Storm is nigh,
The Clouds first gather in the low'ring Sky,
Then roll the Thunders, and the Light'nings fly.
Thus whilst the Goddess with Resentment fir'd;
The blushing Nymph with conscious Shame retir'd;
Trembling, dismay'd, receedes behind the rest;
Droop'd her declining Head, and heav'd her Breast.
She dreads the weight of irritated Pow'r,
And apprehensive Tears the Cause deplore:
Yet to the inmost Corners of her Heart,
The faithfull Words a mingled joy impart.
But unrestrain'd, the madd'ning Queen no more
The Mask of Patience, on her Anger wore;
Nor wise Deceit, nor decent Pride controul;
Unloos'd was all the Fury of her Soul:
So headlong Streams, check'd in their rapid Course,
The Dam born down, rush with redoubled Force.
They roar, they foam, regardless of all bound,
And wander, diverse, o'er the Meads around.
'Tis thus the Passions of Despair and Love,
The Guard of Reason broke, the Goddess move.
Whilst ranging through the Fields unguided stray,
Her heedless Feet, and urge a casual way.[102]
Still on her Steps attend the frighted Train
And devious through the Woods the Bow'r they gain.

102. *urge a casual way*: at this point Fénelon compares Calypso to a lioness that has lost her young; Hervey translated the passage (*Les Avantures* (Tonson), VII. 136) but deleted the couplet in his manuscript.

There Mentor, fast beside the Myrtle-Gate,
Upon a purple Bank of Violets sate;
Hot with the toilsome Labours of the Noon,
H' enjoy'd the Cool of the declining Sun;
The eastern Shades forbid the baffled Beams,
The Breezes fan him from the passing Streams.[103]
When thus, the Goddess with a threat'ning Look,
The Sage, accosted and opprobrious, spoke.

'Hence, impious Strangers! from this sacred Shore,
'Hence, where Calypso ne'er may see you more.
'Oh! that you both had perish'd in the Seas,
'Nor found that Safety which has cost my Peace.
'Thou grey-hair'd Villain, with a specious Tongue,
'Whom Age has taught to doe deliberate Wrong.
'Far from my Sight thy stubborn Charge convey,
'Nor urge my Fury by the least delay,
'Or if thou dost, thy folly on thy Head;[104]
'Be one short Hour alone thy Flight delay'd,
'Too late repentant shall yee both deplore
'That Insolence which brav'd a Goddess Pow'r;
'For both shall dye; in vain thy hoary Hairs
'Shall Mercy plead, in vain thy tender Years:
'Nor Age shall pity move, nor Beauty charm,
'When Vengeance lifts, and justice guides my Arm.
'Perhaps thy Death my Torments may remove,
'My Rage at least appeas'd, if not my Love;
'Thy Euch'ris too shall see the horrid Deed,
'And at the Lover's Wounds the Mistress bleed;
'To root her Image from thy mangled Heart,

103. *beside the Myrtle-Gate ... the passing Streams*: this characteristic passage of natural description is added by Hervey.

104. *thy folly on thy Head*: cf. 'Lett their Folly fall on their own Head, & their Wickedness on their own Pate' in Hervey's letter to Stephen Fox on 25 December 1731 when he had discovered Anne Vane and the Prince of Wales's deception of him (Halsband, p. 129); and ''Twas thy own fault, thy folly's on thy head', Poem 14 'The Answer to Mr Hammond to Miss Dashwood' (line 35).

'I'll probe around and stab through ev'ry Part:
'Just at the Ebb of thy departing Breath,
'Just in the latest Agonys of Death,
'With cordial Malice shall I see thy Eyes,
'Rowl round aghast, and hear thy dying Sighs;
'Hear them in vain implore just Heav'n's Relief,
'And see my hated Rival dye with Grief.
'Save then thy-self, haste urge thy instant Flight,
'And take thy lov'd – thy hated Image from my Sight.
'Hear Heav'n, and Earth! a solem Oath I take,
'By sacred Styx! inviolable Lake![105]
'(An Oath which makes the World's great Thund'rer shake,)
'By Pray'rs, by Threats, by Promises, no more
'To stop thy Progress to thy native Shore.
'Yet hear me Prince; my lab'ring Bosome glow's
'With Rage prophetick of thy future Woes:
'Tho now thy Life a transient safety find,
'Hope not Repose, nor think a Calm behind:
'Thy Sorrows but begin, and late shall end,
'New Dangers threaten, and new Cares attend:
'Thee, the stern God, (whose wide-extended Sway,
'All Ocean own's and all the Winds obey)
'Pursues implacable with stedfast Hate;[106]
'And injur'd Venus importunes thy Fate.
'To Storms expos'd, thou shalt regrett the Aid
'With fruitless Tears, thy Folly once betray'd;
'Thy Sire too lives; whom vainly thou shalt see,
'Unknown to Him, and he unknown to Thee:
'Nor shalt thou joyn him on thy native Land,
'(So Jove and Fate unchangeable command)
''Till adverse Stars on that ungratefull Head,
'All their Variety of Plagues have shed.

105. *By sacred Styx! inviolable Lake*: after enjoying the support of its goddess in the war with the Titans, Zeus agreed that the oaths of the gods should be taken on the Styx.

106. *the stern God . . . stedfast Hate*: the god is Neptune; *stedfast hate* occurs in book I, line 138, for Telemachus' fate is to resemble Ulysses'.

'Take then my last Adieu: to Heav'n I leave
'My just Revenge; which if the Gods will give,
'These are my Pray'rs; Such torments follow thee,
'(I ask no more) as thou hast left with me,'
She say'd: but soon the Resolution past,
Still some new Transport contradict's the last:
Revenge, and Love, and Pride, by turns oppress'd;
And Thoughts like these lay rowling in her Breast.
"Yet lett him stay, the dear, the cruel Youth!
"Time yet may win him, and persisting Truth;
"His Fault one Day, tho' late, he may percieve;
"Nor God-head nor a Crown can Euch'ris give."
Then black reflexion on the Oath she took,
Revolves averse; her Soul with Horror shook;
Like fiery Meteors rowl'd her glaring Eyes,
On ev'ry Limb cold Sweat enfeebling lyes.
Fear siez'd Ulisses' Son; nor passed unseen
His inmost Thoughts; for jealous Eyes are keen.
But this contributes to enhance her Care;
Each motion Madness, and each Look Despair.
As the wild Bacchanals, with wine inspir'd,
By Furys, and nocturnal Orgies fir'd,
With yelling Din, and hideous howling Crys,
Traverse the Plains, and rend the Passive Skys,
Till in loud Ecchoes Rhodopé reply's.[107]
So through the joyless Paths of well-known Groves,
A Jav'lin in her Hand Calypso rove's;
Calling her Nymphs to take her frantick Way,
Denouncing Death to all who disobey;
And straight the Nymphs, intimidated all,
Around her crowd, and follow at her Call:
Ev'n weeping Euch'ris too, all pale with fear,
Advances slow, and linger's in the Rear:
But as her Feet reluctant onward move,

107. *the wild Bacchanals . . . in loud Ecchoes Rhodopé reply's*: Hervey refers again to the Orpheus myth, the Rhodope mountains being in Thrace and Orpheus' death at the hand of Thracian women. See book I, note 42.

Her Eyes reverted dwell on him they love.
Through Sorrow's Veil, she shine's with added Grace,
While Tears chase Tears along her dewy Face:
Nor dared the Nymph to speak her last Farewell,
Yet speaking Looks her inward Meaning tell:
More tenderly than words they seem'd to say,
    "Vain be those orders which forbid thy Stay,
    "Think on our Loves, my Rival's Pow'r defy,
    "And fear like me to part, but not to dye."[108]
As fading Stars insensibly decay,
And vanish, gradual, at the Dawn of Day;
So by minute Degrees she glides away.
Whilst motionless the Youth, with eager Care,
And straining Eyes, hangs on the fleeting Fair.
Allready now the Beautys of her Face,
Beyond his Ken, in vain he try'd to trace:
Yet still her Noble Mien, her lengthy Hair,
And ample Robes, that float upheld in Air,
Engross his Eyes, conspicuous from afar.
Now, as he lost the latest Glimpse of all
He thought, because he wish'd, he heard her call:[109]
But vainly list'ning to the fancy'd Sound,
Prone fell the Youth a lifeless Lump to Ground.

    Mentor deplor'd these transports of Despair,
And gently rais'd him with paternal Care;
His Temples chaf'd, and by celestial Art,
With circulating Life new-warm'd his Heart.
With aged Arms the drooping Youth he press'd,
In all the warmth of Friendship, to his Breast:
Prudent he cheer'd, nor flatter'd him in Ill,
But arm'd his Reason to oppose his Will.
Kindly severe, the strongest Terms he us'd,
And Wisdom, God-like, through his Soul defus'd;

108. *Vain be those orders ... but not to dye*: Hervey adds these thoughts, which parallel Calypso's at lines 319–22.

109. *Beyond his Ken ... he heard her call*: Hervey brings this passage forward in the narrative from its place in the interview with Mentor (*Les Avantures* (Tonson), VII. 140).

To point out Safety in unwellcome Truth,
And aid the immaturity of Youth.

'Belov'd of Heav'n' (He add's) 'How mild is Fate,
'When present Ills our future Good create?
'Such is thy Lott; those Tryals doom'd to prove,
'Which the kind Gods inflict on Men they love:
'Since in our weakness and our Frailty known,
'Our Strength is plac'd, our Way to Virtue shown;
'He who has felt, and dreads his Passion's Force;
'Through the known Shelves, with Caution steer's his Course:
'Still diffident, self-conscious, and prepar'd,
'Virtue's allarm'd, and Reason on her Guard.
'Who then distrust's him-self is only wise,
'And safe who fear's his Foe, not who defy's.
'The Gods have led thee to the Mountain's Brow,
'Have shown the dreadfull Precipice below,
'And sav'd thee from the Fall; lett this suffice,
'To prove what ask'd the Wittness of thy Eyes;
'Hadst thou not seen, thou never hadst believ'd,
'By treach'rous Love, how many are decieved:
'In vain had Prudence, or had Wisdom told,
'What bitter Seeds his golden Fruits infold;
'All Joy he seem's, nor congruent with Pain,
'The Loves the Smiles the Graces in his Train;
'Fatal Allurements! these thy Heart betray'd,
'The willing Victim of his Treach'ry made:
'Fond of the charming Road, you run on Fate,
'His Arts assisted, and indulg'd the Cheat:
'Now Death's thy wish; to smooth the raging Pains
'Of fell Despair, that only Hope remain's:
'Infernal Furys have the Queen possess'd,
'And all their Snakes lye hissing in her Breast.
'Whilst such the Woes her Eucharis sustain's,
'That Death him-self assail's with milder Pains.
'These are thy Triumphs, Love! and this, thy Art;
'But hast, my Prince! to extricate your Heart,
'Assert your-self, and act a manly Part:

'Collect your Courage, all your Force employ;
'To Virtue turn, and fly pernicious Joy.'

To whom the Prince: 'Oh! tis a painfull Part;
'To combate nature, and to wean the Heart;
'When the whole Soul by habitt long betray'd,
'Lean's with acquainted fondness to the Maid.
'But thou forget'st, (or hap'ly never knew)
'How hard a Youthfull ardour to subdue:
'Thee, Reason sway'd, and easyly represst
'The weaker Passions in thy even Breast:
'Nor canst thou guess how painfull to remove,
'And break the Cement of commutual Love.[110]

'Yet is it vain I see to urge my Stay,
'Fate and the Gods command, and I obey.
'Too rash Calypso's Oath has left no Room
'To hope I can evade my cruel Doom;
'Yet e'er I goe this humble Boon I crave,
'To see my Love and take eternal Leave.
'Oh! stay! by Friendship I adjure thee stay;
'One Hour, (tis a short Space) one Hour delay;
'That I may tell her,– "Tis the Gods my Fair!
"(Who jealous of those joys I tasted here)
"Force me away; yet by those Gods I swear,
"Whilst the red Stream of Life shall warm this Heart,
"No time, no Change, shall alienate thy Part";
'And sure Calypso might allow me this,
'Such Pain is mingled with the transient Bliss.
'Nor call that Love which Gratitude must claim,
'That tepid remnant of extinguish'd Flame:
'My quiet Heart no longer Beauty charm's,
''Tis Honour prompt's, and Friendship only warms;
'Grant then my Father! Friend! this just Request;
'Or instant plunge thy Dagger in my Breast.'

110. *To whom the Prince . . . break the Cement of commutual Love*: this paragraph, in which Telemachus suggests Mentor's ignorance of his feelings, is Hervey's addition.

So plead's the Youth, whilst Mentor still diswades,
(Each Argument Minerva's Skill evades.)

'Unhappy Prince!' (he cry'd) 'No more I blame:
'These Cares my Pity not my Anger claim.
'Alas! not Gratitude this Thought inspires,
'Tis Love still reigning in untam'd Desires;
'No lambent Warmth, but fierce resistless Fires;
'Still is your Heart enslav'd, and still the same
'That Passion which you gloss with Friendship's Name.
'Call not these warnings of your Friend unkind;
'I chide you not as false, but mourn as blind:
'What you have urg'd, too gladly you believe,
'Nor only Mentor, but your-self decieve:
'Lost to your-self, you ignorantly love,
'Nor feel the subtle Chains whose Force you prove.
'In Feavers, thus, delirious Wretches boast
'Their Health, and Madmen, Reason lost.

'But oh! dear Youth! yet listen to my Pray'r,
'Decline this Tryal, and her Sight forbear;
'The Foe unequal 'tis allowed to fear.
'By Heav'n, my Prince! if you relapse I dye;
'Say, can you yet your Mentor's Suit deny?
'Doubt you my Love or aid? See, down my Cheek,
'Tears Stream in Fondness o'er thee whilst I speak,
'Prove these my Love; my Aid allready prov'd,
'By all those Ills my Counsells have remov'd:
'In vain if now you fall: That I could tell
'What Doubts, what Fears, what Agonys I feel,
'Whilst thus I plead! what I have felt, Heav'n knows;
'(Ev'n She who bore thee, in her sharpest Throes,
'Groan'd underneath the weight of lighter Woes.)
'When forc'd thy Conduct, silent, to deplore,
'I dared remonstrate, or diswade no more.
'Watch'd by the jealous Queen's observant Eyes,
'I drank my Tears, and swell'd with stifled Sighs:
'Yet still I wish'd, thy Fault by thee perciev'd,

'(So much I wish'd it, that I half believ'd.)
'Thou wouldst return to Virtue and to Me:
'Oh! might these Eyes that dear Conversion see!
'Contented would they close in endless Shade,
'My joys compleat, my Sorrows all repay'd.
'Come then my Prince! my Son! (for sure that Name,
'A Father's Love, a Father's Care may claim.)
'Restore the Fugitive these Tears deplore,
'And to him-self Telemachus restore.'

With Mentor's Voice, thus spoke the Heav'nly Maid;
And as she spoke, invisible, she spread
Her sacred Ægis o'er his favour'd Head.
The influence divine his Soul avow'd,
His Heart, dilated, with new Courage glow'd.
When, half-consenting to superior Pow'r,
The secret Goddess lead's him tow'rd the Shore.

Meantime in gloomy Groves Calypso mourn's;
Resentment ebbs, and fluctuate Love return's.
Cupid approach'd with well dissembled Fears,
Swol'n with forc'd Sighs, and wett with bidden Tears.
Her flutt'ring Heart his painfull Presence own'd.
And bled anew at ev'ry widen'd wound,
Whilst thus submiss, the little Flatt'rer spoke,
And Sobs, pathetick, ev'ry Accent broke.

'These Ills inflicted, beauteous Queen! by me,
'The Gods can tell, how penitent I see.
'By Pity mov'd an equal Part I bear,
'And just I should, who minister'd thy Care.
'Yet let the kneeling Penitent find Grace;
'Yet let the counsells of a God find place;
'With tame forbearance weep your Wrongs no more;
'Nor let a feeble Mortal brave your Pow'r;
'Ah! yet detain him on Ogygia's Shore!
'His Liberty, his Life is in your Hand,
'Assume the Queen; determine and command.'

He ceas'd: and as the Goddess thus reply's;
Reproachfull Anger darted from her Eyes.
'Too far I've trusted, and too far believ'd,
'Nor will I listen to be twice deciev'd.
''Twas thy false Arts first broke my settled Peace,
'I liv'd if not in Joy at least in Ease:
'Again thou wouldst betray; and mock my Grief,
'With Hopes fallacious of a vain Relief.
'Have I not sworn to stay his Flight no more?
'By sacred Styx, revered by Jove, I swore;
'That sole Restriction on his boundless Pow'r.'

'If that be all,' (the God exulting cry's
And as he spoke he dry'd his watry Eyes.)
'No Vow has Cupid, or your Virgins made,
'Be neuter You; and lett your Vassals aid:
'My-self this Moment will their Thoughts inspire;
'The next yon Vessel shall consume in Fire.
'How will you then repentant bless my Name?
'And how shall baffled Mentor curse the Flame?'

These Schemes propos'd by sanguine Cupid's Art,
A transient Comfort to the Fair impart.
As Breezes skimming o'er a curling Brook,
With gratefull Cool, revive a fainting Flock,
That parch'd in Summer by the Noon-tide Heat,
Pant on the Margin, drench'd in scalding Sweat.
So sooth'd these Words the burning Lover's Care,
So lull'd awhile the raging of Despair:
Grief grew serene and soften'd in her Face,
And for a Moment ev'n her Heart knew Peace.

Wing'd by the Hopes of Conquest Cupid flys
To find the Nymphs, and finding thus he cry's.

'Why stand yee musing thus, inactive here?
'The useless Images of mean Despair;
'When Aid is wanted, and Occasion fair?

'Yon anchor'd Bark lett instant Flames devour;[111]
'The Prince shall still be Captive to your Pow'r.'

And straight a lighted Torch each Nymph prepares;
Impetuous Euch'ris in the Van appear's:
Whilst to the Shore in horrid Ranks they fly,
And all at once the shining Bane apply.
The Ship, of unresisting Timber made,
With Pitch bedawb'd, with Rosin thick o'er-lay'd,
(Tind'ry, combustable Materials all;)
Catch'd it's bright Ruin, and indulg'd it's Fall.
In sable Sheets the curling Smoaks arise,
And streak'd with ruddy Flames ascend the Skys.
Planks, Sails and Masts promiscuously pertake,
In glowing Heaps convolv'd, a common Wreck.
Auster[112] blew fierce, the Fires and Auster roar,
Upon his wings the flaming Brands he bore,
And strew'd the sparkling Fragments on the Shore.

This, from a Rock, whose Foot the Ocean laves,
Whose craggy Brow o'er-hang's the nether Waves:
The captive Pair with diff'ring Hearts beheld
With Sorrow this, and that with Pleasure fill'd.
New rising-Hopes the Lover's Soul dilate,
It burn's anew with unabated Heat:
As on a glowing Pile of smother'd Fire,
If sudden Gusts it's latent rage inspire;
The Ashes from the surface blown away,
Again the Coals emit a living Ray,
Emergent blaze, and emulate the Day.
So did this Sight the Prince's Passions move,
And fan the reliques of reviving Love.
When to prevent the Evils might ensue,
Him headlong from the Rock his Guardian threw;

111. *lett instant Flames devour*: the episode parallels the attempted burning of the ships by the women at Juno's behest in *Aeneid*, V. 623–63 (Loeb, I, 514–16).

112. *Auster*: the south wind.

And instant follow'd: nor unweigh'd he try'd
The desp'rate Cure; for on the purple Tide,
Far as the bounded Ken of mortal Eyes
Distinct could reach, an anchor'd Bark he spy's;
(None nearer came; no Pilot dar'd explore
This inaccessible, forbidden Shore.)
Thither he purpos'd to direct his Course,
And Stem the Torrent with a manly Force.
But senseless now, and half depriv'd of Breath,
The sinking Youth beheld the Gates of Death:
When ready Mentor's interposing Aid,
Chas'd from his closing Eyes the settling Shade.
Stunn'd by the rapid fall, oppress'd, and weak,
Replete with Brine, he bore him on his Back;
One Hand the Youth sustaind, one dash'd aside
The thronging Billows, as he rode the Tide;
Securely thus the distant Ship they gain,
The friendly Sailors lift 'em from the Main.

Meantime the baffl'd Nymphs, in wild Despair,
Beat their soft Breasts, and rend their flowing Hair.
Like Sheep dispers'd by Wolves in Search of Prey,
They range the Field and o'er the Mountains stray.

Not so abandon'd Euch'ris complains,
But fix'd in silent, solemn Grief remain's,
Whilst freezing Horror thrill's through all her Veins.
So look'd proud Niobe, her Children slain,
By vengefull Phoebus on the Theban Plain;
When many a Life her impious Vaunts attone,
And all her Body stiffen'd into Stone.[113]

Cupid, desponding on this last Defeat,
Avoid's reproaches by a prompt Retreat:

113. *Not so abandon'd Euch'ris … her Body stiffen'd into Stone*: Niobe, daughter of Tantalus and Amphion, boasted to Latona that she had more children than she did. As a consequence the children were slain by Apollo and Diana, and Niobe wept until she turned to stone. Fénelon, his interest being in Telemachus' political development, has nothing to say about Eucharis at this point.

On silken wings he quitt's th' Ogygian Isle,
Sublime he soar's, and makes to Ida's Hill.

Enrag'd Calypso curs'd the Traytor Love,
And like a Lyon bellowing through the Grove,
Call'd on the Prince; her Griefs to Madness rise,
And distant Hills reverberate her Crys.

'Curs'd be the Day on which he came' (she say'd)
'But doubly curs'd the Day on which he fled:
'Where-e'er he turn's lett Clouds deform the Sky;
'Lett Thunders rowl, and blasting Light'nings fly.
Oh! may the Climate where the Wretch shall dwell,
Be fill'd with Plagues, and prove an Earthly Hell!
May the soft Change of Seasons ne'er appear,
But in eternal Winter rowl the Year!
Lett Desolation, Famine, waste the Land,
Red with the Slaughters of some Tyrants Hand.
And thou, great God! Oceanus! give Ear!
Propitious listen to thy Daughter's Pray'r!
If e'er a Fathers fondness warm'd thy Heart,
Assert my Cause; and act a Father's Part:
Revenge, Revenge, I ask, the Pow'r is thine;
No Rest allow to him who poison'd mine;
Tho' safe his Life by partial Jove's Decree,
Long hold him wand'ring on the stormy Sea.
And lett the Villain's conscious Guilt declare
These Ills the Vengeance of Calypso's Care.'[114]

The End.

114. *Curs'd be the Day . . . Vengeance of Calypso's Care*: Fénelon does not share Hervey's focus on Calypso and gives her no words.

# 66 Agrippina, a Tragedy

***Source.*** British Library, MS Egerton 3787: 'John, 2nd Baron Hervey: "Agrippina, a Tragedy", etc.; *circa* 1709–1744. Hervey's unpublished play forms the main text in a notebook of miscellaneous material that is transcribed in a single unidentified hand. Armorial bookplate (f. ii), after 1756, of the Earl of Ilchester inside front cover.' The play is the fifth and most substantial item in a leather-bound quarto volume. The preceding items are two letters, followed by two items concerning the consecration of a plate for the sacrament in St Margaret's Church, Queen Charlton, Somerset. The first letter is from Dr Thomas Burnet to the Countess of Hertford on the death of her son in 1744; the second her reply (printed in the *Gentleman's Magazine*, July 1762). Frances Seymour (*née* Thynne; 1699–1754), Duchess of Somerset from 1748, was lady of the bedchamber to Caroline (Princess of Wales and later Queen). A poet, letter writer and literary patron, she would have played an important role in the cultural life of the court. The survival of only one copy of the play in the hand of an amanuensis suggests that the material may have been regarded as sensitive because of its relation to the Queen and the Prince of Wales.

***Complementary manuscript sources.*** None known.

***Complementary print sources.*** None known.

***Attribution.*** On the recto of the leaf before the first page of text, in the hand of the transcriber, appears 'This Play was Written by ~~Lord~~ H~~ervey~~', with all the letters of the name struck through, except the 'H'. Horace Walpole in *A Catalogue of the Royal and Noble Authors of England*, says, 'Lord Hervey left several other works in prose and verse in manuscript, particularly "Agrippina, a Tragedy in rhyme"' (II, 142–3). The play incorporates some lines from Hervey's other verse.

***Context and date.*** In a letter to Henry Fox of 4 September 1736, Hervey says he has just finished writing *Aceronia*, and is pleased it has continued to amuse the Foxes at Redlynch after he has left (BL Add. MS 51396 f. 162r). Aceronia is Agrippina's confidante in Hervey's play and probably provided an alternative title for the work, for in a letter to Henry Fox a few days later, 16 September 1736, Hervey says, 'I will get *Agrippina* copied, and send it to you as soon as I return. I desire you will send me your remarks upon it, and your corrections. If you do not; when I am fitter to correct my own faults than I find myself at present, I will correct it myself' (Ilchester, p. 250). Hervey was re-engaged with the play, however, in the summer of the following year, when he wrote to Stephen Fox on 25 June 1737: 'Aceronia you see has made my thoughts so naturally jingle into Rhyme, that I find it is as Difficult to write a letter in plain Prose as a Dancing-Master does to walk into a Room' (BL Add. MS 51345, ff. 77v–78r). It may be that Hervey, seeing something of himself in the role of Aceronia, originally gave her a larger part in the play; as it is, her death, a case of mistaken identity, prefigures that of the Empress.

These dates confirm that the play belongs to a period in Hervey's relations with the Queen when she was compared to Agrippina, and Frederick, Prince of Wales, to the Emperor Nero. In *Some Materials towards Memoirs of the Reign of King George II*, Hervey follows the entry for 28 October 1737 with an extended parallel of the characters of Frederick and Nero: 'The character of Frederick, Prince of Wales, and parallel between his and that of Nero; being part of a separate work entitled "Characters of the Present Royal Family"' (Sedgwick, III, 858–75). The piece was composed, Hervey tells us, at the wish of Queen Caroline, who was willing to be compared with Nero's mother, Agrippina, and the 'Characters' was read to her and Princess Caroline so often, Hervey says, that 'the writer grew more tired of reciting his own work than his auditors of hearing it' (Sedgwick, III, 858). The 'Characters', then, encapsulated the critique of Frederick that had been worked out more subtly in the play written over the previous eighteen months. Its boldness is indicated by the fact that the equivalent pages were removed from the original manuscript of the *Memoirs*; as a note from the first Marquess of Bristol explains, they were 'burnt Nov. 28, 1824. Bristol' (Sedgwick, III, 857, n. 1).

Hervey had earlier been on intimate terms with Frederick. The precise nature of their relationship is difficult to determine. As Hannah Smith and Stephen Taylor point out in an important article, Hervey three times in 1731 referred to himself in letters to the Prince as Hephaestion to his Alexander ('Hephaestion and Alexander: Lord Hervey, Frederick, Prince of Wales, and the Royal Favourite in the 1730s', *English Historical Review*, 124, no. 507 (2009), 283–312 (289)). In November 1731, when he sent him Poem 77, 'For if in Richmond-Morning-Walk', he referred to himself as Pylades ('Pilade'). Both the relation between Hephaestion and Alexander and that between Pylades and Orestes typify devoted friendship, but both could also carry sexual implications. In particular, the love between Pylades and Orestes (in which the former assists the latter in the murder of his mother) has erotic force in Pseudo-Lucian's *Amores*, where they exchange roles. Hervey, if not the Prince, would have been aware of these resonances. However, as Sedgwick explains in a perceptive discussion in his edition of *Some Materials*, in December that year relations cooled. By March 1732, Anne Vane had become the Prince's mistress, replacing Hervey in the Prince's affections, just as the Prince had replaced Hervey in hers. When Hervey sent her a letter threatening to expose her past, the Prince was told and Hervey consequently experienced universal reprobation.

Exile from the Prince's court made it easier for Hervey to sympathise with the King and Queen's growing disapproval of Frederick's behaviour, particularly his attempt to increase his allowance through parliamentary action and his removal of the Princess of Wales from Hampton Court while she was in labour. Debate about the Prince's character grew more intense in December 1736, when it seemed possible that the King had died at sea, returning from Hanover. Hervey had conversations with Walpole and with the Queen in which the Prince's likely behaviour as king, particularly towards his mother, was debated (Sedgwick, II, 625–33). The play may reflect these anxious attempts to imagine the Prince in power. In his conversations Hervey was inclined to predict the new King's reliance on his mother's advice, but 'Agrippina' explores what happens when a period of maternal guidance comes to an end. It is clear from the letters to the Fox brothers that it was being written during this period of anxiety; what is less clear is when the play was finished and whether it was shown to the Queen. She died on 20 November 1737.

***Textual commentary.*** The literary model for Hervey's play was Racine's *Britannicus* (1669). *Some Materials* shows Hervey and Queen Caroline had detailed knowledge of the play. Hervey quotes a couplet from it early in the memoirs, not long after the accession of George II:

> Tous ces présens, hélas! irritent mon dépit,
> Je vois mes honneurs croître, et tomber mon credit.
>
> (Sedgwick, I, 39)

In the Oxford World's Classics version (*Britannicus, Phaedra, and Athalia*, 1987), C. H. Sisson translates:

> I resent all these shows.
> I see my honours rise, my credit fall. (I. 1. 92–3)

The words are the Empress Agrippina's, though here applied amusingly by Hervey to Spencer Compton, raised to the Lords because he was unfit to be Prime Minister. Hervey had earlier translated the couplet (Poem 59) in a letter to his mother, Lady Bristol, dated 26 December [1727]:

> These empty Titles more my Anger raise
> For whilst my Honours grow my Pow'r decay's.

But later in *Some Materials* (17 March 1733) Agrippina's words are applied directly to Queen Caroline, who recognises the allusion and develops the parallel. The Queen had shown Hervey how a remark made by Lord Carteret in the House of Lords might have been rebutted:

> Lord Hervey said he was sorry none of her servants were so capable of answering Lord Carteret on this part of French history as he found Her Majesty would have been; and wished she had been present, to have given any of them this hint, and to have said, like Agrippina:
>
> ———Derière une voile, invisible et présente,
> Je fus de ce grand corps l'âme toute puissante.
>
> The Queen laughed, did not dislike the compliment . . . 'But', said she, 'as you often tell me of my pride, I will now confess to you an instance of it, and

> to carry on the parallel you have drawn between me and Agrippina, will own to you that I very often feel myself in conference *avec ces impertinens*—
>
> Fille, femme, et mère de vos maîtres.
>
> Lord Hervey said he was very glad her pride had so great a pleasure in reflecting on that which all her subjects had so great an advantage in her being. (Sedgwick, I, 144–5)

Both quotations touch on the political power of the Queen. Without George II's realising it, Hervey believed, the Queen ruled the nation, causing the King to take her views for his own. In the early scenes of *Britannicus*, Agrippina declares the power she once exercised over her husband the Emperor Claudius and his Senate ('And, hidden from view, invisible but present, | In its deliberations I was all powerful', I. 1. 98–9) and her authority over her son Nero's advisers ('The daughter, wife, sister, and mother of your masters' (I. 2. 161), though Caroline leaves out 'sœur'). It was precisely this power that, in the event of his father's death, the Prince was expected to resent and resist.

Racine's *Britannicus* marks the turning point in Nero's career. In murdering his step-brother Britannicus at the end of the play, he turns decisively away from the life of virtue and from the influence of his mother. As his adviser Burrhus says,

> You will, my lord, be driven from crime to crime,
> Backing up your severities with other cruelties,
> And dip your hands more deeply still in blood.
> (*Britannicus*, IV. 3. 1360–2)

Hervey's play marks the next major step in this descent, one predicted by Agrippina in *Britannicus*:

> Your hand has begun with your brother's blood;
> I can see you will go on to strike your mother.
> (*Britannicus*, V. 6. 1693–4)

In writing his sequel, Hervey was able to focus his drama, as Racine had, on the love interest. In *Britannicus*, Nero's wickedness is refined into his desire for Britannicus' betrothed, Junia. His indecision, or apparent indecision, over removing Britannicus as the obstacle to its fulfilment, in interviews with Agrippina, Burrhus and Narcissus (the evil counsellor), retards the final fratricide. In 'Agrippina', Nero's desire for Poppæa is obstructed by Agrippina and his marriage, arranged by her, to Britannicus' sister, Octavia, while the final matricide is delayed by Agrippina's lingering power over Nero and his fear of her influence over the army.

The references to Frederick, Prince of Wales, as Nero in *Some Materials* provoke attempts at reading 'Agrippina' as a pièce à clef, but in detail they are unsuccessful. Pallas, as the Queen's close adviser, for example, would seem a possible representation of Hervey himself, perhaps coloured by Walpole in his role as treasurer. But Pallas is quite without the wit that characterises Hervey's self-portrait in his memoirs. Similarly, in Seneca and Burrhus, Nero has two advisers, as Frederick had two in Lord Chesterfield and Bubb Dodington, but their behaviour is shaped by Tacitus' narrative rather than Hervey's negative interpretation of the characters of his contemporaries. Above all, there is no contemporary equivalent to Poppæa. Frederick's relationship with Anne Vane may have been the cause of his breach with Hervey, but it did not enter negatively into his relations with the King and Queen. Vane seems to have been without ambition, and in the period before her death in 1736 became Hervey's lover once more.

That in a broader way the play reflects Hervey's closeness to the Queen and their fears for future relations with her son seems undeniable. The play's portrayal of Nero reflects Hervey's vision of Frederick's decline from early popularity and virtue to folly and vice, culminating in an unnatural hatred of his mother. Its exploration of the mother–son relationship as a struggle for power, reflects a projection forward of the tensions in the Hanoverian court in the 1730s. However, many of the character traits in Hervey's parallel accounts of Frederick and Nero – vanity (particularly in relation to the arts), luxury and social irresponsibility – are not reflected powerfully in the play, where Racine's influence focuses character on a narrow range of personal relationships. Although the play invites sympathy with Agrippina, particularly in her death, Hervey gives Nero, from his own verse, lines in favour of sexual freedom (II. 2. 56–70) that create some balance in the argument. The play focuses on the mother's tragedy and avoids creating a satirical portrait of her antagonist.

At a yet more general level, Hervey's tragedy engages political issues without directly reflecting contemporary events. The debates between Pallas and Agrippina over resistance to an unjust ruler and the relation between familial and national responsibilities resonate with controversies over the 1688 revolution, although Hervey's own view in his *Ancient and Modern Liberty Stated and Compared* (1734) is unequivocal: liberty followed the deposition of James II. Agrippina's contempt for a mercenary Senate surprisingly echoes attacks on Walpole's House of Commons. The scenes in which she asserts her innocence promote a belief in the power of the regal personality and its association with eloquence, while Nero's decline illustrates the dangers of the unfettered expression of such a personality. The play is persistently concerned with the role of advisers and the dangers when they become the instrument of the ruler's passion rather than its curb.

Although the plotting of Hervey's play is shaped by French drama, it is not without English influences and it is not French in its scene structure. Halsband thinks that Hervey might have been involved with the Prince of Wales in writing as well as supporting *The Modish Couple*, a play in the style of Restoration comedy that opened at the Theatre Royal, Drury Lane, in January 1732 (Halsband, pp. 130–2). That experience of the theatre would have been valuable in the planning of 'Agrippina', even if the play had been designed only for reading at Redlynch or the court. The chief influence on Hervey's tragedy, other than Racine, seems to have been Shakespeare. There are echoes of Shakespeare's Roman plays, chiefly *Julius Caesar* and *Antony and Cleopatra*, although Volumnia in *Coriolanus* would have provided Hervey with an example of a powerful mother with waning influence over her son, and Dryden's *All for Love* resonated more with him than did Shakespeare's original. Hervey may have been influenced by English adaptations of Racine, of which Ambrose Phillips's *The Distrest Mother* (1712), based on *Andromaque*, was perhaps the most popular. Katherine E. Wheatley reviews the genre in her *Racine and English Classicism* (Austin: University of Texas Press, 1956). Hervey was, of course free to create an original work. Unlike Racine, he uses soliloquies freely (there is only one, for Burrhus, in *Britannicus*), and the final action is allowed to take place on stage, rather than being a matter of report. Like Racine, Hervey writes in couplets, but in pentameters rather than alexandrines.

***Sources.*** In his comparison of the Prince of Wales with Nero in *Some Materials*, Hervey provides sidenotes acknowledging various sources: Aurelius Victor, *Liber de Caesaribus: Nero*; Tacitus, *Annals*; Suetonius, *Lives of the Caesars: Nero*; Cassius Dio, *Roman History*; and Seneca, *De Clementia*. Seneca's essay, addressed to Nero and contrasting the behaviour of the merciful king and the tyrant, forms a background to Hervey's conception of Nero's rule, though Seneca's arguments rarely come to the fore either in the parallel characters or in the play. The purpose of the parallelism was to blacken the Prince's character, and much of the information taken from Aurelius Victor and Suetonius concerns Nero's vanity over his performances, his extravagance and cruelty. Hervey's indebtedness to Racine in 'Agrippina' excluded much of this material, and as a result he closely follows Tacitus, who provides an action he can trace and enrich with reflection. Examples of close relation to Tacitus are detailed in the notes.

Thomas May's *The Tragedy of Julia Agrippina; Empresse of Rome* was published in London in 1639. Its narrative begins before Claudius' death and ends with Agrippina's. The material Hervey treats constitutes part of its fifth act. There is no discernible influence. The story of Nero and Poppæa is the subject of Monteverdi's *L'incoronazione de Poppea* (1643), with a libretto by Gian Francesco Busenello, but Agrippina plays no part in the opera. Handel's *Agrippina* (Venice, 1709), with a libretto by Vincenzo Grimari, also tells a story of Nero and Poppæa, but sets it during the reign of Claudius. Handel himself never revived the opera and it was not performed in London. Daniel Casper von Lohenstein was the author of a tragedy, *Agrippina* (1665), that drew on Tacitus as a source. However, Lohenstein's conception of Agrippina is very different from Hervey's: central to his play is Agrippina's attempt to seduce her son, something that could not have been countenanced by Hervey or the Queen. The editors are deeply indebted to Professor Hermann Real, who generously read Hervey's play and reported that it could not have been influenced by Lohenstein's. The nature of the play's German would have made it inaccessible to Hervey, and there is no evidence from the *Memoirs* that it was known to him or the court.

***Dramatis Personae with notes.*** Basic information has been drawn freely from *The Oxford Classical Dictionary*, 4th edn, ed. by Simon Hornblower, Antony Spawfoth and Esther Eidinow (Oxford: Oxford University Press, 2012) and from John Hazel's *Who's Who in the Roman World* (London: Routledge, 2001).

PALLAS: Marcus Antonius Pallas (*d.* 62 CE), a Greek freedman; Claudius' financial secretary; Agrippina's counsellor. According to Tacitus, Pallas had the primary role in promoting Claudius' marriage with Agrippina and in the subsequent adoption of Nero as Claudius' son (*Annals*, XII. i–iii and xxv–xxvi). In the later episode, Tacitus suggests that Agrippina and Pallas may have been lovers, but Hervey makes no use of that idea.

SLAVE

ACERONIA: Agrippina's companion. The Roman historians bring her into the narrative at the end of Agrippina's life.

AGRIPPINA: Julia Agrippina (15–59 CE), Roman Empress; fourth wife of the Emperor Claudius (Tiberius Claudius Nero Germanicus, 10 BCE–54 CE) and mother, with her first husband Gnaeus Domitius Ahenobarbus, of Nero. She was the great-granddaughter of the Emperor Augustus (Gaius Octavius, 63 BCE–14 CE), the daughter of Germanicus, the revered Roman general, and the sister of Caligula. She was Claudius' niece. After their marriage in 49 CE, Claudius adopted Nero as his son, giving him precedence over Britannicus (Tiberius Claudius Britannicus, c. 41–c. 56 CE), the son of Claudius and his third wife, Messalina (Valeria Messalina, *d.* 48 CE). According to Tacitus, Agrippina murdered Claudius to prevent the restoration of Britannicus to the succession (*Annals*, XII. lxvi–lxvii). Her early role in influencing Nero's reign, his rejection of her influence, and her death are reported and presented in the play.

ANICETUS: a freedman and naval commander, formerly Nero's tutor. The Roman historians make him Nero's chief aide and killer in his final dealings with Agrippina, partly because her influence with the army ruled out its assistance.

SENECA: Lucius Annaeus Seneca (c. 3 BCE–65 CE), Stoic philosopher, statesman and dramatist. Brought back from exile by Agrippina in 49 CE to become praetor (a magistrate ranking below consul) and tutor to Nero, he became, with Burhus, his chief adviser. After losing favour, he was accused of involvement in Piso's conspiracy and committed suicide.

FIRST SENATOR

SECOND SENATOR

SENATORS

NERO: Lucius Domitius Ahenobarbus / Nero Claudius Caesar (37–68 CE), Roman Emperor (54–68 CE). Son of Agrippina and Domitius Ahenobarbus, he was adopted by Claudius in 50, after Claudius' marriage to Agrippina. He married his step-sister Octavia in 53, murdered his step-brother Britannicus in 55 or 56 and his mother in 59. He divorced and murdered Octavia in 62 and married Poppæa in 63. Blamed for his response to the burning of Rome in 64, he committed suicide in 68, as a result of rebellions throughout the empire 'after a life of self-indulgence, cruelty and self-deception' (Hazel, *Who's Who in the Roman World*).

BURRHUS (Hervey uses Racine's spelling): Sextus Afranius Burrus (*d.* 62 CE). Commander of the Praetorian Guard and tutor and counsellor to Nero. Possibly poisoned after opposing Nero's plans to divorce Octavia.

POPPÆA: Poppaea Sabina (*d.* 65 CE). Daughter of Titus Ollius, quaestor and friend of Sejanus; her mother, of the same name, was the daughter of Poppaeus Sabinus, consul in 9 CE. She married three times: (1) Rufrius Crispinus, commander of the Praetorian Guard before Burrus; (2) Marcus Salvius Otho, Nero's favourite and later Emperor (in 69 CE); (3) Nero (married 63 CE), who exiled Otho to Lusitania to facilitate the union. She died after Nero kicked her while she was pregnant.

FIRST PRIEST

SECOND PRIEST

CHORUS

***Emendations policy and typographic conventions adopted.*** As in the case of the poems, the manuscript text has been transcribed with its spellings, on the whole, retained, but its contractions (including abbreviated numbers and the ampersand) expanded. Initial lower-case letters at the beginnings of verse lines have also been raised to capitals. The manuscript is not a holograph, and some additional changes have been made to spelling and punctuation where the usage is eccentric and very clearly not that found in works in Hervey's own hand: the manuscript frequently confuses 'too' and 'to', 'there' and 'their', and is often incorrect in its use of prefixes pre-, per- and pro-; it is possible that all of these errors are indicative of the play being read aloud by one person to another who transcribed it, and all such confusions have been silently corrected. Long lines sometimes run beyond the page's edge, with the final letter of a word cut through, and any following punctuation missing; in such cases, punctuation required by the sense has been added. Silent correction has also been made to some other aspects of punctuation: a full-stop (or question-mark) has been added at the end of speeches if none is given in the manuscript; a comma at the end of a speech corrected to a full-stop; and a full-stop (or semi-colon, or question-mark) added at the end of a triplet where none is given and where the sense clearly demands it; syllables elided with an apostrophe have been reinstated when the metre demands it. The spelling of proper names has also been silently regularised: in particular, Anicetus and Agrippina are both spelled in several different ways in the manuscript, and after the middle of Act III (and occasionally before that), where italics for proper names have been lost, italicisation has been restored. Apostrophe 's' following a name in italics or small capitals has been consistently brought into confirmity with the type of the surrounding text rather than with the name. Finally, the spelling of 'guard' (often 'gaurd' in the manuscript), 'view' (including 'review' and 'interview', usually

'-veiw' in the manuscript), 'friend' (often 'freind' in the manuscript), 'whom' (frequently 'whome' in the manuscript), 'vengeance' (usually spelled 'vengance' or 'vengence' in the manuscript), 'pursuit' and related words (often spelled with the mistaken opening 'per' in the manuscript), 'altar' ('alter' in the manuscript), 'victim' (almost always 'victom' in the manuscript), 'despair' (usually 'dispair' in the manuscript), 'like' ('Like' has been given erroneously very frequently in the manuscript) and 'usual' (often written as 'usaul') have been silently corrected. (These words have been chosen because of their frequency of occurrence both here and in manuscripts in Hervey's hand.) All other emendations to the manuscript are indicated in the List of Emendations, other than the fact that typographical conventions appropriate to publication of a play have been adopted: act and scene headings have been regularised and numbers suppplied; potentially confusing lines marking the end of sections have been removed; in speech-prefixes and stage directions, characters' names are in small capitals and are spelled out in full, and the punctuation following them is eliminated; stage directions are in italic and in the conventional places; descriptions and entrances are centred; exits are set out full right; interpolated directions are in parentheses.

References to Racine's French text are to *Britannicus*, ed. by Jacques Morel (Paris: Flammarion, 2010). References to Shakespeare are to *The Oxford Shakespeare: The Complete Works*, 2nd edn, ed. by John Jowett, William Montgomery, Gary Taylor and Stanley Wells (Oxford: Clarendon Press, 2005). References to classical texts are, as throughout the edition, to the Loeb texts; in the case of Tacitus, *Annals*, references are by book and paragraph only.

## *Agrippina, a Tragedy*

### *Act First, Scene First*

*Scene Agrippina's Palace. Enter* PALLAS *Speaking to a* SLAVE

PALLAS Let *Aceronia* know I wait her here. *exit Slave*
Tis vain precaution all and fruitless Care:
There is no Safety but in *Neros* Death;[1]
From day to Day, I draw precarious Breath,
Dependant on his Policy and Fear
Which Dare not seize, that Life they would ensnare.
His Avarice views the Wealth I have Amassed
With Greedy Eyes; and all my Service past,

1. *There is no Safety but in Neros Death*: cf. 'It must be by his death', Brutus' decision in *Julius Caesar* (II. 1. 10).

That raised his Fortunes from a private Lot,
To Universal Empire — is Forgot.[2]
Disgraced and Banished his ungratefull Court,
One Day its Idol, and the Next its Sport.[3]
Yet not Contented with my Loss of Pow'r,
Perhaps he Meditates this Very Hour
(To End His Fears, and to Compleat my Shame,)
Mid' these new Plotters to enroll my Name.
This, or some Vile[4] by *Seneca* prepared,
Must take that Life his Coward Mercy Spared. —
And how shall I avert impending Fate?
How, in this impotent, this Wretched State?
Of all the Infl'ence Greatness gives bereft,
It's Envy still, it's dang'rous Odium left?
A Thousand Foes for every Injury done,
And not one Friend for all my Favours Shown:
All Gratitude, where most expected, dead,
And ready Vengeance bursting O'er my Head.

*Enter* ACERONIA

PALLAS How fares the Empress?
ACERONIA ———————— Or she seeks her Rest
Or to conceal 'tis banished from her Breast:
What secret sorrow rankles in her Mind
Afraid to Ask, and impotent to find,
I'm yet to Learn — but till this anxious Hour,
In all the Cares annex'd to Sovereign Power;
In all the Various Fortunes of her Life
As Daughter, Orphan, Sister, Mother, Wife,[5]

2. *my Service … is Forgot*: Pallas refers to his role in securing Claudius' marriage to Agrippina and subsequent adoption of Nero.

3. *Banish'd his ungrateful Court… its Sport*: Pallas is banished by Néron in *Britannicus*, II. 1. Néron's condemnation there of Pallas for poisoning his mother with bad advice comes closer to a critique of Hervey's relation with the Queen than anything in *Agrippina*, though Hervey's banishment from Prince Frederick's court in 1732 may be reflected in this speech.

4. *Vile*: Phial (presumably of poison).

5. *As Daughter … Wife*: echoing 'Moi, fille, femme, sœur et mère de vos maîtres' (*Britannicus*, I. 2. 156), the line alluded to by Queen Caroline in conversation with

Ne'er have I known her Art attempt in Vain,
To feign a Pleasure, or disguise a Pain.

PALLAS How pass'd the Night?

ACERONIA ——————— Beyond Her usual Hour,
Hopeless of Sleep her Quiet to restore,
In Her thin Court, amid her train she try'd,
In Mirth, forced Smiles, and talk, her Care to hide:
The Grosser Herd, these Efforts unperceiv'd,
That Chearfulness, they thought they saw believed;
But these Accustom'd Eyes were not Deceiv'd:
I Mark'd the Wanderings of her Absent Eye,
The unhear'd Question, the unapt Reply,
The unpleas'd Laughter, and unguarded Sigh:
Those Little signs, which nicely watch'd reveal
All that We strive invisibly to feel.

PALLAS Oh! *Aceronia*! well hast thou describ'd
Those tricks of Courts which early She imbib'd![6]
And What Avail's to say what we endure,[7]
Unless the ut'rance wou'd promote our Cure?
To probe is but to irritate the Heart,
Whilst every touch we feel, Augments our Smart.
The Wise in Silence therefore bear each Pain
Or, only where Redress is sure, complain.
Content they seem with Necessary ill,
And what they must submit to, seem to will:[8]
Whilst Babling Fools, their Discontent relate,
Rail at the World, and Murmur against Fate.

Hervey (Sedgwick, I, 145). 'Orphan' has been added in the conversation and reflects the life of Caroline as well as Agrippina.

6. *Those tricks of Courts which early She imbib'd*: Queen Caroline 'was at least seven or eight hours tête-à-tête with the King every day, during which time she was generally saying what she did not think, assenting to what she did not believe, and praising what she did not approve' (Sedgwick, I, 254).

7. *And What Avail's to say what we endure*: the twelve lines beginning here closely follow Poem 78 'For few or can, or wish to bring Relief' in a letter to Stephen Fox of 25 December 1731. The first couplet is different and the penultimate couplet reverses the order of the lines, but otherwise differences are minor.

8. *what they must submit to, seem to will*: this passage reflects Queen Caroline's response to George II's abusive behaviour: she 'returned every injury with flattery, and every contradiction with acquiescences' (Sedgwick, II, 498).

Ignorant of the Make of Humankind,
Solicit Pity, where Contempt they find.
ACERONIA Not so our Mistress: in Tiberius Reign[9]
That hard, but useful Talent well to Feign,
She first was taught; When force'd without a Tear,
A Fathers, and a Mothers Loss to bear,
She kiss'd the Hand that Drew the Ruin on,
Sooth'd the Old Tyrant with Her Flat'ring Tongue
Nor ever hinted the dissembled Wrong.
With equal skill she felt Mad *Caius* Pow'r[10]
And uncomplaining, ev'ry injury bore.
PALLAS Nor did Prosperity in *Claudius* Reign,
Assign an easyer Burden to Sustain:
When Midst Intrigues, Cabals, and distant Schemes,
Which seem'd at first, but Mad Ambitions Dreams,
Each thwarting Incident, she knew to bend,
From Opposition to promote her End.
ACERONIA And Who had thought, that one great Point obtain'd,
For which those various Labours She Sustain'd,
That all her hardest Tryals but begun,
And when she'd place'd her *Nero* on the Throne
Her last, worst Plague, would be her Darling Son?
PALLAS E'er *Seneca* or *Burrhus* warp'd his Mind,
And to their own, their Prince's Rule Confined;
What Rank, what Honours, in the State she bore;
Uneaqual'd Greatness, and unmeasured Power:
Not More she knew in *Claudius'* passive Reign;
*Lictors* and *Eagles*[11] swel'd her pompous Train:
Lov'd by the People, by the Senate praised,
With the Great Title of Augusta graced
Arches were turn'd, Trophys and Statues rais'd.

9. *Tiberius Reign*: Tiberius Claudius Nero reigned 14–37 CE; his reputation was blackened by Suetonius. Agrippina was the daughter of his nephew Germanicus.

10. *Mad Caius Pow'r*: that of Caligula (Gaius Julius Caesar Germanicus), Agrippina's brother, Emperor 37–41 CE, who exiled her.

11. *Lictors and Eagles*: lictors were officers bearing the fasces (a bundle of rods with projecting axe-blade representing the magistrate's power); eagles were carried as the standards of legions. These honours are detailed in Tacitus, *Annals*, XIII. ii.

Her Virtues, Edicts and inscriptions spoke,
Whilst incenced Altars to her Honor Smoke:
To Her, Embassadors their suit adress'd,
And brought the copious Treasures of the East:
From her the Provinces receiv'd their Laws,
And Kings, were Kings, but when she Prov'd their Cause.

ACERONIA Nor did she with more bounded sway at Home,
Rule the Proceedings of obedient *Rome*.
The Senate Acted but by her Commands,
And for *the Word*[12] the Prætorian Bands,[13]
The Duteous Son, *the best of Mothers*,[14] gave,
Whilst he himself seem'd but her formost Slave.
The *Quæstors, Ediles, Consuls*,[15] were her Choice
Her Lips the Proxy of the Peoples Voice:
To Her, Petitioners their Suit Prefer'd,
At Her Tribunal ev'ry Cause was heard;
*Prætors*,[16] for form alone, in judgment sat
To Draw the Edicts of her love and Hate:
Her favours Right, and her Decision Fate.

PALLAS If to the Crouded *Capitol* She Rode,
In splendor scarce inferior to it's God[17]
On *Agrippina* ev'ry Eye was cast;
The shouts of Myriads hailed her as she Pass'd:
Her Progress known, the Streets were all prepared;
Flow'rs strew'd the way, an army was her Guard:
Whilst to receive her, through the Valves of Gold,[18]
The Lawrel'd Priests, the Temple Gates unfold;

12. *the Word*: i.e. the password.

13. *Praetorian Bands*: in 27 BCE Augustus established a permanent elite force, under the Emperor's personal command, of nine cohorts (each of 500 or 1,000 men), serving with superior conditions for sixteen years. Three cohorts were stationed in Rome.

14. *the best of Mothers*: according to Tacitus the password given by Nero to the praetorian guard (*Annals*, XIII. ii.).

15. *Quæstors, Ediles, Consuls*: magistrates with financial responsibilities; magistrates responsible for public works (aediles); chief magistrates.

16. *Prætors*: magistrates ranking below consul.

17. *Capitol . . . it's God*: the Capitol was the smallest of the Roman hills, on which was built the temple to Jupiter Optimus Maximus, Juno and Minerva; a citadel and a symbol of Roman power, it was the place where triumphal processions finished with sacrifice.

18. *Valves of Gold*: i.e. Latin *valvae*, folding doors, of gold.

By Rights[19] divine, the solem Pomp was rais'd,
The Victims Bleeding whilst the Incence blaz'd:
By her White Steeds the Sacred Pavement press'd;
She Looked more like the Godess than the Guest
When on the Shrine her Sacrifice She lay'd,
Serv'd with more adoration than she pay'd.

ACERONIA But soon alas these transient Honors passed,
This Noon of Glory by thick Clowd's o'er cast
The acts of *Claudius* were revere'd no More,
That first Infringment of her tot'ring Power:
The Apostate Senate summon'd at her Call
Within her hearing, in Augustus' Hall,
Annulled those Acts, by *Nero* unreprov'd —
From *Cæsars* Palace next she was remov'd:
Shut from his Confidence, and of her Guard
That Pagentry of Pow'r, at last debar'd:[20]
And had the Cause at first been truly known,
Your fall was but the prelude of her Own.

PALLAS Why *Aceronia* doest thou wound my Ear
With sounds like those, to agravate Despair?
Oh! Yet upon My Cheek the Blush remains,
And Mem'ry recent still the Grief retains;
When forc'd the Stripling's order to Obey,
Through his Curs'd Court I took my exil'd way;
Whilst from the Window, as I pass'd the Croud,
Of my Disgrace, and his Injustice proud,
Insulting thus he Mark'd my parting Hour: —
*See Pallas abdicating Sovereign Power.*
Nay even those my former Bounty fed,
Accumulating Shame upon my head,
Fawning on him, from my resentment safe,
Join'd in the Sneer and the oprobious Laugh,
For who is Gratefull to the falling Friend?
Th' Attachments which on Favorites Attend,
With their Prosperity begin and End:

19. *Rights*: i.e. rites.

20. *From Caesars Palace next she was remov'd . . . and of her Guard . . . at last debar'd*: this account draws on Tacitus, *Annals*, XIII. xviii.

In Craft alone those seeming Leagues are Made,
From the same cause cemented and betray'd.

ACERONIA Tis true, but thence let your distracted Mind
At least this Comfort in it's Sufferings find;
These Slaves the same to *Nero*'s Self had done,
Had you prefer'd his Rival to the Throne,
And given the World to Messalina's Son.[21]

PALLAS There is no Comfort for the Loss of Power,
But in some hope its being to Restore:
'Tis Thus, like me, your Royal Mistress mourn's
Thus with Ambition and Resentment burn's.

ACERONIA But Why this Night should her distracted breast,
Seem with this added Load of Grief opress'd?

PALLAS So long thy faith and Secrecy I've try'd,
That Nothing from thy Eyes I mean to hide.
Know then our Spys, who constantly resort
To bring Intelligence from *Nero*'s Court
Thus from his Midnight Banquet make report:
Late as he sat at the protracted Feast,
With each debauched, indecent, vicious Guest,
*Senica* and Petronius[22] and the Rest;
His Favorite *Paris*, with unusual haste,
Enter'd the Hall: to *Cæsars* Couch he pass'd;[23]
Not with the gay accostings of His Trade,
With Dance or Song, but trembling and Dismay'd:
He gave a Paper which as *Nero* read,
Full of Amazement, Rage, Confusion, Dread,
His Color chang'd; his Glowing Eyes shot fire:
But see the Empress Moves this way.

*Enter* AGRIPPINA *and her Train, Who seeing* PALLAS *says to the rest*

21. *Messalina's Son*: Britannicus (41–c. 55 CE), Nero's step-brother.

22. *Senica and Petronius*: Seneca (see Dramatis Personae); Gaius Petronius (*d.* 66 CE), an indolent and amoral courtier, may also have been the author of the *Satyricon*.

23. *Paris . . . to Cæsars Couch he pass'd*: Paris, called by Cassius Dio a 'pantomimic dancer' (*Roman History*, LXII (Loeb, VIII, 167)), relays the charge that Agrippina had incited Rubellius Plautus to revolt. The episode is from Tacitus, *Annals*, XIII. xx.

AGRIPPINA ———————— Retire.

Exeunt all but PALLAS and AGRIPPINA

Are all these bold Conspirators yet known?

PALLAS Of all Accus'd for certain only one,
*Plautus*, 'tis sure the daring Faction led
A Num'rous Faction and a powerful Head:
His birth, his popularity, his Name,
Scarce second to the Rank of *Cæsars* Fame;[24]
His known Attachment to our State and Laws,
Have drawn so many to espouse his Cause,
That half our Youth, 'tis say'd compos'd the band,
Talk'd of *Old Rome* and under his Command,
Design'd once More to free their Native Land.

AGRIPPINA What, art thou grown this Plautus' Flat'rer too?
Or Does thy erring judgment think it true?
So long the Master of the Reins of Pow'r,
With Skill to Judge, Accuteness to explore;
Cans't thou beleive, in this corrupted State,
Where base materials all *Rome*'s Strength create;
Cans't thou weak Man!, who try'd, who found, who prov'd
These *Romans* serv'd, one whom they never lov'd:
That Proud *Patricians* couch'd beneath those Feet,
They'd seen in Slav'ry naked tread the Street,
Cans't thou beleive, that this Degenerate Brood
These purled Slaves,[25] these Dregs of Roman Blood,
To *Rome*, to Principle or Glory true,
The *Decii*, or the *Fabii*'s Scheme pursue,[26]
Or Pant for freedom which they Never knew?

PALLAS Yet some there are —

24. *Plautus ... Scarce second to the Rank of Cæsars Fame*: Gaius Rubellius Plautus (33–62 CE), a potential rival to Nero; through his mother great-grandson of Tiberius Caesar, and descended from Mark Antony and Augustus' sister Octavia.

25. *These purled Slaves*: those wearing the bordered toga praetexta as a mark of distinction.

26. *The Decii, or the Fabii's Scheme pursue*: families notable for their devotion to Rome. The Decii were Publius Decius Mus, father (C4 BCE) and son (C4–3 BCE), who both deliberately sacrificed themselves in battle for Rome. The Fabii were an eminent patrician family or gens, notable for the sacrifice of over over 300 family members at the Battle of Cremena (477 BCE). Cato refers to the families with reverence in Addison's *Cato*, IV. iv.

AGRIPPINA ——————— I tell thee there are none
To whom these Maxims or these Pathes are known.
Behold what Men in Senates now Preside;
Who govern *Rome* and this great Empire Guide:
Whose Institution is abroad adored,
Whose Acts, and Characters at home abhor'd:
An Abject, servile, Mean abandon'd Crew,
Nor to their Prince, Nor to their people True,
Voting for pay, and speeching for Applause,
O'erturning Right, and trampling on the Laws,
Whilst the best bidder has the Justest Cause.
And What these Grov'ling Wreches should reclaim?
Unurg'd by Honor and uncheck'd by Shame?
In Slavery born, they Court Despotick sway,
And like our Mercenary Troops obey,
Quiet from fear, and Loyal for their Pay.
Nor longer *Romans* but by name, Disgrace
The Ancient Line of an Illustrious Race:
By int'rest guided, whilst affecting Fame,
Their Cry the Publick Good; their own, their Aim.

PALLAS But Grant too Quick my Caution makes me fear,
And that these Slaves shall never bravely dare
To break their Chains, and to new mold the State;
(The view too Noble, and the Work too Great)
Yet if Securely you presume too far,
At least tis Safer on my Side to err.

AGRIPPINA In Government[27] our Safety must arise,
From Watchful, not from speculating Eyes:
And ev'ry Hour by present Dangers press'd,
The wise apply to those and risk the rest.—
What steps to Night were taken by the Court?

PALLAS Measures Confused cause a Confus'd Report:
'Tis sure that *Plautus* instantly was seized,
And that Each Hour the fatal List increas'd,
The Guard was doubled on the first Allarms;
And the *Prætorian* Camp watched under Armes.

27. *In Government*: in discretion, management of demeanour.

All Night the Emperor in Council sate,
Marking each Moment with some Bloody Fate,
Whilst Ancient Hate, and New Suspicions join'd,
Double the Native Fierceness of His Mind.
The *Tribuns*, and *Centurions*,[28] who fullfill
The Rigid Mandates of his furious Will,
To blood, to Rapine, and Opression bred,
In their implicit and remorsless Trade,
From House, to House rush with their Ruffian-band,
Whilst the bar'd Gates in vain their Course withstand;
Resistless still they take their Lawless way,
And make the sleeping Lords their easy Prey;
How many Wreches in this dreadfull Night
To Dungens drag'd ne'er to review the Light
In the Destructive chaos of these times,
Weep their Misfortunes, ign'rant of their Crimes.
Not the tremendous Entry of *the Gaul*;[29]
Not *Hannibal* encamp'd beneath our Wall;[30]
*Marius* and *Syllas* feirce conflicting Bands,[31]
Nor the *Triumvirs* red proscribing Hands,[32]
*Tiberius* Vengeance When *Sejanus* fell;[33]
Nor any Havock which our Historys tell;
Diffus'd in *Rome* more universal Dread,
Than the Confusion which this Night has spread —
Uproar and Tumult raiging in Each Street,
Dismay and Horror, in each face we meet:
None Guessing from what Cause these Stormes proceed,

28. *The Tribuns, and Centurions*: commanders and officers in the Roman army.

29. *Entry of the Gaul*: in c. 387 BCE a Gallic army under Brennus entered and burnt much of Rome.

30. *Hannibal . . . Wall*: Carthaginian general (247–182 BCE) who attacked Rome in the second Punic War (218–201 BCE).

31. *Marius and Syllas . . . Bands*: Gaius Marius (157–86 BCE), seven times consul, and the general Lucius Cornelius Sulla (c. 138–78 BCE; 'Sylla' is the French spelling) fought a civil war (88–86 BCE).

32. *Triumvirs red proscribing Hands*: the second triumvirate (Octavian, Mark Antony and Lepidus) carried out a purge after the assassination of Julius Caesar (44 BCE).

33. *Tiberius . . . Sejanus fell*: the Emperor Tiberius (42 BCE–37 CE), after allowing Lucius Aelius Sejanus (20 BCE–31 CE) to assume power in Rome, had him arrested and executed.

Who has offended, or who next must bleed.  
AGRIPPINA With all his faults may Heaven protect my Son.  
PALLAS Nor Heav'n, nor Earth can keep him on the Throne.  
AGRIPPINA What canst thou Mean by that vain idle Threat?  
PALLAS That in these hourly Tumults of the State,  
The Man who rules, let Him be e'er so great,  
Treads but a steeper Precipice of Fate.[34]  
Nor are they these Calamitys alone,  
That draw the Ruin of your *Nero* on;  
Conflicting Causes seem to urge his Fate,  
For 'tho these Opposites, Contempt and Hate,  
In the same Object rarely are compris'd,  
Your Son's at once both hated and Dispised;[35]  
Mankind his Cruelty with Horror View,  
Whilst all his Follys—  
AGRIPPINA —Hold; suppose this true,  
Who should dispute the Empire with my Son?  
PALLAS Many there are, this *Plautus*-Self is one.  
*Piso* or *Sylla* who of *Julius* Race,[36]  
Alike with *Nero* from that Fountain trace  
Their boasted Blood: but granting there were None,  
When *Caius* bled, he left a vacant Throne.[37]  
AGRIPPINA The Anarchy of *Rome* when *Caius* bled,  
Show'd her unwieldy Limbs requir'd a head  
And to the yoke she bends her willing Neck.[38]

34. *a steeper Precipice of Fate*: cf. 'Who wishes may stand in power | on a palace's slippery peak' (Seneca, *Thyestes*, lines 391–2 (*Tragedies* (Loeb), II, 265)).

35. *hated and Dispised*: in *Some Materials*, the French Minister in England, Chavigny, says in 1731 that the King, not the Prince of Wales, has the rare achievement of being despised and hated by all his subjects (Sedgwick, II, 522).

36. *Piso or Sylla ... of Julius Race*: Gnaeus Calpurnius Piso, who 'sprung from the Calpurnian house, and, by his father's high descent, uniting in his own person many families of distinction', was the centre of an unsuccessful conspiracy against Nero in 65 CE (Tacitus, *Annals*, XV. xlviii–lxxi) and Cornelius Sulla Felix, son-in-law of Claudius, was accused of conspiracy with Pallas (Tacitus, *Annals*, XIII. xxiii and xlvii).

37. *Caius bled ... vacant Throne*: a reference to the death of Caligula (Gaius Julius Caesar Germanicus) in 41 CE. Claudius, whose claim to the throne was through his grandmothers, owed his appointment to the Praetorian Guard.

38. *she bends her willing Neck*: Hervey plays with Caligula's wish that 'the Roman people had but a single neck' (Suetonius, *Lives*, Caligula, para. xxx, I, 453).

PALLAS Yet may her sons a Milder Master Seek.
AGRIPPINA No! her mean sons are only rul'd by fear.
PALLAS Fear push'd too far may turn into Despair.
AGRIPPINA The Army's his; the People dare not move.
PALLAS Tis sure these hate; and Armys Seldom love.
AGRIPPINA They love their Interest; he on that depends
And makes them by that strongest Tye his friends.
PALLAS Suppose them such, your ruin still is sure
Be *Nero*'s Greatness tot'ring or secure:
*Seneca, Burrhus, Anicetus,* all,
Wish, urge, contrive, precipitate your fall;
And not declining *Acte*[39] long enjoy'd,
Whose favours have her Influence destroy'd,
You have to Combate, but a Potent Dame
Who warm's your Son in no ignoble Flame;
High born *Poppæa* beautifull and young
Whose strength's more dang'rous as she feels she's strong;
Who not for *Nero* but the empire burn's,
And *Agrippina*'s very being Mourn's:
For whilst she covets *Cæsar*'s bed and throne,
And knows how weak *Octavia*'s Pow'r alone,
You she esteem's in all her Lover's Court,
Her Rival's single Friend and sole support:
But think not Long your Succor can avail,
The Mistress soon shall turn the Mothers Scale,
Then ——
AGRIPPINA —— You may spare the Sequel of the tale:
All Thou wouldest urge, too faithfully I find
Suggested by my own prophetic Mind:
Then shall my Laurels bind *Poppæa*'s brow;
For her the fruit of all my Labors Grow:
By her my Glory's and my Honor's worn;
Whilst I, the Object of the Publick Scorn,
In Birth, Rank, Titles, impotently great,
Shun'd in the Court, a Cypher in the State,

39. *Acte*: a freedwoman who became Nero's mistress but was losing her place to Poppæa (Tacitus, *Annals*, XIII. xii and n. and xlvi; XIV. ii).

All Intrest in my *Nero* must forego,
And only Left to his indifference —

PALLAS ——————— No;
Those whom we never lov'd may keep their State,
But whom we cease to love we quickly hate.
And cou'd you read the purpose of his Breast,
These Wrongs are but the Prologue to the Rest;
Favours compar'd to what you may expect;
The time will come, you'll wish for his Neglect;
When Fear, Remorse, Affection, Duty fled, —

AGRIPPINA Peace cruel Man! why with that Ravens Note,[40]
Dost thou constrain Me to recall a thought,
Which for one Lucky Moment I'd forgot?

PALLAS That You may see the Danger that you run.

AGRIPPINA The Sight my Friend gives not the Power to Shun.
Be to that end thy Care, thy skill employed,
Those Rocks you show, the Pilot to avoid:
Is there alas! no way?

PALLAS ——————— There is but one.

AGRIPPINA Name it, my Oracle.

PALLAS ——————— Give up your Son.

AGRIPPINA Oh! never, never, tho thy Earth born Mind,
To it's own Int'rest narrowly Confin'd,
Was taught ignobly from thy earlyest Youth
To change its views, and Shift its Venal Truth;
And cou'd, as each New Master bore Command,
Transfer thy Plyant faith from Hand to Hand;
Thinkest thou my Breast with no affection glows?
That my cool Heart no fond Attachment knows?
No fear, no Hope, no Grief, no joy, I've known,
Since — first I was a Mother, but my Son:
Great Minds pursue some uniform Design,
And *Nero*'s Welfare has been ever mine,
I wish'd him Happy, and I wish'd Him great,
I wish'd him Master of the Roman State;

40. *Ravens Note*: 'Came he right now to sing a raven's note | Whose dismal tune bereft my vital powers' (*2 Henry VI*, III. 2. 40–1); 'Peace with that Raven's Note' (Dryden, *All for Love*, III. 1. 393 (Dryden, *Works*, XIII, 68)).

And when I ask'd if Heav'n espouse his cause,
From Sacred Oracles, — the answer was. —
"If *Agrippina* in this Scheme Succeed
"In Fate's unchanging Volume tis decreed,
"The Mother by the impious Son shall bleed."[41]
Yet still to Mine his Int'rest I Prefer'd
Nor Preists, nor threatening Oracles deter'd;
If Parricide,[42] I cry'd, his Hand must stain,
Dye *Agrippina* but let *Nero* Reign.

PALLAS And Heav'n forbid you may not find too late,
Unwarn'd by Wrong'd *Britannicus*'s Fate,
That as no Favours can his Love engage,
So Parricide it Self can't check his Rage.

*Enter* ACERONIA

ACERONIA Oh! Empress! for your Safety quick provide,
Before all Means of Safety are deny'd.

AGRIPPINA What dost thou Mean?

ACERONIA ——————— The Palace is beset;
One band of Soldiers lines the guarded Street;
And whilst another throng's the Marble Hall:
All who oppose their Course their Victims fall.
Feirce *Anicetus* thunder's at their Head.
Where, where's the Empress? furiously he say'd:
With Terror struck at What I saw and hear'd,
The Brazen Gates I Order'd to be bar'd
That lead to this Apartment; and then run —

PALLAS Hark! Now they force the Door. — Whats to be Done?

ACERONIA *(to the Empress)* One only way for your escape is left:
A Minute more and you're of that bereft;
From yon pavilion through the Garden haste,
And seek some Refuge till this Tumult's passed.

41. *The Mother by the impious Son shall bleed*: Hervey here follows Tacitus, *Annals*, XIV. ix; no firm source for Tacitus' narrative has been identified, though Cassius Dio reports a possible Sibylline prophecy: 'Last of the sons of Aeneas, a mother-slayer shall govern' (*Roman History*, LXII (Loeb, VIII, 117)).

42. *Parricide*: a word of doubtful derivation, used correctly by Hervey to refer to the killing of family members.

Perhaps they have not seiz'd the Postern Gate
Fly my Lov'd Mistress and leave us to wait
Alone the Issue of Impending Fate.

AGRIPPINA No let the Coward and the Guilty fly,
I'll face that Tempest, all it's Rage defy,
Or in the Dignity I've liv'd, will dye. *Exeunt*

End Of The First Act

## *Act Second, Scene First*

*Scene Agrippina's Palace. Enter* AGRIPPINA, PALLAS, ACERONIA, *and the rest of the Empress's Train*

PALLAS Yet be advised it is on Death you run.

AGRIPPINA If Pain be What our Nature most would Shun,
Tis better once to Meet that Death we fear,
Than by avoidance of each fancy'd Snare,
To Make our Life but one long Anxious Care.[43]

PALLAS By *Hirtius*, and by *Pansa*[44] well advised,
Their warning slighted and their fears despis'd,
Thus fatally, like you, great *Julius* thought
But this false Courage his Destruction wrought,
When by Dismission of his *Spanish* Guard,
He planed the way[45] to what his foes prepar'd,
And Chuseing in false Friendship to Confide
A treach'rous Son's deluded Victim dy'd.[46]

ACERONIA Her Resolution Staggers — press Her more.

PALLAS Fly to the Army. Yet tis in Your Power.

AGRIPPINA Can I who could command them now implore?

43. *To Make our Life but one long Anxious Care*: cf. 'For it's better to die once | Than spend all one's days suffering miserably' lines 750–1 (Aeschylus, *Prometheus Bound*, ed. and trans. by A. J. Podlecki (Oxford: Aris & Phillips, 2005), p. 131). As appears from Pallas' reply, Hervey is conscious of a parallel with Caesar's 'Cowards die many times before their deaths | The valiant never taste of death but once' (*Julius Caesar*, II. 2. 32–3). For Hervey's treatment of this theme, see Overton, 'Death and Futurity'.

44. *Hirtius, and … Pansa*: Aulus Hirtius (c. 90–43 BCE) and Gaius Vibius Pansa Caetonianus (*d.* 43 BCE) were generals, close associates of Julius Caesar and made consuls by him.

45. *He planed the way*: He cleared the path.

46. *A treach'rous Son's deluded Victim dy'd*: Marcus Junius Brutus (c. 85–42 BCE) was favoured by Caesar as a son.

PALLAS Command them still, *Germanicus's* Name,
That Aid which others court, or buy, shall claim —
ANICETUS *(without)* Pain of your Lives let no one pass the Door.
PALLAS Tis now too Late —
AGRIPPINA ——————— The Conflict then is o'er,
The Dye is thrown and I shall doubt no more.

*Enter* ANICETUS *with a Guard.*

ANICETUS *(Speaks entring)* Not one who makes the least Resistance Spare,
The Person of the Empress is my care.
AGRIPPINA Say Whence this outrage, and by whose Command,
Backed by the Fury of that Hostill Band,
You dare tumultuous, with those impious Feet
To break the Quiet of this calm Retreat,
And thus prophane your Empress' hallow'd Seat?
How comes it these (My Safety once their Care)
No more my Birth, my Rank, or Frown revere,
And you my Slave pretend to Lord it here?
ANICETUS I know what distance to your Rank is Due,
But know my Duty to the Emperor too,
And What ev'n you to *Cæsars* Mandates owe.
For tho you once possess'd imperial Sway,
You now, like us, must *Nero's* Will Obey:
The Wife's usurp'd Authority is done,
And the Proud Mother must Obey the Son;
His orders then I come to execute,
Which I must not neglect nor you dispute.
AGRIPPINA How low my State, when such a Wretch shall dare
To Treat me thus — tis Needless to declare:
But to expostulate with one so base,
Would be to agravate my own disgrace;
To sink my Falling Dignity yet Low'r
But that's a shame beyond ev'n *Cæsars* Pow'r
Who still shall find, whate'er my wretched State
I can Submit but not descend to Fate. —
Declare at once then all thy black Intent,
And to what guilty Purpose thou art sent.
ANICETUS To seize your Person, nor depart your Sight,

But with my Life to answer for your Flight.
AGRIPPINA For what to whom? or whither should I fly?
But I forget — Nor Ask you to reply.
Yet if My Person Sacred is declar'd;
The Senate's and the people's Acts my Guard;
Acts which for *Tribunes* and for *Censors* made[47]
In Tumults and Seditions were Obeyed,
Whilst faction couch'd, and Treason hid her head;
If by these Rights protect'd, and by those
More Sacred Still, which Nature's Laws dispose,
A Right which I, to spare your Prince's Shame
Avoid to Mention and forbear to Claim;
If with these Double Privileges graced,
By Gods and Men in an Asylum placed;
Whilst thus he breaks divine and Human Laws
Were you not Order'd to declare some Cause,
At least some plausible, tho false Pretence,
To gild, if not to justify th' Offence?
ANICETUS Another for that Office is prepar'd,
I am not sent to Judge you, but to Guard.
AGRIPPINA Why comes not this great Judge, that I may clear,
To all the World my Fame?
ANICETUS ———————— Behold him here.

*Enter* SENECA *attended*[48]

AGRIPPINA Is *Agrippina*'s Fortune sunk so low,
That to this base Tribunal she must bow?
Is her forgetfull, and ungratefull Son,
So careless of her Fame, and Intrest Grown
That she must stoop to delegated Pow'r,
And justice from her Vassals Hands implore?
At any Judgment Seate but *Cæsars* heard,
Some Infamy I feel, ev'n whilst I'm clear'd.
SENECA Oh! Never by my Empress be it thought,
That this employment by Her Slave was Sought.

47. *for Tribunes and for Censors made*: the tribunes representing the plebeians; the censors being responsible for the census and for public morality.

48. In the scene in Tacitus from which Hervey draws his materials, the charges are put by Burrus in the presence of Seneca (*Annals*, XIII. xxi).

When *Cæsar* bids, what *Roman* dare refuse?
Our Part is to Submit and not to chuse.
And whilst my Duty points this painful way
The Charge allotted by his Sovereign sway
Resign'd I take; yet blush whilst I Obey.

AGRIPPINA Can any Blush upon that Cheek remain
Which not Ingratitude it self could stain?[49]
Or thinkest thou *Agrippina* is so blind
As to beleive thy close, intriguing Mind
Mourn's an Event, it's Own dark Schemes design'd?
Me would'st thou hope with these stale tricks to Cheat,
Seen through by every Novice in the State?
The very Rudiments of Power and Pride,
Which on your Bondmen vainly would be try'd,
Ev'n they their Suit in terms like these refused;
Would only think they Doubly were abused,
Whilst Your own Dupe, you'd fancy them deceiv'd
Because they fear'd to show they disbeliev'd.

SENECA Not words alone, my Actions shall declare
How much my Benefactress is my Care;
That still for you and, for your cause, I feel
Unalter'd Love and Unabated Zeal;
And whilst I execute the Emperor's will,
Revere You as my Royal Mistress still.

AGRIPPINA That Title once my Due, is Now abuse
To me no soothing, for thee no Excuse.
Once I esteem'd thee gratefull, upright Just,
Graced thee with favor, honor'd thee with Trust;
But if untry'd thy Virtue I believ'd,
Think not my weakness can be twice deceiv'd.

SENECA Those Gods before whose shrine the *Romans* Bow,
Who all the inmost Thoughts of Mortals know,
Can tell if ever in your Noon of Pow'r,
My Soul with more Devotion sought —

AGRIPPINA ——————————No more;
You mock my Mis'rys, and you waste the time;

49. *not Ingratitude it self could stain*: Agrippina had arranged Seneca's recall from exile and appointment as praetor and tutor to Nero (Tacitus, *Annals*, XII. viii).

Perform your Office, and relate my Crime.
SENECA This is the Crime your Enemys relate:
That you have purposed to Subvert the State,
Conspir'd with *Plautus* to depose your Son
And made your bed the purchase of the Throne.
AGRIPPINA Is then my Son so ready to beleive
His Mothers Guilt, that tales like these deceive?
Tis like a Plot concerted for the Stage.
What Shallow Politician forg'd this Lye,
As easy to refute as to deny?
Careless of Truth, determin'd to Accuse,
Knew they no Crime more probable to Chuse?
SENECA If false the Charge, do Justice to your fame.
AGRIPPINA To justice then, for I no favor Claime,
My first demand, is my delator's Name.[50]
SENECA Nor this, tho Favour, *Cæsar* will deny;
With all you ask'd he Charg'd me to comply.
Reluctant to beleive the high Offence
Ready to hear and Credit your Defence.
AGRIPPINA Be this my first Command then streight obey'd.
SENECA The Charge *Domitia* and *Silana*[51] lay'd
And to Your Son, by *Paris* twas convey'd;
*Iturius* and *Calvisius* too possess'd
Of Means to prove these crimes which those Suggest,
Are Ready on your tryal to appear:[52]
But first Your answer I was Sent to hear,
Your Innocence not more your own than *Cæsars* Care.

50. *my delator's Name*: the name of the person informing on me.

51. *Domitia* and *Silana*: Domitia Lepida (c. 19 BCE–59 CE) was the sister of Nero's father; in 33 she married Gaius Sallustius Crispus Passienus but in 41 they were required to divorce so that Crispus could marry Agrippina (a possible cause of antagonism); Domitia had cared for Nero while Agrippina was in exile in the reign of Caligula (*Annals*, XIII. xix). Junia Silana had been married to Gaius Silius, but had been driven out by Messalina, who wanted him for herself (Tacitus, *Annals*, XI. xii). She was an ally of Agrippina, until Agrippina deterred Sextius Africanus from marrying her by describing her as 'a woman of no morals and uncertain age' (*Annals*, XIII. xix).

52. *Iturius and Calvisius* ... *appear*: clients of Silana, who were suborned to make the accusation. They told Atimetus, a freedman of Domitia, who told Paris (not Pallas, as in Loeb translation), another of her freedmen (*Annals*, XIII. xix–xx).

AGRIPPINA To one so mean I blush to plead my Cause
Scorning the Judge tho I revere the Laws:
The Laws of Heav'n, of Nature, and of *Rome*;
I fear to Merit, not to Meet my Doom:
For if my Life were all depending now
My Pride would bid that worthless Trifle go,
My Course of happyness and Glory run
Untimely stop'd by an ungratefull Son:
Who owes his Share of both to me alone;
But for the Sake of *Agrippina*'s Fame,
Unsully'd as I'd leave the Mothers Name;
Be Mine and my Accuser's Story heard,
And then Our Mutual Merit be declar'd,
Nor will I stoop this foolish Tale to Clear
But speak the Inventors worth and leave it there.

PALLAS *(aside)* By Heaven she takes it on a Noble Strain
By Dangers Threats and wrongs oppress'd in vain.

AGRIPPINA That the Affections of a Mother's Breast,
By one who that fond title never blest,
Should ill be understood, I marvel not;[53]
Or that the Barren, old *Silana* — thought
Those Tyes could be disolv'd, that Love forgot.
Far other Cares I know her Thoughts employ,
Her Bosom warm with other sence of joy;[54]
She thinks the Tenure in a Mothers Breast
Like That in Wanton Harlots is possess'd;
And fond Attachments to a Child belov'd,
Like those to trancient Minions are remov'd;
Farther to speak her prostituted Fame,
Would blush my glowing Cheek with glowing Shame
Since all the youth of *Rome* proclaim the Rest,
In the loose Novels[55] of each drunken Feast.

SENECA *Calvisius* and *Iturius* both declare —

53. This speech and the one following elaborate on the one reported by Tacitus, *Annals*, XIII. xxi.

54. *Far other Cares . . . sence of joy*: cf. 'Far other dreams my erring soul employ, | Far other raptures, of unholy joy' (Pope, 'Eloisa to Abelard', lines 223–4; Pope, *Twickenham*, II, 338).

55. *Novels*: news, gossip.

AGRIPPINA Her Minions, Tools and Parasites they are;
I wonder not this suit shou'd be their care.
Her fortune Squander'd and her Coffers drain'd,
They thought this Confiscation still remain'd
(When by my Son her Portion should be pay'd
To recompense the Welcome Lye she'd made)
For a Recruit,[56] to know her only Charms,
And for the Price, when Love no Longer Warms
Requir'd to fill Her Unalluring Arms.

SENECA Of great *Augustus'* line, and to your Son
So near ally'd, *Domitia* still has shown
A Fondness there scarce second to your own.
What Motive for distrust could *Cæsar* see
In Love and Care so try'd?

AGRIPPINA ——————— Her hate to me.
Yet if that hate was for my *Nero*'s sake,
There's no allowances I could not make
To any Rival, Who had only strove,
Who best should serve him or who most could Love.
Tho tis not rare such forward friends to find
For one already Master of Mankind;
In every Court such little insects Swarm,
In the Bright sunshine that first breeds them, Warm.
But Whilst his Fortunes Step by step I wrought
With Dang'rous Vigilance, and Anxious Thought,
When He was given to *Octavias* Bed,
And of the Roman Youth declar'd the Head,
In *Claudius'* House by an adoption placed,
And with proconsulary Honors[57] graced;
Where was *Domitia* then and What her Care?
Her Baths, her Gardens and a fav'rite Play'r
The Int'rest of this Darling quite forgot,
In distant rural Scenes her joy was sought:
With Sports and Banquets winging ev'ry Hour,
She cool'd some Grot, or deck'd some am'rous Bower;

56. *Recruit*: supplement, a fresh or additional supply of money (*OED*).

57. *proconsulary Honors*: the honours of a proconsul; 'proconsulare ius' in Tacitus, *Annals*, XIII. xxi. 36.

To Groves and Lakes by turns her Nets apply'd
Her lov'd *Adonis* ever by her side:[58]
Thus whilst with faction and with Fate I strove,
Her Days were Luxury, her Nights were love.[59]

ANICETUS Such Genral Charges tis not hard to lay,
And in this Point if Characters should weigh,
What Might not *Rome* imagine to be true,
Of that Ambition She has seen in You?

AGRIPPINA Neither to Thee nor *Seneca* I Speak:
No justice from determin'd Minds I seek.
In vain to you my Conduct I should Clear,
For You, like other Parasites, would bear
Such Tidings only as wou'd best avail,
To Strengthen some before Concerted Tale,
And breath such sounds into your Princes Ear
As 'twas your single Intrests he should hear.
Is it to — these, to these I would be clear'd?
*(pointing to the Soldiers)*
Be these my Judges who were meant my Guard?

ACERONIA *(to* PALLAS *aside)* May Heaven assist the Greatness of her Mind!

PALLAS *(aside to* ACERONIA*)* And to Reward it make these Ruffians kind.

AGRIPPINA *(to the Soldeirs)* Born in the Camp and in that Nurs'ry bred[60]
When my great Sire, your Conqu'ring Eagles led,
My Godlike Sire, your common Parent too

58. *Groves and Lakes … Adonis ever by her side*: Cassius Dio says Nero hastened Domitia's death because he envied 'her estates at Baiae and in the neighbourhood of Ravenna' (*Roman History*, LXII (Loeb, VIII, 73)). 'Adonis' is here a generic name for a handsome young man; Tacitus names Atimetus as her lover (Tacitus, *Annals*, XIII. xxi).

59. *Her Days were Luxury, her Nights were love*: the line is echoed in Hervey's letter of 17 August 1739 wishing Montagu success in her pursuit of Algarotti: 'Your Days all Luxury, your Nights all Love' (Poem 91, line 15).

60. *Born in the Camp and in that Nurs'ry bred*: Agrippina was born in Ara Ubiorum in Germany (15 CE) and she, her mother and siblings travelled with her father Germanicus in his military campaigns until his death (19 CE). While Empress she had her birthplace renamed Colonia Agrippinensis (modern day Cologne) and emphasised her family's role in building the empire (Tacitus, *Annals*, XII. p. xxvii and xxxvii).

Proud of Your love, and to your Int'rest true,
In Dayly Marches, in the Nights Allarms,
You have beheld me in my Mothers Arms;
Close by the side of her's and your Great Lord.
To every Danger which yourselves explor'd
Alike expos'd; no fears for us he knew,
But what were jointly watchfull over You;
And whilst You shar'd the Glory of His wars,
We shared your Dangers and partook your Cares.

PALLAS *(aside to* ACERONIA*)* Mark how they Listen to her soft'ning Song,
Charm'd by the flat'ry of that Artful-Tongue.

AGRIPPINA He says I was Ambitious,[61] grant it true.
Was not *Germanicus* ambitious too?
But 'twas Ambition, suited his high Blood,
And Mine, like his, Ambition to do good;
I Wedded *Claudius* but by all 'twas say'd
If Birth gave Claim to the imperiel Bed
None cou'd the widow'd *Claudius'* Choice upbraid.
For where the Blood of the *Augustan* Line,
That flow'd more pure, or was inriched like Mine?
Through the Cæsarean Dynasty ally'd,
To ev'ry Prince you've serv'd or deify'd,[62]
So Much the Senate of this Choice approv'd,
That all Objection was by Law remov'd.

ANICETUS What was your Conduct when you'd Gain'd the Throne?

AGRIPPINA Be that too Judg'd; but be it truly known.
Twas the Prosperity of *Rome* I Sought;
First in my Care, and ever in my thought,[63]
And could my Sanguine Wishes have beleiv'd

61. *He says I was Ambitious*: the play with 'ambitious' and 'ambition' in the following lines echoes Antony's address to the people in *Julius Caesar*, III. 2.

62. Agrippina was the great-granddaughter of Augustus, great-niece and adopted granddaughter of Tiberius, sister of Caligula and niece of Claudius.

63. *First in my Care, and ever in my thought*: cf. 'First in my care, and nearest at my heart', Theobald's address to Dulness in *Duniad Variorum*, I. 144 (*The Poems of Alexander Pope, III*, ed. by Valerie Rumbold (Harlow: Pearson Education, 2007), 195). Pope subsequently revised 'nearest' to 'ever'.

This Empire, from my Ancestors receiv'd,
Won by their Arms, and by their skill secured,
Could the Slack Reins of Freedom have endur'd;
If my Erronious Policy had thought,
(Nor by Experience nor our Records taught)
That this vast, turbulent, Rich Factious State,
By it's Own Strength so dangerously great,[64]
This Empire by our-selves alone Confin'd,
The Envy, Fear, and Wonder of Mankind,
Could have subsisted long without a Lord,
When *Claudius* dy'd, her freedom I'd restor'd.
I had pursued *Germanicus*'s Plan[65]
(I lov'd the Parent, I ador'd the Man:)
But When her Ancient Historys I read
Ponder'd her Case, her Circumstances weigh'd,
I found since first the *Gracchi* shooke the state,[66]
Her Laws were force, and Slavery still her Fate.
*Sylla* and *Marius* bore alternate Sway,[67]
Why Need I Name Who forced her to obey?
Successive Conqu'rors seiz'd supreme Command,
To plunder and depopulate the Land:
And till unribuk'd, Great *Augustus* reign'd,
No peace *Rome* knew, no respight she obtain'd:
The Power her Tyrants lost she never gain'd,
By Different Jaylors, only Scourg'd and Chain'd.
From hence the Genius of the *Romans* known, }
I Judg'd their Intrest to be rul'd by one, }
And as a Mother wish'd that one my Son. }

SENECA Anew my soul by this recital fir'd,
Avows that Worth it allways has admir'd.

64. *This Empire ... great*: These seven lines are repeated in the MS with variant accidentals; see List of Emendations.

65. *Germanicus's Plan*: although Germanicus might have been a rival to Tiberius (Tacitus, *Annals*, II. xliii), he is not usually associated with the restoration of 'republican' rights.

66. *Gracchi ... State*: Tiberius Sempronius Gracchus (Tribune 133 BCE) and Gaius Sempronius Gracchus (Tribune 123 and 122 BCE) both attempted controversial reforms to improve the lot of the plebeians; both lost their lives in violent conflict.

67. *Sylla ... Marius ... Sway*: see above, note 31.

AGRIPPINA Virtues like these you never can approve,
Nor Comprehend what you affect to love.
The short Pursuits of thy Mean Grov'ling Mind
To it's pecuniary, low Views Confin'd
No happyness in Publick-good can find.
Obscurely born, Accustom'd to obey,
Thou thinkest to snatch some little Branch of Sway,
Boil'd by some casual Ferment in the State,
Up to the Top, can constitute Thee great;
Whilst Wealth, and Purple, and a Slavish Crou'd,
Thronging thy Dome, can make thy Folly proud?
Not so the Princes born to Wealth and Power,
They know that Glory lyes in something more.
They know the only valuable Fame,
Is the rare Grandeur of a spotless Name:
And the true Pleasure of the Noble Mind,
Not to Command but benefit Mankind.

ANICETUS I Bless the Chance that Made my Master great,
But did the Welfare of the *Roman* State
Engage you to foment Domestick Jars,
To sow the sanguine seeds of Civil Wars,
When you Transfer'd Succession to the Throne,
From *Claudius*' House to place it in your own?

AGRIPPINA For that important stake in care and strife
If I consum'd my Treasures, risk'd my Life,
Should *Nero* or should *Nero*'s Friends reprove,
The fond Excesses of Maternal Love?
But if Adoption and the Female Blood,
Could make a Title to the Empire good,
What better title was there to the Throne,
Than Might be urg'd by *Agrippina*'s Son?
Came not *Octavius* from the female Line?
And did not *Livia*'s Son succeed like mine?[68]

68. *Came not Octavius from the female Line? … Livia's Son succeed like mine?*: Gaius Octavius, Augustus Caesar (63 BCE–14 CE) was the son of Atia, Julius Caesar's niece; the Emperor Tiberius (42 BCE–37 CE), who succeeded Augustus, was the son of the first marriage of Augustus' wife Livia Drusilla (58 BCE–29 CE) and Tiberius Claudius Nero (*d.* 33 BCE).

When great *Augustus* dying gave the Throne
(The Vices of the young *Agrippa*[69] known)
From his own Blood to an adoptive Son?
Besides: if *Messalina*'s Son[70] had Reign'd
Who knows what Slaughters had th' Accession stain'd.
What retrospective Schemes had been pursued?
What heaps of forfeiture, What seas of Blood:
When Vengeance for a Mother's he might plead,
In each prescription which his wrath decreed?

ANICETUS Tis Vain, whilst glorious Motives thus You boast,
To hope the True, are in the Specious Lost:
Say that You thought to govern by your Son;
To make him but your Proxy on the Throne;
But When You found that, loos'd from Your Command,
He rul'd with an emancipated Hand,
And that he was your Master not Your Slave
You purpos'd to resume that Sway You Gave.

AGRIPPINA Dost thou indeed imagine me so weak,
That safety from such Methods I should Seeke?
If Those determin'd and inveterate Foes,
Who envy even this obscure repose,
At the Sons throne the Mother dare accuse,
And hope even filial Justice to abuse,
Must I not Fear in any other Reign,
What they Attempt, too well they would maintain?
And if I stood on any weaker Ground,
That Many more assailants would be found?

ANICETUS In Schemes concerted by vindictive Rage,
Tis not with Caution always we engage;
And whilst revenge on *Nero* claim'd your Thought,
You more his Ruin than your safety sought.

AGRIPPINA If I had purpos'd to embroil the State,
And careless of my own to urge his Fate;

69. *Young Agrippa*: Marcus Vipsanius Agrippa Postumus (12 BCE–14 CE) was the grandson of Augustus through his daughter Julia. He was banished in 9 CE and executed at around the time of Augustus' death. His vices are not recorded; Tacitus says he was guiltless of virtue (*Annals*, I. iii).

70. *Messalina's Son*: Britannicus, who had been replaced by Nero as heir.

Thinkst thou from dark Cabals I'd sought releif;
Plotted in Corners, whisper'd out my Greif?
No! to my Father's Legions I had fled,
And Spoke my Inj'rys at an Army's head;
Nor when *Germanicus*'s Name I us'd,
Had fear'd whate'er my Suit to be refus'd,
Him, tho they trembled at *Tiberius*' Name
Their Emperor they offered to proclaim:
Again when in *Pannonia* they rebell'd,
His single Intrest their Sedition Quell'd,[71]
Nor would they now that Honour'd Name forsake
But guard the Daughter for the Father's sake
And where the Credit should have Counter weigh'd;
Or ev'n their Progress to the Palace stray'd?
A beardless, dissolute, voluptuous band;
Under a Pedant's, or a Boy's Command?
Or say that *Burrhus* had his Cohort's led
And Lent his Arm to Aid this Pedant's Head
Opposed to me what Figure had you Made?
When by my Grace ye Lord it in the state,
Respected as my Choice, and by my Favor great.
Perpetual Exile else had been thy Lot,
He in some distant Colony forgot:[72]
Nor would one Vet'ran have espous'd Your cause,
'Gainst Honor, Gratitude, and Dutys Laws,
Ev'n those (behold them) whilst my wrongs I speak,
From Eyes, unus'd to weep, their Sorrow break,
And trace unpractised Channals down their Cheek.
Whilst to their General's Glorius mem'ry True,
They only wait my Nod to seize on You.

71. *Him … Their Emperor … their Sedition Quell'd*: Tacitus reports that Tiberius' accession after the death of Augustus in 14 CE was followed by rebellions in the army in Pannonia (*Annals*, I. xvi–xxx) and Germania (I. xxxi–xxxv). Germanicus rejected attempts to proclaim him emperor, and the agreements he made were accepted in Pannonia as well as in Germania.

72. *Perpetual Exile … Colony forgot*: Agrippina had recalled Seneca from exile in Corsica to become praetor and Nero's tutor, and had made Burrhus commander of the Praetorian guard. This speech incorporates some of the speech given by Tacitus to Agrippina before the murder of Britannicus (*Annals*, XII. viii and xiv).

ANICETUS They're not so easyly to Treason Won,
Nor are their Oaths to You but to your Son.
SENECA For ever may your Int'rest be the same,
And may this end in Your Accusers Shame.
Is there aught else you'd urge to clear your Fame?
AGRIPPINA This farther answer only will I make:
That I will see my son. — Go bear it back.
ANICETUS We came not here Your Orders to Obey.
SENECA *(aside to* ANICETUS*)* These Slaves are stagger'd[73]
and we must give way
And where the risk?
ANICETUS ——————— Her flight may be prepar'd.
SENECA The Palace is surrounded by a guard
And every Passage to Escape is bar'd. —
*(To* AGRIPPINA*)* I to the Emperor will that answer bear;
Whilst *Anicetus* waits at distance here.
GUARDS. Long live the Empress!
AGRIPPINA ——————— To my friends Farwel.
*Exeunt* SENECA ANICETUS*; and Guards*
PALLAS These Prayers your Interest in the Army tell
And happyly this Cloud of Danger past,
I see new Lustre o'er your Fortunes cast.
Nor know I to admire your virtues more,
In care, Prosperity, Disgrace or Power.
AGRIPPINA Alas, thou Seest not where these dangers tend,
Which I can ne'er avert, 'tho I suspend.
To think me guilty, He must wish me so
And What He wishes may pretend to know.
In vain we boast that Innocence is Ease,
When Pow'r can wound, and Calumny can teaze:
I can no more this rising Greif Controul,
My Eyes are Woman still, 'tho not my Soul:
And Spight of all the Fortitude I boast,
I find My peace of Mind forever lost.
*Exeunt*

73. *stagger'd*: shaken in their commitment, purpose, or opinion (*OED*).

## *Act Second, Scene Second*

*Scene a Hall in Nero's Palace where the Senate is assembled. Enter* NERO *Attended by* BURRHUS *preceded by Lictors*[74] *and the rest of the imperial Ensigns and Retinue. Drums and Trumpets.* NERO *seats him-self on a Throne*

FIRST SENATOR Hail! Mighty Cæsar! at whose call we meet
Waiting for orders at our Sov'reigns Feet.
NERO Fathers,[75] for me and for the Publick Weal,
I know your Love, your Duty, and your Zeal,
Nor could you ever your Assistance grant,
When I should more your Skill and Vigor want:
For never were my Counsels more distress'd,
More different Cares revolving in my Breast;
Our last advice informs us from the East,
That *Parthia* is in Arms, Armenia seized[76]
And Our Allys (the Legions there too weak)
In Vain the Succor of the *Romans* seek;
Recruits[77] must then be sent. — But foreign Wars
Are not my first Concern: Domestick Cares
Press on my Quiet with far heavyer weight:
Against our Person, and against the state,
Conspiracys are form'd; the treason Spread
(As by my first Intelligence 'tis Say'd,)
Where I should least have wish'd, or you have thought,
Nor must we yet beleive, till Proof be brought;
Be then my task the Inquiry to pursue;
Tis yours to punish if the Charge be true.
SECOND SENATOR They Merit Death who'er th' Offenders are.
ALL SENATORS This is our gen'ral Voice we all declare:
They Merit Death whoe'er th' Offenders are.

74. *Lictors*: officers bearing the fasces (a bundle of rods with projecting axe-blade representing the magistrate's power).

75. *Fathers*: the Senate was addressed as *patres et conscripti*, later *patres conscripti*. Originally the *patres* were heads of patrician families; the *conscripti* those enrolled at the beginning of the republic.

76. *Parthia is in Arms, Armenia seized*: Tacitus gives an account of this conflict (*Annals*, XIII. xxxiv–xli).

77. *Recruits*: reinforcements.

NERO Fathers tis well: but when the time shall come
To Judge these Criminals, and fix their Doom,
Forget Your Prince and only think on *Rome*.
Think what her safety and her peace demands
And by those Dutys only guide your hands.

NERO *rises and comes Forward in Conference With* BURRHUS; *Whilst the Senators go out Bowing to* NERO *as they pass*

BURRHUS A Mother and unheard, it could not be;
*Rome* had rebell'd against the harsh Decree.
NERO Was I not Grown, (so long her Pride I'd borne)
At once my Subjects' Pity and their Scorn?
BURRHUS These might be reasons to withdraw your Love,
To curb her Party, and her Court remove;
But Treason, e'er you Punish, you must prove.
NERO Is She not always leaguing with my Foes?
Does She not Now what most I wish Oppose?
Why am I call'd the Master of Mankind,
More than the Meanest Citizen Confin'd?
They as they hate, or love, repudiate, wed,
And those who warm their Hearts, possess their bed;
Whilst, I remain Indissolutly ty'd,
To a Cold, joyless, *hated, barren* Bride.
BURRHUS What *Roman* weary of the Nuptial Chain,
Can quit the Wife and yet the Dow'r retain?
The Empire Yours, *Octavia* still may Plead,
Whatever Charms first Won You to her Bed,
And Claim a Right (the World through her possess'd)
To share Your Throne tho Banish'd from Your Breast;
All Privilige of Taste or Choice deny'd,
To cut that knot which Intrest only ty'd; NERO *frowns*
Not that My Sovereigns Pleasure I dispute,
But wou'd not prematurely pluck the Fruit.
NERO Happy the Pairs, who in each feild, and Grove[78]
Chuse, woo, caress, and with promiscuous Love,
As Choice and Nature prompt, adhere or Rove;

78. *Happy the Pairs, who in each feild, and Grove*: with some minor changes, the fifteen lines of this speech are found as lines 92–106 of Poem 7 'To the Same [Stephen Fox]. From Hampton-Court, 1731'. Sentiments that there appear to be Hervey's own are here given to Nero.

They meet with pleasure, and with ease they part,
For they are only Coupled by the Heart:
The Body still accompany's the Mind
And When this wanders that is unconfin'd;
That Love that Joyn'd the Sated Pair once fled,
They change their Haunts, their Pasture and their Bed.
No four-legg'd Ideots drag, with Mutual Pain,
The Nat'ral Cement pass'd,[79] an Artfull Chain;
Th' Effect of Passion ceases with the Cause,
Clog'd with no after-weight of Forms or Laws:
To no dull Rules of Custom they Submit,
Like us they cool, but when they Cool, they Quit.

BURRHUS To Cross or to obstruct my Princes will,
Far be from me: I live but to fulfill
Your Wish: Yet sometimes, wisely to pursue,
We must Obliquely gain the point in view:[80]
Time may perhaps accomplish your Design —

NERO Talk not of time to Eagerness like Mine;
To Wed *Poppæa* now, this very hour —

BURRHUS Would you relinquish your *Octavia*'s Dow'r?

NERO I would: wealth, Pow'r, and Empire, I'd resign,
And Life itself, when she's no Longer mine.
But why to thee my fond Distress declare
Nor form'd to feel nor to concieve my Care?
Can the Slow streames that creep along thy veins
Enable thee to Guess the throbs, the Pains,
My swelling Heart in ev'ry Pulse sustains?
Can we compute by *Tibur*'s gentle course
The Cataracts of *Nile*'s impetuous Force?
Or from the Southren Gale that fans our Strand
The Hurrican's that toss the *Libian* Sand?

79. *The Nat'ral Cement pass'd*: once the erotic bond has lapsed; in this period, the stress is on the first syllable of 'Cement'.

80. *We must Obliquely gain the point in view*: cf. 'Obliquely waddling to the mark in view', *Dunciad Variorum*, I. 150 (*The Poems of Alexander Pope III*, ed. by Rumbold, 195).

In Vain to Age and Phlegm I would Suggest
What Youth and Passion kindle in this Breast,
It's Greifs unfelt, unpity'd, unredress'd.

BURRHUS By Heav'n my Prince so much your joy is mine
No weary March, no Danger I'd decline,
From Distant *Ganges* to *Britannia*'s Shore,[81]
To feed your Pleasure or extend your Power;
And if I thought all Efforts would be vain
To quell this Passion or to blunt it's Pain —

NERO Is there a Method I have left untry'd,
To Check the Rage of this impetuous tide?
To Sports and Shows in vain I now Repair,
The *Circus* or the Theatre my Care;
Amid the Heat and fury of the Race,
My Fancy wanders on that Angel face:
My Absent Eye forgets to mark the Goal,
Nor Shouting Miryads animate my Soul:
Her form, her voice, her ev'ry charm I find
Unexil'd for one Moment from my Mind;
Musick I sought, but as I play'd or sung,
Her Name on ev'ry Note unvary'd hung,
*Poppæa* tuned my Voice, my harp *Poppæa* strung.
Remains there aught my Quiet to restore
Yet unessay'd?

BURRHUS ——————— Yes.

NERO ——————————What can I do more?

BURRHUS If Poysons other Poysons will remove,
Why may not Love be Chaced by other Love?[82]

NERO Go Bid the *Syrian*, plant his Native Rose

81. *From Distant Ganges to Britannia's Shore*: cf. 'whether he makes his way to distant India ... or ... the formidable Britons, remotest of men', Catullus, XI. 1 (Loeb, pp. 15–17).

82. *If Poysons other Poysons ... Love be Chaced by other Love*: alluding to Dryden, *All for Love*, IV. 1. 136–7, 'And Love may be expell'd by other Love, | As Poysons are by Poysons' (Dryden, *Works, XIII: Plays*, p. 76). Cf. 'As Poysons other Poysons will remove, | So Love may be expel'd by other Love' in Poem 55, 'Verse Dialogue between Hervey and Montagu', lines 50–1, firmly datable to September 1736. Grundy and Halsband identify the reference to Dryden (*Essays & Poems*, p. 288).

On *Sylla*'s Rocks, or *Scytha*'s barren Snows;[83]
Bid Rivers from the Vale o'er Mountains flow,
And frozen *Caucasus* like *Ætna* glow;
Bid the fond Mother smiling o'er her Son,
Adopt another and forsake her own:
Then bid these sleepless Eyes regain their Rest
On any pillow but *Poppæa*'s *Breast*.

BURRHUS As on the Verge of Libia's western Sand,
In *Cyprus Isle* and in the Marsian Land
People there are who have the secret found,
To suck the Venom from the Aspic's wound;
Think you my Prince there is no Roman fair
Whose Lip might heal the Venom of your Care?

NERO When great *Augustus* these fam'd *Psylla*[84] sought
For *Cleopatra*'s wound, in Vain they brought
Their Boasted Antidote; No Means Prevail'd.
The healing Lip and vocal Medcine fail'd;
As vainly too with ev'ry amorous art
The *Roman* fair assail'd her Lovers heart;
Nor those could Life Restore with all their Charms
Nor these seduce my Grandsire from her Arms.
Thus I a wound unmed'cinable mourn,
Thus in a Flame unalterable Burn,
And would like *Antony* this Moment Chuse,
Were I *Poppæa* or the World to Lose.[85]

BURRHUS To sooth your Ills these Palliatives apply'd,
Awhile at least the Fever would subside.

NERO In Vain I sought my once lov'd *Acte*'s Arms.
The Transient Solace of her weaken'd Charms

83. *Go Bid the Syrian, plant his Native Rose . . . Scytha's barren Snows*: Cowley's 'Go bid the *Needle* his dear *North* forsake', in '59. My Fate', in *The Mistress* (*The Collected Works of Abraham Cowley*, ed. by Thomas O. Calhoun *et al.*, 2 vols. (Newark: University of Delaware Press; London: Associated University Presses, 1989–93), II, 91) begins one example of this common form of adynata.

84. *To suck the Venom from the Aspic's wound . . . Psylla*: the Psylla had the power to suck out venom from wounds made by the asp or vipera aspis; they are discussed by Cassius Dio, *Roman History*, LI. xiv (Loeb, VI, 41).

85. *the World to Lose*: an allusion to the subtitle of Dryden's *All for Love: or, The World Well Lost.*

Small Ease afforded, tho the fair was led,
With Each Luxurious Trapping to my Bed;[86]
Odors of ev'ry kind my Slaves prepar'd,
*Judea*'s Balm and *India*'s richest *Nard*;
All *Ethiopia*'s fragrant harvest yeild,
Or the sweet plunder of *Sabæa*'s field;
The Cinnamon, and Cedars mix'd perfumes,
*Egyptian* Unguents and *Arabian* Gums.
She from the Bath, I from the Banquet came;
Whate'er could raise her Beauty or my Flame
Was call'd in aid; with mirtle and with Flowers
My Couch was shaded, like the *Cyprian* Bow'rs;
She, like their Queen, was wantonly array'd
In purple, Gems, and Gold; Her Breast Display'd
Beneath her curling hair, that half unbound
Escap'd the Blooming wreath her Temples Crown'd;
Yet Whilst her Cheek upon my Bosom Lay,
Revolting from those Charms my wishes stray,
And in the Dalliance of her Close embrace
The Beautys of a Dearer Object Trace. —
See — from yon Golden Portal, like the Day
Ev'n now she breaks; and hither bends her way.[87]
Their Blooming Gifts there Youth and Beauty blend,
And Dignity and Grace her Steps attend.
Ev'n now my *Burrhus* at that fatal View,
I feel my op'ning Wounds all Bleed anew,
I cannot bear this tumult in my breast;
By Fears and Wishes, Pain and joy oppressed:
Oh! Say, my friend, say how shall I appease
This raging Passion? Give my soul some ease. —
My Blood, my Heart, my Brain, is all on fire
It's Agony and Madness of Desire.

86. *With Each Luxurious Trapping to my Bed*: the following account is reminiscent of scenes of seduction in Delarivier Manley's *Secret Memoirs and Manners ... from the New Atalantis* (London: for John Morphew and J. Woodward, 1709), e.g. pp. 21–2, 33, 71, but with added sophistication.

87. *from yon Golden Portal ... bends her way*: cf. 'what light though yonder window breaks? | It is the east, and Juliet is the sun' (*Romeo and Juliet*, II. 1. 44–5).

No Longer then Obstructive Measures try,
Thy Prince My *Burrhus*! must possess or Dye.

*Enter* POPPÆA *Attended*

POPPÆA Beset with dangers, and allarm'd with Fears,
Why am I left a Prey to all these Cares?
Cares, Dangers, Fears, occasion'd all by You
And yet in all, by You abandon'd too:
Uncertain what to dread or what expect
Told of Your Love yet proving your Neglect;
Is it a Hard Request my Sorrows make,
Or to protect me Quite or quite forsake?

NERO Reproach me not; nor absent from thy sight,
Imagine that I seek or find Delight;
I look on ev'ry Moment as destroy'd,
A painfull Burden, or a tedious Void,
In Crouds unpleas'd and joyless on a Throne
I feel no commerce[88] Gratefull but your own;
Constraint, not choice, makes other Pathes my Care,
For ev'ry line of Pleasure centers there;
And Whilst a Thousand Objects I pursue
They're all as tasks, or Debts to Custom Due,
I practice others, but I live with You.

POPPÆA When I no other Marks of Love receive
Can I this Verbal Evidence beleive?

NERO By Heav'n tis true, nor Beauty's open Arms,[89]
Nor Friendship, Int'rest, nor Ambition's Charms,
Defrauds thy Empire of the smallest part
In this engross'd,[90] this undivided Heart,
You rule unshaken on that Worthless Throne
My Life the Tenure and the whole your own.

POPPÆA From *Ovid* and *Propertius*'[91] plaintive Strain,

88. *commerce*: communication, or intercourse.

89. *By Heav'n tis true, nor Beauty's open Arms*: the six lines beginning here closely follow Poem 74 'For not the Joy of Beauty's open Arms' sent to Stephen Fox on 16 September 1731.

90. *engross'd*: wholly possessed.

91. *Ovid and Propertius*: Publius Ovidius Naso (43 BCE–17 CE) author of the *Ars Amatoria* and other amatory verse, and Sextus Propertius (c. 54/47–2 BCE) author of four elegies, the first to his mistress, Cynthia.

To Talk with Quiet Hearts, of Wounds and Pain,
Is the soft stile of all our *Roman* Youth
Who boast in tender tales, fictitious Truth,
And Daily Catch our unexperienced fair.

NERO Seem then my Sufferings but fictitious Care?

POPPÆA What Proof of Real Love or Truth is shown,
When I can ask, or you can grant but one,
And that's witheld? ——

NERO —————————— Withheld but not deny'd.
My Heart still willing tho my Hands are ty'd.

POPPÆA If all Mankind from you their fortune prove,
Your hate their Ruin, their Success your Love;
If thrones to Slaves and Chains to Kings you give,
Can my resign'd Credulity beleive
That your own Fate alone you can't Command,
Nor where you give Your Heart can give Your hand?

NERO Ungrateful and Unjust: for You alone
That very caution which you Blame was shown;
I ne'er had weigh'd my Int'rest in the state
But to preserve the Power to make you great,
Had bid *Octavia* take her slighted Dow'r —

POPPÆA You fear not hers but *Agrippinas* pow'r:
Who of an Emperor ment you but the Name,
Nor dare You more, than she designs you, claim,
Your Pow'r Reproach, and Eminence your Shame.
Whilst a tame Emperor, tho a Duteous Son,
You court her smile and tremble at Her Frown;
Nor know the Pow'r you worship is Your own.

NERO Her frown not *Nero* but his council fear'd;
Yet even they against Her power declared:
And won me to postpone my fixed design,
To Plain the way and to secure you mine.

POPPÆA Mere Art, the Common Policy of those
Who fear their Prince directly to oppose
And gaining time divert him from that End,
To Which he's told their winding measures tend.

BURRHUS If I have counsel'd ——

NERO —————————— I will hear no more:

Give your cold Prudence and tame Caution oer;
And if your care was for her sake alone
By Your Obedience now as fully shown:
Be *Neros* Happyness no more delay'd;
So Wills *Poppæa*; be her will Obey'd.
Tho Life and Empire in this cause I stake,
The cause deserves the Sacrifice I make:
But What from *Agrippina* can we fear?
Her forfeit Life must now engross her care:
*This very Day be my Devorce* declared:
The Preists and Temples instantly prepar'd
For my new Nuptials; that to morrows Sun
May See *Poppæa* seated on a Throne
And Night the Wishes of her *Cæsar* crown.
Oh! How I long to strain thee in my Arms,
Sink on thy Bosom, riot in thy Charms;
That Bosom fairer than *Sythonian* Snow,
Sweet as *Cyrene*'s Roses when they Blow;[92]
A Thousand times in Raptures I'll repeat
She's Mine *Poppæa*'s Mine, then Bless my Fate;
Swear endless Truth, and Heaven it Self disclaim,
Unless it's scenes[93] and Pleasures are the same:
Unless these Beauty's shall my Heart employ,
Which taught me first existance was a joy.

*Exeunt* NERO *and* POPPÆA

BURRHUS *alone.*

BURRHUS To What Confusion, these excesses tend?
And Where will these entangled Measures end?
Throughout the City Constirnation reigns,
The fall of *Plautus, Agrippina*'s Chains,
Have urg'd already half our Foes to arm;
*Octavia*'s Party Next will catch the allarm:
And by a Union of their strength may gain

92. *Sythonian Snow ... Cyrene's Roses when they Blow*: Sithonia is a Greek peninsula noted for snow (see Horace, *Odes*, III. xxvi (*Odes and* Epodes, ed. by Niall Rudd, Loeb, p. 205)); Cyrene is a Greek city near Shahhat, Libya.

93. *scenes*: reading uncertain.

A Force which ununited had been vain.
Tis what I fear'd; before a Prosperous Gale
His Youthfull passions crouding all their Sail,
May find that freight precipitately lost
Which slowly steer'd, had safely reached the Coast.[94]
Oh Prudence what avail thy peircing Eyes?
Cautious in vain, unprofitably wise?
When by those very Means thy Power's destroy'd,
Which thou hadst Skill to see and not avoid.

*Exit* BURRHUS

End of The Second Act

## *Act Third, Scene First*

NERO*'s Palace*
*Enter* SENECA *and* ANICETUS *Meeting.*

ANICETUS Where have you left the Empress?
SENECA ——————————— With her Son:
In his Apartment they Confer alone.
ANICETUS On this important Interview depends
Your Fate and Mine, and all the Emp'rors Friends';
For shou'd the Mother once again prevail,
(No Matter by what arts she turn the Scale,)
The Conquest, be it gain'd by fear or Love,
To us will equally destructive prove.
SENECA I wish our Master had been more prepar'd ——
Did she seduce, or did she Scape the Guard?
ANICETUS Soon as you left the Place, the haughty Dame,
Again in tryumph to the Soldiers came,
Flush'd with her Late Success; and proudly said,
That *Agrippina*'s Cause herself would plead
And as an Empress ought, in *Cæsar*'s sight;
For absent none, she cry'd, are in the right;
Why longer then imprudently depend
On Distant Justice from a Doubtfull friend?

94. *before a Prosperous Gale . . . had safely reached the Coast*: Roger Lonsdale provides helpful notes on a similar metaphor in Gray's 'The Bard' (1755), lines 71–6, but no lines are very close to Hervey's (*The Poems of Gray, Collins and Goldsmith* (London: Longman, 1969), pp. 191–2).

To *Seneca*'s Reports no more I'll trust,
To me ungratefull, to my Son unjust, —
The Soldiers all aplauding what she say'd,
She bad them Streight to *Nero*'s Palace lead,
Whilst they with joy, and I through fear obey'd.

SENECA How, in the tumult, did the gaping Throng
Accost this Meteor as it glanced a long?

ANICETUS Not our old Heros cover'd o'er with Scars,
And Crown'd with Lawrel in successfull Wars,
E'er came with louder Acclamations Home;
When joy and tryumph fill'd the Streets of *Rome*
So great the press, the Sweating Slaves who bore
Her Litter, Scarce could pass; the deaf'ning Roar
Of shouting Crouds, pursu'd her March even here;
Hark! At the Gate the Peals now rend the Air.[95]

SENECA This tow'ring Spirit must be made more tame.

ANICETUS Or *Nero* is our Sov'reign but in Name.

SENECA Nay more, should she resume her wonted sway,
And *Rome* this Mistress once again obey,
Her Minion *Pallas* is of course restor'd.

ANICETUS And we shall feel that manumitted Lord[96]
Hard to be soften'd, less to be withstood;
Washing the stains of his Disgrace in Blood.

SENECA What Might not all from such a Union dread,
His Rage to work, her Influence to Aid?

ANICETUS Me only gen'ral Vengeance would pursue,
But Vengeance, Policy, and Intrest too
Would turn his first, and Surest Stroke on you;
When of some new Vicissitude afray'd,
His own Security would ask Your Head.

SENECA Tis true: and yet all Efforts to restrain
These dangerous Schemes, by open force, were vain:
The Empress' Faction to Octavia's joyn'd,
And the profusion of her Wealth, to bind,

95. *Peals now rend the Air*: Tacitus says no more than that she demanded an interview with her son (*Annals*, XIII. xxi), but Hervey enhances the drama with this account of her popularity.
96. *manumitted Lord*: a slave set free, now in a position of authority.

By frequent Donatives the Army's love,
With this late incident, too plainly prove
How much her safety is the Soldiers' Care;
How much her Rank, and Person they revere;
A Rank which in this Capital before,
The proudest of her Matrons never bore;
Her cause the people too, and Nobles own,
And love the Mother whilst they fear the Son.

ANICETUS Yet in the Zenith of Her former power,
How have they curs'd that Name they now adore?

SENECA Among the populace a common Fate,
Who, when they cease to Envy, cease to hate;
But oft'ner still, no benifit design'd
(Such is the Make and temper of Mankind)
With seeming Pity, and with Real Rage,
We see the clam'rous Multitude engage,
And only fight the cause of the Distress'd
To wound th' Opresser, careless of th' Opress'd.

ANICETUS Does *Seneca* then think the Soldiers' Care
For *Agrippina* mix'd with hatred here?

SENECA That's a harsh term: but Oh! my Friend, I dread
To ask My self how wide the Cause may spread. —
Do you Seek *Burrhus* — and expect me here;
I'll to *Poppæa*, and alarm her Fear;
On her for present safety I depend,
Yet see the Hazards which that road attend.
The Politician's, like the Leeche's Art,[97]
At best can only find the infected part:
Dangers they know, but Remedys apply'd
Success is Chance, Conjecture is their Guide:
And tho both see which way destruction's sure,
They walk in Darkness when they try to cure.

*Exeunt severally.* SENECA *and* ANICETUS

97. *the Leeche's Art*: alluding to both a leech's blood-sucking to remove surplus blood or infected tissue, and more generally to the healing art, medicine.

## *Act Third, Scene Second*

*Scene draws and discovers* NERO *and* AGRIPPINA *Siting at a table*

AGRIPPINA My Short Defence you have already heard,
My Accusers are condemn'd and I am clear'd:
You err'd in haste, and on your cooler thought,
Repent of Steps, I've pardon'd and forgot.

NERO I grant 'tis plain from all that you relate,
These Accusations upon Crimes of State,
Were merely the Result of private hate:
And am convinc'd, whate'er their Zeal pretends,
That your delators[98] were not *Nero*'s Friends;
In ev'ry step and Circumstance I see
Rancour to You, and no Regard for Me;
Whom only as their instrument they chose,
Careless alike of Mine, and Rome's repose.
But as their first injustice is to you,
Declare what Punishment you think is Due,
And Whatsoe'er your Vengeance shall decree,
The Sentence shall be ratify'd by me.

AGRIPPINA I seek not Vengeance on so base a Train
Nor of their Tales, but Your beleif complain. —
But I have done; — No more Reproaches fear,
Those useless Sallys of intemperate Care;
Too well I know their teazing influnce vain;
Whom kindness could not keep, they ne'er regain:
But whilst they urge the Hardships we endure,
Augment the Ill they are apply'd to cure:
Not only fail Indiff'rence to remove
But add Aversion to the want of love.
Were it as easy to correct as Blame
And that Repentance always follow'd shame,
Barely to Mention Inj'rys would Suffice;
But from ourselves compunction must arise;
In Vain the injur'd point the glaring Wrong,
The Charge, at once, as impotent, as strong,

98. *your delators*: informers against you.

When the accus'd, unable to defend,
Admit the Errors which they never mend.

NERO Of my past Faults this Image to convey,
Is to reproach me the severest way.

AGRIPPINA Unkindly answer'd; for your Faults to me
Tho not the last perhaps that I should see
Are not the first, My *Nero*, I would mend,
Nor those whose Poyson most I aprehend;
Those to your Self, to *Rome*, and to the State
My first Concern, and strongest Fears create;
To see your Throne precariously enjoy'd
Perhaps the Labours of my Life destroy'd
Whilst you the ripen'd Harvest cast away,
Of ev'ry sleepless Night, and Anxious Day.

NERO The Benefits you've heap'd upon your Son;
The toils you've borne; The Dangers you have run
For *Nero*'s sake, tis needless to recall
To his Remembrance, he avows them all.

AGRIPPINA Nor was it these I purpose to suggest,
I left that Office to Your own kind Breast.
When those we have oblig'd we once upbraid,
The Debt of obligation which we lay'd,
Acquiting them, is by ourselves repay'd:
And all the merit which our pride would boast,
Is, in the Manner which we claim it, lost.
By Words perhaps small Merits must be shown,
But real favours ever speak their own;
Nor can recitals e'er successfull prove,
Where not the Benefits themselves can move,
Experience always shows these Maxims true;
Upon these Maxims I have dealt with You;
And When this Conduct of it's Force shall fail,
By any other hope not to prevail,
When most I Suffer'd from your cold Neglect,
I ne'er complain'd, but left you to reflect;
I bid My Heart it's Wrongs in silence bear
That hardest Lesson to Affliction's Ear,

And left the Work for Truth and time to Mend;
I knew the first, and hope'd the Last my friend.

NERO Th' Event has shown, with Judgement you rely'd[99]
Upon those Aids; and all Attacks defy'd;
In your own Heart and mine you place'd your Trust,
Conscious that Your's was guiltless, mine was just,
And your Disgrace now turn'd upon Your Foes,
Points out the Wisdom of the part you Chose.

AGRIPPINA These were the Methods Prudence bid me take,
When my own Int'rest only was at stake;
But When for you and for the State I fear,
A Diff'rent course that Prudence bids me steer,
Then I must speak, and *Nero* then should hear.
Nor think whilst I remonstrate, that I Chide;
From all but You, Your Failings I would hide;
Nor would to You those Irksome Truths relate,
But to prevent Your knowing them too Late:
When all Those Ills which Flat'ry would conceal,
And Friendship should disclose, unwarn'd you feel.

NERO Where are these Dangers which Surround Your Son?

AGRIPPINA The greatest is You apprehending none;
When Dangers, were you Suffer'd to look round,
From ev'ry Quarter Menace and abound.
Complaints at Home, And Insults from abroad,
With Odium and Disgrace your Counsels load:
And whilst the Foes of *Rome* contemn your Pow'r
The *Romans* only feel it, and Deplore.
How is Your Reign dishonour'd, when each Day
Revolting Provinces forsake our Sway?
From East to West Our Infamy is told,
The rising, and the seting, Sun, behold
The tarnish'd Lustre of the *Roman* Name;
Whilst *Britain* and *Armenia*, both disclaim

99. *Th' Event has shown, with Judgement you rely'd*: 'Judgement' has been added editorially. The line is short and it is clear that Nero is speaking in a conciliatory tone; a word, probably a cognate of the 'Wisdom' and 'Prudence' that Agrippina is credited with in lines 78 and 79, appears to have dropped out in the transcription.

That Yoke our conquering Ancestors impos'd,[100]
From Tribute free'd and from Subjection loos'd:
A Fate unknown till Now, our Eagles meek
Trampled in Scorn beneath Barbarian Feet:
Such our degen'rate State's inverted Doom
Tis Dang'rous Now to be in League with *Rome*;
They pass unpunish'd who her peace annoy,
And no Protection her allys enjoy.
The Legions you Command (a Num'rous Host)
Their Ancient Discipline and Vigor Lost;
Tis we, and not Our Foes, have Cause to Fear,
In Peace unruly, and unfit for War;
The Publick-Treasure to suport them drain'd;
And Yet the Publick Honour unmaintain'd.

NERO In part the facts which You advance are true;
I grant them Evils too, but Nothing New;
And tho they may my indignation Move,
Nor my Neglect, Nor Ignorance they prove:
For to the Senate I the Whole declar'd,
And Remedys already are prepar'd.

AGRIPPINA Who call them such their weakness seek to hide,
And know these trancient Palliatives apply'd,
Are bare Suspensions of aproaching Fate,
Whilst all these Wounds that fester in the State
Lightly skin'd o'er, you'll probe when tis too Late.

NERO When did the Hardy *Britons* own our Pow'r?
Or Who unpunish'd e'er assail'd their Shore?
Even *Julius* thence a Doubtfull Lawrel bore.[101]
Or When was *Parthia* by our Arms subdued;
Her Plains so often fat with *Roman* blood?
Our Legions lost in *Crassus*'s Defeat,

100. *Britain and Armenia, both disclaim | That Yoke … impos'd*: Hervey probably has in mind the campaigns detailed by Tacitus in *Annals*, XIII. xxxiv–xli; XIV. xxiii–xxvi; and XIV. xxix–xxxviii.

101. *Julius thence a Doubtfull Lawrel bore*: Julius Caesar's first invasion of Britain in 55 BCE took him little beyond the coast; the second, in 54 BCE, made more progress but he had to return to subdue revolts in Gaul.

And Baffled *Anthony*'s Confus'd Retreat;[102]
With many other overthrows declare
*Parthia* ne'er bent beneath our Pow'r in War.

AGRIPPINA E'er *Crassus* fell, And *Anthony* retir'd,
These Cheifs at least, by Love and Glory fired,
First Bravely fought, tho with successless Care,
And only prov'd the Common Chance of War:
But You regardless of *Rome*'s Fame or Ease,
Nor waging War, Nor yet Maintaining Peace,
Commit the shatter'd State a double Prey,
To foreign Insults and domestic Sway.
Thus in Opression all Your Pow'r employ'd,
And no Protection from your Care enjoy'd
The very End of Government's destroy'd:
Each feature of Society defaced,
And the Great Name of Magistrate disgrace'd —
Silent, the Grave and wise such times Lament;
The factious stir the people's discontent,
And tho their Murmurs reach not to your Ear,
Guarded around by Ministerial Care,
Their Wrongs they feel, and what they feel Declare;
And justly still impute them to the Hand
That Negligently bears supreme Command.

NERO Clamor and Faction trouble ev'ry Reign.

AGRIPPINA Make one unjust, the other will be vain:
But if with wanton and destructive Rule,
Princes themselves alone will ne'er controle,
Consulting only how they may fulfill
The Dictates of their own Licentious will;
If Princes, lost in Luxury and Ease,
Will irritate the Land with Wrongs like these;[103]

102. *Crassus's Defeat, | And Baffled Anthony's Confus'd Retreat*: Marcus Licinius Crassus (c. 115–53 BCE) was a general and, with Caesar and Pompey, a member of the first triumvirate ruling Rome; his campaign against Parthia ended in defeat and his death at the Battle of Carrhae. Mark Antony's disastrous campaign in Parthia in 37 BCE and his retreat through Armenia (in which he lost a quarter of his force) marked the break up of the second triumvirate.

103. *Will irritate the Land with Wrongs like these*: 'the Land' added editorially; the line is short, something relating to the views of the common people about bad princes having dropped out of the transcription.

With fatal Weapons, Faction then they Arm,
And to the Will, supply the Pow'r to harm.
And by these Methods, even you my Son,
Great as You are, even you may be undone. ——
The glorious steps of him, from whose high Race
You sprung, the great *Augustus* ill you trace;[104]
The Virill Robe[105] his Shoulders sacred bore,
When bent on Empire, and the Sov'reign Pow'r;
With Industry and Skill he knew to gain
What You, enthron'd, had only to Maintain:
He to that Rule, each Moment plain'd[106] the Way,
Which you each Moment Suffer to Decay.

NERO Ambition's Prize, *Augustus*, Who begun
A Private Man, tis true with Labor won,
Through Sanguine Oceans wading to the Throne:[107]
But I, my Birth, and you, and fate my friend,
Began my Race where he aspir'd his End.

AGRIPPINA And Therefore was *Augustus'* task more hard,
Forced to erect those steps you found prepar'd:
But yet *Augustus* seated on the throne,
By Art establish'd what by Arms he'd Won:[108]
And after rough and haughty Measures try'd,
Took *Livia*'s milder counsel for his Guide:
In vain had *Fannius* and *Murena* bled,[109]

104. *the great Augustus ill you trace*: for Augustus' progress after Julius Caesar's death to command of an empire, see Cassius Dio, *Roman History*, XLV–LVI (Loeb, IV–VII); *trace*: follow.

105. *Virill Robe*: the toga virilis worn by adult Romans; Augustus was not at Julius Caesar's death an office holder.

106. *plain'd*: i.e. planed, smoothed.

107. *Through Sanguine Oceans wading to the Throne*: the metaphor is found in Shakespeare *Richard II*, I. 3. 132; *King John*, II. 1. 42; *Macbeth*, III. 4. 136.

108. *Augustus seated on the throne, | By Art establish'd what by Arms he'd Won*: cf. Anchises' address to Augustus, 'these shall be thine arts—to crown Peace with Law, to spare the humbled, and to tame in war the proud' (Virgil, *Aeneid*, VI. 852–3 (Loeb, I, 567)). The following ten lines closely summarise the argument of Seneca's *De Clementia*, recommending mercy though the example of Augustus, I. ix (Loeb, pp. 380–6).

109. *Fannius and Murena bled*: Fannius Caepio, about whom little is known, and Aulus Terentius Varro Murena were executed for conspiracy in 22 BCE. During the trial of Marcus Primus, Murena his defender had accused Augustus of usurping the powers of the Senate.

Conspiracy still rear'd her Hydra-Head;
And till at *Livia*'s Suit, and Her's alone,
To *Cinna*'s Treason Clemency was Shown;[110]
Till he assail'd his Foes with gentler arts,
Not trampled on their Necks, but sooth'd their Hearts.
Till *Rome* beheld him sheath his Angry Sword,
He reign'd her dreaded, but her trembling Lord.

NERO *Rome*, at that time to Servitude unus'd,
Thought her proud Neck by the New yoke abus'd;
But through five Reigns of Arbitrary Sway,
And a whole Century fashion'd to obey;
Her restif Sons, now patiently endure
The pinching Curb, and Stimulating Spur.

AGRIPPINA *(Looking some time fixedly on her Son after a pause speaks)*
Maxims like these *Caligula* pursued,
But pay'd his Crimes and Errors with his Blood.

NERO To shining Mischiefs, seated on a Throne,
Did you then purpose to betray Your Son?
And was your Gift of Empire but a Snare
To latent Evils and to Splendid Care?
Must I forever wake and Watch and fear?
If so, what meddling, proud, ambitious Fool,
Would Covet Empire and aspire to rule?
If at the Goal, thus fattaly possest
Of all He had pursued, the joys of Rest
Could in his cheated Breast no more find Place,
Than in the Anxious Moments of the Race,
Would he his Labour and his Skill employ,
Only to gain what he must ne'er enjoy?[111]
His watchfull Eyes forbidden still to close,
And his sad Heart a Stranger to Repose.

110. *To Cinna's Treason Clemency was Shown*: Gnaeus Cornelius Cinna Magnus was the grandson of Pompey and an ally of Mark Antony. In 4 CE he was found guilty of conspiring against Augustus with Aemilia Lepida but pardoned. Corneille makes him the protagonist in his play celebrating royal power, *Cinna ou la clémence d'Auguste* (1639).

111. *Would he his Labour and his Skill employ . . . what he must ne'er enjoy*: cf. ''Tis strange, the Miser should his Cares employ, | To gain those Riches he can ne'er enjoy', Pope, *Epistle to Burlington*, lines 1–2 (Pope, *Twickenham*, III. ii, p. 134).

AGRIPPINA If by Repose, Security you Mean,
Danger is there most fatal, as least seen:
A Prince's Safety's never at a Stand,
It ask's a Constant interposing Hand;
And he, who vainly hopes t' establish Pow'r,
Till it shall want his Vigilance no more;
Might hope as well each Apetite to feed,
Till craving never should again succeed;
Nature ordains, as ev'ry Day we prove,
In fluctuation all Her Works shall move;
All, All, my Son, by Care must be suply'd,
To all unwatch'd is Permanence deny'd.

NERO — Where then th'Advantage of my boasted Pow'r?

AGRIPPINA Exemption from the Ills which those deplore,
Who Subject to another's Irksome Sway,
Capricious and oppressive Laws obey:
Or weep beneath some Milder Prince's Rule,
Some insolent Vicegerent's harsh Controle.

NERO These are the Negative Effects of Pow'r,
It's Charms who'd covet, were they Nothing More?

AGRIPPINA Who build on more, but vainly hope to find
A Lot not Man deserves, nor Heaven design'd
To bless our ev'ry way imperfect Kind.

NERO Imperial Prospects, shadow'd o'er you see,
Through the false Medium of Your Fears for me.

AGRIPPINA That for Your Sake I am alarm'd is true,
But speake as well from what my Self I knew
As from the tender Fears I feel for You.

NERO The Sov'reign Lord of *Rome* in empty State
Can never be thus impotently great.[112]

AGRIPPINA How great soe'er, a Sov'reign is but One;
Nor can he rule, nor can subsist alone:
And if in Others, all his Strength must lye,
The intrested Prince, if Wise will try
By Gentle Conquests, and by honest Arts,

112. *The Sov'reign Lord of Rome . . . impotently great*: Pope's 'Prologue to Mr. Addison's Tragedy of Cato' presents Caesar as 'Ignobly vain and impotently great', line 29 (Pope, *Twickenham*, VI, 96).

To fix his Empire in his Subjects' Hearts:
And if from them Support he would receive
Must to their Intrest his protection give;
Must cherish Virtue, and Discorage Vice,
Favour the Upright, and Consult the Wise:
Must bribe with Love, by Dignity must awe;
And by Example give a Strength to Law. —
Are These the Methods *Nero* has employ'd?
Are these the Rights the *Romans* have injoy'd?
What is their Good, or Glory in Your Reign?
What is their Civil, or their Martial Gain?
What Do the Forum, or the Rostra boast?
Their Eloquence forgot, their Justice lost:
Whilst in a calling all your Pride you place,
Where Excellence it-self is a Disgrace;
And only strive the *Romans* to engage
As the first Harper on the *Roman* Stage.[113]
Well may Your friends this Character deplore,
When Your worst Foe can never wish you Low'r:
What are the people that compose your Train?
The Loose, the Profligate, the Lewd, the Vain,
Songsters, and Dancers; a Buffoon, or Play'r,
Who all by Turn their Prince's favor share;
Pandors and Harlots, Wretches lost to Shame
And Others of a Trade I blush to Name:
Tis such, and Such alone, who dayly taste
Your Guilty Bounty, and Your Treasures waste:
And to recruit this Charge to Plunder'd *Rome*,
What Spoils from conquer'd Realms have you Brought Home?
Or Whilst Your Vet'rans count their honest Scars,
Receiv'd for *Rome* in honourable Wars;
What are the Mighty Deeds, their Prince has wrought?
What Dangers has he run, what Battles fought?
What can they Mention with your wounds and Toils;
But Drunken Outrage and Nocturnal Broils?

113. ***the first Harper on the Roman Stage***: this and the following lines summarise the view of Nero presented in the parallel with the Prince of Wales (Sedgwick, III, 858–75).

Whilst Crimes, On Which in Judgment you should sit
To punish Others, You Your Self Commit;
Nor only to Licentious Ruffians show
That Lawless Riot shall unpunish'd go,
But by the Choice of your Companions prove,
Who most Offend, are those whom most you Love. —
I see you mov'd — I Wish as much as You,
That you could prove the Grating Tale untrue.

NERO Rumor for truth too Lightly you receive,
And Each exaggerated Tale beleive.

AGRIPPINA The *Milvian Bridge* and the *Flaminian Way*,[114]
Your Haunts by Night for Acts that Shun the Day,[115]
Can Witness that the Charge is not unjust;
Nor are the loose Associates whom you trust,
Careful to hide, but to divulge your shame;
Proud to enrol their Own with *Nero*'s Name.
In the Wild Havock of this Ruffian War
Nor Rank, Nor Sex, Nor Youth, Nor Age You spare;[116]
From the Rude Touch of their Offensive hands,
The Noble Virgin unprotected Stands:
Nor can the wealthy Matron's num'rous Train,
Her Decent Steps from Violence maintain.
The hoary Senator, as vainly bears
The Double Sanction of his Robe and years:
And ensign'd Magistrates themselves endure
Those Wrongs their Office was design'd[117] to cure:
Nor Safety those, Nor these Respect can Boast;
All order banish'd, all Distinction lost.
In Vain the Nightly Watch or City-Guard

114. *The Milvian Bridge and the Flaminian Way*: the Milvian Bridge (now Ponte Flaminia) crossed the Tiber in northern Rome; the Flaminian Way (Via Flaminia) went from Rome to Rimini and had been under the special care of Augustus.

115. *Acts that Shun the Day*: this speech is based on Tacitus (*Annals*, XIII. xxv) and Suetonius (*Lives*, Nero, para. xxvi, II, 123–4).

116. *Nor Rank, Nor Sex, Nor Youth, Nor Age You spare*: cf. 'Nor Age, nor Sex, nor Thrones, nor Graves revered' (Poem 22 *To the Imitator*, line 41).

117. *Office was design'd*: emended from 'Office design'd'.

Station'd, or Marching to protect each Ward,
And some mask'd Courtier wispers in their Ear
*Your aid is Treason, Cæsar revels there.*
Others, perhaps, where *Cæsar* never came,
Your presence feign; and from that very Name
Such Villains ought to dread, a Passport claim.
Thus all the Outlets and the Streets of *Rome*,
Like *Afric*'s Babr'rous desarts are become,
Where all who urge their Miserable Way,
Fall, in the Midst of Horror and dismay,
The Robber's Plundder, or the Murd'rer's Prey.

NERO Oh! spare my Blushes, and no more repeat
The Errors of a Prince so meanly great.

AGRIPPINA O! think not I delight to wound your Ear
It pains me more to speak, than you to hear.
Others perhaps in counselling my Son,
May Serve some Latent Intrest of their own;
To ask no Boon, to press no Suit I come,
I only plead for *Nero* and for *Rome*:
I want no fleets, nor Armys to Command;
To Squeeze no Province with a plundering hand;
When *Burrhus*, or when *Seneca*, advise,
Tho grave their Words, tho plausable and wise,
They have a Sep'rate Intrest of their own;
Tis to their prince they speak; I to my Son;
And What their Faith and Gratitude will be,
*Nero* may Guess by what they've shown to me;
In love and Truth my every Motive Lyes,
And all my Rhet'rick is my Tears and Sighs.

NERO I see Your Love, Your Wisdom I avow;
Shame Dyes my Cheeks, and Conquest Crowns your Brow;
Yes you have Conquer'd and my follys past,
Be sure, whate'er they were, shall be the last:
But show your Mercy as you've shown your power,
And with my fame, my Quiet to restore;
Forgive my Faults and Mention them no more.

AGRIPPINA[118] By Heaven I never will, I swear to Jove;
And for my Curse, if perjur'd I should prove,
May Heaven again withdraw my *Nero*'s Love.
Come to my Arms thou Darling of my heart,[119]
Once more to meet, and never more to part:
Oh! rather may the bounteous Gods destroy
My health, my Life, rob me of any Joy[120]
But this; and torture me with any pain,
But that of seeing thee unkind again.

NERO This flood of goodness *Agrippina* Spare.
Your wrath I could, I can't your kindness bear,
The Wounds that makes 'twere meaness not to fear.

AGRIPPINA My Words I can comand, but Tears will rise,
And float uncheck'd these fond, these faithfull Eyes;
These Eyes, till you were great, forbid to sleep;
And ever since by You Condemn'd to weep;
Tho other Transports now their streams bestow
No more from Greif, but from my Joy they flow;
Yet to my *Nero*, and his Intrest true,
Whate'er the Passion, still tis rais'd by you.

NERO If *Nero* in his turn a Suit should move,
Might he not hope from *Agrippina*'s Love —

AGRIPPINA There is but one that I can never grant.

NERO If ev'ry wish should center in that Want —

AGRIPPINA To certain Ruin should those wishes tend
Would the Indulgent, be the faithfull Friend?
If Justice, Honnor, Safety, Intrest, all
That is most Sacred held, or That we call
Most dear oppose: By them, who lend their Aid,
You are not Serv'd, but speciously betray'd. —
But let this theme some other Hour employ,
Oh! let me taste unmix'd the present joy.

118. AGRIPPINA: the speech-prefix is missing in the manuscript.

119. *Come to my Arms thou Darling of my heart*: cf. 'Come to my Arms thou Dear Deserving Youth', an erotic line in Poem 2 'Flora to Pompey' (line 100), but also 'Come to my Arms thou Aid, thou Dear releif' (Nero to Anicetus, IV. 1. 150, below).

120. *any Joy*: 'any' added editorially; the line is short without this emendation.

NERO It shall be so as you have better Chose:
And now pronounce the Sentence on your foes.
AGRIPPINA Wretches like those my Sone, below my thought
Intent on you already I'd forgot.
Show that the being *Agrippina*'s Friend
You think no Crime, tis all that I pretend.
NERO Some Punishment, tho unrequir'd by You,
Is to their Guilt, and to my Justice due.
AGRIPPINA Then, tho their Guilt might ask a harder dome,[121]
Let it Suffice, that they be banish'd *Rome*.
NERO Their Exil shall this Instant be declar'd:
And trust my Care your followers to reward.
Within there.——

*Enter* SENECA, BURRHUS, ANICETUS, ACERONIA *and the Rest of* NERO*'s and* AGRIPPINA*'s Retinue: after Which* NERO *Continues to Speak.* ——

NERO ————I have heard and strictly weigh'd
Whate'er th' Accusers and th' Accused say'd;
And find the Charge by Lying Malice Lay'd.
A Complicated Guilt: the publick peace
Disturb'd: their Prince's Int'rest and his Ease
To gratify their Rage, alike forgot;
And Duty, Truth, and Justice set at Nought;
Against my Self, what more flagitious Wrong
Could they Commit? What Treason half so strong,
As this Attempt to turn my wrath on one
Where every mark of favour should be shown?
From whom not barely privileged to live,
A Barren tasteless being I receive,
But every Good and honor I derive.
And since for Less Offences,[122] every Day,
The forfeit of their lives Delinquents pay;

121. *dome*: i.e. doom.

122. *Offences*: the manuscript reads 'Offence is', an error which, like the other mistaken homophones, suggests that the play was read aloud by one person while another transcribed it. An alternative emendation to the couplet is 'And since for Less Offence, as every Day, | The forfeit of their lives Delinquents pay,'.

How Mild must *Agrippina*'s Suit be thought,
Who injur'd as she is, my Power besought
That Banishment alone might be their Lot?
But if tomorrow's Sun See's them in *Rome*
That Mercy is recall'd and Death their Doom.
To *Agrippina*'s Friends, my gratefull hand
Means to dispence Wealth, Honors, and Command.
This is our Pleasure. — Be it too declar'd
That *Cæsar*'s Mother have her Usual Guard.

ANICETUS *(aside)* Too much I have heard, too plainly see our fate
But to *Poppæa* must the Whole relate.

*Exit* ANICETUS

NERO To *Concord*'s sacrad Temple[123] I'll repair
Her Peacefull Altars let her Preists prepare
And *Agrippina*, meet her *Nero* there.
There in the sight of *Rome*, I will renew
My Vows to peace, to Gratitude, and You.

*Exit* NERO *leading* AGRIPPINA, *follow'd by their Train, Guards etc Manent* SENECA *and* BURRHUS

SENECA All, All, is lost ——

BURRHUS ——————Even worse than we could fear.

SENECA There Lyes my hopes: —

BURRHUS ————————What hopes appear
From thence? —

SENECA ————— That all this Conduct is meer art
To Quiet Her's, and to Disguise his Heart;
This Turn's too sudden after what has past.

*Enter* ANICETUS *hastily*

ANICETUS Where, Where's the Emperor?

SENECA ——————————What Means this Haste?

BURRHUS Behold him here returning and alone.

*Re enter* NERO

NERO At Length the tedious irksome Task is done.

ANICETUS Oh that my Lips, dread *Cæsar*, could impart

123. *Concord's sacrad Temple*: the lavish marble temple dedicated to Concordia in the forum.

Their fatal tale with ev'ry softing Art.
*Poppæa* ——

NERO ——— Oh! My Fears! — She is not dead?

ANICETUS To you for ever.

NERO ——— How to me?

ANICETUS ——— She's fled.

NERO Fled? — Whither? — When? — to Whom? —

ANICETUS ———— Soon as She heard
The fatal tiding of your dread award
On *Agrippina*'s Foes, with Tears She say'd
That She was ruin'd, lost, undone, betray'd,
Complain'd of *Nero*, and her cruel fate,
In terms your servant dares not to repeat.
Then in the Midst of Sorrow, Rage, Affright,
Cry'd all her Hopes of Safety was in Flight,
That *Agrippina* Thirsted for her Blood
But that the Am'rous *Otho* could, and would
Defend her still from wrong, with all the force
Of *Lusitania*, where she bends her Course.[124]

NERO Am I with all my Care then Come too Late?
And can one Moment's feigning work my fate?
Curse on my temporizing skill
That dared not try my Pow'r, nor show my Will:
This is the Conquests your tame Counsels boast,
What boot's the Conquest when the Prize is lost?
Fearing *Poppæa* might mistrust my Heart,
I hasten'd back it's Secrets to impart —
But wherefore do I longer here delay? —
I will my-Self with Legions cross her Way.
Proclaim her Empress at the Army's head,
And Chace the loath'd *Octavia* from my Bed.

*(is going out)*

SENECA *(kneeling before* NERO*)* Oh! Emperor one Moment yet give Ear,
And Listen to your faithfull Vassal's praye'r. ——

124. *Otho ... Lusitania, where she bends her Course*: Marcus Salvius Otho (32–69 CE), Nero's favourite and Poppæa's divorced husband, had been exiled as governor of Lusitania (Portugal and part of Spain). He was later Emperor (69 CE).

NERO Thinkest thou for Life, or Empire I will Lose
The Object of my Love?

SENECA ——————— What I propose
Is my great Master's pleasure to secure
By Safer Methods only, not less sure;
Go not in person, Let a Chosen Band
Of Horse, Streight under *Burrhus*'s Command,[125]
Not as you sought her love, but fear'd her hate,
Arrest her as a Prisoner to the State.
Be it divulg'd, that She was fled in Rage
Young *Otho* in Rebellion to engage;
Thus time is gain'd; the tale will be beleiv'd;
And *Agrippina* shall be still deceiv'd,
Whose quick Suspicion should you now alarm.
You know not what you risk, nor whom you arm;
Her Power just Shown, her Innocence declar'd;
Follow'd by Crouds; encircled by a Guard;
All, All, th' Advantage which your Art has won
By this Rash Step would be at Once o'erthrown.

ANICETUS To the *Aurelian Road* if *Burrhus* haste
She cannot yet the City Gate have past.

NERO *Burrhus* shall go: — *(to* BURRHUS*)* fly then and think my Friend,
My joy and Life on thy Success depend.

SENECA There is no Danger Prince he must succeed. *exit* BURRHUS

NERO From *Agrippina*'s Tyranny once freed,
Let but *Poppæa* to my Arms be given,
I ask no other Aid, or taste of Heav'n.

The End of the Third Act

## *Act Fourth, Scene First*

*Scene* NERO*'s Palace*
*Enter* POPPÆA *follow'd By* NERO

NERO Hear me but speak —

125. *Streight under Burrhus's Command*: 'under' is added editorially; the line is short. Thanks to Valerie Rumbold for the suggestion of the likely omitted word.

POPPÆA ——————Would I had never heard;
My shame and *Nero*'s Guilt had then been Spared.
NERO If Love be Guilt, —
POPPÆA —————— That Guilt you may disclaim;[126]
Talk not of Love, you but prophane the Name;
By Sparkes of Transient Passion only fir'd,
You never knew what real love inspir'd;
But fashion'd for Your Bondmaid's mean Embrace,
Deform it's Image, and it's Laws disgrace.
NERO Judg of my Love, when Pride like mine can bear,
From those dear Lips ev'n these Reproofs to hear;
Should any else in this opprobrious Strain —
POPPÆA The Injur'd sure have Licence to complain.
NERO By Heaven since first I saw you, to this Hour —
POPPÆA You have abus'd my weakness and Your Power;
Nor think the Triumph great, when we believe
With willing Minds tis easy to deceive:
My Sanguine Wishes lent your Treach'ry Aid,
Or this firm Heart you never had betray'd:
I knew my Birth was equal to my Throne,[127]
And fondly Judg'd your Passion by my Own:
Beleiv'd your love unbounded as your Pow'r,
And your tame Terrors of a Mother O'er.
NERO If tricks of Policy, and Arts of State,
Forced me to temporise with one I hate;
Did false Apearences so far deceive
*Poppæa* too, that She could once beleive,
A Lover and a Prince so mean would Prove
To yeild his Pow'r and Sacrifice his Love?
POPPÆA If all her Foes are foes to *Rome* declared,
And your's (because her Creatures) you reward,
If to her rage you Sacrifice each friend,
And None Who have opos'd her, dare defend;
Must I not fear, reviewing what has pass'd,

126. *disclaim*: 'repudiate a connection with or interest in' (*OED*).

127. *my Birth was equal to my Throne*: many of Poppæa's reproaches in this scene derive from Tacitus, *Annals*, XIV. I, which includes a reference to her 'grandsires with their triumphs'.

My Ruin, tho' postpon'd, will be the Last?
I know she Thirsts for your *Poppæa*'s Blood,
And see her will in nothing is withstood;
See you, despis'd, Obey her haughty Call,
And at the feet that Spurn you meanly fall.

NERO To use me thus — Judg, all you Powers above!
Oh! Judg between us, could She ever Love?

POPPÆA As I am used, I blush to own I can
Still Love you, yet I do, prefidious Man!
Prompted by Love, not by Ambition Sway'd,
And by my Heart, and not my Pride betray'd,
Once, too, tis true, I wish'd to be Your Wife
But fear prevails, and I compound for Life,
Like other Dames that for Convenience wed;
Yet let me seek my Slighted *Otho*'s Bed;
This little Beauty which in vain I boast,
Since all I wish'd it should engage, is lost;
By You contemn'd, but still by *Otho* sought
Tho cruel, lov'd; tho absent, not forgot;
From One I've wrong'd shall that Protection find,
Which vainly I implor'd from You, tho kind;
When with repentant Tears I Bath his feet,
With open Arms this Fugitive he'll meet;
Your helpless outcast happy to receive,
And proud that Succour you deny'd, to give.

NERO Why wilt thou drive me to despair this way? —
You cannot mean the Cruel things you say.

POPPÆA Yes, since I never can be happy here,
Let me at least be safely joyless there.
Absence and time, tho they can never cure,
One day may Lighten what I now endure:
But Spare my Eyes at least the Constant Pain
Of seeing the false Prince I ne'er can gain;
Spare *me* that Greif, and spare Your-self the Shame,
With which *Poppæa*'s Blood will stain your Name.
I own your Mother's Hate and Pow'r I dread,
Ready to fall on this devoted head;
Nor think by Middle ways her schemes can fail,

By force she'll conquer, or by Art prevail:
This only Choice is left; or I must fly,
Or *Agrippina*, or *Poppæa* dye.

NERO And canst thou think one Moment I'll debate,
Between the Loss of what I love, or hate?
Long in my Mind these truths I have revolv'd,
And long in Secret have her Death resolv'd.
Didst thou then know so Little of my Heart,
To think this Reconcilement aught but Art;
Safely to Guide the purpose of my Breast
Which must be frustrate if avow'd or prest?
And have I known so little of thy Mind,
Who still beleiv'd thee faithfull, just, and kind,
Yet see my Heart thus easyly resign'd?
A thousand Deaths Your *Nero* would have prov'd
Before he had abandon'd her he lov'd;
Whilst on a bare suspicion, rashly you
(Deaf to my Vows and to your own untrue)
Would rob my eager wish of all thy Charms,
And Give them to my happier Rival's Arms.

POPPÆA If that Rash Step, resulting from despair,
Was urg'd in haste, and dictated by fear,
And to preserve my Life was all my care;
Should you my flight as Crimanal reprove,
Or call my Cowardice a want of Love?
Or can you Blame me If I took th' allarm,
Beneath a feirce Pursuer's lifted Arm?

NERO So Quick to fear, so ready to depart,
May *I* not fear some Byas in your Heart?

POPPÆA When Hunted Savages[128] forsake the wood,
And Desparate plunge into the hated flood,
With all the Dangers of the Chace beset,
They Quit that lov'd abod they ne'er forget,
Seek what they loath, and fly what they regret;
Impell'd by Nature, prompting still to save
By Genral Laws, that being which she gave;

128. *Savages*: wild animals.

So I to *Otho*'s Arms for Safety flew,
And all I lov'd forsook, forsakeing You.
NERO Yes thou art True, and kind as thou art fair,
Begon Suspicion, Jealousy, and Fear;
But since, deceiv'd, we both have been to Blame,
Our Error, and Our Innocence the same;
Each *Otho*'s Guilt too ready to beleive
A Mutual Pardon let us take and give.
POPPÆA Tis *Agrippina*'s Death alone can prove
*Poppæa*'s Safety, or her *Nero*'s Love.

*Enter* ANICETUS

ANICETUS The Hour, great *Cæsar*, fix'd by your command,
To Meet in *Concord*'s Temple is at Hand;
And Messengars from *Agrippina* Say,
The Empress is already on her way.
NERO Would I were never to behold her more!
ANICETUS And can that wish be vain to *Cæsar*'s Power?
NERO I have determin'd that She shall not live;
Oh! could thy ready wit the Means contrive,
How I might safely take this hated Life
Which thus embbitters Mine with endless Strife;
And combating my ev'ry least command,
Shakes the precarious Sceptre in my hand.
For such a Service — what would I not pay?
ANICETUS Pronounce her Doom. She shall not live to Day.
NERO The Means I want,[129] to perpetrate that Doom,
To free your Prince without alarming *Rome*:[130]
By force 'twere hazardous, by Law 'twere Vain;
And Subtlest Poysons would appear too plain;
The Example of *Britannicus*'s Fate,
Recent and known, the Secret would relate;
And All our factious Foes on that pretence,
Might draw Rebellion's Sword upon their Prince.
I'd have my Vengeance, like the Aspic's[131] Wound,

129. *want*: lack.

130. *The Means I want . . . without alarming Rome*: the following arguments, and Anicetus' proposal, closely follow Tacitus, *Annals*, XIV. iii.

131. *Aspic's*: of the vipera aspis or asp, Cleopatra's chosen means of suicide.

Mortal and Quick, and yet no traces found.

ANICETUS On the Pretence of Sport, or festive Sight,
To the Mock-Image of some naval-Fight,
On *Tiber*'s Stream, or on the *Lucrine Lake*,[132]
If you could tempt her Caution to forsake
The Shore; as Cæsar's Gallys I command,
Her fate (and therefore Sure) is in my Hand.
The Vessels that convey'd her from the Shore,
Should never to the Strand it's freight restore.

NERO Come to my Arms thou Aid, thou Dear releif,
In ev'ry Danger and in ev'ry Greif;
But say my Friend? how shall thy dextrous Care,
Make this our Deep Design like Chance appear?

ANICETUS I have it; — thus — hold — aye; — this very Night,
This credulous Sacrifice you shall invite,
To celebrate a reconcileing Feast
In the Naumachia;[133] leave me to the rest:
With diligent dispatch and secret Care,
A Gally for this Victim I'll prepare,
Whose Keel shall on the Slightest Touch give way;
And to the Bottem all it's Freight convey.
At the same time a Canopy of Lead
Shall on the Deck crush her devoted Head:[134]
Few Slaves I'll trust, and those of Faith aprov'd
By Whom these springs, and Engines shall be mov'd.
Their Work once done, by plunging in the wave,
Thier Lives by Swiming easily they'll Save:
And More that perish of th' untrusted Crew
The More Our Tale of Accident seems true.

NERO It can not fail; — thou shalt about it streight;
Like Heav'n concerting and directing fate.

ANICETUS Apoint the Banquet late; the Hunted prey
When the Carousels of a Drunken Day

132. *Lucrine Lake*: Lucrinus Lacus in the Campania, a famous fishery and site for holiday villas.

133. *Naumachia*: the arena for staging naval battles as an entertainment.

134. *crush her devoted Head*: the details of the plot come from Tacitus, *Annals*, XIV. iii, supplemented with para. v.

Have made her Train less capable of Aid,
Will surer fall, and easyer be betray'd.

NERO *(to* POPPÆA*)* Does not this Scene my Fair dispelle thy Cares?

POPPÆA Whilst She has Life *Poppæa* must have fears.

ANICETUS If, When the Goblet shall be drain'd by You,
You feign'd a suden Illness and withdrew,
In that Confusion all will Quit the feast,
And we may turn Suspicion on your Guest;
Your friends shall whisper Poyson was design'd,
The tale amid the Croud shall Credit find,
And the kind Gods who make Our Prince their Care
With this Disaster seem to punish her:
You May with filial Honors grace her tomb,
And with feign'd sighs deceive aplauding *Rome*.

NERO Thou best of Servants: how shall I repay,
In all my Life, the Service of this Day?

ANICETUS Employ'd for You my Prince! What'er the Task
Success is all the Recompence I ask.

NERO Whate'er advantages *Augustus* knew,
From two fam'd Counsellers unite in you,
Bold as *Agrippa*, as *Mæcenas* true.[135]

ANICETUS Did I deserve the Praises you bestow,
My Service would be short of What I owe;
When to such Honour you have rais'd your Slave,
That Freedom is the Meanest Boon you gave. —
But to th' apointed Fane[136] great *Cæsar* haste,
All *Rome* expects You, and the Hour is Past;
And to Suspicion's Eye a longer stay
May seem some Change or Coldness to betray.

POPPÆA Tis well advis'd; farwell; you must be gone,
Nor change your Conduct till the work be done;
Disguis'd in smiles your Vengeance still pursue,
Stifle Your Anger, and Your Pride subdue.

135. *Bold as Agrippa, as Mæcenas true*: Marcus Vipsanius Agrippa (64/63–12 BCE) a general who led Augustus' armed forces and became his son-in-law; Gaius Cilnius Maecenas (70–8 BCE), adviser, diplomat and patron of poets, including Horace and Virgil.

136. *Fane*: temple (*OED*).

And if Success attend this great Design
I ask no more of fate, for *Nero*'s Mine.

NERO He's wholy yours; — but with that flat'ring Tongue,
Charm me no more, if you would have me gone;
On, then my friend, to *Concord*'s Temple lead,
And that unguess'd, our purpose may succeed,
With added favours and new Honours there,
I'll load this Cheat'd Victim I prepare:
Whilst she Confiding in the flat'ring Preist,
In Gaudy Ruin ignorantly dress'd;
Shall, when she feels the Blow, perceive too late
Each proud Distinction mark'd her out for fate.

*Exeunt* NERO *and* ANICETUS

POPPÆA *alone.*

POPPÆA My Heart is lighter; smiling Hope again
Has chase'd Despair, and soften'd ev'ry pain,
Again the throne is open to my View,
Again invit'd, I again pursue;
And thou, fair *Venus*![137] whose benignant Power
With joy we follow, not through fear adore;
Whose Genial Edicts, and Whose grateful[138] Sway,
People the Realms of Earth and Air, and Sea;
Kind to my Wish, and to thy Vot'ry just:
Assert my Cause, in thee alone I trust:
Prove to thy Honnor on *Poppæa*'s Foes,
That none Successfull thy Allys opose;
Prove whilst you combate force, and Baffle Art,
The Seat of real Strength is in the Heart;
And Whilst thy Troops their garrison'd prevail,
Thy Aid in ev'ry Contest turn's the Scale. *Exit* POPPÆA.

## *Act Fourth, Scene Second*

*The Temple of Concord*

137. *And thou, fair Venus*: Poppæa's succeeding lines encapsulate something of the opening address to Venus in Lucretius, *De Rerum Natura* (Loeb, pp. 3–7).

138. *grateful*: welcome (*OED*).

*Trumpets Sound*

*Enter on one Side,* NERO, SENECA, BURRHUS, ANICETUS, *and the Emperor's Train: on the Other,* AGRIPPINA, PALLAS, ACERONIA, *and the rest of Agrippina's Train; the Emperor Seats himself on one side of the Theatre, and the Empress on the other, whilst the following Hymn is Sung to the Goddess Concord*

CHORUS To *Concord* all your voices raise,
Invoke her aid, resound her praise:
To *Concord* Io Pæan[139] sing,
Your sacred Gifts to *Concord* Bring.

FIRST PREIST Nor with Blood of Victims slain;
Let your Zeal her Shrine prophane,
These would Shock the gentle Maid:
Let the Soldeir rough with Scars,
Offer these to Stubborn *Mars*,
Emblems of His Bloody Trade.

CHORUS To *Concord* then your voices raise,
Invoke her Aid, resound her praise.

SECOND PRIST Bring *Arabia*'s rich perfumes,
Roses, Spices, fragrant Gums,
These, to *Concord*'s shrine belong;
And with Musick, Dance and Song,
Let the Beautifull and Young,
Lead the Sportive Train along.

CHORUS To *Concord* then your voices raise,
Invoke her Aid, resound her praise.

FIRST PREIST Hail! *Concord*! Smiling Goddess, Hail!
Here ever may thy Laws Prevail:
Here let the peacefull Olive reign,
Whilst Laurels crown *Bellona*'s [140] Fane,
Whose Glory 'tis to Guide those Woes,
Tis *Concord*'s Glory to Compose.

CHORUS To *Concord* Io pæan Sing,
Your sacred Gifts to *Concord* bring.

SECOND PREIST In vain the hardy Sons of *Rome*,
Secure from distant foes,

139. *Io Pæan*: 'Io' is an exclamation of joy (Ho!) and a 'pæan' a festive hymn.
140. *Bellona*: goddess of war.

Would bring their conquering Eagles home,
And *Janus'* Temple close.[141]
To Woe betray'd,
Without thy aid,
They'd only find remoter Wars
Exchang'd for feirce domestick Jars:
Intestine Broils,[142]
For foreign Spoils,
Would Blast the fruit of all their Toils:
Disquiet still would vex the Land,
And torn by Faction, weeping *Rome*,
From her own offspring's murd'rous Hand,
Would Meet a Paricidal Doom.

CHORUS To *Concord* then your Voices raise,
Invoke her Aid, resound her Praise.

FIRST PREIST To spread thy Worship through the State
Should all our thought and Care employ;
'Twill make us happy, keep us great
Tis publick Strength, and private Joy.

SECOND PREIST Gratefull Friendship's Silken Band,
Must be fasten'd by thy Hand:
Love Himself in Beauty's Arms,
Can profess but half her Charms,
If thy Absence damp his taste;
To Compleat and make it last,
*Concord*'s Cement we must prove
Or in Friendship or in Love.

BOTH PREISTS Without thy Blessings then Below,
No Happyness can mortals know;
Without thy Blessings Mighty *Jove*
Him-Self would reign unpleas'd above:
Without thy Fiat and thy Sanction Given
Nor joy on Earth, nor Peace can reign in Heav'n.

141. *Janus' Temple close*: Janus, facing both ways, was the god of gates and doorways; his temple in the forum had doors at both ends and they were closed only in times of peace, which were rare.

142. Intestine Broils: cf. 'intestin broiles', *Paradise Lost*, II. 1001 (Milton, *Poetical Works*, I. 51).

CHORUS To *Concord* then your Voices raise
Invoke her Aid, resound her praise.
To *Concord* Io pæan Sing,
Your Sacred Gifts to *Concord* Bring.

*After this Hymn the* HIGH PREIST *of Concord kneels before the Altar lays Incence there and Whilst it is Burning Speaks thus on his knees*

HIGH-PREIST Whilst at thy Shrine my Adoration's pay'd,
And Humbly here this little off'ring lay'd,
Goddess of Peace! examine well my Breast,
And as thy Laws are reverenced by thy Preist,
So crown his Days with Ease, his Grave with rest.

*(He rises and standing by the Altar goes on thus)*

Now let those Votarys aproach, who find
No rest of Malice rankling[143] in their Mind,
By such alone be adoration pay'd;
By such be Offrings on this altar Lay'd;
For only those our Deity shall hear,
The Vows of others are despersed in Air[144]
Or Vengeance waits their desecrating Pray'r.

*Here a Slave gives a little Censer of Incence to* ACERONIA, *who gives it on her knee to* AGRIPPINA. *After which* AGRIPPINA *rises, comes forward, and speaks*

AGRIPPINA Behold, thus summon'd, a fond Mother here,
Whose Heart thus try'd, to *Concord* makes it's Prayer;
Upon these terms my Worship here I pay,
And on this Shrine maternal Off'rings lay.

*Here* AGRIPPINA *lays her Insense on the Altar, Then kneels before it, and Whilst the Incense Burns Thus Speaks on her kneeling*

AGRIPPINA Yee Powers who made, and rule this World below,
Who Judg our Actions, and our Motives know;

143. *rankling*: the manuscript has 'rankring', which could be a mis-hearing for 'rankling', or 'rancouring' ('With inanimate subject (often a feeling): to rankle; (also) to fester' (*OED*)).

144. *The Vows of others are despersed in Air*: in Pope's *Rape of the Lock* half the Baron's prayer is granted, 'The rest, the Winds dispers'd in empty Air' (II. 46); Pope refers to Virgil's *Aeneid*, XI. 794–5 (Pope, *Twickenham*, II, 162; Loeb, II, 290).

Who stripp'd of ev'ry Veil Our Words impart
Can penetrate the Breast and read the Heart,
With All Our Pride disguises to Mankind,
And all Our Vanity neglects to find;
Oh! Search my Soul, nor Pardon if you View
One Wav'ring thought to these my Vows untrue;
But as I wish the Welfare of my Son,
In that Degree, just Heaven! promote my own.

AGRIPPINA *rises and* NERO *comes forward and Speaks after receiving a censer of Incense from* SENECA *who delivers it kneeling.*

NERO Indulgent Goddess whose Auspicious Power,
None who sincerely ask, in vain implore;
See at the Altar *Cæsar* suppliant stand,
He brings thee Off'rings with a filial Hand;
And as his Vows to *Concord* are Sincere,
May Heav'n reject, or greet his Warmest Prayer.

*(He lays the Incense on the Altar then kneels and continus speaking)*

Thou great Protector of the *Julian* Race![145]
Whose Smile is Glory, and whose Frown Disgrace,
Revered, omnipotent, immortal, *Jove*!
Ruler of Earth beneath, and Heav'n above!
If *Rome*'s imperial Lord be worth thy Care,
Look down, Attend, and Judg me whilst I swear,
That *Agrippina* to my Soul is Dear.
And if remaining in my Heart you find
A smother'd enmity, a thought unkind,
Oh! Give Me to Remorse, Contempt, and Shame,
Guilt wound my Peace, Dishonour blast my Name.
Dart your red light'nings on this perjur'd Head,
Afflict me living and torment me Dead:
Of Pow'r depriv'd, from *Rome* an Exile driv'n,
And an unbury'd Ghost forbid your Heav'n.

145. *Julian Race*: the Julian (sometimes the Julio-Claudian) dynasty includes the five Roman Emperors from Augustus to Nero.

*As soon as* NERO *has done Speaking the stage grows dark by an Eclipse of the Sun:*[146] *all appear in the greatest Surprise and Consternation.*

HIGH-PREIST Yee Awfull Pow'rs! What Means this sudden Night?
Why droops the Chearful World debar'd of Light,
Whilst yet above remain's the mounted Sun,
And little more than half his race is run?
Each darkling Bird, the Bat, and Midnight Owl,
Wing the Black Air; the Wolves begin to howl.
What does inverted Nature thus portend?
Has any impious Mortal dared to offend
The Gentle Goddess of this peacefull House,
With Gifts Deceitfull, and fallacious Vows?
Avert these Omens; and let all repair
T' appease the Gods by Sacrifice and Prayer.

SENECA Peace, Rev'rend Coward, and conceal thy Shame,
Nor for thy own defects the Guiltless Blame.
Say why this Awful Exhortation given
To Deprecate the Wrath of Angry heav'n?[147]
Because our Preists, who to instruct us pay'd,
Neglect the Essence of their Sacred Trade?
And bent alone on profit and on pow'r
Neither the Will nor ways of Heav'n explore?
Is it for this Our Altars we must load,
And Suplicate for this our Guardian-God?
Because Our teachers ignorant and Proud
Tho Blind themselves, would lead a Blinded Croud?[148]

146. *Eclipse of the Sun*: in Tacitus, *Annals*, I. xxviii, a mutiny is ended by an eclipse of the moon, with a discussion of the validity of interpretations.

147. *the Wrath of Angry heav'n*: cf. the first scene of Dryden's *All for Love*, where Alexas rebukes the priest Serapion for his vision of the destruction of Egypt (I. 1. 32–9), a vision the play ultimately supports, and also the debate about heavenly portents in *Julius Caesar*, I. 3. For changing attitudes to astrology in the period, see Patrick Curry, *Prophecy and Power: Astrology in Early Modern England* (Princeton, NJ: Princeton University Press, 1989), esp. pp. 138–52.

148. *Tho Blind themselves, would lead a Blinded Croud*: cf. 'they be blind leaders of the blind. And if the blind lead the blind, both shall fall into the ditch' (Matthew 15: 14, also Luke 6: 39).

HIGH-PREIST When daring Men, with impious words like these,
And Brutal Outrage, fill the House of Peace;
When Heav'n's high Ministers insulted stand,
Nor at the Altar can Respect Command;
Well may the Gods these Marks of Anger show;
But him who execute their will below,
To them Obeident, and to Man a friend
Their Justice in that province will defend.

SENECA Is it the Province of Mild *Concords* preist
To sow Suspicion in her Vot'rys Breast?
Suspicion is your Goddess' deadlyest Foe,
And wounds her deepest, tho it strikes no Blow.
Your Province is to calm those Minds you fright,
And to compose our passions, not excite.
And were you not in Sloth and Ignorance bred,
No Dangers from these Incidents you'd dread;
But when you saw the Effect, would know the Cause,
The Cause as consonant to Nat'ral Laws,
As When the Various Seasons take their turn,
As When Our Winters Chill, or Summers burn.
By certain Revolutions, if the Moon,
At Stated Periods, intercepts the Sun
From this Our Earth; Why should that Suden Gloom
Be more portentous to the Sons of *Rome*,
Than when his parting or returning light
Makes Night succeed to Day, or Day to Night?
Experience teaches this to ev'ry Clown,
Were't not[149] by Industry or study known:
Each Night the sky in Darkness is involv'd;
You'd Start, and think all Nature was Disolv'd;
For as you're govern'd not by Sense but sound,
Uncommon with Unnat'ral you confound;
And think because Eclipses are more rare
Than Night or Winter, that they more declare
The Imediate Influence of the Powers above,

149. *Were't not*: the manuscript says 'Were it', which does not make sense. Thanks to Valerie Rumbold for suggesting this emendation.

More want their Aid, and more their being prove —
*(the stage here grows light again)*
But Whilst I speak, behold returning Day,
Again the Sun resumes his Golden Ray;
Again the Gay Horison stands confess'd,
Clear's ev'ry Brow, and Gladen's ev'ry Breast;
Whilst fear and Wonder like the Shadows fly,
And Quiet and Content their Place supply.

NERO Thanks to My *Seneca*, who calm and Wise
Taught his instructed Master to despise
These Preistly Terrors, and Restor'd that Rest
I felt suspended in my Anxious Breast.

SENECA I did my Duty, speaking this my Sence,
At Once to truth, to *Rome*, and to my Prince.

NERO Thus oft the Mind by pious Errors caught,
Thinks when deluded only, that 'tis taught:
Whilst timid Virtue aprehends a Sin,
Which Conscience ne'er suggest'd from within.
Oh! *Agrippina*! tho I knew my Soul,
With Love, with Gratitude, and Duty full,
A Thousand fears were Busy in my Mind,
Lest thou shouldst *prove*, or I should *seem* unkind,

AGRIPPINA Banish My *Nero* those ill-grounded fears,
And heal thy own, as thou hast heal'd my Cares:
Nor think that one Short Moment I beleiv'd
Who Credit *Nero* ever are Deceiv'd:
Failings in Mortal beings there must be,
But treach'ry's one, can ne'er reside in thee:
No, When thy Heart by false Suggestions Sway'd
In partial Scales my upright Conduct weigh'd
I was neglected, but was ne'er betray'd:
Not even when the harshest Thought took place,
When you were push'd to load me with Disgrace,
You were unkind, but you wer never base.
Then not to Omens or to Preists I trust,
But from Experience of thy Worth, am just.
Such is thy Noble Nature, such thy truth,
Tho prejudice may blind thy hasty youth,

Tho Right and wrong thy passions may confound,
And Urge to Hate, that Hate will still be own'd:
And When thy Lips a Softer Message bear,
'Tis still the Language of a Soul sincere;
Be this or that the Sentiment profess'd
Each is the genuine feeling of thy Breast.

NERO Enough: my fears are hush'd, my Heart at Ease
Thy kindness has restor'd it's exil'd Peace.
Oh! *Agrippina* when I thought thee lost,
Nor joy my Days, nor Rest my Nights could boast.
From others, as I pleas'd, my ample Pow'r
Could Chace Distress and Whiten[150] ev'ry Hour;
But for my-Self in Vain it's force I try'd,
I found it Bounded to *my* Griefs; apply'd
To the fond Cares of *Rome*'s deject'd Lord,
Nor Remedy nor Ease it could Afford;
I found You could embitter all you gave,
And that the World's prou'd Master was your Slave;
Whilst from my Sight, but not my Heart remov'd,
You were at once by *Nero*, wrong'd and lov'd.

AGRIPPINA To Gladness give, my Son, the present Hour,
And wound remembrance with these thoughts no more.

NERO It shall be so, be all as You ordain;
To Day let Universall Gladness reign:
To sports and Shows, and to a gen'ral feast,
Tis *Cæsar* Bids and *Rome* shall be the Guest.
Whate'er the Earth, the Air and Seas afford,
Shall with promiscuous Plenty load the Board,
*Falernias* Vintage[151] through each Street shall rowl,
And ev'ry *Roman* quaff the festive Bowl;
Whilst at His Door each Citizen shall load
The Lawrel'd Altar of his Guardian God.

PALLAS *(aside to* AGRIPPINA*)* When Fear relaxed the Guard of his Disguise
I watch'd his conscious Cheek, and guilty Eyes;

150. *Whiten*: 'to free from evil, guilt, disgrace, etc.'; or 'to provide with a specious appearance of honesty, respectability, rectitude, etc.' (*OED*).

151. *Falernias Vintage*: wine made from grapes grown on the slopes of Mount Falernus, especially a heavy sweet white wine, considered the best.

Be cautious how you come within his Power;
We are Observ'd. I have not time for More.

NERO And When Yon Azure Sky Resign's it's Light,
Wrapt in the sable Mantle of the Night,
My Slaves the Royal Banquet shall prepare
In the Naumachia, and Conspicuous there,
Whilst in the Center of the Ambient Tide
Our floating Palace shall at Anchor ride,
Whilst Lamps and Torches with a Mingled Ray
Shall beam around their Artificial Day,
From the throng'd Shores, collected *Rome* shall view
The Honours by her Sov'reign pay'd to You;
When at the Table you Vouchsafe to grace,
*Cæsar* shall only fill the Second Place.
Then let the World, by faction torn, rejoice
At this Our league, with one applauding Voice,
For not to us it's Blessings are confine'd,
Tis peace to *Rome*, and Safety to Mankind *(Exeunt)*

End of the Fourth Act

## *Act Fifth, Scene First*

*Scene* POPPÆA*'s Apartment* in NERO*'s Palace*
*Enter* POPPÆA *alone*

POPPÆA What various Passions in my anxious Breast
Usurp the Empire of this Hour of Rest?
Rage, Hate, Ambition, Hope, and fear
Wage in a Doubtful Feild a Medly War:
By Turns their varying infl'ence they impart,
Throb in each pulse, and flutter round my Heart. —
Even now the Mighty Lot that must decide
*Poppæa*'s Fate, is in the Balance try'd: —
A Double Horrer sits upon the Gloom
Of this important Night, and Wakefull *Rome*,
Unconscious of the Ruin we prepare,
Seems in the Progress of our Schemes to share;
Whilst Riot, Uproar, and Confusion joyn'd
Rage in each Street and agitate each Mind.

Eager to know, and yet to Ask Affraid
(Our Secrets oft by busy Care Betray'd),
No Mesages I dare to risk; no Spys
To trust; but Often cast my cheated Eyes
From yonder Window, hopeing to discern
From Passing Objects what I never learn.
That thickning Croud bespeaks the Emp'ror near —
*(Looking from the window)*
Those Num'rous Torches too — his Guards apear,
Tis He — Great Gods! — the Mighty Work's begun; —
Tis now in Act: perhaps already Done; —
Perhaps miscarry'd; inauspicious thought,
By fear adminstred, with Horrer fraught.
Where, Where is *Anicetus* now to give
That Ease my Soul is wanting to receive?

*Enter* ANICETUS *Hastily*

POPPÆA Thou Welcome Guest! — is *Agrippina* Dead?
ANICETUS Oh! cursed Chance: She is escap'd and fled.
POPPÆA Distraction: Hell! and dost thou Dare,[152]
Villian, to Live such tideings to declare?
Fiends blast thy Lips; Perdition on thy Head;
Oh fatal Scheme! is this thy Vaunted aid?
Is this the Skill and Courage which you boast,
To which *Poppæa* trusted and is lost?
ANICETUS Oh! Blame not *Anicetus* or his Care.
She had not Scap'd with Life had I been there.
POPPÆA Why were you not?
ANICETUS ————————The Emperor thought this way
The Source of all less likely to betray.
POPPÆA Lame Coward Policy! that none might know
By whom the Stroke was urg'd, you miss the Blow.
Thus ever those, who will be over wise
Unfit for any daring enterprise,
When they should make anothers Ruin Sure,

152. *Distraction … Dare*: short line (if 'Distraction' is not given four syllables), perhaps including a dramatic pause.

Are thinking how they may themselves secure;
And by the Weakness of a Double View,
Fail in the Single Point they should pursue;
But Quick thou clumsy Minister of Fate
The Progress of thy Blundering Schemes relate.

ANICETUS This was the Dark Account[153] the Luckless Slave
I chiefly trusted, of the Progress gave:
That on the Stated Signal, when at first
The Roof with all it's Leaden Ruin burst;
Tho crushed to Atoms at the Empress's Side,
Her freedman *Gallus*[154] instantaneous Dy'd;
A Shelter She and *Aceronia* found
Beneath one Part, which, Hollow from the Ground,
Some broken fragment o'er the rest sustain'd
Above the fractur'd Deck, and there remain'd.
The Dissolution of the Ship below
Did not as was propos'd, succeed the Blow;
The Chance by which it fail'd he did not know.
Confusion thus comenced among the Crew
Neither the trusted nor untrusted knew
Or what they should avoid or what pursue:
But interfering with each others Aim
Conflicting Orders all around proclaim
Whilst *Aceronia*, fraudfull and Affraid,
Cry'd, I'm the Empress *Cæsar*'s Mother. Aid!
But this Expedient fatally She try'd
And by the Means She Sought her Safety, dy'd,
Since what she vainly purpos'd Should employ
Their Care to Save her, urg'd it to destroy;
For by this Fraud our faithfull friends deceiv'd,
O'erwhelm'd with Blows the imposter they believ'd.
Then all their Force, and All their art Apply'd
To sink the tott'ring Vessel on one Side
At once they bore the Whole beneath the tide;

153. *Dark Account*: based on Tacitus, *Annals*, XIV. v.

154. *Gallus*: Crepereius Gallus, described by Tacitus as standing not far from the tiller, while Aceronia bends over Agrippina's feet.

When each himself alone intent to Save
Crys fill'd the Air and Ruin spread the Wave.
POPPÆA What then became of *Agrippina*?
ANICETUS ————————————None
For Certain could inform me: this alone
(After the first Report that She was Dead)
I learn'd in Haste, that She was Safe and fled.
POPPÆA Without Connivance this could Never be
And ev'ry Step speak's Treachery to me:
The Slave you Trusted must have lent her Aid
And what he says Miscarry'd, he betray'd.
ANICETUS The Cause of that distrust he soon remov'd,
For Whilst in Wrath his Conduct I reprov'd,
Without the least Reply, an angry Tear
Burst from his Eye, and instant in despair
He plung'd a Knife, with these reproaches fir'd,
Into his Breast, and at my feet expir'd.
POPPÆA Perhaps twas Consious Guilt that gave the stroke
And that he fear'd the torture whilst you spoke.
ANICETUS I've known him long, and did not judg it so: —
But that's a useless vain enquiry now.
Our care must be these Errors to retrieve.
POPPÆA Force must be used, we can no more deceive.
ANICETUS Of *Nero*'s Love so strongly prepossess'd
Who knows if yet Our Counsels have been guess'd?
Perhaps She may not think the ruin Meant
And only Fortune's casual Hand Lament.
POPPÆA Canst thou beleive her sanguine Hope so blind
To Doubt a Moment of Her Death design'd?
If She suspect'd not the Toils were set,
Can She Yet Doubt, intangled in the Net?
In vain on this deceitfull Plan you'd buil'd,
That one like her, in Courts and Courtiers skill'd,
Whose Comprehensive penetrating Sight
Can bring their Darkest Policy to light;

By Nature Quick and by experience Wise,[155]
In path's of Moles can See with Linx's Eyes
Will in her judgment at this Crisis err,
And Want Conviction on a Point so clear:
When scarce I fear, there's one refineing fool,
In wise conjectures straining to be dull,
That loiter's[156] in the Forum, whose coarse Brain,
Will not as well as *Œdipus* explain
Riddles like these;[157] and tho restrain'd by fear,
In Whispers only to Rebellion's Ear
'Twill first be told; the fatal time will come
The Palace Walls shall Eccho it through *Rome*,
When joyn'd to *Agrippina*'s strengthend Band
Revolting Legions Vengeance shall demand.

ANICETUS We must prevent these Mischeifs you foresee.

POPPÆA No other Counsel shall be given by me,
Than at all Hazards, not to let her live, —
But say how *Nero* did this News receive.

ANICETUS At first like *Niobe* to Marble struck[158]
He seem'd; then in to Rage like Madness Broke;
Upon his Couch his trembling Limbs he threw,
And, as a Dagger from his side he drew,
Beg'd that some friend wou'd sheath it in his Breast
The only Method to restore it's Rest.
His Freedmen at this wild excess amazed,
For *Seneca* and *Burrhus* sent in haste,
Who in his Closet with the prince alone,
Are now consulting what is to be done:
This passing I colected as I flew
To bring this fatal History to You;

155. *By Nature Quick and by experience Wise*: cf. 'By Nature honest, by Experience wise' (Pope, *Epistle to Dr. Arbuthnot*, line 400; Pope, *Twickenham*, IV, 126).

156. *loiter's*: loter's MS; reading doubtful.

157. *as well as Œdipus explain | Riddles like these*: in Sophocles' *Œdipus the King*, Œdipus has saved Thebes by solving the riddle of the Sphinx.

158. *Niobe to Marble struck*: Niobe was the mother of seven daughters and seven sons slain by Diana and Apollo; she wept until she turned to stone.

Nor did I dare his angrey Eyes to Meet
Or throw this Wretch for Pardon at his feet.

POPPÆA In my Protection safe, dismiss that fear:
I'll to his Closet instantly repair,
And tell him all is lost unless she dyes:
If other Measures, other friends advise
And Doubts, Demurs and Difficultys Make,
Do you the Execution undertake;
Nor can you fail his Pardon to obtain,
When what through you he lost, by you he shall gain.

*Exeunt*

## *Act Fifth, Scene Second*

*Scene,* NERO*'s Closet, Draws and Discovers* NERO *sitting at a Table* SENECA *on One Side and* BURRHUS *on the other.* NERO *rises comes forward and Speaks*[159]

NERO Talk not of Patience, tis for lighter Care;
I'm all Confusion, Horror, and Despair:
The *Caspian Sea*, whose Billows ne'er Subside,[160]
Expos'd to Urging Stormes on either Side,
Enjoys, compared to those in *Nero*'s Breast,
The Softest Calm, and the profoundest Rest;
Nor all the Monsters that her Woumbe Contain,
Let loose at once cou'd aggravate my Pains.
Whate'er our Legends or our Poets tell
Afflict the Damn'd and Constitute their Hell,
The *Furys* Scourges, or their Scorpion Hair;[161]
The ever Labouring, ever frustrate Care;
*Prometheus'* Vulture, and *Ixion*'s Wheel[162]

159. This scene elaborates on Tacitus, *Annals*, XIV. vii, which it follows especially in the advice given by Burrhus, but Poppæa's role is added.

160. *The Caspian Sea, whose Billows ne'er Subside*: Nero contradicts Horace 'nor do gusty squalls always whip up the Caspian Sea' in an ode recommending moderation (*Odes*, II. ix. 2–3 (*Odes and* Epodes, ed. by Niall Rudd, Loeb, p. 113)).

161. *The Furys Scourges, or their Scorpion Hair*: the Furiae or Dirae avenged wrongs, especially within the family; they are depicted as flying hags with serpents in their hands or hair.

162. *Prometheus' Vulture, and Ixion's Wheel*: for stealing a spark of fire and giving it to man, and for keeping from Jupiter the secret of the oracle, Prometheus was chained to a rock in the Caucasus and an eagle/vulture fed daily on his liver; Ixion was chained to a perpetually revolving wheel in Hades as a punishment for attempted seduction of Juno.

Would be an easy Change to what I feel.
Why was I single'd out by Partial *Jove*,
These Manicles[163] in Misery to prove?
For what but interposing Gods could Save
This distin'd Victim from the Liquid Grave?
And rescue thus from intercepted Fate
The constant Object of my Dread and hate?

SENECA The time is precious, *Cæsar*, which You Waste
In these Reflections upon what is past:
You only grieve what you shou'd try to cure;
That She's escap'd (no matter how) is sure,
And how things might have been, or how they were
Prudence forever deems a useless care,
She only well examines how they are;
And to this Knowledge, all her skill apply'd
With Judgment for the future will provide;
Avert the Consequence we apprehend,
Or regulate the means to gain our end,
Your Love, Your empire, and Your Life's at Stake,
And bid You Quick, and Vig'rous Measures take,
For when irresolute we act too late,
We after partially Complain of fate
Or our own Errers upon fortune Lay'd,
Her Nuetral Pow'r unjustly we upbraid.

NERO Yet When the Waves, the Winds, and Thunders roar
Who but regrets he ever left the Shore?
And what avail thy cooler *Argus'* Eyes,[164]
Who warn, and hint, but Nothing Dare advise?
I know my Danger imminent and great,
Too far advance'd to think of a retreat,
By ev'ry way our Conduct[165] she'll resent,
That Fury can suggest or Rage invent.

163. *Manicles*: emended from 'Maricles'. The thought may be that Nero is manacled to his mother as Prometheus to the rock or Ixion to the wheel. An alternative reading would be 'Miracles'.

164. *Argus' Eyes*: the many-eyed herdsman who guarded Io for Hera.

165. *our Conduct*: the manuscript omits 'our', but the line is a syllable short without a pronoun. Another possibility is 'my Conduct', consistently with 'my throne' in line 49.

The Senate, People, Even Slaves she'll Arm;
The Legions and the Provinces alarm;
And any Cheif who will her Vengeance own,
For his reward, She'll Place upon my throne.
Then my Opinion in few words receive:
I can't be Safe, and *Agrippina* live.
And from Your Counsels only seek to know
The Surest, safest Way to Strike the Blow.
Speak then. ——— (SENECA *and* BURRHUS *stand Silent for some time looking at one another Then at* NERO)

SENECA ——— Does *Burrhus* think that these Commands
*Cæsar* may trust to the *Pretorian* Bands?

BURRHUS I must be plain, and Own I Doubt it much;
For the *Cæsarean* Blood their Rev'rence such,
Such their regard to *Agrippina*'s Name;
And to their Lov'd *Germanicus*'s Fame,
That Whatsoe'er these Orders should convey
Tho *Cæsar*'s Self, I think they'd disobey;
Perhaps Each Foe converted to a friend,
That Life You would Assail, they would Defend;
They are not Apt to Act a Nuetral Part.

NERO Then what remain's but to transfix my Heart
If I am left defenceless and alone,
And None their Wretched Emperors Cause will Own?
Supose again a Softer Method try'd
That I should Sooth her wrath and court her pride;
If at her feet Submissive I should fall
In feign'd Repentance, and avowing all,
Offer to Dye if She my Death comand,
And yeild the Reins of Empire to her Hand?

SENECA The worst of all the Methods you can try;
The fact Once own'd, you never can deny;
And as her Mercy Vainly You'll implore,
Her Rage unblunted, you'd increase her Pow'r.

*Enter* POPPÆA

NERO What then is to be done? — *Poppæa* here?
Her Presense used to Soften every Care,
But now it Serves to Sharpen my despair.

POPPÆA Why do you waste the time, in Vain Cabals?
When Ruin imminent to Action calls?
For *Agrippina*'s comeing do you wait,
To Ask for Vengeance at the Palace Gate?
Tis force, and Open force, must now be try'd
And fraud and Stratigem no more applied.
Who counsels You one Moment to suspend
Her fate, is Her Confed'rate not your Friend;
The populace around her Palace swarm,
And only wait the comeing Dawn to Arm;
When in avow'd Rebellion, at their head,
Even the Multitude enrag'd she'll lead:
And *Nero* Shall become, her Wrongs declar'd,
No more the Prince, but Prisn'r of his Guard;
The Senate too those Venrable Knaves,
Of Shifting fortune, still the Shifting Slaves;
Who will as power and force enjoin, decide,
Their Idol, intrest, and Success their Guide
Who oft to Day with imprecation load
Whom Yesterday they Worship'd as a god;
An Enemy adjudg'd, to Death may Doom
Whom late they hail'd imperial Lord of *Rome*:
And When expir'd in torments and in Shame,
Blot from their Annals Your detested Name.

NERO All You have Urg'd too firmly I beleive,
And instant Orders for her Death would Give;
But where to find the Hand to execute?

POPPÆA And Who the Emperor's Order shall dispute?
Or Claims a Right to ask if they are just?

NERO The Soldeirs, *Burrhus* is affraid to trust.

POPPÆA Are then Your Troops of Traytors all Compos'd?
If that's the Case, already You're deposed. —
Be *Anicetus* charg'd with this Command,
To take his own imperfect work in hand.

BURRHUS This Execution with no cause Assign'd,

The Source of potent discontents you'll find;
Nor will the Empress' death her Influnce end.

POPPÆA I know that Dangers every way attend;
But None Avenge so well as they Defend.
In private Cases oft, of those we've lov'd
The Influnce Lessens from our Sight remov'd;
But factions ever, When their Leader's dead
Lose all their Strength, like Limbs without a head.

*Enter* ANICETUS *hastily*

ANICETUS From *Agrippina, Cæsar*, at the Door
Waits *Agerinus* ——

NERO ——To defy my Pow'r.
Say, does he come to tell me I'm betray'd
And that revolted *Rome* her cause will aid?

ANICETUS In Courteous Speech, he does to all relate
Her late disaster, as the Work of fate
And says to *Nero* he is only Sent
To tell his Mistress's Safety, and prevent
As Yet your comeing; Whilst she seekes her rest,
By a Slight Wound and with Fatigue opress'd.

POPPÆA Tis to gain time that She employs this Art,
And to Disguise the purpose of her Heart.

ANICETUS This art Might I advise, should cost her Dear.

NERO As how? — the Meaning of thy Words declare.

ANICETUS That we may Turn the Parricide on her.
As *Agerinus* shall to you repeat
His Tale, I'll Drop this Dagger at his feet
The Pains of treason Instant let him Meet;
Whilst wee, at Court, and *Rome*, will tell
That from his Robe, ill-hid the Weapon fell;
And as the Poyson at the Banquet fail'd,
That *Agrippina* thus your Life Assail'd:
Then with a few on whom I can depend
I'll fly, her Life and *Nero*'s farce to End;
The People thus amus'd,[166] Shall not resent

166. *amus'd*: beguiled, deluded.

Her Death, but call it a just Punishment
And the full Senate vote a publick Pray'r
To thank those Gods who Made our Prince their care.

NERO Thou dost again my drooping Spirits Lift,
Dispatch her, and the Empire as thy Gift
I'll ever Own.

BURRHUS ——— If realy She's deceiv'd,
And Chance the Cause of her late Wreck beleiv'd;
Twere better yet this Murder were defer'd;
I own by me it's Consequence is fear'd:
Nay tho You thought She Slightly might Suspect
Her fate design'd; thus prompted to reflect
Upon her Danger; you may after find
More tame and tractable her haughty Mind.

POPPÆA *(to* NERO*)* If on her fear or Ign'rance you presume,
You'll find her Mistress of your Fate and *Rome.*
My Counsel is Dispatch.

BURRHUS ——— And mine delay.

NERO Suppose a While I take a Middle Way.
Hear *Agerinus*; and if I perceive
His Mesage Art and fraud, the Signal give
For *Anicetus'* Plot; — it shall be so: —
Great Gods in what perplexity I goe!
I can no longer bear this Anxious State.
Know your own purpose, and decide my fate.

*Exeunt Omnes*

## *Act Fifth, Scene Third*

*Scene draws and discover's* AGRIPPINA *Lying on a Couch* PALLAS *standing by her*

PALLAS What daring, what stupenduous Guilt: The Whole
With Horror and amazement fills my Soul:
But midst Assassins on the Surges tost,
That you should scape the Wreck, and reach the Coast,
Of all I've heard excites my wonder most.

AGRIPPINA Awhile, unwet, my floating Robe sustain'd
These wreched Limbs, till casually[167] I gain'd

167. *casually*: by chance.

The Shallow'r part; Where strugling faint and Weak,
Nor knowing what to Shun, or whom to seek
I labor'd on, of all Aproach afray'd,
And Utter'd not one Word: to call for Aid,
By hapless *Aceronia*'s Fate I found,
Was to direct the Hand that wish'd to Wound.
Thus through the Gallys unobserv'd I pass'd
Tho all around, the Moon refulgent cast
With torches and with Lamps, a Mingled Light,
That in the Robe of Noon aray'd the Night.
At last Assisted by some friendly hand,
Strech'd in Compassion from the crouded Strand,
When quite exhausted, and a Moment More
Had ended all my cares, I made the Shore.

PALLAS The Pow'r to Act in this Surprise and fear
With the Calmn Caution of Delibrate Care,
Shows all the Virtues of your Splendid Race,
The Conduct of their great decendant graced.
Not cool *Augustus* more in Counsel skill'd;
Or brave *Agrippa* firmer in the feild;
Oh! Why yee Gods! is their Success alone
To this great Heiress of thier Worth unknown;
And All her Virtues by Misfortune shown?

AGRIPPINA Were these Encomiums on thy Mistress true
And all thy Partial Friendship gives, my due,
Yet What would Skill, or fortitude avail,
When Hate, and power, are in the adverse Scale?

PALLAS To Combate ills when others would Despair.

AGRIPPINA And to involve me in a fruitless Care.

PALLAS What with regard to *Nero* have you done?

AGRIPPINA No signs of Anger or Suspicion shown,
Seeming to think it Chance, I've sent to tell
This Monster of a Son, his Mother's Well.

PALLAS To hope it could be Chance were weak and Vain;
From ev'ry Circumstance the treason's plain;
His previous Kindness in that flow of Love,
Those perjur'd Vows his penitence to prove;
The treach'rous banquet to disperse your Train,

His Quick Departure on pretended pain;
To Cause Confusion and employ the Guard,
Th' Insidious Gally by his fraud prepar'd;
All, All, evince, tho slighted my Distrust,
My Apprehensions of his Guilt were just.

AGRIPPINA No More my fond Credulity upbraid,
I own tis Manifest the whole was lay'd;
I see my Error, but I see too late,
Tis vain discernment to look back on fate.

PALLAS Add not a Second Error to the first,
But since You fear, provide against the Worst.

AGRIPPINA What can the weak provide against the Strong
Or Who the Life that Pow'r has doom'd Prolong?

PALLAS The Slavish Senators perhaps may fear
To Make the justice of Your Cause their Care,
But for revenge and Safety would You deign
Where others sure[168] would follow, to Complain?
The People yet and the *Pretorian* Bands
Shock'd at his Crimes and fond of Your commands,
By force would save You from his impious hands;
Would Hurl Distruction back upon your Foes
And Him they rais'd for You, for You depose.

AGRIPPINA Did Safety or Revenge deserve my Care,
I might excite the Romans to this War:
But what is safety when Content is gone?
And ev'ry Hope of Its Return's o'erthrown?
Or from Revenge what joy can we receive,
When Crimes we should resent, we only greive?

PALLAS Can then Your love so far Your Wrath appease,
That you could ever Pardon Crimes like these?

AGRIPPINA No; tis because I never can forgive,
That I no longer strive or wish to live:
If *Nero*'s Love, and *Nero*'s Int'rest sought,
In ev'ry Action and in ev'ry thought,

168. *Where others sure*: emended from 'Where sure'.

Through my past Life have ev'ry Hour employ'd,
That Single Plan of Happyness destroy'd,
The World beside is one wide useless Void.
And could I now my former Pow'r renew,
I cannot frame a wish I would pursue;
Why then tenacious of a wretched Life
Should I involve thee, *Rome*, in civil Strife?
Why pave thy Streets with thy own offspring slain,
And with Domistick Blood the *Tiber* stain?[169]
Against her-self this mighty Empire arm?
All Our Allys and Provinces alarm?
To Warrant Rapine and Exactions there
And Give a loose to New Proscriptions here?
From this Confusion what could I forsee,
But Woe to *Rome* and No relief to me?
For say our Party should the Victory gain,
That I should be secure, and *Nero* slain;
What profit would result from all this Strife,
But some few hated Years of Added Life?
To weep the Cause of this disastrous War,
To Curse the Lawrels I should blush to wear,
And find the fruit of Conquest was Despair.

PALLAS Were such forbearing Principles to Weigh,
When Tyranny on Innocence would Prey;
The More exalted, and the greater those
Who feel the Wrong, the Less they should oppose.
By Your great Ancestors Example taught,
Think against Whom, the two first *Cæsars* fought;
Had *Julius*, or *Octavius*, thought like You
A Son or Brother Neither could pursue,
They Never thought of Kindred or of *Rome*,
But each averting an unrightous Doom,
Reflected he was wrong'd, nor cared by Whom.

AGRIPPINA In *Thesaly*[170] tis true when *Julius* fought

169. *And with Domistick Blood the Tiber stain*: cf. 'Wars, grim wars I see, and Tiber foaming with streams of blood' (Virgil, *Aeneid*, VI. 86–7 (Loeb, p. 513)). The warning against civil war echoes Anchises' in the same poem (VI. 832–5 (Loeb, p. 565)).

170. Julius Caesar defeated Pompey at Pharsalus in central Greece in 48 BCE.

Each other's Life a Son and father sought;
And *Actium*[171] doom'd to give the World a Lord,
A Brother's Sheild oposed a Brother's Sword;
But these Alliances by Intrest made
As Intrest changed, were broken and betray'd.
They Wounded Names; but Nature's-Self would start,
To see a Mother peirce her Offspring's heart;
Or to behold a Son returning Death,
In parricidal payment for his breath.

PALLAS Self preservation must dissolve all Tyes,
And Makes what you term cruel, only Wise;
Makes all these ills, permited ills; who fight
For life, if not for Empire, have a right
All other Claims of Nature to suspend;
All Means are lawfull, for a Lawful end,
And none forbid our being to defend;
And even Childrens Blood by Parents spilt
The Child th' Agressor, his is all the Guilt.

AGRIPPINA In Vain with judgment, Eloquence and Art,
You try to recommend the rig'rous Part;
They take the slightest Plea, who rigor Chuse
Who like it not the strongest will refuse;
No *Pallas*; no, my ev'ry future hour
Chance shall decide, for I will strive no more.

PALLAS Just at this Crisis leaving Chance to rule,
Is, tho unvanquish'd, giving up the Whole;
For not resisting, you invite the Blow;
Call up the Courage of a trembling Foe,
And to your self your own Misfortune owe.

AGRIPPINA When all we know of being is Distress,
Not being will at least our Greifs supress
Nor should be call'd Misfortune, but Redress.

PALLAS Whatever of this joyless World I thought,
I would not to the Butcher hold my Throat,
Or like a senceless Victim tamely Bleed,
As Pride, Caprice, or Prejudice decreed;

171. Augustus Caesar defeated Mark Antony in the naval battle at Actium in 31 BCE.

No, tho I deem'd my Life not worth my Care,
Yet to My foe I'd ever sell it dear,
Like hunted Panthers fiercer from my Wound,
I'd Dye reveng'd and deal Destruction round.
On each Assailant Mutual Death retort,
And Make their ruin, what they meant their Sport.

AGRIPPINA I tell thee Vengeance has no Charms for me
An Added Horror in her Gifts I see:
There is in Nature but one certain Cure;
For these perplexing Conflicts I endure:
But to avow the Weakness of my Heart,
Tho Well, too Well, I know the only Part
Thy Mistress ought to Act; Yet still I find
Falacious Hope with tardy fear combin'd
Suspend the purpose of my Wav'ring Mind;
Then full of Black presage, Despair again,
Relys on Death alone to ease my Pain.
Nor ask I heaven my shatter'd Bark to save
But Quick to plunge it in the Murd'rous wave.
Since Life with ease is thought a Grace too high,
Yee, ruling Powers! grant me at least to Dye;[172]
And tho my own slack, useless, Coward Hand,
By Instinct Check'd, my Judgment can't command;
Oh! let the Wretch you've made, from you receive
That friendly Stroke I want, but dare not give,
And end the Double Horror of these woes,
By takeing what I dread to keep or lose.

PALLAS Think not I combate your design through fear
This Willfull Ruin you embrace to share;
To change and not opose your will I plead;
Resolv'd to follow where so e'er you lead:
Takeing that Share in Your decline of Power,
Which in the Zenith of it's Race I bore;
And ev'n in Death resolv'd, nay proud to join,
The greatest Name that *Rome* e'er know, with Mine.

172. *grant me at least to Dye*: for Hervey's treatment of this theme, see Overton, 'Death and Futurity'.

AGRIPPINA Oh! let me not, whatever I resolve,
The Ruin of a Friend in mine involve:
When I am sunk to nothing but a Name,
*Pallas* shall Live the Guardian of my Fame;
When *Nero*'s Flat'rers shall my Memory load
Thy Care shall be to Chase Aspersion's Cloud,[173]
To give each Virtue's intercepted Ray,
To the full Lustre of it's genuine Day;
And prove, of great *Germanicus*'s Race
Degen'rate *Nero* was the first Disgrace.

PALLAS What in my former Conduct have you seen,
That tells you I would act a part so Mean?
That any Views, when you shall cease to live
That even these, can tempt me to Survive?
In such a Case, whoe'er prolongs his Breath,
Whatever his pretence, tis fear of Death;
Tho on my Birth Heaven stampt the Name of Slave,
A Soul Superior to that Birth it gave:
Not that those fabling flat'rers I beleiv'd
Who, from *Arcadia*'s Kings my Blood deriv'd.
No, tis to inborn Principles I owe,
What no descent of titles can bestow;
A Mind that each ignoble act disdains,
Nor knows to blush for any other Stains
And with a Concious Glory can look down,
On all that's Base tho mounted on a throne.
A Faithfull Heart to its Professions true
Is all of great or good I ever knew:
And this, with stedfast and becoming Pride,
I have and will preserve, however try'd.
Tis this, Whilst I have Life shall make me true,
And ev'n relinquish Life to follow You.

AGRIPPINA Since Words are all that I have left to give
The useless Payment of my Thanks receive:
Be the Professions of the Hollow Breast,

173. *When I am sunk . . . to Chase Aspersion's Cloud*: cf. 'Wilt thou not live, to speak some good of me? | To stand by my fair Fame, and guard th'approaches | From the ill Tongues of Men?' (Antony to Ventidius, Dryden, *All for Love*, V. 1. 300–2 (Dryden, *Works*, XIII, 107)).

In pompous Phrase, and glaring Colors drest;
The Native dictates of a worthy Heart
Want no adorning, and employ no Art:
I have a sense of all thy Service Past
And joy to find thee faithfull to the last.—
Hide not thy Face; — tis a becoming Tear; —
You weep a Friend, and Benefactress' Care;
And When this thinking faculty, the Mind,
Shall leave releas'd her Earthly load behind,
Perhaps, my *Pallas*! we may meet again,
With added joy from our divested Pain.

PALLAS I wish I could injoy that pleasing Thought,
It would be comfort, but 'tis vainly Sought;
I think 'tis fable and Illusion, all
That Pride and Sanguine Hope here after call.
Suns in Succession as they set may rise,
And chase the transient Darkness of the skys;
But When our feeble Lamp of Life decays,
There's no toomorrow for those wasted Days,
No Second Dawn restores their ravish'd Light
Unwak'd as Sleep in one perpetual Night.[174]
What Noise is that? *(Trampling without)*

AGRIPPINA ——— Returning from my Son
Perhaps tis Agerinus: — quickly known,
My Fate will then unfold.

PALLAS ——— The Noise is such
It Indicates, I fear, no Friends Approach.

*Enter* ANICETUS *with a Band of Men disguis'd He speaks whilst entering to some of them who retire, and then advances with the rest*

ANICETUS Bar ev'ry pass, and line it with a guard:
*Cæsar* this Service amply shall reward.

174. *But When our feeble Lamp . . . perpetual Night*: 'heav'ns great lampes doe dive | Into their west, and strait againe revive, | But, soone as once set is our little light, | Then must we sleepe one ever-during night' (Thomas Campion, 'My sweetest Lesbia', a version of Catullus, *Carmina* 5, lines 4–6, *The Works of Thomas Campion*, ed. by Walter R. Davis (New York: Doubleday, 1967), p. 18).

AGRIPPINA *(to* ANICETUS*)* If from my Son on friendly Terms you're sent
Go tell Him I am well: — if Ill be meant,
I'll not believe it authorised by him;
Forg'd is the Mandate, and your own the Crime.

ANICETUS He sends a Mesage not to be express'd
In Words, but bid me Write it in Your breast.

PALLAS *(Drawing his Sword)* If that's thy Mesage, Villian, Turn thee Here,
And pass through Mine before you Write it there.

ANICETUS That prating Hero from my Sight remove
And let his Zeal the fate it Merits prove.

(*They fight* PALLAS *retreating off the stage; Whilst they are fighting* AGRIPPINA *Speaks*)

AGRIPPINA Seest thou not, *Pallas*! tis in vain to strive?
I Charge thee Hear, desist, and yeild, and live.

ANICETUS 'Twas his Own fault: I did not now pursue
His Life; my only Business is With You.

AGRIPPINA Since *Nero*'s Counsel have my Death decree'd,
And by the Son the Mother's Doom'd to bleed;
I ask you not this destin'd Life to spare,
You know no Mercy, and I know no fear:
But in your Crulty this Justice Show;
Turn from my honest heart the impious Blow,
And Plunge thy Sabre in the guilty Womb,
That Gave this Monster to Afflicted *Rome*.

ANICETUS Whilst *Nero* Arms, and you direct my Hand
Thus I obey both his and your Command.
(*Runs his Sword through Her Body*)

AGRIPPINA Oh! — go then — tell him — that the Work is done
His Mother's Slain — my Race of Life is run
And I shall weep no more it e'er begun.
He cannot hope my Pardon to receive —
No Heart is made such Injurys to forgive: —
Yet Dying I implore no vengeance due; —
But leave, just Gods! — The Parricide to you. —
My Soul is on the Wing; — but where it goes? —

We guess, — Doubt, — hope — and fears: — Heaven only knows. *(Dyes)*

ANICETUS At Length this Dreaded Rival is no More:[175]

The End of the Fifth Act

175. The declaration of the end of the Act that follows this incomplete couplet suggests it is deliberate, but the colon might suggest an error on the transcriber's part. Given the frequency with which the transcriber ends speeches with commas, though (silently emended throughout), the presence of a colon here is not strong evidence of incompleteness.

# EMBEDDED ORIGINAL VERSE

# INTRODUCTION TO EMBEDDED ORIGINAL VERSE

Embedded original verse is verse composed as an integral part of a personal letter. It is distinct from verse quotations, which occur quite often in cultured correspondence of the Restoration and eighteenth century, including quotations from verse by the writer himself or herself.[1] It is also distinct from verse composed beforehand and inserted at an appropriate point, though for obvious reasons such a distinction is more difficult to establish. Set pieces of that kind also occur occasionally in letters of the period. Sometimes placed at or near the end of a letter, they may run to appreciable length, as in the correspondence of the Countesses of Hertford and Pomfret.[2] The original verse that Hervey embedded in his correspondence is distinctive for several reasons. In particular, it is more frequent than verse quotations from other writers, especially in letters to his most intimate correspondents; it usually appears to have been improvised; and it is capable of striking emotional directness. It is for these reasons, and in order to represent his verse-writing activities as fully as possible, that it is not only included in this edition but given its own section.

There seem to have been two main reasons why Hervey put verse into prose letters. The first he gave to his most intimate correspondent, Stephen Fox. Excusing a letter that has not been preserved and that appears to have been wholly in verse, he claimed: 'tis some days so much more natural to me to write in verse than prose, that I did it for my ease; and 'twas only want of time that hindered me putting it into a common epistolary form' (SRO 941/47/4, p. 73). Similarly, in a letter to Fox several years later, he inserts

1. See Bill Overton, 'Embedded Extempore Verse in the Intimate Letters of John, Lord Hervey (1696–1734)', *MLR*, 110 (2015), 379–98.

2. *Correspondence between Frances Countess of Hertford (afterwards Duchess of Somerset) and Henrietta Louisa Countess of Pomfret*, 3 vols. (London: for R. Philips, 1805; 2nd edn, 1806). E.g. each contributed one letter all or almost all in verse and one partly so (II, 139–51, 259–62; I, 306–8; III, 69–71). Part of one such verse passage (I, 307–8) is reprinted by Roger Lonsdale (ed.), in *Eighteenth-Century Women Poets: An Oxford Anthology* (Oxford: Oxford University Press, 1989), pp. 109–10; for further details, see Overton, *Verse Epistle*, pp. 54–5.

three quatrains, and remarks, with reference to the verse tragedy he was writing: 'Aceronia you see has made my thoughts so naturally jingle into Rhyme, that I find it is as Difficult to write a letter in plain Prose as a Dancing-Master does to walk into a Room; but as I have not time to ask my second thoughts, you must e'en take them hopping as they come at first'.[3] The second reason is implicit in a parallel remark the year before in a letter to another intimate friend, Francesco Algarotti: 'as my thoughts, without any affectation, fall some Days so naturally into Rhyme, that I am forced to think twice to put them into Prose, and that I never constrain my Nature when I write or speak to you, forgive the Inconveniency of my Sincerity for the sake of that Affection which occasion's it' (JMA Letter 5, ff. 3v–4r; copy at SRO 941/47/4, p. 587). Hervey suggests here not only that he sometimes writes verse more easily than prose, but also that, for him, verse is the natural form for expressing affection. More generally, in the same way that shifts into verse in prose drama of the Restoration and earlier eighteenth century tend to suggest heightened emotion, he seems to have used verse in his letters to express ideas or feelings of particular force or complexity. Perhaps for the same reason, on several occasions he quoted lines from his own unpublished verse. In two cases the likelihood that the poems were already known to his correspondent increases the sense of an intimate confidence.[4]

Hervey's claim is borne out by the amount of original verse that he put into his letters. However, as he suggests in the remarks just quoted, he included verse in correspondence only with those to whom he felt close, and who he knew would appreciate it. Among the 130-odd of his letters to Stephen Fox that have survived, eleven contain verse of this kind, including one that has two such passages, producing a total of 65 lines; among forty-six letters to Montagu, ten have passages of embedded verse, amounting to 100 lines; among thirty-one to Algarotti, nine, amounting to 45 lines; among seventy-two to Henry Fox, only two, amounting to 4.5 lines; and a single couplet among the two extant letters to his doctor, George Cheyne. The paucity of embedded verse in his letters to Henry Fox

3. BL Add MS 51345, ff. 77v–78r (25 June 1737), repr. in part in Ilchester, p. 266. 'Aceronia' almost certainly refers to his verse tragedy 'Agrippina' (Poem 66), which was never printed but survives in a single manuscript copy (BL MS Egerton 3787, ff. 13r–49v).

4. See, for example, notes to Poem 20 *A Satire in the Manner of Persius*, lines 57–9; Poem 28 'Verses to the Memory of my Dearest Sister the Lady Elizabeth Mansel', lines 17–18; and Poem 24 *The Difference between Verbal and Practical Virtue*, lines 146–55.

is explained by an apology early in their correspondence for having written to him in verse: 'I won't reproach you with not having writ to me this fortnight, since I acknowledge it to have been my fault; for who would not (like you) rebuke an unconscionable Correspondent who, not content with persecuting you in prose, extends his Cruelty yet farther and inflicts himself upon you in Rhyme: however, he has will enough (which I fear you will have some Difficulty to believe) to take the Hint of your tacit reproof, good nature enough to give you his word, to offend no more, and honesty enough to keep it' (SRO 941/47/4, p. 43). The letter or letters to Henry to which this remark refers do not appear to survive. They must have been among the twenty-six pages of Hervey's letter-book that have been torn out – probably, as Halsband remarks, 'by the first Marquess of Bristol, who edited Hervey's *Memoirs* in similar fashion' (p. 91n).[5]

Hervey's apology to Henry Fox for subjecting him to verse, and his repeated claim to be able to write in that form as easily as in prose, suggest that the original verse he embedded in letters was composed extempore. Two further kinds of evidence support this. First, living at a period when facility at verse composition was much valued, he showed an aptitude for improvising verse when in company. Several of his poems that circulated in manuscript are identified as having been composed extempore (see for example Poems 5, 41, 49), and he was adept at producing verse to entertain those close to him. For instance, in 1729 he wrote a verse letter of 229 lines to his wife about his travels in Italy that ends with the remark that, apart from the value it may have for its reader, it is only 'the poor Offspring of a Day, | Just to be read and thrown away' (Poem 16). He also wrote two poems, one in French, to entertain Frederick, Prince of Wales, and two for Queen Caroline (Poems 62, 105; 19, 56). That such verse could be and often was improvised is shown by the verse dialogue of seventy-five lines that he wrote with Lady Mary Wortley Montagu (Poem 55).[6]

Second, there is manuscript evidence that verse that he embedded in those of his letters that are not scribal copies was composed during the process of writing. For example, a mysterious note probably referring to

5. Halsband refers to Frederick William Hervey (1769–1859), who became fifth Earl in 1803 and first Marquess in 1826. For details of the excisions from Hervey's manuscript memoirs, see Sedgwick, I, xi–xiv.

6. Harrowby MS 81, pp. 216–17, repr. in Lady Mary Wortley Montagu, *Essays & Poems*. Hervey copied some of the lines (SRO 941/47/2, pp. 70–1). For discussion of another copy of lines 44–73 that casts light on how the dialogue was composed, see Grundy, 'New Verse'.

Montagu's feelings for Algarotti ends with a triplet in the first line of which two words have been transposed; and a letter to Algarotti has a compliment on the latter's *Il Newtonianismo per le dame*, heavily corrected (Poems 79 and 82). Evidence from the large number of Hervey's letters that have been preserved only as copies in his letter-book is more difficult to interpret. In several such copies, however, lines set out as prose, either in his own hand or in that of an amanuensis, have been identified as verse by underlining or by deletion and reformatting. This may even suggest that, in the original document, the lines were not set out as verse at all.[7] Such corrections may constitute evidence that, as Ilchester suggests (pp. xiii, 6), Hervey intended his letters, or selections from them, to be published at some future time. If this is the case, there is no evidence that the verse was written specifically for publication. It is, instead, part of the fabric of the letters into which it was embedded. The possibility cannot be excluded, of course, that some lines that appear to constitute embedded verse are quotations from poems by Hervey that have not come to light, and that future scholarship on Hervey's verse will establish that.

Most of Hervey's letters containing embedded verse are preserved at SRO, but there are also some in the John Murray Archive, and a few others among the Holland House Papers at the British Library. Those at SRO are in a copyist's hand, though some have autograph corrections. Those at the British Library and in JMA are autograph. In order to indicate the role played by each verse item in each letter, the immediate context is provided. The arrangement is chronological, date of composition being inferred in the few cases where the letter is undated. Original spelling and punctuation are retained in order to reflect the character of familiar correspondence in the period.

7. 28 December 1728 to Stephen Fox (SRO 941/47/4, p. 63); 20 June 1728 to Stephen Fox (SRO 941/47/4, p. 78); 2 October 1731 to Stephen Fox (SRO 941/47/4, p. 239); 30 October 1736 to Algarotti (SRO 941/47/4, p. 582). Verse in the copied letters is usually written in a larger hand.

# 67 But learn wise Youth thy Happyness to know

***Main source.*** SRO 941/47/4, p. 63, copy by an amanuensis in Hervey's letter-book with autograph corrections. The first page has traces of a seal, perhaps related to its position as the first in what was, before they were bound together, the second of ten books that make up the collection. The paper is blotted at the edges, apparently from water, impairing legibility in places. No other copy is known. Hervey's corrections reformat, as verse, lines that the copyist had written out in prose. The fact that they required reformatting may suggest that they were not set out as verse – or not obviously so – in the original letter.

***Complementary source.*** Similar lines appear in Poem 65, 'Telemachus', Book I, lines 189–96.

***Date, addressee and context.*** 28 December 1727 to Stephen Fox. Hervey had met Fox at the end of January, after his friendship with Stephen's younger brother Henry had cooled (Halsband, p. 68; Ilchester, p. 15). Stephen, who enjoyed life in the country, especially for hunting, was at Redlynch, the family estate in Somersetshire; Hervey was in London, hoping to persuade Stephen to move there (Halsband, p. 75; Ilchester, p. 25). Most of the letter worries about Stephen's apparently lower emotional temperature towards Hervey. It ends with the sentence following the eight verse lines given below, which serve as a kind of valediction. If these verse lines were composed impromptu, during the composition of the letter, Hervey was to reuse them for Poem 65, 'Telemachus' (I. 189–96), where they appear for the first time in his final draft of that poem. It is possible, alternatively, that the verses here are self-quotation, perhaps with the implication that Fox was already familiar with the poem and might recognise that context, where Calypso is addressing the 'Sweet Youth' Telemachus (I. 164).

***Textual commentary.*** In the transcription that follows, Hervey's corrections and interpolations have been silently incorporated in the prose text; the page is blotted, and some letters have been supplied silently and some editorial explanation has been added in brackets. Except for the expansion of contractions ($y^e$, $w^{th}$, $y^t$), which are frequent enough in the poem to marginally interfere with a clear reading, the verse has been transcribed without alteration.

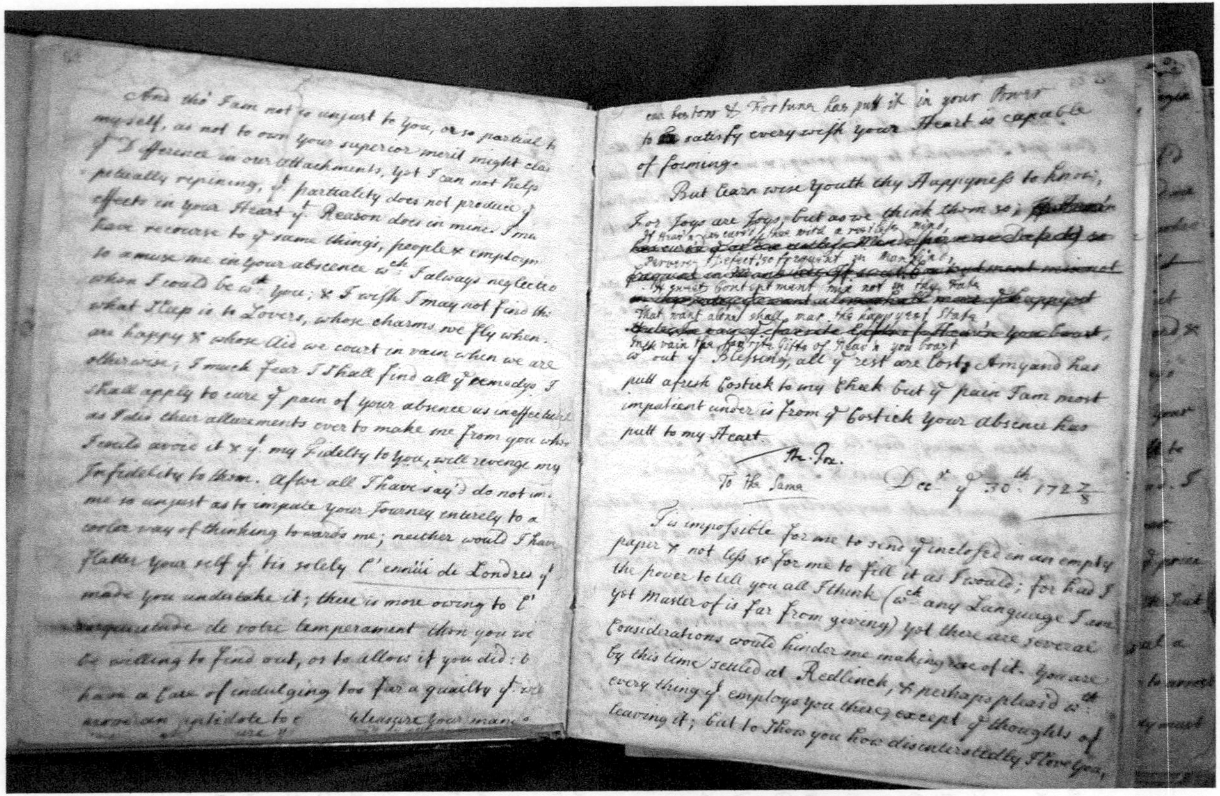

**Figure 3** Letter to Stephen Fox 28 December 1727, in Hervey's letter-book, with autograph corrections to show correct lineation for embedded verse for Poem 67, 'But learn wise Youth thy Happyness to know'.

**Verse in its letter context**

After all I have say'd do not imagine me so unjust as to impute your Journey [to Redlynch] entirely to a cooler way of thinking towards me; neither would I have you flatter your self y$^{t}$ 'tis solely *l'ennüi de Londres*[1] y$^{t}$ made you undertake it; there is more owing to *l'inquietude de votre temperament*[2] then you would be willing to find out, or to allow if you did: but have a Care of indulging too far a quailty [sic] that will prove an antidote to every pleasure your many [line mostly obliterated and consequently illegible] can bestow & Fortune has putt it in your Power to satisfy every wish your Heart is capable of forming.

But learn wise Youth thy Happyness to know,
For Joys are Joys, but as we think them so;
If Heav'n has curs'd thee with a restless Mind,
Perverse Defect! so frequent in Mankind,
If sweet Contentment mix not in thy Fate
That want alone shall mar the happyest State,
In vain the fav'rite Gifts of Heav'n you boast,
With out that Blessing, all the rest are lost:

Amyand[3] has putt a fresh Costick[4] to my Cheek but y$^{e}$ pain I am most impatient under is from y$^{e}$ Costick Your absence has putt to my Heart.

1. *l'ennüi de Londres*: boredom with London.
2. *l'inquietude de votre temperament*: literally, 'your characteristic disquiet'.
3. *Amyand:* Claudius Amyand, Principal Surgeon and Sergeant-Surgeon in Ordinary to George I and II from 1715 to 1740 (*Daily Courant*, 2 December 1715; *Daily Courant*, 9 October 1727; *Gentleman's Magazine*, X [July 1740], p. 358).
4. *Costick*: caustic.

# 68 Make her curl her Nose

***Source.*** SRO 941/47/4, p. 78, copy by an amanuensis in Hervey's letter-book. The letter is incomplete and is headed 'Fragment' in a different hand, which is probably Hervey's own. Although the lines are not set out as verse, the rhyme suggests that that is what they are. Perhaps Hervey omitted to reformat them, as he had done with the longer Poem 67 ('But learn wise Youth').

***Date, addressee and context.*** 20 June 1728 to Stephen Fox, not long before Hervey's departure with Fox on 12 July for an extended visit to Italy.

## Verse in its letter context

For 'tis no more like me than 'tis like Heidegar;[1] I beg my Compliments to Miss;[2]

> make her curl her Nose, repeat my Name, & say,
> *well I do love him Ste: tho he does carry you a way.*

tell Mr Hill[3] I expect he should observe the Lent[4] I have imposed upon him as strictly as ever he did that enjoyn'd him by the Rubrick;[5] and for his encouragement tell him the reward I promise is in present not in reversion,[6] and tho' mine is but a Lease and 'tother in perpetuity yet bid him remember 'tis for Life, and no bad tenure 'till 'tother can commence.[7]

1. *For 'tis . . . like Heidegar*: further context is lacking, because the fragment begins here, but Hervey presumably refers to a portrait or drawing of himself; Johann Jakob Heidegger (1666–1749) was an impresario renowned for his ugliness.

2. *Miss*: Charlotte Fox (later Digby), Stephen's sister, born in 1708, for whom Hervey had great affection and with whom he subsequently corresponded (Ilchester, p. 11).

3. *Mr Hill*: Samuel Hill, the clergyman at Redlynch and a favourite of the Fox family (Ilchester, p. 78n).

4. *the Lent*: 'a time of fasting and penitence, in commemoration of Jesus's fasting in the wilderness' (*OED*), here presumably referring to some humorous form of abstinence prescribed by Hervey.

5. *the Rubrick*: 'The rule of a religious order' (*OED*).

6. *in reversion*: 'Conditional upon the expiry of a grant or the death of a person' (*OED*), presumably referring to the benefits of the abstinence prescribed, perhaps concerning Hill's physical health.

7. *commence*: the full-stop here replaces a colon in the manuscript, which rolls on for another page of jocularity on various matters.

# 69 Each hour my Spirits, and my strength decay

***Main source.*** SRO 941/53/1, pp. 212, 214, the commonplace book of William Hervey (1732–1815), Hervey's fourth son, where it is headed 'Part of a letter written when I was ill at Naples – feb. 1729'. This copy is chosen because its source must have been a manuscript held by the Hervey family that has not been preserved. It is clear and quite carefully punctuated, so no emendations have been made.

***Complementary source.*** The lines seem first to have been printed in *The European Magazine*, 32 (July–December 1797), 412. As there are substantive variations in this text from William Hervey's, it may have come from a manuscript that is not extant or that has not been traced. Subsequent texts reprint this one (e.g. *Walker's Hibernian Magazine*, January 1797, p. 88; *The Annual Register . . . for the Year 1799* [1801], p. 471).

***Date, addressee and context.*** Hervey was with Stephen Fox in Italy from November 1728 to September 1729. The two left Rome for Naples on 29 December 1728 (Halsband, p. 81), but the weather there was poor. Hervey describes the experience and the illness that resulted in 'An account of my own constitution and illness, with some rules for the preservation of health; for the use of my children', written in 1731 (SRO 941/47/16) and printed in Sedgwick, III, pp. 961–87 (975–8). The addressee of the letter, which has not been preserved, is not known, but the presence of the lines in the commonplace book of one of Hervey's sons suggests that it may have been a member of his family. It seems unlikely to have been his wife Mary, to whom he addressed a much more cheerful verse letter about his and Stephen Fox's journey on their return to England from Florence to Lyons (Poem 16). Because the poem as copied by William Hervey is given no letter context, no context is given here.

Each hour my Spirits, and my strength decay,
    Each hour my cares and all my Ills encrease,
In pain and lassitude I drag the day
    Bankrupt of joy a stranger e'en to ease.

And when the World's great Esculapius[1] Sleep,
    His healing balm distil's thro' ev'ry breast,

1. *Esculapius*: Aesculapius was the Roman god of medicine.

Forbids Calamity awhile to weep,
  And gives Despair herself a transient rest:

My Eyes alone, rebellious to his Pow'r,
  Refuse his friendly mandates to obey,
All night the Rigour of my fate deplore,
  Long for the Dawn, yet dread the coming Day.

# 70 My Heart's Delight

***Source.*** SRO 941/47/4, p. 102, copy by an amanuensis in Hervey's letter-book.

***Date, addressee and context.*** 25 November 1729 to Stephen Fox. The letter is dated from London, and begins with Hervey mentioning that he had just 'left the Country', in other words his family's estate at Ickworth. It ends as below with a reference to a pamphlet enclosed with the letter, two lines of verse and an incongruous postscript. Hervey kept the Fox brothers supplied with books, pamphlets and other topical material when he was in London and either of them was not. Most of the letter, including its embedded verse, is printed in Ilchester, pp. 39–40.

## Verse in its letter context

the inclosed, & the tale of a Tub[1] are indisputably written with a vast deal of Spirit & vivacity, but I think he deserves to be hang'd for one, & to have his Gown pull'd over his Ears[2] for t' other. Adieu

> My Heart's Delight in whom alone I find
> All that at once improves & charms the Mind.

poor L. Ab.[3] is brought to bed and there is a report to Day that She's dead.

1. *the inclosed, and the tale of a Tub*: a new pamphlet, evidently by Swift and most likely *A Modest Proposal*, published a few weeks before and here compared by Hervey to *A Tale of a Tub*, published twenty-five years earlier.
2. *to have ... his Ears*: to be unfrocked as a priest; the *Tale* had attracted less serious retribution in that Swift never received the ecclesiastical preferment he expected in England. In a letter a few days later, Hervey remarked that he both liked and disliked the pamphlet 'in a great Degree' (SRO 941/47/4, p. 107).
3. *L. Ab.*: Katharine, Lady Abergavenny, who had been discovered *in flagrante delicto* with her lover Richard Lyddel by servants of her husband on 8 November and had been ejected from the family home, dying a few weeks later after having given birth to a son. As Hervey's letter is dated 25 November, two days after her death, it was indeed recent news. Hervey informed his mother as well as Fox about what had happened (SRO 941/47/2, pp. 232–3, 237–8; 941/47/4, pp. 88–90, 108), and discussed it with Lady Mary Wortley Montagu (SRO 941/47/2, pp. 46–7, 49–51). See further Grundy, pp. 296–7. Both Montagu and Hervey wrote poems about Lady Abergavenny and her death. For the one that is probably by Hervey, see Poem 29 'On the Late Lady Abergavenny'.

# 71 In dull equality, the Sandy Store

***Source.*** SRO 941/47/4, p. 10, copy by an amanuensis in Hervey's letter-book.

***Date, addressee and context.*** 2 December 1729 to Stephen Fox. Most of the letter is about the absurdities of London life, an example of which Hervey offers in the shape of Thomas Coke of Holkham (1697–1759), created Baron Lovel in 1728. The verse lines end the letter, serving as an ardent valediction. Excerpts from the letter, including the embedded verse, are printed in Ilchester, pp. 41–2.

## Verse in its letter context

From Lord Lovel[1] to You is no very natural transition, any otherwise than as 'tis always a natural one to my thoughts to recur thither from any other Subject. lett me tell you then before I bid you Adieu that you are always dear to me, always appear aimiable, to deserve my best wishes and services and shall always have them as fully as you can deserve them: on Saturday, thank God I Shall see You,

In dull equality, the Sandy Store  
Of Time, still parcel's out the measur'd Hour;  
Could I in Absence cut the tedious Day,  
With Intrest when we meet the Debt I'd pay.

1. *Lord Lovel*: earlier in the letter Hervey calls Lovel 'the darling idol of the professed wits of this good city, tout ridicule qu'il est'; the French phrase ('wholly ridiculous as he is'), he added to the copy in his own hand. A. A. Hanham mentions Lovel's 'dissolute ways', including 'persistent and open infidelity', but observes, charitably: 'His high-spirited, boisterous nature was too deeply ingrained to keep him from the gaming table, the chase, the cockfighting arena, or from adding to his magnificent collections of art, manuscripts, and books' (*ODNB*).

# 72 What Joys I have

***Source.*** SRO 941/47/4, p. 120, copy by an amanuensis in Hervey's letter-book.

***Date, addressee and context.*** 21 August 1730 to Stephen Fox. The context is Hervey's wish that he and Fox could live together, responding to Fox's apparent discomfort over what he supposed were the pleasures of a court life. The letter is given complete in Ilchester, pp. 52–3. It begins on the page before the poem, on p. 119. The first line of the verse, above dashes, is a quotation from Matthew Prior's 'The Ladle'.[1] Unlike Prior, who is arguing that to be contented, people need to appreciate the worth of what they already have, Hervey is asserting passionately his need for Fox's company, while rejecting any suggestion that there is a pleasure at court that cannot be equally well obtained at Fox's estate in the country.

## Verse in its letter context

What are the Royal pleasures you talk of my dear dear Ste: which are not given equally to every Subject? do the trappings of Royalty make the amusements of the Country more agreable? Are our Chaises easyer or our Boats safer for being gilt? is the Air sweeter for a Court, or the Walks pleasanter for being bounded with Centinels? what Entertainment does Windsor afford that can not be found at Redlinch? but transpose that Question and I should quickly answer, the greatest Joy I ever did or can know: do not then ungratefully to me and unjustly to your-self any more Imagine but that the privation of that dear something unpossessed

corrodes and leven's all the rest

— — — — — — — — — —

What Joys I have you may pertake
And all I tast 'tis you must make.

For this reason I beg you would not encourage your-self in supposing that the Walks of Life we are thrown into have so few paths of communication that one of us must go out of his way whenever we meet; why should we only see one another by Visits, but never have a common home . . .

1. *The Literary Works of Matthew Prior*, ed. by H. Bunker Wright and Monroe K. Spears, 2 vols., 2nd edn (Oxford: Clarendon Press, 1971), I, 207 (line 166).

# 73 Whilst I maintain my Empire in that Breast

***Source.*** SRO 941/47/4, p. 147, copy by an amanuensis in Hervey's letter-book.

***Date, addressee and context.*** 12 December 1730 to Stephen Fox. Hervey is led to discuss absurdities by a new tragedy he has just witnessed, Charles Johnson's *Medea*, having specified the main ones about the play and performance in the paragraph immediately before. (Hervey was not alone in his low estimation of the production: the play ran for only three nights, 11, 12 and 14 December; see *London Stage*, pp. 101–2.) The second part of the letter, including the text below but not the closing endearment in French, is printed in Ilchester, p. 62.

## Verse in its letter context

I never hear any absurditys of any kind (and God knows I am seldom without hearing 'em of some kind or other), that I am not astonish'd how Creatures of Your Species can be guilty of so many, or that you who are of their's, can be exempt from them: there is but one I know belong's to You; which is the being capable of feeling a Kindness that I know no Mortal on Earth but your-self ever deserv'd; but 'tis some Consolation to me for not being like You, to think you could not love me better if I were. to what purpose then should I wish it? and what good could it do me.

Whilst I maintain my Empire in y$^{t}$ Breast
Each wish is answer'd, and each Good possess'd.

Je meurs d'envie de vous revoir.[1]

1. *Je meurs d'envie de vous revoir*: I am dying from need of seeing you again.

# 74 For not the Joy of Beauty's open Arms

***Source.*** SRO 941/47/4, p. 180, copy by an amanuensis in Hervey's letter-book.

***Date, addressee and context.*** The letter is to Stephen Fox and is dated 16 September 1731. Ilchester, pp. 88–90, includes part of the letter, but not its ending which includes the verse and the text that immediately precedes it. The main significance of the verse is its expression of total dedication to Fox during a period when Hervey was deprived of his company and desperate to see him. Like much amatory verse of the period, it uses the metaphor of political power for that dedication. The lines appear, only slightly modified, in a speech by Nero addressed to Poppæa in Poem 66 'Agrippina', II. 2. 201–6 (thought to have been written five years later), where the interest in political power is more immediate. All the same, in the context of Hervey's absorption in court life, such reassurances must have felt all the more necessary for Stephen: 'Ambition's Charms' had more influence over Hervey than the verse admits. After the verse, the letter proceeds and ends with a complete change of subject: 'I have not sent you the Numbers of Your ten Lottery Tickets because they are still mix'd with others in Mr Hoare's Hands [a banker, presumably Hervey's; see *ODNB*], but any time before the Drawing I conclude will be early enough to do it. Adieu ——'.

## Verse in its letter context

I am Just come back from walking w$^{th}$ y$^{e}$ Queen in Order to breakfast & dress; upon my Return I found on my table a delightfull long, entertaining, kind Letter from You but it is too late (being publick-Day[1]) for me to answer it by this post. – The Court leaves this place[2] y$^{e}$ 12th of next Month: I want to know if I came y$^{t}$ Night to Basingstoke whether it would be pleasant or easy to you to meet me there when I should be obliged to come back next Day to Richmond. Mais enfin je ne puis vivre jusqu'a Novembre sans vous voir.[3]

1. *publick-Day*: a holiday, in this case a Sunday according to the Gregorian calendar.

2. *this place*: Hampton Court, from where the letter was sent.

3. *Mais enfin … sans vous voir*: 'But in short I cannot live till November without seeing you'. A letter to Fox dated 30 September indicates that they arranged to meet instead near Basingstoke on 8 October (SRO 941/47/4, pp. 225–32; printed in Ilchester, pp. 95–8 (98)).

For not the Joy of Beauty's open Arms,
Nor other Friendships, nor Ambition's Charms,
Defraud thy Empire of the smallest part
In this engross'd,[4] this undivided Heart:
You rule unshaken on that worthless Throne
My Life the tenure, and the Whole[5] thy own.

4. *engross'd*: 'To gain or keep exclusive possession of; to concentrate (property, trade, privileges, functions) in one's own possession (often with the notion of unfairness or injury to others); to "monopolize"' (*OED*).

5. *the Whole*: Hervey has corrected the phrase in his own hand from 'The Soul' in the manuscript.

# 75 'Tis You alone my Fears and Wishes make

***Source.*** SRO 941/47/4, p. 239, copy by an amanuensis in Hervey's letter-book.

***Date, addressee and context.*** The letter, part of which is printed in Ilchester (pp. 100–1), is dated 2 October 1731 and is to Stephen Fox. It begins with arrangements for meeting at Hartford Bridge, a place in Hampshire near to Bagshot and Basingstoke and between their respective locations, so that they could each reach it relatively easily. Hervey returns to the topic of the meeting-place near the end of the letter, so the immediate context of the verse is the anxiety caused by the strength of his desire to see Fox. Despite the closing sentence of the passage below, the letter ends with another piece of embedded verse, Poem 76 ('And sure I am').

## Verse in its letter context

I write to You from y$^{e}$ Dutchess of Richmond's; where I am to dine, she has a Belly up to her Chin & looks mighty well, his Grace is in great Anxity for her Welfare and a Boy:[1] I am so for fear of any unforeseen Accident preventing our meeting on Friday;

> 'Tis You alone my Fears & Wishes make,
> From you my Thoughts their various Tincture take.
> With every Good, whilest you are[2] present, blest,
> Of all, when you are absent, dispossesst.
> Each hour at best a Blank; not one enjoy'd;
> A tedious Waking, or a sleeping Void.
> And whilest the present I should strive to tast,
> I wish the Future or I weep the past.

It is ridiculous to say one writes in a Hurry when one writes in Rhyme; but 'tis true; & you know I do not lye when I say I sometimes can write as fast in Verse as I can in prose. Adieu Dinner is on y$^{e}$ Table.

1. *a Boy*: The Duke was to be disappointed in his second hope but not his first. The baby, born on 6 October, was to be Emilia Mary, later Duchess of Leinster (1731–1814) and political hostess (*ODNB*). A son, Charles, had lived for only two months after his birth in the previous year. The couple already had one daughter, Georgiana Carolina, born in 1723; their wishes for a male heir were satisfied only in 1735. This son, also named Charles, succeeded his father as Duke in 1750 (*ODNB*; *Complete Peerage*, X, 838).

2. *you are*: here, and in the line below, the phrase has been altered in Hervey's hand from 'thou art'.

# 76 And sure I am

***Source.*** SRO 941/47/4, p. 239, copy by an amanuensis in Hervey's letter-book.

***Date, addressee and context.*** The couplet occurs at the end of a letter to Stephen Fox dated 2 October 1731 that also contains other embedded verse (Poem 75, ''Tis you alone my Fears and Wishes make'). Ilchester, who prints part of the letter including the other passage of embedded verse, omits this closing endearment. It suggests that Hervey could not bear tearing himself away even from the partial and imperfect contact of a letter. As 2 October, the date the letter was written, was a Saturday according to the Julian calendar that the two used between them, and as they were to meet on 8 October (SRO 941/47/4, p. 232), they had six days to wait.

The passage follows immediately, with a small overlap, the context of Poem 75. Hervey is looking forward to the meeting the two have arranged.

## Verse in its letter context

Adieu Dinner is on y$^{e}$ Table. Vendredi Viendra[1]

And sure I am I would not change that Hour
For all the while[2] Ones Fate has in it's power.[3]

1. *Vendredi Viendra* – 'Friday will come'. Hervey probably liked the play of sound in the phrase, especially in light of his facility at writing verse to which he has just referred (see Poem 75 ''Tis you alone my Fears and Wishes make').

2. *the while*: the time (*OED*).

3. *And sure . . . it's power*: The amanuensis had written the two verse lines as continuous prose, but Hervey has corrected them in his own hand to verse, underlining them to make the alteration stand out.

# 77 For if in Richmond-Morning-Walk

***Source.*** SRO 941/47/4, pp. 270–1, copy by an amanuensis in Hervey's letter-book, printed in *Some Materials* (Sedgwick, I, xxxvi–xxxviii). Because the copy is not part of the original letter, the question arises as to whether or not the verse it contains should be regarded as embedded. The fact that it follows on directly from the prose introduction suggests that it should be. As it is a copy, it cannot be expected to show evidence of extempore composition. It is presented with four minor corrections to punctuation to increase clarity, as indicated in the List of Emendations, which also provides details of some manuscript corrections in Hervey's hand.

***Date, addressee and context.*** 6 November 1731, to Frederick, Prince of Wales. Writing from the Fox brothers' country estate at Redlynch, Hervey is doing his best to entertain his royal correspondent whose friendship he was making every effort to cultivate at this time. Like much of his embedded verse, the poem occurs at the end of the letter, though it has been preceded by two other pieces of verse (see Poem 62 'No more my Eyes thy Beauty charms', and Poem 105 'Quant al Padrone'). It is introduced by a self-depreciating remark about the quality of entertainment he has given the Prince, most of which consists of a description of life at Redlynch.

## Verse in its letter context

Upon reading over this Galimatias[1] I feel some Doubts arising whether I ought to send It or no, especially without covenanting that It shall be expos'd to no[2] Eyes but Your Own.

> For if in Richmond-Morning-Walk,
> In want of other Theme for Talk;
> The Queen, Your-self, and Sisters three,
> (My letter brought on the Tapis)[3]
> Should set in Judgment on poor me;
> Methinks I hear my Sentence pass,

1. *Galimatias*: 'Confused language, meaningless talk, nonsense' (*OED*).
2. *no*: corrected from 'now', which is presumably a scribal error unnoticed by Hervey when he checked the transcription.
3. *on the Tapis*: 'on the table-cloth, under discussion or consideration' (*OED*).

*Griffon*,[4] and looking like an Ass.
The Queen, who does not love Abuse,
But likes us Chamberlains to Souse,[5]
Will Say – My God that is so dull –
*Why Fretz!*[6] *Your Pilade*[7] *is turnd Fool.*
*Ah! L'Ignorant ah! Franchipan!*[8] —
*I pray you show that to the Anne*;[9]
She (*whom I love and fear*) will say, *Esprit.*[10]
A Word which as She uses it,
One may interpret Fool, or Wit.
The next is Princess Amilie,[11]
For ever partial against me,
And as Your Royal Highness knows,
So like thro'out to the gay Rose;
That as her Cheek It's Bloom adorns,
Her Satyr's tip'd with all It's Thorns.
Dolce-piccante[12] It contains,
And both at once delights and pains.
Last Speaks the Princess Caroline,[13]
Where Justice, Sense and sweetness joyn:
To all She's affable and kind,

4. *Griffon*: 'the Griff', Hervey was to write in *Some Materials*, 'was a Nick-name the King had long ago given the Prince' (SRO 941/47/14, f. 321r; Sedgwick, III, 804).

5. *Souse*: stew (figuratively).

6. *Fretz*: another familiar name for Prince Frederick (the English equivalent would be 'Fred').

7. *Pilade*: Pylades, in Greek mythology, the bosom friend of Orestes, the two being often cited as patterns of male friendship.

8. *Franchipan*: this seems a nonce-word out of court-French for a foolish person.

9. *the Anne*: Anne, Princess Royal (1709–59); the use of the definite article before a first name is idiomatic in conversational German.

10. *Esprit*: the more usual meaning is 'wit'.

11. *Princess Amilie*: Amelia (Emily) (1711–86), the second of the royal daughters; Hervey was less guarded about her in *Some Materials*, where he wrote that she 'was glad of any back to lash, and the sorer it was the gladder she was to strike' (Sedgwick, I, 275).

12. *Dolce-piccante*: literally, sweet-sharp (bitter-sweet).

13. *Last . . . Princess Caroline*: in keeping with etiquette, the youngest royal daughter, Caroline Elizabeth (1713–57) does not speak before her sisters; she had a tenderness for Hervey, who wrote in *Some Materials* that 'She had affability without meanness, dignity without pride, cheerfulness without levity, and prudence without falsehood' (Sedgwick, I, 276).

And dumb to Faults, tho' never blind.
If then the Rose[14] should cry, *Strange Stuff*,
She'll Say, *no, no, 'tis well enough*
But when they come to pull and hawl It,
To Shrug, to criticise, and maul It:
You Sir in pity to Your Friend,
Who wont condemn, Yet can't defend,
Will think *vous aviez tort*[15] to Show It,
And wish that Hervey ne'er may know It.

14. *the Rose*: i.e. Princess Amelia. 15. *vous aviez tort*: 'you were wrong'.

# 78 For few or can, or wish to bring Relief

***Source.*** Letter of 25 December 1731 to Stephen Fox, from St James's Palace. SRO 941/47/4, pp. 328–30 (330) (Ilchester, p. 128).

***Complementary manuscript sources.*** None known.

***Complementary print sources.*** None known.

***Attribution.*** No other source identified.

***Context and date.*** In this letter Hervey writes to Stephen Fox about his hurt and anger at having detected the affair between Frederick, Prince of Wales, and his own mistress, Anne Vane. At a time when George Bubb Dodington (1691–1762) was becoming the Prince's chief adviser, Hervey felt he had been betrayed both in his friendship with the Prince (the precise nature of their intimacy is unclear) and in his affair with Anne. This letter, discussed by Halsband, p. 129, and Moore, pp. 137–8, marks the end of Hervey's confidence in the Prince. The lines appear, with some modifications, in Pallas' account of the Queen in Poem 66 'Agrippina' (I. 1. 51–62).

***Textual commentary.*** In the transcription that follows, Hervey's corrections and interpolations have been silently incorporated in the prose text, which is in the hand of an amanuensis with autograph corrections; except for the expansion of contractions, the poem has been transcribed without alteration. The verse ends the letter.

## Verse in its letter context

I have almost every Day fresh Instances of the Falsehood as well as Folly of the Prince,[1] & since it is impossible to correct the first, wherever it is so natural; I am not very solicitous as you may imagine to rectify the Errors of the Last. Lett their Folly fall on their own Head, & their Wickedness on their own Pate. they neither know nor suspect that I have detected them, nor ever shall: for the easyest, the most natural & the justest Revenge one can take upon People who imagine they impose upon one, is to let them fancy they do; & instead of being their Dupe, let them make themselves their own. I have fretted at their Conduct a good deal, but for the future I am resolv'd to think of it as little as I can & not speak of it at all; many

1. *the Prince*: inserted in Hervey's hand above a dash in the transcription by the amanuensis.

Reasons will make me silent on this Occasion but I think People with common Judgment or common Prudence, would keep their Grievances to them-selves as much as their Distempers; & never trust the recital to any Body but those who were to cure them. I would no more divulge my being vex'd than you would formerly have done your being clap'd.[2]

For few or can, or wish to bring Relief,
And every touch we feel augments our Grief:[3]
To probe is but to irritate the Heart,
And to divulge is to encrease our Smart.
The Wise in silence therefore bear their Pain
Or, only where Redress is sure, complain.
Content they seem with necessary Ill,
And what they must submit to, seem to will.
Whilst babling Fools, repining at their Fate,
Their Wrongs, their Wants, their Discontents relate,
And Ign'rant of the Make of Humankind,
Solicit Pity where Contempt they find.

2. being clap'd: having gonorrhoea.

3. *For few or can ... augments our Grief*: 'Hear, then, and let your Song augment our Grief, | Which is so great, as not to wish Relief' (Edmund Waller, 'Thyrsis, Galatea' in *The Poems of Edmund Waller*, ed. by G. Thorn Drury, 2 vols. (London: Routledge; Boston: Dutton, 1905), I, 40–2, lines 13–14).

# 79 When the gay Sun no more his Rays shall boast

***Main source.*** John Murray Archive, Letter 2, [ff. 3v–4r], autograph. The verse was adopted by Algarotti as one of the commendatory poems prefacing his book, along with others by Lady Mary Wortley Montagu, Robert Symmer and Benjamin Stillingfleet. Despite their inclusion in the Italian edition, none of these poems appears in any of the eighteenth-century English translations.

***Complementary source.*** Francesco Algarotti, *Il Newtonianismo per le dame* (Naples: Giambatista Pasquali, 1739), sig. A6r. This is a more polished version, including significant changes that suggest an intermediate source, presumably resulting from Hervey's undertaking to correct the lines subsequently.

***Date, addressee and context.*** 16 August 1736 to Count Francesco Algarotti. Introduced to Hervey by a letter from Voltaire that he brought with him, Algarotti (1712–64) came to London in March 1736 while he was writing *Il Newtonianismo per le dame* (1737; translated by Elizabeth Carter in 1741 as *Sir Isaac Newton's Philosophy Explain'd for the Use of the Ladies*). Having entranced Montagu as well as Hervey by his intelligence, charm and good looks, Algarotti left London on 6 September. Hervey's first three letters to him were written while he was staying with Stephen Fox at Redlynch and Algarotti was still in London. In this letter, the second, he ends by complimenting Algarotti on his Newtonian dialogues, which Hervey must have seen in manuscript, by advising changes to two passages he thought risqué, and by redoubling the compliments. Apart from a few phrases in Italian and the Latin quotation, the letter is in French. The original English verse it contains is of special interest because Hervey's corrections indicate that it was composed in the process of writing the letter.

## Verse in its letter context

Ovid, il me semble en quelque endroit, parlant du Poeme de Lucrece dit.[1]

Carmina sublimis tunc sunt peritura Lucreti,
Exitio terras cum dabit una Dies.[2]

1. *Ovid ... dit*: 'Ovid, it seems to me, somewhere, speaking of Lucretius' poem, says.' The Lucretius poem in question, *De Rerum Naturae* (*On the Nature of Things*), is a long philosophical work written in the first century BCE. Like other intellectuals of his generation, Hervey was much influenced by Lucretian thinking.

2. *Carmina ... Dies*: 'The verses of sublime Lucretius will perish then when a single day shall give the earth to doom' (Ovid, *Amores*, I. xv. 33–4 (Loeb, p. 379)).

& moi je dirais de vos Dialogues[3]

When the gay Sun no more his Rays shall boast,
And human Eyes their Faculty have lost:
Then shall thy writings on those Subjects dye
Thy Wit and Learning in Oblivion lye,[4]
England shall cease to boast her *Newton's* Head,
And Algarotti's Works no more be read.

Voilà des tres mauvais Vers sur un tres beau Sujêt; & dans lesquels je dis mal en six lignes fades & flasques ce que le Romain a dit tres bien en deux. mais n'importe je les corrigerai une autre fois; je hais les choses trops etudiées, & quand on a tort il faut mieux qu'on soit capable de dire qu'on laisse sans ỳ penser.[5]

3. *et moi . . . Dialogues*: 'and for my part, I would say of your dialogues'.

4. *Then . . . lye*: these lines replace two previous attempts at the line, both deleted and the first including a false second try at rephrasing: 'Then shall thy Colours too and thy Optics and thy Optics | Thy Colours and thy Optics too shall dye'.

5. *Voilà . . . penser*:

> There are some very bad verses on a very fine subject; and in them I say badly in six insipid and flaccid lines what the Roman has said very well in two. But it does not matter. I will correct them another time; I hate things that are too studied, and when one is wrong it is better that one is capable of saying that it has been let go without thinking about it.

# 80 But what avails our own Defects to find?

***Source.*** BL Add. MS 51396, f. 162r, holograph letter.

***Date, addressee and context.*** The letter is to Henry Fox and is dated 4 September 1736; most of it is printed in Ilchester, pp. 247–9. The immediate context for the two lines of verse is Hervey's expression of relief at finding himself feeling better on his return to London from Fox's country estate at Redlynch than he had expected. The couplet is followed by a change of subject to the play Hervey had just finished writing, 'Agrippina' (Poem 66, though he calls it *Aceronia*), saying 'I am glad to hear *Aceronia* kept her ground after I was gone'. He expresses his relief that it had continued to amuse those at Redlynch after he had left.

## Verse in its letter context

I was glad on my first coming to town to find my-self so much easyer than I expected to be, & say'd like Anthony — *Gods I thank you I form'd the Danger greater than it was, & now tis near, tis vanish'd.*[1] I am proud of this, & if I was not ashamed of what follow'd I would relate it. I know you say now of me in your Heart, what I say'd in black & white on another Body. *Idem manebat neque Idem decebat.*[2] tis true.

But what avails our own Defects to find?
If impotent to cure, 'twere better we were blind.

1. *Gods I . . . tis vanish'd*: Dryden, *All for Love*, II. 1, 238–40, slightly misquoted ('Gods, I thank you: | I form'd the danger greater than it was, | And now 'tis near, 'tis lessened' (Dryden, *Works*, XIII, 47). The danger appears to be that of illness, but Hervey's actual motive for returning to London was probably to see Algarotti before his departure from England.

2. *Idem manebat neque Idem decebat*: 'He stayed the same, when the same was not fitting'. The original source is Cicero, *Brutus*, where the remark has a different form: *remanebat idem nec decebat idem* (Loeb, p. 284). The different wording suggests that Hervey is quoting from Francis Bacon, 'Of Youth and Age', where the wording is the same; see *Francis Bacon: The Essays*, ed. and introd. by John Pitcher (Harmondsworth: Penguin, 1985), p. 188. The letter gives no evidence of the identity of the man to whom Hervey had applied the remark.

# 81 Whose Meaning still in Riddles is express'd

***Source.*** SRO 941/47/2, p. 15, holograph letter.

***Date, addressee and context.*** The letter is to Lady Mary Wortley Montagu, and is undated except for 'Saturday 3. a' clock' written below it, but Halsband dates it 18 September 1736 (*Montagu Letters*, II, 108). It clearly refers to Montagu's confused feelings about Algarotti shortly after he had left England following his first visit there. Montagu's invitation for the following Saturday must therefore be to the meeting in late September that produced their extempore verse dialogue, Poem 55, though it is possible that it took place on the Tuesday instead. The acerbity of Hervey's tone at the start of the first sentence may be explained not just by the freedom of expression that a long friendship often enables, but by his irritation at the fact that Algarotti had spent his last evening in England with Montagu rather than with himself, though he had told Hervey he had done so with someone else (for more detail, see Poem 82 and Grundy, p. 360). The whole letter and the lines of embedded verse that end it are reproduced here.

## Verse in its letter context

It is not strange that any body who labour's as much as you to be unintelligible should be misunderstood, but if you will send me word what hour to night I may see you, I will call upon you for better information, if it be but for a minute, to show you that at least, it is not *willfully* (as you say) that I misunderstand. — at all hazards I accept of the Summons for next Saturday & will wait on you then at seven.

Whose Meaning still[1] in Riddles is express'd,
May sometimes vainly try to show their Breast,
And when they wish it least perhaps, be guess'd.

1. *Whose Meaning still*: the expression is elliptical, the words 'a person' being implied before it; as often in early-modern usage, 'still' means 'always'.

# 82 In black & white whilst Chloris' Mind you trace

***Source.*** John Murray Archive, Letter 4, f. 2r, holograph letter (in French except for embedded verse).

***Date, addressee and context.*** 20 September 1736 to Francesco Algarotti. The context is Hervey's rivalry with Montagu for Algarotti's affections. Algarotti had spent his last evening in England with Montagu rather than with Hervey, though he had told Hervey that his host had been Martin Folkes, a Fellow of the Royal Society with whom he shared scientific interests. Rather than reprove his friend for lying, Hervey criticises Montagu, for she had, he claims, boasted publicly of her success. He goes on to provide what he represents as a true portrait of what is at issue, introducing the embedded verse with the words: 'Pourtant je crois que veritablement voici le Portrait fidel de ce Comerce' ('However, I believe that here is the true picture of this business'). This is to suggest that Montagu is trying to court Algarotti by letter – as indeed she was – now that she can no longer do so in person. Even so, the verse compliments her on her verbal skills as well as criticising her for her ageing complexion and the cosmetics she uses to improve it.

After the verse, the letter continues, in French, in a similar vein, including a further three lines of embedded verse complimenting Algarotti on his own poetry. See the next item, Poem 83, 'So well the merit of your Words is known'.

## Verse in its letter context

vous avez agi en vrai descendant d'Adam, & faisant voir selon son exemple fui que pour la gouter d'un peu de fruit de cette Arbre dangereuse de la Science, vous voudrez donner votre Corps au grand Diable, & risquer de faire naitre toute votre Posterité (comme lui la sienne) en Corruption. Pourtant je crois que veritablement voici le Portrait fidel de ce Comerce.[1]

1. *vous avez . . . ce Comerce*:

You have acted as a true descendant of Adam, and made seen, according to his shunned example, that in giving her the taste of a little of the fruit of that dangerous Tree of Knowledge, you would give your Body to the Devil, and risk having all your Posterity born (like he his) in Sin. However, I believe that here is the true picture of this business. (literal translation mine)

In black & white whilst Chloris'[2] Mind you trace,
With red and white whilst she adorns her Face;
'Tis true she trys by Nature and by Art,
Each way to force a Passage to your Heart;
But for her Vows compleat Success to find,
To make her Lover pleas'd, as well as kind,
She should be never mute, You always blind.

2. *Chloris*: a name from pastoral verse, though Montagu's usual soubriquet in Hervey's correspondence with Algarotti, despite the associations Pope had given it, was 'Sappho'.

# 83 So well the merit of your Words is known

***Source.*** John Murray Archive, Letter 4, f. 2r, holograph (almost all in French except for embedded verse and quotations in Italian and Latin).

***Date, addressee and context.*** 20 September 1736 to Francesco Algarotti. The verse follows on closely from Poem 82, 'In black & white whilst Chloris' Mind you trace'. Hervey introduces it with the remark that he cannot say more to Algarotti on the subject than the latter knows already, with affirmations of his friendship for him, and with a quotation from one of Algarotti's own poems affirming his friendship for Hervey. A literal translation of the Italian lines that begin the extract, which come from a poem to Hervey, is

I am a hundred times the happiest man,
Oh the happiest among all mortal men
Who breathe this air will I be
If this bond never breaks!

Hervey concludes the letter by quoting lines 5–8 from the third ode of Horace's first book, along with instructions as to the address by which to write to him, but the main significance of the valediction printed here is the further evidence it provides of what embedded verse meant to Hervey, and how easily it came to him.

## Verse in its letter context

je ne vous puis rien dire pourtant sur ce Chapitre que ce que vous savez deja; c'est a dire que je vous aime de tout mon Coeur, & que je vous supplie de n'oublier jamais l'amitié que je vous porte, ni de laisser affoiblir celle que vous m'avez temoignée[1]

O beatissimo me cento volte,
O beatissimo sovra mai quanti
Quest' aria spirano uomin mortali,
Se mai per sciogliersi fià tal nodi.[2]

1. 'I cannot say anything more to you however under this heading than what you know already; that is to say, that I love you with all my Heart, & I beg you never to forget the friendship I hold for you, nor to let that which you have witnessed to me weaken.'

2. *Opere del conte Algarotti*, 10 vols. (Cremona: per Lorenzo Manini, 1778–85), IX (1783), 325. Bill Overton's colleague Arianna Maiorani kindly provided the basis for the translation given earlier.

So well the merit of your Words is known,
It can't seem strange (or strange to You alone)
When I would have *mine* please, I take your own.

Vous allez me dire encore que je pense en vers; il est sur que quand je vous ecris je pense sur le papier, & que si c'est des Vers, de la Prose, du François, de l'Anglais, du Latin, ou l'Italien, que j'ai ce moment en tête, je vous donne les *rough Diamonds* justement comme je les puise, sans attendre pour les tailler & les rafiner en Brillants; je vous laisse ce soin, & j'attends que votre Amitié faira la même chose pour moi quand vous me lisez, que votre esprit a fait pour notre Païs quand vous l'avez depeint.[3]

3. 'You are going to tell me again that I think in verse; it is certain ['sur' should be 'sûr'] that when I write to you I think on paper, and that whether it is verse, prose, French, English, Latin or Italian, that I have in my head at the moment, I give you *rough Diamonds* just as I extract them, without trying to cut and refine them into jewels; I leave that trouble to you, and I expect that your friendship will do the same thing for me when you read me, as your wit has done for our country when you have described it.'

# 84 As Travellers still think of Day by Night

***Source.*** John Murray Archive, Letter 5, f. 1v, holograph. There is a copy by an amanuensis in SRO, 941/47/4, pp. 582–3; only the later parts of the letter, not including the part provided below, are printed in Ilchester, pp. 253–5.

***Date, addressee and context.*** 30 October 1736 to Francesco Algarotti. The embedded verse is introduced by an expression of how much Hervey misses his friend. After the verse, the letter continues for a sentence in a similar vein until Hervey changes the subject:

> If a Place in my Heart is what you think worth preserving, you need be in no Pain about losing it; it is like what you quote of the Field round Rome, when it was besieged by the Carthaginians; and you are the Roman to whom the Property of that terrain still remains, whatever Hannibal may seem to take Possession of it by a temporary Encampment.

## Verse in its letter context

You cannot imagine how often I think of you, how often I take Occasion to speak of you, with how much regret I think of your Absence, & with how steady an affection, & perpetual Admiration I remember every mark of Partiality you express'd towards me, as well as all those Merits that leave no Room for partiality in me towards you. there is no agreable Quality I meet with in any Body, that does not put me in mind of You by Resemblance, and no disagreable one that does not do it by Comparison, –

As Travellers still think of Day by Night
And long in thickest Darkness, most for Light.[1]

1. *And long . . . Light*: Hervey initially wrote: 'in the midst of Darkness, long for Light' before correcting the line, so providing evidence that the verse was composed in the process of writing the letter. In the SRO copy, the amanuensis wrote the two verse lines as prose and Hervey returned the layout to verse in his own hand.

# 85 Of all who feel how few so well declare

***Source.*** John Murray Archive, Letter 5, f. 1v, holograph. There is a copy by an amanuensis in SRO, 941/47/4, pp. 597–606 (604–6). A much abbreviated version, not including the verse, is printed in Ilchester, pp. 262–3.

***Date, addressee and context.*** 27/16 January 1737 to Francesco Algarotti. The context is a humorous reproof from Hervey that Algarotti underestimates the quality of some verse by Montagu ('Sapho') that Hervey had sent him. This begins a new subject and paragraph, as given below. After the verses, Hervey remarks, 'It is high time to conclude this *Potpourris*, but I can not do it Without renewing my Petition to you to return to England'.

## Verse in its letter context

I do not think you Commend Sapho enough for the verses I sent you of her's; You who do not know that they were most of them taken out of *Priors Solomon*,[1] Should have been more Lavish in Your Praises.

Of all who feel how few so well declare,
The Doubts, the Lassitude, Distaste, & Care,
Which on each thought & each employment wait,
Through this dark, tedious, irksom, mortal State,
Where Providence by such perverse Degrees,
(Too small for pleasure, & too great for ease,)
Has so dispers'd her Gifts to Humankind,
Has so disposed our Body & our Mind,
And Mixed so ill the Angel & the Brute,
That hardly ever the Ingredients suit:
Our Sence of Happyness so much refin'd,
Our means of Gaining it so much confined,
That the According Point we never know,

1. *Priors Solomon*: Matthew Prior's *Solomon; Or, the Vanity of the World: A Poem in Three Books*, first published in 1718, is the most serious of his poems, relating Solomon's unsuccessful attempts to find happiness and meaning in knowledge, erotic pleasure and power. Hervey admired his work (as did Montagu). Nonetheless, the twenty lines that follow provide an overview of the poem that distances Hervey both from it and from the lines by Montagu that he claims it inspired.

But still by this too high, by that too low,
To unpermitted Blessings turn our Eyes,
Condemn'd to Occupations we despise.

A Picture of the World in Strains like these
Sappho from *Prior* coppy'd at her Ease,
For She in Verse like *Seneca*[2] in Prose
Enjoys it's Pleasures whilst she paints it's Woes.

2. *Seneca*: Lucius Annaeus Seneca (c. 4 BCE–65 CE), philosopher, orator and playwright.

# 86 Why doest thou ignorantly mourn his Fate (to Montagu)

***Source.*** SRO 941/47/2, pp. 57–8, holograph.

***Date, addressee and context.*** 23 June 1737 to Lady Mary Wortley Montagu from Ickworth. The context is Hervey's response to news from his correspondent of the death of John Hedges (Treasurer and Receiver General to the Prince of Wales), and some verse she wrote on the subject. Montagu's letter survives only in part, but her lines, from 'Conclusion of a Letter to Lord H—— giving an Account of the Death of Mr. Hedges Treasurer to his *R. H.*' (*c.* 20 June 1737), are printed in *Montagu Letters*, II, 112–13:

——This is wrote with Tears,
Tears for our loss, it is not his I mourn,
Who past all Care sleeps in his peace-full Urn;
Or crown'd with Roses in Elysian Groves
With bright Ophelia now renews his Loves;
Where Purer Light and happier Feasts they share
With Ovid, Congreve, Sapho, Delawar,
Perhaps with Pity at a distance view
The Paths poor Poets militant persue.

About three months later, on 17/28 September 1737, Hervey sent a longer, considerably revised, version of his own verses on the subject to Algarotti from Hampton Court (Poem 89). His more immediate response to Montagu is introduced and followed by an explanation of what had evoked it, when he reflects: 'This is a Subject that I really think inexhaustable, but luckyly for you the Post will not allow me to say half what I could and would say upon it. Adieu then, continue to write to me whilst I stay, and when I come to town let us meet as often as we can before we grow to be our own Ghosts, before we become the walking Sepulchres of our own Merits and Pleasures, and are exposed to all the disagreable Circumstances from which poor Hedges by a happyer Fate has been rescued.'

**Verse in its letter context**

– the news of poor Hedges's Death[1] & your Comments upon it, enlarg'd *and raised my Imagination*, as you call it,[2] more than any Leisure, or the reality of the finest Landskips[3] Claude Lorain[4] ever painted could do in seven years: nothing I own affects my Mind much, but human Creatures, & Black and White.

Why doest thou ignorantly mourn his Fate,
And wish his scanty Lease a longer Date?
His[5] gone, his Honors green upon his Brow,
The Lover's Myrtle, and the Poet's Bough;
Unwasted yet to Ashes either Fire,
Nor dwindled into Dotage from Desire:
In the full Vigor of his Blood & Mind
He drank of Life, & left the Dregs behind:
Exempt from all th' Infirmitys of Age,
Nor doom'd to totter on Life's latest Stage;
(Where many breath, tho they no longer live,
And all worth living for, despised survive:)
Sure too the Reccord of his Fame to save,
For Lady Mary writes upon his Grave.

1. *Hedges*: John Hedges (1688–1737) was MP for three Cornish constituencies successively from 1722 till his death, and Treasurer and Receiver General to the Prince of Wales, 1728–37, a post that caused him great trouble because of the poor relations between the Prince and his parents. See Romney Sedgwick (ed.), *The History of Parliament: The House of Commons 1715–54*, 2 vols. (London: HMSO, 1970), II, 125. Hedges wrote a humorous will in verse that survives in a number of manuscripts, for example BL Add. MS 63648, f. 31v, and that bears out the account of his death given by Hervey. Despite its tone and the quite considerable estate it bequeathed, the will was proven.

2. *raised* … *call it*: the letter in which Montagu used this phrase appears not to have survived. Hervey had already referred to the phrase in a letter dated 18 June 1737 (*Montagu Letters*, II, 112).

3. *Landskips*: landscapes.

4. *Claud Lorain*: Claude Lorrain (c. 1600–82), the name by which Claude Gellée, the famous Baroque landscape painter, was usually known.

5. *His*: presumably an error for 'He's, which is what Hervey revises the word to in Poem 89, repeating and expanding his verses when writing to Algarotti.

# 87 Not that in Dogs or Horses I delight

***Source.*** BL Add. MS 51345, ff. 77v–78r, holograph.

***Date, addressee and context.*** 25 June 1737 to Stephen Fox. A shortened form of the letter, including the verse, is printed in Ilchester, p. 266. The context is Hervey's expression of pleasure at the peace and quiet he is enjoying at Ickworth Park. Immediately after the three stanzas Hervey refers again to his facility in writing verse, and to the tragedy in verse on which he was working, presumably Poem 66, 'Agrippina', though, as elsewhere, he does not use that title. The few remaining lines of the letter are damaged and therefore difficult to make out, but they continue in the same vein.

## Verse in its letter context

I really feel so settled & so easy here that I begin to think I am fitter to live in the Country than I thought I was; not that I think of the common Pleasures of a Country at all differently from the manner in which I used to think of them.

Not that in Dogs or Horses I delight;
  That Country Sports or Bus'ness I pursue;
That Lawns or Woods or Waters feast my Sight,
  Or Landskips[1] fair as Claud Lorain[2] e'er drew:

I own, my Friend! my only Pleasures lye
  In human Creatures, and in Black and White;
Whilst in my Conduct still I only try,
  To reconcile what's pleasant with what's right

Nor need I blush whilst in these Paths I tread,
  Since (as in Xenophon's grave Page[3] you read)

1. *Landskips*: landscapes.
2. *Claud Lorain*: Claude Lorrain (c. 1600–82), the name by which Claude Gellée, the famous Baroque landscape painter, was usually known.
3. *Xenophon's grave Page*: Xenophon (c. 430–c. 350 BCE) was a student of Socrates who recorded some Socratic dialogues as well as personal accounts of the philosopher, and whose *Anabasis* is a history of the expedition of the Younger Cyrus, and of the retreat of the Greeks who formed part of his army.

These Paths great Socrates him-self once led
    And by this Rule his ev'ry Action weigh'd.

Aceronia you see has made my thoughts so naturally gingle into Rhyme, that I find it is as difficult to write a letter in plain Prose as a Dancing-Master does to walk into a Room: but as I have not time to ask my second thoughts, you must e'en take them hopping as they come at first . . .

# 88 In these wise Trifles and important Joys

***Source.*** SRO 941/47/4, p. 610, copy by an amanuensis in Hervey's letter-book.

***Date, addressee and context.*** 17/28 September 1737 to Francesco Algarotti. A shortened version of the letter, including the embedded verse, is printed in Ilchester, pp. 271–3; the original letter is not among the manuscripts in the John Murray Archive. The context is a reference to what is going on at court and the inappropriateness of relating it.

## Verse in its letter context

You talk to me of my being taken up with the publication of the Peace; but you mistake my Occupations extreamly if You think foreign Peace[1] has had half so great Share in them as domestic Wars.[2] The two Courts of the K[ing] & the P[rince] over w$^{ch}$ a Cloud has hung for some time, are at last quite seperated by a Storm, that has broke out upon the Lying in of the Princess: the Detail of this Rupture would be little interesting to you, improper for me & tedious for both.

> In these wise Trifles and important Joys,
> Your busy'd Friend his useless Hours employs.

When will you come and enable me to pass my Hours more Agreeably than any body who knows you, can ever do without you?

1. *foreign Peace*: a reference to the British policy of non-intervention in the War of the Polish Succession that had broken out in 1733; although a preliminary peace had been reached in 1735, the war would be formally ended only by the Treaty of Vienna in 1738.

2. *domestic Wars*: as the phrase 'Lying in of the Princess' goes on to indicate, the reference is in part to the furore that broke out when Augusta, Princess of Wales, had gone into labour and the Prince had insisted on her being removed from Hampton Court, where the King and Queen were resident, to St James's Palace, where she had given birth to a daughter; the resulting breach in the royal family became irreparable when, in September 1737, Frederick established his own court, initially at Norfolk House. Hervey gives a detailed account of what happened in *Some Materials* (Sedgwick, III, 757–839).

# 89 Why dost thou Ignorantly weep his Fate (to Algarotti)

***Source.*** SRO 941/47/4, pp. 612–13, copy by an amanuensis in Hervey's letter-book.

***Date, addressee and context.*** 17/28 September 1737 to Francesco Algarotti. The lines occur later in the same letter as Poem 88, 'In these wise Trifles and important Joys'. Part of the letter, not including the poem given below, is printed in Ilchester, pp. 271–3. Although Hervey refers to the poem as a transcript of the one he had written to Montagu (Poem 86), it is actually a longer version, considerably revised. Both facts mean that it is not, strictly speaking, an example of embedded verse, for there is no evidence that it was composed, or revised, during the process of writing the letter in which it occurs. It is kept in this section for purposes of comparison with Hervey's first thoughts on the subject, Poem 86. Hervey explains the context in introducing the poem.

**Verse in its letter context**

As you love Verses I will transcribe some Written to Lady M. W. about three months ago in answer to some of her's on the death of Mr. Hedges[1] a Friend of mine, who was Treasurer to the Prince; one you have often seen at Court and often heard me speak of: I have not the Copy of Lady Mary's at Hampton Court or I would send you those too.

Why dost thou Ignorantly weep his Fate
And Wish his Scanty Lease a longer Date?
He's gone; – his Honors green upon his Brow,
The Lover's Myrtle, and the Poets Bough;
Unwasted yet to ashes either Fire,
Nor dwindled into Dotage from Desire:
In the full Vigour of his Blood & mind,
He drank of life, & left the Dregs behind
Exempt from all th'Infirmitys of Age
Nor doom'd to drag through Life's last dirty Stage:

1. *Mr. Hedges*: for details about Hedges and the unusual circumstances of his death, see the letter in Poem 86.

Where many breath, tho' they no longer live,
And all worth living for, despised survive
He knew to purge the Courtier from y^e^ Knave,
The faithfull Servant from y^e^ fawning Slave;
Could entertain the Gay, forgive the Dull,
And keep his Wit within so Just a Rule
That no good man repined he was no Fool
None cursed his nature whilst they own'd his Art
Nor grudg'd so good a Head to Such a Heart:
His vanity not Narrowly confined,
To please the Malice only of Mankind;
For he could make the present always laugh:
And yet the Absent Friend was ever safe:
No altars on vile steps he Sought to raise,
Nor from bad Passions ever borrow'd Praise:
But could all vices of the Species tell,
Yet serve & wish the Individuals well:
Exposing generall faults he wish'd to mend,
Not more our Comentator than our Friend,
These were the Merits of his noble mind,
Endow'd by Nature & by Art refin'd.
So could I live, & so tho' early dye,
Let none prophane my Fun'rals with a Sigh,
No ill-Judg'd fond Regret, no streaming Eye.
For few to Pleasure live, and none to Fame
Dye premature, who leave an honor'd Name.

I have lately Received a Letter and a vast Packet of verses from Voltaire without any date, or any thing that makes me guess where he is, or where I can send him any Answer. Adio, Carissimo.

## 90 By an instinctive Folly still we choose

***Source.*** SRO 941/47/4, p. 620, copy by an amanuensis in Hervey's letter-book.

***Date, addressee and context.*** 31 January 1738 to Dr George Cheyne. The context is an expression of regret by Hervey that nothing can be done, even by Cheyne, to mitigate the deterioration of 'Sources of all Pleasure [that] begin to slacken their Supplys' at his time of life (p. 617). Cheyne (1671/2–1743) was a physician and occasional correspondent of Hervey's who had been advising him on his health since 1725, after he had read and been impressed by his book *An Essay of Health and Long Life*, first published in 1724 (*ODNB*; Halsband, pp. 56–7). Part of the letter, including its embedded couplet, is quoted by Moore, p. 298. Hervey remarks on the decline of sources of pleasure with increasing age.

### Verse in its letter context

without refining or philosophizing at all, I seriously think a Life after forty, like a Lottery in which there are no Prizes; where a Blank is the best Ticket you can hope for, & every Ticket which is not a blank is a Tax: yet to continue in this Annihilation of Joy, without an Exemption from Pain, —

> By an instinctive[1] Folly still we choose
> Unpleased possessing, what we fear to lose.

When you say the Beef & Claret Rioters[2] might be Happy if they would, I think you say too much, if you only Say'd they might be free from many additional uneasynesses they bring upon themselves you would say true, & you compliment the understanding of nine Parts in ten of my acquaintance full as much, when you Suggest that any Dyet could give them a clear or a reasonable Head; you might as well affirm, that because mellons may dye for want of watering, that you could water a Cucumber till it grew a Mellon.

1. *instinctive*: the word appears in error as 'insinctive', and was not corrected by Hervey.
2. *Beef and Claret Rioters*: the reference is to those of Hervey's class who eat and drink to excess without fear of the likely consequences.

# 91 Since all the Pray'rs of weeping Friends were vain

***Source.*** SRO 941/47/2, p. 75, holograph.

***Date, addressee and context.*** 17/28 August 1739 from Kensington, to Lady Mary Wortley Montagu. Part of the letter, not including the embedded verse, is printed by Halsband in *Montagu Letters*, II, 145–6; further, describing the poem as 'a generous benediction in verse', Halsband quotes its last six lines in *Lord Hervey*, p. 249. Some changes to phrasing in lines 12 and 14 of the poem indicate that it was probably composed spontaneously during the writing of the letter; see List of Emendations. The poem's general context is Hervey's response to Montagu's departure for Italy. Montagu had left England on 25 July 1739 in the hope of joining Algarotti, who, unbeknownst to her, was about to set off for Russia. She was not to return until 1762 (Grundy, pp. 390–5, 613). The immediate context is a series of pleasantries on Montagu as a kind of pilgrim.

## Verse in its letter context

You are in the right to take the Pilgrim's Staff in your Hand, and travel with Shells upon your Garment,[1] but I who should have nothing but the journey for my Pains,[2] may as well stay at home; not forgetting (according to the Custom of the Country[3] you at present inhabit) to throw up an ejaculation for the Soul of my departed Friend, and that the Purgatory you are to pass through before you enter the Gates of that Heaven your Piety deserves, may not be of long duration.

Since all the Pray'rs of weeping Friends were vain,
To stay your hated Passage o'er the Main,
Suffer at least our wishes to pursue
That charming Object which eludes our View,
And take from real Grief this fond Adieu.

1. *Shells upon your Garment*: scallop shells had become badges of pilgrimage as a result of pilgrims to the shrine of Saint James of Compostela gathering them.

2. *nothing but the journey for my Pains*: referring to Montagu's hope of joining Algarotti, known only to Hervey.

3. *Custom of the Country*: Roman Catholicism; the phrase introduces a humorous metaphor in which Montagu's journey to join Algarotti is a transition through Purgatory to Paradise.

Where'er you dwell, where'er you bend your way,
Or fix'd by Land, or roving o'er the Sea,
Be yours each Pleasure (more you can not find,)
Which Those regret whom you have left behind:[4]
May all the Transports[5] jealous Minds suggest
Are tasted in a happy Rival's Breast,
And all the Envious fancy we enjoy,
Gild ev'ry Scene, & ev'ry Sense employ;
May ev'ry Hour in gay Succession move,
Your Days all Luxury, your Nights all Love.[6]

But to return from Verse and Fancy to prose and Busyness I must ask if you have no Codicil to ad to your last Will which you left with me when you departed this Life and took your Flight to another World? you will see by the inclosed that I have hitherto been a carefull Executor.[7]

4. *Be yours ... left behind*: may you enjoy as much pleasure – more would be impossible – as you deny your friends in leaving them.

5. *Transports*: 'The state of being "carried out of oneself", i.e. out of one's normal mental condition; vehement emotion (now usu. of a pleasurable kind)' (*OED*).

6. *Your Days all Luxury, your Nights all Love*: when Agrippina compares her own political action for her son with his Aunt Domitia's self-indulgence, she declares, 'Her Days were Luxury, her Nights were love' ('Agrippina', II. 1. 216).

7. *no Codicil ... Executor*: evidently enclosing a letter from Algarotti in accordance with a prior agreement, Hervey is asking whether Montagu has any other requests or instructions concerning him.

# 92 But whilst in foreign Climes admired you rove

***Source.*** SRO 941/47/2, p. 80, holograph. Part of the letter is printed by Halsband in *Montagu Letters*, II, 160, without the verse.

***Date, addressee and context.*** 2/13 November 1739 to Montagu. The context is Hervey's explanation of why he is giving political news only in broad terms – partly, he claims, because Montagu is not interested, and partly because if he did his letters would not reach her (implicitly because they would be intercepted). The poem segues, however, into a compliment to Montagu; there is no further text after this, verse or prose.

## Verse in its letter context

I send you no news of our political world for two Reasons, the first & the best is that you do not care about it, & the other that if you had any Curiosity that way & that I should endeavour to satisfy it, it would be the most effectual Method I could take to prevent my Letter being permitted ever to reach you;[1] all I shall say in general is, that our great good Luck in the Spanish Prizes[2] we have taken, has extremely clear'd up the Countenances of us Courtiers, & lengthen'd those of our Adversarys.

> But whilst in foreign Climes admired you rove,
> And what our western World produces, prove:

1. In a subsequent letter to her that includes Poem 93, in late June or early July 1740, he indeed reflects:

> I will send you no account of public Affairs, since it would be the sure way to prevent your ever recieving my Letter, for as this Paper must pass through as many Hands, & be prostituted to as many Ravishers as the Fiancée du Roi de Garbe, if they found any thing in it that could be of use to them, they would not, like those Violaters, ever suffer it at last to come to those for whom it was design'd. (SRO 941/47/2, p. 85)

See also a similar valediction to her dated 20/31 May 1743 (SRO 941/47/2, pp. 139–42 (141)).

2. *Spanish Prizes*: War had been declared on Spain on 19 October 1739 after prolonged commercial disputes. It became known as 'The War of Jenkins's Ear', after the injury inflicted on Captain Robert Jenkins of the merchant navy by a Spanish commander off Havana (*ODNB*).

Were all that Danvers[3] writes of England true,
Her sinking Fame should still revive in You;
Like Greece, her Cimons & her Phocions[4] lost,
Tho Arms or Patriots she no more could boast;
For Wit & Science[5] still Maria's Name,[6]
Should deck our Island in Athenian Fame;
Superior Genius there Mankind should view;
From what you taste should stamp the Standard true,
And call all Barbarous compared with You.

3. *Danvers*: 'Caleb Danvers of Gray's Inn' was the fictitious editor of the leading anti-Walpole newspaper *The Craftsman*, which ran from 1726 until 1752 and in its heyday was 'the most important newspaper in circulation in England'. See Simon Varey, 'The Craftsman', *Prose Studies*, 16 (1993), 58–77 (58).

4. *her Cimons & her Phocions*: Cimon was an Athenian military leader (510–450 BCE), who distinguished himself at the battle of Salamis and elsewhere; Phocion was an Athenian statesman (c. 402–318 BCE), renowned for his virtues in both public and private life.

5. *Science*: knowledge in general, the usual sense at this period.

6. *Maria's Name*: Montagu's, in humorously formal style.

# 93 Too high the Value of such Acts you raise

***Source.*** SRO 941/47/2, pp. 86–7, holograph.

***Date, addressee and context.*** Late June/early July 1740. The letter begins by stating that Hervey received Montagu's letter on 20 June while staying with the Duke of Richmond at Goodwood. A letter to Algarotti dated 17/28 June indicates that he was back in London by then. On 12 July he would accompany Sir Robert Walpole to his estate at Houghton (Halsband, p. 261). The poem is in part an extended compliment, but it also returns to a theme frequent in Hervey's correspondence, the struggle between the demands of political ambition – he had been appointed Lord Privy Seal at the beginning of May (Halsband, p. 255) – and the pleasures of civilised conversation, including epistolary conversation. The poem ends the letter, the correspondence having long since become sufficiently close as to render such formalities as a valediction superfluous, especially in a context when they had to assume that their letters might be opened and read by others (see headnote to Poem 92).

## Verse in its letter context

You rather make me ashamed than proud, when you give me such undeserv'd thanks for writing to you so often,

Too high the Value of such Acts you raise,
I plead no Merit, & deserve no Praise:
When Zealots bend the interested[1] Knee,
Deserve their Vows the Name of Piety?
Some useless Incense at the Shrine they give,
To bribe some solid Boon they would recieve.
As they to Heav'n I to Maria bow,
And only ask the Pleasures You bestow:
To You, my Thoughts, my Pen,[2] or Time apply'd,
Tis Inclination is their only Guide.
Nor think it strange deserting Pomp & Pow'r,
That I should seek a pleasurable Hour;

1. *interested*: in the common eighteenth-century sense of pursuing personal advantage.

2. *Pen*: the word replaces 'Time', which has been deleted, so providing possible evidence of extempore composition.

When meer Ambition steers our rugged Course,
We feed an Appetite's impelling Force;[3]
Her Morsels may a hungry Rage appease,
But tis my Taste your Commerce[4] knows to please.
And sated with Ambition's grosser Fare,
I find my Luxury is only there:
By One employ'd, by tother I'm improv'd,
That only covetted, but This belov'd.

3. *an Appetite's impelling Force*: an illegible deletion before 'impelling' offers further possible evidence that the poem was written in the course of writing the letter.
4. *Commerce*: 'Interchange (esp. of letters, ideas, etc.)' (*OED*).

# 94 Subjects would bless the salutary Sway

***Source.*** John Murray Archive, Letter 20, f. 1r, holograph.

***Date, addressee and context.*** 7 October 1740 to Algarotti. The context is Hervey's response to Frederick the Great's *Anti-Machiavel*, published the month before, not long after Frederick had become king. Algarotti had sent Hervey the book without disclosing its authorship. *Anti-Machiavel* is a systematic rebuttal of Machiavelli's *The Prince* (1513; first printed 1532), and Hervey expresses agreement with both its form and content. He suggests, however, with characteristic scepticism, that its ideas would be unlikely to pass the test of exposure to the real world. Hervey would have taken an even greater interest in the book, had he known who wrote it, because of the indications it might have given him about Frederick's future policies. But, instead of continuing the discussion, he ends the letter – which is brief – by looking forward to Algarotti's visiting England, and by doing his best to encourage him to do so.

## Verse in its letter context

if all Princes were in his way of thinking, or follow'd his Rules in their way of acting, there would be no such thing remaining in the World as a Republican by Principle or a Rebel in Practice.

> Subjects would bless the salutary Sway,
> And even England willingly obey.

# 95 When the Philosophers attempt to scan

***Source.*** Letter of 16 May 1741 to Lady Mary Wortley Montagu from Ickworth Park, SRO 941/47/2, pp. 86–7, holograph.

***Date, addressee and context.*** The letter begins with news of Hervey's mother's death, which had taken place on 1 May 1741, a fortnight before writing ('Hervey, John, first earl of Bristol', *ODNB*). As a consequence Hervey has been staying with his father in the country; he praises the simplicity of life there and claims an ability to 'see things just as they are'. He turns from a critique of fine dress to soldiers and war. Walpole had reluctantly entered the 'War of Jenkins's Ear' in 1739, and the difficulties of prosecuting the war were undermining confidence in his ministry. The letter was sent after the catastrophic failure of the assault on Cartagena (9 May 1741), but it would have been written in ignorance of the outcome. The general sentiments echo those of Poem 7 'To the Same. From Hampton-Court, 1731' and Poem 106 'Chanson au Curé —', which characterise the rejection of appetite as folly. For a considered response in verse by Montagu, see *Montagu Letters*, II, 238–9.

***Textual commentary.*** In the transcription that follows, Hervey's corrections and interpolations have been silently incorporated in the prose text; the poem has been transcribed without alteration.

## Verse in its letter context

I see all the Princes in Europe, & all their Ministers in their correspondent Habits to Flannel Pettycoats; I see all the poor Devils that they set to cutting one anothers throats, to try what Robber shall plunder this Country & what Opressor shall harass t'other; marching in red & yellow Coats with Ears[1] as long as their Musquets. I have infinitely a higher Esteem for the Understanding of a fighting Cock, than I have for a fighting common Soldier; for the Cock may think when he gets rid of another Cock that he may have more Hens & more Grains of Wheat to his own Share; but for 50000, Cocks to fight with 50000, more, that some other one Cock, that none of them go shares with, may have all the Hens & Wheat in that Neighbourhood, is a superlative Piece of Folly which no fether'd Cock ever

1. *Ears*: possibly *lapels*.

was guilty of, & which no Species ever thought of but that, which our own Ideocy, and Ignorance of ourselves, has christen'd rational.

When the Philosophers attempt to scan
The Motives of infatuated Man,
Let them no more define, & judg by Rule,
But solve each Riddle by that one Word Fool:
And when by Chance (tho distant far) you hear
Of all the Nothings that employ my Care,
This one remaining Mark of Sense you'll see,
I'll own you're just, when you cry Fool to Me.

When I tell you that since I came hither my Father has made me a Present of ten thousand Pounds you will think perhaps that has contributed more than Country Air to the good Spirits I brag of: & as I know the Part you take in every thing that benefits or pleases me I make no excuse for inserting this Family Transaction.

# 96 How must we think the Gods esteem Mankind

***Source.*** Letter of 26 July 17[41] to Lady Mary Wortley Montagu from Grosvenor Street, London. SRO 941/47/2, p. 114. The letter is given in part in *Montagu Letters*, II, 244–5, but without the verse, and by Grundy, p. 443.

***Date, addressee and context.*** Montagu was at this time living in Genoa and concerned about a dispute between Britain and Genoa, over a ship Britain had seized, violating Genoese neutrality (*Montagu Letters*, II, 242, n. 1; Halsband, p. 277). Montagu had supported Genoa and was concerned about any implications for her own position. As Hervey reports, a British decision had been made in favour of Genoa (see Grundy, pp. 442–3).

***Textual commentary.*** The poem and its surrounding prose text, which end this letter, appear exactly as in the Suffolk Record Office manuscript.

## Verse in its letter context

The Genoese Affair has been under our Consideration & very proper Directions in my Opinion have been given for the termination of it, w$^{ch}$ I make no doubt will be comply'd with, & prevent your being any way inconvenienced by a farther dispute between our Court & that Republic. I fear this is the only Squabble in Europe of w$^{ch}$ you will soon hear of any Conclusion; & wish rather than[1] hope that you may not quickly hear of many important new ones breaking out.

> Delirunt Reges (& Reginae) plectuntur Achivi.[2]
> How must we think the Gods esteem Mankind
> Viewing the Hands to whom they are consign'd.

I dare trust my-self no farther on this Subject and therefore must bid you Adieu.

1. This word ends p. 114, which has at the bottom in the left margin, in ink but not the same hand, two names one above the other: 'Ds: [illegible] and 'Ld. Shelburne'.

2. *Delirunt reges . . . Archivi*; 'When kings (and queens) go mad, the people take a beating', Hervey's adaptation of *quidquid delirant reges, plectuntur Achivi*, a line from Horace's *Epistles* (I. ii. 14) that had become proverbial.

# 97 These kind auxiliary Recruits should bring

***Source.*** Letter written 1/12 September 1741 to Lady Mary Wortley Montagu from Grosvenor Street, London, SRO 941/47/2, p. 115.

***Date, addressee and context.*** The letter responds to one written from Genoa in which Montagu discussed her new circle of friends, including a friend of Hervey's, the 'Marquis de Mari' (Grundy, p. 440). According to Charles de Sainte-Maure, Esteban Mari y Centurión, Marqués de Mari (1683–?1749) was a 'General Officer in the *Spanish* Service' (*A New Journey through the Kingdoms and Provinces of Italy, Greece, Egypt, and Palestine* (London: for J. Osborn, 1739), p. 134). Born in Genoa, the Marquis had taken part in several naval campaigns and was anxious to be active in the War of Jenkins's Ear. His was probably the collection of paintings from which two Gaspard Poussins and a Claude found their way to Walpole's Houghton Hall (see *Ædes Walpolianæ* (London: [printed by John Hughs], 1752), p. 94). Hervey's reference to 'recruits' in the first line of verse relates troops to fresh company.

***Textual commentary.*** The verse and its letter context are taken without alteration from the Suffolk Record Office manuscript.

## Verse in its letter context

I laugh'd at y^r^ last two Letters relating to the Marquis di Mari, with as much real cherfullness, as if I were still at y^e^ Age he first knew me: I am glad to hear there is so little Alteration in his Spirits & am not at all surprised that in such a Climate to make them ferment, & such a Companion as y^r^ self to keep them in Play

> These kind auxiliary Recruits should bring
> To his autumnal Life a second Spring
> That Spirits even under Wrinkles flow
> And in Flesh Ashes Love's warm Fire should glow.[1]

Pray make my Compliments in the best Manner to this envyable Composition & do not undecieve him in the Opinion he seems to entertain of my being as handsome & as gay as I was a quarter of a Century ago; but in 52. Degrees of Latitude I know of no return of such Jubilees. Adieu I set out for y^e^ Bath to morrow.

1. *And in Flesh Ashes Love's warm Fire should glow*: echoing 'In me thou seest the glowing of such fire | That on the ashes of his youth doth lie' (Sonnet 73, *Shakespeare Works*, p. 788).

# 98 This world was made for Fools who can compound

***Source.*** Letter of 16 November 1741 to Lady Mary Wortley Montagu from London. SRO 941/47/2, p. 121.

***Date, addressee and context.*** Hervey was ill at this time, suffering from a 'very acute Complaint of a most malignant Fever'. The illness and Hervey's state of mind are discussed by Halsband (p. 278) and Moore (pp. 291–2).

***Textual commentary.*** In the transcription that follows, Hervey's corrections and interpolations have been silently incorporated in the prose text; in all other respects, the poem and its letter context have been transcribed without alteration from the Suffolk Record Office manuscript.

## Verse in its letter context

I send you these few Lines only to tell you I received y^e two Letters you wrote me from Genoa & was pleased with them at a time when I am sure nothing else entertain'd me & when I thought I was not entertainable, in short y^e Day after I came from y^e Bath (a month ago) I fell ill of a violent Fever & vomiting which nothing for three Days could stop, I have been five times blooded & never less than 9 ounces, sometimes 12. the fever is off, but I am weaker in Body than any of my Court-acquaintance in mind: & from an instinctive unaccountable impulse try to live, even tho my coolest Judgment tell's me that living upon y^e terms I do, is buying mellow Apples, & mealy Potatos at a Guinea a piece instead of a penny a dozen.

> This world was made for Fools who can compound[1]
> For a small crop on a hard-labor'd Ground
> I find the Growth of Pleasure is so small
> I long to tear my Lease & spurn it all.[2]

Adieu. I write this from a Couch to which I am still confin'd.

1. *compound*: settle or compromise.

2. For an analysis of this theme in Hervey's verse, see Overton, 'Death and Futurity', and Poems 1 *Monimia to Philocles*, 4 'Roxana to Usbeck', 86 'Why doest thou ignorantly mourn his Fate' and 89 'Why doest though Ignorantly weep his Fate'.

# 99 Did Men (who ne'er act right) inspect with Care

***Source.*** Letter to Lady Mary Wortley Montagu (probably from Ickworth, though not explicitly stated), SRO 941/47/2, p. 129. Letter paraphrased and quoted by Halsband, p. 292–3; prose quoted by Moore, pp. 291–2.

***Date, addressee and context.*** The letter to Montagu is dated 19 September 1742. Hervey left public office in the summer of 1742, surrendering the Privy Seal on 12 July. He had hoped that his personal relations with George II would enable him to survive the fall of Walpole's ministry. His resentment at the King's failure to retain him in office is expressed in Poem 27 *The Patriots Are Come*. In this letter, renunciation of ambition is followed by an attack on the new government.

***Textual commentary.*** In the transcription that follows, Hervey's corrections and interpolations have been silently incorporated in the prose text; his two revisions to the poem are recorded in the List of Emendations.

## Verse in its letter context

You do me great Injustice if you imagine I want your Advice (w$^{ch}$ I confess to be excellent) with regard to checking the Dictates of Ambition; since I can assure you after seeing by whom y$^{e}$ first Employments are often held, I could no more be proud, or desirous of obtaining them, than if I was a Lady, I could be solicitous to have my Name inserted in a List of Toasts where I had not one Companion there in twenty, younger than my Lady Notingham[1] or handsomer than y$^{e}$ Ds. of Devonshire;[2] & should no more imagine such an exaltation a Proof of my Understanding or my Merit; than an Athenian could have thought it of his adress or his Strength to carry away the Prize at the Olympic Games if a Boy of fiveteen had born y$^{e}$ Palm y$^{e}$ year before. 'Sr.G.P.'[3]

1. *Lady Notingham*: Anne Finch (*née* Hatton), Dowager Countess of Nottingham, in her seventy-fifth year (1668–1743).

2. *Ds. of Devonshire*: Catherine Cavendish (*née* Hoskins), wife of the third Duke (c. 1700–77); there is a portrait of her by Charles Jervas at Chatsworth House.

3. *Sr.G.P.*: 'Sir George Pembroke?' is written in a different hand in the left margin on p. 128 and, accompanied by a vertical line from line 1 to line 12, on p. 129. Sir George, or another who is referred to, has not been identified.

Did Men (who ne'er act right) inspect with Care,
What Blockheads often Fortune's Favors wear;
The G — ns and N — es of the Age,[4]
The last of Men, the first upon the Stage;
Of Things call'd Honors who could then be proud
Possess'd by Folly and by Chance bestow'd?
Or ev'n of Homage to great Monarchs pay'd,
When Claudius[5] once the kneeling World obey'd?
Pass oer our happy Isle, and see what Things
Now despicably bear the Name of Kings,
You have a Judgment and a Taste so true,
You'll give those Cæsars what is Cæsar's due;[6]
I've read a tenet in our Law maintains,
The Crown's a Cleanser washes out all Stains;[7]
Oh! were it Providence or Nature's Law,
That Royalty should banish ev'ry Flaw;
What Changes through all Europe would be shown,
In ev'ry Court and State (except our own)
When Vice and Folly were expell'd each Throne.

4. *The G — ns and N — es of the Age* – probably referring to Charles Fitzroy, second Duke of Grafton (1683–1757), Lord Chamberlain 1724–57; and Thomas Pelham-Holles, first Duke of Newcastle (1693–1768), a minister in Walpole's government from 1730 (*ODNB*). Hervey despised both.

5. *Claudius*: Claudius (10 BCE–54 CE) became Emperor of Rome in 41 CE when Caligula was assassinated, despite suffering from physical disabilities that included a limp and a speech impediment.

6. *give those Cæsars what is Cæsar's due*: 'Render therefore unto Caesar the things that are Caesar's; and unto God the things that are God's' (Matthew 22: 21, also Mark 12: 17 and Luke 20: 25).

7. *The Crown's a Cleanser washes out all Stains*: 'it is a Maxim of our Law, that the King can do no Wrong' (Hervey, *An Examination of the Facts and Reasonings Contain'd in a Recent Pamphlet* (London: sold by J. Roberts, 1739), p. 6); 'The King's Dignity consists . . . In his absolute Perfection' (William Blackstone, *An Analysis of the Laws of England* (Oxford: Clarendon Press, 1756), p. 13).

# VERSE IN LATIN AND IN FRENCH

# INTRODUCTION TO VERSE IN LATIN AND IN FRENCH

In Hervey's time Latin was still the language of formal social record, while French was the language of the court. The two Latin poems in this section concern the accession of a king and the death of a queen. 'Ad Regem' (Poem 100) is a poem in a volume published by Cambridge University to commemorate the death of Queen Anne and the accession of George I. Hervey takes his place in the first half of the volume as one of the aristocrats at the University. We cannot be certain, but he may have been one of the few aristocrats to write his own poem. The epitaph on Queen Caroline (Poem 107), equally formal, was written at the request of the King. The importance of shaping opinion of the royal house is indicated by there being a second edition provided with an English translation.

Hervey's French verse, in contrast to his Latin, is particularly relaxed, tending to naughtiness. In that respect it may reflect the mores of the court, but at other times it may have been designed to protect daring material from prying eyes. Two poems (101 and 102) spring directly out of court writing, responding to Lady Bolingbroke's attack on Walpole, while another (Poem 105) is addressed to the Prince of Wales and implicitly contrasts the pleasing dullness of Redlynch with the life at court. Perhaps a similar cross-evaluation is attempted in the couplet (Poem 103) where Hervey tells Stephen Fox in French that he should enjoy what he can. In another intimate letter, it seems likely that the four insulting lines in French addressed to his brother after 'Adieu' are merely designed to be comic, but the French of 'Chanson au Curé de —' (Poem 106) may have a more serious purpose. Like Poem 54 ('Reveillez vous'), it seems to have been addressed to Parson Samuel Hill, but this is one of Hervey's most daring poems, treating the Trinity with ribald contempt and arguing a libertine morality. Its French may have been intended to protect it from the eyes of visitors or servants.

# 100 Ad Regem

***Source.*** *Mœstissimæ ac Lætissimæ Academiæ Cantabrigiensis Carmina Funebria et Triumphalia. Illis Serenissimam ac Desideratissimam Reginam Annam Repentina Morte Abreptam Deflet. His Augustissimo Potentissimoque Regi Georgio Britannicum Solium Optimis Auspiciis Ascendenti Gratulatur* (Cambridge: s.n., 1714), sig. D1r

***Complementary manuscript sources.*** None known.

***Complementary print sources.*** None known.

***Attribution.*** Identified as Hervey's on the page.

***Context and date.*** This collection of Latin and Greek verse laments the death of Queen Anne and congratulates King George on his ascent of the throne; the University is most sorrowful (*moestissima*) and most joyful (*laetissima*). The folio volume was advertised for sale in London by G. Innys in the *Daily Courant*, 4050 (16 October 1714). Queen Anne died on 1 August 1714; George I arrived in Great Britain on 18 September and was crowned on 20 October 1714. If Innys was supplied with copies at the same time as the collection was published in Cambridge, publication was timed for the coronation.

Such collections of Latin and Greek verse were made in Cambridge and Oxford to mark events in the royal house or to celebrate a royal visit to the University. After two introductory poems, the verse is presented in order of precedence of the writers. Hervey's poem is preceded by those of the sons of the Duke of Kent (two), the Duke of Somerset, and the Earl of Nottingham (two). In each case the seniority of the son is declared. Hervey himself is followed by the fifth son of a Baron and the sons of a Baronet and a Knight before the collection descends to Henry James, the Regius Professor of Sacred Theology and President of the Queen's College.

It seems unlikely that all the poems were actually written by the aristocrats who claimed them, rather than by tutors or hired hands. Hervey's, however, shows considerable individuality, with an argumentative structure and playing with counterfactuals that is characteristic of some of his later verse.

***Textual commentary.*** The text is taken without alteration (except for expansion of the ampersand) from the Cambridge printing. For the translation that follows it we are indebted to Dr Llewelyn Morgan, Fellow of Brasenose College, Oxford.

## *Ad* Regem

Si non qui lapsam posset fulcire Coronam,
Qui leges, populumque suum, qui jura tuendo
Arceret falsosque Deos et vinc'la minantem,
Vindice jam rerum Brittanni et Rege carerent;
Si Gens prima novi statuens cunabula Regni
Quæreret imperio dignum; Tibi debita, Princeps,
Virtutique Tuæ gauderet tradere Sceptra.
Non Te tam generis Splendor, quàm plurima menti
Insita vis, ad Regna vocat; non Stemmata tantum,
Quantum animi dotes, titulis et honoribus augent.
Indole sublimis scandis fastigia rerum,
Ingenioque potens regnas; Te regia Virtus
Evexit, Solioque locat, redimitque Coronâ.
Dumque alios decorant Fasces, Diademata, Sceptra,
Imperio titulisque novis et laude nitentes;
Tu quibus es cinctus lauris nova lumina spargens
Ipse decus lumenque tuis insignis honores
Majores longe, quam quos acceperis, addis.

*Joh. Hervey*, Aul Clar. A.M. Honoratissimi Domini
*Johannis Hervey* Baronis de *Ickworth* Filius Natu Secundus.

## Translation

If he were not a man who could support a fallen crown,
a man who by protecting the laws, his people and justice,
could keep at bay false gods and one threatening chains,
Britons would now be without a champion of their interests and a king.
If the first race, establishing the cradle of a new kingdom,
were seeking a man worth of sovereignty, to you, Prince,
and to your virtue it would happily hand the sceptre as your right.
It is not so much the glory of your birth as the immense strength
innate to your mind that calls you to kingship; not ancestry so much as
the gifts of the soul that exalt you with titles and honours.
By natural genius you scale the summits of the world on high;
you rule with the power of your inborn talent. It is royal virtue

that has raised you up, and places you on the throne and girds you with a crown.
And while others are ennobled by fasces,[1] diadems, sceptres,
gleaming with authority and novel honours and praise,
you, scattering new light from the laurels with which you are crowned,
yourself an ornament and light to your people, in your eminence bestow
on them honours far greater than those you have received.

Joh. Hervey, Clare Hall, M.A. of the most honourable Lord John Hervey, Baron of Ickworth Second Born Son

1. *fasces*: 'A bundle of rods bound up with an axe in the middle and its blade projecting. These rods were carried by lictors before the superior magistrates at Rome as an emblem of their power' (*OED*).

# 101 Pult'ney soyez en allegresse

***Source.*** Letter of 17 August 1731 to Stephen Fox, from Hampton Court. SRO 941/47/4, pp. 158–9 (Ilchester, p. 77). A letter-book in a scribal hand, with corrections by Hervey.

***Complementary manuscript sources.*** None known.

***Complementary print sources.*** None known.

***Attribution.*** Hervey does not claim this verse as his, but it adapts a stanza by Lady Bolingbroke in a song that we know he responded to in Poem 102 'D' Hamton Cour a Milady B.' The attention he gives to these lines in his letter also suggests they are his. Reticence about authorship would have been in keeping with aristocratic modesty, especially for so slight a pleasantry.

***Context and date.*** Hervey wrote to Stephen Fox on Friday, describing events of the previous Saturday, 11 August 1731. The lines by Lady Bolingbroke to which these are a response provide a stanza in her song 'Or ecoutez ma noble Histoire'. Lady Bolingbroke was French (Marie Claire des Champs (1675–1750)) and the language of the court was French.

William Pulteney (1684–1754) was in opposition to Walpole and had quarrelled violently with Hervey earlier that year, when they had engaged in a duel in which they were both slightly wounded (25 January 1731).

***Textual commentary.*** The text is from the Suffolk Record Office manuscript. Contractions are expanded and insertions incorporated in the transcription of the prose; the verse is taken without alteration from the Suffolk Record Office manuscript.

## Verse in its letter context

We began hunting last Saturday in Richmond park; I never saw the Hounds, but rode as usual the whole time by the Queen's Chaise; Sir Robert recieved the King at the park-Gate dress'd in Green and Gold and a Cap as Ranger, with the Leash cross his Shoulders, which gave occasion to a Joke which I Shall transcribe, and that we all sung the whole Day. You know the Stanza in Lady B.'s Song,[1]

1. *Lady B.'s Song*: Lady Bolingbroke was the second wife of Henry St. John, first Viscount Bolingbroke (1678–1751). As a Lady of the Bedchamber, she was close to Queen Caroline, who notoriously had considerable influence over George II. The full

Caroline ma douce Maitresse
partage mes bons tours de main
Nous menons son Mari en Lesse
Et nous nous moquons du Genre humain.

It was thus turn'd upon this Occasion

Pult'ney soyez en allegresse
Du beau Triomphe de ce Jour
Nous menons Sr. Robert en Lesse
Il faut que chacun ait son tour.[2]

I dined after the Chase with her Grace,[3] where I had the pleasure of talking of you, and finding my tast so well confirm'd, that every body's good Opinion of you is proportion'd to the Degree to which they are acquainted with You.

## Translation

Pulteney be joyful
about today's great triumph
we lead Sir Robert on a leash
everyone has to have his turn.

song from which these lines are taken is reprinted with Poem 102 'D' Hamton Cour a Milady B.', which is Hervey's response to it. These lines mean: 'Caroline my sweet mistress | shares in my clever tricks | We lead her husband on a leash | And we laugh at the human race.'

2. *Pult'ney . . . son tour*: Pulteney was in bad odour with the court at this time owing to his opposition to Walpole's administration. He had been removed from the list of Privy Councillors and the commission of the peace on 1 July (*ODNB*), and the duel with Hervey had generated sentiment in Hervey's favour (Halsband, p. 115). The leash is the one worn by Sir Robert in his dress as a Park Ranger.

3. *her Grace*: As Ilchester notes (p. 77), the Duchess of Richmond (Lady Sarah Cadogan (1705–51)).

# 102 D' Hamton Cour a Milady B

***Source.*** BL Add. MS 51441, ff. 24r–v. Part of a loose collection of leaves in 'Vol. CXXIL Verses and literary [sic] of 1st Lord Holland'. Many items are from the 1750s or later; some have notes by Horace Walpole (identified by subsequent annotation).

***Complementary manuscript sources.*** None known.

***Complementary print sources.*** None known.

***Attribution.*** The song 'By Lady Bolingbroke' and Hervey's reply are on a single sheet, folded once vertically. On the fourth and final page is written horizontally in a hand which might be that of one of the Fox brothers or Horace Walpole, 'Lord Hervey'. The two previous items (Poem 106 'Chanson au Curé de —', ff. 21–22r and 54 'Reveillez vous', f. 22r) are also attributed to Hervey.

***Context and date.*** Hervey's verses are a response to the satirical attack on Walpole by Lady Bolingbroke that precedes them in the manuscript. She alleges that Walpole is a corrupt first minister who uses his influence with the Queen to control the King. A stanza from Lady Bolingbroke's poem is also the basis of the verses, probably by Hervey (Poem 101), that were sung by the Queen's party on 17 August 1731. This time again the language is French because Lady Bolingbroke was French (Marie Claire des Champs (1675–1750)).

Between 5 September 1730 and 22 May 1731, her husband, Henry St John, first Viscount Bolingbroke (1678–1751), former Tory minister and leader of the non-parliamentary opposition to Walpole, had published, in *The Craftsman*, 'Remarks on the History of England. From the Minutes of Humphry Oldcastle', a history that had criticised Walpole's government by analogy. The Lancastrian kings, for example, had subjected Parliament to the control of the government, and Cardinal Wolsey had exercised excessive power as Henry VIII's first minister. Hervey sees Lady Bolingbroke as pursuing her husband's campaign by other means. Composition in the summer of 1731 seems likely.

***Textual commentary.*** The lines are taken from the British Library manuscript, and presented just as they appear there, with footnotes indicating errors in the French. A literal translation then follows.

## Lady Bolingbroke's Song

Or ecoutez ma noble Histoire[1]
  Je vous la donne en raccourçî
Avant George d'heureuse memoire
  Je vivois sur un grand-merci

Depuis ce Prince de bonnaire
  Me fît son Ministre d'Etât
J'ai brouillis[2] toutes ses affaires
  Et l'ai recu de pecula't[3]

Pour decroisser mon petit Frere
  Meprise[4] malgrè ma Faveur
Au Detriment de l'Angleterre
  J'en ait fait un Ambassadeur.[5]

Caroline ma douce Maitresse
  Partagea mes bons tours de main
Nous menons son Mari en Lesse
  Et nous mocquons du genr' humain.

Ne vous offensez pas beau Sire[6]
  Si nous paroißons agir mal
Nos traites n'etoient que pour rire
  Adieu notre cher Cardinal.[7]

1. The speaker is Sir Robert Walpole (1676–1745), first minister to George I and George II.

2. *brouillis*: correctly, this should read 'brouilli'.

3. *pecula't*: a word rather blotchy and difficult to read, but probably an allusion to corruption. Cf. 'Each Purse by Peculate and Rapine drain'd', meaning 'peculation' (Poem 24, *The Difference between Verbal and Practical Virture*, line 64).

4. *Meprise*: correctly, this should read 'Mepris' if it refers to 'Frere', as it seems to.

5. *un Ambassadeur*: Horatio Walpole, first Baron Walpole (1678–1757) was envoy extraordinary and minister plenipotentiary in Paris from 1723 to 1730.

6. *beau Sire*: Walpole; the courtiers writing the verse now address him.

7. *cher Cardinal*: an allusion to Cardinal Wolsey, advisor to Henry VIII, with whom Walpole was compared by Bolingbroke in *The Craftsman* and by other writers (see Urstad, p. 18), with the French Cardinals Richelieu and Mazarin, first ministers to Louis XIII and XIV, in the background.

## Translation of Lady Bolingbroke's Song

Now listen to my noble story
I give it to you in brief
Under George of blessed memory
I lived in a state of thanksgiving.

Since this Prince of happiness
Made me his Minister of State
I have muddled all his affairs
And I have profited from peculation.[8]

To diminish my little brother
Scorned in spite of my favour
To the detriment of England
I have made him an ambassador.

Caroline my sweet mistress
Shared in my clever tricks
We lead her husband on a leash
And we laugh at the human race.

Do not take offence good sir
If we appear to act badly
Our business was only a joke
Adieu our dear cardinal.

## Hervey's Verse
## D' Hamton Cour a Milady B.

Nous chantons tous votre Satire
Elle est tant a la mode icy
Elle pique tant qu'elle fait rire
N'at Elle pas bein[9] reussi.

Walpole cet insolent s'en mocque
Lui même au Roi il l'a donnè

8. *peculation*: appropriation of public money or property by one in an official position (*OED*).
9. *N'at Elle pas bein*: correctly, this should read 'N'a-t-elle pas bien'.

J'ai peur que cet advis vous choque
  Qui l'a use[10] jamais soupçonne.

Le Roi malgrè votre colere
  Ne paroit pas mal satisfait
Helas! qu'importe votre guerre?
  Il tient toute l'Europe en paix.[11]

La Reine doit être glorieuse
  De pouvoir tant sur tel Epoux
Madame, que vous seriez heureuse
  S'il etoit de meme chez vous.

Pourtant Madame enc une[12] Chose
  Asses[13] d'accord vous paroisses
Vos Vers discut[14] que dit sa prose
  Madam Oldcastle en Francois.

Peu vous peutêtre voules[15] rire
  Du Dailey Conseil sur ce Ton
C'est Finemènt Madame leur dire
  Leur Esperance est un Chanson[16]

## Translation of Hervey's Verse

We all sing your satire
  It's so much in the fashion here
It stings as much as it causes laughter
  Hasn't it done well.

10. The reading at this point is unclear. There may be a reference to suspicion about the identity of the author or merely surprise that Walpole would show the attack to the King.

11. *Il tient toute l'Europe en paix*: for an analysis of the relation of literature to Walpole's peace policy, see the chapter on 'The "Pax Romana" and the "Pax Brittanica"' in Howard Weinbrot, *Britannia's Issue: The Rise of British Literature from Dryden to Ossian* (Cambridge: Cambridge University Press, 1993).

12. *enc une*: correctly, perhaps 'encore une'; the manuscript is unclear and a syllable seems to be missing.

13. *Asses*: translated as 'assez'; the manuscript frequently uses 's' where 'z' is required.

14. *discut*: correctly, 'discutent'. 15. *voules*: correctly, 'voulez'.

16. *un Chanson*: correctly, 'une Chanson'.

Walpole, that insolent man, only laughs
He has given it to the King himself
I'm afraid this warning shocks you
Who never have suspected it.

The King in spite of your anger
Doesn't appear dissatisfied
Alas, what does your war matter
He holds all Europe in peace.

The Queen must be glorious
To have such power over her spouse
Madam, how happy you would be
If it was the same in your house.

However, Madam, in one thing
Agreed enough you appear
Your verse discusses what his prose says
Madame Oldcastle in French.[17]

Perhaps you little wish to laugh
At the daily counsel in this key
It's for Madame to tell them delicately
Their hope is a song.[18]

17. *Madame Oldcastle in French*: Lady Bolingbroke writes as if she is the wife of Oldcastle, repeating his message in 'Remarks on the History of England' in *The Craftsman*.

18. *Their hope is a song*: possibly a reference to the phrase 'going for a song', that is, almost worthless, but Hervey may have in mind 'chansons que tout cela' meaning 'poppycock'.

# 103 Quand on ne peut pas

***Source.*** Letter of 27 September 1731 to Stephen Fox [from Hampton Court?], SRO 941/47/4, p. 213 (Ilchester, p. 93). A letter-book in the hand of an amanuensis.

***Complementary manuscript sources.*** None known.

***Complementary print sources.*** None known.

***Attribution.*** No known source.

***Context and date.*** Hervey is responding in this letter of 27 September 1731 to Stephen Fox's expressed dislike of writing. The letter is quoted and discussed at some length by Moore (pp. 155–7), but she is not concerned with this part.

***Textual commentary.*** The verse and its letter context are taken without alteration from the Suffolk Record Office manuscript.

## Verse in its letter context

I had time last post to thank you but very slightly & can never thank you enoug for $y^e$ agreable Letter I $y^t$ Morning reciev'd from Maddington. As to Your dislike of writing, I think one can no more in general say one loves or hates it, than one can say in general one love or hates eating or Kissing, both which, depend intirely on $y^e$ Food and $y^e$ Object. one hates talking to people one dislikes, but to those one does not dislike it is pleasent even to talk upon Paper, & the only Reason why it is less pleasent to speak to their Eyes than to their Ears, is that one is forced to speak slower, & a little more constrain'd, from being more afray'd of being overlook'd, than one is of being overheard. But because one has not all $y^e$ Liberty one wishes, is $y^t$ a Reason why one should not enjoy all one possesses? I could no more deny my-self $y^e$ Satisfaction of writing to one I loved when I had no other way of conversing $w^{th}$ them, than if I was a prisoner I would always stay Stifling in my Dungeon, because I had only a little Garden of two or three Acres within my Limits allow'd me to walk in;

> Quand on ne peut pas ce qu'on veut,
> Il faut vouloir ce qu'on peut.'[1]

1. His maxim appears to adapt one later recorded by Lewis Chambaud in *The Idioms of the French and English Languages* (London: for J. Nourse, 1751), p. 217: 'Quand on ne peut

## Translation

When one cannot do what one wants,
One has to want what one can.

pas faire comme on veut, il faut faire comme un peu', translated as 'They who cannot do as they will, must do as they can'.

# 104 rien mieux

***Source.*** Letter of 30 September 1731 to Felton Hervey [no place stated, but possibly from Hampton Court, where his letter two days later to Sir Robert Smyth is sent from], SRO 941/47/4, p. 194 (not included by Ilchester). A letter-book in the hand of an amanuensis.

***Complementary manuscript sources.*** None known.

***Complementary print sources.*** None known.

***Attribution.*** No other source identified.

***Context and date.*** A jocular and affectionate letter, largely concerned with a suit of clothes Hervey has ordered for his brother Felton, with some teasing about the fact that the suit's 'Inside is much better than the Out', the reverse supposedly being true of Felton himself. The lines form a humorous valediction, following a pun concerning their sister Louisa's marriage the week before, on 23 September 1731, to Sir Robert Smyth.[1]

***Textual commentary.*** In the transcription that follows, Hervey's corrections and interpolations have been silently incorporated in the prose text; the poem has been transcribed without alteration from the Suffolk Record Office manuscript.

### Verse in its letter context

Raillery apart I wish you Joy both of Your new Coat & Your new Brother; make my Compliments to $y^e$ Lady with $y^e$ new Name, & tell her I would certainly have writt to her on this Occasion, but $y^t$ I conclude she desires no Body to give her Joy in *Sheets* but $S^r$ Robert. Adieu.

rien mieux
que Fourb & Fou
baise mon Cul:
encore. Adieu.

This Sort of poetry is call'd a Roundeau: live & learn.[2]

1. See the biographical essay on Louisa Hervey, later Lady Louisa Smyth (1715–70), in D[oris] A[lmon] Ponsonby, *Call A Dog Hervey* (London: Hutchinson, [1949]), pp. 181–4 (182).

2. This is probably a further joke by Hervey, as the rondeau, in the form established by Renaissance French poets, has thirteen lines. His rudimentary version reads more like the refrain to a drinking song.

## Translation

Nothing better
than a rogue[3] and mad
kiss my arse:
once more. Goodbye.

3. *rogue*: the French 'Fourb' (correctly, fourbe) carries an additional resonance of hypocrisy, picking up on Hervey's teasing during the letter, about whether his brother, like his new clothes, is finer on the inside than the out, or vice versa.

## 105 Quant al Padrone, Signor Ste

***Source.*** Letter dated 6 November 1731 to Frederick, Prince of Wales, from Redlynch, SRO 941/47/4, pp. 268–9. This is a copy by an amanuensis in Hervey's letter-book, printed in Sedgwick, I, xxxvii; and Ilchester, p. 108.

***Complementary manuscript sources.*** None known.

***Complementary print sources.*** None known.

***Attribution.*** No other source identified.

***Context and date.*** In November 1731 Hervey visited the country. He went first to the Earl and Countess of Pembroke at Wilton and then to stay with Stephen Fox at Redlynch. The lines on Stephen Fox are introduced by a discussion of Mrs Digby and followed by an apology for their poor quality. Mrs Digby was Stephen's sister, Charlotte. She had married the Hon. Edward Digby in 1729 (Ilchester, p. 10). After the apology, the letter continues after a short linking passage, in which Hervey refers to himself as Hephaestion, with the translation 'No more my Eyes thy Beauty charms' (Poem 62), and ends with Poem 77 'For if in Richmond-Morning-Walk'.

***Textual commentary.*** In the transcription that follows, Hervey's corrections and interpolations have been silently incorporated in the prose text; the poem has been transcribed without alteration from the Suffolk Record Office manuscript.

### Verse in its letter context

It has rained Incessantly, ever Since I left London . . . all our employments eating & drinking chatting & Reading we might pray if we would for my Dear Friend & Patient, parson Hill is allways at hand: But I like him much better in his Lay Calling than his Ecclesiastical Vocation. And give him his Due I believe he had rather act in one than t'other tho' he is really not only a Good Companion but a good Man. As for M$^{rs}$ Digby y$^{e}$ only Woman we have here, I know no fault She has but loving her Husband better than any other Man, & likeing her Children better than any other Company. According to La Bruyere's Doctrine She Should be one of the most agreeable Creatures in y$^{e}$ World for He says y$^{e}$ prettiest human Composition is une Polie femme qui avoutes les bonnes Qualités d'un honête Homme.[1] And as far as my Skill goes I think She Seems to be made by y[t] Recept.[2]

Quant al Padrone, Signor Ste,
Le petit Drol, mon cher Ami,
Il peste un Peu contre la Pluï,
Mais d'une Humeur badin, Joli,
Amusant, Polisson, poli,[3]
Fait les Delices de nôtre vie,
Rit, cause, et chante, & chasse l'Ennüi.

Voila un Crambo[4] qui ne vaut rien mais n'importe.

## Translation

As for the Master, Signor Ste,
The little Rascal, my dear Friend,
He curses the Rain a Little,
But in a playful Mood, Attractive,
Amusing, Naughty, polite,
Makes the Pleasures of our life
Laughs, chats, and sings, and chases away Boredom.

There's a Crambo worth nothing; but never mind.

1. *une Polie femme … d'un honête Homme*: alluding to La Bruyère's observation, 'A Beautiful Woman that has the Qualities of an Accomplisht Man, is of all the Conversations in the World, the most delicious. In her is to be found all the Merit of both Sexes' (Jean de La Bruyère, *The Characters, or the Manners of the Age* (London, 1702), p. 48).

2. *Recept*: recipe.

3. *badin … poli*: these adjectives should, correctly, be in the feminine form to agree with 'Humeur', not in the masculine (agreeing with 'cher Ami', dear Friend).

4. *Crambo*: 'A game in which one player gives a word or line of verse to which each of the others has to find a rhyme'; transf. 'Rhyme, rhyming: said in contempt' (*OED*).

# 106 Chanson au Curé de —

***Source.*** BL Add. MS 51441, ff. 21r–22r. Part of a loose collection of leaves in 'Vol. CXXIL Verses and literary [sic] of 1st Lord Holland'. Many items are from the 1750s or later; some have notes by Horace Walpole (identified by subsequent annotation). The hand in which the poem is written is very clear and legible, possibly that of Henry Fox, and it is an almost entirely clean copy. There is no lineation.

***Complementary manuscript sources.*** None known.

***Complementary print sources.*** None known.

***Attribution.*** Under the title someone (probably Hervey himself) has written in a different hand and ink from that of the poem 'by Ld Hervey'. The poem is on a single sheet folded vertically, producing four pages. Three of these contain the poem, and on the fourth is written horizontally, apparently in the same ink and hand as those of the attribution, 'Lord Hervey'. The two following poems (Poem 54 'Reveillez vous', f. 22r, and Poem 102 'D' Hamton Cour a Milady B.', ff. 24r–24v) are also attributed to Hervey.

***Context and date.*** The daring irreverence of the poem echoes that of the poem that precedes it in the Holland papers, Poem 54 'Reveillez vous', though it goes further by mocking the Trinity. If the 'Curé' Hervey had in mind is Samuel Hill, the clergyman at Redlynch, the Fox brothers' country estate in Somerset, the poem may belong to the period of his visit there in November 1731, the year to which the poem that follows in the collection, 'D' Hamton Cour a Milady B.', also belongs. The following year Hervey published *Some Remarks on the Minute Philosopher* (advertised in the *Grub-street Journal*, 145, 12 October 1732), a hostile response to George Berkeley's *Alciphron*. Through the persona of a country clergyman, Hervey argues that the doctrines of Christianity do not survive rational analysis and that Berkeley's arguments only serve to draw attention to that inadequacy. In a passage that ends the main discussion, Hervey presents a viewpoint that underlies his verses. He begins by quoting a passage in Berkeley where Euphronor challenges inadequate argument:

> *Pray hold, and let me see if I understand you; for if your Foundation is not clear, and your Premises what I comprehend, I shall never admit any Conclusions or Consequences from them, tho' never so justly drawn.*

I defy any *Free-thinker*, in so few Words, to make a stronger Objection to *the whole System of Christianity*: What more forcible can be urged in behalf of *Sceptical* inquisitive Minds? What can strike deeper into the Tenets and

> Doctrines of a Religion, whose *Foundation* is *Mystery*; and whose *Premises*, the *Trinity in Unity*, the *immaculate Conception*, the *mortal Immortality*, and the *coeval Existence of a Father and a Son*? (*Some Remarks on the Minute Philosopher* (London, 1732), pp. 64–5)

Hervey confuses the immaculate conception (the doctrine that Mary was conceived without original sin) with the virgin birth, but *Some Remarks* suggests that he was a free-thinker (not an atheist) who believed that Christianity had social utility but that it taught doctrines that were irrational and unworthy of credence. The verses might have preceded or followed the pamphlet, but they probably belong to 1731–2.

***Textual commentary.*** The poem is taken from the British Library manuscript. In the manuscript the first few lines are apparently laid out in couplets, though sometimes the space between them is very small. As the rhyme scheme is of quatrains, that structure is adopted here. Lineation has been supplied.

## Chanson au Curé de —

Je ne puis croire aucune[1] mystere
  Aucune sainte absurditè
Un bon Dieu Fils, un bon Dieu Pere
  Et un bon rien en Trinitè

Et comme ta Doctrine chocque
  De mortelle Immortalitè[2]
Aussi cher Curè Je me mocque
  De l'intacta Fecondite[3]

Sur ces choses quand tu babilles
  Au lieu de me faire devot
Je trouve aucun de la Famille
  De tes grands Dieux qui n'est pas sot.

Selon Ovid plus raisonnable
  Quand ses Dieux descendoient ici

1. *aucune*: correctly, 'aucun', because 'mystère' is masculine.

2. *mortelle Immortalitè*: the reference may be to the granting of human immortality in 1 Corinthians 15: 53: 'For this corruptible must put on incorruption, and this mortal must put on immortality.' This verse is the source of the juxtaposition 'mortal, immortality' in many contemporary sermons. Hervey may allude to the doctrine of the atonement: that Christ, though immortal, died for the human immortality Paul refers to in 1 Corinthians.

3. *l'intacta Fecondite*: usually, in English, the virgin birth.

C'etait pour quelque objet aimable
La Terre etoit un Paradis
Mais pour plaisir bon Dieu le Pere
Dans son Amour n'en avoit pas
Car il n'a point baisè la Mere
Et d'un Fils avoit l'Embarras.

Selon cette sotte maniere
Le Vice ennuit comme la Vertu
Ayant un Enfant sans le faire
Le Gallant est comme le Cocu

Aupres de la Belle que j'aime
Si j'etais Dieu il m'auroit plû
De renverser ce beau Systeme
Et sans Enfants avoir ———

Le Fils autant sot que son Pere
Pour une Partie de Plaisir
Est descendu sur cette terre
Par la main d'un Bourreau mourir

Quand tu les Qualités rassemble
De ton bizarre S^t Esprit
Beacoup[4] plus beau son Rang me semble
Que son Emploi ou son Credit.

Quand Jupiter pour belle Lede
Se transforme dans un Oiseau
Ou pour le Cul de Ganimede[5]
Son Amusement etoit beau.

Mais ton Dieu Pigeon, sotte Bête,
Fit seul enrager un Veillard[6]

4. *Beacoup*: correctly, 'Beaucoup', much more.

5. *Quand Jupiter . . . Ganimede*: Jupiter consummated his relation with Leda, Queen of Sparta, in the form of a swan; he transformed himself into an eagle in order to carry Ganymede off to Mount Olympus, where he became cupbearer to the gods.

6. *Veillard*: correctly, Vieillard (old man). The Holy Spirit assured Simeon 'that he should not see death, before he had seen the Lord's Christ' (Luke 2: 26). His 'Lord, now lettest thou thy servant depart in peace' has a prominent role in Evensong.

Et voltigeant de tête en tête
  Rendit douze autres Babillards.[7]

Voila a terre sa sotise
  Au Ciel il fait ni mal ni bien
Il est comme le Doge a Venise
  Par titre Dieu mais ne fait rien.

Ainsi cher Curé il me semble
  Tes Dieux ont perdu la Raison
Chassez les donc du Ciel ensemble
  Logez les aux petites-Maisons

Renonce une foi qui nous gene
  Et ta bizarre Trinitè
Prenez pour l'avenir la mienne
  Le Vin, l'Amour, et l'Amitiè

Voilà les Dieux qu'il faudroit suivre
  Arbitres doux de notre sort
Sous leur Auspices je veux vivre
  Quand ils me quittent – vient la Mort.

## Translation

## Song to the Vicar of —

I cannot believe any mystery
  Any holy absurdity
A good God the Son, a good God the Father
  And a good nothing in the Trinity

And as your Doctrine shocks
  Of mortal Immortality
Also dear Vicar I mock
  The intact Fecundity

7. *Mais ton Dieu Pigeon ... Rendit douze autres Babillards*: the Holy Spirit descended as tongues of fire at Pentecost, when the twelve apostles were given the gift of tongues (Acts 2:1–4).

When you babble about these things
  Instead of making me devout
I can find no one in the Family
  Of your great Gods who isn't stupid

According to the more reasonable Ovid
  When his Gods descended here
It was for some pleasing end
  The Earth was a Paradise

But as for pleasure, good God the Father
  Had none of it in his Love
For he never even kissed the Mother
  And had the Embarrassment of a Son.

According to this stupid way of doing things
  Vice is as boring as Virtue
Having a child without the deed
  The Gallant is like the Cuckold

Beside the Woman I love
  If I were God it would have pleased me
To invert this fine system
  And without Children to have ———

The Son just as daft as his Father
  To have Some Fun
Came down to this earth
  To die by the hand of an Executioner.

When you gather together the Qualities
  Of your bizarre Holy Spirit
His Rank seems to me much more attractive
  Than his Job or his Credit.

When Jupiter, for the beautiful Leda,
  Transforms himself into a Bird
Or for the Arse of Ganymede
  His Amusement was fine.

But your Pigeon God, silly Animal,
  Just put an Old Man in a passion

And fluttering from head to head
  Made twelve others Babblers.

Behold his folly on earth
  In Heaven he does neither ill nor good
He is like the Doge in Venice
  By title God, but does nothing.

So dear Vicar it seems to me
  Your Gods have lost their Reason
Drive them then from Heaven together
  Lodge them in Mad-houses

Renounce a faith that embarrasses us
  And your bizarre Trinity
Take for the future mine
  Wine, Love, and Friendship

Those are the Gods one should follow
  Sweet arbiters of our fate
Under their Auspices I wish to live
  When they leave me – Death comes.

# 107 Epitaphium Reginae Carolinae

***Main source.*** *Epitaphium Reginæ Carolinæ. The Second Edition, Corrected. With an English Translation* (London: for T. Cooper, 1738).

***Complementary manuscript sources.*** Copies of the Latin epitaph were sent to Algarotti, Middleton, Lord Bristol and Mrs Digby, Stephen Fox's sister (Halsband, p. 228), but none is known to have survived.

***Complementary print sources.*** The first edition, without the English translation, *Epitaphium Reginae Carolinae* (London: for T. Cooper, 1738). ESTC T32895.

***Attribution.*** The epitaph is discussed in Hervey's correspondence (Halsband, p. 228). The Cambridge University Library copy has a manuscript attribution, in ink and in what looks like an eighteenth-century hand, under 'English Translation': 'by Lord Hervey'.

***Context and date.*** Queen Caroline died on 20 November 1737. According to Halsband, Hervey wrote the epitaph at the King's request. The Latin one cost him 'great Pains' but the English version flowed easily; Conyers Middleton sent some corrections to the Latin text (Halsband, pp. 228 and 233). Publication was advertised in the *Daily Gazetteer* on 26 January 1738 and in the *London Evening-Post* on 2 February 1738. No advertisement for the second edition, which adds the translation, has been found. Hervey's father Lord Bristol, in a letter to Hervey dated 12 June 1738, discusses Henry Hervey's chances of preferment through a verse translation of the epitaph: 'Or may you not modestly enough urge the zealous affection he so early discoverd to the memory of that truly great woman and your particular friend and patroness, (and for which I lovd her also,) the late Queen, by attempting, and not without success, an imitation of your Latin epitaph in English verse? which if it was ever in Princess Caroline's hands, I know by your character of her would have made some generous use of it for his service' (*Letter-Books*, III, 209).

The view of the Queen in the epitaph is very much in keeping with Hervey's presentation of her in the *Memoirs*, though any reservations he might have had are suppressed. The interest the *Memoirs* take in her final illness, treating it in great detail (Sedgwick, III, 877–917), is reflected in the epitaph. Pope attacked the tribute for want of honesty in his *Epilogue to the Satires. Dialogue I*, lines 65–82 (Pope, *Twickenham*, IV, 302–4), perhaps implying that Hervey had been helped by Conyers Middleton and Henry Bland.

The epitaph is not in conventional verse (in Latin or English), but neither is it in conventional prose. It follows the pattern of what Joshua Scodel calls a *carmen lapidarium*:

> an inscriptional or pseud-inscriptional form whose lineation underlines the meaning of the inscription rather than follows either the normal practices of prose or the requirements of meter. Used by the ancients and popularized by Italian humanists for brief sepulchral inscriptions, the *carmen lapidarium* first became popular in England in the seventeenth century. In England, however, the form was most often used for extended, florid praise, and beginning in the late seventeenth century lengthy *carmina lapidaria* became popular, like Pindaric funerary odes, for grand-style panegyric of the dead.
>
> (*The English Poetic Epitaph: Commemoration and Conflict from Jonson to Wordsworth* (Ithaca: Cornell University Press, 1991), p. 257)

The form is treated as poetry in *The Art of Poetry on a New Plan*, compiled by John Newbery and revised by Oliver Goldsmith, 2 vols. (London: for J. Newbery, 1762): 'We are now come to that sort of Epitaph which rejects Rhyme, and has no certain and determinate measure; but where the diction must be pure and strong, every word have weight, and the antithesis be preserved in a clear and direct opposition' (I, 65).

***Textual commentary.*** The text is taken from the second edition, which supplies the English translation, and makes two minor additions to the Latin text, resulting in its being one line longer.

## EPITAPHIUM
## REGINÆ CAROLINÆ
## H. S. E.

Serenissima Principissa CAROLINA,
Ex antiquâ et illustrissimâ Brandenburgi Onoltzbacensis Stirpe orta,
Augustissimi et potentissimi Georgii II. D.G. Mag. Britanniæ, Franciæ, et Hiberniæ Regis
Fidei Defensoris;
Ducis Brunsvici et Luneburgi, S. R. I. Archi-Thesaurarii et Principis Electoris,
REGINA CONSORS.
Ortu splendida, Conjugio splendidior, Virtute splendidissima:
Sine Fastu magna, sine Levitate pulchra,
Sine Asperitate proba, sine Arrogantia sapiens,
Sine Ostentatione munifica,
Summam Dignitatem suam, cum Decore, Humanitate, et Modestia sustinuit.
Omnium Artium, Scientiarum, Litterarumque humaniorum
Cultrix et Patrona.

Bene merentes apte distinxit, remuneravit amplè:
Immerentium Errata siluit, potius quàm ignoravit:
Liberalitate scilicèt, quàm metu, Imperium exercere,
Et ignoscere quàm vituperare,
Naturâ promptior.
Amicitiâ paucos, Beneficentiâ multos, omnes Benevolentiâ,
Injuriâ neminem prosequebatur.
In alloquio tam blanda et affablilis, ut nemo ei suadenti posset resistere,
Sed singulis quamquam benigna,
Nunquam non bonum publicum privato omni anteposuit.
Christianam Religionem sincerè, sanctéque coluit;
A Superstitiosorum imbecillitate, et Infidelium audaciâ,
Æquè remota.
In Proposito sanctissima, et Propositi tenax;
Rectè fecit, non ut facere videretur, sed Recti gratiâ:
Nempè Amore Virtutis unicè capta, et Oculo irretorto sequens
Quò Jus, et Fas, et Gloria duxerunt.
In Negotiis, adeò habilis et acuta, tanquam nihil aliud curasset;
Rebus tamen in domesticis assidua, quasi in Negotiis nunquam versata,
Liberos ad Virtutem formavit, Præceptis imbuit, excitavit Exemplo.

Eam utilia præcipuè spectantem, nec dulcia spernentem,
Ad utraque aptam,
Nec mollia corrumpebant, nec terrebant aspera:
Cum omni enim Lepore et Hilaritate perelegantis Ingenii,
Vim etiam sagacissimi possidebat:
Et sicuti in rebus quotidianis muliebri Comitate utebatur,
Ita in arduis, Viri fortissimi Fortitudinem præstabat.
REGIO CONSORTI,
In sollicitis Lenimen, in onerosis Auxilium, in prosperis Decus et Deliciæ,
In omnibus felicissimi sui Ingenii Opem ferens,
In quo nihil futile erat, nihil parvum, nihil imbecillum:
Per omnia denique Conjux et Comes, utilis, placens, fida, perjucunda:
Regiæ nempè Voluntati (suæ nimirùm facilimè oblita) perindè adeò dedita,
Acsi aliam secum agendi Rationem nunquam iniisset:

His Artibus Regis Amorem demeruit, his expressit suum.
Amicos habuit, et meritò; Inimicos, si immeritò; quid mirum?
Cælum ipsum Stultitiâ suâ Profani impetunt.
Sed Inimicis quidem
(Periculi non Injuriæ memor, et Salutem non Ultionem quærens,)
Nihil præter lædendi Licentiam eripere optavit.

Eam tantis ornatam Virtutibus,
Rex Germaniam proficiscens, Custodem Regni quater reliquit:
Tum Consilii plena, et Artium omnium regnandi perita,
Seditiones vel jam obortas sine clade compescuit;
Vel nascentibus tempestivè occurrit et obstitit:
De instantibus nimirùm verissimè Judicare,
Et de futuris callidissimè conjectare assueta,
Curâ, Vigilantiâ, Patientiâ, Sagacitate, et Celeritate Ingenii,
Superavit omnes et omnia;
Ac populo pacato, sacrum Depositum Regi integrum reddidit:
Non minus læta, eo optatò redeunte, summæ Potentiæ Splendorem Honoresque deponere,
Quam pro eo Curas et Labores suscepisse.

Morbo diù et supra modum discruciante Corpus,
Mens interea manebat inturbata:
Quid potuere præcellens Animi Magnitudo, et rectissima Indoles
Virtutis Vi, Integritatis Conscientiâ munitæ atque auctæ,
Tum temporis eluxit;

Dum omnis officii, dum solitæ Humanitatis,
Dum Patientiæ, dum Pietatis,
Etiam et Dignitatis suæ memor,
Suos non minùs curans, quàm à suis curata,
Dolores, heu! acerrimos! penè sine Gemitu toleravit:
Et saucia Vulneribus, medicantem manum, frustrà molestam, Questu nullo admisit.
Mortem inevitabilem à Medicis indictam
Sine Trepidatione audivit;
Jam in horas appropinquantem,

Inconcussa expectavit;
Constantiâ Antiquis penè inaudita, apud nos prorsùs ignotâ, et vix credibili Posteris.

Rapta demùm ineluctabili fatorum Vi,
Diem obiit supremum, 20 Nov. 1737. Anno Æt[s]. suae 55.
Regio Conjuge inconsolabili;
Liberis acerbissimè plangentibus;
Aulicis summo Mærore affectis;
Et universo illachrymante Populo.

## TRANSLATION of the foregoing *Epitaph*, in which is contained the Character of the QUEEN

Here lie the Remains of Queen CAROLINE,
A Princess of the Ancient and Illustrious House of Brandenberg Anspach,
Queen Consort to GEORGE II. of Gr. Britain, Fr. and Ir[d]. King, Defender of the Faith,
Duke of Brunswick and Lunenberg, and Arch-Treasurer, and Prince Elector
Of the Empire.
She was eminent by Birth, more eminent by Marriage, but most eminent by her Virtues.
Great without Pride, Beautiful without Vanity,
Just without Rigor, Knowing without Arrogance,
And Liberal without Ostentation;
She sustained her high Rank with Grace, Dignity and Moderation.
The Learned she loved; the Industrious she encouraged; and both she protected.
Merit of all kind she distinguished and rewarded: Errors she cou'd pardon:
And tho' some Faults escaped her Censure, none escaped her Discernment:
But disposed by Nature, confirmed by Principle, and accustomed by Habit,

She always chose to gain by Benefits, rather than intimidate by Severity,
To exercise her Power in Rewards, rather than Punishments,
And to forgive Injuries, rather than revenge them.

Fond only of a few, she was beneficent to many, benevolent to all, and unjust to none:
In her Address so easy and engaging, that her Persuasion none cou'd withstand:
Her Favor to Particulars was extensive, but interfered not with Justice;
And the first Object of her constant Care *the Publick Good*;
To that Great Point, that Noble End,
Uniform in her Conduct, alarm'd by no Dangers, repulsed by no Obstacles,
Undeviating She adhered.
The Christian Religion she firmly believed, and strictly practised.
From the implicit Blindness of Superstition and the wilful Blindness of Unbelief
Equally free.
Upright in her Purposes, and steady in the Pursuit of them,
She did Right, not for the sake of seeming to do so, but for the sake of Right it self;
Constantly pursuing those Paths where Justice, Truth, and Glory led the way.
In Business she was as conversant, as skilful, and indefatigable,
As if Business had engross'd all her Time and all her Thoughts,
Yet in domestic Duties as assiduous, as if she had attended to no other;
Forming the Minds of her Children to great and good Affections,
Fortifying them by Precept, and animating them by Example.

Thus chiefly intent on useful Views, yet not despising the smoother Paths of Pleasure,
And form'd for both,
Luxury did not corrupt, nor Difficulties stagger her;
For with all the agreeable chearful part of the most pleasing Understanding,
She possess'd the Force of the most Penetrating, and the Clearness of the most Judicious;

Joining to female Sweetness and Affability in ordinary Occurrences,
The Fortitude of the firmest Man, on those important Occasions
Where Dangers threatned, or Exigencies press'd.

Loving the King, beloved by him, and both with Reason;
She was an Ease to his Cares, an Assistant in his burdensome Employments,
His chief Delight in Health, his only Comfort in Sickness,
And as much the Cause as Partner of all his Felicity:
On every Occasion watchful of his Interest, and applying in the Promotion of it,
Every Faculty of that happy Genius,
In which there was nothing mean, nothing trifling, nothing cou'd be spared, and nothing wanting.
In Her united thus, He found all the different Characters
Of an amiable and agreeable Companion, an able and faithful Friend,
A tender and observant Wife;
For in every Action she was so regardful of his Will and so forgetful of her own,
That her Obedience seem'd to be her only Ambition, and her Compliance her only Inclination;
Such were the ways she took to gain the King's Love, such the means she used to manifest her own.
She had many Friends, and deservedly, and if undeservedly she had some Enemies,
Where is the Wonder?
Providence it self has its blind Upbraiders, Heaven its impious Blasphemers.
Yet could not her worst Foes deceive, hurt, or provoke her;
The Danger she knew, and averted; the Injury she saw, and forgave;
Seeking Security, not Revenge, and endeavouring to disarm, but not to wound.
Adorned with all these Virtues, the King in his Absence, left her four Times Guardian of the Realm,
When skill'd in every Art of Policy and Government, many Seditions already rais'd she suppress'd

By her Sagacity foreseeing, and by her Caution preventing many more:
In this manner, by a ready Judgment on what was, nor less just Conjectures on what wou'd be,
She overcame all Difficulties, dispell'd all Dangers:
And by her Vigilance, Patience, Perseverance, Penetration, and Resolution,
Restored the Kingdom in Tranquility to the King:
Not less willing, on his wish'd Return, to quit the Pomp and Splendor of supreme Command,
Than she had been for his sake, to undergo its Cares and its Fatigues.

In her Illness,
During twelve tedious Days, and sleepless Nights, in frequent Sickness and in constant Pain,
Her Mind remained unweaken'd and serene:
In those afflictive Hours might be seen and learn'd, what strong Support
True Courage, unchangeable Opinions, well-grounded Principles,
Exalted Virtue, and conscious Innocence afford:
Whilst mindful of every Duty, and every Affection,
With a Fortitude which no Terrors cou'd shake; a Patience which no Tryals could exhaust,
A Calmness no Distress cou'd ruffle, and a Dignity that claim'd at once Compassion and Respect,
She bore the heavyest Sufferings without Remission, yet without a Groan,
Submitted to the most painful Operations, without Hope, and yet without Complaint;
And with a Mildness which nothing cou'd suspend, and an Attention which nothing cou'd divert,
Seem'd not less careful of all about her than they of her.

The fatal Sentence of inevitable Death pronounced by her Physicians
She heard without a Sigh:
Its nearer Approach she perceived without a Tear:
And waited the last Stroke, neither with Fear nor Impatience, but with a Composure and a Constancy
Scarce heard of by Tradition from Antiquity, unknown among the present Generation,

And hardly credible to Posterity.
Thus at last taken away by the irresistable Force of Fate,
She expired on the 20th of Nov. in the 55th Year of her Age;
Leaving the King her Husband inconsolable, her Children in the deepest Affliction,
All her Servants in Lamentation, and a whole People in Tears.

# DESCRIPTIONS OF MANUSCRIPT SOURCES

## *Bodleian Library*

Unless otherwise indicated, descriptions are quoted from or based on those in Falconer Madan and others, *A Summary Catalogue of Western Manuscripts in the Bodleian Library at Oxford Which Have Not Hitherto Been Catalogued in the Quarto Series* (7 vols. in 8 (Vol. II in 2 parts), Oxford, 1895–1953; repr. with corrections in vols. I and VII, Munich: Kraus-Thomson, 1980), cited as *SC1*; and Mary Clapinson and T. D. Rogers, *Summary Catalogue of Post-Medieval Western Manuscripts in the Bodleian Library Oxford: Acquisitions, 1916–75*, 3 vols. (Oxford: Clarendon Press, 1991) (*SC2*).

**MS Eng. misc. b. 48**: 'Miscellaneous papers of general and political interest, mainly English verse, mid-18th cent., copied by various hands on separate sheets . . . i + 147 leaves' (*SC2*, I, 405).

**MS Eng. misc. b. 169**: 'Miscellaneous papers, 18th–19th cent., including *a* (fols. 1–175) verse, and *b* (fols. 176–246) printed ephemera' (*SC2*, I, 293). For further details see Grundy, 'New Verse'.

**MS Eng. misc. c. 399**: 'Letters and papers of James West (1704?–1772) including (fols. 1–16) catalogue of manuscripts, numbered 1–396, at Alscot, Glos., in the hands of West and of an amanuensis' (*SC2*, I, 526–7). Contains a letter from one of the cataloguers dated 2 March 1744.

**MS Eng. misc. f. 79**: 'Volume containing extracts and notes, many relating to grammar and language, with copies of verse in several hands, mainly from printed sources, 18th cent. Verse in *Crum*. ii + 185 pages; calf. / Inscribed "Miscellanies. Robert Trail" (p. 1)' (*SC2*, I, 676).

**MS Eng. poet. e. 40**: 'Collection of verse, epitaphs and riddles, copied by Gabriel Lepipre, mid-18th cent., with a list of contents on fols. 166$^{v}$–71$^{v}$' (*SC2*, II, 713). Contains verse going back at least to 1720; the last entry before the index is: 'GL – finish'd this Volume at M$^{r}$ Vere's at Kensington on Sunday November the 12 – 1749' (f. 166r).

**MS Firth b. 4**: 'Pieces from an 18th-cent. scrap-book, including satires in verse and prose' (*SC1*, II, 755). A miscellaneous collection in various hands; the majority of items are prose.

**MS Firth b. 22**: copy of 'Adelphi' (f. 34v) Volume of eighteenth-century ballads, some print, some manuscript.

**MS Firth c. 16**: 'Collection of similar verses [i.e. to previous item, 'Collection of political verses and satires, 1672–92, copied in one hand; some printed in *State Poems*, 1683–1707'], entitled "Astrea's book for songs and satyrs, Bhen's & Bacon, 1686", copied in two hands, with (pp. 307–8) satires dated 1738' (*SC2*, II, 753). For further details see Mary Ann O'Donnell, 'A Verse Miscellany of Aphra Behn: Bodleian Library MS Firth c. 16', *English Manuscript Studies 1100–1700*, II (1990), 189–227. Only a few items are eighteenth-century.

**MS Montagu e. 13**: 'English poems in three volumes, the first (fol. 4) containing songs chiefly amorous, the other two (foll. 75, 152) longer poems, poetical epistles, political verses and the like. The range of dates is 1744–61. The name of Mary Tadwell occurs on each volume, and that of John Watson Tadwell on the first two; the former seems to have written all as far as fol. 175$^{v}$; perhaps the latter added the rest. Each volume has an index, the third being added by Montagu, in 1852' (*SC1*, V, 117).

**MS Rawl. poet. 152**: 'Miscellaneous poems of the 17th and early part of the 18th cent., mainly on political subjects, some amorous' (*SC1*, III, 315). A collection in various hands; not all the items are verse.

## *British Library (BL)*

Where available, descriptions are quoted from or based on those in the online British Library Manuscripts Catalogue (BLMC).

**Add. MS 5822**: From the collection of the antiquarian William Cole (1714–82). 'Vol. 21 Visitation for Cambridgeshire in 1684[.] General for all my MS Volumes to April 1754. This was taken out, & this Volume new bound & fresh Paper added to it in 1779 at Cambridge. The Index was new made & is a separate Volume by itself / Wm. Cole 1780.'

**Add. MS 8127**: A miscellaneous collection, mostly legal, antiquarian and political. The political items include copies of letters between the King, Queen, and the Prince and Princess of Wales during the crisis over the delivery of the latter couple's first child, some of which Hervey transcribed in *Some Materials* (Sedgwick, III, 778, 802–3, 823–4). The only verse items are two epigrams by Hervey.

**Add. MS 21544**: 'Miscellaneous poems, songs, elegies, etc'; eighteenth and nineteenth centuries.

**Add. MS 22629**: 'Original letters written by various persons of distinction to Henrietta Hobart, Countess of Suffolk, during the reigns of King George the First, George the Second, and George the Third [with drafts of Mrs. Howard's replies, and other papers]'. The last volume of five.

**Add. MS 28095**: 'Correspondence and papers of the family of Godolphin-Osborne, Dukes of Leeds ... Political, amatory and other verses, with a few pieces in prose, and, at the end, cuttings from newspapers.' In various hands.

**Add. MS 28101**: '"The Family Miscellany;" a collection of poems and prose pieces formed by Ashley Cowper, Clerk of the Parliaments, nephew of the first earl Cowper and uncle of William Cowper, the poet; consisting partly of extracts from authors of the second quarter of the 18th century, and partly of compositions by the collector himself and members of his family' (*BLMC*). The manuscript appears to have been compiled between the later 1730s and 1747. Cowper favoured accurate punctuation and heavy use of italics.

**Add. MS 31152**: 'Official and private correspondence and papers of Thomas Wentworth, Lord Raby and Earl of Strafford ... Political and other pieces in verse, chiefly relating to the early part of the 18th century. MS. *and printed.* At f. 22 is a printed copy of the "Vicar of Bray." With a few miscellaneous papers at the end.' In many different hands.

**Add. MS 32463**: 'Political and other pieces, in verse, connected with events from 1711 to 1731.' A prefatory description by the compiler calls this 'the Employment of some leisure Hours' and remarks that 'several of the Pieces have since appear'd in Print, among them the Political of each Party'. The contents, which are all in the same hand and mostly verse, are arranged chronologically, and there is a meticulous list of contents at the end.

**Add. MS 35335**: 'Original letters, political verses and miscellaneous papers, chiefly relating to Sir Robert Walpole; *circ.* 1700–1783. From Horace Walpole's collections.' In various hands.

**Add. MS 37683**: 'P. A. Taylor Papers. Vol. II. Poetical collections, chiefly of the 18th century.' In many different hands.

**Add. MS 46916**: 'Album of Marianne Spencer Stanhope, Containing copies in her hand of verses and a few letters, etc.; compiled circ. 1812 – circ. 1832.' At f. 9 is a copy of 'Verses by, on his sister, Lady Elizabeth Hervey' (Poem 30, Epitaph on Lady Elizabeth Mansel).

**Add. MS 47127**: 'Egmont Papers ... collected by the lst Lord Egmont. Arranged in each volume under subject-headings. Indexes are included at the end of Vols.... Vol. CCVIII (ff. i+181). Egmont MS. 101.' A commonplace book in more than one hand in which prose greatly predominates over verse. Topics are diverse, and the order seems chronological.

**Add. MS 47128**: 'Egmont Papers ... Vol. CCIX (ff. i+186) Egmont MS. 102.' Also contains prose items; most of the verse is social and political.

**Add. MS 51345**: Holland House Papers (not yet fully indexed). Holograph letters from Hervey and his wife Mary to Stephen Fox, with two from Fox to Hervey and one from Lady Hervey to Lady Ilchester. Contains one item of embedded verse, and a copy of Hervey's letter from Italy to his wife.

**Add. MS 51396**: Holland House Papers. Holograph letters to Henry Fox, including a large number from Hervey, some with verse enclosures, and a copy of Hervey's Will.

**Add. MS 51441**: Holland House Papers. An unbound collection of loose sheets entitled 'Vol. CXXIL Verses and literary [sic] of 1st Lord Holland [Henry Fox]'. Many items are from the 1750s or later; some have notes by Horace Walpole.

**Add. MS 57836**: Supplementary Grenville Papers. 'Vol. XXXIV (ff. 146). 1. ff. 1–125v. "Poems and verses, some published; circa 1729 – circa 1801."'

**Add. MS 59439**: 'Dropmore Papers. Correspondence and papers of William Wyndham Grenville (b.1759, d.1834) . . . Vol. DLXXXV (ff. 109). Miscellaneous literary papers.' Originally in loose sheets, with a table of contents. Most items are from the later eighteenth or earlier nineteenth centuries.

**Add. MS 63648**: 'Commonplace books c. 1725–68 of Sir Peter Thompson (1698–1770), FRS, MP. Partly printed. Partly Latin and French.'

**Add. MS 70454**: 'Vol. CCCCLIV (29/352). "Miscellanies": epigrams and poetry in the handwriting of Lord Oxford and Adrian Drift.'

**Add. MS 71125**: 'John Whaley: seven letters from John Whaley (b.1710, d.1745), Fellow of King's College Cambridge and poet, to Horace Walpole, afterwards 4th Earl of Orford; 1735–1744 . . . The whole text of these letters and poems is printed in *The Yale Edition of Horace Walpole's Correspondence*, vol. xl (*Horace Walpole's Miscellaneous Correspondence*, vol. i), ed. by W. S. Lewis and John Riely (Oxford, 1980), pp. 8–17, 22–3, 42–4, 48–50.'

**Add. MS 75381**: 'Althorp Papers. Vol. lxxxi. "Miscellanies in Prose and Verse"; late 18th cent. Consisting chiefly of political verse and ballads, tempp. William III–George III.'

**Add. MS 78522**: 'Evelyn Papers. Vol. ccclv. (ff. 212). Miscellaneous occasional verse, partly political, religious and amatory; *temp.* William III–1809, n.d. Mostly *copies*. Partly *printed*. The arrangement is roughly chronological by date of composition (ff. 1–184), with some pieces of uncertain date reserved to the end (ff. 185–211). The writers include Isaac Hawkins Browne, Mary Chandler, George Granville, Alexander Pope, Horace Walpole, Sir Charles Hanbury Williams and Edward Young.' In various hands.

**Egerton MS 23**: the ninth folio in a series of thirteen (Egerton MS 15 – Egerton MS 27) of miscellaneous letters and papers arranged alphabetically. An index of writers is given at the beginning of each of the thirteen volumes (description provided by Jeff Kattenhorn, British Library).

**Egerton MS 3787**: 'John, 2nd Baron Hervey: "Agrippina, a Tragedy", etc.; *circa* 1709–1744. *Copies*. Hervey's unpublished play forms the main text in a notebook of miscellaneous material that is transcribed in a single unidentified hand. Armorial bookplate (f. ii), after 1756, of the Earl of Ilchester inside front cover.'

**Harley MS 7318**: Contains a large number of poems and some prose on political and social topics, written in the same neat hand. '7316–7319. Four Quarto Books, containing Miscellaneous Poems, of the same period ['the age of Charles IId and after']; very fairly transcribed. The second is entitled "Satyrs & Lampoons." In these 5 volumes there are many repetitions, & much trash'

(*Catalogue of the Harleian Manuscripts in the British Museum*, 4 vols. [London: 1808–12], III [1808], 525).

**MS Stowe 972**: 'Collections of poems and verses by various authors . . . ff. 32. XVIIIth cent.' Appears to be all in the same small, neat hand.

## *Brotherton Collection*

In the Special Collections Department, Leeds University Library.

**Lt 12**: 'Poetical commonplace book, partly in the hand of George Scott[.] Mainly poetical miscellany or commonplace book, in two hands, one c.1728–1750, the other seemingly that of George Scott, c.1766–1779. Fols 89v–90r: "Latin Proverbs with English Ones that answer to them."'

**Lt 24**: 'Poetical commonplace book, compiled by Benjamin Coles.'

**Lt 35**: 'Commonplace book of English and Latin verse and prose . . . c.1713–1740.'

**Lt 119**: 'Anthology of eighteenth-century verse, compiled by Mary Capell. Comprises an anthology of over eighty manuscript poems, of which some are dated from 1740 to 1751, with a six-page index at the end.'

**Lt q 20**: 'Collection of English verse, begun on March 26th 1732 by William Jermy of Norfolk, 1732–ca. 1741 . . . Written by two main scribes.'

## *Chester Record Office, Cheshire*

**DCC/16/101**: Contained within 'Folder entitled "William Cowper (Dr.). Correspondence, poetry, miscellanea and Cholmondeley Papers", containing a series of newspaper wrappers and loose items' (TNA).

## *Delany manuscripts*

At the Lilly Library, Indiana University, Bloomington, Indiana. Entitled 'The Delany mss., 1728–1760', they include a collection of poems described by Richard C. Frushell in 'Swift's 6 August 1735 Letter to Mary Pendarves Delany: "All other days I eat my chicken like a king"', *Philological Quarterly*, 74 (1995), 415–41 (430–3). In this collection, dated 1728, Frushell finds 'at least four hands, uniformly neat' (p. 430).

## *Folger Shakespeare Library*

Descriptions kindly provided by Jennifer Keith.

**V.a.399**: '[A]n octavo with a range of materials transcribed, including devotional poems, sermons, bawdy poems, and epigrams.'

**W.b.11 (1–10)**: Within a leather folder entitled 'Prologues & Epilogues / 18th Century'. 'The interior folder has the following note: "All of the mss with the cs no. 6643 are in the hand of John Ward."' Ward (1678/9–1758), an antiquary and biographer, was a trustee of the British Museum.

## *Harrowby Manuscripts Trust*

At Sandon Hall, near Stafford, the Harrowby Muniments Rooms contain among other important papers the great majority of the private papers of Lady Mary Wortley Montagu.

**MS 81**: A collection of verse, including some by Montagu, mostly in manuscript and in various hands. Contains a typewritten index compiled by Isobel Grundy and annotated by Dudley Ryder, sixth Earl of Harrowby, and briefly by Robert Halsband that in some cases includes additional bibliographical data.

**MS 255**: A collection of verse in Montagu's hand some of which is by her and some by other writers including Hervey. Not indexed.

## *Harvard University (Houghton)*

**MS Eng 834**: George Wiley Sherburn collection of English ballads, songs and poems (c. 1700–1850).

## *John Murray Archive (JMA)*

Located in Albemarle Street, London, JMA contains twenty-eight autograph letters from Hervey to Count Francesco Algarotti, some of which contain embedded verse, as well as letters to Algarotti from Lady Mary Wortley Montagu. A few of Hervey's letters were also copied into his letter-book now at the West Suffolk Record Office. The provenance of the Montagu and Hervey letters is described by Halsband, *Life of Lady Mary Wortley Montagu*, pp. 291–2.

## *John Rylands Collection, University of Manchester*

**GB 133 Eng MS 737, f. 65r**: 'Papers primarily concerning the collectors and collections in Lancashire responding to the Queen's request on behalf of Charles I for financial aid from Catholics . . . The papers also include miscellaneous items related to Catholics in Lancashire and the Towneley family in particular, dating from the late seventeenth to the early nineteenth centuries.' (Description from the John Rylands Library Catalogue.)

## ***Longleat*** **see** *Portland Papers (Longleat)*

## *Newport Reference Library*

**M411 012**: Correspondence, literary MSS and papers of Sir Charles Hanbury Williams.
**q M416.6/012/DEL**: Manuscript Letters of Mrs Mary Delany, 7 vols.

## *Portland Papers (Longleat)*

At Longleat House, Wiltshire; available on microfilm. 'Correspondence and papers, political and private, of the family of Harley, chiefly of Robert Harley, 1st Earl of Oxford (cr.1711, d.1724), of Edward Harley, 2nd Earl of Oxford (d.1741), and of Margaret, daughter and heir of the latter and wife (1734) of William Bentinck, 2nd Duke of Portland, together with a few letters, etc., of members of the families of Cavendish and Holles' (*National Archives* record, www.archives.gov/research/).

**PO XVIII**: 'Miscellaneous Verses, copies of letters, etc., in various hands, collected apparently by the Duchess of Portland, into quarto common-place books, now bound together in one volume.' Most items are eighteenth-century, the latest dated 1760, but a few are earlier.
**PO XIX**: 'Vers de Société and other short and fugitive pieces, apparently collected by Margaret, Duchess of Portland, and her mother Henrietta, Countess of Oxford; arranged alphabetically according to the first lines, A–Th.' Although the catalogue gives the dates 1700–1748, one item, 'To Stella — — — Night; by the Milk Woman [Ann Yearsley]' ('At this late hour when Nature silent lies', ff. 21r–24v), was first printed in 1785.
**PO XX**: 'Vers de Société, etc., continued, Ti – Y; with a few pieces in French; followed by Epitaphs (f.138) and Riddles (f.187) in prose and verse.' Most items are from the earlier eighteenth century, but a few are earlier and some later, the latest date provided being 1781.

## *Portland Papers (Nottingham University)*

In the Portland (Welbeck) Collection of the Special Collections Department of Nottingham University Library. Consists of 'several series of literary, personal and official papers from the Library of the Dukes of Portland at Welbeck Abbey' (online catalogue: http://mssweb.nottingham.ac.uk/catalogue/).

**Pw V 118**: The main part of the volume is 'Lord Viscount Vane / Book of Accounts / 1722–1724'. The volume has been reversed for verse items written in from the end.

**Pw V 270**: A single sheet with writing in an eighteenth-century italic hand only on the recto.

**Pw V 693**: A single sheet folded twice, with writing in an eighteenth-century italic hand only on the first recto and verso.

**Pw V 784**: A single sheet written in a neat hand on both sides.

**Pw2 V 192**: A single folio, with writing on the recto only in an italic hand, tipped into a miscellaneous collection evidently for reasons of preservation.

## ***Rylands*** **see** *John Rylands Collection, University of Manchester*

## *Suffolk Record Office (SRO)*

In Bury St Edmunds, this branch of SRO holds manuscripts from Ickworth House nearby, home of the Hervey family. Descriptions are quoted from or based on those in the Record Office catalogue, available online from the National Archives.

**SRO 941/46/5**: Copy of English paraphrase of an Ode by Horace, by John, later Lord Hervey, with endorsement by the first Earl of Bristol; 1713.

**SRO 941/47/2**: A bound volume of letters, most by Hervey and in his own hand, the majority of which are to Lady Mary Wortley Montagu and to his mother Elizabeth, Countess of Bristol. The letters to Montagu contain some of Hervey's embedded verse.

**SRO 941/47/4**: A bound collection of eight volumes of Hervey's letter-books. These are scribal copies, but some carry corrections or annotations in his hand. They constitute the other main source of his embedded verse.

**SRO 941/47/13–14**: '"Manuscript of the Memoirs of the Reign of George II from 1727–1737" [title on binding] *1727–1737*.'

**SRO 941/47/17**: '"The Adventures of Telemachus in the Island Ogygia, taken from the French of Fenelon: in three Books." [in Hervey's hand] *undated*.'

**SRO 941/53/1**: Commonplace book of Hervey's fourth son William Hervey (1732–1815), dated by him 'Tuesday Feb: 11, 1751' (though 11 February was a Monday in the Julian calendar, and a Thursday in the Gregorian calendar to be introduced in the following year but already in wide use). The verse it contains is indexed as 'Poetry'. Most of it is by Lord Hervey, and it appears to have been copied from texts written out or annotated by him. In some cases these are the only copies known.

## ***Welbeck*** **see** *Portland Papers (Nottingham University)*

## *Windsor Castle*

**Windsor**: 'Some Materials towards Memoirs of the Reign of King George II', RA GEO/MAIN ff. 53672r–53676r, in the Royal Archives at Windsor Castle.

## *Yale University*

### *Charles Hanbury Williams Collection, Yale University, vol. 84*

No permanent call number, but currently Phillips 84–11402; a miscellaneous volume acquired as part of Phillips collection containing both verse and school exercises (details from private correspondence with the archivist).

### *Yale Osborn Collection (James M. and Marie-Louise Osborn Collection)*

At the Beinecke Rare Book and Manuscript Library, Yale University

**c.53**: '[Commonplace book] [late 18th century].' Anonymous ms. 'Collection of English verse, epitaphs, copies of letters, and descriptions of voyages to Germany.'

**c.83/1**: '[Commonplace book] [late 18th century]. Contain[s] more than 1100 numbered extracts from works by various authors; a number of the poems are signed or initialed by William Warren Porter (1776–1804) or his sister, so possibly the books were compiled by a member of the Porter family.'

**c.83/2**: '[Commonplace book] [late 18th century]. To the memory of Lady B. Mansell.'

**c.130**: '[Commonplace book], 1781–ca. 1785. Autograph inside front cover: Anne Heigham 1781. Manuscript, in a single hand, of a collection of 39 primarily sentimental and occasional poems.'

**c.138**: 'Commonplace book, circa 1787. Manuscript, in a single hand, of a collection of 8 primarily melancholy poems copied from various authors.'

**c.152**: 'Commonplace book, *c.* 1737. Manuscript, in multiple hands, of a collection of about 25 primarily satirical or light-hearted poems, many on the subject of women and love.'

**c. 154**: '[Commonplace book] [early 18th century]. Manuscript, in a single hand, of a collection of fifteen 18th-century satirical poems, epigrams, and epitaphs.'

**c.175**: '[Commonplace book] 1775–1794 Poems from the latter half of the 18th century, as well as copies of letters.'

**c.188**: '[Collection of poems . . . circa 1760] Manuscript, in multiple hands, of a collection of 35 poems, bound in together.'

**c.229/2**: 'Miscellaneous poems and translations &c. Johnson's collection of poems, MSS. Most of which were never printed . . . by several hands & on various subjects.' Catalogued as Osborn c.299 1/2; Volume/enumeration: Vol. III [Vol. II]. Poem 40, 'Receipt to make an Epigram' 7v.

**c.233**: '[Commonplace book] [early 18th century] Collection of verse by various authors; on p. 100 is the signature of Dr. Thomas Apperley, Fellow of St John's, Oxford.'

**c.392**: '[Commonplace book] [early 18th century] . . . Collection of verse by various authors.'

**fc.51**: Commonplace book belonging to Frances Evelyn Boscawen '(1719–1805)' '[mid-18th century].'

**fc.58**: '[Poems] [ca. 1750].' 'Collection of Jacobite verses; contains approximately sixty poems chiefly referring to political events in 1714–17.' 'Anonymous manuscript in two hands.'

**Yale Osborn Shelves Poetry Box V**: 'The collection consists of manuscript copies of several thousand individual English poems, dating from the sixteenth through the nineteenth centuries.'

**Yale, William Smith Papers, Osborn Collection, OSB MSS 57, Folder 74**: The collection comprises three discrete sections: Series I, Correspondence (folders 1–47); Series II, Poems (folders 48–75); Series III, Personal Papers (folders 76–88). Within Series II, folders 74 and 75 are catalogued as 'Poems by Others.'

# LIST OF PRINT SOURCES

This is a list of printed sources for the poems consulted for this edition, mostly restricted to eighteenth-century imprints, but with a few more modern ones where neither earlier printed nor modern critical editions exist.


Algarotti, Francesco, *Il Newtonianismo per le dame* (Naples: Giambatista Pasquali, 1739)

*As Much as May Be Publish'd of a Letter from the Late B— of R-ch-r to Mr. —. To which Are Added, the Several Advertisements for which Mr. Wilkins Was Assaulted at the Crown Tavern in Smithfield* (London: for A. Moore, [1728]), pp. 25–7 (fictitious imprint)

*The Barber Turn'd* Packer. *A New Ballad. To the Tune of* Packington's *Pound* (London: for A. Moore, 1730) (fictitious imprint)

*The Batchelor's Recantation* (London: printed and sold by A. Dodd, 1731)

*The Bouquet: A Selection of Poems from the most Celebrated Authors* (London: by E. Hodson for J. Deighton, 1792)

*The Chester Miscellany ... From January 1745, to May 1750* (Chester: by and for Eliz. Adams, 1750)

*A Choice Collection of Poetry, by the Most Ingenious Men of the Age*, 2 vols., ed. by Joseph Yarrow (York: by A. Staples, 1738)

*The Choice: Being a Collection of Two Hundred and Fifty Celebrated Songs*, 2 vols. (London: for W. Bickerton, T. Astley, R. Willock and J. Watson, 1733), II

*A Collection and Selection of English Prologues and Epilogues* (London: for Fielding and Walker, 1779)

*A Collection of Epigrams*, 2nd edn, 2 vols. (London: for J. Walthoe, 1733), II

*A Collection of Poems, from the Best Authors*, ed. by James Elphinston (London: by James Bettenham, 1764)

*A Collection of Select Epigrams* (London: for C. Hitch and L. Hawes, and W. and J. Flackton, 1757)

*Colley Cibber's Jests* (Newcastle: for W. Charnley, 1761)

*A Complete Collection of Old and New English and Scotch Songs*, 2 vols. (London: by T. Boreman, 1735), II, 172, and same page of four-volume 1736 edn; A Collection of Epigrams, 2 vols. (London: for J. Walthoe, 1735), II

*A Complete Collection of Old and New English and Scotch Songs*, 4 vols. (London: by T. Boreman, 1736), IV

*Court Whispers: or, a Magazine of Wit* (London: for W. Webb, 1743)

*The Craftsman*, 14 vols. (London: for R. Francklin, 1731–7)

[Curll, Edmund?], *Faithful Memoirs of the Life, Amours and Performances, of that Justly Celebrated, and Most Eminent Actress of her Time, Mrs. Anne Oldfield* (London: n.p., 1731)

*Daily Courant*, 5 February 1731

*The Difference between Verbal and Practical Virtue Exemplify'd, In some Eminent Instances both Ancient and Modern. With a Prefatory Epistle from Mr. C—b—r to Mr. P.* (London: for J. Roberts, 1742)

Dodsley, Robert, *A Collection of Poems by Several Hands*, 3 vols. (London: by J. Hughs for R. Dodsley, 1748 [1st edn], 1748 [2nd edn], 1751); 4 vols. (London: by J. Hughs for R. and J. Dodsley, 1755); 6 vols. (London: by J. Hughs for R. and J. Dodsley, 1758; London: for J. Dodsley, 1782)

*Echo or Edinburgh Weekly Journal*, 3 March 1731

*An Elegy to a Young Lady, in the Manner of Ovid. By – – – – – –. With an Answer: By a Lady, Author of the Verses to the Imitator of Horace* (London: [Sam Aris] for J. Roberts, 1733)

*An Epistle from a Nobleman to a Doctor of Divinity: In Answer to a Latin Letter in Verse. Written from H——n-C—t, Aug. 28. 1733* (London: [Sam. Aris] for J. Roberts, 1733)

*Epitaphium Reginae Carolinae* (London: for T. Cooper, 1738)

*Epitaphium Reginæ Carolinæ. The Second Edition, Corrected. With an English Translation* (London: for T. Cooper, 1738)

*The European Magazine*, Vol. 32 (July–December 1797)

*Faithful Memoirs of the Grubstreet Society* (London: for the Grubstreet Society, 1732)

*The False Patriot's Confession, or B——k's Address to Ambition* (London: for R. Charlton, 1737)

*Fog's Weekly Journal*, 7 November 1730

*The Foundling Hospital for Wit*, I (London: for G. Lion, 1743)

Gage, John, *The History and Antiquities of Suffolk. Thingoe Hundred* (London: by Samuel Bentley, 1838)

*Gentleman's Magazine*, 1 (January 1731); 1 (November 1731); 2 (July 1732); 3 (November 1733); 6 (June 1736); 6 (September 1736); 7 (October 1737); 7 (December 1737); 8 (December 1738); 15 (June 1745)

*Grub-street Journal*, 25 November 1731; 13 December 1733

*The History of the House of Lorraine* (London: [for E. Curll], 1731)

*Humours of the Times* (London: s.n., 1771)

Ireland, Samuel, *Picturesque Views on the River Thames*, 2 vols. (London: by T. and J. Egerton, 1792), II, 131

*Joe Miller's Jests: or, the Wits Vade-Mecum* (London: for T. Read, 1743)

*The Journalists Displayed, A New Ballad. To the Old Tune of Lilleburlero* (London: by Peter Wiseacre in the Old Bailey, 1731) (fictitious imprint)

*The Journalists Displayed, A New Ballad. To the Old Tune of, Lullebullero* (London: for J. Johnson, 1731)

*The Ladies Complete Pocket-Book, for the Year of our Lord 1760* (London: for John Newbery, 1760)
*The Lady's Curiosity, or, Weekly Apollo* (London: by C. Sympson, 1752)
*The London Evening-Post*, 13–15 November 1733; 19 January 1731; 24 January 1745
*London Journal*, 31 January 1730; 6 February 1731
*London Magazine*, 2 (September 1733); 14 (February 1745); 19 (February 1750); 19 (November 1750); 22 (September 1753)
*The Masquerade* (London: for J. Bouquet, 1752)
*Miscellanea Nova et Curiosa* (Dublin: by S. Powell, 1749)
*Mœstissimæ ac Lætissimæ Academiæ Cantabrigiensis Carmina Funebria et Triumphalia* (Cambridge: s.n., 1714)
*Monimia to Philocles* (Dublin: s.n., 1726)
*Monimia to Philocles ... To which is added, Glotta a poem* (Dublin: by S. Powell for J. Thompson, 1728)
*The Museum: Or the Literary and Historical Register*, 3 vols. (London: for R. Dodsley, 1746–7)
*A New C—t Ballad* (Dublin [London?]: by James Stone, 1742)
*New Foundling Hospital for Wit*, III (London: s.n., 1769); IV (1771)
*New Foundling Hospital for Wit*, 6 vols. (London: for J. Debrett, 1784), I
*The New Ministry. Containing a Collection of All the Satyrical Poems, Songs, &c. since the Beginning of 1742* (London: for W. Webb, 1742)
*A New Miscellany in Prose and Verse* (London: for T. Read, 1742)
*The Norfolk Poetical Miscellany*, 2 vols., [ed. by Ashley Cowper] (London: for the author, sold by J. Stagg, 1744)
*The Nut-Cracker* (London: for J. Newbery, 1751)
*The Orrery Papers*, 2 vols., ed. by the Countess of Cork and Orrery (London: Duckworth, 1903), II
*The Patriots Are Come; Or, a New Doctor for a Crazy Constitution. A New Ballad. To the Tune of Derry Down* (London: for W. Webb, 1742)
*The Poetical Farrago*, 2 vols. (London: by G. Stafford for J. Deighton, 1794), I
*The Prompter*, no. 164, 1 June 1736
*Read's Weekly Journal*, 6 February 1731; 11 December 1736
'Roxana to Philocles', in *The Museum*, III, 378–80 (no. 36, 1 August 1747)
*The S—te M—r's Are Come: Or a New Doctor for a Crazy Constitution. A New Ballad to the Tune of Derry Down* ([London?]: s.n., 1742)
*A Satire in the Manner of Persius: in a Dialogue between Atticus and Eugenio. By a Person of Quality* (London: for J. Clarke and J. Robinson, 1739)
*A Satyr in the Manner of Persius. In a Dialogue between the Poet and his Friend. By a Certain English Nobleman* (London [i.e. Dublin]: s.n., 1730)
*The Scarborough Miscellany: for the Year 1734* (London: by J. Wilford, 1734)
*Scots Magazine*, 7 (February 1745)
*A Select Collection of English Songs*, 3 vols. (London: for J. Johnson, 1783), I
*Select Collection of Modern Poems* (Edinburgh; sold by A. Donaldson, 1759)

*Select Poems from Ireland* (London: for T. Warner, 1730)
*The Sports of the Muses*, 2 vols. (London: by M. Cooper, 1752), II
*To the Imitator of the Satire of the Second Book of Horace* (London: [Sam Aris] for J. Roberts, 1733)
Topham, Edward, *The Life of the Late John Elwes, Esquire* (London: by John Jarvis for James Ridgway, 1790)
*The Ulster Miscellany* ([Dublin?]: s.n., 1753)
*Universal Magazine*, 7 (October 1750)
*Universal Spectator*, 11 July 1730
*The Universal Spectator and Weekly Journal*, 26 March 1737
*Verses Address'd to the Imitator of the First Satire of the Second Book of Horace. By a Lady* (London: for A. Dodd, 1733): 1st edn, Foxon V39 (Dodd A); 2nd edn, Foxon V41 (Dodd B), and '5th edn' (1735), Foxon V44 (Dodd C)
Voltaire, F. M. Arouet de, *Letters Concerning the English Nation* (London: for C. Davis and A. Lyon, 1733)
*The Warbling Muses* (London: for G. Woodfall, 1749)
*The Weekly Amusement: or, The Universal Magazine* (15 March 1734; London: for J. and T. Dormer, 1735), II
*Whitehall Evening-Post*, 19 January 1731
*The Windsor Medley*, 'The third edition' (London: for A. Moore, 1731; ESTC T069084)
Winstanley, John, *Poems Written Occasionally by the Late John Winstanley . . . with Many Others*, 2 vols., ed. by George Winstanley (Dublin: by S. Powell, for the editor, 1751), II
*The Works of the Right Honourable Lady Mary Wortley Montagu*, 5 vols., ed. by James Dallaway (London: for Richard Phillips, 1803), V

# TEXTUAL INTRODUCTION

Hervey's verse has never before been collected and edited. The unavailability of his work has shaped the editorial policy of this edition, which has been to provide a text that is scholarly but accessible to undergraduates and general readers as well as to specialists. The primary aim has always been to invite the reading of Lord Hervey's verse and thus to secure a fresh assessment of him as a personality and as a poet. Our interest, therefore, is first of all in what he wrote and not in the practices of manuscript circulation in his circle, interesting though those are. We have sought to provide clear and intelligible texts, though we have always recorded details of our sources in the apparatus.

The headnote to each text provides a list of all contemporary witnesses and later ones where they are suspected to have authority. Hervey's verse survives in autograph manuscripts, copies by amanuenses, copies by family, friends and members of his wider circle (and copies they had made), individual printed editions in London and Dublin, journal publication and miscellanies. Substantive readings from all authoritative witnesses are recorded in the historical collation.

Of Hervey's extant poems, the three-book 'Telemachus' and his share of a verse exchange with Lady Mary Wortley Montagu survive in his hand, as does some of the poetry embedded in letters. These surviving manuscript texts have been chosen as copy. Hervey's writing, as evidenced by his letters as well as the poems, is generally careful and correct. The texts have been emended only to expand contractions that can prove distracting in print and to eliminate errors that might have troubled the reader: occasional slips of the pen or failure to provide punctuation. The expansion of contractions is silent but otherwise emendations are recorded. In the case of the verse exchange with Montagu, the initials of the two participants have been provided from another manuscript: what was self-evident to them is not to today's reader.

The edition has generally preferred manuscript to printed copy, it being highly unlikely in most cases that Hervey approved the printing. The aim in selecting copy has been to choose the manuscript closest to Hervey's original (the copy of a relative or close friend, for example), and then to repair its defects through consultation of other witnesses and, rarely, through editorial conjecture. Substantive emendation is rare, but coherent punctuation and capitalisation have frequently been supplied. The emendations are recorded in order to enable readers to reconstruct the source manuscript. The historical collation provides substantive but not accidental variants. The possibility of more radical intervention – to create the text that Hervey himself might have seen through the press – was considered very carefully, but it was rejected as involving too many editorial judgements upon an inadequate basis. There were advantages too in providing readers with a sense of the manuscript culture through which this verse circulated, even though the practices of the transcribers were not always Hervey's own.

Hervey's five-act tragedy, 'Agrippina', has been treated slightly differently from the rest of the material. The manuscript, elegantly written, shows frequent mistakes of spelling and punctuation that are clearly not Hervey's. They have been corrected and the layout of the play and the stage directions have been regularised to improve its intelligibility.

On two occasions, *A Satire in the Manner of Persius* and *To the Imitator*, revised printed texts have been chosen as copy. They demonstrate a close attention to the text that cannot confidently be ascribed to either the extant manuscript or the earlier printed editions.

Although generally manuscript copy has been preferred, in a small number of cases, its quality proved to be so poor that printed copy was chosen instead. The headnote in each case explains the basis on which the judgement has been made.

# LISTS OF EMENDATIONS AND HISTORICAL COLLATIONS

Details of emendations made to the main source for poems in this edition are followed by the poem's historical collation. Each poem is identified by its poem number (not its page number) in this volume.

The abbreviations used in these lists are specific to each poem (though broadly consistent with one another), and are given at the start of the list of emendations for the poem in question. See 'Descriptions of Manuscript Sources' for brief further details of the collections.

## *Emendations to 1 Monimia to Philocles*

**main source** *Harrowby*: Harrowby MS 255, pp. 79–88
**complementary sources** *Dublin 1726*: *Monimia to Philocles* (Dublin: s.n., 1726)
*Dublin 1728*: *Monimia to Philocles . . . To which is added, Glotta a poem* (Dublin: by S. Powell for J. Thompson, 1728)
*Delany*: Delany MS [1], item 23
*GM*: *Gentleman's Magazine*, 15 (June 1745), 325–6
*Add. 28101*: BL Add. MS 28101, ff. 221v–223v
*LM*: *London Magazine*, 22 (September 1753), 433–5
*Osborn c.392*: Yale, Osborn Collection c.392, pp. [1]–7 (first page misnumbered 3)
*Osborn fc.51*: Yale, Osborn Collection fc.51, pp. 146–54
*Dodsley*: Dodsley, *Collection* (1755), IV, 82–9, collated with 1782 edn (IV, 86–93).

| | |
|---|---|
| **1.1** | Pain,] *Dublin 1726, 1728, Add. 28101*; Pain *Harrowby* |
| **1.2** | complain?] *Dublin 1726, 1728, GM, Add. 28101, LM, Osborn c.392, fc.51, Dodsley*; complain, *Harrowby* |
| **1.3** | Woman's] *Dublin 1726, 1728*; Womans *Harrowby* |
| | Distress] *Dublin 1726, 1728*; distress *Harrowby* |
| **1.4** | love] *Dublin 1726, 1728, Delany, GM, LM, Osborn c.392, fc.51, Dodsley*; Love *Harrowby* |
| | plead,] *Dublin 1726, 1728, Delany, GM, LM, Osborn fc.51, Dodsley*; plead *Harrowby* |
| | Redress] *Dublin 1726, 1728, Delany, Add. 28101*; redress *Harrowby* |
| **1.6** | Message] *Dublin 1726, 1728, Add. 28101*; message *Harrowby* |
| **1.7** | Grief] *Dublin 1726, 1728*; greif *Harrowby* |
| **1.8** | wretched] *Dublin 1726, 1728, Delany, GM*; Wretched *Harrowby* |
| | Hand] *Dublin 1726, 1728, Delany*; hand *Harrowby* |
| **1.11** | abandon'd] *all complementary sources*; abandonn'd, *Harrowby* |

forlorn,] *Dublin 1726, 1728, Delany, GM, LM, Osborn c.392, fc.51, Dodsley*; forlorn *Harrowby*

1.12 Reproach] *Dublin 1726, 1728*; reproach *Harrowby*

1.13 Mirth] *Dublin 1726, 1728, Delany*; mirth *Harrowby*

Comfort] *Dublin 1726, 1728, Delany*; comfort *Harrowby*

you] *all complementary sources*; You *Harrowby*

1.14 too,] *GM, Osborn c.392, Dodsley*; too. *Harrowby*

1.15 What Refuge] *Dublin 1726, 1728*; what refuge *Harrowby*

try?] *Dublin 1726, 1728, Delany, Osborn c.392*; try *Harrowby*

1.17 Hope,] *Delany, GM, LM, Dodsley*; Hope *Harrowby*

Wretch's] Wretches *Harrowby*

resort,] *GM, LM, Dodsley*; resort *Harrowby*

1.19 frail Dependance] *Dublin 1726, 1728*; Frail dependance *Harrowby*

1.20 Rules:] *Dublin 1726, 1728*; Rules! *Harrowby*

1.23 Reflections] *Dublin 1726, 1728, Add. 28101*; Refflections *Harrowby*

1.24 revolving] *all complementary sources*; revolveing *Harrowby*

Prey,] *Dublin 1726, 1728, Delany, Add. 28101*; prey *Harrowby*

1.27 Relief] *Dublin 1726, 1728*; releife *Harrowby*

1.28 my self] *Dublin 1726, 1728, Delany, Osborn fc.51*; my selfe *Harrowby*

1.29 due,] *Dublin 1726, 1728, Delany, GM, LM, Dodsley*; due *Harrowby*

1.30 you;] *Dublin 1726, 1728, Osborn c.392, fc.51*; You. *Harrowby*

1.31 receive,] *Dublin 1726, 1728, Delany, GM, LM, Dodsley*; receive *Harrowby*

1.32 hapless] *Delany, LM, Dodsley*; helpless *Harrowby*

1.33 command,] *Dublin 1726, 1728, Delany, LM, Osborn c.392, Dodsley*, command *Harrowby*

1.34 Hand] *Dublin 1726, 1728, Delany, Add. 28101*; hand *Harrowby*

1.36 implicitly] *all complementary sources*; implicitely *Harrowby*

obeys.] *GM, Osborn c.392*; obeys, *Harrowby*

1.37 *new paragraph Harrowby*

shewn,] *Dublin 1726, 1728, Osborn c.392, Dodsley*; shewn *Harrowby*

1.38 known.] *Dublin 1726, 1728, Delany, GM, LM, Dodsley*; known *Harrowby*

1.39 *no new paragraph Harrowby*

1.40 after-witness] *Dublin 1726, 1728, GM, LM, Dodsley*; after Wittness *Harrowby*

Shame;] *Add. 28101*; Shame *Harrowby*

1.41 Thought,] *Dublin 1726, 1728, Add. 28101*; Thought *Harrowby*

1.42 half] *all complementary sources*; halfe *Harrowby*

1.43 Reason's] *Dublin 1726, 1728*; Reasons *Harrowby*

1.44 my self] *Dublin 1726, 1728*; my selfe *Harrowby*

said:] *Delany, GM, Osborn fc.51*; said. *Harrowby*

1.45 *new paragraph Harrowby*

Maid] *Dublin 1726, 1728, Delany, Add. 28101*; maid *Harrowby*

o'er,] *Dublin 1726, 1728, Add. 28101, LM, Osborn fc.51, Dodsley*; o're *Harrowby*

1.46 the Wrong] *Dublin 1726, 1728, Add. 28101*; the wrong *Harrowby*

ne'er] *Add. 28101*; ne're *Harrowby*

that Wrong] *Dublin 1726, 1728, Add. 28101*; that wrong *Harrowby*

1.48 Pain] *Dublin 1726, 1728, Add. 28101*; pain *Harrowby*

1.50 desart] *GM, LM, Osborn c.392, fc.51, Dodsley*; Desart *Harrowby*
1.53 Tho'] *Dublin 1726, 1728, Delany, GM, LM, Osborn fc.51, Dodsley*; Tho *Harrowby*
Wishes] *Dublin 1726, 1728, Add. 28101*; wishes *Harrowby*
1.54 Wretch] *Dublin 1726, 1728, Add. 28101*; wretch *Harrowby*
tho'] *Dublin 1726, 1728, Delany, GM, LM, Osborn fc.51, Dodsley*; tho *Harrowby*
1.56 'twas Love] *Dublin 1726, 1728, Osborn fc.51*; twas Love, *Harrowby*
1.57 *new paragraph Harrowby*
1.58 Pleasure,] *Dublin 1726, 1728, Delany*; Pleasure *Harrowby*
1.59 World] *Dublin 1726, Delany, Add. 28101*; World, *Harrowby*
1.61 lieu] *all complementary sources*; leiu *Harrowby*
Roofs] *Dublin 1726, 1728, Delany, Add. 28101*; roofs *Harrowby*
gay,] *Dublin 1728, Delany, GM, LM, Dodsley*; gay *Harrowby*
1.62 Day,] *Dublin 1726, 1728, Add. 28101*; Day *Harrowby*
1.63 *new paragraph Harrowby*
Court,] *Dublin 1726, 1728, Delany, Add. 28101*; Court *Harrowby*
1.64 Brutes)] *Dublin 1726, 1728*; Brutes,) *Harrowby*
resort:] resort *Harrowby*
1.65 yes,] *Dublin 1726, 1728, Delany, GM, LM, Dodsley*; yes *Harrowby*
Change] *Dublin 1726, 1728*; Change, *Harrowby*
see,] *Dublin 1726, 1728, Delany, GM, LM, Osborn fc.51, Dodsley*; see *Harrowby*
1.66 thee;] *Dublin 1726, 1728, LM*; thee. *Harrowby*
1.67 *new paragraph Harrowby*
1.68 Fortune,] Fortune *Harrowby*
1.71 rest,] *Dublin 1726, 1728, Delany, GM, LM, Osborn fc.51, Dodsley*; rest *Harrowby*
1.72 Breast;] Breast. *Harrowby*
1.73 Pleasure] *Dublin 1726, 1728, Delany, Add. 28101*; pleasure *Harrowby*
Pain] *Dublin 1726, 1728, Delany, Add. 28101*; pain *Harrowby*
1.74 Sense] *Dublin 1726, 1728*; sense *Harrowby*
1.75 Wrongs distressful] *Dublin 1726, 1728, Delany*; Wrongs, distressfull, *Harrowby*
repeat,] *all complementary sources*; repeat *Harrowby*
1.76 Say,] *Dublin 1726, 1728, Delany, LM, Osborn fc.51, Dodsley*; Say *Harrowby*
1.80 part?] *Dublin 1726, 1728, LM, Osborn c.392, fc.51, Dodsley*; part. *Harrowby*
1.81 Throb, one] Throb? One *Harrowby*
1.84 Remorse] *Dublin 1726, 1728, Delany, Add. 28101*; remorse *Harrowby*
humane] *Delany, GM, LM, Osborn c.392, fc.51, Dodsley*; Humane *Harrowby*
feel;] feel, *Harrowby*
1.87 *new paragraph Harrowby*
prevail,] *Dublin 1726, 1728, Delany, GM, LM, Dodsley*; prevail *Harrowby*
1.88 Scale,] Scale *Harrowby*
1.89 licentious Crew,] *Dublin 1726, 1728*; Licentious Crew *Harrowby*
1.91 Chance] *Dublin 1726, 1728, Delany, Add. 28101*; chance *Harrowby*
Choice,] *Dublin 1726, 1728, Add. 28101*; Choice *Harrowby*

**1.92** leagu'd] *Dublin 1726, 1728, Delany, GM, LM, Dodsley*; league'd *Harrowby*
social Vice] *Dublin 1726, 1728*; Social vice *Harrowby*
**1.93** indigent] *Dublin 1726, 1728, Delany, GM, LM, Dodsley*; Indigent *Harrowby*
Shame,] *Dublin 1726, 1728, Delany, Add. 28101*; Shame *Harrowby*
**1.94** Crimes] *Dublin 1726, 1728*; Crimes, *Harrowby*
name;] *Dublin 1726, 1728, LM, Dodsley*; name, *Harrowby*
**1.95** mov'd,] *Dublin 1726, 1728, GM, LM, Dodsley*; mov'd *Harrowby*
**1.96** Unprincipl'd] *Dublin 1726, 1728, GM, LM*; Unprinciple'd *Harrowby*
**1.97** Vows,] *Dublin 1726, 1728, Add. 28101*; vows *Harrowby*
**1.98** Boasts] *Dublin 1726, 1728, Delany, Add. 28101*; boasts *Harrowby*
**1.99** elude] *LM, Osborn c.392, fc.51, Dodsley*; evade *Harrowby*
Harm,] *Dublin 1726, 1728, Delany*; harm *Harrowby*
**1.100** Charm,] *Dublin 1726, 1728, Add. 28101*; Charm *Harrowby*
**1.102** languish] *Dublin 1726, 1728, Delany, GM, LM, Dodsley*; Languish *Harrowby*
Flame,] *Dublin 1726, 1728, Delany, Add. 28101*; Flame *Harrowby*
**1.103** Scandal] *Dublin 1726, 1728, Delany, Add. 28101*; scandal *Harrowby*
Name,] *Dublin 1726, 1728, Delany, Add. 28101*; Name *Harrowby*
**1.104** And, baffl'd] And baffle'd *Harrowby*
o'er] *all complementary sources*; o're *Harrowby*
**1.105** Youth,] *Dublin 1726, 1728, Delany, Add. 28101*; Youth *Harrowby*
**1.106** Truth,] *Dublin 1726, 1728, Delany*; Truth *Harrowby*
**1.107** Mirth] *Dublin 1726, 1728, Add. 28101*; Mirth, *Harrowby*
prophane,] *GM, LM*; prophane *Harrowby*
**1.108** Friendship's Band] *Delany, Add. 28101*; Freindships band *Harrowby*
Hymen's] *Add. 28101*; Hymens *Harrowby*
Chain.] chain, *Harrowby*
**1.110** Religion's] *Dublin 1726, 1728, Add. 28101*; Religions *Harrowby*
Head;] *Delany, Add. 28101*; Head, *Harrowby*
**1.111** Divine] *Add. 28101, Osborn c.392*; Divine, *Harrowby*
Laws,] *Dublin 1726, 1728, Delany, Add. 28101*; Laws *Harrowby*
**1.113** *new paragraph Harrowby*
**1.114** Heart;] *Add. 28101*; Heart *Harrowby*
**1.115** Hour,] *Dublin 1726, 1728, Delany*; Hour *Harrowby*
**1.116** Virtue] *Dublin 1726, 1728, Add. 28101*; virtue *Harrowby*
Nature's Power;] natures power *Harrowby*
**1.117** deface,] *Dublin 1726, 1728, Delany*; deface *Harrowby*
**1.118** Place] *Dublin 1726, 1728, Add. 28101*; place *Harrowby*
**1.119** *no new paragraph Harrowby*
Delight,] *Dublin 1726, 1728*; delight *Harrowby*
**1.120** lewd] *GM, LM, Osborn c.392, Dodsley*; Lewd *Harrowby*
**1.121** Peace);] peace) *Harrowby*
**1.122** Arguments] *Delany, Add. 28101*; arguments *Harrowby*
**1.123** Reason] *Add. 28101*; reason *Harrowby*
admit,] *Add. 28101*; admit *Harrowby*
**1.124** dazzl'd] *Dublin 1726, 1728, GM, LM*; dazle'd *Harrowby*
Wit;] *Dublin 1726, 1728, Delany*; Wit *Harrowby*

**1.125** Ill] *Delany*; ill *Harrowby*
throws,] *Dublin 1726, 1728, Delany*; throws *Harrowby*
**1.126** shows;] *GM, LM*; shows *Harrowby*
**1.127** gilds] *Dublin 1726, 1728, GM, LM, Osborn c.392, fc.51, Dodsley*; gilds, *Harrowby*
Wrong] *Dublin 1726, 1728*; wrong *Harrowby*
depreciating] *Dublin 1726, 1728, GM, LM, Osborn c.392, fc.51, Dodsley*; depreciateing *Harrowby*
Right,] *Dublin 1726, 1728, Add. 28101*; right *Harrowby*
**1.128** Judgment,] *Dublin 1726, 1728, Add. 28101*; Judgment *Harrowby*
Sight] *Dublin 1726, 1728*; sight *Harrowby*
**1.129** *new paragraph Harrowby*
cheated] *Dublin 1726, 1728, GM, LM*; Cheated *Harrowby*
**1.130** Trifle] *Dublin 1728*; Triffle *Harrowby*
Dye;] *Add. 28101*; Dye. *Harrowby*
**1.131** glows,] glows *Harrowby*
**1.132** Mirror] *Dublin 1726, 1728, Add. 28101*; mirror *Harrowby*
shows;] *Delany, GM, LM*; shows *Harrowby*
**1.133** Scenes] *Dublin 1726, 1728, Delany, Add. 28101*; scenes *Harrowby*
lye,] lye *Harrowby*
**1.134** o'er] *Dublin 1726, 1728, Delany, GM, Add. 28101, LM, Dodsley*; o're *Harrowby*
Sky;] *Add. 28101*; sky *Harrowby*
**1.136** gaudy] *Dodsley*; Gaudy *Harrowby*
**1.138** Word] *Dublin 1726, 1728, Delany, Add. 28101*; word *Harrowby*
kind.] *Dublin 1726, 1728, GM*; kind, *Harrowby*
**1.139** oh] *Delany, LM, Osborn c.392, fc.51, Dodsley*; Oh *Harrowby*
pay,] *Osborn fc.51*; pay? *Harrowby*
**1.140** Pleasures] *Dublin 1726, 1728, Add. 28101*; pleasures *Harrowby*
**1.141** love] *Dublin 1726, 1728, LM, Osborn c.392, fc.51, Dodsley*; Love *Harrowby*
**1.143** *new paragraph Harrowby*
Disposition] *Add. 28101*; disposition *Harrowby*
Fate,] Fate *Harrowby*
**1.144** Date;] *Dublin 1726, 1728, Add. 28101*; Date *Harrowby*
**1.145** Reflection] *Dublin 1726, 1728, Delany, Add. 28101*; Refflection *Harrowby*
**1.146** after-sting] *Dublin 1726, 1728, GM, Dodsley*; after sting *Harrowby*
**1.147** immoral] *Dublin 1726, Delany, GM, LM, Dodsley*; Immoral *Harrowby*
**1.148** Pledges] *Dublin 1726, 1728*; pledges *Harrowby*
**1.149** afford,] *Dublin 1726, 1728, Delany, Add. 28101, Dodsley*; afford *Harrowby*
**1.150** Heart] *Dublin 1726, 1728, Delany, Add. 28101*; Heart, *Harrowby*
Word;] *Dublin 1726, 1728*; word, *Harrowby*
**1.151** Sighs] *Dublin 1726, 1728, Delany, Add. 28101*; sighs *Harrowby*
**1.152** Eyes;] *Delany, Add. 28101*; Eyes, *Harrowby*
**1.153** vain,] *Dublin 1726, 1728, GM, LM, Dodsley*; vain *Harrowby*
**1.154** Syllable] *Dublin 1726, 1728, Delany, Add. 28101*; Sillable *Harrowby*
retain),] retain) *Harrowby*
**1.155** Passions] *Dublin 1726, 1728, Add. 28101*; passions *Harrowby*
and] *all complementary sources*; a *Harrowby*

**1.156** Fears] *Dublin 1726, 1728*; fears *Harrowby*
**1.157** constant] *Dublin 1726, 1728, GM, LM, Osborn c.392, fc.51, Dodsley*; Constant *Harrowby*
**1.158** half] *Dublin 1726, 1728, GM, LM, Osborn fc.51, Dodsley*; halfe *Harrowby*
Joys] *Dublin 1726, 1728, Delany, Add. 28101*; Joys, *Harrowby*
**1.159** taste] *Dublin 1726, 1728, GM, LM, Osborn fc.51, Dodsley*; tast *Harrowby*
Pleasures] *Dublin 1726, 1728, Add. 28101*; pleasure *Harrowby*
receive,] *Dublin 1726, 1728, GM, LM, Dodsley*; receive *Harrowby*
**1.161** which] *Dublin 1726, 1728, Delany, LM, Add. 28101; Osborn c.392, fc.51, Dodsley*; we *Harrowby*
know,] *Dublin 1726, 1728, Delany, LM, GM, Add. 28101; Dodsley*; know *Harrowby*
**1.162** bestow] *Dublin 1726, 1728, GM, LM, Osborn fc.51, Dodsley*; Bestow *Harrowby*.
**1.163** *new paragraph Harrowby*
**1.166** Deceit:] *Dublin 1726, 1728*; Deceit *Harrowby*
**1.167** return,] *Dublin 1726, 1728, Delany, GM, LM, Dodsley*; return *Harrowby*
**1.169** Part] *Dublin 1726, 1728, Delany, Add. 28101*; part *Harrowby*
**1.170** stab] *all complementary sources*; stab, *Harrowby*
**1.171** Life] *Dublin 1726, 1728, Add. 28101*; Life, *Harrowby*
**1.172** Pain;] *Add. 28101*; Pain *Harrowby*
**1.174** Fate;] *Add. 28101*; Fate. *Harrowby*
**1.175** Life's] *Dublin 1726, 1728, Add. 28101*; Lifes *Harrowby*
Stage,] *Dublin 1726, 1728*; stage *Harrowby*
**1.176** Cruelties] *Delany, Add. 28101*; Cruelty *Harrowby*
Age.] *Dublin 1726, 1728, Add. 28101*; Age; *Harrowby*
**1.177** Grief] *Dublin 1726, 1728, Osborn fc.51*; Greife *Harrowby*
Sails] *Dublin 1726, 1728*; sails *Harrowby*
o'er] *all complementary sources*; 'ore *Harrowby*
**1.178** shore,] *Dublin 1726, Delany, GM, LM*; shore *Harrowby*
**1.180** Charms,] *Dublin 1726, 1728*; Charms *Harrowby*
**1.181** last] *all complementary sources*; Last *Harrowby*
Arms,] Arms *Harrowby*
**1.182** Eye,] *Dublin 1726, 1728*; Eye *Harrowby*
**1.183** live] *Dublin 1726, 1728, GM, Dodsley*; live, *Harrowby*
dye;] *Osborn fc.51*; dye *Harrowby*
**1.185** store.] *Dublin 1726, 1728, Osborn c.392, Dodsley*; store, *Harrowby*
**1.186** 'tis] *Dublin 1726, 1728, GM, Add. 28101, LM, Osborn fc.51, Dodsley*; tis *Harrowby*
what] *all complementary sources*; What *Harrowby*
**1.187** nor] *all complementary sources*; or *Harrowby*
kind;] *Dublin 1726, 1728*; kind *Harrowby*
**1.188** 'tis . . . 'tis] *Dublin 1726, 1728, GM, LM, Osborn fc.51, Dodsley*; Tis . . . tis *Harrowby*
farewell!] *GM*; Farewell *Harrowby*
**1.189** Agonies] *Dublin 1726, 1728, Add. 28101*; Agonys *Harrowby*
feel!] *Dublin 1726, 1728, GM, Add. 28101, Dodsley*; feel? *Harrowby*
**1.191** Pains] *Dublin 1726, 1728, Delany, Add. 28101*; pains *Harrowby*

**1.193** 'Tis] *Dublin 1726, 1728, Delany, GM, Add. 28101, LM, Osborn fc.51, Dodsley*; Tis *Harrowby*
Eternally] *Dublin 1726, 1728, Delany, Add. 28101, Osborn fc.51*; Etternally *Harrowby*
Adieu.] *Dublin 1726, 1728*; Adieu *Harrowby*

## *Historical collation to 1 Monimia to Philocles*

**1.** *title* Philocles] Lothario *Delany*. Followed by an epigraph in *Dublin 1726, 1728*; see headnote
**1.3** Yet] But *Osborn c.392, fc.51, Dodsley*
**1.5** Ignorance] innocence *Delany, Add. 28101*
thou'lt] you'll *GM*; you'l *Osborn c.392*
**1.7** feign'd cold] cold feign'd *GM*; cold *Osborn fc.51*
**1.8** wretched] hapless *GM, Osborn c.392, fc.51, Dodsley*
**1.9** force me] force *Osborn c.392*
**1.10** them] it *Dodsley*
with] by *Delany, Add. 28101*
**1.13** Mirth] joy *Osborn fc.51*
and Comfort] or comfort *LM, Osborn c.392*
**1.15** shall] can *Dublin 1726, 1728, GM, LM, Osborn c.392, fc.51, Dodsley*
**1.20** On] Or *Delany, LM, Osborn c.392*
or] on *Osborn fc.51*
**1.21** in] are *Dublin 1726, 1728*
**1.22** Belinda's False] *Monimia*'s lost *Dublin 1726, 1728, GM, Add. 28101*; *Amyntor*'s lost *Delany*; Monimia's faln *Dodsley*
Philocles] *Harriot* proves *Delany*
**1.23** slow-wearing] slow weary *Delany*; slow weaning *Osborn c.392*
**1.25** ungentle] ungratefull *Osborn c.392*
**1.26** my] this *GM*
**1.29** One moment sure may be at least] One moment sure at least may be *GM*; One moment sure may be at last *Delany*; For sure one moment is at least *LM, Osborn c.392, fc.51*
**1.30** for] to *LM*
**1.32** hapless] hopeless *Dublin 1726, 1728, GM*; helpless *Harrowby*; fatal *LM, Osborn c.392, fc.51*
**1.33** this I would] would I this *Osborn c.392, fc.51*
**1.35** nor Interest] or int'rest *Osborn c.392*
**1.39** wrote] writ *all complementary sources*
and] as *GM*
**1.40** this] the *GM*
**1.42** Beauties] Beauty *Dublin 1726, 1728, GM*
my] thy *GM*
**1.43** those] these *Dublin 1726, 1728, GM*
of] for *Dublin 1726, 1728, Delany, Add. 28101, LM, Osborn c.392, fc.51, Dodsley*
**1.45** Remonstrance] remonstrances *Osborn fc.51*
**1.46** act] acts *GM, Osborn c.392*

that] the *Osborn fc.51*
**1.48** form] form'd *Dodsley*
**1.49** flinted] flinty *GM, Osborn c.392, fc.51, Dodsley*
was] be *GM*; is *Dodsley*
**1.50** Tygers] Tygress *Delany*
the] a *Dublin 1726, 1728*; some *GM*
**1.52** That] A *GM*
to] for *GM, Osborn c.392*; of *Dodsley*
**1.53** no] in *Dublin 1728*
**1.55** while] whilst *all complementary sources*
count] court *Dodsley*
**1.56** and] of *Delany*
thee] Thou *Dublin 1726, 1728*
**1.57** habituated] habituate *Osborn c.392, Dodsley*
**1.58** the] this *all complementary sources*
**1.59** retire] retreat *Dublin 1726, 1728*
**1.60** In bloom of Life, and warm with young desire] Forsake at once my Pleasure, Friends and State *Dublin 1726, 1728*
**1.61** Splendor] splendors *LM, Osborn fc.51*
**1.63** Beasts] Beast *Delany*
**1.64** Or] And *GM*
**1.65** this] the *Dodsley*
could] can *GM*
**1.66** found] find *Dublin 1726, 1728, GM, Add. 28101, LM, Osborn c.392, fc.51, Dodsley*
**1.67** centers] center *all complementary sources*
**1.68** mourn] weep *Delany, GM, LM, Osborn c.392, fc.51, Dodsley*
not] and *LM*
**1.69** all] courts *GM*
**1.70** gilded] stateliest *GM*
**1.72** in my] in my own *Osborn fc.51*
**1.76** with] in *Dublin 1726, 1728, GM, Osborn c.392, fc.51*
**1.77** know Peace] live pleas'd *GM*
**1.80** one] a *Osborn c.392*
take my part] speak my smart *GM*
**1.81** repentant] repenting *GM*
gratefull] tender *GM*
**1.82** thy Eye] thine Eye *Dublin 1726, 1728, GM*
**1.83** cool] cold *GM*
**1.84** nor Remorse] no remorse *Osborn c.392*
nor Thought humane] nor human Thought *Dublin 1726, 1728*; nor humane thought *Osborn c.392*
canst] can *Delany*
**1.86** thy] the *Osborn c.392*
**1.87** Fraud and Guilt] guilt and fraud *Dodsley*
**1.88** the Scale] her Scale *Dublin 1726, 1728, Add. 28101, LM, Osborn c.392*
**1.91** mix] joyn *GM*
**1.92** Not] Nor *Dublin 1726, 1728, Delany, LM, Osborn c.392, fc.51, Dodsley*

| | |
|---|---|
| | but in] but its *Delany* |
| **1.93** | Merit] honour *LM, Osborn c.392, fc.51, Dodsley* |
| | or] as *GM* |
| **1.94** | Avow those] Glory in *LM, Osborn c.392, fc.51, Dodsley*; Avow the *GM* |
| **1.95** | right] wright *GM* |
| **1.97** | trust] trusts *all complementary sources* |
| **1.98** | Falsehood] falsehoods *GM, Osborn fc.51* |
| | still] yet *GM* |
| **1.99** | elude] evade *Harrowby*; escape *GM* |
| **1.100** | she] her *GM* |
| | spurns] scorns *Add. 28101*; shuns *Dodsley* |
| **1.101** | fail] fall *GM* |
| **1.102** | with] in *all complementary sources* |
| **1.103** | Scandal] slander *Dodsley* |
| | to] on *Delany, Add. 28101, LM, Osborn c.392, fc.51, Dodsley* |
| **1.104** | baffl'd] ruffled *Osborn c.392* |
| **1.105** | are] were *GM* |
| | thy] the *GM* |
| **1.106** | 'Twas these Seducers] These vile seducers *GM, Dodsley* |
| | laugh'd] caught *Osborn c.392* |
| **1.107** | Mirth] jests *Osborn c.392, fc.51, Dodsley* |
| | all] at *Delany* |
| **1.108** | Band] Bond *Dublin 1726, 1728* |
| **1.113** | that] the *Dublin 1726, 1728* |
| **1.117** | the Goddess in thy Soul deface] the Goodness of thy soul deface *Delany, Add. 28101*; that goddess in the soul debase *GM*; the goodness of the soul efface *Dodsley* |
| **1.119** | Delight] delights *Delany, Add. 28101, Dodsley* |
| **1.120** | Night] Nights *Delany, Add. 28101, Dodsley* |
| **1.121** | fatal Commerce] commerce fatal *GM* |
| **1.122** | Their Arguments convince, because they please] Unarm'd you listen, weakly trust to these *Dublin 1726, 1728, GM* |
| **1.123** | While Sophistry for Reason you admit] Sophistic Arguments for Proof admit *Dublin 1726, 1728*; Sophistic arguments for proofs admit *GM*; Whilst Sophistry for Reason you admit *Delany*; Whilst you for reason sophistry admit *LM, Osborn c.392*; While you for reason sophistry admit *Osborn fc.51*; Whilst sophistry for reason they admit *Dodsley* |
| **1.124** | And wander] A wanderer *Osborn c.392* |
| | by] in *Osborn c.392, fc.51* |
| **1.125** | specious] spacious *Dublin 1726, 1728* |
| **1.128** | while] whilst *Dublin 1726, 1728, LM* |
| | feasts] feast *LM* |
| **1.129** | So] Thus *LM, Osborn c.392, fc.51* |
| | Prism] Prison *Dublin 1728* |
| | cheated] deluded *Osborn c.392, fc.51, Dodsley* |
| **1.130** | pictur'd] worthless *GM* |
| | the] a *all complementary sources* |
| | Rainbow] rainbow's *GM* |

1.131 shining] gaudy *Dublin 1726, 1728, GM, LM, Osborn c.392, fc.51*
1.132 And] But *Dublin 1726, 1728, GM, LM, Osborn c.392, fc.51*
1.134 The Lawns] And lawn *Osborn c.392*; And lawn's *Osborn fc.51*
o'er] shade *Osborn c.392, fc.51*
nether] neither *Delany*
1.135 we meet] are met *Osborn c.392*
1.136 But] For *Dublin 1726, 1728*
gaudy] shining *Dublin 1726, 1728, GM, LM, Osborn c.392, fc.51*
is] of *Dublin 1726, 1728*
1.137 this] my *GM*
1.138 spoke] spake *Dublin 1726, 1728*
1.140 Pleasures] pleasure *LM, Osborn c.392, fc.51*
Cares] Pain *Dublin 1726, 1728*
1.141 love] loved *Delany, GM*
1.142 Oh] Ah *Dublin 1726, 1728, Delany, GM, Add. 28101, LM, Osborn fc.51, Dodsley*
1.143 Disposition] Dispensation *Dublin 1726, 1728*
1.144 is] are *Osborn fc.51, Dodsley*
1.145 their Taste] them back *Osborn c.392, fc.51, Dodsley*
1.146 gives] brings *Dodsley*
1.147 immoral] immortal *Dublin 1728, Osborn c.392, fc.51*
1.148 Pledges] Pleasures *Delany*; Treasures *Add. 28101*
1.151 glowing] beating *Dublin 1726, 1728*
throb'd] swell'd *Dublin 1726, 1728*
1.152 rush'd] gush'd *Dodsley*
1.155 Care] cares *Dublin 1726, 1728*
1.156 Fears are Greif] Tears are Grief *Delany, GM, Add. 28101, LM, Osborn c.392*; fears are griefs *Osborn fc.51*; Fears, my Grief *Dublin 1726, 1728*; joys and grief *Dodsley*
Transports are] transport is *GM*; transports and *Dodsley 1755*; transport and *Dodsley 1782*
1.157 all Tyes] the ties *Dodsley*
1.158 his] its *Dodsley*
1.160 When sure] *part-line blank Delany*; But sure *GM*
1.161 which] we *Harrowby*; that *GM*
1.162 Joy] bliss *LM, Osborn c.392, fc.51, Dodsley*
1.163 emulate] imitate *GM*
1.165 yet intercept] and intercept *Osborn c.392*
1.166 and] I *Dublin 1726, 1728*
1.167 As soon the Dead shall from the Grave return] First vital warmth shall to the dead return *Osborn c.392, fc.51*
1.168 As] E'er *Osborn c.392, fc.51*
1.169 to act] but act *Dublin 1726, 1728*
1.170 this] my *Osborn c.392*
1.171 to] for *Dodsley*
1.172 A] Ah *Dublin 1726, 1728, Osborn fc.51*
Author of] Usher to *Dublin 1726, 1728, Delany*; Usher of *Delany, GM, Add. 28101*; sharpning every *LM, Osborn c.392, fc.51*

| | |
|---|---|
| **1.175** | on] out *GM, Add. 28101* |
| **1.176** | Cruelties] Cruelty *Harrowby* |
| **1.177** | speed] waft *Dublin 1726, 1728* |
| **1.178** | *line omitted Osborn fc.51* |
| | long'd for] quiet *LM, Osborn c.392, Dodsley* |
| **1.180** | thy] those *Dublin 1726, 1728, GM, LM, Osborn c.392, fc.51* |
| **1.183** | where] when *Osborn c.392* |
| **1.184** | My soften'd] Relenting *GM* |
| **1.186** | gleam] gleams *Osborn fc.51* |
| **1.187** | When] Where *Dublin 1726, 1728* |
| **1.190–91** | *lines omitted LM, Osborn c.392, fc.51, Dodsley* |
| **1.191** | Pains] pain *GM* |
| | they] this *GM* |

## *Emendations to 2 Flora to Pompey*

**main source** *Delany*: Lilly Library, Delany MS [1], item 17
**complementary sources** *Welbeck*: Portland Papers (University of Nottingham), Pw V 118/4 (p. 134 rev.)
*Museum*: 'Flora to Pompey', in *The Museum*, I (1746), 92–5 (no. 3, 26 April)
*Dodsley*: Dodsley, *Collection* (1755), IV, 95–101
*Dodsley 1782*: Dodsley, *Collection* (1782), IV, 99–108

| | |
|---|---|
| **2.** | Introduction 1. Pompey,] *Museum, Dodsley*; Pompey *Delany* |
| | *young*] *Museum, Dodsley*; Young *Delany* |
| | Introduction 1. Flora,] *Museum, Dodsley*; Flora *Delany* |
| | Introduction 4. Geminius (Pompey's *Friend*)] *Museum, Dodsley*; Pompey's Friend *Delany* |
| | Introduction 5. *she*,] she *Delany* |
| | Introduction 5. Pompey,] Pompey *Delany* |
| | Introduction 6. *Pompey*,] *Museum, Dodsley*; Pompey *Delany* |
| | Introduction 9. *following Letter*] Following letter *Delany* |
| **2.2** | made,] made *Delany* |
| **2.7** | Paper] *Museum*; paper *Delany* |
| **2.8** | read] *all complementary sources*; read, *Delany* |
| **2.16** | Grace] Grace: *Delany* |
| **2.20** | tell] *Museum, Dodsley*; tell, *Delany* |
| **2.24** | *Pompey*,] *Museum, Dodsley*; Pompey *Delany* |
| | Pain,] *Museum, Dodsley*; Pain *Delany* |
| **2.25** | bespoke: "Say] *Museum, Dodsley*; bespoke; "say *Delany* |
| **2.30** | 'tis] *Museum, Dodsley*; tis *Delany* |
| **2.31** | excess,] *Museum, Dodsley*; excess *Delany* |
| **2.32** | less!"] less! *Delany* |
| **2.35** | late,] *Museum, Dodsley*; late *Delany* |
| **2.38** | Rival's] *Museum, Dodsley*; Rivals *Delany* |
| **2.40** | no Kin] *Museum, Dodsley*; no=Kin *Delany* |
| **2.41** | self] *Museum, Dodsley*; self, *Delany* |
| | ungrateful] *Museum, Dodsley*; ungratfull *Delany* |

art!] *Museum, Dodsley*; art *Delany*
2.45 you;] *Museum, Dodsley*; you *Delany*
2.48 abuse,] *Museum, Dodsley*; abuse *Delany*
2.56 Friend,] *Museum*; Friend *Delany*
2.61 *Geminius'*] *Museum, Dodsley*; Geminiu's *Delany*
2.66 Hypocrisy] *Museum, Dodsley*; Hippocrisy *Delany*
2.67 deceit.] *Dodsley*; deceit *Delany*
2.72 decree,] *Dodsley*; decree *Delany*
2.74 *Geminius'*] *Museum, Dodsley*; Geminius *Delany*
2.82 He,] *Museum, Dodsley*; He *Delany*
made,] *Museum, Dodsley*; made *Delany*
2.89 Part,] *Museum, Dodsley*; Part *Delany*
2.95 thy] *Museum, Dodsley*; my *Delany*
2.99 he Doats] Doats *Delany*
2.102 him] *Museum, Dodsley*; thee *Delany*
2.103 him] *Museum, Dodsley*; thee *Delany*
2.104 thy despair.] *Museum, Dodsley*; his despair *Delany*
2.105 'tis] *Museum, Dodsley*; tis *Delany*
2.108 dissolve] *Museum, Dodsley*; disolve *Delany*

## *Historical collation to 2 Flora to Pompey*

2. *title*] *Museum, Dodsley*; *no title Delany, Welbeck*; The Plan of the following Poem *Delany*
*prose introduction*] *not in Welbeck*
*Introduction 5. in Favour of*] *with a passion for Museum, Dodsley*
*Introduction 6. up*] *him Museum, Dodsley*
*Introduction 8. have written*] *write Museum, Dodsley*
2.2 That] (That *Welbeck*
made,] made;) *Welbeck*
2.5 Bed floats with my Tears] eyes o'erflow with tears *Dodsley*
Trembling Hand] trembling *Welbeck*
2.8 my self] myself *Museum, Dodsley*
2.10 your self] your-Self *Welbeck*; yourself *Museum, Dodsley*
2.11–108 *not in Welbeck*
2.15 (Whose] Whose *Museum*
2.16 Grace)] Grace *Museum*
2.19 Peice] work *Dodsley*
2.22 my] thy *Museum, Dodsley*
2.31 to] in *Museum, Dodsley*
2.33 cure that] cure thy *Museum*; ease that *Dodsley*
2.41 thy self] thyself *Dodsley*
2.60 in] of *Museum, Dodsley*
2.71 thy] your *Museum, Dodsley*
2.73 art] are *Museum, Dodsley*
base] false *Dodsley*
2.78 a] your *Museum, Dodsley*
2.90 my Self] myself *Dodsley*

**2.94** my] the *Museum*
**2.99** he Doats] Doats *Delany*
**2.103** fading] faded *Museum, Dodsley*
**2.104** thy Vows] his Vows *Museum*; his vows *Dodsley*

## *Emendations to 3 Arisbe to Marius Junior*

**main source** *Welbeck*: Portland Papers (University of Nottingham), Pw V 118/2 (pp. 138–41 rev.)
**complementary sources** *Bodley*: Bodley MS Montagu e. 13, ff. 105r–109r
*Museum*: 'Arisbe to Marius junior', in *The Museum; Or, The Literary and Historical Register*, 3 vols. (London: for R. Dodsley, 1746–7), II (1746), 14–19 (no. 14, 27 September)
*Dodsley*: Dodsley, *Collection* (1755), IV, 95–101
*Dodsley 1782*: Dodsley, *Collection* (1782), IV, 99–108

**3.** *title* From Fontenelle] *Museum, Dodsley*; *no subtitle Welbeck*
*Introduction* 3. *Hiempsal,*] *Hiempsal Welbeck*
*Introduction* 5. *junior,*] *Museum, Dodsley*; *junior Welbeck*
**3.2** Say,] *all complementary sources*; Say *Welbeck*
**3.15** search] *all complementary sources*; seach *Welbeck*
**3.21** *new paragraph*] *Bodley*; *no new paragraph Welbeck*
**3.41** *new paragraph*] *Bodley*; *no new paragraph Welbeck*
**3.67** Yourself] *all complementary sources*; Your-Self *Welbeck*
**3.71** He] Me *Welbeck*
**3.72** breathe] *Museum, Dodsley*; breath *Welbeck*
**3.77** *new paragraph*] *Bodley*; *no new paragraph Welbeck*
**3.80** and] *all complementary sources*; a *Welbeck*
**3.93** *new paragraph*] *Bodley*; *no new paragraph Welbeck*
**3.97** tasteless] *Museum, Dodsley*; tastless *Welbeck*
**3.103** struck] *all complementary sources*; stuck *Welbeck*
**3.109** *new paragraph*] *Bodley*; *no new paragraph Welbeck*
**3.111** upbraid,] *all complementary sources*; upbraid *Welbeck*
**3.112** Whose fatal] *all complementary sources*; Whose *Welbeck*
**3.121** would] *all complementary sources*; wou'd *Welbeck*
**3.131** no] *all complementary sources*; not *Welbeck*
boast] *Bodley*; bost *Welbeck*

## *Historical collation to 3 Arisbe to Marius Junior*

**3.** *title* From Fontenelle] *no subtitle Welbeck, Bodley, Museum*
*Introduction*] *preceded by* The Argument *Bodley, Museum*
*Introduction* 2. *(who*] who *Bodley*
*Introduction* 2. *him)*] him *Bodley*
*Introduction* 5. *to*] *as to Museum*
*and give*] to give *Bodley, Dodsley*
*Introduction* 6. *'Twas*] It was *Bodley*
*Introduction* 7. *writ*] wrote *Bodley, Museum*
*Introduction* 8. *Letter*] Epistle *Bodley*

| | |
|---|---|
| **3.1–132** | *divided into numbered quatrains Museum, Dodsley* |
| **3.3** | my] its *all complementary sources* |
| **3.10** | scarce] not *Bodley* |
| **3.14** | too] to *Bodley* |
| **3.17** | Wouldst] Would *Bodley* |
| **3.24** | wish no] disclaim *Museum, Dodsley*; disdain *Bodley* |
| **3.28** | Bring] Brings *Bodley* |
| **3.31** | was] is *Bodley* |
| **3.33** | ah!] oh *Bodley* |
| **3.40** | be thy] be the *Museum, Dodsley* |
| | and] but *Bodley* |
| **3.53** | most I] I *Bodley* |
| **3.64** | Africk] Africk's *Dodsley* |
| **3.65** | which] that *Bodley* |
| **3.71** | He] Me *Welbeck* |
| **3.72** | sighs] sigh *all complementary sources* |
| | breathe] breath *Welbeck* |
| **3.79** | in] an *Dodsley 1782* |
| **3.80** | and] a *Welbeck* |
| **3.92** | him] thee *Museum, Bodley* |
| **3.96** | Flutterer] Flatterer *Bodley* |
| **3.103** | struck] stuck *Welbeck* |
| **3.110** | th'Injustice] the Injustice *Bodley* |
| **3.112** | Whose fatal Diligence] Whose Diligence *Welbeck* |
| **3.123** | Ah!] oh! *Bodley* |
| **3.128** | o'er pay] repay *Bodley, Museum* |
| **3.129** | those] these Dodsley |
| **3.131** | no] not *Welbeck* |
| | boast] bost *Welbeck* |
| **3.132** | for] to *Dodsley 1782* |

## *Emendations to 4 Roxana to Usbeck*

**main source** *Dodsley 1755*: Dodsley, *Collection* (1755), IV, 102–6
**complementary sources** *Museum*: 'Roxana to Philocles', in *The Museum*, III, 378–80 (no. 36, 1 August 1747), repr. in *The Chester Miscellany*, 1 September 1747
*Dodsley 1758*: Dodsley, *Collection* (1758), IV, 98–102
*Dodsley 1782*: Dodsley, *Collection* (1782), IV, 106–10

| | |
|---|---|
| **4.** | *title* Usbeck] *Dodsley 1758, 1782*; Philocles *Dodsley 1755* |
| | *Introduction* 3. *eunuch,*] *Dodsley 1782*; *eunuch Dodsley 1755* |
| **4.21** | joy,] *Dodsley 1758, 1782*; joy *Dodsley 1755* |
| **4.26** | atone] *Dodsley 1782*; attone *Dodsley 1755* |
| **4.49** | possess'd] *Dodsley 1782*; possess'd, *Dodsley 1755* |
| **4.66** | soul,] soul *Dodsley 1755* |
| **4.90** | aversion] aversion, *Dodsley 1755* |
| **4.91** | soul,] *Dodsley 1782*; soul *Dodsley 1755* |

## *Historical collation to 4 Roxana to Usbeck*

| | |
|---|---|
| **4.** | *title* Usbeck] Philocles *Dodsley 1755* |
| **4.4** | tears] Fears *Museum* |
| **4.13–54** | *not in Museum* |
| **4.56** | harsh] hard *Museum* |
| **4.59** | knew] know *Museum* |
| **4.62** | knew] know *Museum* |
| **4.75** | thy] the *Dodsley 1782* |
| **4.95** | profess'd] possess'd *Dodsley 1758, 1782* |
| **4.108** | a while] awhile *Museum* |

## *Emendations to 5a To a Young Lady who desired to know her Fortune*

**main source** *Delany*: Lilly Library, Delany MS [1], item 36
**complementary sources** *Add. 32463*: BL Add. MS 32463, f. 121r
*London Journal*: *London Journal*, 19 June 1731, p. 3
*Orrery*: *The Orrery Papers*, 2 vols., ed. by the Countess of Cork and Orrery (London: Duckworth, 1903), II, 321–2
*Brotherton*: Brotherton Lt q 20, f. 82r
*Longleat*: Portland Papers (Longleat) Vol. XVIII, ff. 295r–296r
*BL Harley*: BL Harley MS 7318, f. 127v
*Yale Poetry Box*: Yale Osborn Shelves Poetry Box V/12

| | |
|---|---|
| **5a.1** | Forbear, my dear Nymph,] *Add. 32463, London Journal*; Forbear my Dear Nymph *Delany* |
| | fruitless Desire] *Add. 32463, London Journal*; Fruitless desire *Delany* |
| **5a.2** | conceal'd] Conceal'd *Delany* |
| **5a.6** | perhaps is] *all complementary sources*; perhaps *Delany* |
| **5a.10** | cure] *Add. 32463, BL Harley*; Cure *Delany* |
| **5a.11** | freed,] *all complementary sources*; freed? *Delany* |
| **5a.12** | false] *Add. 32463, BL Harley*; False *Delany* |
| | those Ills be] *Add. 32463, London Journal, Orrery, Yale Poetry Box*; those be *Delany* |
| **5a.16** | confined] Confined *Delany* |
| **5a.18** | a Moment's cut] *Add. 32463, London Journal*; A Moment's Cut *Delany* |
| **5a.21** | swift] *Add. 32463*; Swift *Delany* |
| | dear] *Add. 32463*; Dear *Delany* |
| **5a.22** | hereafter] Hereafter *Delany* |

## *Historical collation to 5a To a Young Lady who desired to know her Fortune*

| | |
|---|---|
| **5a.** | *title*] To A Young *Lady*, who wanted to know her *Fortune Add. 32463, London Journal*; an extempore Answer by Ld Hervey upon his Lady's asking him what He shd be: that time twelvemonth *Brotherton*; To a Lady. Upon her asking the Author where he thought he should be that time twelve Months. (Written off hand.) *Orrery*; To a Lady upon her asking the |

Author where he thought he should be that time twelve Month, Written off hand *BL Harley*; To a Lady upon her asking the Auther where he thought he should be that time twelve month *Longleat, Yale Poetry Box.*

**5a.1** Forbear ... Desire] Forbear Dearest with a fruitless desire *Brotherton*; Forbear Dearest Nanny with a fruitless desire *Longleat*; Forbear Dearest —— with a fruitless desire *Orrery, BL Harley*; Forbear Dearest ... with a fruitless desire *Yale Poetry Box*

**5a.3** Who] To *Longleat*
anticipate] anticipates *BL Harley*
Pleasure] Pleasures *Add. 32463, London Journal, Longleat*
destroy] destroys *BL Harley*

**5a.4** And] They *Brotherton, BL Harley*
Disappointment] Disappointments *Add. 32463, London Journal, BL Harley*
Joy] joys *BL Harley*

**5a.5** are] were *BL Harley*

**5a.6** Or] And *Yale Poetry Box*
my] their *Orrery, Longleat, Yale Poetry Box*

**5a.7** Credulous] the credulous *Add. 32463, London Journal, Orrery, Longleat, BL Harley, Yale Poetry Box*
Fools] fool *Longleat, BL Harley, Yale Poetry Box*

**5a.8** Exult] Or exult *Orrery*; Exalt *Brotherton, BL Harley*

**5a.9** All Ills] All our Ills *Orrery*; all ill *Brotherton*
easiest] eas'est *Delany*; better *Orrery*; easyer *Longleat*; easiest's *Yale Poetry Box*

**5a.10** could] can *all complementary sources*

**5a.11** from Ills by] by Ills from *Add. 32463, London Journal*; from ill by *Brotherton*; from Ills from *Yale Poetry Box*
that] their *Brotherton, Orrery, Longleat, BL Harley, Yale Poetry Box*

**5a.12** Since] When *all complementary sources*
those] our *Brotherton*

**5a.13–14** *not in Longleat*

**5a.13** on] *not in Brotherton*

**5a.14** live] lives *Brotherton*; live but *Orrery*

**5a.15** and] or *Brotherton, BL Harley*
Hope] hopes *BL Harley*
no Comfort] little Pleasure *all complementary sources*

**5a.16** thy] the *Yale Poetry Box*

**5a.17** whilst I'm writing] while I write *Brotherton*; while I scribble *Orrery*; whilst I write *Add. 32463, London Journal, Longleat, BL Harley, Yale Poetry Box*

**5a.17** our] my *Orrery*

**5a.18** Moment's cut] moment cuts *Brotherton, Orrery*; moment cut *Yale Poetry Box*

**5a.18** thy] this *Brotherton.*

**5a.19** To day's] As To-day's *Orrery*; Too day's *BL Harley*
Treasure] Pleasure *Brotherton*

**5a.20** For] *not in Brotherton*

come] gain'd *Add. 32463, London Journal, Longleat, BL Harley, Yale Poetry Box*; captur'd *Orrery*
Yesterday's] yesterday *Brotherton*

**5a.21** seize] seize on *Brotherton*; annex *Orrery*; secure *Longleat*; enjoy *Yale Poetry Box*
swift] dear *BL Harley*
enjoy] and enjoy *Brotherton*
dear] clear *Orrery*

**5a.23** And expect not what Fate will hereafter bestow] And take, not expect, what Hereafter'll bestow *Add. 32463, London Journal, BL Harley, Yale Poetry Box*; And take not accept what hereafter may Do *Brotherton*; And receive – not expect – what Hereafter'll bestow *Orrery*; Neither ask nor expect what hereafter'll bestow *Longleat*

## *Emendations to 5b Horace Ode XI. Lib. I. Imitated.* The *Advice. To S—n F—x. Esq.*

**main source** *GM*: *Gentleman's Magazine*, 6, 351 (June 1736)
**complementary sources** *Prompter*: *The Prompter*, no. 164, 1 June 1736
*New Miscellany*: *A New Miscellany in Prose and Verse* (London: for T. Read, 1742), pp. 40–1
*Museum*: *The Museum*, I, 132 (no. 17, 8 November 1746)
*Masquerade*: *The Masquerade* (London: for J. Bouquet, 1752), p. 225
*Yale*: Yale Osborn Collection c.138, f.29

**5b.** *title* Esq] Esq; *GM*
**5b.7** astrologers] *Masquerade*; astrologets *GM*

## *Historical collation to 5b Horace Ode XI. Lib. I. Imitated. The Advice. To S—n F—x. Esq.*

**5b.** *title*] The Advice. To S—n F—x, Esq; *Prompter*; HORACE, Book I, Ode xi. *Imitated New Miscellany; Imitation of Ode* XI. *Book* I. *of* Horace *Museum*; Hor. Ode XI. Lib. I. *Imitated Masquerade*; The late Lord Hervey to Mr Fox *Yale*

**5b.1** *S—n*] S—n *Prompter, Strephon New Miscellany*; Friend *Museum, Masquerade*; Stephen *Yale*
fruitless] such earnest *Masquerade*; a fruitless *Yale*

**5b.2** which are] w$^{ch}$ are *GM*; that are *Masquerade*; which a *Yale*
**5b.3** anticipate care] anticipates Ills *Yale*
**5b.5** me] you *Museum, Masquerade*; us *Yale*
**5b.6** their] your *Museum, Masquerade*; our *Yale*
**5b.7** astrologers] astrologets *GM*
**5b.8** *Exalt*] Exult *New Miscellany, Yale*; Expect *Museum, Masquerade*
they] those *Museum*
**5b.10** could] can *Yale*
**5b.11** *their art*] their Arts *New Miscellany, Masquerade*; such Arts *Museum*
**5b.12** *false*] fate *Masquerade*

**5b.13** Even] E'en *New Miscellany, Masquerade*
whilst] while *New Miscellany, Museum, Masquerade, Yale*
I write] I'm writing *Masquerade*
our] my *New Miscellany*; thy *Museum, Masquerade*
**5b.14** moment's cut] moment is off *Masquerade*
**5b.15–16** *not in Yale*
**5b.17** poor] we *Museum, Masquerade*
**5b.17–18** *positioned after line 12 Yale*
**5b.18** For] Our *Masquerade*
*gain'd*] come *Yale*
*yesterday's*] our yesterday's *Masquerade*
**5b.19** seize the] seize y$^{e}$ *GM*
swift] Sweet *Yale*
enjoy the dear *now*] away with all sorrow *Masquerade*
**5b.20** *take*] receive *Yale*
not *expect*] but expect not *Museum*
hereafter'll] hereafter's *Yale*
*take*, not *expect*, what hereafter'll bestow] load not to-day with the care of to-morrow *Masquerade*

## *Emendations to 5c An Imitation of the Eleventh Ode of the First Book of Horace*

**main source** *Dodsley*: Dodsley, *Collection* (1755), IV, 109
**complementary sources** none

*no emendations made*

## *Historical collation to 5c An Imitation of the Eleventh Ode of the First Book of Horace*

*none; only one witness exists; see, though, the Historical Collation to all three versions*

## *Historical collation to all three versions: 5a To a Young Lady who desired to know her Fortune (base-text), 5b Horace Ode XI. Lib. I. Imitated. The Advice. To S—n F—x. Esq and 5c An Imitation of the Eleventh Ode of the First Book of Horace*

**5a.** *title* To A Young Lady who desired to know her Fortune] To A Young *Lady*, who wanted to know her *Fortune Add. 32463, London Journal*; an extempore Answer by Ld Hervey upon his Lady's asking him what He shd be: that time twelvemonth *Brotherton*; To a Lady. Upon her asking the Author where he thought he should be that time twelve Months. (Written off hand.) *Orrery*; To a Lady upon her asking the Author where he thought he should be that time twelve Month, Written off hand *Harley*; To a Lady upon her asking the Auther where he thought he should be that time twelve month *Longleat, Yale Poetry Box*; Horace Ode XI. Lib. I. Imitated. *The* ADVICE. To S—n F—x. Esq; *GM*; The Advice. To S—n F—x, Esq; *Prompter*; HORACE, Book I, Ode xi. *Imitated New Miscellany; Imitation of Ode* XI. *Book* I. *of* Horace *Museum*; Hor. Ode XI. Lib. I. *Imitated Masquerade*; The late Lord Hervey to Mr Fox *Yale*; An Imitation of the Eleventh Ode of the First Book of Horace *Dodsley*

**5a.1** my dear] Dearest *Brother, Longleat, Orrery, BL Harley, Yale Poetry Box*

Nymph] *not in Brotherton*; Nanny *Longleat*; — *Orrery, BL Harley*; . . . *Yale Poetry Box*; S—n *GM, Prompter*; *Strephon New Miscellany*; Friend *Museum, Masquerade*; Stephen *Yale, Dodsley*

a] *not in GM, Prompter, New Miscellany, Museum*; such *Masquerade*

fruitless] earnest *Masquerade*

**5a.2** which are] that are *Masquerade*; which a *Yale*

**5a.3** Who] To *Longleat*

anticipate] anticipates *BL Harley, Yale*

Care] Ills *Yale*

Pleasure] Pleasures *Add. 32463, London Journal, Longleat*

destroy] destroys *BL Harley*

Who . . . destroy] *becomes line 7 Dodsley*

**5a.4** And] They *Brotherton, BL Harley*

Disappointment] Disappointments *Add. 32463, London Journal, BL Harley*

Joy] joys *BL Harley*

And . . . Joy] *becomes line 8 Dodsley*

**5a.5** are] were *BL Harley*

me] you *Museum, Masquerade*; us *Yale, Dodsley*

Perhaps . . . Fate] *becomes line 3 Dodsley*

**5a.6** Or] And *Yale Poetry Box*

my] their *Orrery, Longleat, Yale Poetry Box, Dodsley*; your *Museum, Masquerade*; our *Yale*

Or . . . Date] *becomes line 4 Dodsley*

**5a.7** Credulous] the credulous *Add. 32463, London Journal, Orrery, Longleat, BL Harley, Yale Poetry Box, Dodsley*

Fools] fool *Longleat, BL Harley, Yale Poetry Box*

Astrologers] astrologets *GM*

Let . . . Cheat] *becomes line 5 Dodsley*

**5a.8** Exult] Or exult *Orrery*; Exalt *Brotherton, BL Harley, GM, Prompter*; Expect *Museum, Masquerade*

they] those *Museum*

Exult . . . deceit] *becomes line 6 Dodsley*

**5a.9** All Ills] All our Ills *Orrery*; all ill *Brotherton*;

easiest] eas'est *Delany*; better *Orrery*; easyer *Longleat*; easiest's *Yale Poetry Box*

**5a.10** could] can *Add. 32463, London Journal, Orrery, Brotherton, Longleat, BL Harley, Yale Poetry Box, Yale*

**5a.11** from Ills by] by Ills from *Add. 32463, London Journal*; from ill by *Brotherton*; from Ills from *Yale Poetry Box*
that Art] their Art *Brotherton, Orrery, Longleat, BL Harley, Yale Poetry Box, GM, Dodsley*; their Arts *New Miscellany, Masquerade*; such Arts *Museum*

**5a.12** Since] When *all complementary sources*
false] fate *Masquerade*
those] our *Brotherton*

**5a.13–14** *not in Longleat, Yale, Dodsley; becomes lines 15–16 GM, Prompter, New Miscellany, Museum, Masquerade*

**5a.13** on] *not in Brotherton*

**5a.14** live to] lives to *Brotherton*; live but to *Orrery*; build on *GM, Prompter, New Miscellany, Museum, Masquerade*

**5a.15–16** *not in GM, Prompter, New Miscellany, Museum, Masquerade, Yale*

**5a.15** and] or *Brotherton, BL Harley*
Hope] hopes *BL Harley*
no Comfort] little Pleasure *Add. 32463, London Journal, Brotherton, Orrery, Longleat, BL Harley, Yale Poetry Box*; little comfort *Dodsley*

**5a.16** thy] the *Yale Poetry Box*

**5a.17–18** *become lines 13–14 GM, Prompter, New Miscellany, Museum, Masquerade, Yale; become penultimate couplet Dodsley*

**5a.17** Even] E'en *New Miscellany, Masquerade*
whilst I'm writing] while I write *Brotherton, New Miscellany, Museum, Yale*; while I scribble *Orrery*; whilst I write *Add. 32463, London Journal, Longleat, BL Harley, Yale Poetry Box, GM, Prompter, Yale, Dodsley*
our] my *Orrery, New Miscellany*; thy *Museum, Masquerade*

**5a.18** Moment's cut] moment cuts *Brotherton, Orrery*; moment cut *Yale Poetry Box*; moment is off *Masquerade*
thy] this *Brotherton*

**5a.19** To day's] As To-day's *Orrery*; Too day's *BL Harley*
Treasure] Pleasure *Brotherton*
poor] we *Museum, Masquerade*

**5a.20** For] *not in Brotherton*; Our *Masquerade*
come] gain'd *Add. 32463, London Journal, Longleat, BL Harley, Yale Poetry Box, GM, Prompter, New Miscellany, Museum, Masquerade, Dodsley*; captur'd *Orrery*
Yesterday's] yesterday *Brotherton*; our yesterday's *Masquerade*

**5a.21** seize the] seize on the *Brotherton*; annex *Orrery*; secure *Longleat*; enjoy *Yale Poetry Box*; seize y[e] *GM*
swift] dear *BL Harley*; Sweet *Yale*
enjoy] and enjoy *Brotherton*
dear] clear *Orrery*
enjoy the dear Now] away with all sorrow *Masquerade*

**5a.22** And expect not what Fate will hereafter bestow] And take, not expect, what Hereafter'll bestow *Add. 32463, London Journal, BL Harley, Yale Poetry Box, GM, Prompter, New Miscellany, Dodsley*; And take not accept what hereafter may Do *Brotherton*; And receive – not expect – what Hereafter'll bestow *Orrery*; Neither ask nor expect what hereafter'll bestow *Longleat*; And take, but expect not, what Hereafter'll bestow *Museum*; And load not to-day with the care of to-morrow *Masquerade*; And receive, not expect, what hereafter's bestow *Yale*

## *Emendations to 6 To Mr. Fox Written at Florence 1729*

**main source** *Harrowby*: Harrowby MS 81, ff. 66r–66v
**complementary sources** *Harley*: BL Harley MS 7318, ff. 130r–131r
*Portland*: Portland Papers (Longleat) XIX, ff. 329r–331r
*Brotherton*: Brotherton Lt 119, ff. 99–101 (rectos only)
*Windsor Medley*: *The Windsor Medley*, 'The third edition' (London: for A. Moore, 1731; ESTC T069084), pp. 3–5, collated with three other editions of the same year (ESTC N025099, T058887, N025098)
*GM*: *Gentleman's Magazine*, 7, 628 (October 1737)
*Dodsley*: Dodsley, *Collection* (1748), III, 181–3, collated with later editions up to 1782 (III, 194–6)

| | |
|---|---|
| **6.1** | dearest] *Harley, Portland, Windsor Medley, GM, Dodsley*; Dearest *Harrowby* |
| **6.3** | Int'rest] Intrest *Harrowby* |
| **6.4** | Heart] *Brotherton, Windsor Medley*; heart *Harrowby* |
| **6.5** | soothe] Soothe *Harrowby* |
| | entertain] *all complementary sources*; Entertain *Harrowby* |
| **6.6** | of my Health] *Windsor Medley*; of health *Harrowby* |
| **6.7** | Life seem'd] *Portland, Brotherton, Windsor Medley*; life Seem'd *Harrowby* |
| **6.8** | Disease anticipated] *Harley, Portland, Windsor Medley*; disease Anticipated *Harrowby* |
| | Age;] *Windsor Medley*; Age *Harrowby* |
| **6.10** | Æsculapius'] *Harley, Portland*; Asculapius' *Harrowby* |
| | vain] *Harley, Portland, Windsor Medley, GM, Dodsley*; Vain *Harrowby* |
| **6.11** | desperate,] *Dodsley*; desperate *Harrowby* |
| | explore] *all complementary sources*; Explore *Harrowby* |
| **6.13** | steady] *all complementary sources*; Steady *Harrowby* |
| | with] *all complementary sources*; With *Harrowby* |
| **6.14** | gay] *all complementary sources*; Gay *Harrowby* |
| **6.15** | employs] *all complementary sources*; Employ's *Harrowby* |
| **6.16** | Int'rest] *GM*; Intrest *Harrowby* |
| | softer Joys] *Brotherton, Windsor Medley*; Softer Joy's *Harrowby* |
| **6.17** | weary] *all complementary sources*; Weary *Harrowby* |
| | Misery to attend] *Windsor Medley*; misery to Attend *Harrowby* |
| **6.18** | share] *all complementary sources*; Share *Harrowby* |
| **6.19** | snowy] *Portland, Windsor Medley, GM, Dodsley*; Snowy *Harrowby* |
| | stray] *all complementary sources*; Stray *Harrowby* |
| **6.21** | thro'] *Brotherton, GM*; thro *Harrowby* |
| **6.23** | unrepining, still you] *GM, Dodsley*; unrepineing, Still You *Harrowby* |
| **6.25** | alone] *all complementary sources*; Alone *Harrowby* |
| **6.27** | past] *all complementary sources*; Past *Harrowby* |
| **6.28** | me] *all complementary sources*; me, *Harrowby* |
| **6.29** | lov'd] *Harley, Portland, Windsor Medley, GM, Dodsley*; Lov'd *Harrowby* |

| | |
|---|---|
| | delightful] *all complementary sources*; Delightful *Harrowby* |
| 6.30 | Pleasure] *Windsor Medley*; Pleasures *Harrowby* |
| 6.33 | trifle] *Windsor Medley, GM, Dodsley*; triffle *Harrowby* |
| | away] *all complementary sources*; Away *Harrowby* |
| 6.34 | Life's] *Harley, Portland, Windsor Medley*; life's *Harrowby* |
| 6.35 | World's intrusion] *Harley, Portland*; world's Intrusion *Harrowby* |
| 6.36 | with Love, with Beauty, and with] *Harley, Portland, Windsor Medley*; With Love, With Beauty, and With *Harrowby* |
| 6.37 | no Wish yet] *Harley, Portland, Windsor Medley*; No Wish Yet *Harrowby* |
| 6.38 | Breast:] *Harley, Portland*; breast; *Harrowby* |
| 6.39 | Fortune's shining] *Harley, Portland, Windsor Medley, Dodsley*; fortune's Shining *Harrowby* |
| 6.40 | sue] *Harley, Portland, Windsor Medley, GM, Dodsley*; Sue *Harrowby* |
| | Splendour] *Harley, Brotherton, Windsor Medley*; Splender *Harrowby* |
| 6.41 | scornful] *all complementary sources*; Scornful *Harrowby* |
| 6.42 | Pleasures] *Harley, Portland, Windsor Medley*; Pleasure's *Harrowby* |
| 6.43 | still] *Brotherton, Windsor Medley, GM, Dodsley*; Still *Harrowby* |
| 6.44 | she] *Brotherton, Windsor Medley, GM, Dodley*; She *Harrowby* |
| | destroys] *all complementary sources*; Destroy's *Harrowby* |
| 6.45 | envy] *all complementary sources*; Envy *Harrowby* |
| 6.46 | self directing] *Harley, Portland, Brotherton, Dodsley*; Self Directing *Harrowby* |
| | Fate;] Fate, *Harrowby* |
| 6.49 | sinister, still] *Harley, Portland*; Sinister, Still *Harrowby* |
| 6.52 | attract] *all complementary sources*; Attract *Harrowby* |
| 6.53 | attend] *all complementary sources*; Attend *Harrowby* |
| 6.54 | his Memory] *Brotherton, Windsor Medley*; His Memory *Harrowby* |
| | you] *Harley, Portland, Brotherton, Windsor Medley, Dodsley*; You *Harrowby* |

## *Historical collation to 6 To Mr. Fox Written at Florence 1729*

| | |
|---|---|
| 6. | *title*] To Mr. Fox at Florence *Harley, Portland*; To Mr: F – x at Florence *Brotherton*; *Lord* H—rv—y, *To Mr.* S. F—x. *Written at* Florence. *In Imitation of* Horace. Ode *the 6th*, Book II *Windsor Medley*; *To Mr* F—— *in Imitation of the 6th Ode of the 2d Book of* Horace. *Written in* Florence *in 1729. By the Rt Hon. Ld* H—— *GM*; To Mr. *FOX*, written at *Florence*. In Imitation of *Horace*, Ode IV. Book 2 *Dodsley incorrect numbering never rectified* |
| 6.2 | Pleasures] real pleasure *Brotherton* |
| 6.3 | Where] When *Dodsley 1748, 1751, 1755* |
| | Deceit] design *Brotherton, Dodsley, Windsor Medley* |
| 6.4 | of] from *Harley, Portland*; to *Windsor Medley T069084, GM* |
| 6.5 | know'st] knows *Brotherton* |
| 6.6 | of my Health] to my heart *Harley*; of my heart *Portland, Brotherton* |
| | to] of *Brotherton, Dodsley* |
| 6.7 | failing] fainting *Harley, Portland* |
| 6.9 | wasting] warring *Harley, Portland* |
| | afflictive] afflicted *Dodsley 1763* |

**6.10** Æsculapius' Sons] Asculapius' Sons *Harrowby*; Esculapius Son *Brotherton*; *Esculapius'* Sons *Windsor Medley, GM, Dodsley*
**6.15** or] and *Harley, Portland*
**6.16** softer Joys] soft Joys *Harley, Portland*
**6.20** Carthage] *Carthage' hero GM*
the venterous way] the way *GM*
**6.21** Air of Rome's] Air Rome's *Brotherton*
**6.22** resides] presides *Brotherton*
Superstition] Superstitions *Brotherton*
**6.24** dangerous] threat'ning *GM*
various] varying *GM*
**6.25** thy] your *Windsor Medley*; their *Windsor Medley N025098*
**6.27** Heaven] Heavens *Windsor Medley*
those] these *Brotherton, Windsor Medley, Dodsley*
**6.28** Ickworth] *I——th GM*
Rest, and Health] health, and rest *Harley, Portland*
**6.29** my] (my *Harley, Portland*
**6.32** bestow;] bestow:) *Harley, Portland*
**6.33** trifle, carelessly] innocently wear *Harley, Portland*
**6.34** Life's clouded] Life's Cloudy *Harley, Portland*; a Clouded *Brotherton*
**6.35** intrusion] intrusions *Brotherton*
**6.37** farther] further *GM*
**6.38** this] the *GM*
**6.40** or] and *Harley, Portland*
**6.41** unactive] inactive *Windsor Medley*
**6.43** Let them still] Still let them *Harley, Portland*
Goddess' falser] Goddess's false *Harley, Portland*
**6.44** whilst] while *Harley, Portland, Brotherton, Dodsley*
**6.45** foremost] firmest *Windsor Medley*
**6.46** Walpole's] Warpole's *Brotherton*; *W——le's Windsor Medley, GM*
Fate] State *Windsor Medley*
**6.47** Still let him] Let Him still *Harley, Portland*
**6.50** Ickworth] *I——th GM*
**6.52** Sight] light *GM*
**6.53** Then] The *Harley*; There *Portland*
**6.54** you lov'd] thou lov'st *GM*

## *Emendations to 7 To the Same. From Hampton-Court, 1731*

**main source** *Dodsley 1748*: Dodsley, *Collection*, 2nd edn (1748), III, 183–90
**complementary sources** *Dodsley 1st*: Dodsley, *Collection*, 1st edn (1748), III, 183–9; similar lines appear in Poem 66 Agrippina, II. 2. 56–70; the lines are collated in the apparatus of that poem
*Dodsley 1782*: Dodsley, *Collection* (1782), III, 197–204

**7.56** please,] *Dodsley 1782*; please. *Dodsley 1748*
**7.70** Nature] *Dodsley 1782*; nature *Dodsley 1748*
**7.79** giv'n] *Dodsley 1782*; given *Dodsley 1748*

| | |
|---|---|
| **7.111** | they, like us,] *Dodsley 1782*; they like us *Dodsley 1748* |
| **7.121** | strife,] *Dodsley 1782*; strife *Dodsley 1748* |
| **7.129** | with-hold] *Dodsley 1782*; withold *Dodsley 1748* |
| **7.133** | flood,] *Dodsley 1782*; flood; *Dodsley 1748* |
| **7.137** | withstood.'] withstood. *Dodsley 1748* |

## *Historical collation to 7 To the Same. From Hampton-Court, 1731*

| | |
|---|---|
| **7.14** | undigested] indigested *Dodsley 1st* |
| **7.134** | or] and *Dodsley 1782* |

## *Emendations to 8 The Countess of — to Miss —*

**main source** *Add. 78522*: BL Add. MS 78522, ff. 191r–194v
**complementary sources** *Harrowby 255*: Harrowby MS 255, pp. 72–6
*Add. 22629*: BL Add. MS 22629, ff. 195r–195v (lines 65–78, 81–102 only)

| | |
|---|---|
| **8.** | *title*] *Harrowby 255*; Lady — to Miss — *Add. 78522* |
| **8.5** | thee (Charming Fair)] *Harrowby 255*; thy modest Heart *Add. 78522* |
| **8.6** | plaintive] *Harrowby 255*; plainer *Add. 78522* |
| **8.7** | Soul,] *Harrowby 255*; Soul; *Add. 78522* |
| **8.9** | Heart] *Harrowby 255*; Heart, *Add. 78522* |
| | unexperienced Maid] *Harrowby 255*; unexperienc'd Maid! *Add. 78522* |
| **8.11** | every] *Harrowby 255*; ev'ry *Add. 78522* |
| | you read] *Harrowby 255*; You read, *Add. 78522* |
| **8.15** | Charms; how] *Harrowby 255*; Charms: How *Add. 78522* |
| **8.16** | Heat!] heat! *Harrowby 255*; Heat, *Add. 78522* |
| | inspires!] *Harrowby 255*; inspires? *Add. 78522* |
| **8.17** | Oh] *Harrowby 255*; Oh! *Add. 78522* |
| | Breast] *Harrowby 255*; Breast! *Add. 78522* |
| **8.18** | distress'd:] *Harrowby 255*; distress'd! *Add. 78522* |
| **8.21** | fears] *Harrowby 255*; Fears *Add. 78522* |
| **8.22** | Man, who] Man; who *Harrowby 255*; Man that *Add. 78522* |
| | you] *Harrowby 255*; thee *Add. 78522* |
| | destroy] *Harrowby 255*; destroy, *Add. 78522* |
| **8.23** | Joy:] *Harrowby 255*; Joy. *Add. 78522* |
| **8.25** | Friend.] Friend; *Add. 78522* |
| **8.26** | we] *Harrowby 255*; We *Add. 78522* |
| **8.27** | Night,] Night; *Add. 78522* |
| **8.29** | you] *Harrowby 255*; You *Add. 78522* |
| **8.31** | Name.] *Harrowby 255*; Name: *Add. 78522* |
| **8.32** | its] *Harrowby 255*; it's *Add. 78522* |
| **8.35** | Maid,] *Harrowby 255*; Maid! *Add. 78522* |
| | shalt] *Harrowby 255*; shall't *Add. 78522* |
| **8.41** | Man] *Harrowby 255*; God *Add. 78522* |
| **8.42** | form] *Harrowby 255*; Form *Add. 78522* |
| **8.44** | The harmless Gift undaunted then] The harmless gift undaunted then *Harrowby 255*; Undaunted then the harmless Gift *Add. 78522* |

| | |
|---|---|
| **8.47** | hireling Priests] Hireling-Priests *Add. 78522* |
| **8.48** | the] *Harrowby 255*; that *Add. 78522* |
| **8.53** | Shame,] *Harrowby 255*; Shame; *Add. 78522* |
| **8.54** | glose] *Harrowby 255*; gild *Add. 78522* |
| **8.57** | betray'd, by] *Harrowby 255*; betray'd and *Add. 78522* |
| **8.58** | Bed,] *Harrowby 255*; Bed! *Add. 78522* |
| **8.59** | Still] *Harrowby 255*; Should *Add. 78522* |
| | Charms] *Harrowby 255*; Charms, *Add. 78522* |
| **8.62** | Veins,] Veins *Add. 78522* |
| **8.64** | your] *Harrowby 255*; thy *Add. 78522* |
| **8.65** | St Evremont] *Harrowby 255*; S$^{t}$ ——d *Add. 78522* |
| **8.66** | fat Fit—n] *Harrowby 255*; fat ——n *Add. 78522* |
| | Arms.] *Harrowby 255, Add. 22692*; Arms *Add. 78522* |
| **8.68** | Coarse as it is] *Harrowby 255*; Homely as 'tis *Add. 78522* |
| | was;] *Add. 22629*; was: *Add. 78522* |
| **8.70** | bloom'd,] *Harrowby 255*; bloom'd *Add. 78522* |
| **8.78** | inspire:] inspire. *Add. 78522* |
| **8.81** | agree,] *Add. 22629*; agree? *Add. 78522* |
| **8.82** | and] *Harrowby 255*; as *Add. 78522* |
| | thee] *Harrowby 255, Add. 22629*; Thee *Add. 78522* |
| **8.83** | Beauty] *Harrowby 255, Add. 22629*; beauty *Add. 78522* |
| | Face] *Add. 22629*; Face, *Add. 78522* |
| **8.86** | Lesbian] *Harrowby 255*; Lesbians *Add. 78522, Add. 22629* |
| | kind;] *Add. 22629*; kind! *Add. 78522* |
| **8.87** | Fate,] *Harrowby 255*; Fate; *Add. 78522* |
| **8.91** | St— s] *Harrowby 255*; St—es *Add. 78522* |
| | Lowth— rs] *Harrowby 255*; Rich—ds *Add. 78522* |
| **8.93** | Dal— h] *Harrowby 255*; Dal—th *Add. 78522* |
| **8.94** | In] *Harrowby 255*; With *Add. 78522* |
| **8.95** | even H— gh might fire] *Harrowby 255*; might H—rb—gh's breast inspire *Add. 78522* |
| **8.96** | demi-Man] Demi-Man *Add. 78522* |
| | Desire,] Desire; *Add. 78522* |
| **8.97** | 'Tis you] Tis You *Add. 78522* |
| | in you] *Harrowby 255, Add. 22629*; in You *Add. 78522* |
| **8.98** | Kind] *Harrowby 255, Add. 22629*; kind *Add. 78522* |
| **8.100** | Transitory] *Harrowby 255*; transitory *Add. 78522* |
| **8.102** | thee] *Harrowby 255, Add. 22629*; Thee *Add. 78522* |

## *Historical collation to 8 The Countess of — to Miss —*

| | |
|---|---|
| **8.** | *title*] *Harrowby*; *no title Add. 78522*; Countess — to Miss — *Add. 22629* |
| **8.1–64** | *not in Add. 22629* |
| **8.5** | thee (Charming Fair)] *Harrowby 255*; thy modest Heart *Add. 78522* |
| **8.6** | plaintive] *Harrowby 255*; plainer *Add. 78522* |
| **8.22** | who] that *Add. 78522* |
| | you] *Harrowby 255*; thee *Add. 78522* |
| **8.29** | Sex] *above deleted* selfe *Harrowby 255* |

**8.35** shalt] *Harrowby 255*; shall't *Add. 78522*
**8.38** the Young] young *Harrowby 255*
**8.41** Man] *Harrowby 255*; God *Add. 78522*
**8.44** The harmless Gift undaunted then] *Harrowby*; Undaunted then the harmless Gift *Add. 78522*
**8.48** the] *Harrowby 255*; that *Add. 78522*
**8.54** glose] *Harrowby 255*; gild *Add. 78522*
**8.57** by] *Harrowby 255*; and *Add. 78522*
**8.59** Still] *Harrowby 255*; Should *Add. 78522*
**8.64** your] *Harrowby 255*; thy *Add. 78522*
**8.65** St Evremont] *Harrowby 255*; S[t] ——d *Add. 78522*; S[t] E——nt *Add. 22629*
**8.66** fat Fit—n] *Harrowby 255*; fat ——n *Add. 78522*; Dear F——n *Add. 22629*
wallow'd] languish'd *Add. 22629*
**8.68** Coarse as it is] *Harrowby 255*; Homely as 'tis *Add. 78522, Add. 22629*
**8.70** bloom'd] shone *Add. 22629*
**8.76** Myrtle and Lawrel on my Temples] My Brow with Lawrell and with Myrtle *Add. 22629*
**8.77** touch'd] Struck *Add. 22629*
**8.79–80** *not in Add. 22629*
**8.79** Breast] *above deleted* heart *Harrowby 255*
**8.82** and] *Harrowby 255*; as *Add. 78522, Add. 22629*
**8.86** Lesbian] *Harrowby 255*; Lesbians *Add. 78522, Add. 22629*
**8.87** their] there *Add. 22629*
**8.91** St— s] *Harrowby 255*; St—es *Add. 78522*; St—e's *Add. 22629*
Lowth— rs] *Harrowby 255*; Rich—ds *Add. 78522*; G——r's *Add. 22629*
**8.93** Dal— h] *Harrowby 255*; Dal—th *Add. 78522*; D—k *Add. 22629*
**8.94** In] *Harrowby 255*; With *Add. 78522, Add. 22629*
**8.95** even H— gh might fire] *Harrowby 255*; might H—rb—gh's breast inspire *Add. 78522*; might Harb—hs breast inspire *Add. 22629*
**8.96** And warm that demi-Man into] Or warm a Hermitt into loose *Add. 22629*

## *Emendations to 9 To Molly on Easter Eve*

**main source** *Harrowby 81*: Harrowby MS 81, ff. 148r–v
**complementary sources** *Harrowby 255*: Harrowby MS 255, pp. 77–8
*Fog's*: *Fog's Weekly Journal*, 7 November 1730 (lines 1–2, 5–6, 9–10, 26–7 only)

9. *title* Molly] *Harrowby 255*; Molly — *Harrowby 81*
9.1 Prudes (who] *Harrowby 255*; Prudes, who *Harrowby 81*
good),] *Harrowby 255*; Good, *Harrowby 81*
9.2 disciplin'd] *Harrowby 255*; Disciplin'd *Harrowby 81*
9.3 preparing] *Harrowby 255*; Preparing *Harrowby 81*
spiritual Feast] Spiritual Feast, *Harrowby 81*
9.4 Dispens'd] *Harrowby 255*; Dispense'd *Harrowby 81*
9.5 credits] *Harrowby 255*; Credits *Harrowby 81*
9.6 playing] *Harrowby 255*; Playing *Harrowby 81*

| | |
|---|---|
| 9.7 | us] *Harrowby 255*; uss *Harrowby 81* |
| | dear] *Harrowby 255*; Dear *Harrowby 81* |
| | Molly,] Molly *Harrowby 81* |
| | improve] *Harrowby 255*; Improve *Harrowby 81* |
| | Night,] Night *Harrowby 81* |
| 9.8 | season] *Harrowby 255*; Season *Harrowby 81* |
| | Delight;] Delight, *Harrowby 81* |
| 9.9 | us] *Harrowby 255*; uss *Harrowby 81* |
| | Fate] *Harrowby 255*; fate, *Harrowby 81* |
| 9.11 | us] *Harrowby 255*; uss *Harrowby 81* |
| | Fire] *Harrowby 255*; fire *Harrowby 81* |
| 9.12 | supper retire] *Harrowby 255*; super Retire *Harrowby 81* |
| 9.13 | singing] *Harrowby 255*; singing, *Harrowby 81* |
| 9.14 | Watchman] *Harrowby 255*; watchman *Harrowby 81* |
| | Taste] Tast *Harrowby 81* |
| 9.15 | ignorant Crew,] Ignorant Crew *Harrowby 81* |
| 9.16 | neglect] *Harrowby 255*; Neglect *Harrowby 81* |
| | persue,] *Harrowby 255*; Persue: *Harrowby 81* |
| 9.17 | Future employ] *Harrowby 255*; future Employ *Harrowby 81* |
| 9.18 | compounding] *Harrowby 255*; Compounding *Harrowby 81* |
| | Ease] ease *Harrowby 81* |
| 9.19 | Speculation] *Harrowby 255*; specculation *Harrowby 81* |
| 9.20 | Wretches we pity] *Harrowby 255*; wretchess wee Pity *Harrowby 81* |
| | despise,] *Harrowby 255*; Dispise *Harrowby 81* |
| 9.22 | us riot] *Harrowby 255*; uss Riot *Harrowby 81* |
| | prove] *Harrowby 255*; Prove *Harrowby 81* |
| 9.23 | possessing] *Harrowby 255*; Possessing *Harrowby 81* |
| | Love.] Love, *Harrowby 81* |
| 9.24 | us crown] *Harrowby 255*; uss Crown *Harrowby 81* |
| | Wish] *Harrowby 255*; wish *Harrowby 81* |
| | give] *Harrowby 255*; Give *Harrowby 81* |
| 9.25 | quench] *Harrowby 255*; quench, *Harrowby 81* |
| | Fire,] Fire. *Harrowby 81*. |
| 9.26 | tir'd] *Harrowby 255*; Tir'd *Harrowby 81* |
| 9.27 | dream] *Harrowby 255*; Dream *Harrowby 81* |
| | 'tis possess'd] *Harrowby 255*; tis Possess'd *Harrowby 81* |

## *Historical collation to 9 To Molly on Easter Eve*

| | |
|---|---|
| 9. | *title* Molly] *Harrowby 255*; Molly — *Harrowby 81*; *no title Fog's, but introduced as one of two enclosed* Imitations of *Horace, Ode* 28 *Lib.* 3 |
| 9.1–2 | *replaced by* Whilst well disciplin'd Maids wrapt up in a Hood, \| Are List'ning, and staring, at one they call good; *Fog's* |
| 9.1 | Whilst] While *Harrowby 255* |
| | will] would *Harrowby 255* |
| 9.2 | their] a *Harrowby 255* |
| 9.3–4 | *not in Fog's* |

**9.5** who credits the Nonsense] so dull to believe what *Fog's*; who credits *above deleted* so dull *Harrowby 81, Harrowby 255*
**9.6** conscious] knowing *Fog's*
what farces he's] what farce he is *Harrowby 255*; the Farce he is *Fog's*
**9.7–8** *not in Fog's*
**9.9** seize on] haste to *Fog's*
here] us *Fog's*
**9.10** those] them *Fog's*
**9.11–25** *not in Fog's*
**9.16** Pleasure] pleasures *Harrowby 255*
**9.26** thy] your *Fog's.*
**9.27** my Heaven, where awake 'tis] the Blessing I waking *Fog's*

## *Emendations to 10 Verses Sent to —*

**main source** *Harrowby 81*: Harrowby MS 81, ff. 141r–v
**complementary sources** *Harrowby 255*: Harrowby MS 255, pp. 88–9
*Museum*: 'A Song', in *The Museum*, III, 289–90 (no. 34, 4 July 1747)

**10.1** Time] *Harrowby 255, Museum*; time *Harrowby 81*
Absence] *Harrowby 255, Museum*; absence *Harrowby 81*
**10.2** Night] *Museum*; night *Harrowby 81*
**10.3** waste] *Museum*; wast *Harrowby 81*
Hours] *Museum*; hours *Harrowby 81*
**10.10** its] *Harrowby 255, Museum*; it's *Harrowby 81*
gave,] *Museum*; gave; *Harrowby 81*
**10.11** disdain] *Harrowby 255, Museum*; desdain *Harrowby 81*
**10.14** Tyrant's Part] *Museum*; Tyrants part *Harrowby 81*
**10.17** Monarch's Pow'r] *Museum*; Monarchs pow'r *Harrowby 81*
**10.20** Sway] *Museum*; sway *Harrowby 81*
**10.21** Invader's] *Museum*; Invaders *Harrowby 81*
Arms] *Harrowby 255, Museum*; Arms, *Harrowby 81*
**10.23** Glory's] *Museum*; Glorys *Harrowby 81*
**10.24** conquers] *Museum*; conquer's, *Harrowby 81*
**10.26** its] *Harrowby 255, Museum*; it's *Harrowby 81*
Pain,] *Museum*; Pain; *Harrowby 81*
**10.28** Chain;] *Museum*; Chain *Harrowby 81*
**10.29** grieve] *Museum*; grieve, *Harrowby 81*

## *Historical collation to 10 Verses Sent to —*

**10.** *title*] *Harrowby 255*; *no title Harrowby 81*; A Song *Museum*
**10.3** might] should *Harrowby 255*
**10.12** Or] and *Harrowby 255*
like] *above deleted* love *Harrowby 81*
**10.13** Nymph] *above deleted* Youth *Harrowby 81*; Nymph *Harrowby 255*; Youth *Museum*

**10.16** rule] rules *Museum*
**10.24** May] Should *Museum*
she] *corrected from* he *Harrowby 81*; she *Harrowby 255*; he *Museum*
**10.27** Shall] Should *Museum*
**10.28** hers] *Harrowby 255*; hers *corrected from* his *Harrowby 81*; his *Museum*
**10.31** her] *Harrowby 255*; her *corrected from* him *Harrowby 81*; him *Museum*

## *Emendations to 11 Epistle to —*

**main source** *Harrowby*: Harrowby MS 255, pp. 90–3
**complementary sources** *LM*: *London Magazine*, 19 (February 1750), 89
*Dodsley*: Dodsley, *Collection* (1755), IV, 110–12, and subsequent editions

**11.5** obey] *LM, Dodsley*; obey, *Harrowby*
**11.7** constant] *LM, Dodsley*; Constant *Harrowby*
**11.10** Ardour] *Dodsley*; Ardour, *Harrowby*
**11.13** Scruples] Scrupules *Harrowby*
**11.14** implicitly] *LM, Dodsley*; implicitely *Harrowby*
**11.15** decide,] *LM, Dodsley*; decide *Harrowby*
**11.19** move,] *LM, Dodsley*; move *Harrowby*
**11.20** indulge] *LM, Dodsley*; Indulge *Harrowby*
'tis] *LM, Dodsley*; tis *Harrowby*
**11.27** decay;] *LM, Dodsley*; decay *Harrowby*
**11.29** Nature's] *Dodsley*; Natures *Harrowby*
blows,] *LM, Dodsley*; blows *Harrowby*
**11.31** Eyes,] Eyes *Harrowby*
Love,] Love *Harrowby*
**11.35** be;] *LM, Dodsley*; be *Harrowby*
**11.37** For tho'] *LM, Dodsley*; (For tho *Harrowby*
alienate] *LM, Dodsley*; Alienate *Harrowby*
Flame,] Flame *Harrowby*
**11.38** same,] *LM, Dodsley*; same) *Harrowby*
**11.43** say,] *LM, Dodsley*; say *Harrowby*
Sickness] sickness *Harrowby*
Woe,] Woe *Harrowby*
**11.44** allow;] *LM, Dodsley*; alow *Harrowby*
**11.45** Charms,] Charms *Harrowby*
**11.46** himself] *LM, Dodsley*; himselfe *Harrowby*
**11.47** would thou then] would then *Harrowby*
**11.49** future] *LM, Dodsley*; Future *Harrowby*
Day,] Day *Harrowby*
**11.52** Happiness] Happyness *Harrowby*
**11.56** Now] Now, *Harrowby*
**11.57** like] *LM, Dodsley*; Like *Harrowby*
**11.60** languish'd] *LM, Dodsley*; Languish'd *Harrowby*
**11.63** strain'd] *LM, Dodsley*; strain'd, *Harrowby*
Foe] Foe, *Harrowby*
**11.68** half … half] *LM, Dodsley*; halfe … halfe *Harrowby*

**11.71** caress'd] *Dodsley*; carress'd *Harrowby*
**11.76** know,] *LM, Dodsley*; know *Harrowby*

## *Historical collation to 11 Epistle to —*

**11.** *title* Epistle To —] A LOVE-LETTER. *To ———. Written by the late Lord* HERVEY *LM*; A LOVE LETTER *Dodsley*
**11.7** *no new paragraph LM, Dodsley*
thy] this *Dodsley*
**11.8** that] which *LM, Dodsley*
**11.9** thy present] the languid *LM, Dodsley*
**11.11** these] those *LM, Dodsley*
**11.13** Scruples] Scrupules *Harrowby*; scruple *LM, Dodsley*
**11.22** their Cup] the cup *LM, Dodsley*
**11.27** *no new paragraph LM, Dodsley*
**11.31** the] those *Dodsley*
**11.36** shallst] shalt *LM, Dodsley*
**11.38** Whilst] While *Dodsley*
**11.47** would thou then] would then *Harrowby*; wouldst thou then *LM, Dodsley*
**11.49** *no new paragraph LM, Dodsley*
**11.50** Live while] Live whilst *LM, Dodsley*
happy while] happy whilst *LM, Dodsley*
**11.64** when] whilst *LM, Dodsley*
**11.68** While] Whilst *LM, Dodsley*
**11.72** *no new paragraph LM, Dodsley*

## *Emendations to 12 Epistle to a Lady*

**main source** *Longleat*: Portland Papers (Longleat), XX, ff. 63r–64v
**complementary sources** *LM*: *London Magazine*, 2 (September 1733), 472
*Dodsley*: Dodsley, *Collection*, 2nd edn (1748), pp. 193–6, and subsequent editions
*Winstanley*: *Poems Written Occasionally by the Late John Winstanley . . . with Many Others*, ed. by George Winstanley, 2 vols. (Dublin: by S. Powell, for the editor, 1751), II, 218–21

**12.1** heart] *LM, Dodsley*; Heart *Longleat*
grief] *LM, Dodsley*; Grief *Longleat*
**12.3** flatt'rer] *LM, Dodsley*; Flatt'rer *Longleat*
**12.4** smart,] *LM, Dodsley*; smart *Longleat*
lament] *all complementary sources*; Lament *Longleat*
wound] *LM, Dodsley*; Wound *Longleat*
**12.5** me,] *LM*; me *Longleat*
last] *all complementary sources*; Last *Longleat*
**12.6** sorrow] *LM, Dodsley*; Sorrow *Longleat*
**12.7** friendship] *LM, Dodsley*; Friendship *Longleat*
**12.9** miser,] *LM, Dodsley*; miser *Longleat*
pierc'd] *all complementary sources*; (pierc'd *Longleat*
inward] *all complementary sources*; Inward *Longleat*

pain,] *LM, Dodsley*; pain) *Longleat*
12.10 horror] *LM, Dodsley*; Horror *Longleat*
troubled main;] *LM*; Troubled main *Longleat*
12.11 rocky coast,] *LM, Dodsley*; Rocky coast *Longleat*
12.12 treasures] *LM, Dodsley*; Treasures *Longleat*
tempest lost;] *LM, Dodsley*; Tempest Lost *Longleat*
12.14 ashore,] *all complementary sources*; ashore *Longleat*
12.15 forlorn] *all complementary sources*; Forlorn *Longleat*
12.16 life] *LM, Dodsley*; Life *Longleat*
its pomp] *LM, Dodsley*; it's Pomp *Longleat*
scorn] *LM, Dodsley*; Scorn *Longleat*
12.17 sweetener] *Dodsley*; Sweetness *Longleat*
busy scene;] *LM, Dodsley*; Busy Scene *Longleat*
12.18 joy without,] *LM, Dodsley*; Joy without *Longleat*
within.] *all complementary sources*; within *Longleat*
12.19 you] *LM, Dodsley*; you, *Longleat*
ally'd,] *all complementary sources*; ally'd *Longleat*
12.20 one,] *all complementary sources*; one *Longleat*
dy'd;] *Dodsley*; dy'd *Longleat*
12.21 killing store;] *LM, Dodsley*; Killing store *Longleat*
12.22 add,] *all complementary sources*; add *Longleat*
more.] *all complementary sources*; more *Longleat*
12.23 view'd] *all complementary sources*; viewd *Longleat*
fire,] *LM, Dodsley*; fire *Longleat*
12.24 angels mingle,] *LM, Dodsley*; Angels mingle *Longleat*
admire;] *all complementary sources*; admire *Longleat*
12.25 passion] *LM, Dodsley*; Passion *Longleat*
part,] *LM, Dodsley*; part *Longleat*
12.28 sex] *LM, Dodsley*; Sex *Longleat*
beauty] *LM, Dodsley*; Beauty *Longleat*
12.29 join'd,] *all complementary sources*; Join'd *Longleat*
12.30 softness,] *LM, Dodsley*; Softness *Longleat*
12.31 conquer evils] *LM, Dodsley*; Conquer Evils *Longleat*
endure] *all complementary sources*; Endure *Longleat*
12.32 pain] *LM, Dodsley*; Pain *Longleat*
cure.] *all complementary sources*; cure *Longleat*
12.33 Scandal, a busy fiend] *Dodsley*; Scandal a Busy Fiend *Longleat*
truth's] *LM, Dodsley*; Truths *Longleat*
12.35 tale] *LM, Dodsley*; Tale *Longleat*
12.37 pity] *LM, Dodsley*; Pity *Longleat*
12.38 credit] *all complementary sources*; Credit *Longleat*
12.39 evil] *LM, Dodsley*; Evil *Longleat*
12.40 scale,] *LM, Dodsley*; Scale *Longleat*
12.41 wish,] *all complementary sources*; wish *Longleat*
least] *all complementary sources*; Least *Longleat*
justice] *LM, Dodsley*; Justice *Longleat*
prevail.] *all complementary sources*; prevail *Longleat*

12.42 Insinuates] *all complementary sources*; Insinuat'es *Longleat*
lyes] *LM, Dodsley*; Lyes *Longleat*
12.43 hypocrite] *LM, Dodsley*; Hipocrite *Longleat*
12.44 innocence] *LM, Dodsley*; Innocence *Longleat*
12.45 honour bleed,] Honour bleed *Longleat*
prey] *LM, Dodsley*; Prey *Longleat*
slander's tongue] *LM, Dodsley*; Slanders Tongue *Longleat*
12.46 fate,] *LM, Dodsley*; Fate *Longleat*
distress] *LM, Dodsley*; Distress *Longleat*
12.47 suffer] *all complementary sources*; Suffer *Longleat*
12.48 joy,] *LM, Dodsley*; Joy *Longleat*
sensible] *all complementary sources*; Sensible *Longleat*
pain] *LM, Dodsley*; Pain *Longleat*
12.49 complain] *all complementary sources*; Complain *Longleat*
12.50 injure] *all complementary sources*; Injure *Longleat*
12.51 pity] *LM, Dodsley*; Pity *Longleat*
12.52 remains,] *all complementary sources*; remains *Longleat*
drop] *all complementary sources*; Drop *Longleat*
claim] *LM, Dodsley*; Claim *Longleat*
12.53 conduct justify] *Dodsley*; Conduct Justifye *Longleat*
flame] *LM, Dodsley*; Flame *Longleat*
12.54 dear bands] *LM, Dodsley*; Dear Bands *Longleat*
heart-strings] *LM, Dodsley*; Heart-strings *Longleat*
join,] *all complementary sources*; Join *Longleat*
12.55 sacrifice my peace] *LM, Dodsley*; Sacrifice My Peace *Longleat*
purchase] *all complementary sources*; Purchase *Longleat*
12.56 mother] *LM, Dodsley*; Mother *Longleat*
delirious eyes] *all complementary sources*; Delirious Eye's *Longleat*
12.57 babe] *LM, Dodsley*; Babe *Longleat*
12.58 strains] *all complementary sources*; Strains *Longleat*
transport] *LM, Dodsley*; Transport *Longleat*
arms] *LM, Dodsley*; arm's *Longleat*
12.59 its lips] *LM, Dodsley*; it's Lips *Longleat*
its charms] *LM, Dodsley*; it's Charms *Longleat*
12.60 Pleads] *all complementary sources*; Plead's *Longleat*
slumbers] *all complementary sources*; Slumbers *Longleat*
12.61 little cherub live] *LM, Dodsley*; Little Cherub Live *Longleat*
12.62 heart] *LM, Dodsley*; heart, *Longleat*
12.63 torture constancy] *LM, Dodsley*; Torture Constancy *Longleat*
sadden love] *LM, Dodsley*; Sadden Love *Longleat*
12.64 image] *LM, Dodsley*; Image *Longleat*
12.65 Fancy] *all complementary sources*; Fancy, *Longleat*
12.66 phantom] *LM, Dodsley*; Phantom *Longleat*
idolize] *all complementary sources*; Idolize *Longleat*
12.67 substance] *LM, Dodsley*; Substance *Longleat*
12.68 idle] *all complementary sources*; Idle *Longleat*
12.69 joy's imagin'd] *LM, Dodsley*; Joy's Imagin'd *Longleat*

| | |
|---|---|
| | despair] *LM, Dodsley*; Dispair *Longleat* |
| **12.72** | prospect] *LM, Dodsley*; Prospect *Longleat* |

## *Historical collation to 12 Epistle to a Lady*

| | |
|---|---|
| **12.17** | sweetener] Sweetness *Longleat* |
| **12.22** | she can] can she *Dodsley* |
| | I can] can I *Winstanley* |
| **12.33** | fiend] Friend *Winstanley* |
| **12.39** | hope] hopes *Dodsley, Winstanley* |
| **12.62** | move] prove *Dodsley* |

## *Emendations to 13 Mr Hammond to Miss Dashwood*

**main source** *Brotherton*: Brotherton Lt 119, ff. 70r, 71r
**complementary sources** *Add. 57836*: BL Add. MS 57836, f. 113r
*Roberts*: *An Elegy to a Young Lady, in the Manner of Ovid. By ------. With an Answer: By a Lady, Author of the Verses to the Imitator of Horace* (London: [Sam Aris] for J. Roberts, 1733)
*Dodsley*: Dodsley, *Collection* (1755), IV, 77–9, collated with edns to 1782
*Yale c.83/1*: Yale Osborn Collection c.83/1, no. 114
*Yale c.130*: Yale Osborn Collection c.130, pp. 81–3
*Yale c.175*: Yale Osborn Collection c.175, p. 54

| | |
|---|---|
| **13.** | *title* Mr. H— to Miss D—] Mr. H——d to Miss D——d *Brotherton* |
| **13.1** | say,] *Roberts, Dodsley*; say *Brotherton* |
| **13.7** | Beauties] *Add. 57836, Yale c.175, Roberts*; Beauty's *Brotherton* |
| **13.8** | more.] *Yale c.175, Roberts*; more, *Brotherton* |
| **13.15** | day,] *Yale c.83/1, c.130, Dodsley*; day *Brotherton* |
| **13.16** | say;] *Yale c.130, Dodsley*; say, *Brotherton* |
| **13.18** | Heart's] *Add. 57836, Roberts*; Hearts *Brotherton* |
| **13.22** | Shame,] Shame *Brotherton* |
| **13.24** | dispis'd?] dispis'd, *Brotherton* |
| **13.27** | words,] *Roberts, Dodsley, Yale c.83/1, Yale c.130*; words *Brotherton* |
| **13.29** | Ears,] *Roberts*; Ears *Brotherton* |
| **13.34** | fair:] *Roberts*; fair, *Brotherton* |
| **13.39** | Lore,] *Roberts*; Lore: *Brotherton* |
| **13.40** | feels,] *Add. 57836, Yale c.83/1, Yale c.130 Roberts, Dodsley*; feels *Brotherton* |
| **13.41** | Trade,] *Roberts, Yale c.83/1*; Trade *Brotherton* |
| **13.43** | deceive,] *all complementary sources*; deceive *Brotherton* |
| **13.47** | woe,] *Roberts, Yale c.83/1*; woe *Brotherton* |
| **13.48** | thy] *all complementary sources*; the *Brotherton* |

## *Historical collation to 13 Mr Hammond to Miss Dashwood*

| | |
|---|---|
| **13.** | *title*] The first Elegy to Delia *Add. 57836*; An ELEGY TO A Young LADY, in the Manner of *OVID Roberts*; ELEGY to Miss D- - -W- - -D. |

| | |
|---|---|
| | In the Manner of Ovid. *By the late Mr.* Hammond *Dodsley*; An Elegy to a Young Lady *Yale c.83/1*; Elegy to Miss Dashwood By Mr. Hammond *Yale c.130*; Emma or the Child of Sorrow *Yale c.175* |
| **13.2** | Where is] Where now's *Dodsley, Yale c.130*; Where's now *Yale c.83/1, Yale c.175* |
| | boasted] wonted *Yale c.175* |
| **13.3** | I once] once I *Yale c.83/1* |
| **13.5–6** | *not in Yale c.175* |
| **13.6** | Abroad uneasy, nor content] Joyless abroad; yet Restless when *Add. 57836* |
| **13.8** | feel] I feel *Yale c.83/1* |
| | worth] Charms *Add. 57836* |
| **13.9–10** | *not in Add. 57836* |
| **13.9** | and] or *Roberts, Dodsley, Yale c.83/1, Yale c.130*; I *Yale c.175* |
| **13.10** | not there] *Yale c.175 ends after this line* |
| **13.11** | former] formal *Add. 57836, Roberts, Dodsley, Yale c.130* |
| **13.12** | Their Wit and Wisdom can't] Not all their Wisdom can *Add. 57836*; Nor wit, nor wisdom, can *Dodsley, Yale c.130* |
| **13.13** | can't decieve] cannot cheat *Add. 57836* |
| | I now] that I *Add. 57836* |
| **13.14** | Wisdom] Reason *Add. 57836* |
| | Ills] Ill *Roberts, Dodsley, Yale c.83/1, Yale c.130* |
| | the Ills without the] thy Merit, not my *Add. 57836* |
| **13.15** | from thy] far from *Add. 57836* |
| | Face] Thee *Add. 57836*; sight *Dodsley, Yale c.130* |
| **13.16** | thousand] thousands *Yale c.83/1* |
| | schemes I form, and things] Things my Heart resolves *Add. 57836* |
| **13.17** | when] in *Add. 57836* |
| | gives the time I seek] all Resolves are weak *Add. 57836* |
| **13.19** | speak with Eloquence and ease] tell thee all my hapless Flame *Add. 57836* |
| **13.20–28** | *not in BL Add. 57836, which substitutes [Tear in ms]*d I plead for what I ought to blame: \| *[Tear in ms]* Want thy beauteous Spring invade, \| And cloud thy Lustre with my Fortune's Shade? |
| **13.22** | Excuse] Expose *Roberts, Dodsley, Yale c.83/1, Yale c.130* |
| **13.23** | these] those *Roberts, Dodsley, Yale c.83/1, Yale c.130* |
| **13.26** | wrong] wrongs *Roberts, Dodsley, Yale c.83/1, Yale c.130* |
| **13.28** | what I writ] all I write *Roberts, Dodsley, Yale c.83.1, Yale c.130* |
| **13.29** | My humble sighs shall only reach] No selfish Sigh shall e'er disturb *Add. 57836* |
| **13.30** | And all my Eloquence shall be my] Nor shall thy pitying Nature see these *Add. 57836* |
| **13.31** | And now (for more I never must pretend.)] Yet to my sober Wish at least Attend. *Add. 57836* |
| **13.32** | Deaf to the Lover, Listen to the] Hear me not as thy Lover, but thy *Roberts, Dodsley, Yale c.83/1, Yale c.130*; And tho you shun the Lover, hear the *Add. 57836* |
| **13.33** | would] will *Roberts, Dodsley, Yale c.83/1, Yale c.130* |
| | little] youthful *Add. 57836* |

**13.34** For without danger none like thee are] (For oh like Thee how dangerous to be) *Add. 57836*
**13.36** the] thy *Yale c.130*
become] adorn *Add. 57836*
Fame] flame *Yale c.130*
**13.37** And not] Nor yet *Dodsley, Yale c.130*
And not dispise 'tho' void of winning] But thou prefer, tho' unadorned by *Add. 57836*
**13.38** honest] silent *Add. 57836*
**13.39–40** *after line 36 and before line 37 Add. 57836*
**13.40** Tho'] The *Add. 57836*
please and flatter] sooth the ear the *Add. 57836*
**13.41–2** *not in Add. 57836*
**13.43** Lips so knowing] Vows so practisd *Add. 57836*
**13.45** Tears] Looks *Add. 57836*
**13.46** thaw the icy Coldness] touch the unguarded Softness *Add. 57836*
**13.47** Oh! shut thine Eyes to such deceitfull] Ah shut thy Ear to their deluding *Add. 57836*
**13.48** by] with *Add. 57836*
thy] the *Brotherton*
**13.49** do not] cannot *Add. 57836*

## *Emendations to 14 The Answer*

**main source** *Brotherton*: Brotherton Lt 119, ff. 72, 73, 74 (rectos only)
**complementary sources** *Roberts*: *An Elegy to a Young Lady, in the Manner of Ovid. By ------. With an Answer: By a* LADY, *Author of the Verses to the Imitator of Horace* (London: [Sam Aris] for J. Roberts, 1733)
*Dodsley*: Dodsley, *Collection* (1755) IV, 79–82, collated with edns to 1782
*Yale c.83/1*: Yale Osborn Collection c.83/1, no. 114
*Yale c.130*: Yale Osborn Collection c.130, pp. 83–5

**14.3** say,] *all complementary sources*; say *Brotherton*
Love?] *Roberts*; Love *Brotherton*
**14.4** hope,] *Roberts, Dodsley, Yale c.130*; hope? *Brotherton*
**14.6** vain] *all complementary sources*; Vain *Brotherton*
**14.8** shame;] *Dodsley, Yale c.130*; shame *Brotherton*
**14.9** gild] *all complementary sources*; yeild *Brotherton*
Wife,] *Roberts, Yale c.130*; Wife *Brotherton*
**14.11** chain,] *Dodsley, Yale c.83/1, Yale c.130*; chain *Brotherton*
**14.16** frown'd;] *Dodsley, Yale c.130*; frown'd, *Brotherton*
**14.19** truth,] *Dodsley, Yale c.83/1, Yale c.130*; truth *Brotherton*
**14.20** Youth;] *Roberts*; Youth *Brotherton*
**14.21** Ambition's] *Dodsley, Yale c.130*; Ambitions *Brotherton*
**14.27** *no new paragraph Brotherton*
kind,] *Roberts, Yale c.83/1*; kind *Brotherton*
**14.29** breast,] *Yale c.83/1*; breast *Brotherton*

**14.34** dread,] *all complementary sources*; dread *Brotherton*
**14.35** folly's] follys *Brotherton*
**14.37** pities] *all complementary sources*; pitty's *Brotherton*
**14.39** act] *all complementary sources*; acts *Brotherton*
**14.43** Clodios] *all complementary sources*; Clodias *Brotherton*
**14.45** People] *all complementary sources*; Peoples *Brotherton*
disease.] *Dodsley, Yale 83/1, Yale c.130*; desease: *Brotherton*
**14.50** sense] sence, *Brotherton*
**14.52** deviate,] *Roberts*; deviate *Brotherton*
**14.53** Name's] *Roberts*; Names *Brotherton*
**14.54** *no new paragraph Brotherton*
**14.58** blown] *all complementary sources*; blown, *Brotherton*
flame] *all complementary sources*; flame, *Brotherton*
**14.59** friend's] *Dodsley*; friends *Brotherton*
**14.66** Hear] *Roberts, Dodsley, Yale c.130*; Hear, *Brotherton*
**14.67** one] *all complementary sources*; one, *Brotherton*

## *Historical collation to 14 The Answer*

**14.** *title*] *The* ANSWER *to the foregoing* ELEGY: *By the Author of the Verses to the Imitator of* HORACE *Roberts*; Answer to the foregoing Lines. *By the late Lord* HERVEY *Dodsley*; The Lady's Answer *Yale c.83/1*; An Answer to the forgoing Lines By Lord Hervey *Yale c.130*.
**14.9** gild] yeild *Brotherton*
honour] Ruin *Roberts*; ruin *all other complementary sources*
**14.16** when] where *Dodsley, Yale c.130*
**14.19** Thine] Thy *all complementary sources*
**14.21** nobler] noble *Yale c.83/1*
**14.22** name] fame *Dodsley, Yale c.130*
thy] that *all complementary sources*
**14.24** might] wou'd *Dodsley, Yale c.130*
**14.28** inly] only *Dodsley, Yale c.83/1, Yale c.130*
or] and *all complementary sources*
**14.29** Demons] Demon *Yale c.83/1*
**14.31** tell what] all that *Dodsley, Yale c.130*
**14.32** added Grief] added – Grief *Roberts*; added Grief – *Yale c.83/1*
**14.35** fault] deed *Roberts, Dodsley*
folly's] folly *all complementary sources*
**14.39** act] acts *Brotherton*
a] the *Roberts, Yale c.83/1*
**14.42** interest] Interest's *Roberts*
**14.43** Timons] Simons *Brotherton*
bosom] bosoms *Dodsley, Yale c.130*
**14.45** People] Peoples *Brotherton*
**14.47** And] Whilst *all complementary sources*
their] the *Dodsley, Yale c.130*
**14.50** sense or worth] worth or sense *Roberts, Dodsley, Yale c.83/1, Yale c.130*
is] be *Dodsley, Yale c.83/1, Yale c.130*

| | |
|---|---|
| **14.60–1** | *replaced by* And only as a friend on you believe, \| I might, upon that score, my heart deceive *Yale c.83/1* |
| **14.63** | silent] latent *all complementary sources* |
| **14.66** | Hear] Here *Yale c.83/1* |
| | take] make *all complementary sources* |
| **14.69** | honour, nor to interest] int'rest, nor to honour *Dodsley, Yale c.130* |
| **14.70** | triumph] Triumphs *Roberts, Yale c.83/1* |

## *Emendations to 15 Written as from Lady Mary Wortley to Monsieur Algarotti*

**main source** *Egerton*: BL Egerton MS 23, ff. 239r–v
**complementary sources** none

| | |
|---|---|
| **15.** | *epigraph* formam] forman *Egerton* |
| **15.1** | design'd] desinged *Egerton* |
| **15.2** | cramp] crams *Egerton* |
| **15.6** | Love.] Love, *Egerton* |
| **15.13** | with] With *Egerton* |
| **15.14** | tho'] tho *Egerton* |
| | despise.] despise, *Egerton* |
| **15.15** | forc'd] forcd *Egerton* |
| **15.16** | 'tis] tis *Egerton* |
| **15.17** | could] coul *Egerton* |
| **15.20** | Force] force *Egerton* |
| **15.28** | Cause.] Cause, *Egerton* |
| **15.30** | Force] Forte *Egerton* |
| **15.32** | say'd] Say'd *Egerton* |
| **15.33** | unhappy] un happy *Egerton* |
| **15.35** | unmoor'd] un moor'd *Egerton* |
| **15.36** | like] Like *Egerton* |
| **15.37** | deplore".] deplore. *Egerton* |
| **15.41** | dull Churls] dull' Churls *Egerton* |
| **15.42** | vain] Vain *Egerton* |
| **15.43** | we not] We not *Egerton* |

## *Historical collation to 15 Written as from Lady Mary Wortley to Monsieur Algarotti*

*none; only one witness exists*

## *Emendations to 16 Verse Letter to Lady Hervey from Italy*

**main source** *Add. 51345*: BL Add. MS 51345, ff. 18r–23r
**complementary sources** *SRO*: SRO 941/47/4, p. 40 (lines 42–56 only)

*Voltaire*: Voltaire, *Letters Concerning the English Nation* (London: for C. Davis and A. Lyon, 1733), pp. 195–6 (lines 42–56 only, rendered loosely in French)

**16.7** shine] *written after deleted* fi, *perhaps eye-slip from* fine *in line 8 Add. 51345*
**16.28** Since] *above deleted* When *Add. 51345*
**16.37** so] *after deleted* a *Add. 51345*
**16.45** Distress] *after deleted* oppr *Add. 51345*
**16.56** He] *above deleted* They *Add. 51345*
Want.] Want *Add. 51345*
**16.98** gett] *after deleted* k *Add. 51345*
**16.101** Groat.'] Groat. *Add. 51345*
**16.112** each] *above deleted* we *Add. 51345*
**16.123** ev'ry] *above deleted* all the *Add. 51345*
**16.126** Countrys] *above deleted* City *Add. 51345*
**16.152** Factions] *after deleted* Pe *Add. 51345*
**16.172** He's lov'd] *after deleted* He's lov'd even *Add. 51345*
He's] *above deleted* He'es *Add. 51345*
**16.178** our] *after deleted* ho *Add. 51345*
piteous] pteous *Add. 51345*
**16.182** a] *after deleted* our *Add. 51345*
**16.184** beneath our] *above deleted* they grown *Add. 51345*
**16.204** Cascades and Rivers] *above deleted* Rivers Cascades & *Add. 51345*
**16.210** self] *above deleted* had b *Add. 51345*
**16.211** Fear.] Fear *Add. 51345*
**16.214** is] *above deleted* was *Add. 51345*
**16.215** Welfare] *above deleted* Safe *Add. 51345*
**16.216** But all our frights and dangers] *above deleted* At length each Difficulty *Add. 51345*
**16.217** last;] last *Add. 51345*
**16.224** prove,)] prove, *Add. 51345*

## *Historical collation to 16 Verse Letter to Lady Hervey from Italy*

**16.1–41** *not in SRO, Voltaire*
**16.45** Distress, and] Oppression *SRO*
**16.57–229** *not in SRO, Voltaire*

## *Emendations to 17 To Mr. Poyntz upon returning him Dr. Secker's Sermon*

**main source** *SRO*: SRO 941/53/1, p. 122
**complementary sources** *Bod*: Bod. MS Rawl. poet. 152, ff. 218r–219r
*BL*: BL Add. MS 28101, f. 206r
*LEP*: *The London Evening-Post*, 13–15 November 1733, p. 2
*GM*: *Gentleman's Magazine*, 3, 602 (November 1733)
*NFH*: *New Foundling Hospital for Wit*, IV (1771), 119–20 (reprinted 1784: I, 240–1; 1786: I, 242–3)

| | |
|---|---|
| **17.** | *title* Poyntz] *Bod, BL, LEP, NFH*; Pointz *SRO* |
| **17.4** | mild,] *all complementary sources*; mild *SRO* |
| **17.5** | child.] *Bod*; child *SRO* |
| **17.7** | Know] *all complementary sources*; Know, *SRO* |
| **17.9** | please;] *BL, GM, NFH*; please. *SRO* |
| **17.12** | strengthen] *LEP, GM, NFH*; strengthen, *SRO* |
| **17.17** | engage:] *BL, LEP, GM, NFH*; engage *SRO* |
| **17.21** | smile:] *BL, GM, NFH*; smile, *SRO* |
| **17.29** | Poyntz's] *BL, GM, NFH*; Pointz's *SRO* |

## *Historical collation to 17 To Mr. Poyntz upon returning him Dr. Secker's Sermon*

| | |
|---|---|
| **17.** | *title*] Verses sent to Stephen Poyntz Esq[r]. with Dr Seckers Sermon on Education *Bod*; L[d]. Harvey to Mr Poyntz – w[th] Dr. Secker's Sermon on Education *BL; From Lord* H——Y *to Mr.* POYNTZ, *with Dr.* SECKER'S Sermon *on Education LEP, GM*; TO MR. POYNTZ, WITH DR. SECKER'S SERMON ON EDUCATION, PREACHED BEFORE THE UNIVERSITY OF OXFORD, July 8, 1733 *NFH* |
| | Poyntz] Pointz *SRO* |
| **17.2** | to] on *all complementary sources* |
| **17.5** | Can] Canst *all complementary sources* |
| **17.9** | Can] E'en *all complementary sources* |
| | ev'n] can *all complementary sources* |
| **17.14** | toil] Toils *all complementary sources* |
| **17.18** | days] years *all complementary sources* |
| **17.19** | to] with *all complementary sources* |
| | Virtues] Virtue *all complementary sources* |
| | add] give *all complementary sources* |
| **17.21** | both Minerva's] each Minerva *all complementary sources* |
| | fortunes] fortune *BL, LEP, GM, NFH* |
| **17.22** | Senates] Senate *GM, NFH* |
| **17.23** | that] this *Bod* |
| **17.24** | or] and *all complementary sources* |
| **17.26** | Truth] rule *all complementary sources* |
| **17.27** | from] by *all complementary sources* |

## *Emendations to 18 To Dr Sherwin in Answer to a Latin Letter in Verse*

**main source** *BL:* BL Add. MS 51396, ff. 99r–102v
**complementary sources** *Roberts: An Epistle from a Nobleman to a Doctor of Divinity: In Answer to a Latin Letter in Verse. Written from H——n-C—t, Aug. 28. 1733* (London: [Sam. Aris] for J. Roberts, 1733)
*Ickworth:* copy of Roberts annotated in Hervey's hand, National Trust at Ickworth, shelf-mark 18.B.4.8

| | |
|---|---|
| **18.8** | *Greek*] *Roberts*; Greek *BL* |

| | |
|---|---|
| | *Latin*] *Roberts*; Latin *BL* |
| **18.9** | *Doctor Freind*] *Roberts*; Doctor Friend *BL* |
| **18.10** | *Gradus, Lexicon*] *Roberts*; Gradus, Lexicon *BL* |
| | Rule;] *Roberts*; Rule *BL* |
| **18.12** | *Doctor King*] *Roberts*; Doctor King *BL* |
| **18.13** | *John-Trot*] *Roberts*; John-Trot *BL* |
| **18.14** | *English*] *Roberts*; English *BL* |
| | Stead:] Stead. *BL* |
| **18.15** | forgive] *Roberts*; forgive, *BL* |
| **18.19** | says, That] *Roberts*; says that *BL* |
| | Cat,] *Roberts*; Cat *BL* |
| **18.21** | recieve] recieve, *BL* |
| **18.23** | Reason] *inserted above the line BL* |
| | then,] *Roberts*; then *BL* |
| | Friend,] *Roberts*; Friend *BL* |
| **18.28** | *England's*] *Roberts*; Englands *BL* |
| **18.29** | Nay,] *Roberts*; Nay *BL* |
| **18.31** | Mother,] *Roberts*; Mother *BL* |
| **18.33** | Groat,] *Roberts*; Groat; *BL* |
| **18.34** | *our*] *Roberts*; our *BL* |
| | dress and] *Roberts*; dress, and, *BL* |
| **18.35** | Great] *Roberts*; great *BL* |
| **18.37** | bely,] *Roberts*; bely *BL* |
| **18.49** | understood.] *Roberts*; understood: *BL* |
| **18.50** | *the Great:*] *Roberts*; the Great *BL* |
| **18.51** | *wit*] wit *BL* |
| | shown,] *Roberts*; shown; *BL* |
| **18.54** | *wit*] wit *BL* |
| **18.56** | *common Sense*] *Roberts*; common Sense *BL* |
| **18.57** | For,] *Roberts*; For *BL* |
| | Prudence,] *Roberts*; Prudence *BL* |
| | Parts,] *Roberts*; Parts *BL* |
| **18.59** | *Last*] *Roberts*; Last *BL* |
| **18.60** | *First*] *Roberts*; first *BL* |
| **18.66** | *Wit*] *Roberts*; Wit *BL* |
| **18.67** | Brain,] Brain; *BL* |
| **18.78** | Aid,] *Roberts*; Aid; *BL* |
| **18.81** | *Monkeys*] *Roberts*; Monkeys *BL* |
| **18.84** | please,] *Roberts*; please *BL* |
| | surprise;] *Roberts*; surprise, *BL* |
| **18.90** | attentive] *Roberts*; atentive *BL* |
| **18.91** | commend,] *Roberts*; commend *BL* |
| | adore.] *Roberts*; adore, *BL* |
| **18.95** | proud,] proud. *BL* |
| **18.97** | *Coxcomb*] *Roberts*; Coxcomb *BL* |
| | *Fool*] *Roberts*; Fool *BL* |
| **18.99** | *Religion*] *Roberts*; Religion *BL* |

| | |
|---|---|
| | *Marriage-Chain*] *Roberts*; Marriage-Chain *BL* |
| **18.105** | Deceit] *Roberts*; deceit *BL* |
| **18.109** | Bubble] *Roberts*; Buble *BL* |
| | Cheat".] Cheat. *BL* |
| **18.111** | his] *above deleted* this *BL* |
| | Store] *Roberts*; store *BL* |
| **18.112** | *Solomon*] *Roberts*; Solomon *BL* |
| | more:] *Roberts*; more. *BL* |
| **18.114** | *Walpole's*] *Roberts*; Walpole's *BL* |
| **18.115** | *Senates*] *Roberts*; Senates *BL* |
| | *the State*] *Roberts*; the State *BL* |
| **18.116** | *England*'s] *Roberts*; England's *BL* |
| | *Europe*'s] *Roberts*; Europe's *BL* |
| **18.123** | *Pope*] Pope *BL* |
| **18.128** | thought:] *Roberts*; thought *BL* |
| **18.130** | Name,] *Roberts*; Name; *BL* |
| **18.132** | *Dictionary*] *Roberts*; Dictionary *BL* |
| **18.135** | thus,] *Roberts*; thus *BL* |
| **18.139** | see] *after deleted illegible word BL* |
| **18.141** | Works,] *Roberts*; Works *BL* |
| **18.145** | *Hatter*] *Roberts*; Hatter *BL* |
| | *Head*] *Roberts*; Head *BL* |
| **18.150** | but] *inserted above the line BL* |
| **18.154** | wrote] *Roberts*; wrote, *BL* |
| **18.156** | On] *above deleted* From *BL* |
| | model built his] *above deleted* Labours borrow'd *BL* |
| | Fame] *inserted above the line BL* |
| **18.157** | sold *Broome's* Labours, printed with *Pope's*] *above deleted* printed Lady Mary's with his *BL* |
| **18.161** | *School-Boys*] School-Boys *BL* |
| | *Girls*] *Roberts*; Girls *BL*; *followed by deleted* So much for Pope, nor this I would have say'd \| Had not the Spider first his venom shed \| For who begins can ne'er be a good Friend \| Nor a wise Foe who thus attack'd will end *BL* |
| **18.164** | try] *inserted above the line BL* |
| | into] *followed by deleted* a *BL* |
| **18.168** | *Courts*] Courts *BL* |
| **18.170** | *lounge*] *Roberts*; lounge *BL* |

## *Historical collation to 18 To Dr Sherwin in Answer to a Latin Letter in Verse*

| | |
|---|---|
| **18.** | *title*] *An Epistle from a Nobleman to a Doctor of* Divinity*: In Answer to a* Latin *Letter in Verse. Written from* H——n-C—t, Aug. *28. 1733 Roberts* |
| **18.4** | Busyness] Bus'ness *Roberts* |
| **18.10** | From] By *Roberts* |
| **18.26** | Lords] L—ds *Roberts* |
| **18.39** | Which] That *Roberts* |

**18.46** Still] I *Roberts*
**18.48** my-self] myself *Roberts*
**18.50** *no new paragraph Roberts*
**18.64** squander'd all on Trifles or Abuse] still on Trifles squander'd, or Abuse; *Roberts*
**18.65** as] and *Roberts*
**18.70** *no new paragraph Roberts*
**18.72** is] such *Roberts*
**18.77** would] they *Roberts*
**18.99** *new paragraph Roberts*
**18.113** thin] weak *Roberts*
**18.123** *Pope*] *P—e Roberts*
**18.124** *Lord Fanny*] *His Lordship Roberts*
**18.125** *Pope*] *P—pe Roberts*
**18.131** No better is when you examine it] A Judge of writing would no more admit *Roberts*
**18.133** gives you nothing] nothing gives you *Roberts*
it's own] *deleted and replaced by* the Brain's *Ickworth*
**18.134** But a few modern Words for ancient Sense] *deleted and replaced by* replete with Words and indigent of Sense *Ickworth*
**18.135** 'Tis thus] *deleted and replaced by* 'Tis Hence *Ickworth*
*Pope*] P—pe *Roberts*
**18.137** For] "For *Roberts*
**18.141** *Pope*] P—pe *Roberts*
**18.156** On] *above deleted* From *BL*
model built his] *above deleted* Labours borrow'd *BL*
**18.157** sold *Broome's* Labours, printed with *Pope's*] *above deleted* printed Lady Mary's with his *BL*
**18.162** *Pope*] *P—pe Roberts*; *marginal marks to insert deleted:* So much for Pope, nor this I would have say'd | Had not the Spider first his Venom shed | For who begins can ne'er be a good Friend | Nor a wise Foe who thus attack'd will end *BL*; *marginal marks to insert deleted:* So much for Pope – nor this I would have say'd | Had not the Spider first his Venom shed | For the first Stone I ne'er unjustly cast | But who can blame the Hand that throw's the Last | And if one comon Foe a Wretch has made, | Of all Mankind – his Folly on his Head | And now dear Doctor *Ickworth*
**18.164** I now would try] *deleted beneath* I'd try, tho late *Ickworth*
**18.168** *Courts*] *C—ts Roberts*

## *Emendations to 19 To the Queen*

**main source** *Windsor*: 'Some Materials towards Memoirs of the Reign of King George II', Windsor Castle RA GEO/MAIN ff. 53672r–53676r
**complementary source** *SRO*: 'Manuscript of the Memoirs of the Reign of George II from 1727–1737', SRO 941/47/13–14 (14), ff. 115r–119r

**19.3** *ducktisk*] ducktisk *Windsor*
*teufflish*] *SRO*; teufflish *Windsor*

| | |
|---|---|
| **19.4** | *raccomode*] *SRO*; raccomode *Windsor* |
| **19.8** | *Midas'*] *SRO*; Midas' *Windsor* |
| **19.12** | *Labour*] *SRO*; Labour *Windsor* |
| **19.25** | *Sundon*] *SRO*; Sunden *Windsor* |
| **19.33** | She] *SRO*; she *Windsor* |
| **19.52** | *Greek* or *Roman*] *SRO*; Greek or Roman *Windsor* |
| **19.53** | *Plato, Socrates*, or*Tully*] *SRO*; Plato, Socrates or Tully *Windsor* |
| **19.54** | *Philosophers* or *Moralists*] *SRO*; Philosophers or Moralists *Windsor* |
| **19.67** | *most*] *SRO*; most *Windsor* |
| | *none*] *SRO*; none *Windsor* |
| **19.76** | *Eden*] *SRO*; Eden *Windsor* |
| **19.85** | heard] *SRO*; hear'd *Windsor* |
| **19.88** | *mine*] *SRO*; mine *Windsor* |
| **19.97** | *Pon*] Pon *Windsor* |
| | *troll*] *SRO*; troll *Windsor* |
| **19.102** | *grinning horrible a ghastly Smile*] *SRO*; grinning horribly a ghastly Smile *Windsor* |
| **19.104** | *that two and two he's sure makes four*] *SRO*; that two & two he's sure makes four *Windsor* |
| **19.105** | *SRO*; *not underlined Windsor* |
| **19.115** | *From*] *SRO*; From *Windsor* |
| | *to*] *SRO*; to *Windsor* |
| **19.120** | *old-China*] *SRO*; old-China *Windsor* |
| **19.130** | *Augustus*] *SRO*; Augustus *Windsor* |
| | *Horace*] *SRO*; Horace *Windsor* |
| **19.131** | *Trajan*] *SRO*; Trajan *Windsor* |
| | *Pliny*] *SRO*; Pliny *Windsor* |
| **19.133** | *Pliny's*] *SRO*; Pliny's *Windsor* |
| | *Horace*] *SRO*; Horace *Windsor* |
| **19.139** | *Schutz* and *Lifford*] *SRO*; Schutz & Lifford *Windsor* |
| | bear.] *SRO*; bear? *Windsor* |
| **19.140** | *Slone*] *above deleted* Stone *Windsor* |
| **19.141** | *dry'd Fly*, and *Hamstead-Stone*] *SRO*; dry'd Fly & Hamstead-Stone *Windsor* |
| **19.146** | State.] *SRO*; State *Windsor* |
| **19.147** | *Ever-Green his*] *SRO*; Ever-Green his *Windsor* |
| **19.156** | *Hamlet*] *SRO*; Hamlet *Windsor* |
| **19.157** | *Walpole*'s] *SRO*; Walpole's *Windsor* |
| **19.158** | Strain] *SRO*; Stain *Windsor* |
| **19.162** | Oak.] *SRO*; Oak *Windsor* |
| **19.169** | *Stone*] *SRO*; Stone *Windsor* |
| | *his Grace*] *SRO*; his Grace *Windsor* |
| **19.170** | *Pomfret*'s] *SRO*; Pomfret's *Windsor* |
| **19.172** | Servant's] *SRO*; Servants *Windsor* |
| **19.192** | *any Rule of Court*] *SRO*; any Rule of Court *Windsor* |
| **19.198–200** | *no triplet brace Windsor* |
| **19.213** | *Walpole*] *SRO*; Walpole *Windsor* |
| | *Newcastle*] *SRO*; Newcastle *Windsor* |

| | |
|---|---|
| **19.215** | *Cæsar*] *SRO*; Cesar *Windsor* |
| | *Cæsar's*] *SRO*; Cesars *Windsor* |
| **19.225** | *Cabinet*] *SRO*; Cabinet *Windsor* |
| **19.230** | *Gold-Keys*] *SRO*; Gold-Keys *Windsor* |
| **19.231** | *Willmington*] *SRO*; Wilmington *Windsor* |
| **19.234** | *Harrington*] *SRO*; Harrington *Windsor* |
| **19.236** | *Argyle*] *SRO*; Argyle *Windsor* |
| **19.245** | *comment le va?*] *SRO*; comment le va *Windsor* |
| | *how you do*] *SRO*; how you do *Windsor* |
| **19.247** | *hit it off*] *SRO*; hit it off *Windsor* |
| | *did well*] *SRO*; did well *Windsor* |
| **19.250** | *Schutz*] *SRO*; Schutz *Windsor* |
| | chatter,] *SRO*; chatter *Windsor* |
| **19.254** | *Palladio*] *SRO*; Palladio *Windsor* |
| **19.258** | *Huntsman*] Huntsman *Windsor* |
| **19.259** | *Mason-Husband*] *SRO*; Mason-Husband *Windsor* |
| **19.260** | *Corinthian*] *SRO*; Corinthian *Windsor* |
| **19.261** | *his*] *SRO*; his *Windsor* |
| | *Ionic*] *SRO*; Ionic *Windsor* |
| **19.264** | end] *SRO*; send *Windsor* |
| **19.274** | *Europe's*] *SRO*; Europes *Windsor* |
| | Pow'r:] *SRO*; Pow'r *Windsor* |
| **19.279** | *can*] *SRO*; can *Windsor* |

## *Historical collation to 19 To the Queen*

| | |
|---|---|
| **19.3** | *ducktisk*] *ducktick SRO* |
| **19.6** | Like Hellebore so long 't has] *autograph insertion above deleted* That has so long like Rhubarb *SRO* |
| **19.20** | *Brudnal*] *autograph insertion in blank space SRO* |
| **19.25** | *Sundon*] *autograph insertion in blank space SRO* |
| **19.47** | In] *autograph correction from* I *SRO* |
| **19.71** | Constraints] Constraint *SRO* |
| **19.75** | Court Animal] Court-Animal *SRO* |
| **19.94** | more] worse *SRO, autograph insertion above deleted* more |
| **19.98** | name] *autograph insertion above deleted* neam *SRO* |
| **19.102** | *horrible*] *SRO*; horribly *Windsor* |
| **19.135** | Masters] Mesters *SRO* |
| **19.137** | *Le Behn*] *autograph insertion of* ehn *after* Le B *SRO* |
| **19.139** | *Schutz*] *autograph insertion in blank space SRO* |
| | *Lifford*] *autograph insertion in blank space SRO* |
| **19.140** | *Slone*] *autograph insertion in blank space SRO*; *above deleted* Stone *Windsor* |
| **19.144** | hear] *autograph insertion above deleted* here *SRO* |
| | *Montandre*] *autograph insertion in blank space SRO* |
| **19.158** | Strain] Stain *Windsor* |
| **19.160** | *Clermont*] *autograph insertion in blank space SRO* |
| **19.162** | Oak.] Oak *SRO* |

**19.166** *Kent*] *autograph insertion of* ent *after* K *SRO*
*Stone*] *autograph insertion of* tone *after* S *SRO*
**19.168** Envy will] will Envy *SRO*
**19.169** *Stone*] *autograph insertion of* tone *after* S *SRO*
*Grace*] *autograph insertion in blank space SRO*
**19.170** *Backenswants*] *autograph insertion in blank space SRO*
*Pomfret's*] *autograph insertion in blank space SRO*
**19.213** *Newcastle*] *autograph insertion in blank space SRO*
**19.223** *Shaw*] *autograph insertion in blank space SRO*
**19.225** *Cabinet*] *autograph insertion in blank space SRO*
**19.228** *Teed*] *autograph insertion in blank space SRO*
*Purcel*] *autograph insertion in blank space SRO*
**19.230** *Gold-Keys*] *autograph insertion in blank space SRO*
**19.231** *Willmington*] *autograph insertion in blank space SRO*
**19.234** *Harrington*] *autograph insertion in blank space SRO*
*Ilay*] *autograph insertion in blank space SRO*
**19.236** *Argyle*] *autograph insertion of* rgyle *after* A *SRO*
**19.238** *Hare*] *autograph insertion in blank space SRO*
**19.240** *Sherlock*] *autograph insertion of* herlock *after* S *SRO*
**19.242** *Gibson*] *autograph insertion of* ibson *after* G *SRO*
*Potter*] *autograph insertion in blank space SRO*
**19.243** *Grantham*] *autograph insertion of* rantham *after* G *SRO*
*Grafton*] *autograph insertion in blank space SRO*
**19.244** Let one] *above deleted* Whilst that *SRO*
**19.246** T'other] *above deleted* Let This *SRO*
**19.248** *Selkirk*] *autograph insertion of* elkirk *after* S *SRO*
**19.250** *Schutz*] *autograph insertion in blank space SRO*
**19.252** *Pembroke*] *autograph insertion in blank space SRO*
**19.254** *Palladio*] *autograph insertion in blank space SRO*
**19.258** *Huntsman*] *Hunstman SRO*
**19.264** end] send *Windsor*
**19.277** to trifles] *autograph insertion above the line SRO*
**19.279** He] *autograph emendation from* he *SRO*
**19.284** Whose] *autograph insertion above deleted* Whilst *SRO*

## *Emendations to 20 A Satire in the Manner of Persius*

**main source** *1739*: *A Satire in the Manner of Persius: in a Dialogue between Atticus and Eugenio. By a Person of Quality* (London: for J. Clarke and J. Robinson, 1739)
**complementary sources** *Delany*: Delany MS [1], item 22, Lilly Library, Indiana University
*Add. 28101*: BL Add. MS 28101, ff. 6r–8v
*Longleat*: Portland Papers (Longleat), XX, ff. 86r–91v
*1730*: *A Satyr in the Manner of Persius. In a Dialogue between the Poet and his Friend. By a Certain* E*NGLISH* N*OBLEMAN* (London [i.e. Dublin]: s.n., 1730)
*Select Poems*: *Select Poems from Ireland* (London: for T. Warner, 1730), pp. 1–14
*Norfolk*: *The Norfolk Poetical Miscellany* (London: for the author, 1744), pp. 147–60

*SRO*: SRO 947/53/1, pp. 194–202
*Dodsley*: Dodsley, *Collection* (1758), V, 147–55

**20.7** *That,*] *That 1739*
**20.56** discern,] *Add. 28101, 1730, Dodsley*; discern *1739*
**20.110** thought] *all complementary sources*; Thought *1739*
**20.172** refin'd?] *Delany, Add. 28101, Longleat, Select Poems, Norfolk, Dodsley*; refin'd. *1739*
**20.176** loath] *all complementary sources except SRO*; loth *1739*

## *Historical collation to 20 A Satire in the Manner of Persius*

**20.** *title*] A Dialogue between the Poet and his Friend *Delany, Add. 28101, Norfolk Miscellany*; The Poet and his Friend: a Dialogue *Longleat*; A Satyr. In the Manner of *PERSIUS*. In a Dialogue between the POET and his FRIEND. By a Certain English Nobleman *1730*; A Satyr in the Manner of *PERSIUS*, in a Dialogue between the POET and his FRIEND. By an English Nobleman *Select Poems*; A SATIRE in the Manner of PERSIUS, in a Dialogue between ATTICUS and EUGENIO. By the late Lord HERVEY *Dodsley*; A Satire in the manner of Persius. *1739*. Atticus, Eugenio. *SRO*.
**20.1** ATTICUS] Poet *all complementary sources except SRO*
**20.4** hath] has *Delany, Add. 28101, Longleat, 1730, Select Poems, Norfolk*
**20.8** the] these *Longleat*
**20.9–11** *not in Longleat, Norfolk*
**20.10** and] or *Delany, Add. 28101*
Poor] meek *Delany, Add. 28101, Dodsley*; Weak *1730, Select Poems*
**20.14** reek] wreck *Delany*; wreak *Add. 28101, Longleat, Norfolk*; wrack *1730*; rack *Select Poems*; reck *Dodsley*
**20.17** O'er] On *1730, Select Poems*
**20.19** Hath] Has *Add. 28101, Longleat, 1730, Select Poems, Norfolk*
hungry] Haughty *Longleat, Norfolk*; angry *Select Poems*
**20.20** Member] ****** *1730*
**20.21** acts] Act *Delany*
**20.22** Int'rest] Int'rests *Longleat, Norfolk*
**20.26–32** not in *Longleat, Norfolk*
**20.26** Senate's] ****** *1730*; S——s *Select Poems*
**20.28** partial Judges] hireling Judges *Delany, Add. 28101, Dodsley*; —— —— *1730*; hireling J——s *Select Poems*
**20.29** hath] has *Delany, Add. 28101, 1730, Select Poems*
**20.30–31** What then? | They have] What then? They've *Delany, Add. 28101, 1730, Select Poems*
**20.32** Wrong that bears] wrongs that bears *1730*; Wrongs that bear *Select Poems*
**20.33** Besides, such Thoughts] Such Thoughts as these *Longleat, Norfolk*
**20.36** our] her *Delany, Add. 28101, Longleat, 1730, Select Poems*
**20.40** youthful] grateful *1730, Select Poems*
**20.42** Pleasures] pleasure *Delany, Add. 28101, Longleat, 1730, Select Poems, Norfolk*
despise] Disguise *Select Poems*

20.45 soon] still *Delany, Longleat, 1730, Select Poems, Norfolk*
shalt] shall'st *Longleat*
20.50 thou] you *all complementary sources except SRO*
20.51 when] then *1730*
thou] you *all complementary sources except SRO*
length] last *Add. 28101, Longleat, 1730, Select Poems, Norfolk*
20.52 Men] they *Delany, Add. 28101, Longleat, 1730, Select Poems*
your] thy *1730, Select Poems*
20.53 never their Demerits] their Demerits never *Select Poems*
20.55 Mischief] Mischiefs *Longleat, 1730, Select Poems*
20.59 Injuries] injury *Delany, Add. 28101, Longleat, Norfolk*
20.60 And] Or *Delany, Add. 28101, Longleat, 1730, Select Poems, Norfolk*
Evils] Evil *Delany, Add. 28101, Norfolk*
20.61 EUGENIO] Friend *Delany, Add. 28101, Longleat, 1730, Select Poems, Norfolk*
20.62 the] this *Longleat*
20.66 on] in *Longleat*
20.67 Store] Pow'r *Delany, Add. 28101, Longleat, 1730, Select Poems, Norfolk*
20.68 these] their *Longleat*
no more] *followed by* No more let past Events survive in you, | In Lights too faithful usher'd to my View *Delany, Add. 28101, Longleat, 1730, Select Poems, Norfolk*
20.69 dislodge] but drive *Longleat, Norfolk*
my Breast] the Breast *Add. 28101, 1730, Select Poems*
20.70 And] Or *Delany, Add. 28101, Longleat, 1730, Select Poems, Norfolk*
her] the *Select Poems*
20.73 unfeign'd Afflictions] from real Causes *Delany, Add. 28101, Longleat, 1730, Select Poems, Norfolk*
20.74 our Cure] the Cure *Add. 28101, Longleat, Norfolk*
20.81 should be light, who am for all prepar'd] shou'd, who am for all Events prepar'd *1730*; should not gall, who am for all prepar'd *Select Poems*
20.82 Disappointments] disappointment *Delany, Add. 28101, Longleat, Norfolk*
20.83 hath] has *all complementary sources except SRO*
all Hopes] the hope *Delany, Add. 28101, Longleat, 1730, Select Poems, Norfolk*
20.89 where] when *Delany, Add. 28101, Longleat, 1730, Select Poems, Norfolk*
20.90 In] I *Select Poems*
20.91 the Heart's] their Heart's *Delany, Longleat*
the same.] *followed by* This shews the Foe, that hides it in the Friend, | The Road is various, but the same's the End *Delany, 1730, Select Poems*; This shews the Foe — That hides within the Friend — | The Road is various — but the same, the End *Add. 28101*; This shews the Foe, that hides it in the Friend, | The Road is various, but the same the End *Longleat, Norfolk*
20.93 On] So *Longleat*; For *Select Poems*
20.94 That] It *Longleat*
20.95 And hence] And thence *Delany, Add. 28101, Norfolk, Dodsley*; From it *Longleat*; From this *Select Poems*
honey'd] Honey *Longleat*
20.96 suspected what at last] suspect what at the last *1730*

| | |
|---|---|
| **20.97** | 'em] them *Longleat, 1730* |
| **20.99** | learn'd] earn'd *Add. 28101, Longleat, Norfolk* |
| | Science] Silence *1730, Select Poems* |
| **20.100** | dear] high *Delany, Add. 28101, Longleat, 1730, Select Poems, Norfolk* |
| **20.101** | by] my *Delany, Add. 28101, Longleat, 1730, Norfolk, Dodsley* |
| **20.103** | an Human] a human *Add. 28101, Longleat, 1730, Select Poems, Norfolk, Dodsley* |
| **20.104** | specious] spacious *1730* |
| | Wile] wiles *Longleat* |
| **20.105** | Smile] Smiles *Longleat* |
| **20.107** | That] Who *Delany, Add. 28101, Longleat, 1730, Select Poems, Norfolk* |
| **20.111** | Th'effects] Th'Effect *Longleat* |
| **20.113** | their Children's] the Children's *SRO* |
| **20.124–5** | *not in 1730, Select Poems; follows lines 126–7 Delany, Longleat, Norfolk* |
| **20.124** | Who talks on any] Discussing ev'ry *Delany, Add. 28101, Longleat, Norfolk* |
| **20.127** | and] or *Delany, 1730, Select Poems, Dodsley* |
| **20.128** | Of him, as] Him as the *Delany, Add. 28101, Longleat, 1730, Select Poems, Norfolk* |
| | Thought] Thoughts *1730* |
| **20.130** | cautionless] cautiously *Dodsley* |
| **20.131** | Treasures] Treasure *Delany, Longleat, 1730, Select Poems, Norfolk* |
| **20.134** | the] an *Add. 28101, Norfolk* |
| **20.137** | Sorrows] sorrow *Add. 28101, Norfolk* |
| **20.139** | Men] Man *Add. 28101, 1730, Select Poems* |
| **20.140** | season] seasons *1730, Select Poems* |
| **20.141** | Hope, nor Fear] hopes, not fears *1730*; Hopes, nor Fears *Select Poems* |
| **20.142** | Enjoy] Enjoys *Select Poems* |
| | risque] risques *Select Poems* |
| **20.143** | These] Him *Select Poems* |
| | Luxury of slothful Ease] Slothful Luxury of Ease *Delany, Add. 28101, Longleat, 1730, Select Poems* |
| **20.144** | downy Beds] beds of down *Delany, Add. 28101, Longleat, 1730, Select Poems, Norfolk* |
| **20.145** | While] Whilst *Delany, 1730, Select Poems* |
| **20.146** | Sorrows] Honors *Longleat* |
| **20.148** | ev'n those] the poor *Select Poems* |
| **20.150** | still] long *Select Poems* |
| **20.153** | that] when *Delany, Add. 28101, Longleat, 1730, Select Poems, Norfolk* |
| **20.155** | while] whilst *Delany, Add. 28101, 1730, Select Poems* |
| | Contest] Contests *Delany, Add. 28101, Longleat, 1730, Select Poems, Norfolk* |
| **20.156** | apposite] opposite *1730, Select Poems* |
| **20.158** | Zest] Test *Select Poems, Dodsley* |
| | lengthen'd] learned *1730* |
| **20.159** | said] cry'd *Add. 28101, Longleat, Norfolk* |
| **20.160** | Breast] heart *Delany, Add. 28101, Longleat, Norfolk* |
| **20.164** | Friendships] Friendship *Select Poems, Dodsley* |
| **20.165** | judg'd] judge *Delany* |

| | |
|---|---|
| **20.166** | Soul] Heart *Delany, Add. 28101, Longleat, 1730, Select Poems, Norfolk* |
| **20.171** | who] whom *Delany, Add. 28101, Longleat, 1730, Select Poems, Norfolk* |
| **20.172** | such] those *all complementary sources except SRO* |
| **20.174** | Death] Wound *Delany, Add. 28101, Longleat, 1730, Select Poems, Norfolk* |
| **20.175** | when] whilst *Delany, Add. 28101, 1730, Select Poems* |
| **20.179** | mean] main *1730, Select Poems* |
| **20.180** | prospers, but] prospers best *1730, Select Poems* |
| **20.181** | ATTICUS] Poet *Delany, Add. 28101, Longleat, 1730, Select Poems, Norfolk* |
| **20.182** | the Friendships] and Friendships *Delany*; the Friendship *Select Poems, Dodsley, SRO* |
| **20.183** | EUGENIO] Friend *Delany, Add. 28101, Longleat, 1730, Select Poems, Norfolk* |
| **20.184** | ATTICUS] Poet *Delany, Add. 28101, Longleat, 1730, Select Poems, Norfolk* |
| | I hope] and hope *all complementary copies except SRO* |
| **20.185** | steddy] stable *Delany, Add. 28101, Longleat, 1730, Select Poems, Norfolk, Dodsley* |
| **20.185–7** | who view with steddy Eyes, \| This shifting Scene; who, temp'rate, firm, and wise] who temp'rate, firm and wise; \| Can view this shifting Scene with stable Eyes *Add. 28101, Longleat, Norfolk* |
| **20.186** | This shifting] The shifting *Delany, Dodsley*; This trifling *Select Poems* |
| **20.187** | bear] stand *Delany, 1730, Select Poems*; brave *Add. 28101, Longleat, Norfolk* |
| **20.188** | look] looks *1730* |
| | Disappointments] disappointment *Delany* |
| **20.189** | consequential] necessary *1730, Select Poems* |
| **20.194** | Heav'n thus rightly] Heaven rightly *1730*; Heav'n once rightly *Select Poems* |
| **20.198** | Gives a] It gives *Delany, Add. 28101, 1730, Select Poems*; Opens *Longleat, Norfolk* |
| | Prospect] prospects *Delany, Add. 28101, Longleat, 1730, Select Poems, Norfolk* |
| **20.199** | thence] hence *Delany, Add. 28101, Longleat, Norfolk*; here *1730, Select Poems* |
| **20.201** | sooths] smooths *Delany, Add. 28101, Longleat, Norfolk*; calms *1730, Select Poems* |
| **20.202** | this] his *SRO* |
| | Pain] Care *1730, Select Poems* |
| **20.204** | *Freind*] Hulse *Longleat, Norfolk* |
| | have] hath *1730* |
| **20.205** | and] or *Delany, Add. 28101, Longleat, 1730, Select Poems, Norfolk* |
| **20.209** | He] Who *1730, Select Poems* |
| **20.210** | Nor] Not *1730* |
| **20.214** | are] is *Delany, Add. 28101, Longleat, Norfolk* |
| | Comforts] Comfort *Delany, Add. 28101, Longleat, Norfolk* |
| **20.215** | Comforts] Comfort *Delany, Add. 28101, Longleat, Norfolk* |
| **20.216** | Foundation] Foundations *1730, Select Poems* |
| **20.217** | unsubject] not subject *Add. 28101, Longleat, Norfolk* |
| **20.221** | the] thy *1730, Select Poems* |
| **20.222** | my Friend] elate *Delany, Add. 28101, Longleat, 1730, Select Poems, Norfolk* |
| | fondness] Kindness *1730, Select Poems* |
| **20.223** | on] in *Longleat* |

**20.224** With Patience each capricious Change] Submissive each Vicissitude *1730*; Submissive such Vicissitude *Select Poems*
**20.227** grand Precept] Reflection *1730, Select Poems*
wav'ring] wand'ring *1730, Select Poems*
**20.229** rashly] slightly *1730, Select Poems*
his] her *all complementary sources except SRO*
**20.230** he] she *all complementary sources except SRO*
**20.231** his] her *all complementary sources except SRO*
**20.233** His] Her *all complementary sources except SRO*
his] her *Add. 28101, Longleat, 1730, Select Poems, Norfolk, Dodsley*

## *Emendations to 21 Lord Bolingbroke, to Ambition In Imitation of Horace. Ode I, Lib. 4.*

**main source** *Welbeck*: Lord Bolingbroke to Ambition, In Imitation of Horace to Venus. Ode 1st. Book 4th., Portland Papers (Nottingham University), Pw V 784
**complementary sources** *Harley*: BL Harley 7318, ff. 22r–23r
*1728*: 'Harry Gambol's Soliloquy. In Imitation of Horace. Ode I. Lib. 4', in *As Much As May Be Publish'd of a Letter from the* Late B— of R-ch-r to Mr. —. *To which Are Added, the Several Advertisements for which Mr. Wilkins Was Assaulted at the Crown Tavern in Smithfield* (London: for A. Moore, [1728]), pp. 25–7; fictitious imprint
*1731*: 'Ode to Ambition', in *The History of the House of Lorraine* (London: [for E. Curll], 1731)
*1737*: *The False Patriot's Confession, or B—k's Address to Ambition* (London: for R. Charlton, 1737)

*no emendations made*

## *Historical collation to 21 Lord Bolingbroke to Ambition In Imitation of Horace. Ode I, Lib. 4.*

**21.** *title*] *Harry Gambol*'s Soliloquy. *In Imitation of* HORACE. Ode I. Lib. 4. *1728*; Ode to Ambition *1731*; *The False Patriot's Confession*; *or, B—k's Address to Ambition 1737*
**21.1** Oh!] Ah! *1728*; O *1731, 1737*
**21.4** should] shall *1731*
**21.5** Thankfull] Joyful *1728*
I have] I've *1728, 1731, 1737*
thy] the *1728, 1737*
**21.6** to] now *1728, 1737*
**21.9** Anna] A—a *1737*
**21.11** even] ev'n *1728, 1737*; e'en *1731*
Brunswicks] *B—k's 1737*
**21.12** this] the *1728*
**21.13** But] And *1737*
**21.14** Arts] Art's *1728*;
Falsehoods] Falshood's *1728*; Falshood *1731*

| | |
|---|---|
| **21.18** | Thy] My *1731, 1737* |
| **21.19** | I in] *not in Harley* |
| | Parliaments] Parliament *1728, 1737* |
| **21.20** | Royal] Regal *1728, 1731, 1737* |
| **21.21** | this] the *1728* |
| **21.22** | Me] The *Harley* |
| **21.23** | Let George, or James, then wear] Whatever Monarch wears *1731*; G——e or J——s *1737* |
| **21.25** | Credulous] cred'lous *1728, 1737*; luscious *1731* |
| | or] and *1737* |
| **21.26** | now] then *1731* |
| **21.27** | Dawley's homely] D- - - -'s humble *1728*; *Dawley's* Rural *1731*; *D——y's* homely *1737* |
| **21.29** | Assert] Assist *1728* |
| | King] King's *1737* |
| | Laws] Cause *1728, 1731, 1737* |
| **21.32** | by Cursed Chance] the dire Mischance *1731* |
| **21.33** | Walpole's] *W- - - -*'s *1728*; *W——le*'s *1737* |
| **21.38** | And jumble] And publish *1728*; With humble *1737* |
| **21.41** | I've wrote] I'm at *1728*; I've wrought *1731, 1737* |
| **21.42** | alas] alike *1728* |

## *Emendations to 22 To the Imitator of the First Satire of the Second Book of Horace*

**main source** *Ickworth: To the Imitator of the Satire of the Second Book of Horace* (London: [Sam Aris] for J. Roberts, 1733), annotated by Hervey and bound up as the second item in a collection of five held by the National Trust at Ickworth, 18.B.4.8
**complementary sources** *Add. 35335*: BL Add. MS 35335, ff. 53r–54v
*Add. 31152*: BL Add. MS 31152, 25r–26v
*Bodley*: Bodleian MS Eng. misc. c. 399, ff. 76r–77v
*Longleat*: Portland Papers (Longleat), PO XIX, ff. 149r–150v
*Welbeck*: Portland Papers (Nottingham University), Pw V 118/6, pp. 128–31 rev.
*SRO*: SRO 941/53/1, pp. 37–40
*Roberts*: *To the Imitator of the Satire of the Second Book of Horace* (London: [Sam Aris] for J. Roberts, 1733)
*Dodd A, B, C*: *Verses Address'd to the Imitator of the First Satire of the Second Book of Horace. By a Lady* (London: for A. Dodd, 1733): 1st edn, Foxon V39 (*Dodd A*); 2nd edn, Foxon V41 (*Dodd B*), and '5th edn' (1735), Foxon V44 (*Dodd C*)

| | |
|---|---|
| **22.** | *To the Reader* 8. insinuate] insinua *page and thereby rest of word cropped Ickworth* |
| | *To the Reader* 10. greatest] greates *page and thereby rest of word cropped Ickworth* |
| | *To the Reader* 16. *this.*] *this Ickworth* |
| | *title* First] first *Ickworth* |
| **22.21** | *followed by autograph* ——Thine is just such &c —— *with cross in margins* |
| **22.34** | *confin'd,*] *confin'd: Ickworth* |

**22.57** *Head.*] *Bodley, Welbeck, SRO*; *Head Ickworth*
**22.96** sleep.] sleep *Ickworth*

## *Historical collation to 22 To the Imitator of the First Satire of the Second Book of Horace*

**22.** *title*] *To the Imitator of the Satire of the Second Book of Horace Roberts*; *Verses Address'd to the Imitator of the First Satire of the Second Book of Horace. By a* Lady *Dodd A–C*; To the Imitator of the 1st. Satire of the 2d: Book of Horace *Add. 35335*, *Add. 31152*; To the Imitator of the 1st. Satire of the 2d: Book of Horace. Ldy M W. Mountagu *Bodley*; To The Imitator of the 1st. Satire of the 2d. L. Horace Mr. P—pe by L—y Ma–y W—ly Describ'd by the Name Sappho *Longleat*; Verses Addres'd to the Imitator of the 1st. Satire of the 2d. Book of Horace by a Lady *Welbeck*; Verses addressed to the imitator of the first satire of the Second book of Horace. – – by a Lady. (Lady M. Wy. and Ld. H–y) *SRO*
*followed by epigraph*] *Si Natura negat, facit Indignatio versus Dodd B, C*
*To the Reader*] *not in all complementary sources*

**22.1** Columns] Volumes *Welbeck*
**22.7** views] view *Dodd A–C, Welbeck, SRO*
**22.8** mean] *above deleted* dull *Ickworth*; dull *all complementary sources*
**22.9–12** *lines above deleted* That *Spirit* he pretends to imitate, | Than heretofore that *Greek* he did translate *Add. 35335, Ickworth*; That Spirit he pretends to imitate, | Than heretofore that Greek he did translate *Roberts, Dodd A–C, Add. 31152, Bodley, Welbeck*; That Spirit he pretends to imitate, | That heretofore that Greek he did translate *Longleat*
*followed by* Broome would have told thee and have told thee true | That whilst the Paths of Horace you pursue *Add. 35335*
**22.13** is clear] and clear *Longleat*
**22.16** thy] than *corrected to* thy *SRO*
**22.17** *Dodd C adds footnote* *See Mr. *Pope*'s Epistle to Dr. *Arbuthnot*, p. 19; *SRO adds footnote* *See Mr. *Pope*'s Letter to Dr. *Arbuthnot*. p. 19
**22.19** like] the *Bodley*
**22.21** Weeds] Weed *Bodley*
**22.22–6** *following line 10 and preceding line 13 all complementary sources*
**22.24** Where] Whilst *Welbeck*
**22.25** Sign-Post] Sign=pott *Add. 31152*
**22.28** scarcely felt or seen] neither felt nor Seen *Longleat*
**22.29** is] like *Add. 31152*
**22.30** of] to *Dodd B–C, SRO*
**22.31** in *Hate*] the *Hate Welbeck*
**22.38–9** *lines not in Bodley*
**22.38** and] a *Add. 31152*; ang *corrected to* and *SRO*
**22.39** Bow] blow *Add. 31152*; Brow *Welbeck*
force] forge *Add. 31152*

| | |
|---|---|
| **22.40** | No] Nor *Dodd B, C, Add. 35335, Add. 31152, Bodley, SRO*; Nor *corrected to* No *Ickworth* |
| **22.40–41** | *lines not in Roberts, Dodd A, Longleat, Welbeck* |
| **22.41** | Thrones, nor Graves] Graves, Nor Thrones *Bodley* |
| **22.42** | *line preceded by* Nor only Justice vainly we demand, \| But even Benefits can't rein thy Hand; \| To this, or that, alike in vain we trust, \| Nor find thee less ungrateful than unjust *Roberts, Dodd A–C, Bodley, Longleat, Welbeck, SRO*; *followed by the same lines except* in vain we *becomes* we vainly *Add. 31152* |
| **22.42** | Not] Nor *Add. 31152* |
| | and] nor *Bodley* |
| **22.43** | thy] the *corrected to* thy *SRO* |
| **22.44** | soften] Softer *Longleat* |
| **22.53** | He] He'd *Roberts, Add. 35335, Longleat* |
| | *keyed to footnote* See Mr. *Pope*'s letter to Dr. *Arbuthnot*, p. 16 *Dodd C*; *keyed to footnote* See Mr. *Pope*'s Epistle to Dr. *Arbuthnot*, p. 16 *SRO* |
| **22.55** | *everlasting*] *perpetual corrected to everlasting SRO* |
| **22.56** | that] the *all complementary sources*; that *above deleted* the *Ickworth* |
| **22.57** | *your*] thy *Bodley* |
| **22.59** | (The] The *Dodd A–C, Welbeck, SRO* |
| | Offence:)] Offence. *Dodd A–C, Welbeck, SRO* |
| **22.61** | to libel] libel *corrected to* to libel *SRO* |
| **22.62** | draw'st] draws *Add. 31152* |
| | the Law] of Law *Bodley*; thy Law *SRO* |
| **22.70** | and] what *Bodley* |
| **22.71** | *Porcupines*] *Porcupine Dodd B, C, SRO* |
| **22.72** | Backs] Back *Dodd B, C, Add. 31152, SRO* |
| | shoot] shoots *Dodd B, C, SRO* |
| **22.75** | Whilst] While *Dodd C, SRO* |
| **22.76** | unwounding] unwounded *Bodley* |
| **22.77–80** | *lines deleted Add. 35335* |
| **22.78** | *little*] *puny Dodd B, C, SRO* |
| | *side note*] *not in all complementary sources* |
| | *line followed by* One over-match'd by ev'ry Blast of Wind, \| Insulting and provoking all Mankind. *Roberts, Dodd A–C, Add. 31152, Bodley, Longleat, Welbeck, SRO* |
| **22.79** | to keep Mankind] that keeps the world *Add. 31152* |
| **22.84** | we're] we are *Bodley* |
| **22.85** | then] do *Dodd A–C, Welbeck, SRO*; thou *Add. 31152* |
| **22.85–6** | *lines not in Bodley* |
| **22.86** | *side note*] *not in all complementary sources except Add. 35335* |
| **22.88** | as are] as *SRO* |
| **22.89** | yet] but *Add. 31152* |
| **22.92** | they] the *Add. 31152* |
| | prized] prais'd *Roberts*; prized *above deleted* prais'd *Ickworth* |
| **22.95–6** | And to thy Books shall ope their Eyes no more, \| Than to thy Person they would do their Door *all complementary sources* |

**22.98** When left forlorn] That leaves Thee thus *all complementary sources*; *above deleted* That leaves Thee thus *Ickworth*
**22.101** Whilst then] Then whilst *all complementary sources*; *above deleted* Then whilst *Ickworth*
**22.103** Assassin's] Assassin *Bodley*
**22.104** or] nor *Welbeck*
**22.107** thy] the *Longleat*
**22.108** through] thrô all *Longleat*

## *Emendations to 23 Dr Sherwin's Character design'd for his Epitaph*

**main source** *Sherwin*: BL Add. MS 51396, ff. 110r–111v
**complementary source** *Ford*: BL Add. MS 51396, ff. 112r–113r

**23.** *title* Sherwin's] Sherwyns *Sherwin*
Epitaph] Epita *at page-edge Sherwin*
**23.1** awkward] aukard *inserted above the line Sherwin*
**23.2** morals sound] morals than sound *than deleted Sherwin*
**23.3** travel'd] travelld *Sherwin*
Life's] *Ford*; lifes *Sherwin*
**23.5** Life,] *Ford*; Life *Sherwin*
**23.7** right,] right *Sherwin*
**23.8** talk'd,] talk'd *Sherwin*
**23.10** blame;] blame *Sherwin*
**23.11** at] at *above deleted* to? *Sherwin*
door,] door *Sherwin*
**23.12** Pow'r;] Power, *Sherwin*
**23.13** rule:] rule *Sherwin*
**23.15** good,] good *Sherwin*
**23.16** understood;] understood *Sherwin*
**23.17** deceived,] deceived *Sherwin*
**23.18** beleiv'd;] beleiv'd *Sherwin*
**23.19** pay,] pay *Sherwin*
**23.20** 'prentice] prentice *Sherwin*
**23.21** 'twixt] twixt *Sherwin*
**23.22** 'Tis] Tis *Sherwin*
**23.24** hold,] *Ford*; hold. *Sherwin*
**23.26** of ev'ry] of *before deleted* of *Sherwin*
Mind.] *Ford*; Mind *Sherwin*
**23.27** abject,] abject *Sherwin*
ranc'rous] rancorous *Sherwin*
**23.29** could,] could *Sherwin*
**23.30** Blood,] Blood *Sherwin*
**23.31** taste,] taste *Sherwin*
**23.33** recommend,] recommend *Sherwin*
**23.36** to ev'ry man] *above deleted* an equal *Sherwin*
**23.38** whore,] whore *Sherwin*

| | |
|---|---|
| **23.39** | times,] times *Sherwin* |
| **23.40** | Historian's] Historians *Sherwin* |
| | Poet's] Poets *Sherwin* |
| | Rhymes;] Rhymes *Sherwin* |
| **23.41** | swerv'd,] swerv'd *Sherwin* |
| **23.43** | rever'd,] *Ford*; rever'd *Sherwin* |
| **23.44** | spar'd;] spar'd *Sherwin* |
| **23.45** | Monk,] *Ford*; Monk *Sherwin* |
| **23.46** | drunk,] *Ford*; drunk *Sherwin* |
| **23.47** | control,] controul *Sherwin* |
| **23.48** | Soul;] Soul *Sherwin* |
| **23.49** | alike] a like *Sherwin* |
| **23.51** | Guest;] Guest *Sherwin* |
| **23.53** | safe;] *Ford*; safe. *Sherwin* |
| **23.55** | to] to *above deleted* from *Sherwin* |
| **23.56** | scurrilous,] scurrilous *Sherwin* |
| | Priest,] Priest *Sherwin* |
| **23.57** | caress'd] *Ford*; caresd *Sherwin* |

## *Historical collation to 23 Dr Sherwin's Character design'd for his Epitaph*

| | |
|---|---|
| **23.** | *title.*] Dr Sherwyns Character design'd for his Epita *Sherwin*; Parson F—d's Epitaph *Ford* |
| **23.1** | awkward] clumsy *Ford* |
| | Short] large *Ford* |
| **23.2** | Constitution more than morals sound] Morals and in Health alike unsound *Ford* |
| **23.3** | whilst he travel'd through] tho he touch'd not on *Ford* |
| **23.4** | The chearfullness of youth ran on to] His vicious Youth anticipated *Ford* |
| **23.16** | He ne'er considered, car'd, or] None by his Conduct thought he *Ford* |
| **23.17** | Nor others with stale Priestly tales] With priestly Tales he no man e'er *Ford* |
| **23.23** | fam'd] feign'd *Ford* |
| **23.27** | ranc'rous, sordid] and licentious *Ford* |
| **23.28** | He ly'd, he cheated, he defam'd, he stole] No Tye could bind him and no Law controll *Ford* |
| **23.30–1** | virtuous Blood, \| His] virtuous Blood; \| By wine, and Pox ennervated at Last \| His *Ford* |
| **23.32** | *line below deleted* The Wretch at last was impotently Chast *Ford* |
| **23.50** | He'd call] He dealt *Ford* |
| **23.55** | Condemn'd to ridicule, he's sav'd from] Expos'd to our Contempt he scap'd our *Ford* |
| **23.56** | scurrilous] profligate *Ford* |

## *Emendations to 24 The Difference between Verbal and Practical Virtue Exemplify'd*

**main source** *The Difference between Verbal and Practical Virtue Exemplify'd, In some Eminent Instances both Ancient and Modern. With a Prefatory Epistle from Mr. C—b—r to Mr. P.* (London: for J. Roberts, 1742)
**complementary sources** none

*no emendations made*

## *Historical collation to 24 The Difference between Verbal and Practical Virtue Exemplify'd*

*none; only one witness exists*

## *Emendations to 25 The Barber Turn'd Packer*

**main source** *Moore: The Barber Turn'd* Packer. *A New Ballad. To the Tune of* Packington's *Pound* (London: for A. Moore, 1730); fictitious imprint
**complementary sources** none

**208.4** *no emendations made*

## *Historical collation to 25 The Barber Turn'd Packer*

**main source** *The Barber turn'd* Packer. *A New Ballad. To the Tune of* Packington's *Pound* (London: for A. Moore, 1730); fictitious imprint
**complementary sources** none
*none; only one witness exists*

## *Emendations to 26 The Journalists Displayed*

**main source** *Wiseacre: The Journalists Displayed, A New Ballad. To the Old Tune of Lilleburlero* (London: by Peter Wiseacre in the Old Bailey, 1731); fictitious imprint
**complementary sources** *Johnson*: *The Journalists Display'd. A New Ballad. To the Old Tune of, Lullebullero* (London: for J. Johnson, 1731)
*Add. 51441*: BL Add. MS 51441, ff. 58r–58v
*Daily Courant*: *Daily Courant*, 5 February 1731
*London Journal*: *London Journal*, 6 February 1731
*Read's Weekly*: *Read's Weekly Journal*, 6 February 1731
*Brotherton*: Brotherton Lt 24, ff. 37r–v from back

**26.** *title* Lillebullero] *Johnson*; Lilleburlero *Wiseacre*

**26.2** *line in italics*] *all printed complementary sources*; *no italics Wiseacre*; *Flash;*] *Johnson, Daily Courant, London Journal, Read's Weekly*; Flash, *Wiseacre*

| | |
|---|---|
| **26.3** | rung] *Johnson, Brotherton, Daily Courant, London Journal, Read's Weekly*; sung *Wiseacre* |
| **26.4** | *line in italics*] *all printed complementary sources; no italics Wiseacre* |
| | *Trash;*] *Johnson, Daily Courant, London Journal, Read's Weekly*; Trash, *Wiseacre* |
| **26.10** | *line in italics*] *all printed complementary sources*; *no italics Wiseacre* |
| | *Flash;*] *Johnson, Read's Weekly*; Flash *Wiseacre* |
| **26.12** | *line in italics*] *all printed complementary sources*; *no italics Wiseacre* |
| **26.14** | Some-body's] some-body's *Wiseacre* |
| **26.18** | *line in italics*] *all printed complementary sources*; *no italics Wiseacre* |
| **26.20** | *line in italics*] *all printed complementary sources*; *no italics Wiseacre* |
| **26.22** | Some-body's] some-body's *Wiseacre* |
| **26.26** | *line in italics*] *all printed complementary sources*; *no italics Wiseacre* |
| **26.28** | *line in italics*] *all printed complementary sources*; *no italics Wiseacre* |
| **26.30** | Some-body's Fall] some-body's fall *Wiseacre* |
| **26.34** | *line in italics*] *all printed complementary sources*; *no italics Wiseacre* |
| **26.36** | *line in italics*] *all printed complementary sources*; *no italics Wiseacre* |
| **26.38** | Some-body's Fall] some-body's fall *Wiseacre* |
| **26.42** | *line in italics*] *all printed complementary sources*; *no italics Wiseacre* |
| **26.43** | well,] *Johnson*; well *Wiseacre* |
| **26.44** | *line in italics*] *all printed complementary sources*; *no italics Wiseacre* |
| | *Trash;*] *all printed complementary sources*; Trash. *Wiseacre* |
| **26.45** | no] *all complementary sources*; ro *Wiseacre* |
| | Bribery] *all complementary sources*; Brlbery *Wiseacre* |
| **26.46** | Some-body's] some-body's *Wiseacre* |

## *Historical collation to 26 The Journalists Displayed*

| | |
|---|---|
| **26.** | *title*] *no title Add. 51441* |
| | *Old Tune*] Tune *Brotherton* |
| | *of*] of, *Johnson, Daily Courant, London Journal, Read's Weekly* |
| | Lillebullero] Lilleburlero *Wiseacre* |
| **26.3** | rung] sung *Wiseacre, Brotherton*; rang *Johnson* |
| **26.4** | *Treasondom*] treasonum *Add. 51441* |
| **26.5** | Knavery] Knavey *Johnson* |
| **26.8** | the Devil] and the Devil *Johnson, Daily Courant, London Journal, Read's Weekly*; & y$^{e}$ D—l *Brotherton* |
| **26.9** | a] one *Add. 51441* |
| **26.10** | *Scribbledum, Fribbledum, Flash;*] &c *Add. 51441* |
| **26.11** | *Saturdays*] Saturday *Add. 51441.* |
| **26.12** | *Traytorum, Treasondum, Trash;*] &c *Add. 51441* |
| **26.13–16** | Popery Slavery &c &c *Add. 51441* |
| **26.16** | the Devil] and the Devil *Johnson, Daily Courant, London Journal, Read's Weekly*; & y$^{e}$ D—l *Brotherton* |
| **26.18** | *Scribbledum, Fribbledum, Flash;*] &c *Add. 51441* |
| **26.19** | when you've] when you have *Brotherton* |
| | them] 'em *Johnson, London Journal, Reed's Weekly* |
| **26.20** | *Traytorum, Treasondum, Trash;*] &c *Add. 51441* |

| | |
|---|---|
| **26.21–4** | Popery Slavery &c &c &c *Add. 51441*; Popery, Slavery, &ca. *Brotherton* |
| **26.24** | the Devil] and the Devil *Johnson, Daily Courant, London Journal, Read's Weekly Journal* |
| **26.26** | *Scribbledum, Fribbledum, Flash;*] &c *Add. 51441* |
| **26.28** | *Traytorum, Treasondum, Trash;*] &c *Add. 51441* |
| **26.29–32** | Popery Slavery &c &c *Add. 51441*; Popery, Slavery, &ca. *Brotherton* |
| **26.29** | *Bribery*] Bravery *Johnson.* |
| **26.32** | the Devil] and the Devil *Johnson, Daily Courant, London Journal, Read's Weekly Journal* |
| **26.33** | That the] The *Brotherton* |
| **26.34** | *Scribbledum, Fribbledum, Flash;*] &c *Add. 51441* |
| **26.35** | 'Twas just the same] The same that was *Add. 51441* |
| **26.36** | *Traytorum, Treasondum, Trash;*] &c *Add. 51441* |
| **26.37–40** | Popery Slavery &c &c *Add. 51441*; Popery, Slavery, &ca. *Brotherton* |
| **26.37** | *Bribery*] Bravery *Johnson.* |
| **26.40** | the Devil] and the Devil *Johnson, Daily Courant, London Journal, Read's Weekly Journal* |
| **26.41** | Complainants] Complaints *Johnson* |
| **26.42** | *Scribbledum, Fribbledum, Flash;*] &c *Add. 51441* |
| **26.43** | Give all of them Places] Give 'em Pensions and Places *Add. 51441* |
| | them] 'em *Johnson, London Journal* |
| **26.44** | *Traytorum, Treasondum, Trash;*] &c *Add. 51441* |
| **26.45** | no] ro *Wiseacre* |
| | Bribery] Brlbery *Wiseacre* |
| **26.46** | Irruption, Corruption] Irruptions Corruptions *Add. 51441* |
| **26.47** | Royalty] Loyalty *Johnson, Brotherton* |

## *Emendations to 27 The Patriots are Come*

**main source** *Walpole*: Horace Walpole, *A Collection of Letters from Horace Walpole, youngest son of Sr Robert Walpole Earl of Orford to Horace Mann resident at Florence, 1741–1786*, The Lewis Walpole Library, Yale University, I, letter 53 (16 October 1742)
**complementary sources** *Bodley*: Bodley MS Eng. misc. b. 48, f. 2
*PAC*: *The Patriots Are Come; Or, a New Doctor for a Crazy Constitution. A New Ballad. To the Tune of Derry Down* (London: for W. Webb, 1742)
*NCB*: *A New C—t Ballad* (Dublin [London?]: by James Stone, 1742)
*NM*: 'The Patriots are Come; Or, a Doctor for a Crazy Constitution. A New Ballad. To the Tune of, Derry Down', in *The New Ministry. Containing a Collection of All the Satyrical Poems, Songs, &c. Since the Beginning of 1742* (London: for W. Webb, 1742), pp. 20–5
*SMC*: *The S—te M—r's Are Come: Or a New Doctor for a Crazy Constitution. A New Ballad to the Tune of Derry Down* ([London?]: s.n., 1742)
*FHW*: 'The Patriots are Come; Or, a Doctor for a Crazy Constitution. A New Ballad. To the Tune of, Derry Down', in *The Foundling Hospital for Wit*, I (London: for G. Lion, 1743), pp. 20–4

| | |
|---|---|
| **27.** | *title*] *no title Walpole* |
| **27.20** | home."] home. *Walpole* |
| **27.28** | 'tis] *all printed complementary sources*; tis *Walpole* |

**27.42** can't] *all printed complementary sources*; cant *Walpole*
**27.49** can't] *all printed complementary sources*; cant *Walpole*
**27.53** Tho'] *all printed complementary sources*; Tho *Walpole*
**27.64** can't] *all printed complementary sources*; cant *Walpole*
**27.73** should] *NCB*; shoud *Walpole*
**27.80** tho'] *all printed complementary sources*; tho *Walpole*
**27.88** tho'] *PAC, NM, FHW*; tho *Walpole*
can't] *all printed complementary sources*; cant *Walpole*
**27.92** tho'] *all printed complementary sources*; tho *Walpole*
**27.100** review."] review. *Walpole*
**27.105** tho'] *all printed complementary sources*; tho *Walpole*

## *Historical collation to 27 The Patriots are Come*

*please note that the printed sources that lack some names replace these either with dots (NM sometimes), with dashes (NCB, SMC, NM sometimes) or with rules of varying lengths (PAC, FHW; NCB, SMC, NM sometimes); these have all been represented as rules in the list that follows*

**27.** *title*] *no title Walpole*; A New Ballad to the old Tune of Derry-down *Bodley*; *A New C—t Ballad NCB*; The Patriots are Come; Or a Doctor for a Crazy Constitution. A New Ballad. To the Tune of *Derry down PAC, NM, FHW*; The S—te M—r's Are Come: Or a New Doctor for a Crazy Constitution. A New Ballad to the Tune of Derry down *SMC*
**27.1** O] Old *NCB*
England] *E—g—d PAC, NM, SMC, FHW*
while] whilst *PAC, NCB, SMC*
**27.2** Rehearsing] And rehearse *NCB*
and the conduct] and conduct *NCB*
**27.3** And since] Since *NCB*
**27.4** I am] I'm *Bodley, PAC, NCB, NM, SMC, FHW*
think that] think *PAC, NCB, NM*
hint at] hint of *Bodley*
King] — *PAC, NCB, NM, SMC*
*followed by Derry down Bodley, PAC, NM, SMC, FHW*
**27.5** Son] S—n *PAC, NCB, NM, SMC, FHW*
Robin] R— *NCB*
**27.6** King] — *PAC, NCB, NM, SMC, FHW*
**27.7** But] And *NCB*
**27.8** *followed by Derry down PAC, NM, FHW*; *followed by &c. SMC*
**27.9** in] at *NCB*
St James's] St *J—s's PAC, NM, SMC, FHW*; *St. J— NCB*
**27.10** these] those *NCB*; the *FHW*
Ministers] M—rs *PAC, NCB, NM, SMC, FHW*
**27.11** think] reflect *Bodley, PAC, NCB, NM, SMC, FHW*
**27.12** They have made] They made *Bodley, PAC, NCB, NM, SMC, FHW*
King] —— *PAC, NCB, NM, SMC, FHW*

| | |
|---|---|
| | *followed by Derry down PAC, NM, FHW; followed by &c. SMC* |
| **27.15** | murmuring] murmurous *NCB* |
| **27.16** | these] the *NCB*; those *SMC* |
| | *followed by Derry down PAC, NM, FHW; followed by &c. SMC* |
| **27.17** | Cart'ret] C—— *PAC, NCB, NM, SMC, FHW* |
| | spoke thus] thus spoke *PAC, NM, FHW* |
| **27.20** | *followed by Derry down PAC, NM, FHW; followed by &c. SMC* |
| **27.21** | King] —— *PAC, NCB, NM, SMC, FHW* |
| | Lord] L—d *PAC, NM, SMC, FHW*; L— *NCB* |
| **27.23** | now bring] bring *NCB* |
| | whom] who *PAC, NM, SMC* |
| **27.24** | Let but me] Let me *PAC, NM, SMC, FHW* |
| | Walmoden] *W—d—n PAC, NM, SMC, FHW*; *W—n NCB* |
| | *followed by Derry down PAC, NM, FHW; followed by &c. SMC* |
| **27.25** | Walmoden] *W—d—n PAC, NM, SMC, FHW*; *W—n NCB* |
| **27.27** | I have] I've *Bodley* |
| | Son] S—n *PAC, NM, SMC, FHW* |
| **27.28** | *followed by Derry down PAC, NM, FHW; followed by &c. SMC* |
| **27.29** | howe'er-little] howe'er so little *NM* |
| | King] —— *PAC, NCB, NM, SMC, FHW* |
| | you] you are *PAC, SMC*; you're *NCB, NM, FHW* |
| **27.32** | King] —— *PAC, NCB, NM, SMC, FHW* |
| | *followed by Derry down PAC, NM, FHW; followed by &c. SMC* |
| **27.33** | your Admiralty] the A–l–y *PAC, NM, SMC, FHW*; your A—y *NCB* |
| | Treasury] T—y *PAC, NCB, NM, SMC, FHW* |
| **27.34** | save] have *NCB* |
| **27.35** | God] G—d *PAC, NCB, NM, FHW* |
| | both] C—rt *Bodley* |
| **27.36** | Walpole's] *W—p—*'s *PAC, NM, FHW*; *W—*'s *NCB, SMC* |
| | cyphers] Cyphers entire *FHW* |
| | Gasherry's vassals to] *Ga—ry's* to *PAC, NM, FHW*; *Ga—y's* to *SMC*; G —— Vassals to *NCB* |
| | *followed by Derry down PAC, NM, FHW; followed by &c. SMC* |
| **27.37** | Prince's] P—es *PAC, NM, SMC, FHW*; P—'s *NCB* |
| | Statesmen] St—s—n *PAC, NM, FHW*; St—sm—n *SMC* |
| **27.38** | So, as] So *FHW*; Though *NCB* |
| | long yours] long as yours *PAC, NCB, NM, FHW*; long you *SMC* |
| **27.39** | court-crew] Old Crew *PAC, NCB, NM, SMC, FHW* |
| | we'll] we *Bodley, PAC, NM, SMC* |
| **27.40** | Who] Whom *FHW* |
| | *followed by* Derry down *PAC, NM, FHW; followed by &c. SMC* |
| **27.41** | Grafton] *G—n PAC, NCB, NM, SMC, FHW* |
| **27.44** | *followed by Derry down PAC, NM, FHW; followed by &c. SMC* |
| **27.45** | court] C—t *PAC, NM, SMC, FHW*; C— *NCB* |
| **27.46** | Schutz] *S—z PAC, NCB, NM, SMC, FHW* |
| | Hanover] *H—r PAC, NM, SMC, FHW*; *H— NCB* |
| | tool] Fool *Bodley, PAC, NCB, NM, SMC, FHW* |
| **27.48** | Deloraine] *D—ne PAC, NM, SMC, FHW*; *D— NCB* |

*followed by Derry down PAC, NM, FHW*; *followed by &c. SMC*
27.49 all your] your *FHW*
court-nobles] C—t Nob—s *PAC, NM, SMC, FHW*; C—t Nobles *NCB*
27.50 courts] C—ts *PAC, NM, SMC, FHW*
27.51 parliament-Swiss] parliament-Switzers *Bodley*; P——t Swisses *PAC, NM, SMC, FHW*; P——t Switzes *NCB*
vote] v—e *NCB*
27.52 *followed by Derry down PAC, NM, FHW*; *followed by &c. SMC*
27.53 Newcastle's] N——'s *PAC, NM, SMC, FHW*; N—— *NCB*
he's] he is *NCB*
27.54 By] Thy *NCB*
Robin] R— *NCB*
27.56 Yet I] Yet I'll *Bodley, PAC, NCB, NM, SMC, FHW*
but I] but I'll *Bodley, PAC, NCB, NM, SMC, FHW*
*followed by Derry down PAC, NM, FHW*; *followed by &c. SMC*
27.57 is as] is a *NCB*
27.58 no more] less *NCB*
27.59 coward] C—d *PAC, NM, SMC, FHW*
27.60 call'd him a] call'd him once *Bodley, PAC, NM, SMC, FHW*; once call'd him *NCB*
rascal] R—l *PAC, NM, SMC, FHW*
use] treat *Bodley, PAC, NCB, NM, SMC, FHW*
*followed by Derry down PAC, NM, FHW*; *followed by &c. SMC*
27.61 since] as *NCB*
Elections] E—s *PAC, NM, FHW*; E—ns *SMC*
27.63 fool] F—l *PAC, NM, SMC, FHW*
27.64 fear, so his] fear, his *PAC, NM, FHW*
use] chouse *NCB*
*followed by Derry down PAC, NM, FHW*; *followed by &c. SMC*
27.65 Hardwicke] H—— *PAC, NCB, NM, SMC, FHW*
courts] C—t's *PAC, SMC*; C—rs *NM, FHW*
27.66 his law] the Law *SMC*
27.67 foreign] F—gn *PAC, NM, SMC, FHW*
27.68 I'll] I will *NCB*
and will cry] and cry *PAC, NM, SMC, FHW*
*followed by Derry down PAC, NM, FHW*; *followed by &c. SMC*
27.69 Countess] C—ss *NCB*
Wilmington] *W——n PAC, FHW, NCB, NM, SMC*
excellent] like your old *Bodley, PAC, NCB, NM, SMC, FHW*
27.70 trust with] trust at *Bodley, PAC, NM, SMC, FHW*
treasury] *T—y PAC*; T—y *NCB, NM, SMC, FHW*
not with it's] but not with the *NCB*
27.71 I've] I'm *Bodley, PAC, NM, SMC, FHW*; I am *NCB*
27.72 that] the *NCB*
throne] T—e *PAC, NM, FHW*; T— *NCB, SMC*
*followed by Derry down PAC, NM, FHW*; *followed by &c. SMC*
27.73 Perhaps now you] Perhaps you *NCB*
I should] I now should *NCB*

27.75 But we're] But we've *PAC, NM, SMC, FHW*; We've *NCB*
27.76 hands] H—ds *PAC, NM, SMC, FHW*
*followed by Derry down PAC, NM, FHW*; *followed by &c. SMC*
27.77 Pultney] P—y *PAC, NCB, NM, SMC, FHW*
27.78 great noble nothing] N—e, for nothing *PAC, NM, SMC, FHW*
27.80 *followed by* Derry down *PAC, NM, FHW*; *followed by &c. SMC*
27.81 Pultney] *P—y PAC, NCB, NM, SMC, FHW*
27.82 did] to a *NCB*
27.84 *followed by* Derry down *PAC, NM, FHW*; *followed by &c. SMC*
27.85 gaz'd] geer'd *NCB*
27.88 hand, tho' 'tis plain] hands tho' 'tis plain *Bodley, SMC*; Hands, but that *NCB*
*followed by Derry down PAC, NM, FHW*; *followed by &c. SMC*
27.89 foreign] F—gn *PAC, NM, SMC, FHW*
27.92 *followed by Derry down PAC, NM, FHW*; *followed by &c. SMC*
27.93 Walpole] *W—p—e PAC, NM, FHW*; *W— NCB*; *W—e SMC*
27.95 fleets] Fl—ts *PAC, NM, SMC, FHW*
provide and great] provide, great *PAC, NM, FHW*
armies] A—y's *PAC, SMC*; A—s *NCB*; A—mies *NM, FHW*
27.96 make] pay *NCB*
*followed by Derry down PAC, NM, FHW*; *followed by &c. SMC*
27.97 Monarch's] M—s *PAC, SMC*; M— *NCB*; M—'s *NM, FHW*
27.99 raptures] Rapture *NCB*
Lord] L—d *PAC, NM, SMC, FHW*
27.100 troops] T—ps *PAC, NM, SMC, FHW*; T—s *NCB*
review] r—w *PAC, NM, SMC, FHW*
*followed by Derry down PAC, NM, FHW*; *followed by &c. SMC*
27.101 England] Country *PAC, NM, SMC, FHW*; Country *above deleted* England *Bodley*; *E—d NCB*
thy state] your Fate *NCB*
27.102 thee] the *SMC*
thy fate] your State *NCB*
27.103 thou art] thou'rt *PAC, NM, SMC, FHW*
27.104 Whilst] With *PAC, NCB, NM, SMC, FHW*
Oppression] Opp—ss—n *PAC, NM, SMC, FHW*
Slav'ry's] Sl—v—y *PAC, NM, SMC, SMC, FHW*; Slavery *NCB*
Whilst Faction, Oppression] With Faction oppress'd *Bodley*
*followed by Derry down PAC, NM, FHW*; *followed by &c. SMC*
27.105 you have made] you made *NCB*
rogue] R—e *NCB*
Walpole] *W—e PAC, NM, SMC, FHW*; *W— NCB*
27.106 You are] You're *Bodley, PAC, NCB, NM, SMC, FHW*
27.107 I'm] I am *NCB*
27.108 where] were *SMC*
these] those *NCB*
changes] Ch—ges *PAC, NM, SMC, FHW*
*followed by Derry down PAC, NM, FHW*; *followed by &c. SMC*

## *Emendations to 28 Verses to the Memory of my Dearest Sister the Lady Elizabeth Mansel*

**main source** *SRO*: SRO 941/53/1
**complementary sources** *Yale*: 'Verses to the Memory of my dearest Sister Lady Barbara May; by Lord Hervey', Yale Osborn Shelves Poetry Box V/10

| | |
|---|---|
| **28.10** | paid;] paid, *SRO* |
| **28.12** | choice:] choice, *SRO* |
| **28.32** | Praise,] Praise *SRO* |
| **28.41** | Walks] *Yale*; walks *SRO* |
| **28.50** | with what] *Yale*; which *SRO* |
| | breath,] breath *SRO* |
| **28.63** | each] Each *SRO* |

## *Historical collation to 28 Verses to the Memory of my Dearest Sister the Lady Elizabeth Mansel*

| | |
|---|---|
| **28.** | *title*] Verses to the Memory of my dearest Sister Lady Barbara May; by Lord Hervey *Yale* |
| | *epigraph*] *not in Yale* |
| **28.4** | Fictitious] Fictious *Yale.* |
| **28.24** | *followed by additional couplet* The last faint Thought that lingers in my Mind \| Shall bear thy name, with dear Maria's join'd, *Yale* |
| **28.32** | merit] Virtues *Yale* |
| **28.33** | grace her] tune my *Yale* |
| **28.34** | her] my *Yale* |
| **28.35** | thy tomb] the Shrine *Yale* |
| **28.37** | inscribe] enroll *Yale* |
| **28.50** | with what] which *SRO* |
| **28.60** | conduct] convey *Yale* |
| **28.66** | fond] vain *Yale* |
| **28.70** | unending] Eternal *Yale* |

## *Emendations to 29 Poem on Lady Abergavenny*

**main source** *Yale*: Charles Hanbury Williams Collection, Yale University, vol. 84, f. 5r (no permanent call number, but currently Phillips 84–11402)
**complementary sources** *Add. 32463*: BL Add. MS 32463, f. 116r
*Harley*: BL MS Harley 7318, f. 128r
*Portland*: Portland Papers (Longleat), XX, f. 116r
*Universal Spectator*: *Universal Spectator*, 18 April 1730
*Grub-street Journal*: *Grub-street Journal*, 4 May 1730
*Poetical Magazine*: *Poetical Magazine* (London: by Dryden Leach for J. Coote, 1764), 5 (May 1764), 204

*Additions*: *Additions to the Works of Alexander Pope*, 2 vols. (London: for H. Baldwin, T. Longman and others, 1776), I, 155–6
*Hanbury Williams*: *The Works, of the Right Honourable Sir Chas. Hanbury Williams*, 3 vols. (London: Edward Jeffery and Son, 1822), I, 122–3

**29.2** care;] *Grub-street Journal, Poetical Magazine, Additions, Hanbury Williams*; Care *Yale*
**29.3** kindness] *Harley, Portland, Grub-street Journal, Poetical Magazine, Additions, Hanbury Williams*; Kindness *Yale*
**29.4** indulge the dictates] *Harley, Grub-street Journal, Poetical Magazine, Additions, Hanbury Williams*; Indulge the Dictates *Yale*
heart;] *Grub-street Journal, Poetical Magazine, Additions, Hanbury Williams*; heart *Yale*
**29.5** solicited] *Add. 32463, Additions, Hanbury Williams*; Solicited *Yale*
**29.6** envied] *Harley, Additions, Hanbury Williams*; Envied *Yale*
desir'd,] *Portland*; desird *Yale*
**29.7** torn,] *Add. 32463, Portland, Universal Spectator, Grub-street Journal, Poetical Magazine, Additions, Hanbury Williams*; torn *Yale*
**29.8** forlorn,] *Add. 32463, Portland, Universal Spectator, Grub-street Journal, Poetical Magazine, Additions, Hanbury Williams*; forlorn *Yale*
**29.9** talkers, insults] *Additions*; talkers Insults *Yale*
scorn;] *Poetical Magazine, Additions, Hanbury Williams*; Scorn *Yale*
**29.10** every idle] *Add. 32463, Universal Spectator, Poetical Magazine, Hanbury Williams*; Every Idle *Yale*
story told,] *Poetical Magazine, Additions, Hanbury Williams*; Story told *Yale*
**29.11** novel] *Grub-street Journal, Poetical Magazine, Additions, Hanbury Williams*; Novel *Yale*
lecture] *all complementary sources*; lectures *Yale*
old.] *Grub-street Journal, Additions*; old *Yale*
**29.12** scoffer] *Poetical Magazine, Additions, Hanbury Williams*; Scoffer *Yale*
relate] *all complementary sources*; relete *Yale*
**29.13** fate,] *Harley, Poetical Magazine, Additions*; fate *Yale*
**29.14** nature still] *Harley, Grub-street Journal, Poetical Magazine, Additions, Hanbury Williams*; Nature Still *Yale*
soft] *Harley, Poetical Magazine, Additions, Hanbury Williams*; Soft *Yale*
**29.15** fault;] *Poetical Magazine*; fault *Yale*
**29.16** conduct] *Harley, Grub-street Journal, Poetical Magazine, Additions, Hanbury Williams*; Conduct *Yale*
some steps] *Add. 32463, Harley, Grub-street Journal, Poetical Magazine, Additions, Hanbury Williams*; Some Steps *Yale*
**29.17** virtue's] *Harley, Poetical Magazine, Additions, Hanbury Williams*; Virtues *Yale*
**29.18** Yet] *all complementary sources*; Yett *Yale*
still] *Add. 32463, Harley, Universal Spectator, Grub-street Journal, Poetical Magazine, Additions, Hanbury Williams*; Still *Yale*
show'd] *Poetical Magazine, Hanbury Williams*; showd *Yale*

29.19 survive] *Add. 32463, Harley, Portland, Universal Spectator, Grub-street Journal, Poetical Magazine, Additions, Hanbury Williams*; Survive *Yale*
guilt] *Harley, Grub-street Journal, Additions, Hanbury Williams*; Guilt *Yale*
29.20 proved,] proved *Yale*
29.21 dearer] *Add. 32463, Harley, Portland, Universal Spectator, Grub-street Journal, Poetical Magazine, Additions, Hanbury Williams*; Dearer *Yale*
man] *Grub-street Journal, Poetical Magazine, Additions, Hanbury Williams*; Man *Yale*
lov'd] *Add. 32463, Harley, Universal Spectator, Grub-street Journal, Poetical Magazine, Additions, Hanbury Williams*; lovd *Yale*

## *Historical collation to 29 Poem on Lady Abergavenny*

29. *title*] On the Late Lady Abergavenny, Daughter of General Tatton *BL Add. 32463*; On Lady A *Harley*; *no title Portland*; *A Copy of Verses on —— Universal Spectator*; Verses on —— *Grub-street Journal*; Epitaph on Lady A****Y *Poetical Magazine*; *On Lady* A. *Additions*; ON LADY ABERGAVENNY *Hanbury Williams*
29.4 her] the *Additions, Hanbury Williams*
29.6 woman] Women *Add. 32463, Universal Spectator, Grub-street Journal, Poetical Magazine, Additions, Hanbury Williams*
man] Men *Add. 32463, Portland, Universal Spectator, Poetical Magazine, Additions, Hanbury Williams*
29.9 talkers] censures *Poetical Magazine*; talk, to *Hanbury Williams*
want] wants *Poetical Magazine*
29.11 the lecture] the lectures *Yale*; and Lecture *Add. 32463, Universal Spectator, Grub-street Journal*
the old.] *followed by additional couplet* Whil'st luckier Dames, their Thefts yet unbetray'd, | By conduct warrant what their Lips upbraid *Portland*
29.13 rigour or despight] rigour, or despise *Portland*; rigour's utmost force *Additions, Hanbury Williams*
29.14 soft] kind *Add. 32463, Universal Spectator, Grub-street Journal*
29.15 her ruin] the Ruin *Add. 32463, Portland, Universal Spectator, Grub-street Journal, Poetical Magazine*
whilst] while *Poetical Magazine, Additions, Hanbury Williams*
her fault] the Fault *Add. 32463, Portland, Universal Spectator, Grub-street Journal, Poetical Magazine*
29.17 virtue's] virtuous *Add. 32463, Universal Spectator, Grub-street Journal*
rules] rule *Harley, Poetical Magazine, Additions, Hanbury Williams*
too] so *Poetical Magazine*
29.19 her guilt] the Guilt *Add. 32463, Portland, Universal Spectator, Grub-street Journal*; the thought *Poetical Magazine*
though] but *Harley, Additions, Hanbury Williams*
her shame] the Shame *Add. 32463, Universal Spectator, Grub-street Journal, Poetical Magazine*
29.21 But] And *Add. 32463, Harley, Portland, Universal Spectator, Grub-street Journal, Additions, Hanbury Williams*

than them] far than *Add. 32463, Harley, Portland, Universal Spectator, Grub-street Journal, Poetical Magazine, Additions, Hanbury Williams*
man] Men *Harley*

## *Emendations to 30 Epitaph on Lady Elizabeth Mansel*

**main source** *Concise Description*: *A Concise Description of Bury St. Edmund's: And its Environs* (London: Longman, 1827 [1825–7]), pp. 203–4
**complementary sources** *SRO*: SRO 941/53/1, p. 218
*Rylands*: Special Collections, John Rylands University Library, University of Manchester, GB 133 Eng MS 737, f. 65r
*Yale fc.51*: Yale Osborn Collection fc.51, p. 223
*Topham*: Edward Topham, *The Life of the Late John Elwes, Esquire* (London: by John Jarvis for James Ridgway, 1790), p. 109
*Yale c.83/2*: Yale Osborn Collection c.83/2, no. 402
*Add. 46916*: BL Add. MS 46916, f. 9
*Gage*: John Gage, *The History and Antiquities of Suffolk. Thingoe Hundred* (London: by Samuel Bentley, 1838), pp. 317–18
*Ickworth*: *Ickworth Parish Registers. Baptisms, Marriages and Burials: 1566–1890*, ed. by S[ydenham] H[enry] A[ugustus] H[ervey] (Wells: Ernest Jackson, 1894), pp. 73–4

**30.** *title*] *no title Concise Description*
**30.2** dear,] *Topham, Yale c.83/2*; dear *Concise Description*
one,] *Rylands, Yale c. 83/2*; one *Concise Description*
**30.3** fair,] *Yale fc.51, Topham, Yale c. 83/2*; fair; *Concise Description*
**30.9** Mind,] Mind *Concise Description*
**30.15** Its] *Yale fc.51, Topham, Yale c. 83/2, Add. 46916*; It's *Concise Description*
its] *Yale fc.51, Topham, Yale c. 83/2, Add. 46916*; it's *Concise Description*

## *Historical collation to 30 Epitaph on Lady Elizabeth Mansel*

**30.** *title*] *no title Concise Description*; Epitaph on Lady Betty Mansel, on her Tomb-Stone in Ickworth Church *SRO*; Epitaph on Lady Eliz: Mansel by her brother Lord Hervey *Rylands*; By the late Lord Harvy, upon L$^{dy}$ B$^{y}$ Mansel *Yale fc.51*; To the Memory of *Lady E. Mansell*, Niece to the Mother of Sir Hervey Elwes *Topham*; To the memory of Lady E Mansell. true to the Mother of S$^{r}$ Hervey Elwes *Yale c.83/2*; On Lady Elizth Harvey by her brother L$^{d}$ Harvey *Add. 46916*; *no title Concise Description*
*epigraph*] *not in SRO, Rylands, Yale fc.51, Yale c.83/2, Add. 46916*
*a Templis*] e templis *Topham*
*trahet*] trahat *Topham*
*epigraph followed by Poem 60 before the current poem Topham, Yale c.83/2*
**30.5** social Paths of] paths of social *Yale fc.51*; social calls of *Topham, Yale c.83/2*
**30.6** and] or *Add. 46916*

| | |
|---|---|
| **30.7** | the] in *Gage, Ickworth* |
| **30.9** | Pious, Patient, Affable] pious, affable *Rylands* |
| **30.10** | Happy in] Happy thro' *Add. 46916* |
| **30.11** | those golden] her glorious *Add. 46916* |
| **30.12** | e'er] and *Add. 46916* |
| **30.13** | Fate] death *Add. 46916* |
| | untimely] for ever *Topham, Yale c.83/2* |
| **30.15** | when] whilst *Rylands*; while *Add. 46916* |

## *Emendations to 31a Epitaph on John, Duke of Marlborough*

**main source** *Dallaway: The Works of the Right Honourable Lady Mary Wortley Montagu*, ed. by James Dallaway, 5 vols. (London: for Richard Phillips, 1803), V, 156
**complementary sources** none

| | |
|---|---|
| **31a.4** | saw,] saw; *Dallaway* |
| **31a.5** | Gaul;] Gaul, *Dallaway* |

## *Emendations to 31b Epitaph on Anne Oldfield*

**main source** *GM: Gentleman's Magazine*, 1 (January 1731), 23
**complementary sources** *LEP*: *London Evening-Post*, 19 January 1731, p. 2
*WEP*: *Whitehall Evening-Post*, 19 January 1731
*Faithful Memoirs*: [Edmund Curll?], *Faithful Memoirs of the Life, Amours and Performances, of that Justly Celebrated, and Most Eminent Actress of her Time, Mrs. Anne Oldfield* (London: n.p., 1731), Appendix, p. 21
*Choice Collection*: *A Choice Collection of Poetry, by the Most Ingenious Men of the Age*, ed. by Joseph Yarrow, 2 vols. (York: by A. Staples, 1738), I, 21
*Folger*: Folger Shakespeare Library, W.b.11 (8)

*no emendations made*

## *Historical collation to 31a Epitaph on John, Duke of Marlborough*

*none; only one witness exists; but see collation of 31a and 31b below*

## *Historical collation to 31b Epitaph on Anne Oldfield*

| | |
|---|---|
| **31.a** | title *Epitaph on Anne Oldfield*] *Another [An Epitaph on Mrs.* OLDFIELD*] GM, Faithful Memoirs, LEP, Folger*; *On the Death of Mrs.* Oldfield *Choice Collection* |
| | *title* followed by Epigraph] Here lies the Body of ANNE OLDFIELD, the most celebrated Actress not only of her own Time, but of any other *LEP, Faithful Memoirs* |

## *Historical collation to 31a Epitaph on John, Duke of Marlborough (base-text) and 31b Epitaph on Anne Oldfield Anne Oldfield*

**31a.1–10** *not in GM*
**31a.14** hours] life *GM, LEP, WEP, Faithful Memoirs, Choice Collection, Folger*
him] her *GM, LEP, WEP, Faithful Memoirs, Choice Collection, Folger*

## *Emendations to 32 Epitaph on the Queen*

**main source** *Gentleman's Magazine*, 7 (December 1737), 759
**complementary sources** none

*no emendations made*

## *Historical collation to 32 Epitaph on the Queen*

*none; only one witness exists*

## *Emendations to 33 Lord Hervey's Epitaph upon the Earl of Bristol*

**main source** *Add. 5822*: BL Add. MS 5822, ff. 95v–96v
**complementary sources** *Gage*: *The History and Antiquities of Suffolk. Thingoe Hundred* (London: by Samuel Bentley, 1838), pp. 296–7, a modernised text of the BL manuscript

*no emendations, other than to remove underlinings of almost every phrase in the poem*

## *Historical collation to 33 Lord Hervey's Epitaph upon the Earl of Bristol*

*none; only one witness exists*

## *Emendations to 34 Lord Hervey's Epitaph on Himself*

**main source** SRO 941/53/1, p. 210
**complementary sources** none

*no emendations made*

## *Historical collation to 34 Lord Hervey's Epitaph on Himself*

*none; only one witness exists*

## *Emendations to 35 Epilogue Design'd for* Sophonisba

**main source** *Dodsley*: Dodsley, *Collection*, 1755, IV, 107–8
**complementary sources** *Select Collection*: *Select Collection of Modern Poems* (Edinburgh: sold by A. Donaldson, 1759), pp. 56–7
*Collection and Selection*: *A Collection and Selection of English Prologues and Epilogues* (London: for Fielding and Walker, 1779), vol. IV, 49–50

**35.23** charms] *Select Collection, Collection and Selection*; charm *Dodsley*

## *Historical collation to 35 Epilogue Design'd for* Sophonisba

**35.21** did she] did not *Select Collection, Collection and Selection*
the way] that way *Collection and Selection*
that sword] the sword *Collection and Selection*
**35.23** charms] charm *Dodsley*

## *Emendations to 36 Mr* Harvey's *Answer to a Lady, Who Ask'd Him,* What Is Love?

**main source** *Stowe*: BL MS Stowe 972 f. 4v(b)–5r
**complementary sources** *GM*: *Gentleman's Magazine*, I (July 1731), 305
*Brotherton*: Brotherton Lt 12, p. 26
*Complete Collection*: *A Complete Collection of Old and New English and Scotch Songs*, 4 vols. (London: by T. Boreman, 1736), IV, 184
*Universal Spectator*: *The Universal Spectator and Weekly Journal*, 26 March 1737
*Warbling Muses*: *The Warbling Muses* (London: for G. Woodfall, 1749), p. 185
*Winstanley*: *Poems Written Occasionally by the late John Winstanley . . .with Many Others*, ed. by George Winstanley, 2 vols. (Dublin: S. Powell, 1751), II, 266–7
*Collection of Poems*: *A Collection of Poems, from the Best Authors*, ed. by James Elphinston (London: by James Bettenham, 1764), p. 172
*Select Collection*: *A Select Collection of English Songs*, 3 vols. (London: for J. Johnson, 1783), I, 90–1
*Poetical Farrago*: *The Poetical Farrago*, 2 vols. (London: by G. Stafford for J. Deighton, 1794), I, 54–5

**36.12** Want] *Warbling Muses, Winstanley*; want *Stowe*
**36.15** 'Tis] *all complementary sources except Collection of Poems*; Tis *Stowe*
**36.16** 'Tis] *all complementary sources*; Tis *Stowe*

## *Historical collation to 36 Mr* Harvey's *Answer to a Lady, Who Ask'd Him,* What Is Love?

**36.** *title*] An Answer to What is love? *Brotherton*; *On* LOVE *GM*, *Winstanley*, *Collection of Poems*; *What is* LOVE? *Universal Spectator, Select Collection*; Song CLXXXIII. Blest as th' immortal gods *Complete Collection*; Song CCCCXLVII *Warbling Muses*; LOVE *Poetical Farrago*

**36.** *numbering*] *the stanzas in Brotherton are numbered in Arabic; those in all other texts except Stowe are unnumbered*

**36.2** of raging] or raging *Brotherton*

**36.3** That] Which *GM, Complete Collection, Universal Spectator, Warbling Muses, Winstanley, Collection of Poems, Select Collection, Poetical Farrago*
grows a] turns to *Brotherton*

**36.5** Not] Nor *Complete Collection*

**36.6** Who] That *GM, Complete Collection, Winstanley, Collection of Poems, Select Collection*

**36.7** dismal] senseless *Warbling Muses*

**36.8** only Heart] heart alone *GM, Complete Collection, Winstanley, Collection of Poems, Select Collection*; Sense alone *Universal Spectator*; heart so much *Poetical Farrago*
but] as *Poetical Farrago*

**36.9** is it centred] does it center *GM, Complete Collection, Winstanley, Collection of Poems, Select Collection, Poetical Farrago*

**36.10** in Order] by order *Brotherton, Select Collection*

**36.11** all consists] Sense appears *Universal Spectator*

**36.12** And] Who *Poetical Farrago*

**36.15** know] feel *GM, Complete Collection, Winstanley, Collection of Poems, Select Collection, Poetical Farrago*

**36.16** feel] know *GM, Complete Collection, Winstanley, Collection of Poems, Select Collection, Poetical Farrago*

## *Emendations to 37 To a Lady Who Ask'd,* What Is Love?

**main source** *Stowe*: BL Stowe 972 f. 12v(b)
**complementary sources** *Brotherton*: Brotherton Lt q 20, f. 34v
*Add. 75381*: BL Add. MS 75381, p. 82
*GM*: *Gentleman's Magazine*, 2 (July 1732), 870
*Craftsman*: *The Craftsman*, 1 July 1732 (repr. in 'Caleb D'Anvers', *The Craftsman*, 14 vols. (London: for R. Francklin, 1731–7), IX (1732), 162–3)
*Scarborough*: *The Scarborough Miscellany: for the Year 1734* (London: by J. Wilford, 1734), p. 54
*Warbling Muses*: *The Warbling Muses* (London: for G. Woodfall, 1749), pp. 187–8
*Miscellanea*: H.C., *Miscellanea Nova et Curiosa* (Dublin: by S. Powell, 1749), p. 341
*Lady's Curiosity*: 'Nestor Druid', *The Lady's Curiosity, or, Weekly Apollo* (London: by C. Sympson, 1752), p. 11
*Bouquet*: *The Bouquet: A Selection of Poems from the most Celebrated Authors* (London: by E. Hodson for J. Deighton, 1792)

*no emendations made*

## *Historical collation to 37 To a Lady Who Ask'd,* What Is Love?

**37.** *title*] To one who ask'd what Love is by Ld Hervey *Brotherton*; a Discription of Love *Add. 75381*; *To a Lady, who ask'd, what is* Love? *GM,*

*Craftsman, Miscellanea, Lady's Curiosity*; *To Miss* F— D—g, *who ask'd what is Love. By Mr.* Greenaway *Scarborough*; Song CCCCLIII *Conjectures concerning* Love *Warbling Muses*; *What Is Love? Bouquet*

**37.3** Subtle] sudden *Warbling Muses*

**37.4** Which Heaven did with] With which Heav'n did *Warbling Muses*

**37.6** while] whilst *Add. 75381, GM, Craftsman, Scarborough, Miscellanea, Lady's Curiosity, Bouquet*

**37.10** its] it *Add. 75381*

## *Emendations to 38 The Answer to a Receipt to Cure Love*

**main source** *Add. 47127*: BL Add. MS 47127, f. 172r

**complementary sources** *Recantation*: 'John Single', *The Batchelor's Recantation* (London: printed and sold by A. Dodd, 1731), pp. 11–12

*Miscellany*: *The Ulster Miscellany* ([Dublin?]: s.n., 1753), pp. 319–20

*Pocket-Book*: *The Ladies Complete Pocket-Book, for the Year of our Lord 1760* (London: for John Newbery, 1760), p. 16

**38.1** Physician,] *Recantation*; Physician *Add. 47127*

**38.9** knew,] *all complementary sources*; knew *Add. 47127*

**38.10** due.] *all complementary sources*; due, *Add. 47127*

**38.13** apply'd] *all complementary sources*; apply'd, *Add. 47127*

**38.14** Cure,] *Recantation*; Cure *Add. 47127*

**38.16** it's] *Pocket-Book*; its *Add. 47127*

**38.17** Cure,] *Recantation*; Cure *Add. 47127*

**38.19** Light,] *Recantation*; Light *Add. 47127*

**38.20** Furnace] *Recantation*; Furnace, *Add. 47127*

**38.21** View,] *all complementary sources*; View *Add. 47127*

**38.28** Air.] *Recantation*; Air *Add. 47127*

**38.30** upon the] *all complementary sources*; upon *Add. 47127*

restless] *all complementary sources*; Wrestless *Add. 47127*

## *Historical collation to 38 The Answer to a Receipt to Cure Love*

**38.** *title*] *Answer Recantation*; *a Receipt to Cure* LOVE *Miscellany*; *The Answer Pocket-Book*

**38.1** O] Ah! *Recantation, Miscellany*; Oh! *Pocket-Book*

**38.2** Of] But *Pocket-Book*

**38.3** apply] employ *Recantation, Miscellany*

**38.5** Perfections] *Perfection Recantation*

has] hath *Recantation*

just] such *Pocket-Book*

**38.6** And thaws] As warms *Pocket-Book*

**38.8** Blessings they] all they can *Miscellany*

**38.10** affords] can give *Miscellany*

**38.11** Speak] Bid *Pocket-Book*

**38.12** He] She *Add. 47127*

Torments] Torment *Recantation*

| | |
|---|---|
| | Pangs] rack *Miscellany* |
| **38.13** | Pains] Pain *Recantation, Pocket-Book* |
| **38.14** | There is no Cure alas! in Herbs] Alas in herbs there is no cure *Miscellany*; In herbs, alas! there is no cure *Pocket-Book*; *keyed to footnote Hei mihi quod nullis Amor est medicabilis herbis* Ov. *Recantation.* |
| **38.15** | has] hath *Pocket-Book* |
| **38.16** | it's] its *Add. 47127*; 'tis *Recantation, Miscellany* |
| **38.18** | 'em] them *Miscellany, Pocket-Book* |
| **38.19–20** | *not in Pocket-Book* |
| **38.19** | Wind puts] winds put *Miscellany* |
| **38.20** | But] And *Recantation* |
| | blaze] shine *Recantation* |
| **38.23** | for] her *all complementary sources* |
| | Favours] favour *Pocket-Book* |
| **38.24** | And I'm a] I am her *Recantation* |
| **38.28** | in Ermines] on Ermine *Recantation, Pocket-Book*; in ermine *Miscellany* |
| | tinge] catch *Pocket-Book* |
| **38.29** | the Art to be no more her] no more to be her humble *Miscellany* |
| **38.30** | upon the restless] upon Wrestless *Add. 47127* |
| **38.31** | you must] he must *Miscellany* |
| | ere you can find] e'er I can find *Recantation*; who'er conceits *Miscellany* |
| **38.32** | Fault] Faults *Recantation* |
| | Fault in her Person, blemish in her Mind] He can prescribe in Love, and write receipts *Miscellany* |
| | *followed by* My *Estimate* I have maturely scann'd, \| And chang'd Opinion on the better hand *Recantation* |

## *Emendations to 39 Extempore Epigram on Voltaire*

**main source** *Newport*: Holograph letter from Mary Pendarves, later Delany, to her sister Charlotte, 29 February 1728, Newport Reference Library, q M416.6/012/DEL
**complementary sources** none

*no emendations made*

## *Historical collation to 39 Extempore Epigram on Voltaire*

*none; only one witness exists*

## *Emendations to 40 A Receipt to Make an Epigram*

**main source** *Add. 70454*: BL Add. MS 70454, f. 63v
**complementary sources** *Yale 229/2*: Yale Osborn Collection c.229/2, ff. 7v–8r
*GM*: *Gentleman's Magazine*, 1 (November 1731), 495

*Grub-street Journal*: *Grub-street Journal*, 25 November 1731, repr. in *Faithful Memoirs of the Grubstreet Society* (London: for the Grubstreet Society, 1732), p. 139
*Weekly Amusement*: *The Weekly Amusement: or, The Universal Magazine* (15 March 1734; London: for J. and T. Dormer, 1735), II, 477
*Read's*: *Read's Weekly Journal*, 11 December 1736
*Yale c.152*: Yale Osborn Collection c.152, p. 37
*Joe Miller*: *Joe Miller's Jests: or, the Wits Vade-Mecum* (London: for T. Read, 1743), p. 141, and many reprints
*Nut-Cracker*: *The Nut-Cracker* (London: for J. Newbery, 1751), pp. 8–9
*Sports of Muses*: *The Sports of the Muses*, 2 vols. (London: by M. Cooper, 1752), II, 192

**40.4** Strong;] *Yale 229/2*; Strong *Add. 70454*
**40.6** quicker,] *Yale 229/2, GM, Grub-street Journal, Weekly Amusement, Nut-Cracker, Sports of Muses*; quicker *Add. 70454*
**40.11** flow.] *Yale 229/2, GM, Grub-street Journal, Weekly Amusement, Joe Miller, Yale c.152, Sports of Muses*; flow *Add. 70454*
**40.13** all-collected] *GM, Grub-street Journal, Yale c.152*; all collected *Add. 70454*
**40.14** observ'd,] *GM, Grub-street Journal, Weekly Amusement, Read's*; observ'd *Add. 70454*
Epigram's] *all complementary sources*; Epigrams *Add. 70454*

## *Historical collation to 40 A Receipt to Make an Epigram*

**40.** *title*] A Reciept to make an Epigram By the Right Honble Philip Earle of Chesterfield after the manner of the Cento Nuptialis of Ausonius Inscribed to his Frd Paul published by Dr James Tolliver in 8° Var *Yale 229/2; A* Receipt *to make an* Epigram: *By a* Noble Lord *Read's*; *A Receipt to Make an Epigram; said to be wrote by Lord Chesterfield Yale c.152*; *A* Receipt *to make an* EPIGRAM. *By the Right Hon. the late Lord* Hervey *Joe Miller, Nut-Cracker*; *A Receipt to make an* Epigram. *By Lord* Hervey *Sports of Muses*
**40.2** by] with *Joe Miller, Nut-Cracker, Sports of Muses*
**40.3** be] and *Read's*
**40.4** too] be *Nut-Cracker*
**40.5** In] For *Yale 229/2*
Numbers] *Measure Read's*
Use] chuse *Yale c.152, Read's*
**40.6** quicker] *slower Read's*
Slower] *quicker Read's*
choose] use *Yale 229/2, Read's*
**40.8** Thoughts] Thought *Read's*; That *Yale c.152*
**40.10** you] you'll *Yale c.152, Joe Miller, Nut-Cracker, Sports of Muses*
**40.11** For there not Wit alone] There all your Parts *Read's*
**40.12–13** *lines transposed Read's, Yale c.152; lines missing Yale 229/2, Joe Miller, Nut-Cracker, Sports of Muses*
**40.13** all] whole *Read's*

**40.14** These Rules observ'd] Observing these *Joe Miller, Nut-Cracker, Sports of Muses*
observ'd] observe *Yale c.152*

**40.15** And Sure to please] Nor fear 'twill tire *Joe Miller, Nut-Cracker, Sports of Muses*
altho' ten] tho' seven *Joe Miller, Nut-Cracker, Sports of Muses*

## *Emendations to 41 Note on Chiswick*

**main source** *Chatsworth*: letter addressed to the Countess of Burlington at Bath, Chatsworth House
**complementary sources** *Pw V 693*: Portland Papers (Nottingham University), Pw V 693
*Pw2 V 192*: Portland Papers (Nottingham University), Pw2 V 192
*Add. 8127*: BL Add. MS 8127, f. 71r
*GM*: *Gentleman's Magazine*, 6 (September 1736), 548
*Collection*: *A Collection of Select Epigrams* (London: for C. Hitch and L. Hawes, and W. and J. Flackton, 1757), p. 37
*NFH*: *The New Foundling Hospital for Wit*, IV (London: for J. Almon, 1771), 121–2

**41.** *title*] Not on Cheswick *Chatsworth*
**41.3** let] *Pw V 693, GM, Collection, NFH*; lett *Chatsworth*
**41.4** dwell.] *all complementary sources*; *dwell Chatsworth*

## *Historical collation to 41 Note on Chiswick*

**41.** *title*] Not on Cheswick *Chatsworth*; Not on Ch—sw—ck *Pw V 693*; *no title Pw2 V 192*; Verses *on the E— of* B—n *and his house at* Ch—k, *by the Author of* The Nobleman's Epistle to a Dr. of Divinity *GM*; Verses on the E— of B —, & His House at C—k. By the Author of the Noblemans Epistle to Dr Sherwyn *Add. 8127*; CXXXI *Collection*; Extempore Epigram on the Earl of Burlington and his House at Chiswick. By Lord Hervey *NFH*
*preceded by*] Atria longa paten. sed nec cænantibus usquam | Nec somno locus est, quam bene non habitas *Pw2 V 192*
**41.1** for] of *Pw V 693*
**41.2** to] too *GM*
**41.3** flattery] flatterers *Pw2 V 192*

## *Emendations to 42 Inscribed to Mr. Kent,*

**main source** *Chatsworth*: letter addressed to the Countess of Burlington at Bath, Chatsworth House
**complementary sources** *Pw V 693*: Portland Papers (Nottingham University), Pw V 693
*Pw2 V 192*: Portland Papers (Nottingham University), Pw2 V 192
*Add. 8127*: BL Add. MS 8127, f. 71r
*GM*: *Gentleman's Magazine*, 6 (September 1736), 548

*NFH*: *The New Foundling Hospital for Wit*, IV (London: for J. Almon, 1771), 121–2

**42.1** Architect] *Pw V 693, Pw2 V 192, Add. 8127*; Architeck *Chatsworth*
**42.3** spoil their] *Pw V 693, Pw2 V 192, GM, NFH*; spoile theire *Chatsworth*
fool,] *Add. 8127, GM, NFH*; fool *Chatsworth*
**42.4** we] *Pw V 693, Pw2 V 192, GM, NFH*; wee *Chatsworth*
**42.5** give!] *GM, NFH*; give, *Chatsworth*
**42.6** we] *Pw V 693, Pw2 V 192, GM, NFH*; wee *Chatsworth*
**42.9** Irreconcileable] *Pw V 693, Pw2 V 192, GM, NFH*; irreconciliable *Chatsworth*
**42.10** groping] *all complementary sources*; gropeing *Chatsworth*
**42.11** Lynxes'] Linx's *Chatsworth*
read;] *Pw V 693, GM, NFH*; read, *Chatsworth*
**42.13** close;] *Pw V 693, Pw2 V 192, GM, NFH*; close, *Chatsworth*
**42.14** inverting] *Pw V 693, Pw2 V 192, GM, NFH*; inventing *Chatsworth*
they] *all complementary sources*; the *Chatsworth*
**42.15** let] *Pw2 V 192, GM, NFH*; lett *Chatsworth*
cold;] *Pw2 V 192, GM, NFH*; cold, *Chatsworth*
**42.16** possest] *Pw V 693, Pw2 V 192*; posses't *Chatsworth*
**42.17** tho'] *Pw V 693, Pw2 V 192, GM, NFH*; thô *Chatsworth*
Guest;] *Add. 8127*; Guest, *Chatsworth*
**42.18** Stairs] *all complementary sources*; Staires *Chatsworth*
Mortal] *Add. 8127*; Mortall *Chatsworth*
go] *all complementary sources*; goe *Chatsworth*
**42.19** crown;] *Pw V 693, Pw2 V 192, GM, NFH*; crown, *Chatsworth*
**42.20** shape,] *Pw V 693, Pw2 V 192, GM, NFH*; shape *Chatsworth*
part,] *Pw V 693, Add. 8127, GM, NFH*; part *Chatsworth.*
**42.21** We] *Pw V 693, Pw2 V 192, GM, NFH*; Wee *Chatsworth*
**42.22** Yet] *all complementary sources*; Yett *Chatsworth*
Divine,] Divine *Chatsworth*
**42.24** been] *all complementary sources*; bin *Chatsworth*
**42.25** would] *all complementary sources*; *would Chatsworth*
can] *all complementary sources*; *can Chatsworth*

## *Historical collation to 42 Inscribed to Mr. Kent*

**42.** *title*] To Mr Kent *Pw2 V 192*; *no title Pw V 693*; Verses on Second Thoughts *GM, Add. 8127*; Verses on Second Thoughts on the Same Subject *NFH*
**42.7** design'd] assigned *all complementary sources*
**42.10** Halls] Hall *Pw V 693*
should] can *Pw2 V 192*
**42.11** where] were *GM*
eyes] eye *Pw V 693*
**42.14** inverting] inventing *Chatsworth*
they] the *Chatsworth*

| | |
|---|---|
| **42.15** | nor] or *GM, Add. 8127, NFH* |
| **42.16** | of full] full of *GM, Add. 8127, NFH* |
| **42.17** | to warm] warm *Pw2 V 192* |
| **42.18** | or] and *NFH* |
| **42.23** | When] We *Pw V 693* |
| **42.24** | amongst] among *Pw V 693, GM, Add. 8127, NFH* |

## *Emendations to 43 Response to Compliment from John Whaley*

**main source** *Add. 71125*: BL Add. MS 71125, f. 10v
**complementary sources** none

| | |
|---|---|
| **43.** | *title*] *no title Add. 71125* |

## *Historical collation to 43 Response to Compliment from John Whaley*

*none; only one witness exists*

## *Emendations to 44 Norfolk House*

**main source** *Add. 51441*: BL Add. MS 51441, f. 56r
**complementary sources** *Add. 28095*: BL Add. MS 28095, f. 72r
*Firth*: Bodley MS Firth c. 16, p. 307
*Newport Public Library*: Newport Reference Library M411 012 WIL, [f. 1r]
*Houghton*: Harvard University Library Houghton MS Eng 834, folder 71
*Yale c.154*: Yale Osborn Collection c.154, pp. 9, 11
*Yale Poetry Box*: Yale Osborn Shelves Poetry Box V/12
*Court Whispers*: *Court Whispers: or, a Magazine of Wit* (London: for W. Webb, 1743), pp. 8–9

| | |
|---|---|
| **44.1** | Lords,] *Yale c.154, Court Whispers*; Lords *Add. 51441* |
| **44.2** | Britain's] Britains *Add. 51441* |
| | Heir.] Heir *Add. 51441* |
| **44.3** | Crew,] *Firth, Court Whispers*; Crew *Add. 51441* |
| **44.4** | Blue;] *Firth*; Blue *Add. 51441* |
| **44.5** | Applause,] *Court Whispers*; Applause *Add. 51441* |
| **44.6** | Laws.] *Houghton, Yale c.154, Court Whispers*; Laws *Add. 51441* |
| **44.7** | despise,] *Firth, Yale c.154, Court Whispers*; despise *Add. 51441* |
| **44.8** | lyes.] *Houghton*; lyes *Add. 51441* |
| **44.9** | Country's] *Add. 28095, Firth*; Countrys *Add. 51441* |
| | Smart,] *Houghton, Yale c.154, Court Whispers*; Smart *Add. 51441* |
| **44.10** | Head,] *Firth, Yale c.154, Court Whispers*; Head *Add. 51441* |

## *Historical collation to 44 Norfolk House*

| | |
|---|---|
| **44.** | *title*] By Ld Harvey 1738 *Firth*; By the same *Yale Poetry Box*; N——k House *Court Whispers*; *no title Newport Public Library, Houghton* |

**44.1** Norfolk] *N——k Court Whispers*
Squires] Beaux *Firth*
**44.2** view] see *Yale Poetry Box*
Great Britain's] G B's *Newport Public Library*
**44.3** It fawns and grins] Who grins and fawns *Newport Public Library*
and grins] it grins *Add. 28095, Firth, Yale c.154, Court Whispers*; ——— *Yale Poetry Box*
and prattles] it prattles *Yale c.154, Court Whispers*
**44.4** whispers mighty Threats] threatens mighty things *Yale Poetry Box*
**44.5** Then] It *Yale Poetry Box*
struts and nods] nods and struts *Newport Public Library, Yale c.154*
**44.6** Truth] Faith *Firth*
**44.9** Avert Ye Gods our Country's] Ye Gods Avert G B's *Newport Public Library*
Country's] C——y's *Court Whispers*
**44.10** its Head] his Head *Yale Poetry Box*
ten times worse] worse far worse *Houghton*
its Heart] his heart *Yale Poetry Box*

## *Emendations to 45 Adelphi*

**main source** *Add. 51441*: BL Add. MS 51441, f. 95r
**complementary sources** *Add. 28095*: BL Add. MS 28095, f. 72r
*Add. 63648*: BL Add. MS 63648, f. 123r
*Add. 21544*: BL Add. MS 21544, f. 152v
*Firth c.16*: Bodley MS Firth c. 16, p. 306
*Firth b.22*: Bodley Firth b. 22, f. 34v
*Newport Public Library*: Newport Reference Library M411 012 WIL, [f. 1r]
*Houghton*: Harvard University Library Houghton MS Eng 834, folder 71
*Yale c.154*: Yale Osborn Collection c.154, p. 9
*Yale fc.58*: Yale Osborn Collection fc.58, p. 132
*Yale Poetry Box*: Yale Osborn Shelves Poetry Box V/12
*Court Whispers*: *Court Whispers: or, a Magazine of Wit* (London: for W. Webb, 1743), p. 9

**45.1** hopeful] *Yale fc.58, Court Whispers*; hopefull *Add. 51441*
George's] *Firth c.16, Yale fc.58, Yale Poetry Box*; Georges *Add. 51441*
Loyns,] *Yale fc.58*; Loyns *Add. 51441*
**45.2** Shines.] Shines *Add. 51441*
**45.3** Freddy's] *Firth c.16, Newport Reference Library, Yale Poetry Box*; Freddys *Add. 51441*
flows,] *Yale c.154, Yale fc.58, Court Whispers*; flows *Add. 51441*
**45.4** goes.] *Firth b.22, Houghton, Yale c.154, Yale fc.58, Court Whispers*; go's *Add. 51441*
**45.6** Sleep.] *Firth c.16, Yale fc.58*; Sleep *Add. 51441*
**45.8** Great,] *Firth c.16*; Great *Add. 51441*
**45.9** Say,] *Firth c.16, Yale c.154, Yale fc.58, Court Whispers*; Say *Add. 51441*
Britons,] *Yale fc.58*; Britons *Add. 51441*
Head,] *Yale c.154, Yale fc.58, Court Whispers*; Head *Add. 51441*

## *Historical collation to 45 Adelphi*

**45.** *title*] The Adelphi *Add. 63648, Yale Poetry Box*; Epigram *Add. 21544*; Adelphi 1738 *Firth b.22*; Par Nobile Fratrum 1738 *Firth c.16* ['in the hands of the noble brothers']; The Brothers *Yale c.154*; *no title Yale fc.58*; The Two Brothers *Court Whispers*; *followed by P. of W. and D. of C Yale Poetry Box*

**45.1** hopeful Sons] Royal Youths *Firth c.16*; hopefull Youths *Add. 63648, Firth b.22, Yale c.154, Yale fc.58*; royal Youths *Add. 21544*
are sprung] we boast *Add. 21554, Firth c.16*
George's] G—'s *Add. 21554, Newport Reference Library, Yale c.154*; —— *Court Whispers*

**45.2** And one] The one *Add. 63648, Yale fc.58, Yale Poetry Box*; The first *Add. 21544, Firth c.16*; As one *Yale c.154*
one in] last in *Add. 21544, Firth c.16*

**45.3** Freddy's Lips] Fredericks Tongue *Add. 63648, Yale c.154, Yale fc.58*; Feddy's Tongue *Add. 21544*; *F–d–k's* Lips *Court Whispers*; Freddy's tongue *Firth b.22, Firth c.16*
Royal] Princely *Add. 21544, Firth c.16*; R— *Court Whispers.*

**45.4** And Fools] While Beaux *Add. 21544, Firth c.16*
Ladies] flatterers *Add. 64648, Yale fc.58*

**45.5** Will] *W–ll Court Whispers*

**45.6** Navys] Nations *Add. MS 63648*

**45.7** But Oh! when by] But When by our *Newport Reference Library*

**45.8** Monarch rots] Mon— rots *Newport Reference Library*; M—— rots *Court Whispers*; King shall rot *Yale fc.58*
*with*] by *Add. 63648, Yale c.154*
Caroline] C—— *Newport Reference Library, Court Whispers*

**45.9** Britons] B—ns *Court Whispers*
which then] who then *Add. 63648, Yale fc.58*; whether *Court Whispers*
your] the *Add. 63648, Yale c.154*

**45.10** The prattling Monkey] The Chattering monkey *Add. 21544, Firth c.16*; *Yale Poetry Box*; A pratling Monkey *Yale c.154*; The Prating Coxcomb *Houghton*
*the Lump*] a lump *Yale c.154*
*followed by* Duke of Cumberland and Prince Frederick *Yale fc.58*

## *Emendations to 46 On Health*

**main source** *Dodsley*: Cancelled page in Dodsley, *Collection*, IV (1755), 113, repr. in Dodsley, I, 167
**complementary sources** *SRO*: SRO 941/53/1, p. 203
*Add. 59439*: BL Add. MS 59439, f. 25r
*Firth b. 4*: Bodley MS Firth b. 4, f. 50r
*London Evening*: *London Evening-Post*, 24 January 1745
*London Magazine 1745*: *London Magazine*, 14 (February 1745), 99

*Scots Magazine*: *Scots Magazine*, 7 (February 1745), 75
*Universal Magazine*: *Universal Magazine*, 7 (October 1750), 184
*London Magazine 1750*: *London Magazine*, 19 (November 1750), 515
*Select Epigrams*: *Collection of Select Epigrams*, ed. by John Hackett (London: for C. Hitch and L. Hawes; Canterbury: for W. and J. Flackton, 1757), pp. 42–3
*Colley Cibber*: *Colley Cibber's Jests* (Newcastle: for W. Charnley, 1761), pp. 90–1
*New Foundling 1769*: *New Foundling Hospital for Wit*, III (London: s.n., 1769), 84–5
*Humours*: *Humours of the Times* (London: s.n., 1771), pp. 350–1
*New Foundling 1784*: *New Foundling Hospital for Wit*, 6 vols. (London: for J. Debrett, 1784), I, 240–1

*no emendations made*

## *Historical collation to 46 On Health*

| | |
|---|---|
| **46.** | *title*] *no title Add. 59439*; *On* Health, by *Lord* H—y *London Evening, London Magazine 1745*; *On* Health, *by the late Lord* Harvey *Universal Magazine, London Magazine 1750, New Foundlng 1769*; CXLVIII. *Health Select Epigrams*; *On* HEALTH, *by Lord* HARVEY *Colley Cibber*; *On* HEALTH. *By the late Lord* HERVEY *Humours, New Foundling 1784* |
| **46.2** | whilst] while *Select Epigrams, Colley Cibber* |
| **46.5** | force or fraud] Fraud, or Force *Select Epigrams, Colley Cibber* |
| **46.6** | from] by *Add. 59439* |
| **46.7** | Hanover] H——— *London Evening, London Magazine 1745, London Magazine 1750, Scots Magazine, Universal Magazine* |
| **46.9** | Or] And *Add. 59439* |
| **46.10** | shake] shape *Universal Magazine, London Magazine 1750, New Foundling 1769, Humours, New Foundling 1784* |
| **46.11** | Or] And *Add. 59439* |
| | fools] F—ls *London Evening, London Magazine 1745, London Magazine 1750, Scots Magazine, Universal Magazine* |
| **46.12** | e'er] have *all complementary sources* |
| **46.13** | To beggar'd] With beggar'd *Add. 59439*; To Beggar *SRO* |
| **46.15** | Who] That *SRO* |
| **46.17** | fools] f—ls *London Evening, London Magazine 1745, London Magazine 1750, Scots Magazine, Universal Magazine* |
| | *make*] made *Scots Magazine* |
| **46.21** | richer] Richest *SRO* |

## *Emendations to 47 Riddle*

**main source** *Bodley*: Bodley MS. Eng. misc. b. 169, f. 59v
**complementary sources** *Grundy*: Grundy, 'New Verse', p. 239, and *Essays & Poems*, p. 382

| | |
|---|---|
| **47.** | *title*] *no title Bodley* |
| **47.1** | beer] *corrected from* bear *Bodley* |

**47.2** World] Word *Bodley*
they say what's] they what's *Bodley*

## *Historical collation to 47 Riddle*

**47.** *title*] *no title Grundy*
**47.2** World] Wor[l]d *Grundy*
they say what's] they [say] what's *Grundy*

## *Emendations to 48 Written on the Gilded Statue*

**main source** *SRO*: SRO 941/53/1, p. 208
**complementary sources** none

**48.15** 'Twill do for her] 'Twill for her *SRO*

## *Historical collation to 48 Written on the Gilded Statue*

*none; only one witness exists*

## *Emendations to 49 Written Impromptu to a Lady Stung by a Bee*

**main source** *Delany*: Lilly Library, Delany MS [1], item 9
**complementary sources** *Bodley*: Bodley MS Eng. poet. e. 40, f. 48r
*SRO*: SRO, 941/53/1, p. 208
*Yale*: Yale William Smith Papers, Osborn Collection, Folder 74/19, p. 1
*Windsor Medley*: *Windsor Medley* (London: for A. Moore [fictitious], 1731), p. 8, and two other editions of the same year
*The Choice*: *The Choice: Being a Collection of Two Hundred and Fifty Celebrated Songs*, 2 vols. (London: for W. Bickerton, T. Astley, R. Willock and J. Watson, 1733), II, 60
*Complete Collection*: *A Complete Collection of Old and New English and Scotch Songs*, 2 vols. (London: by T. Boreman, 1735), II, 172, and same page of four-volume 1736 edn
*Collection of Epigrams*: *A Collection of Epigrams*, 2 vols. (London: for J. Walthoe, 1735), II, unpaginated, sig. H3r
*Choice Collection*: *A Choice Collection of Poetry*, ed. by Joseph Yarrow, 2 vols. (York: by A. Staples, 1738), II, 49

*The poem continued to be reprinted frequently either as a song or as an epigram throughout the century.*

**49.2** Delia's] *SRO, Complete Collection, Collection of Epigrams, Choice Collection*; Delias *Delany*

## *Historical collation to 49 Written Impromptu to a Lady Stung by a Bee*

**49.** *title*] A Song. given me by the most Excellent Lady and Charming Beauty the Widow Carbonnel in her Coach, when I had the Happiness of waiting on Her to Drury Lane Play House on Monday March the 7 – 1747–8 in her own Hand-Writing *Bodley*; On Delia Stung by a Bee, extempore by Ld. Hy. *SRO*; *no title Yale*; *An EPIGRAM on Miss* K. A–ls–n. *By Mr.* H. *Windsor Medley*, Song XLIX. *The Choice*; Song CCXVIII. *As Celia near a Fountain lay. Complete Collection*; CLV. *On a* Lady, *stung by a* Bee, *Collection of Epigrams*; *An EPIGRAM Choice Collection*

**49.1** the] a *Bodley, SRO, Yale, Choice Collection*
a] the *Complete Collection*

**49.2** Delia's] Chloe's *Bodley*; Cloe's *Yale*; *Kitty's Windsor Medley, The Choice*

**49.3** His Honey on] Honey on *Yale*; The Honey on *Choice Collection*; It's Honey to *Complete Collection, Collection of Epigrams*; Honey upon *Bodley, Windsor Medley, The Choice*
on her Cheek] on her lips *Yale, Choice Collection*; upon her lips *Windsor Medley*; to the wound *Complete Collection*; to the part *Collection of Epigrams*

**49.4** bid] bad *SRO, Yale, Collection of Epigrams, Choice Collection*

**49.6** Imbib'd both] Suck'd both the *SRO, Complete Collection, Collection of Epigrams*
Sweet] Cure *Yale*

**49.7** His] The *all complementary sources*
lips] Lip *SRO*

**49.8** Within] went to *SRO*; went thro' *Choice Collection, Collection of Epigrams*

## *Emendations to 50 Written on a Lady's Fan Who Had her Lover's Picture Painted on It*

**main source** *SRO*: SRO 941/53/1, p. 208
**complementary sources** none

*no emendations made*

## *Historical collation to 50 Written on a Lady's Fan Who Had her Lover's Picture Painted on It*

*none; only one witness exists*

## *Emendations to 51 Written at the Bottom of a Note from Lady . . . to Ld . . . .*

**main source** *SRO*: SRO 941/53/1, p. 210
**complementary sources** none

*no emendations made*

## *Historical collation to 51 Written at the Bottom of a Note from Lady . . . to Ld . . . .*

*none; only one witness exists*

## *Emendations to 52 On Ickworth Park in Suffolk*

**main source** SRO 941/53/1, pp. 210, 212
**complementary sources** none

*no emendations made*

## *Historical collation to 52 On Ickworth Park in Suffolk*

*none; only one witness exists*

## *Emendations to 53 Lord Harvey on the Dutchess of Richmond*

**main source** *Welbeck*: Portland Papers (Nottingham University), Pw V 270
**complementary sources** *Harrowby*: Harrowby MS 255, pp. 78–9
*Harley*: BL MS Harley 7318, f. 108v
*Add. 32463*: BL Add. MS 32463, p. 230
*Add. 37683*: BL Add. MS 37683, f. 28v
*Add. 47128*: BL Add. MS 47128, f. 42v
*Chester*: Chester Record Office DCC/16/101
*Lt 12*: Brotherton Lt 12, p. 45
*Lt 35*: Brotherton Lt 35, p. 57
*Yale c.53*: Yale Osborn Collection, c.53, pp. 53–4
*Yale c.233*: Yale Osborn Collection c.233, p. 81
*Yale c.188*: Yale Osborn Collection c.188, p. 91
*LJ*: *London Journal*, 31 January 1730
*Universal Spectator*: *Universal Spectator*, 11 July 1730
*Select Poems*: *Select Poems from Ireland* (London: for T. Warner, 1730), pp. 15–16
*Collection of Epigrams*: *A Collection of Epigrams*, 2nd edn, 2 vols. (London: for J. Walthoe, 1733), II, CCCXXIII
*GM*: *Gentleman's Magazine*, 8 (December 1738), 653
*Norfolk Miscellany*: *The Norfolk Poetical Miscellany*, 2 vols. [ed. by Ashley Cowper] (London: for the author, sold by J. Stagg, 1744), I, 171–2

*There are numerous reprints after 1750, especially in collections of epigrams, but also in such well-known sources as the Poetical Calendar (III, 111), the New Foundling Hospital for Wit (1769 edn, p. 114, mistitled 'On the Duchess of Rutland') and Pearch's Collection of Poems (1775 edn, II, 293–4). None of the variants after 1744 is recorded.*

53.2 one's] *Add. 32463, Yale c.233, LJ, Collection of Epigrams, Norfolk Miscellany*; ones *Welbeck*

53.10 Pulteney's] *Add. 32463*; Pulteneys *Welbeck*

## *Historical collation to 53 Lord Harvey on the Dutchess of Richmond*

53. *title*] Verses written by the E. of Chesterfield *[struck through]* Ld Hervey *Harrowby*; Lord Harvey on the Dutchess of Richmond *Harley*; An Epigram *Add. 32463*; On Dutchesse of Richmond by Ld. Chesterfield *Add. 37683*; An extempore Poem by Ld Chesterfeild on the Dutchesse of Richmond Ao 1730 *Add. 47128*; A Complimt to the Dutchess of R—d *Chester*; An Epigram. by the E. of Ch—d *Lt 12*; Inscribed to the Dutchess of Richmond *Lt 35*; On the Dutchess of Richmond by Lord Chesterfield *Yale c.53*; On the Dutchess of Richmond's supping with Mr. Poultney *Yale c.233*; *no title Yale c.188*; An EPIGRAM. *By the* E. of CH——D *LJ*; *On* Lenocia's *going to Supper to* Clarinda's *Universal Spectator*; AN EXTEMPORARY POEM, by Lord *CH——D Select Poems*; CCCXXIII *Collection of Epigrams; On the D——ss of* R—d. (*By L–d* Ch—d.) *GM*; *On the Du—ess of* R—ch—nd *Norfolk Miscellany*

53.1 do] does *Chester*

Astrologers] Astronomers *Harrowby, Chester, Yale c.53, Universal Spectator, GM*; Philosophers *Add. 32463, Add. 37683, Add. 47128, Lt 12, Yale c.233, Yale c. 188, LJ, Select Poems, Collection of Epigrams, Norfolk Miscellany*

53.2 one's head] our Heads *Harrowby, Add. 37683, Lt 35, Yale c.53, Yale c.188, Universal Spectator, Select Poems, GM*; our head *Lt 12*

with] with such *Harrowby, Add. 32463, Add. 37683, Add. 47128, Chester, Lt 12, Yale c.53, Yale c.233, Yale c.188, LJ, Universal Spectator, Select Poems, Collection of Epigrams, Norfolk Miscellany*

53.3 one, Venus] us Venus *Add. 32463, Add. 37683, Lt 35, Universal Spectator, Select Poems, Collection of Epigrams, GM*; that Venus *Yale c.53*

53.4 Shell or a] Shell, with a *Lt 35*

53.5 or Dolphins] a Dolphin *Add. 32463, Add. 47128, Lt 12, Yale c.233, Yale c.188, LJ, Select Poems*; by Dolphins *Universal Spectator*

53.6 And attended] Attended *GM*

by the] by *Chester*

and] or *Yale c.188*

53.7–8 *two lines transposed Select Poems*

53.7 is] are *Chester*

she will] that she'le *Lt 35*

53.8 And her Passport] And a Passport *Add. 32463, Add. 47128, Chester, Lt 12, Yale c.233, Yale c.188, LJ*; And the Pasport *Lt 35*; With a Passport *Select Poems*

Hearts, a] Hearts is a *Add. 32463, Add. 37683, Add. 47128, Lt 12, Yale c.233, Yale c.188, LJ, Universal Spectator*; hearts is the *Lt 35*

Belt] Cest *Add. 37683*; hearts on a *GM*

| | |
|---|---|
| | round] to *Add. 32463, Lt 12, Yale c.233, Yale c.188, LJ, Collection of Epigrams* |
| **53.9** | bustle] Trouble *Add. 32463, Add. 47128, Lt 12, Yale c.233, Yale c.188, LJ, Universal Spectator, Select Poems, Collection of Epigrams* |
| **53.10** | To] When to *Lt 35, Universal Spectator, Select Poems*; At *Yale c.53* |
| | Pulteney's] *Clarinda Universal Spectator*; *P——y's GM*; *P–lt–y's Norfolk Miscellany* |
| **53.11** | no] for a *Lt 35.* |
| **53.12** | for] her *Add. 32463, Add. 37683, Add. 47128, Lt 12, Lt 35, Yale c.233, Yale c.188, LJ, Universal Spectator, Select Poems, Collection of Epigrams, GM* |
| | Flambeau] *flambeaux GM* |
| **53.14** | a Chicken] and Chicken *Harrowby, Add. 32463, Add. 37683, Add. 47128, Lt 12, Yale c.233, Yale c.188, LJ, Universal Spectator, Select Poems, Collection of Epigrams, Norfolk Miscellany* |
| **53.15** | wanted] needed *Harrowby* |
| | the Cestus] She Cestus *Add. 47128, Chester, Lt 12, Lt 35, Yale c.53, Yale c.233, Yale c.188, LJ, Collection of Epigrams*; a Cestus *Select Poems, GM* |
| **53.16** | Richmond] *Lenocia Universal Spectator*; R——D *GM*; *R–ch–nd Norfolk Miscellany* |
| | her her] Venus her *Universal Spectator* |

## *Emendations to 54 Reveillez vous*

**main source** *Add. 51441*: BL Add. MS 51441, f. 23r
**complementary sources** none

| | |
|---|---|
| 54. | *title* Reveillez] Reveilles *Add. 51441* |
| 54.1 | Story,] Story *Add. 51441* |
| 54.2 | Art;] Art *Add. 51441* |
| 54.3 | Tory,] Tory *Add. 51441* |
| 54.6 | Babylon,] Babylon *Add. 51441* |
| 54.7 | Revelation,] Revelation *Add. 51441* |
| 54.9 | reversions] reversion's *Add. 51441* |
| 54.10 | see,] see *Add. 51441* |
| 54.11 | Curtain,] Curtain *Add. 51441* |

## *Historical collation to 54 Reveillez vous*

*none; only one witness exists*

## *Emendations to 55 Verse Dialogue between Hervey and Montague*

**main source** *Harrowby*: Harrowby MS 81, ff. 216r–217v
**complementary sources** *SRO*: SRO 941/47/2, pp. 69–71
*Bodley*: Bodley MS Eng. misc. b. 169, f. 61r–61v

| | |
|---|---|
| **55.** | *title*] *no title Harrowby* |
| **55.1** | L. H.] *no prefix Harrowby* |
| **55.2** | *followed by deleted* A painfull secret should be guess'd not told \| I wish to tell *Harrowby* |
| **55.3** | L. M.] *no prefix Harrowby* |
| **55.5** | L. H.] *SRO*; *no prefix Harrowby* |
| **55.8** | L. M.] *SRO*; *no prefix Harrowby* |
| | Secret] *SRO*; secret *Harrowby* |
| **55.10** | L. H.] *SRO*; *no prefix Harrowby* |
| **55.19** | L. M.] *SRO*; *no prefix Harrowby* |
| | Pain,] *SRO*; pain *Harrowby* |
| **55.19–21** | *no triplet brace Harrowby* |
| **55.20** | explain,] *SRO*; explain *Harrowby* |
| **55.21** | Brain.] *SRO*; brain *Harrowby* |
| **55.22** | L. H.] *SRO*; *no prefix Harrowby* |
| | Brain;] *SRO*; Brain *Harrowby* |
| **55.23** | plain,] *SRO*; plain *Harrowby* |
| **55.24** | read,] *SRO*; read *Harrowby* |
| **55.25** | tread:] *SRO*; tread *Harrowby* |
| **55.26** | Art,] *SRO*; Art *Harrowby* |
| **55.27** | Heart;] *SRO*; Heart *Harrowby* |
| **55.28** | grow,] *SRO*; grow *Harrowby* |
| **55.29** | flow?] *SRO*; flow. *Harrowby* |
| **55.30** | L. M.] *SRO*; *no prefix Harrowby* |
| | Scars] *SRO*; scars *Harrowby* |
| | Wound] *SRO*; wound *Harrowby* |
| **55.31** | Truth] *SRO*; truth *Harrowby* |
| **55.32** | smart,] *SRO*; smart *Harrowby* |
| **55.33** | Heart.] *SRO*; Heart *Harrowby* |
| **55.34** | L. H.] *SRO*; *no prefix Harrowby* |
| **55.44** | L. M.] *SRO*; *no prefix Harrowby* |
| **55.45** | Taper's] Tapers *Harrowby, Bodley* |
| **55.50** | L. H.] *no prefix Harrowby* |
| **55.51** | Love] *Bodley*; love *Harrowby* |
| **55.53** | Won't] Wont *Harrowby* |
| | Med'cines] medcines *Harrowby* |
| **55.54** | L. M.] *no prefix Harrowby* |
| **55.59** | L. H.] *no prefix Harrowby* |
| **55.64** | L. M.] *no prefix Harrowby* |
| **55.68** | L. H.] *no prefix Harrowby* |
| | hate,] hate *Harrowby* |
| **55.69** | eat.] eat *Harrowby* |
| **55.70** | L. M.] *no prefix Harrowby* |
| **55.74** | L. H.] *no prefix Harrowby* |

## *Historical collation to 55 Verse Dialogue between Hervey and Montagu*

| | |
|---|---|
| 55. | *title*] *no title Harrowby, SRO*; Epigram written extempore in a dispute whether Absence ended Love *Bodley* |
| 55.1–4 | *not in SRO* |
| 55.1–43 | *not in Bodley* |
| 55.2 | *followed by* A painfull secret should be guess'd not told \| I wish to tell *SRO* |
| 55.5 | The Preface to your Question] Your Question's plain, this Preface *SRO with* Your *above deleted* The *SRO* |
| 55.7 | your] the *SRO* |
| 55.10 | *followed in left-hand margin by* I'm sure this is wrong but can't make it right *SRO* |
| 55.11 | Ask] I ask *SRO* |
| | shall] should *SRO* |
| 55.12 | Or that your Trust I ever] *below deleted* Fear not your trust I ever shall abuse *and above deleted* Nor that whate'er you ask *SRO* |
| | can] shall *SRO* |
| 55.19 | Question] Question's *SRO* |
| 55.23 | Fearing my Answer] *replacing deleted* For fear that *SRO* |
| | Fearing . . . thought too] *above deleted* But tis because I fear to make it *SRO* |
| 55.32 | to feel th' exstatic] when you may know the *SRO;* know *above deleted* feel *SRO* |
| 55.44 | deserves not passions name] scarce merits &c — You have the rest. *SRO* |
| 55.45–75 | *not in SRO* |
| 55.49 | Even Tempests] *below deleted* A Tempest *Bodley* |
| 55.55 | on] *emended from* in *Bodley* |
| 55.56 | you sooth my] *above deleted* I may expect to find *Bodley* |
| | restless] painfull *Bodley* |
| 55.57 | To] *above deleted* In *Bodley* |
| 55.58 | To meet a second Lovely of the Kind] To meet the best and Loveliest of Mankind *Bodley with* meet *above deleted* To seek another *[word indecipherable]* in Ma. *This line preceded by* Latians were allways Masters of Mankind; Latians *above deleted* Romans *Bodley* |
| 55.62 | you've heard explain'd by] that you have learn'd from *Bodley* |
| 55.63 | they are] we are *Bodley* |
| | they ought] we ought *Bodley* |
| 55.64 | or] nor *Bodley* |
| 55.68 | you talk] we talk *Bodley* |
| | you love] we love *Bodley* |
| 55.69 | For when you're hungry, and have Food you'll] *above deleted* Whate'er the Food the hungry'll always *Bodley* |
| 55.72 | rais'd] *above deleted* gave *Bodley* |
| | I feel] *above deleted* I felt *Bodley, to supply a rhyme for the original following line* |
| 55.73 | Which only one can give, and only One could] *above deleted* Where in soft passions the touch'd soul can melt *Bodley* |

| | |
|---|---|
| | heal] *above deleted* feel *Harrowby*; heal *corrected from* feal *Bodley* |
| **55.74–5** | *not in Bodley* |

## *Emendations to 56 The Griff to the Queen*

**main source** *SRO*: SRO 941/47/13–14 (14), f. 320r
**complementary source** *Windsor*: Royal Archives, Windsor: RA GEO/MAIN/53088–53977 (53871r)

| | |
|---|---|
| **56.1** | Cub,] *Windsor*; Cub *SRO* |
| **56.5** | town —] town, *SRO* |
| | true —] true *SRO* |
| **56.10** | 'tis] *Windsor*; tis *SRO* |
| | said),] said) *SRO* |
| **56.12** | Why,] Why *SRO* |
| | yours] *Windsor*; Your's *SRO* |
| **56.13** | bids] *Windsor*; bid's *SRO* |

## *Historical collation to 56 The Griff to the Queen*

*no variants*

## *Emendations to 57 Written in Algarotti's Book on Sir Isaac Newton's Philosophy of Light and Colours*

**main source** *SRO*: SRO 941/53/1, pp. 202–3
**complementary sources** none

| | |
|---|---|
| **57.** | title Book] book *SRO* |
| | Philosophy] philosophy *SRO* |
| | Colours] colours *SRO* |
| **57.6** | its light] it's light *SRO* |
| **57.7** | Night.] Night *SRO* |
| **57.12** | principles] *above blotted* philosophy |

## *Historical collation to 57 Written in Algarotti's Book on Sir Isaac Newton's Philosophy of Light and Colours*

*none; only one witness exists*

## *Emendations to 58 A Dialogue between Horace and Lydia: Horace, Book III, Ode 9 paraphrased*

**main source** *SRO*: SRO 941/46/5
**complementary sources** none

**58.** *title* paraphrased] paraphased *SRO*
and] & *SRO*

## *Historical collation to 58 A Dialogue between Horace and Lydia: Horace, Book III, Ode 9 paraphrased*

*none; only one witness exists*

## *Emendations to 59 These empty Titles*

**main source** SRO 941/47/2, p. 241
**complementary sources** none

*no emendations made*

## *Historical collation to 59 These empty Titles*

*none; only one witness exists*

## *Emendations to 60 Tho' thy whole life should pass without a stain*

**main source** *SRO*: SRO 941/53/1, p. 202
**complementary sources** none

**60.** *title*] Elegia] El *SRO*
Liber] L *SRO*

## *Historical collation to 60 Tho' thy whole life should pass without a stain*

*none; only one witness exists*

## *Emendations to 61 If equal Charms*

**main source** SRO 941/47/2, p. 45
**complementary sources** none

*no emendations made*

## *Historical collation to 61 If equal Charms*

*none; only one witness exists*

## *Emendations to 62 No more my Eyes thy Beauty charms*

**main source** SRO 941/47/4, 266–71, p. 270

**complementary sources** none

*no emendations made*

## *Historical collation to 62 No more my Eyes thy Beauty charms*

*none; only one witness exists*

## *Emendations to 63 This little House*

**main source** SRO 941/47/2, p. 260
**complementary sources** none

*no emendations made*

## *Historical collation to 63 This little House*

*none; only one witness exists*

## *Emendations to 64 Epigram from Rousseau*

**main source** *SRO*: SRO 941/53/1, p. 206
**complementary source** *Harrowby*: Harrowby MS 255, f. 30v

*no emendations made*

## *Historical collation to 64 Epigram from Rousseau*

| | |
|---|---|
| **64.** | *title*] Epigram *Harrowby* |
| **64.3** | dupe to] Dup'd by *Harrowby* |
| | to Eve] by Eve *Harrowby* |
| **64.4** | recites] has writ *Harrowby* |
| **64.5** | Satire] Moral *Harrowby* |
| | of the] of this *Harrowby* |

## *Emendations to 65 The Adventures of Telemachus in the Island of Ogygia*

**main source** *SRO*: SRO 941/47/17
**complementary sources** none

*re-drafted lines are often unpunctuated, or very lightly so; reference has been made to deleted drafts of lines when making emendations; for details of those deletions, see below*

| | |
|---|---|
| **65.1.4** | Mind,] Mind *SRO* |
| **65.1.24** | stood,] stood *SRO* |
| **65.1.27** | Ship.] Ship *SRO* |
| **65.1.31** | Coast.] Coast *SRO* |
| **65.1.33** | Shore.] Shore *SRO* |
| **65.1.37** | Goddess'] Goddess *SRO* |
| | View,] View; *SRO* |
| **65.1.40** | Goddess'] Goddess *SRO* |
| | won,] won *SRO* |
| **65.1.41** | Son;] Son *SRO* |
| **65.1.43** | Face.] Face *SRO* |
| **65.1.54–71** | *slip bearing these lines is so tightly trimmed that no end-of-line punctuation is visible* |
| **65.1.54** | Goddess'] Goddess *SRO* |
| **65.1.55** | Shore,] Shore *SRO* |
| **65.1.56** | mis-led?] mis-led *SRO* |
| **65.1.57** | dread,] dread *SRO* |
| **65.1.59** | vain;] vain *SRO* |
| **65.1.60** | Storms,] Storms *SRO* |
| **65.1.61** | Sea.] Sea *SRO* |
| **65.1.63** | reveres;] reveres *SRO* |
| **65.1.65** | Chains;] Chains *SRO* |
| **65.1.66** | Friends,] Friends *SRO* |
| **65.1.67** | Eyes.'] Eyes *SRO* |
| **65.1.72** | rever'd'] rever'd *SRO* |
| **65.1.75** | Innocence?] Innocence. *SRO* |
| **65.1.83** | draw,] draw; *SRO* |
| **65.1.92** | Doom.'] Doom. *SRO* |
| **65.1.93** | Father?'] Father? *SRO* |
| **65.1.99** | Ulisses'] Ulisses *SRO* |
| **65.1.106** | Achilles'] Achilles *SRO* |
| **65.1.121** | Wall.] Wall *SRO* |
| **65.1.128** | Ulisses'] Ulisses *SRO* |
| **65.1.143** | Ulisses'] Ulisses *SRO* |
| **65.1.146** | cry,] cry *SRO* |
| **65.1.147** | cast] cast, *SRO* |
| **65.1.155** | Grave?'] Grave. *SRO* |
| **65.1.160** | dart] dart, *SRO* |
| **65.1.163** | spoke.] spoke *SRO* |
| **65.1.173** | feel] feel, *SRO* |
| **65.1.185** | Head.] Head *SRO* |
| **65.1.196** | lost.'] lost. *SRO* |
| **65.1.197** | Plain] Plain, *SRO* |
| **65.1.199** | wait;] wait, *SRO* |
| **65.1.220** | before.] before, *SRO* |
| **65.1.240** | Mine).] Mine) *SRO* |

| | |
|---|---|
| **65.1.242** | Art,] Art; *SRO* |
| **65.1.256** | heard,] heard *SRO* |
| **65.1.257** | Bird;] Bird *SRO* |
| **65.1.259** | Spring;] Spring *SRO* |
| **65.1.263** | flow.] flow *SRO* |
| **65.1.265** | Draught.] Draught *SRO* |
| **65.1.269** | Woodbine, Jasmin, Violet, and Rose.] Woodbine Jasmin Violet and Rose *SRO* |
| **65.1.271** | Flood.] Flood *SRO* |
| **65.1.278** | Elm;] Elm *SRO* |
| **65.1.280** | Pomegranate, Figg,] Pomegranate Figg *SRO* |
| | around,] around *SRO* |
| **65.1.283** | display'd;] display'd, *SRO* |
| **65.1.286** | off'] off *SRO* |
| | 'Retire] retire *SRO* |
| **65.1.301** | not,] not *SRO* |
| **65.1.304** | Heart;] Heart *SRO* |
| **65.1.306** | Sorrow,] Sorrow *SRO* |
| | End.'] End, *SRO* |
| **65.1.313** | sees] sees, *SRO* |
| **65.1.319** | destroy] destroy, *SRO* |
| **65.1.330** | thine,'] thine. *SRO* |
| **65.1.334** | Fame.] Fame *SRO* |
| **65.1.342** | Unknown.'] Unknown. *SRO* |
| **65.1.343** | rather'] rather *SRO* |
| **65.1.363** | Aid.'] Aid. *SRO* |
| **65.1.379** | Fight;] Fight. *SRO* |
| **65.1.380** | Night;] Night. *SRO* |
| **65.1.386** | Ulisses'] Ulisses *SRO* |
| | employ;] employ, *SRO* |
| **65.1.462** | 'Dear] Dear *SRO* |
| | Euridice'] Euridice *SRO* |
| **65.1.463** | 'Euridice'] Euridice *SRO* |
| • **65.1.471** | hast] has *SRO* |
| **65.1.478** | '(For] 'For *SRO* |
| | due),] due, *SRO* |
| **65.1.496** | "Haste] haste *SRO* |
| | Sails";] Sails; *SRO* |
| **65.1.553** | Heart.'] Heart. *SRO* |
| **65.1.591** | due.'] due. *SRO* |
| **65.1.596** | Griefs'] Greifs *SRO* |
| | 'I] I *SRO* |
| **65.1.599** | Urn] Urn, *SRO* |
| **65.1.614** | Land.'] Land. *SRO* |
| **65.1.615** | tire';] tire; *SRO* |

| | |
|---|---|
| | reply'd)] reply'd *SRO* |
| **65.1.616** | Fears' (the] Fears the *SRO* |
| **65.1.645** | Shame,] Shame *SRO* |
| **65.1.687** | Dream.'] Dream. *SRO* |
| **65.2.53** | Thee.'] Thee. *SRO* |
| **65.2.57** | Heart.] Heart *SRO* |
| **65.2.63** | Light,] Light *SRO* |
| **65.2.79** | blaze.'] blaze. *SRO* |
| **65.2.196** | Love.'] Love. *SRO* |
| **65.2.207** | Dart] Dart, *SRO* |
| **65.2.269–70** | *redundant triplet brace* SRO |
| **65.2.270** | Venus'] Venus *SRO* |
| **65.2.272** | love;'] love; *SRO* |
| **65.2.279** | Youth!'] Youth! *SRO* |
| | 'Thou'rt] thou'rt *SRO* |
| **65.2.285** | Hopes,] Hopes *SRO* |
| **65.2.319** | Fair,] Fair *SRO* |
| **65.2.332** | Ill,] Ill *SRO* |
| **65.2.343** | Punishment.'] Punishment. *SRO* |
| **65.2.348** | 'Whither'] 'Whither *SRO* |
| | 'Or] or *SRO* |
| **65.2.363** | Port.'] Port. *SRO* |
| **65.2.364** | thus'] thus *SRO* |
| **65.2.399** | embrace.'] embrace. *SRO* |
| **65.2.406** | Gift'] Gift *SRO* |
| **65.2.408** | scorn'd?'] scorn'd? *SRO* |
| **65.2.420** | Praise;] Praise. *SRO* |
| **65.2.424** | long.'] long. *SRO* |
| **65.2.431** | knew,] knew *SRO* |
| **65.2.468** | Love'] Love *SRO* |
| | 'By] by *SRO* |
| **65.2.470** | Neglect.'] Neglect. *SRO* |
| **65.2.481** | Groves.'] Groves. *SRO* |
| **65.2.482** | no,'] no, *SRO* |
| **65.2.514** | here.'] here. *SRO* |
| **65.2.524** | Field.'] Field. *SRO* |
| **65.2.540** | below,] below *SRO* |
| **65.2.556** | Care.'] Care. *SRO* |
| **65.3.4** | Boy] Boy, *SRO* |
| **65.3.76** | Sorrow,] Sorrow *SRO* |
| **65.3.106** | free.'] free. *SRO* |
| **65.3.134** | dye.'] dye. *SRO* |
| **65.3.163** | Dame] Dame, *SRO* |
| **65.3.186** | Soul.] Soul *SRO* |
| **65.3.208** | bound?'] bound? *SRO* |
| **65.3.216** | Spy.'] Spy. *SRO* |
| **65.3.217** | me!'] me! *SRO* |

| | |
|---|---|
| **65.3.218** | Heav'n;'] Heav'n; *SRO* |
| **65.3.220** | Thee.'] Thee. *SRO* |
| **65.3.268** | deplore] deplore, *SRO* |
| **65.3.314** | me,'] me. *SRO* |
| **65.3.322** | give."] give. *SRO* |
| **65.3.327** | passed] past *SRO* |
| **65.3.353** | dye."] dye. *SRO* |
| **65.3.380** | Heav'n'] Heav'n *SRO* |
| | 'How] how *SRO* |
| **65.3.416** | Joy.'] Joy. *SRO* |
| **65.3.427** | Stay,] Stay *SRO* |
| **65.3.439** | Part";] Part; *SRO* |
| **65.3.447** | Breast.'] Breast. *SRO* |
| **65.3.450** | Prince!'] Prince! *SRO* |
| | 'No] no *SRO* |
| **65.3.490** | Father's] Father *SRO* |
| **65.3.492** | restore.'] restore. *SRO* |
| **65.3.494** | spread] spread, *SRO* |
| **65.3.518** | command.'] command. *SRO* |
| **65.3.527** | more?] more, *SRO* |
| **65.3.529** | Pow'r.'] Pow'r. *SRO* |
| **65.3.530** | all,'] all, *SRO* |
| **65.3.537** | Flame?'] Flame? *SRO* |
| **65.3.554** | Pow'r.'] Pow'r. *SRO* |
| **65.3.573** | fill'd.] fill'd *SRO* |
| **65.3.622** | came'] came *SRO* |
| **65.3.641** | Care.'] Care. *SRO* |

## *Historical collation to 65 The Adventures of Telemachus in the Island of Ogygia*

*none; only one witness exists; instead, because the manuscript is in Hervey's hand and was subject to quite extensive revision, details of those autograph changes follow; lines similar to 1.189–96 are found in Poem 67, where they are collated*

## *Account of the manuscript of 65 The Adventures of Telemachus in the Island of Ogygia*

The manuscript is in three booklets in very pretty red marbled wrappers, with the first leaf of each tightly pasted to the wrapper. Each recto is numbered, and originally the versos were perhaps blank. The lines are numbered in Hervey's hand, and evidence of eyeskip in Book III suggests that the whole is a fair copy. In the first version of the poem in the manuscript, Book I consisted of 607 lines, Book II of 570 lines, Book III of 647 lines. A letter from Lord Bristol to 'My dear Count' dated 3 February 1921 indicates that he had decided to have them bound into a single volume, which they now are.

At some point after Hervey wrote the poem into the little booklets, he began to revise it, sometimes writing his emendations above the original lines, sometimes using the facing verso for the new version and sometimes using a combination of these methods. He did not revise his line numbers to recognise the new material, which is sometimes very extensive. Book I is the most heavily revised – perhaps he put the revision to one side at this point – with the net effect that it grew from the original 607 lines to 718. In that Book, some rectos that hold extensive revisions are crossed through with a vertical line, the revised version either occupying the facing verso or, in more extreme cases, appearing on new, unnumbered sheets that have been tipped in to the original booklet or, in one case, pasted to the deleted recto.

The revisions to Book I are of five basic kinds:

1. lines very lightly revised from the first version, or reappearing verbatim;
2. lines relatively lightly revised, introduced through deletion and writing above the line;
3. lines extensively revised, and so written on the facing verso or on a tipped-in leaf;
4. lines not present in the first version, but added during the revision; most of these are lines of dialogue between Calpyso and Telemachus;
5. lines present in the first version that are deleted by the revision.

In detail, the material on the first few leaves of the manuscript is as follows. **Bold** is used to distinguish final from draft versions in the list.

*Book I*

f1r: pasted firmly to red marbled wrapper

f1v: revised version of **lines 4–5**; otherwise blank

f2r (numbered 1 by Hervey): **lines 1–3, 6–22**, including some crossings-out and revisions above and below the line

f2v: **lines 23–43** revised version, including lines further crossed out and replaced, resulting in five completely new lines (33–7)

f3r (numbered 2 by Hervey): deleted lines 23–41 original version; **lines 44–9** unrevised other than one word

f3v: **lines 50–3** and **lines 72–9** revised version; deleted revised version lines 54–71

f4r (numbered 3 by Hervey): lines 50–96 deleted original version; pasted to this along inside edge of page a slip carrying re-revised version of **lines 54–71** (with some further revisions above some lines); re-revised version increases the length of Calypso's angry speech from four lines to sixteen, and Telemachus' reply from seven lines to twenty-one

f4v: revised version of **lines 80–100**, expanding the length of Telemachus' speech, with further replacement of five lines by four new ones, and a little further revision above other lines

fχ1r (tipped in after f4v): revised version of **lines 101–21**, expanding Telemachus' speech about Ulysses; further revision above the line of just one word

fχ1v: revised version of **lines 122–41**; further revision above the line of two words, and one possible revision to a short phrase left undecided

fχ2r (2nd tipped-in leaf after f4v): revised version of **lines 142–61**; further replacement of one couplet by another, and a little further revision above other lines

fχ2v: blank

f5r (numbered 4 by Hervey): deleted, much shorter, 1st version of lines 106–13 (with a further revision above), lines 136–53 (the latter almost identical to the final version on fχ1v–fχ2r)

f5v: revised version of **lines 162–81**, adding twelve lines to the first draft and revising others further above the line

f6r (numbered 5 by Hervey): deleted first, much shorter version of lines 154–202; and above some of those lines, deleted rough draft of lines 231–45

f6v: revised version of **lines 182–200**, with a small number of further revisions above the line, and the final couplet moved to f2χ1r; expanding Calypso's promises to Telemachus

f2χ1r (tipped in after f6v): revised version of **lines 201–20**, taking in a couplet from f6v, and making a further revision to one couplet

f2χ1v: revised version of **lines 221–40**, presumably copied in part from corner of f7r, making a few further revisions above the line

f2χ2r (2nd tipped-in leaf after f6v): revised version of **lines 241–59**, making a few revisions above the line and deleting a couplet

f2χ2v: revised version of **lines 260–75**; the page began with a version of lines 260–5 that is replaced, above the line, with the version on f7v, and followed by eight new lines; followed by nine lines partially drafted

f7r (probably numbered by Hervey 6, but overwritten): revised version (repeated) of lines 201–2, 205, followed by draft of lines 206–16, 227–39, ten of which lines are unaltered in the final version; and in top right-hand corner, revised version of lines 217–26, copied without substantive revision to f2χ2v

f7v: deleted revised version of lines 260–6 (used to emend version first written on f2χ2v), and a revised version of a discarded line on f8r

f8r (numbered by Hervey 7): deleted version of lines 245–57; and above some of these lines revised version of lines 247–57, with twelve other lines finally discarded, and one reused (revised) for 3.240

f8v: revised version of **lines 276–85**, including one line further revised above the line

f9r (numbered 8 by Hervey): deleted version of lines 266–82, including sixteen lines finally discarded, and one reused (revised) for 1.25

f9v: **lines 286–306**; consisting solely of Calypso's speech, these lines (not numbered by Hervey) are on a verso and replace and expand the deleted five lines of dialogue on f9v and f10r; some revisions above the line

f10r (numbered 9 by Hervey): four deleted lines of dialogue, followed by **lines 307–26**, with some revisions above the line

f10v: **lines 333–6** marked with an asterisk for insertion on the facing page

f11r (numbered 10 by Hervey): **lines 327–32, 337–52**, with some revisions above the line

Thereafter revision is less extensive, being made above the line; the poem is largely confined to rectos, with versos blank, and no further tipped-in sheets. The only exception to this are the following lines, drawn in from the verso facing the appropriate part of the poem: 1.558–65, 1.589; 2.269–70, 2.354, after 2.356 two lines drafted and then marked 'leave out'; 3.185–6, 3.236, 3.359–65. In Books II and III, revisions are almost all made above the line, and quite often, though a phrase or line has been underlined and sometimes a possible substitution considered, no decision has been made; this might be further evidence that the revision was abandoned by Hervey after a period of work on Book I.

Someone – probably a family member, given that the manuscript remained at Ickworth until its transfer to the Suffolk Record Office – has annotated the manuscript's margins, mostly in pencil. These annotations are of five main kinds:

1. pencilled Q (or similar symbol) against some lines, perhaps indicating that the reader believes that something has been quoted from here, or is preparing to quote the line. Q appears in Book I against lines 59, 80, 87, 94, 109, 135, 152–3, 193, 215, 221, 289, 299, 336, 376, 407, 441–2, 462, 480, 509, 515, 520, 524, 652, 711; in Book II against lines 196, 262, 267–8, 283, 290, 295–6, 325, 343, 353, 387, 410; none in Book III;
2. large pencilled dots (sometimes dashes) against some lines, perhaps indicating some interpretation or intention akin to that in (1) above. Large pencilled dots appear in Book I against lines 117, 124, 150, 157, 159, 171, 173, 175, 179, 181, 183, 190, 196, 200, 252, 255, 259, 292, 305, 328, 340, 352, 395, 459, 468, 579, 584, 587, 591, 606, 612, 621, 648, 664; in Book II against lines 37, 147, 229, 270, 333, 340, 368, 424; in Book III against lines 236, 375, 381, 383, 385, 387, 389, 391, 399, 418, 420, 426, 443, 458, 460, 462, 464, 484, 485;
3. underlining in pencil in Book I: line 193 ('sweet Contentment'), line 509 ('at their Post'), line 601 ('Pain is the Lott'), line 602, line 673 ('my Love'), line 711 ('falshood'); in Book II line 129 ('his Sister'); line 133 ('fav'rite'); line 129 ('Sister-Consort'); line 133 ('fav'rite Ganymede');
4. pencilled words in the manuscript: 'Ick', presumably meaning 'Ickworth', against lines 1.64, 1.233–5, 2.252; 'on' above 'to' l. 238; 'All' above 'Earth'

1.601; 'ballanc' above 'byass' l. 652; 'Song' in margin l. 684; 'C.P.' 2.222–3; 'P of' 2.36, perhaps indicating 'Prince of Wales'; 'Donn', perhaps indicating the belief that the lines are reminiscent of lines in Donne's verse, against line 2.59; 'oi' above 'au' of 'paus'd' 2.83; 'C. D.' 2.153; 'P' perhaps indicating 'Prince of Wales' 2.305;

5. ink annotation against 'Poplars' 3.123 'very improper Trees to build Ships with'; and against 3.464 'wants a foot'.

The following list records the alterations in the manuscript. On most of its pages, a fair copy has been subjected to later revisions, but on some pages the poem is at an earlier stage of composition. As indicated above, these sections are not continuous with the narrative of the earlier ones; they are considerably overwritten and are crossed out with a firm vertical line. These sections are noted in the list below. The very large number of diagonal lines in the margin are not recorded.

The following simple descriptions of positions in the manuscript are used:

*above*: the words or words in the lemma are interlined above the specified word or words (generally deleted)
*after*: the word or words in the lemma appear in the same line immediately after the specified word or words (generally deleted)
*before*: the word or words in the lemma appear in the same line immediately before the specified word or words (generally deleted)
*below*: the words or words in the lemma are interlined below the specified word or words (generally deleted)
*over*: the word or letter following *over* replaces the previous one by overwriting

Lemmata follow the edited text, with its expanded contractions; quotations from the manuscript do not use such expansions.

## *Book I*

**65.1.2** close] *above deleted* heal

**65.1.3–5** What . . . unkind] *present line 4 mistakenly deleted in MS, and the two lines that follow and their corrections also deleted; the first of these is illegible; the second reads* She still adores him absent & unkind *above which are several draft revisions: above* see's him absent whom she & loves him tho; *after* absent she sees & loves; *lines 4 and 5 brought in from the facing verso; MS line three* Regrett, despair, & rage distract her Mind *mistakenly left undeleted*

**65.1.4** His Image] *after deleted* For still

**65.1.7** How . . . we] *above deleted* No Deaths so terrible as Death of

**65.1.13** Deplore . . . at] *above deleted* And wish, but dare not to propose,

**65.1.21** once . . . prosp'rous] *above deleted* bless'd abode of her once happy

**65.1.22** Return] *above deleted* Present; *whole line below deleted* Brought all her Sorrows fresher to her View,

**65.1.23** fan] d *of* fan'd *deleted*

**65.1.30** Cables] *after deleted word, possibly planned as* Planks
**65.1.31** were dash'd] were *before deleted* now, *above deleted* were, *above deleted* approached
**65.1.33** *large X in margin*
**65.1.34** Steep . . . spent] *above deleted and reused lines* Steep as it was they climb'd the rough [rough *above* steep] Ascent | They [*before deleted* gain the Sum] climb by craggy steps the rude Ascent | Steep as it was & half their Vigour spent | They gain'd the summit of the rude Ascent [*above deleted* climb w$^{th}$ pain the Mountains rough Ascent] | Craggy & vast: when [*above deleted* &] nearer as they drew | The Summit gain'd; the Queen w$^{th}$ curious View | Examin'd by the Goddess curious View | Each examin'd as they nearer drew
**65.1.36** And gain the Summit] *above deleted* Replete w$^{th}$. Joy: when
**65.1.38** The one a Youth] *underlined*
**65.1.40** The Goddess' Favour soon the younger] *underlined*
won] *after deleted* one
**65.1.43** time] *before deleted* & Care
or Battle scar'd his] *above deleted* his alter'd
*After this line, draft of lines 23–43 deleted:*
And fan'd her half extinguish'd [*above deleted* the dying Embers of her] Flame anew.
Now wrapt in Thought, upon the Beach she stood,
Whilst briny [*above deleted* kindred] Tears encrease the kindred [*above deleted* briny] Flood
Viewing, incessant, where her Eyes lett slip
The last dim Object of Ulisses Ship.
When on a sudden, floating on the Tide [*above deleted* & from far she spy'd,]
Some Ship-wreck Fragments from afar she spy'd [*above deleted* floating on the Tide;]
The Oars, & seats of the late lab'ring Row'r,
The Masts, & Cables, driving tow'rd the Shore.
Nor far remote She soon two Men perceives,
Each well-known Beauty of the Parent [*above deleted* Struggling for Life, & waring w$^{th}$ the Waves:]
By Youth improved was there w$^{th}$ added Grace [*above deleted* Awhile the Sport of adverse Billows toss'd,]
But thrown at last in safety on the Coast.
Beauteous [*above deleted* Charming] the One in bloom of Life appears;
The other rev'rend in decline of Years.
The Younger soon [*above deleted* Youth] the Goddess favour won; [*after deleted* quickly]
For ev'ry Feature spoke Ulisses' [*above deleted* Too like Ulisses not to be his Son.] Son
Spoke what the Father was in youthfull Grace [*above deleted* Nor shone the Offspring w$^{th}$ inferior Grace,]
To the known Beautys of the [*after deleted* his] Parent's Face.
**65.1.44** knew] *above deleted* could

**65.1.52** by] *above deleted* on
right] *above deleted* hope

**65.1.54** 'Come . . .] *the quotation marks are taken from the original lines in the MS*

The next 18 lines, taken in from the next page, replace the following, deleted and beginning with a cross to mark the insertion:

"Rash Mortals know [*before deleted* who] this Island own's my Power,
"Where [*above deleted* And] none unpunish'd touch the sacred Shore:
"Tho press'd by Storms the wretched Pilots steer,
"A distant Course nor hope for Harbour here:

*[three following lines written over the three that follow them]*

For hard the Penalty our law ordains,
if any dares molest these hallow'd Plains,
Tis instant Death or never-ending Chains.

*[following triplet deleted earlier]*

"Half in accessible from Rocks & Sand
"And Interdicted by our strict Command
"They shun the Dangers of this hallow'd Land
Artfully thus w$^{th}$ Menaces she strove,
To check the Dictates of fast-growing Love.
W$^{ch}$ uncontroul'd [*above deleted* in her Looks] & pure [*after deleted indecipherable words and above deleted* impassive of her Art,] of all her Art
Spoke, in her Eyes [*above* uncontoul'd], the Language of her Heart.

*the lines just given also replace an earlier draft on the facing recto, which lies underneath a slip of paper carrying the lines 55–71, which is pasted over a deleted, shorter draft of lines 50–96*

Meantime Calypso w$^{th}$ an inward joy,
Beheld the Son of him who humbled [*above deleted* vanquish'd] Troy:
And thus (as ignorant to whom She spoke)
Advancing tow'ard the Strangers, silence broke.
'Whence are [e *written over* t] yee [*above deleted* thou?] say, & how yee came [*above deleted* thou camst] to dare,
'To sett your [*above deleted* thy] impious Feet unbidden here?
'Rash [*above deleted* Young] Strangers [s *added*] know, who touch this sacrad [*above deleted* venture on this] Shore,
'fall the just Victims to offended [*above deleted* Are justly punish'd by my slighted] Pow'r.
Artfully thus w$^{th}$ [*above deleted* in] Menaces She strove
To check the Dictates of fast [*above deleted* hide her inward joy, &] growing Love:

W$^{ch}$ uncontroul'd, elusive of [*above deleted* in spight of all] her Art,
Spoke in her looks the Language of her Heart.
When [W *written over* T] thus Ulisses' Son. [*above deleted* the pious *followed by indecipherable word*] 'Who-eer you are,
'Goddess or Mortal (yet divinely fair.)
Can you behold, unmov'd, a wretched Son,

'By virtuous Zeal, & filial Love undone?
'Deaf as the Winds by w$^{ch}$ my Ship was born,
'Relentless as the Rocks on w$^{ch}$ twas torn,
'Can you behold me for my Father mourn?
'Who is that Father? (interrupt's the Queen.)
'The best of Fathers & the best of Men:
'A King Ulisses call'd, no little Name
'Nor unrecorded in the Rolls of Fame
*the last two lines above the following deleted couplet* (Weeping replied the Pious Youth again.) | 'A King he was, Ulisses was his Name:
'Among those Heroes (nor the least) he came,

**65.1.56** Sin yee] *above deleted* wander
**65.1.57** the Cause, our] *above deleted* it be the
**65.1.60** press'd] *after deleted* urg
**65.1.61** holds aloof] *above deleted* distant sails
**65.1.62** If] *after deleted* Who
**65.1.64** molest] *above deleted* pollute
**65.1.66** Friends] *before deleted* own lov'd
Friends . . . Parents] *above deleted* distant Country
**65.1.67** permitted] *inserted above with caret*
Eyes] *before deleted* permitted
**65.1.68** Desembling] *above deleted* Deceitfull
**65.1.69** commencing] *above deleted* fast growing
**65.1.71** undisguis'd] *above deleted* uncontroul'd
**65.1.72** Prince] *after deleted* humble
submiss] *inserted above with caret*
**65.1.73–8** *a vertical line through these, presumably by mistake*
**65.1.74** tim'rous urge a weak] *above deleted* fear to urge his own; urge *before deleted* speak; weak *before deleted* strong
**65.1.81** By] *above deleted* Twas
I sought a Refuge here] *above deleted* me to take Shelter here.
**65.1.84** deathfull] *above deleted* mortal
**65.1.86–7** *couplet above deleted* Recieved my Vows, & gave me to obtain | This transient Respight for a Life of Pain.
**65.1.86** still] *after deleted* who but
**65.1.99–100** *couplet above deleted* The Mighty War my Fathers Councils guide, | They chose Ulisses Counsell for their Guide | To him for Aid the King of Kings apply'd.
**65.1.106** Huge] *above deleted* Great
**65.1.127** wait's] *above deleted* guides *which is above deleted* crown's
**65.1.131** on Earth we know] *above underlined* we tast below; *neither deleted*
**65.1.141** Life] *after deleted* Wife
**65.1.143** Ulisses'] *above deleted* My Father's
**65.1.146** They cry] *above deleted* Perhaps
**65.1.147** some] *above deleted* the
**65.1.156–7** *couplet above deleted* He ended here compleating w$^{th}$ his Tongue | The am'rous Conquest w$^{ch}$ his Eyes begun;

**65.1.158** flowing] *above deleted* manly
such] *after deleted* w$^{th}$
manly] *after deleted* decent
w$^{th}$ . . . manly] *above deleted* such Youthfull Grace!
**65.1.161** kindling] *above deleted* melting
*followed by a further page of deleted material, consisting of the first, much shorter version of lines 109–53, with very little revision; and above the first 9 of these, a later draft of lines 106–13*

'Who swore destruction on devoted Troy,
'And vengeance on her lewd, adult'rous Boy.
'But ten Years past of [*over* in] unsuccessful strife,
'To gain the freedom of the Spartan Wife;
'By Stratagem he sack'd the burning Town, }
'It's tow'ry Honours were by Him oerthrown, }
'He wore the Palm of Victory alone. }
'In Greece & Asia is his Story told;
'In Council wary, in the Battle bold.
'But now he roves o'er Neptunes wat'ry Reign,
'Expos'd to all the dangers of the Main:
'That unforgiving God w$^{th}$ stedfast Hate,
'Bar's his Return, & urges him on Fate.
'In vain His Son, his People, & his Wife,
'Make Vows to Jove, for Jove neglects his Life.
'Yee equal Gods! if virtue be your Care,
'My Father's [*above deleted* Ulisses] Friends ought never to despair
'But Fears &c — [*above deleted* But now] perhaps, allready has he breath'd [*above deleted* ev'n now be breaths] his last,
'Choak'd by the Waves: against the Rocks is cast
'His mangled Body: while the hapless Ghost
'Wanders unbury'd on the Stygian Coast.
'Forgive these Tears the Privilege of Grief
'Nor, if tis thine to give, refuse relief.

[*below this couplet a couplet deleted earlier*

Oh! pity the distress to w$^{ch}$ I'm brought,
'Or (if thou canst) remove th'afflicting Thought.]
'If tis allow'd thee (Fair divine!) to read
'What Fate unalterable has decreed;

*above the first 9 of these lines a later draft of lines 106–13*
Great Ajax Strength Achilles matchless Force
From his Direction learn'd to steer their Course
W$^{th}$out it vain: he show'd 'em to destroy [*after deleted* unable to destroy]
The sacred Walls of Heav'n-defended Troy
for ten Years wasted in successless Strife,
for Restitution of the Spartan Wife
When Seas of Blood & mountains of the Slain
had dy'd the Shore & heap'd the Phrygian Plain
He deeply skill'd in war's destructive Art [*after deleted* & in Action]

**65.1.163** *line followed by this deleted couplet* Mute adoration for awhile she pay'd | Insatiate gazing, then benignant say'd:
**65.1.164** sweet Youth] *above deleted* young Stranger well
**65.1.171** Alas] *above deleted* Your Toil[?] Woes
nay I share] *above deleted* & I feel
**65.1.172** Nature] *above deleted* not of Steel
form'd] *above deleted* stamped
**65.1.174** fill'd my gen'rous] *above deleted* bless'd my *followed by two indecipherable words*
**65.1.176** All] *above deleted* What
**65.1.177** Doubt] *above deleted* Fear
in] *above deleted* on
**65.1.178** What] *above deleted* The *with caret*
**65.1.181** *This line is followed by a deleted page of draft material corresponding to lines 154–202, and above those lines a draft of 231–45:*

'Say has it destin'd mercyfull to save?
'Or has it doom'd him [him *inserted above with caret*] to the peacefull Grave?
Calpyso gaz'd enamour'd on his Face,
Charm'd by his eloquence & youthfull Grace.
Insatiate looking She stood mute awhile,
Then thus she answer'd w$^{th}$ a gracefull Smile.
'Thy Father's Fate young Stranger well I know,
'Too long, the Tale to be recounted now.
'Hence [*above deleted* Come] to my Grotto [o *added*], there [there *inserted above with caret*] repose [*followed by deleted*] yourself awhile,
'Refresh your Spiritts, & forgett your Toyl.
'Oyls and the healing Bath we'll straight prepare,
'And Health-restoring Sleep shall lull thy Care.
'Thee will I tend w$^{th}$ more than Mother's Love
'And more than mortal Joy thy Soul shall prove
[*couplet above deleted couplet* 'Like a fond Mother will I cherish Thee | 'For thou my Comfort & my Care shalt be:]
'My former Pleasures all shalt thou pertake,
'And added Pleasures to the former make.
'Incessant Raptures shall in Circles flow,
'And [*below deleted* For] thou art happy, think thy-self but so.
Ulisses' Son the kind command obey'd,
Close by her side; & to the Grott they lead.
Amid her Nymphs She walk'd, but w$^{th}$ a Mien,
That told at once the Goddess & the Queen.
So a tall Oak, the Forest's lofty Pride,
W$^{th}$ Head majestick top's the Plants beside.

*above these lines, a draft of lines 231–44:*
What Beautys [Beautys *underlined,* Prospects *inserted above, neither deleted*] here [here *inserted above with caret*] what blissfull Scenes invite
All court at once & croud upon the Sight
Whereer the Stranger turn their ravish'd Eyes,

New Wonders dazzle & new Beautys [Beautys *over* Wonders] rise
Yet nature her [*inserted above with caret*] spontaneous grace deck'd [*after deleted* grace] the Soil.
Pure of the Builder's or the Gardner's [*after deleted* Labo] Toil
Spontaneous Beautys deck'd the S
The Pomp of Nature pure of Art or Toil
For [*before deleted* Hence] ev'ry Charm spontaneous [*after deleted* there] deck'd the Soil
Here polish'd Gems, nor burnish'd Metals shine
The far sought [*above deleted* borrow'd] Lustre of the Indian Mine
No marble Colums here nor painted Domes ari [*after deleted* in rich order rise]

*after 2 lines above which the revised version of lines 180–1 are written*

Meting the Clouds & climbing on the Skys
Each menial Virgin boasts her sep'rate Bow'r
by shells & Pebles rudlely crusted o'er

*after 1 line above which deleted* For *is written*

Deep in a hollow Rock, a quiet Shade,
That own's nor Architect nor Sculptor's aid
For Tapistry a Vine

**65.1.188** Successive] *above deleted* Incessant
incessant] *above deleted* successive
**65.1.192** in Mankind] *above deleted* to thy kind
**65.1.197** Fair] *above deleted* Queen
**65.1.199** far from] *above deleted* distant at
**65.1.200** *followed by deleted and reused couplet* So, amid the Nymphs she walks but w$^{th}$ a Mien, [*followed by* w$^{th}$ nobler Mien] | That told at once the Goddess & the Queen.
**65.1.211–12** *couplet above deleted* Her Wast was circled by a Golden Zone; | The precious Clasps w$^{th}$ living Saphirs shone,
**65.1.231** Heav'nly Visions here] *above deleted* Prospect here what bliss
**65.1.232** Open] *above deleted* All court
solliciting] *above deleted* & croud upon
**65.1.234** offer] *above deleted* dazzle
**65.1.237** No] *in margin replacing deleted* Here *which replaced deleted* No
here venerable] *above deleted* nor Marble Columns
**65.1.238** Nor marble Columns] *above deleted* In awfull Splendour
**65.1.240** Product] *above deleted* Lustre
**65.1.246** *followed by deleted couplet* Unbidden Plenty in the Orchard [Orchard *above* Fruit-Yard] reign's | And Ceres ripen's on unlabour'd Plains.
**65.1.251** Perfumes scatter'd] *above deleted* Fragrance dropping
**65.1.256** sweet] *above deleted* calm
**65.1.257** soft] *after deleted* swe
Call] *inserted above with caret*
**65.1.260** incessant] *above deleted* some silver
**65.1.261** diverse wander] *above deleted* winds incessant a [wander *after deleted* roll]
down] a *of* adown *deleted*

**65.1.262–5** *above four deleted lines* & floats the Plain beneath [neath *above deleted* low] there whilst it flow's | A thousand nat'ral Baths the Stream bestow's | Limpid & cool, for arching o'er Head | Their verdant Canopys tall Poplers spread

**65.1.263** mazy] *above deleted* limpid

**65.1.264** Warm] *after deleted* A
oft] *after deleted* high

**65.1.271** Ocean] *underlined*

**65.1.272** along] *above* w$^{th}$
the Shore] *after deleted* hollow *and above deleted* hideous Roar
*followed by six deleted lines or part-lines* Huge Liquid Mountains tumbling shake | The Mountain Billows sparkling lash the Shore | & now Serene the curling | Now sudden cease the Winds, | And play amid the Rocks | And play among the Rocks, a harmless Tide.
*After this line there are nine lines imperfectly revised by Hervey, where it is impossible to discern his intentions because they do not link to the lines immediately before or after them; they are excluded from the printed text:*

This to the Setting Sun [Sun *above the line*] oppos'd are seen
Meadows [*after deleted* meadows & w *above* Fair tufted Groves] & Groves & mead of [*? incomplete word* undecu]
The sweet Haunt these [*above* The [The *deleted*] Refuge this [this *deleted*]; *in margin* these] of many a tunefull Bird
And those [*above deleted* that] sweet Pasture for the milky Herd
Beneath the Pliads & celestial [*above deleted* Mountains uncouth beneath the starry] Bear
High Hills [*above deleted* Exclude the balefull North's inclement] objected to the Northern Air
exclude [*after deleted* Mountains obstruct the &] th' Inclement air aloft they rise
& lose [*after deleted* Enormous, vast, Olympus Height they rise] their less'ning Sum

*Then three pages of deleted draft material, the first of these a deleted draft of lines 201–44, with revisions to some lines interspersed, and section 217–26 squeezed into top right-hand corner; main page reads*

As some tall Oak the Forest's lofty Pride
W$^{th}$ Head majestick tops the Plants beside
A Purple Robe she wore w$^{th}$ gracefull Pride *below deleted* Her purple Robes but half her Bosome hide.
Her Hair [*after deleted* Har] behind was negligently ty'd
The Spring was rifled to adorn her brow:
A light Cymar o'erspread her Limbs below,
Whilst busy [*above deleted* warring] Winds oblige the curious Eye
And half permitt the View & half deny.
Her Wast was circled by a golden Zone,
The glitt'ring Clasps wth living Saphirs shone. [*couplet above deleted couplet* A Golden Zone her slender Wast confin'd | And many a Dimond on the border shone. [*after deleted* shin'd]]
In many a Fold collecting from the Plain [In *after deleted* w$^{th}$ cautious *after* ample]
The spotted Beautys of her Ermin Train *below* respect *in margin* in ev'ry Breast an Awe & mix *after deleted* He.

Her Eyes inspire [*below deleted* respect] command yet raise desire
Nor are alone her piercing Eyes [Eyes *inserted above*] but mix emotions of a soft Desire
For temp'ring Sweetness soften's ev'ry Fire.
Th'admiring Youth confess'd a new [Youth ... new *inserted above deleted* was ravish'd at the sigh w$^{th}$] delight,
And felt a secret rapture at the sight. *beneath alternative line* indulged [*after deleted* Yet unacquainted] the raptures of a new Delight:
The Royal Guest whose Virgin Breast before unconscious of [*above deleted* had never felt] the warmth of Beauty's Power Love never warm'd
W$^{th}$ down-cast Looks, nor pleas'd, the hoary Seer,
Lag'd far behind, & pensive, clos'd the Rear:
He see's the Evils of a future Hour,
And joyless to the present gain's the Bow'r.
These Charms unseen [*after deleted* till] before the Prince surprise [*before this line deleted* Amazement seiz'd the Prince *and below* Telemachus was struck at once see, [see *after deleted* at]]
A thousand Beautys crowding on his Eyes
There polished Brass nor burnished Gold was seen [seen *brought in from earlier draft line below* No glittering Gold, no Silver there was seen;]
Nor Paint, nor Statues deck'd the Silvan Scene:
No marble Columns in rich [*above deleted* here by *and followed by deleted* in] Order rise,
Meting the Clouds & climbing on [*above deleted* seem to reach] the Skys.
W$^{th}$in a Rock is hewn each blissful Bow'r,
By Shells & Pebles rudely crusted o'er.

*on same page draft of lines 217–26 squeezed into top right-hand corner and not set as verse, reads:*

w$^{th}$ grace divine celestial Charms display'd
thus proudly as she treads the painted Glade
The Royal Stranger new to Beautys Pow'r
indulg'd [*above deleted* confused] a transport never felt before
wishes & soft inquietudes arose
& warmth unusual in his bosome glows;
his Eyes, his Thought, o'er ev'ry Beauty rove,
w$^{th}$ all the little previous Cares to love,
e'er yet the Conquest testify'd by smart
in its full vigour rages in the Heart.

*next page a deleted draft of lines 260–5*

Or trickling Current of incessant Rills,
That diverse wander down the Rocky Hills;
& wide expanded on the Plains below,
In silver Lakes, or mazy Rivers flow
Warm from the Chace here oft the Goddess sought,
The limpid Bath [*above deleted* Draught], or cool refreshing Draught.

*towards the bottom of the page, linked to the facing recto with a cross*

This to the rising Sun, opposed are seen,

*next page deleted draft of lines 245–57, 271, and above the first 12 of these lines revised version of lines 247–57, with 12 lines later discarded*

No Tapistry but Vines [*after deleted* a]; around each Stone,
The Branches curl'd, the purple Clusters Shone:
Sweet Zephirs here, in spight of Phoebus Heat,
Preserve their coolness & refresh the Seat.
A Citron-Grove there rests its golden Head,
Whose fragrant Blossoms gratefull Odours shed:
Their gaudy Leaves like painted Feathers show,
And in eternal Spring successive [*above deleted* for ever] blow:
Whilst intermix'd the ripen'd Fruits appear,
Loading [*before deleted* And load] the fertile Branches all the Year.
Their leafy Arms close-wove forbid the Light,
And form at Noon an artificial Night.
Nor noise w$^{th}$ in this calm retreat is heard,
Save the soft Carols of some tunefull Bird;
Or tumbling [*above deleted* boiling] Streams, that w$^{th}$ impetuous Force,
Gush from the Rocks, & headlong urge their [*above deleted* shape a headlong] Course.
Upon an easy Hill the Grotto stood,
Within the prospect of the Ocean-flood;
That now becalm'd, & now w$^{th}$ angry Shocks,
Dashes repell'd [*above deleted* in vain] against unshaken Rocks.
This from the East [*above deleted* North], & from the West [*above deleted* South] is seen,
*whole line deleted and marked with cross to bring in line on facing page* This to the rising Sun, opposed are seen,
Slow Rivers vagrant [*above deleted* wandring] o'er a flowry Green.
A thousand nat'ral Baths their Springs prepare,
Than Glass more smooth, than pollish'd Crystal clear.

**65.1.281** Promiscuous Plenty] *above deleted* With glowing Beautys
Plenty] *after deleted* fertile

**65.1.285** *line followed by a page of deleted draft of lines 266–82, including 16 lines finally discarded:*

Whilst over-head a Canopy is made
(Gratefull refreshment!) by the Poplar's shade.
Beneath upon the Shore promiscuous grows,
The Woodbine, Jasmin, Violet, & Rose.
Sometimes the sportive Streams their waves divide,
Forming small Islands, then rejoin their Tide.
Some creep along, in sleepy Currents, slow;
And some precipitately rapid flow.
Whilst others circling w$^{th}$ a middle Force,
Through many a turn pursue their vagrant Course;
And seem their various windings to retrace,
Unwilling to forsake the charming Place.
Northward [North *before deleted* East *and above deleted* From far] Vast Hills & Mountains you descry;

In odd-Shaped Forms they catch the far-stretch'd Eye,
And lose [*above deleted* seem to lose] their Summits mingling w$^{th}$ [*above deleted* in] the Sky.
On southern Mounts [*above deleted* And on the West *with deleted* South *above deleted* West *with caret*] are fruitfull Vinyards sett
Their purple Grapes peep through the curling Nett
Whilst supple Boughs bend wth the luscious weight.
Pomegranate, Figg, & Olive-Trees around,
Are wildly mix'd & own the fertile Ground.
Then native beautys that enrich her Isle
Calpyso shew'd: then, w$^{th}$ benignant smile,
Thus to the wellcome Pair her Words address'd.
'Your late fatigue requires a moment's Rest:

**65.1.294** mantling Vine's autumnal Gifts] *above deleted* Vines beneath the Noon-tide Sun
**65.1.295** spoil] *above deleted* cull
of] *above deleted* pluck
**65.1.297** to soften thy delay] *above deleted* when far from what we love
**65.1.298** *line above deleted* The Hours employ'd, less tedious seem to move
**65.1.303** impart] *before large asterisk in margin, linked to deleted four lines of dialogue on facing page*
**65.1.304** Will] *after deleted* that shall at once
**65.1.306** End,] *before and above large cross in margin. Line followed by four lines deleted with asterisks in right margin* 'Tis time to change these Robes, w$^{ch}$ still retain | The various Vapour [*above deleted* dampness] of the soaking Main. | When next we meet, a Tale [a Tale *above with caret*] I shall [*before deleted* a Tale] impart | Will all thy doubts resolve, & touch thy Heart.
**65.1.309** *line is deleted and has a cross in the right margin, but it is needed for the couplet*
Nymphs] *after deleted word, possibly* hardy
expert] *inserted above with caret*
**65.1.310** Cost] *above deleted* Care
Labour] *above deleted* trouble
**65.1.312** The] *after deleted* Around
round the fire was] *above deleted* airing
**65.1.315** glossey] *above deleted* softest
labour'd] *above deleted* glossey
**65.1.316** Not Snow so] *above deleted* Snow is less
so fine] so *above* less
**65.1.318** *line above deleted* And rich besett w$^{th}$ golden Stars appear.
**65.1.319** When] *above deleted* Then
**65.1.320** *line above deleted indecipherable line including* the weakness of the earlyest
*after deleted* Unprofitable Cates
**65.1.321** 'Is it . . . to] *above* Vain youth (sayd He) is this what you
**65.1.323** on the . . . won] *above deleted* rather on the glorious Race he ran
**65.1.329** endure] *above deleted* despise
**65.1.330** this] *above deleted* that

**65.1.333–6** *lines inserted from facing page* [Lines tother Side], *before deleted couplet* May angry Jove this brittle Fame annull, | E'er Luxury take possession of my Soul.

**65.1.338** offspring, prodigal of ] *above deleted* Son, in Heat of active

**65.1.340** a] *above deleted* his

**65.1.346** atractive] *above deleted* actrive, *possibly an attempt at* atractive

**65.1.350** Doubtfull] *above deleted* Anxious

**65.1.352** will] *after deleted* can *which is above deleted* will

**65.1.353** ever Sanguine] *above* is presuming

**65.1.354** Pursue's all joy, and apprehend's no] *above deleted* He seeks the Pleasure never dread's the

**65.1.355** *line above deleted* He's headstrong, will no obstacles confes

**65.1.361** each] *above deleted* her

**65.1.362** By specious . . . betray'd] *line lightly crossed through*

**65.1.365** for th'] *above deleted* the

**65.1.366** Maids] *above deleted* Nymphs

**65.1.371** tastfull] *above deleted* gratefull

**65.1.388** Herculean Fame his Labours] *after deleted* as a God *above deleted* a Demi-god the Heroe

**65.1.397** ready] *inserted above with caret*

Eyes] *after deleted* brim full

**65.1.400** distress'd] *marginal replacement for* oppress'd

**65.1.405** Where] *above deleted* And

**65.1.407** Like Orpheus-self ] *above deleted* In Strains like his

**65.1.410** count] *above deleted* tell

**65.1.413** vent'rous] *above deleted* lonely

the gates of ] *above deleted* tremendous

**65.1.418** Then all] *inserted above with caret.* In *consequently emended to lower case.*

chaunt] *after deleted* then all

**65.1.424** their solemn] *after deleted* within their *and above deleted* their solemn

show] *marginal replacement for deleted* Show;

**65.1.425** How ten successive] *above deleted* They urge how sev'n long

**65.1.443** ancient] *above* wonted

**65.1.452** rabid] *above deleted* rav'nous

**65.1.454** ten] *above deleted* sev'n

**65.1.460** regardless of the Pains] *above deleted* in the last Agonys

**65.1.464** when to the Youth apart] *above deleted* & terminate the Song

*this line followed by* Nor longer the Repast w$^{th}$ Tunes prolong. | When fair Calypso took the Youth apart,

**65.1.465** The Goddess] *above deleted* And (private)

**65.1.467** thou ungratefull to my Care] *above deleted* for Ulisses sake but thine alone

**65.1.468** Tho dear] *above deleted* Dear was

**65.1.472–3** *with a squiggly vertical line*

**65.1.478** *line above deleted* Beauty he had & Beauty had its due.

**65.1.483** fly] *underlined*

**65.1.487** scarce the shore] *above deleted* just as Land

his] *inserted above with caret*

**65.1.488** When] *above deleted* The

| | |
|---|---|
| **65.1.491** | play] *after deleted* fly |
| **65.1.497** | His Orders perish] *above deleted* His Voice is swallow'd |
| **65.1.505** | bend] *above deleted* Shun |
| | stubborn] *above deleted* shatter'd |
| **65.1.506** | loaded] *above deleted* heavy |
| **65.1.515** | And] *before deleted* desperate *which is above deleted* mourning |
| | desponding] *above deleted* he |
| **65.1.523** | To] *above deleted* But |
| | for Aid] *above deleted* relentless |
| **65.1.532** | fast] *inserted above with caret* |
| **65.1.539** | the gains] *above deleted* th' effects |
| **65.1.541** | And hear] *above deleted* You've heard |
| **65.1.542** | Then by] *above deleted* By all |
| | Frenzy] *above deleted* Fancy |
| **65.1.547** | which] *above deleted* that |
| **65.1.554** | Dissembling] *inserted in space at beginning of paragraph.* Thus *consequently emended to lower case* |
| | Queen] *after deleted* dissembling |
| **65.1.558–65** | *these eight lines are brought in from the facing page to replace* Long was the Hero by the Tempest toss'd; \| But found a Harbour on Pheacia's Coast. *Before them is a deleted rejected line* Tho' Neptune long the vagrant Hero toss'd |
| **65.1.570** | the well-lay'd] *above deleted* each flatt'ring |
| **65.1.583** | marvel] *above deleted* wonder |
| **65.1.584–5** | *couplet is above deleted* A Father lost; and lost the rightfull Crown, \| Inheritance should bring to me his Son. |
| **65.1.590** | *line brought in from facing page, replacing deleted* W$^{ch}$ not the [*above deleted* your] Smiles of Beauty can [*with caret after and above* can wholly yet] redress. |
| **65.1.592** | manly] *above deleted* pious |
| **65.1.595** | pious] *above deleted* deadly |
| **65.1.598** | Ev'n] *above deleted* The |
| **65.1.615** | the modest Youth] *above deleted* thus modestly |
| **65.1.616** | *line above deleted* The blushing Prince) Vain Fear (the Goddess cry'd.) |
| **65.1.629** | *line followed by deleted four lines* Of golden Tissue were [*above deleted* wher] their Garments made, \| Embroider'd some, & some of rich Brocade; \| The labours of their Loomb, & nicely wrought \| W$^{th}$ various Fancy, rul'd by artfull Thought. |
| **65.1.630** | Bow's] *after deleted* Silver *and before and below* unbent *with caret* |
| **65.1.631** | *line followed by deleted couplet* To show how pure a Virgin-Fame they bore, \| Each a fresh Sprig of Agnus castus wore. |
| **65.1.645** | with Shame] *above deleted* at once |
| **65.1.656** | Place] *underlined; alternative written above is* Face |
| **65.1.659** | attended] *after deleted* arising |
| **65.1.669** | quiet] *above deleted* leafy |
| **65.1.670** | even] *above deleted* quiet |
| **65.1.689** | Of . . . irradiate] *underlined* |
| **65.1.692** | *line followed by deleted line,* The hapless Lover mourn'd the Woman fired |

| | |
|---|---|
| **65.1.700** | Close] *above deleted* And |
| **65.1.703** | sought] *above deleted* seeks |
| **65.1.706** | Rang'd] *overwrites indecipherable word* |
| **65.1.708** | Sleep] *after deleted* courted |
| | tho courted still] *entered above with caret* |
| **65.1.713** | Yet] *above deleted* And |

## *Book II*

| | |
|---|---|
| **65.2.7** | To weep] *after deleted* Unseen |
| | unseen] *above deleted* unheard |
| | unhear'd] *inserted above with caret* |
| **65.2.9** | from the] *after deleted* murm'ring |
| **65.2.14** | Fair] *underlined* |
| **65.2.15** | Soul] *above deleted* Grief |
| **65.2.16** | Care] *above deleted* Grief |
| **65.2.19** | Tears can bring] *underlined; below* weeping is*; neither deleted* |
| **65.2.20** | both] *above deleted* the |
| **65.2.25** | first] *underlined; below* great*; neither deleted* |
| **65.2.30** | cooling] *above deleted* gentle |
| **65.2.35** | caused] *inserted from above with caret* |
| **65.2.36** | kind returns are] *above deleted* mark of Thanks is |
| **65.2.37** | *line underlined* |
| **65.2.43** | Despis'd] *above deleted* Contemn'd |
| **65.2.44** | next] *underlined and below* now*; neither deleted* |
| **65.2.46** | Contemn's] *above deleted* Neglects |
| **65.2.47** | Eludes] *above deleted* Eludes |
| | spurn's] *above deleted* slight's |
| **65.2.48** | Yet (gratefull] *after deleted* and*; above* Yet thou (dear |
| **65.2.52** | Immortality] *after deleted* ought could cancel |
| **65.2.53** | Those Racks would doe it which] *above deleted* Sure 'twould be done by what*; deleted indecipherable word before* Racks |
| **65.2.57** | the Heart] the *over* her |
| **65.2.64** | uncurtain'd] d *underlined* |
| **65.2.66** | adorn'd] d *underlined* |
| **65.2.67** | Danced] d *underlined* |
| **65.2.72** | Compassionate behold] *underlined and below* Look with compassion on*; neither deleted* |
| **65.2.82** | white] *after deleted* more |
| | as unsully'd] *above deleted* than Alpine |
| **65.2.85** | burnish'd] *above deleted* polish'd |
| **65.2.86** | beaten] *above deleted* burnish'd |
| **65.2.90** | polish'd] *above deleted* various |
| **65.2.92** | force] *underlined and below* Art*; neither deleted* |
| **65.2.98** | whiter] *above deleted* reining |
| **65.2.100** | Son of Juno] *after deleted* Juno |
| **65.2.101** | *line underlined, with marginal comment* this line mark'd by mistake*; and various crosses on the underlining* |

| | |
|---|---|
| **65.2.107** | On] *underlined and below* By; *neither deleted* |
| **65.2.118** | constant] *underlined* |
| **65.2.123** | Cupids strew] *above deleted* Lovers sport ore |
| **65.2.131** | Which] *above deleted* And |
| **65.2.139** | when] *above deleted* & |
| **65.2.161** | With] *inserted before* Cunning, *with* his *deleted after* Cunning |
| **65.2.163** | ready] *above deleted* idle |
| **65.2.179** | the] *inserted from above with caret* |
| **65.2.182** | seek, Revenge] Revenge *inserted from above with caret obscuring comma after* seek |
| | injur'd] *underlined* |
| **65.2.194** | shall claim but second] *above deleted* stands second for thy |
| **65.2.195** | Tho' Life immortal be] *underlined and below* For tho' immortal Life's; *neither deleted* |
| **65.2.212** | A present Ease but source of] *above deleted* For twas the Source of all her |
| **65.2.233** | fast] *above deleted* quick |
| **65.2.338** | Half] *above deleted* False |
| | recurring] *above deleted* intestine |
| **65.2.269** | *this line and the following taken in from opposite page; cross marks deleted line* Behold the Master-piece of Nature's Art: *Redundant triplet brace deleted by emendation* |
| **65.2.272** | *line before deleted couplet* Lucina's Virtue, Venus's Beauty joyn'd, \| A perfect Body, & a perfect Mind: *marginal bracket and comment in right margin* leave out or insert + above |
| **65.2.281** | slumber'd in] *above deleted* slept |
| | Hour] *after deleted* fatal |
| **65.2.290** | her Right] her *above deleted* the |
| **65.2.291** | Nor fear'd] *underlined* |
| **65.2.295** | pursue] *after deleted* subdue |
| **65.2.302** | leisure] *underlined* |
| **65.2.312** | base] *above deleted* false |
| **65.2.315** | If] *after deleted* By |
| | *this line and the next replace deleted couplet* By Vice, if gross, the Flesh alone is caught \| The reason that [*indecipherable words*] Thought |
| **65.2.332** | real Ill, the seeming] *above deleted* false, insinuating |
| **65.2.333** | to destroy] to *inserted from above with caret* |
| **65.2.337** | Passion] *above deleted* Pleasure |
| **65.2.339** | stand naked] *above deleted* be present |
| | Thought;] *after deleted* Fault *and overwrites comma* |
| **65.2.344** | Age and Wisdome] *above deleted* Prudence |
| | in vain] *after deleted* alas! |
| **65.2.354** | *line underlined, with on facing verso* Say, perhaps willing; should I urge my Flight. *Neither deleted* |
| **65.2.365** | 'When . . . Reign,] *below deleted* 'When prejudice & Passion hold the Rein; |
| **65.2.366** | Appetite] *above deleted* Prejudice |
| **65.2.393** | combate all their Bounty by] *above deleted* urge their Thunder to avenge |
| **65.2.400** | urg'd] *above deleted* spoke |
| **65.2.403** | In civil] *after deleted* And rend |

they rend] *entered from above with caret*
**65.2.407** such] *above deleted* so *with caret*
**65.2.408** to this] *above deleted* when thus
**65.2.410** or] *above deleted* &
**65.2.412** thy Int'rest and thy Fame] *above deleted* and fond Penelope's
**65.2.417** Was it] *above deleted* But not
that] *above deleted* did
preserv'd] *above deleted* protect
**65.2.422** What tho] *underlined; below* & say; *neither deleted*
should] *above deleted* shall
**65.2.424** survives his Virtue live's] *above deleted* outlives Desert has liv'd
**65.2.425** spoke] *after deleted* Mentor
the Friend] *entered from above with caret*
**65.2.431** Nor what to hope] *after deleted* He knew
he knew] *inserted from above with caret*
**65.2.436–7** *between these lines an insertion flourish and in the margin* Two Lines to the Side *On the facing page, but marked* leave out *with a vertical line* The Malice of a Foe less keen we find, | Than irksome Chidings from a Friend too kind.
**65.2.440** *line underlined*
**65.2.449** Charms] r *entered from above with caret*
**65.2.459** how] *underlined; below* 'twas; *neither deleted;*
vain] *inserted from above with caret*
**65.2.463** whilst] *above deleted* e'er
**65.2.469** effect] *after deleted* obtain *above deleted* effect
**65.2.470** Woman, whetted] whetted *underlined; below* Rage and; *neither deleted; consequential* 's
**65.2.503** apt] *above deleted* fitt
**65.2.508** Destraction] a *underlined; below* u; *neither deleted*
**65.2.514** Hell] *inserted from above with caret*
**65.2.540** And You] *underlined; below* Yee Powers; *neither deleted*
**65.2.564** roaring] *above deleted* raging

## *Book III*

**65.3.2** By] *after deleted* Circled
enshrin'd] *entered from above with caret*
**65.3.5** Claim their] *above deleted* Their Eyes
their debates] their *above deleted* &
**65.3.7** To Pallas some and some adhere] *above deleted* Some to Minerva hold, & some
**65.3.21** clad] *above deleted* dress'd
**65.3.53** her-self] *after deleted* our
**65.3.55** private] *underlined*
**65.3.58** the Queen submit] *above deleted* admit to goe
**65.3.106** this Struggle and Calypso's] *above deleted* one hearty Pang & I am
**65.3.109** in] *after deleted* on
**65.3.112** execute] *above deleted* excercise

| | |
|---|---|
| **65.3.119** | assist, avert th' impending] *above deleted* to intercept the threaten'd; avert *above deleted* avoid |
| **65.3.120** | Oppose thy Art] *above deleted* For Shame assist; Art *after deleted* Face |
| **65.3.123** | Poplars] *after a superscript cross connecting to a marginal note in another hand* very improper Trees to build [*above deleted* make] Ships w$^{th}$. |
| **65.3.124** | Tops] *after deleted* di |
| **65.3.131** | Ropes] *entered from above with caret* |
| **65.3.136** | hated] *underlined; below* hatefull; *neither deleted* |
| **65.3.156** | deciev'd] *underlined* |
| **65.3.164** | force] *after deleted* turn |
| **65.3.183** | had left] *above deleted* forsook |
| **65.3.185–6** | *couplet inserted with cross from facing page* |
| **65.3.195** | tott'ring] *after deleted* tre |
| **65.3.197** | her] *inserted from above with caret* |
| **65.3.203** | On] *above deleted* For |
| **65.3.216** | *line below deleted* And all the Friend was bury'd in the Spy<br>latent] *underlined; below* real; *neither deleted* |
| **65.3.226** | in the low'ring] *above deleted* then involve the |
| **65.3.227** | roll] *above deleted* burst |
| **65.3.230** | receedes] *above deleted* She slunk |
| **65.3.236** | *line inserted with cross from facing page, replacing deleted* Now unrestrain'd the furious Queen *above deleted* And now the Goddess unrestrained no more |
| **65.3.243** | diverse] *underlined* |
| **65.3.247** | *line followed by deleted couplet* The Mother Lyoness, her Children slain, \| Revengefull thus, loud bellow's through [*after deleted* oe] the Plain. |
| **65.3.254** | the] *above deleted* his |
| **65.3.256** | When thus, the Goddess with] *above deleted* The Queen, w$^{th}$ transport & |
| **65.3.257** | The Sage] *after deleted* Accost's<br>accosted and] *above deleted* & thus, |
| **65.3.271** | thy] *above deleted* his |
| **65.3.274** | thy] *above deleted* his |
| **65.3.285** | hated] *above deleted* cursed *which is after deleted* hat |
| **65.3.286** | haste] *above deleted* & [*comma supplied by emendation*] |
| **65.3.293** | *line followed by deleted* Thy Sorrows but begin & late shall end, *which Professor Overton takes to be evidence of this MS being a fair copy, the transcriber having skipped a couplet* |
| **65.3.308** | command] *after deleted* decreed |
| **65.3.309** | Stars] *entered from above with caret* |
| **65.3.339** | Death] *entered from above with caret* |
| **65.3.343** | linger's] *above deleted* loiters |
| **65.3.344** | But] *above deleted* And |
| **65.3.347** | dewy] *underlined* |
| **65.3.358** | hangs on] *underlined* |
| **65.3.359–65** | *these lines inserted from the opposite page, with a note in the margin* |

The Lines on the other Side *They replace the following deleted passage* Allready vainly would the Lover trace | The dear lov'd Features of the distant Face [*with scarcely decipherable revisions above* Beyond ... his ... the Beautys of her]; | Yet still her [*above deleted* the] ample Robes & flowing Hair; | (Unbound by Grief) that float upheld in Air, | Engross his Eyes, conspicuous from afar. | And vanish'd now [now *followed by deleted* ex *above*]the latest Glimpse of all | He thought, because he wish'd, he heard her [her *inserted above*] call

| | |
|---|---|
| **65.3.361** | Hair] *after deleted* Hair |
| **65.3.380** | mild] *above deleted* kind |
| **65.3.382** | Such] *above deleted* There |
| **65.3.384** | in] *above deleted* by |
| **65.3.389** | Reason] *capital* R *overwrites lower case* |
| **65.3.391** | not who] *underlined* |
| **65.3.413** | your] *above deleted* thy *with caret* |
| **65.3.415** | Collect] *above deleted* Call all |
| **65.3.424** | in] *underlined; below* of; *neither deleted* |
| **65.3.440** | Calypso might allow] *above deleted* the cruel Queen might grant |
| **65.3.443** | tepid] *above deleted* lukewarm |
| **65.3.453** | reigning in untam'd] *above deleted* raging with resistless F [*Professor Overton interprets as eyeskip to the next line of an earlier copy*] |
| **65.3.455** | your] *above deleted* thy *with caret* |
| **65.3.464** | *underlined; note in margin, not in Hervey's hand* wants a foot |
| **65.3.486** | might] *after deleted* cou |
| **65.3.512** | Penitent] *above deleted* Criminal |
| **65.3.531** | watry] *above deleted* sparkling |
| **65.3.543** | drench'd ... Sweat.] *underlined* |
| **65.3.553** | instant] *above deleted* speedy |
| **65.3.557** | horrid] *underlined* |
| **65.3.567** | Fires] *above deleted* Winds |
| **65.3.580** | Emergent blaze] *above deleted* Blaze to the Sky |
| **65.3.593** | half] *inserted with caret after* & |
| **65.3.607** | complains] *above deleted* speaks her Pains |
| **65.3.637** | poison'd] *underlined; below* ruin'd*; neither deleted* |
| **65.3.639** | Long] *above deleted* Still |

## *Emendations to 66 Agrippina, a Tragedy*

**main source** *Egerton*: British Library MS Egerton 3787
**complementary sources** none; but see Poem 78 for an earlier version of I. 1. 51–62 and see Poem 7, II. 92–106 for an earlier version of II. 2. 56–70

*see end of headnote to this poem for details of emendations made silently, which are additional to those listed here*

| | |
|---|---|
| **I.1.1** | here.] here *Egerton* |
| **I.1.12** | its Idol] it's Idol *Egerton* |
| **I.1.14** | Hour] Hour. *Egerton* |
| **I.1.17** | This,] This *Egerton* |
| **I.1.37** | Hour,] Hour. *Egerton* |

| | |
|---|---|
| **I.1.42** | believed;] believed *Egerton* |
| **I.1.45** | unapt] apt *Egerton* |
| **I.1.47** | reveal] reveal, *Egerton* |
| **I.1.49** | hast] has *Egerton* |
| **I.1.50** | imbib'd!] imbib'd *Egerton* |
| **I.1.56** | Or,] *Poem 78*; Or *Egerton* |
| | sure,] *Poem 78*; sure *Egerton* |
| | complain.] *Poem 78*; Complain *Egerton* |
| **I.1.58** | to,] *Poem 78*; to *Egerton* |
| **I.1.73** | Burden] Burdent *Egerton* |
| **I.1.82** | Son?] Son. *Egerton* |
| **I.1.83** | warp'd] wrap'd *Egerton* |
| **I.1.88** | pompous] pompouse *Egerton* |
| **I.1.91** | Statues] Statutes *Egerton* |
| **I.1.92** | Virtues,] Virtues *Egerton* |
| **I.1.94** | Her,] Her *Egerton* |
| **I.1.99** | *Rome.*] *Rome Egerton* |
| **I.1.102** | gave,] gave *Egerton* |
| **I.1.103** | Slave.] Slave *Egerton* |
| **I.1.104** | *Quæstors,*] *Quæstors Egerton* |
| **I.1.106** | Her,] Her *Egerton* |
| **I.1.130** | Augustus'] Augustu's *Egerton* |
| **I.1.141** | Stripling's] Striplings *Egerton* |
| **I.1.146** | *Power.*] *Power Egerton* |
| **I.1.162** | its] it's *Egerton* |
| **I.1.169** | constantly] consantly *Egerton* |
| **I.1.174** | Rest;] Rest. *Egerton* |
| **I.1.182** | Empress Moves] Empress: — Moves *Egerton* |
| | Retire.] *misplaced at end of* I. 1. 182 SD *Egerton* |
| **I.1.184** | one,] one *Egerton* |
| **I.1.194** | What,] What *Egerton* |
| | Plautus'] Plautus *Egerton* |
| **I.1.197** | Judge,] Judge *Egerton* |
| **I.1.207** | *Decii*] Decu *Egerton presumably a result of mis-dictation, not mis-transcription* |
| | *Fabii's*] Fabu's *Egerton presumably a result of mis-dictation, not mis-transcription* |
| **I.1.218** | Laws,] Laws. *Egerton* |
| **I.1.245** | Council] Concil *Egerton* |
| **I.1.248** | Mind.] Mind, *Egerton* |
| **I.1.256** | Prey;] Prey, *Egerton* |
| **I.1.260** | Crimes.] Crimes *Egerton* |
| **I.1.268** | Than] The *Egerton* |
| **I.1.282** | Opposites,] Opposites *Egerton* |
| **I.1.284** | Dispised;] Dispised, *Egerton* |
| **I.1.291** | None,] None *Egerton* |
| **I.1.299** | Army's] Armys *Egerton* |
| **I.1.306** | fall;] fall *Egerton* |

| | |
|---|---|
| **I.1.308** | destroy'd,] destroy'd *Egerton* |
| **I.1.312** | strong;] strong *Egerton* |
| **I.1.325** | Labors] Labor's *Egerton* |
| **I.1.329** | Court,] Court *Egerton* |
| **I.1.333** | hate.] hate *Egerton* |
| **I.1.343** | Sight] Slight *Egerton* |
| | Shun.] Shun *Egerton* |
| **I.1.344** | Care,] Care *Egerton* |
| **I.1.347** | it,] it *Egerton* |
| **I.1.351** | its views] it's veiw's *Egerton* |
| | its Venal] it's Venal *Egerton* |
| **I.1.352** | cou'd,] cou'd *Egerton* |
| **I.1.353** | Hand;] Hand, *Egerton* |
| **I.1.366** | bleed."] bleed *Egerton* |
| **I.1.369** | cry'd,] cry'd *Egerton* |
| **I.1.371** | late,] late *Egerton* |
| **I.1.387** | left:] left *Egerton* |
| **I.1.390** | Tumult's] Tumults *Egerton* |
| | passed.] passed *Egerton* |
| **I.1.395** | Tempest,] Tempest *Egerton* |
| **I.1.394–6** | *no triplet brace Egerton* |
| **II.1** | *Act Second, Scene First*] Act 2$^{d}$ *Egerton* |
| **II.1.3** | Meet] Meat *Egerton* |
| **II.1.8** | you,] you *Egerton* |
| **II.1.11** | planed] plain'd *Egerton* |
| **II.1.15** | Army.] Army *Egerton* |
| **II.1.18** | buy,] buy *Egerton* |
| | claim —] claim, *Egerton* |
| **II.1.28** | Empress'] Empress's *Egerton* |
| **II.1.33** | Emperor] Emporer *Egerton* |
| **II.1.41** | dare] dare, *Egerton* |
| **II.1.58** | Obeyed,] Obeyed. *Egerton* |
| **II.1.71** | Judge you,] Judge, you *Egerton* |
| **II.1.79** | implore?] implore *Egerton* |
| **II.1.83** | Sought.] Sought *Egerton* |
| **II.1.85** | chuse.] chuse *Egerton* |
| **II.1.92** | Mind] Mind, *Egerton* |
| **II.1.94** | stale] state *Egerton* |
| **II.1.95** | State?] State; *Egerton* |
| **II.1.111** | Trust;] Trust *Egerton* |
| **II.1.120** | relate:] relate *Egerton* |
| **II.1.125** | deceive?] deceive *Egerton* |
| **II.1.126** | Stage.] Stage, *Egerton* |
| **II.1.129** | Truth,] Truth *Egerton* |
| **II.1.133** | delator's] dilator's *Egerton* |
| **II.1.134** | Favour,] Favour *Egerton* |
| **II.1.145** | than] then *Egerton* |
| **II.1.164** | blest,] blest. *Egerton* |

| | |
|---|---|
| **II.1.173** | remov'd;] remov'd, *Egerton* |
| **II.1.179** | Parasites] Parisites *Egerton* |
| **II.1.183** | Portion] Potion *Egerton* |
| **II.1.185** | know] kow *Egerton* |
| **II.1.188** | *Augustus'*] *Augustus Egerton* |
| | line,] line *Egerton* |
| **II.1.189** | ally'd,] ally'd *Egerton* |
| **II.1.194** | make] make, *Egerton* |
| **II.1.196** | Love.] Love, *Egerton* |
| **II.1.200** | Warm.] Warm *Egerton* |
| **II.1.205** | *Claudius'*] *Claudiu's Egerton* |
| **II.1.206** | proconsulary] procunsuly *Egerton* |
| **II.1.208** | Baths,] Bath's *Egerton* |
| **II.1.214** | *Adonis*] Adnis *Egerton* |
| **II.1.224** | Parasites] Parisites *Egerton* |
| | bear] bear, *Egerton* |
| **II.1.229** | clear'd?] clear'd *Egerton* |
| **II.1.231** | Mind!] Mind; *Egerton* |
| **II.1.232** | Ruffians] Ruffains *Egerton* |
| **II.1.242** | You;] You, *Egerton* |
| **II.1.244** | partook] pertook *Egerton* |
| **II.1.250** | good;] good, *Egerton* |
| **II.1.251** | Wedded] Weded *Egerton* |
| **II.1.253** | *Claudius'*] *Claudius Egerton* |
| **II.1.254** | *Augustan*] *Augutan Egerton* |
| **II.1.261** | known.] know, *Egerton* |
| **II.1.264** | beleiv'd] beleiv'd, *Egerton* |
| **II.1.265–71** | *repeated Egerton* This empire, from my Ancestors receiv'd, \| Won by their Arms, and by their skill secur'd; \| Could the Slack Reins of Freedom have endur'd, \| (If my Erronious Policy had thought, \| (Nor by Experience nor our Records thaught) \|That this vast, turbulent, Rich, Factious State, \| By it's own Strength, so dangerously great, |
| **II.1.267** | endur'd;] endur'd *Egerton* |
| **II.1.275** | dy'd,] dy'd *Egerton* |
| **II.1.281** | Fate.] Fate *Egerton* |
| **II.1.286** | *Augustus*] Augustas *Egerton* |
| **II.1.290** | known] know *Egerton* |
| **II.1.296** | love.] love *Egerton* |
| **II.1.300** | Obscurely] Obsurely *Egerton* |
| **II.1.302** | casual] causual *Egerton* |
| **II.1.303** | great;] great. *Egerton* |
| **II.1.313** | State] State, *Egerton* |
| **II.1.316** | When] Wen *Egerton* |
| **II.1.329** | (The] The *Egerton* |
| | known)] known *Egerton* |
| **II.1.331** | Reign'd] Reighn'd *Egerton* |
| **II.1.335** | Mother's] Mothers *Egerton* |
| **II.1.340** | Throne;] Throne *Egerton* |

| | |
|---|---|
| **II.1.341** | that,] that *Egerton* |
| | Command,] Command *Egerton* |
| **II.1.343** | And that he] And he *Egerton* |
| **II.1.352** | maintain?] maintain *Egerton* |
| **II.1.357** | Thought,] Thought *Egerton* |
| **II.1.358** | than] then *Egerton* |
| **II.1.363** | Father's] Fathers *Egerton* |
| **II.1.376** | Pedant's] Pendants *Egerton* |
| **II.1.378** | Pedant's] Pendants *Egerton* |
| **II.1.390** | wait] weight *Egerton* |
| **II.1.395** | aught] Ought *Egerton* |
| **II.1.396** | make:] make *Egerton* |
| **II.1.397** | Go] goe *Egerton* |
| **II.1.407** | past,] past; *Egerton* |
| **II.1.408** | Lustre] Lusture *Egerton* |
| **II.1.414** | know.] know *Egerton* |
| **II.1.416** | Calumny] Calumy *Egerton* |
| **II.2** | *Act Second, Scene Second*] *no new scene number Egerton* |
| **II.2.3** | Fathers,] Fathers *Egerton* |
| **II.2.12** | seek;] seek, *Egerton* |
| **II.2.13** | Wars] Wars, *Egerton* |
| **II.2.14** | Cares] Cares, *Egerton* |
| **II.2.18** | (As] A *Egerton* |
| **II.2.19** | thought,] thought *Egerton* |
| **II.2.20** | brought;] brought *Egerton* |
| **II.2.24** | declare:] declare *Egerton* |
| **II.2.30 SD** | *Senators*] Senetors *Egerton* |
| **II.2.33** | borne] born *Egerton* |
| **II.2.34** | Subjects'] Subjects *Egerton* |
| **II.2.35** | Love,] Love *Egerton* |
| **II.2.36** | remove;] remove *Egerton* |
| **II.2.37** | Punish,] Punish *Egerton* |
| **II.2.41** | than] then *Egerton* |
| **II.2.42** | they] the *Egerton* |
| | wed,] wed *Egerton* |
| **II.2.43** | those] there *Egerton* |
| | bed;] bed *Egerton* |
| **II.2.49** | Bed,] Bed. *Egerton* |
| **II.2.50** | through] throught *Egerton* |
| **II.2.53** | ty'd;] ty'd, *Egerton* |
| **II.2.57** | woo,] *Poem 7*; woo *Egerton* |
| | Love,] love, *Poem 7*; Love *Egerton* |
| **II.2.64** | Bed.] bed. *Poem 7*; Bed *Egerton* |
| **II.2.65** | four-legg'd] *Poem 7*; fore-leg'd *Egerton* |
| | drag,] *Poem 7*; drag *Egerton* |
| | Mutual] mutual *Poem 7*; Mutal *Egerton* |
| | Pain,] pain, *Poem 7*; Pain *Egerton* |
| **II.2.68** | Laws:] laws: *Poem 7*; Laws *Egerton* |

| | |
|---|---|
| **II.2.70** | Cool,] cool, *Poem 7*; Cool *Egerton* |
| **II.2.72** | fulfill] fulfill, *Egerton* |
| **II.2.80** | mine.] mine *Egerton* |
| **II.2.82** | Care?] Care, *Egerton* |
| **II.2.84** | throbs,] throbs *Egerton* |
| **II.2.90** | Suggest] Suggest, *Egerton* |
| **II.2.104** | Angel] Angle *Egerton* |
| **II.2.105** | Goal,] Goal *Egerton* |
| **II.2.107** | form,] form *Egerton* |
| **II.2.108** | Mind;] Mind, *Egerton* |
| **II.2.109** | as] a *Egerton* |
| **II.2.112** | aught] ought *Egerton* |
| **II.2.119** | glow;] glow *Egerton* |
| **II.2.128** | fair] fair; *Egerton* |
| **II.2.133** | fail'd;] fail'd *Egerton* |
| **II.2.137** | Arms.] Arms *Egerton* |
| **II.2.138** | unmed'cinable] medcinable *Egerton* |
| **II.2.144** | *Acte's*] Actes *Egerton* |
| | Arms.] Arms *Egerton* |
| **II.2.145** | Charms] Charms, *Egerton* |
| **II.2.151** | *Sabæa's*] Sabæas *Egerton* |
| **II.2.154** | Bath,] Bath *Egerton* |
| | came;] came, *Egerton* |
| **II.2.155** | Flame] Flame, *Egerton* |
| **II.2.156** | aid;] aid, *Egerton* |
| **II.2.158** | She,] She *Egerton* |
| **II.2.161** | Crown'd;] Crown'd, *Egerton* |
| **II.2.167** | way.] way, *Egerton* |
| **II.2.174** | Say,] Say *Egerton* |
| | friend,] friend *Egerton* |
| | appease] appease, *Egerton* |
| **II.2.177** | Desire.] Desire *Egerton* |
| **II.2.193** | own;] own, *Egerton* |
| **II.2.194** | Constraint,] Constraint *Egerton* |
| **II.2.207** | *Propertius'*] *Propertius Egerton* |
| **II.2.210** | tales,] tales *Egerton* |
| **II.2.218** | Ruin,] Ruin *Egerton* |
| | Love;] Love, *Egerton* |
| **II.2.220** | beleive] beleive, *Egerton* |
| **II.2.224** | shown;] shown, *Egerton* |
| **II.2.227** | Dow'r —] Dow'r *Egerton* |
| **II.2.235** | council] counsel *Egerton* |
| **II.2.238** | the] they *Egerton* |
| **II.2.243** | hear] here *Egerton* |
| **II.2.258** | Arms,] Arms *Egerton* |
| **II.2.259** | Charms;] Charms *Egerton* |
| **II.2.263** | Fate;] Fate *Egerton* |
| **II.2.264** | disclaim] desclaim *Egerton* |

| | |
|---|---|
| **II.2.271** | *Plautus,*] *Plautus Egerton* |
| | *Agrippina's*] *Agrippinas Egerton* |
| **II.2.279** | Coast.] Coast, *Egerton* |
| **II.2.282** | Power's] Powers *Egerton* |
| **III.1.** | *Act Third, Scene First*] Act. 3. Scene 1st. *Egerton* |
| **III.1.4** | Friends'] Friends *Egerton* |
| **III.1.7** | Conquest,] Conquest *Egerton* |
| **III.1.12** | came,] came *Egerton* |
| **III.1.15** | ought,] ought *Egerton* |
| **III.1.16** | none,] none *Egerton* |
| | cry'd,] cry'd *Egerton* |
| **III.1.23** | through] throug *Egerton* |
| **III.1.25** | it] if *Egerton* |
| **III.1.28** | Home;] Home, *Egerton* |
| **III.1.39** | feel] feel, *Egerton* |
| | Lord] Lord, *Egerton* |
| **III.1.49** | restrain] restrain, *Egerton* |
| **III.1.50** | force,] force *Egerton* |
| **III.1.53** | Army's] Armys *Egerton* |
| **III.1.54** | prove] prove, *Egerton* |
| **III.1.55** | safety] safty, *Egerton* |
| | Soldiers'] Soldiers *Egerton* |
| **III.1.58** | Matrons] Matorns *Egerton* |
| **III.1.64** | Who,] Who *Egerton* |
| | Envy,] Envy *Egerton* |
| **III.1.71** | Soldiers'] Soldiers *Egerton* |
| **III.2.** | *Act Third, Scene Second*] *no new scene number Egerton* |
| **III.2.9** | delators] dalators *Egerton* |
| **III.2.20** | Reproaches] Reproache's *Egerton* |
| | fear,] fear; *Egerton* |
| **III.2.22** | vain;] vain, *Egerton* |
| **III.2.27** | love.] love, *Egerton* |
| **III.2.33** | impotent] impotant *Egerton* |
| **III.2.34** | accus'd,] accus'd *Egerton* |
| **III.2.40** | first,] first *Egerton*; |
| | *Nero,*] *Nero Egerton* |
| **III.2.49** | borne] born *Egerton* |
| **III.2.58** | it,] it *Egerton* |
| **III.2.64** | You;] You *Egerton* |
| **III.2.70** | Affliction's] Afflictions *Egerton* |
| **III.2.73** | with Judgement you] with you *Egerton* |
| **III.2.78** | Chose] Chosee *Egerton* |
| **III.2.79** | Methods] Methods: *Egerton* |
| **III.2.81** | fear,] fear *Egerton* |
| **III.2.85** | hide;] hide *Egerton* |
| **III.2.103** | disclaim] disclaim. *Egerton* |
| **III.2.113** | Lost;] Lost, *Egerton* |

| | |
|---|---|
| **III.2.125** | Palliatives] Pallatives *Egerton* |
| **III.2.139** | least,] least; *Egerton* |
| **III.2.151** | Silent,] Silent *Egerton* |
| **III.2.152** | people's] peoples *Egerton* |
| **III.2.156** | Hand] Hand, *Egerton* |
| **III.2.159** | unjust,] unjust *Egerton* |
| **III.2.161** | controle,] controle *Egerton* |
| **III.2.162** | fulfill] fulfill, *Egerton* |
| **III.2.164** | Princes,] Princes *Egerton* |
| **III.2.165** | irritate the Land with] irritate with *Egerton* |
| **III.2.166** | Weapons,] Weapons *Egerton* |
| **III.2.171** | trace;] trace *Egerton* |
| **III.2.174** | gain] gain: *Egerton* |
| **III.2.183** | *Augustus'*] Augustus *Egerton* |
| **III.2.188** | counsel] consell *Egerton* |
| **III.2.190** | Hydra-Head;] Hydra-Head *Egerton* |
| **III.2.192** | *Cinna*'s] Cinnas *Egerton* |
| **III.2.196** | reign'd] reighn'd *Egerton* |
| **III.2.197** | *Rome*,] Rome *Egerton* |
| **III.2.212** | possest] possest, *Egerton* |
| **III.2.240** | find] find, *Egerton* |
| **III.2.247–9** | *no triplet brace Egerton* |
| **III.2.252** | Others,] Others *Egerton* |
| | Strength] Strenght *Egerton* |
| **III.2.255** | Subjects'] Subjects *Egerton* |
| **III.2.263** | injoy'd?] injoy'd *Egerton* |
| **III.2.285** | honourable] honourble *Egerton* |
| **III.2.286** | wrought?] wrought *Egerton* |
| **III.2.291** | Others,] Others *Egerton* |
| | Commit;] Commit *Egerton* |
| **III.2.299** | exaggerated] exagereted *Egerton* |
| **III.2.304** | Careful] Carfull *Egerton* |
| **III.2.309** | Virgin] Virgen *Egerton* |
| **III.2.314** | endure] endure, *Egerton* |
| **III.2.315** | Office was design'd] Office design'd *Egerton* |
| **III.2.317** | lost.] lost *Egerton* |
| **III.2.322** | Others,] Others *Egerton* |
| **III.2.324** | dread,] dread; *Egerton* |
| **III.2.333** | than] then *Egerton*; |
| | hear.] here *Egerton* |
| **III.2.355** | AGRIPPINA] *not in Egerton* |
| **III.2.361** | of any Joy] of Joy *Egerton* |
| **III.2.364** | Spare.] Spare *Egerton* |
| **III.2.371** | other] other, *Egerton* |
| **III.2.372** | flow;] flow, *Egerton* |
| **III.2.374** | Passion,] Passion *Egerton* |
| **III.2.378** | in] I *Egerton* |
| **III.2.381** | Safety,] Safety *Egerton* |

| | |
|---|---|
| | Intrest,] Intrest *Egerton* |
| **III.2.390** | Intent] Intention *Egerton* |
| **III.2.395** | dome,] dome *Egerton* |
| **III.2.403** | Prince's] Princes *Egerton* |
| **III.2.405** | set at Nought] set Nought *Egerton* |
| **III.2.409** | shown?] shown *Egerton* |
| **III.2.413** | Offences] Offence is *Egerton* |
| **III.2.418** | tomorrow's] two morrows *Egerton* |
| **III.2.419** | Doom.] Doom *Egerton* |
| **III.2.423** | *Cæsar's*] Caesars *Egerton* |
| **III.2.426** | *Concord's*] Concordi *Egerton* |
| **III.2.430 SD** | *Train,*] *Train Egerton* |
| **III.2.431** | than] then *Egerton* |
| **III.2.432** | appear] appear. *Egerton* |
| **III.2.434** | Heart;] Heart, *Egerton* |
| **III.2.439** | *Cæsar,*] Cæsar; *Egerton* |
| **III.2.448** | repeat.] repeat *Egerton* |
| **III.2.465** | Army's] Armys *Egerton* |
| **III.2.468** | Vassal's] Vassals *Egerton* |
| **III.2.474** | Streight under *Burrhus's*] Streight Burrhus's *Egerton* |
| **III.2.476** | State.] State *Egerton* |
| **III.2.478** | engage;] engage *Egerton* |
| **III.2.481** | Suspicion] Supicion *Egerton*; |
| | alarm.] alarm, *Egerton* |
| **III.2.487** | haste] haste; *Egerton* |
| **IV.1** | *Act Fourth, Scene First*] Act 4. Scene 1st *Egerton* |
| **IV.1.1** | heard;] heard, *Egerton* |
| **IV.1.3** | disclaim] desclaim *Egerton* |
| **IV.1.6** | inspir'd] insper'd *Egerton* |
| **IV.1.7** | Bondmaid's] Bondmaids *Egerton* |
| **IV.1.11** | opprobrious] oprobious *Egerton* |
| **IV.1.13** | you,] you *Egerton* |
| **IV.1.27** | Prove] Prove, *Egerton* |
| **IV.1.33** | pass'd,] pass'd *Egerton* |
| **IV.1.34** | Last?] Last: *Egerton* |
| **IV.1.36** | withstood;] withstood *Egerton* |
| **IV.1.37** | you,] you *Egerton* |
| | despis'd,] despis'd *Egerton* |
| **IV.1.46** | Life,] Life *Egerton* |
| **IV.1.47** | wed;] wed, *Egerton* |
| **IV.1.49** | in] I *Egerton* |
| **IV.1.58** | deny'd,] deny'd *Egerton* |
| **IV.1.91** | Rival's] Rivals *Egerton* |
| **IV.1.92** | Step,] Step *Egerton* |
| **IV.1.103** | beset,] beset. *Egerton* |
| **IV.1.106** | Nature] nature *Egerton* |
| **IV.1.112** | deceiv'd,] deceiv'd *Egerton* |

| | |
|---|---|
| **IV.1.118** | command,] command. *Egerton* |
| **IV.1.129** | Sceptre] Septer *Egerton* |
| **IV.1.131** | Doom.] Doom *Egerton* |
| **IV.1.162** | Lead] Lead, *Egerton* |
| **IV.1.168** | perish] perish'd *Egerton* |
| **IV.1.178** | If,] If *Egerton* |
| **IV.1.194** | *Agrippa,*] Agrippa *Egerton* |
| **IV.1.211** | *Concord*'s] Concod's *Egerton* |
| **IV.1.217** | late] late, *Egerton* |
| **IV.1.219** | lighter;] lighter, *Egerton* |
| | again] again, *Egerton* |
| **IV.2.** | *Act Fourth, Scene Second*] Scene: *Egerton* |
| **IV.2.1. SD** | *Emperor's*] *Emporer's Egerton* |
| **IV.2.9** | Stubborn] Subborn *Egerton* |
| **IV.2.13** | *line preceded by deleted* Hail! Concord! Smiling Goddess, hail! \| Here ever may thy *Egerton* |
| **IV.2.60** | *Jove*] Jove, *Egerton* |
| **IV.2.74** | rankling] rankring *Egerton* |
| **IV.2.79 SD** | AGRIPPINA.] AGRIPPINA *Egerton* |
| **IV.2.81** | try'd,] try'd *Egerton* |
| **IV.2.86** | stripp'd] strip'd *Egerton* |
| **IV.2.107** | find] find, *Egerton* |
| **IV.2.131** | Preists,] Preists *Egerton* |
| | pay'd,] pay'd *Egerton* |
| **IV.2.141** | Heav'n's] Heav'ns *Egerton* |
| **IV.2.149** | Goddess'] Goddess *Egerton* |
| **IV.2.152** | excite] exite *Egerton* |
| **IV.2.159** | Revolutions,] Revolutions *Egerton* |
| **IV.2.162** | portentous] protentious *Egerton* |
| **IV.2.163** | Than] Then *Egerton* |
| **IV.2.166** | Were't not] Were it *Egerton* |
| | known:] known, *Egerton* |
| **IV.2.167** | involv'd;] involv'd, *Egerton* |
| **IV.2.172** | Than] Then *Egerton* |
| **IV.2.175** | speak,] speak |
| | Day,] Day *Egerton* |
| **IV.2.183** | Rest] Rest, *Egerton* |
| **IV.2.185** | Duty,] Duty *Egerton* |
| **IV.2.194** | thou] though *Egerton* |
| **IV.2.195** | ill-grounded] ill-ground *Egerton* |
| **IV.2.197** | beleiv'd] beleiv'd, *Egerton* |
| **IV.2.214** | sincere;] sincere *Egerton* |
| **IV.2.224** | Griefs; apply'd] Griefs apply'd *Egerton* |
| **IV.2.225** | *Rome*'s] Romes *Egerton* |
| **IV.2.228** | World's] Worlds *Egerton*; |
| | Slave;] Slave, *Egerton* |
| **IV.2.237** | Earth,] Earth *Egerton* |

| | |
|---|---|
| **IV.2.244** | conscious] consicous *Egerton* |
| | Eyes;] Eyes, *Egerton* |
| **IV.2.257** | grace,] grace *Egerton* |
| **V.1.** | *Act Fifth, Scene First*] Act 5$^{th}$. *Egerton* |
| **V.1.3** | fear] fear, *Egerton* |
| **V.1.19** | discern] desern *Egerton* |
| **V.1.20** | learn.] learn *Egerton* |
| **V.1.21** | near —] near *Egerton* |
| **V.1.23** | Work's] Works *Egerton* |
| **V.1.25** | miscarry'd;] miscarry'd *Egerton* |
| **V.1.26** | fraught] frought *Egerton* |
| **V.1.32** | Villian,] Villian: *Egerton* |
| **V.1.33** | Fiends] Finds *Egerton* |
| **V.1.34** | Vaunted] Vanted *Egerton* |
| **V.1.37** | Care.] Care *Egerton* |
| **V.1.46** | secure;] secure *Egerton* |
| **V.1.48** | pursue;] pursue *Egerton* |
| **V.1.56** | Dy'd;] Dy'd, *Egerton* |
| **V.1.58** | which,] which *Egerton* |
| **V.1.62** | Blow;] Blow *Egerton* |
| **V.1.69** | *Aceronia*,] Aceronia *Egerton* |
| **V.1.70** | *Cæsar*'s Mother. Aid!] Cæsars Mothers Aid *Egerton* |
| **V.1.72** | dy'd,] dy'd *Egerton* |
| **V.1.76** | they] the *Egerton* |
| **V.1.85** | Haste] Has *Egerton* |
| **V.1.89** | Miscarry'd,] Miscarry'd *Egerton* |
| **V.1.94** | Knife,] Knife; *Egerton* |
| | fir'd,] fir'd *Egerton* |
| **V.1.98** | known] know *Egerton* |
| **V.1.99** | now.] now *Egerton* |
| **V.1.105** | casual] causual *Egerton* |
| **V.1.108** | set,] set *Egerton* |
| **V.1.109** | Doubt,] Doubt *Egerton* |
| **V.1.113** | light;] light *Egerton* |
| **V.1.120** | loiter's] loter's *Egerton* |
| | Forum,] Forum *Egerton* |
| **V.1.121** | explain] explain, *Egerton* |
| **V.1.123** | Rebellion's] Rebellions *Egerton* |
| **V.1.124** | told;] told, *Egerton* |
| **V.1.131** | receive.] receive? *Egerton* |
| **V.1.133** | Broke;] Broke *Egerton* |
| **V.1.135** | And,] And *Egerton* |
| | drew,] drew *Egerton* |
| **V.1.143** | You;] You *Egerton* |
| **V.2.** | *Act Fifth, Scene Second*] *no scene number Egerton* |
| **V.2.3** | *Sea*,] Sea *Egerton* |
| **V.2.6** | Rest;] Rest, *Egerton* |

| | |
|---|---|
| **V.2.9** | tell] tell, *Egerton* |
| **V.2.13** | Vulture,] Vulture; *Egerton* |
| | Wheel] Wheel; *Egerton* |
| **V.2.16** | Manicles] Maricles *Egerton* |
| **V.2.17** | Save] Save, *Egerton* |
| **V.2.21** | Waste] Waste, *Egerton* |
| **V.2.23** | cure;] cure *Egerton* |
| **V.2.24** | sure,] sure *Egerton* |
| **V.2.28** | Knowledge,] Knowledge *Egerton* |
| | apply'd] apply'd, *Egerton* |
| **V.2.32** | Life's] Lifes *Egerton* |
| **V.2.35** | Complain] Complian *Egerton* |
| **V.2.41** | advise?] advise *Egerton* |
| **V.2.44** | way our Conduct] way Conduct *Egerton* |
| **V.2.46** | Senate,] Seate *Egerton* |
| **V.2.49** | throne.] throne *Egerton* |
| **V.2.53** | Blow.] Blow, *Egerton* |
| **V.2.57** | such,] such *Egerton* |
| **V.2.64** | They] The *Egerton* |
| **V.2.75** | own'd,] own'd *Egerton* |
| **V.2.79** | used] use *Egerton* |
| **V.2.93** | declar'd,] declar'd *Egerton* |
| **V.2.94** | Guard;] Gaurd, *Egerton* |
| **V.2.97** | decide,] decide *Egerton* |
| **V.2.100** | they] the *Egerton* |
| **V.2.103** | Shame,] Shame; *Egerton* |
| **V.2.108** | Emperor's] Emperors *Egerton* |
| **V.2.112** | that's] thats *Egerton* |
| | Case,] Case *Egerton* |
| **V.2.124** | *Agrippina*,] Agrippina *Egerton* |
| **V.2.125** | Pow'r.] Pow'r *Egerton* |
| **V.2.131** | Mistress's] Mistresses *Egerton* |
| **V.2.132** | comeing;] comeing, *Egerton* |
| **V.2.147** | fly,] fly *Egerton* |
| | End;] End, *Egerton* |
| **V.2.153** | her,] her *Egerton* |
| **V.2.168** | *Anicetus'*] Anicetus *Egerton* |
| **V.2.169** | goe!] goe? *Egerton* |
| **V.3.** | *Act Fifth, Scene Third*] *no act and scene number Egerton* |
| **V.3.5** | excites] exites *Egerton* |
| **V.3.6** | sustain'd] sustian'd *Egerton* |
| **V.3.13** | direct] derect *Egerton* |
| | Wound.] Wound *Egerton* |
| **V.3.17** | Night.] Night, *Egerton* |
| **V.3.25** | graced.] graced *Egerton* |
| **V.3.31** | Were] Where *Egerton* |
| **V.3.32** | Friendship] Friendships *Egerton* |
| **V.3.40** | Mother's] Mothers *Egerton* |

| | |
|---|---|
| **V.3.41** | PALLAS] *no new speech-prefix Egerton* |
| **V.3.49** | evince,] evince *Egerton* |
| | Distrust,] Distrust *Egerton* |
| **V.3.54** | discernment] desernment *Egerton* |
| **V.3.55** | PALLAS] *no new speech-prefix Egerton* |
| **V.3.58** | Prolong?] Prolong: *Egerton* |
| **V.3.59** | fear] fear, *Egerton* |
| **V.3.62** | Where others sure] Where sure *Egerton* |
| | Complain?] Complain. *Egerton* |
| **V.3.63** | *Pretorian*] Petorian *Egerton* |
| **V.3.69** | excite] exite *Egerton* |
| **V.3.71** | Its Return's] It's Return is *Egerton* |
| **V.3.73** | greive?] greive. *Egerton* |
| **V.3.74** | appease,] appease: *Egerton* |
| **V.3.80–2** | *no triplet brace Egerton* |
| **V.3.84** | pursue;] pursue, *Egerton* |
| **V.3.86** | thee,] thee *Egerton* |
| | *Rome*,] Rome *Egerton* |
| **V.3.98** | Life?] Life; *Egerton* |
| **V.3.105** | Wrong,] Wrong *Egerton* |
| | oppose.] oppose *Egerton* |
| **V.3.107** | fought;] fought *Egerton* |
| **V.3.110** | or of *Rome*] or Rome *Egerton* |
| **V.3.114** | sought;] sought *Egerton* |
| **V.3.116** | Sword;] Sword *Egerton* |
| **V.3.118** | betray'd.] betray'd *Egerton* |
| **V.3.120** | Offspring's] Offsprings *Egerton* |
| **V.3.123** | dissolve] desolve *Egerton* |
| **V.3.125** | these ills,] these ills; *Egerton* |
| **V.3.132** | Art,] Art; *Egerton* |
| **V.3.135** | refuse;] refuse, *Egerton* |
| **V.3.139** | Whole;] Whole *Egerton* |
| **V.3.140** | Blow;] Blow, *Egerton* |
| **V.3.145** | Misfortune,] Misfortune *Egerton* |
| **V.3.149** | decreed;] decreed, *Egerton* |
| **V.3.152** | fiercer] firceer *Egerton* |
| **V.3.155** | ruin,] ruin *Egerton* |
| **V.3.156** | thee] the *Egerton* |
| **V.3.157** | see:] see *Egerton* |
| **V.3.168** | wave.] wave, *Egerton* |
| **V.3.170** | Dye;] Dye *Egerton* |
| **V.3.171** | slack,] slack *Egerton* |
| **V.3.172** | can't] cant *Egerton* |
| **V.3.173** | made,] made *Egerton* |
| **V.3.179** | opose] opose, *Egerton* |
| **V.3.183** | resolv'd,] resolv'd *Egerton* |
| **V.3.187** | Name,] Name *Egerton* |
| **V.3.188** | Fame;] Fame, *Egerton* |

| | |
|---|---|
| **V.3.190** | Aspersion's] Aspersions *Egerton* |
| **V.3.193** | prove,] prove; *Egerton* |
| **V.3.196** | Mean?] Mean *Egerton* |
| **V.3.198** | Survive?] Survive, *Egerton* |
| **V.3.201** | Slave,] Slave *Egerton* |
| **V.3.204** | deriv'd.] deriv'd *Egerton* |
| **V.3.206** | descent] decent *Egerton* |
| **V.3.210** | that's] thats *Egerton* |
| **V.3.214** | try'd.] try'd *Egerton* |
| **V.3.224** | last.—] last,— *Egerton* |
| **V.3.226** | Benefactress'] Benefactress's *Egerton* |
| **V.3.227** | faculty,] faculty *Egerton* |
| **V.3.232** | Sought;] Sought, *Egerton* |
| **V.3.240** | Night.] Night *Egerton* |
| **V.3.257** | Seest] Sees *Egerton* |
| **V.3.261** | AGRIPPINA] *no speech-prefix Egerton* |
| **V.3.269** | direct] derect *Egerton* |
| **V.3.272** | Mother's] Mothers *Egerton* |

## *Historical collation to 66 Agrippina, a Tragedy*

*none; only one witness exists*

## *Emendations to 67 But learn wise Youth thy Happyness to know*

**main source** *SRO*: SRO 941/47/4, p. 63

*similar lines are found in Poem 65 'Telemachus', 1.189–96*

| | |
|---|---|
| **67.2** | *followed by deleted* If Heaven |
| **67.3** | *in Hervey's hand above deleted* has curs'd ye with a restless Mind, (perverse Defect) so |
| **67.4** | *in Hervey's hand above deleted* frequent in Mankind, If sweet Contentment mix not |
| **67.5** | *in Hervey's hand above deleted* in thy Fate that want alone shall mar the happiest |
| **67.6** | *in Hervey's hand above deleted* State. In vain the fav'rite Gifts of Heav'n you boast |
| **67.7** | *in Hervey's hand above deleted* with out that Blessing, all the rest are lost: Amyand has |

## *Historical collation to 67 But learn wise Youth thy Happyness to know*

| | |
|---|---|
| **67.5** | in] with *Telemachus* 65.1.193 |
| **67.6** | shall] will *Telemachus* 65.1.194 |
| **67.7** | Heav'n] Jove *Telemachus* 65.1.195 |

## *Emendations to 68 Make her curl her Nose*

**main source** SRO 941/47/4, p. 78
**complementary sources** none

*no emendations made*

## *Historical collation to 68 Make her curl her Nose*

*none; only one witness exists*

## *Emendations to 69 Each hour my Spirits, and my strength decay*

**main source** *SRO*: SRO 941/53/1, pp. 212, 214
**complementary source** *European Magazine*: *The European Magazine*, 32 (July–December 1797), 412, reprinted in *Walker's Hibernian Magazine*, January 1797, p. 88; *The Annual Register . . . for the Year 1799* [1801], p. 471

*no emendations made*

## *Historical collation to 69 Each hour my Spirits, and my strength decay*

| | |
|---|---|
| **69.4** | joy a] joy, and *European Magazine* |
| | e'en] ev'n *European Magazine* |
| **69.6** | healing] halcyon *European Magazine* |
| **69.7** | awhile] a while *European Magazine* |
| **69.10** | mandates] edicts *European Magazine* |
| **69.11** | All] At *European Magazine* |

## *Emendations to 70 My Heart's Delight*

**main source** SRO 941/47/4, p. 102
**complementary sources** none

*no emendations made*

## *Historical collation to 70 My Heart's Delight*

*none; only one witness exists*

## *Emendations to 71 In dull Equality, the Sandy Store*

*no emendations made*

### *Historical collation to 71 In dull equality, the Sandy Store*

*none; only one witness exists*

### *Emendations to 72 What Joys I have*

**main source** SRO 941/47/4, p. 120
**complementary sources** none

*no emendations made*

### *Historical collation to 72 What Joys I have*

*none; only one witness exists*

### *Emendations to 73 Whilst I maintain my Empire in that Breast*

**main source** SRO 941/47/4, p. 147
**complementary sources** none

*no emendations made*

### *Historical collation to 73 Whilst I maintain my Empire in that Breast*

*none; only one witness exists*

### *Emendations to 74 For not the Joy*

**main source** *SRO*: SRO 941/47/4, p. 180
**complementary sources** none; similar lines appear in Poem 66, 'Agrippina', II. 2. 201–6

| | |
|---|---|
| **74.4** | engross'd,] *Agrippina* II.2.204; engross'd *SRO* |
| **74.6** | the Whole] *in Hervey's hand above deleted* The Soul |

### *Historical collation to 74 For not the Joy*

| | |
|---|---|
| **74.1** | For not the Joy of] By Heav'n tis true, nor *Agrippina* II.2.201 |
| **74.2** | other Friendships] Friendship, In'trest *Agrippina* II.2.202 |
| **74.3** | Defraud] Defrauds *Agrippina* II.2.203 |

### *Emendations to 75 'Tis you alone my Fears and Wishes make*

**main source** *SRO*: SRO 941/47/4, p. 239
**complementary sources** none

| | |
|---|---|
| **75.4** | you are] *in Hervey's hand above deleted* thou art *SRO* |

## *Historical collation to 75 'Tis you alone my Fears and Wishes make*

*none; only one witness exists*

## *Emendations to 76 And sure I am*

**main source** *SRO*: SRO 941/47/4, p. 239
**complementary sources** none

| | |
|---|---|
| **76.1** | Hour] *followed by deleted* For all the *SRO* |
| **76.2** | For all the while Ones] *in Hervey's hand above deleted* while once *SRO* |

## *Historical collation to 76 And sure I am*

*none; only one witness exists*

## *Emendations to 77 For if in Richmond-Morning-Walk*

**main source** *SRO*: SRO 941/47/4, pp. 270–1
**complementary sources** none

| | |
|---|---|
| **77.7** | *Griffon,*] Griffon *SRO* |
| **77.13** | *Anne;*] Anne *SRO* |
| **77.22** | Satyr's tip'd] *in Hervey's hand above deleted* Satyres tast |
| **77.23** | Dolce-piccante] *in Hervey's hand above deleted* Dolce picato |
| **77.25** | Caroline,] Caroline *SRO* |
| **77.34** | defend,] defend: *SRO* |

## *Historical collation to 77 For if in Richmond-Morning-Walk*

*none; only one witness exists*

## *Emendations to 78 For few or can, or wish to bring Relief*

**main source** *SRO*: SRO 941/47/4, p. 330
**complementary sources** none; similar lines appear in Poem 66, 'Agrippina', I. 1. 51–62

| | |
|---|---|
| **78.9** | repining] *corrected in Hervey's hand from* pining *SRO* |

## *Historical collation to 78 For few or can, or wish to bring Relief*

| | |
|---|---|
| **78.1–2** | *replaced by* And What Avail's to say what we endure, \| Unless the ut'rance wou'd promote our Cure? *Agrippina* |
| **78.4** | And to divulge is to encrease] Whilst every touch we feel, Augments *Agrippina* |
| **78.5** | their] each *Agrippina* |
| **78.9** | repining at their Fate] their Discontent relate *Agrippina* |

| | |
|---|---|
| **78.10** | Their Wrongs, their Wants, their Discontents relate] Rail at the World, and Murmur against Fate *Agrippina* |
| **78.11** | And Ign'rant] Ignorant *Agrippina* |

## *Emendations to 79 When the gay Sun no more his Rays shall boast*

**main source** *JMA*: John Murray Archive, Letter 2, ff. 3v–4r
**complementary source** *NPD*: Francesco Algarotti, *Il Newtonianismo per le dame* (Naples: Giambatista Pasquali, 1739), sig. A6r

| | |
|---|---|
| **79.1** | gay Sun] *above deleted* bright Sun *JMA* |
| | no more] *inserted above with caret after* Sun *JMA* |
| | Rays] *followed by deleted* no more *JMA* |
| **79.2** | And] *above deleted* When *JMA* |
| **79.3** | Then shall thy writings on those Subjects dye] *below deleted* Then shall thy Colours too and thy Optics and thy Optics *JMA* |
| **79.4** | Thy Wit and Learning in Oblivion lye] *below deleted* Thy Colours and thy Optics too shall dye *JMA* |
| **79.6** | Works] *above deleted* shall *JMA* |

## *Historical collation to 79 When the gay Sun no more his Rays shall boast*

| | |
|---|---|
| **79.** | *title*] Di My Lord Hervey *NPD* |
| **79.3** | thy writings on those Subjects] these Colours and these Opticks *NPD* |
| **79.5** | shall cease to boast] no more record *NPD* |
| | Head] Fame *NPD* |
| **79.6** | Algarotti's Works no more be read] *Algarotti* be an unknown name *NPD* |

## *Emendations to 80 But what avails our own Defects to find?*

**main source** BL Add. MS 51396, f. 162r
**complementary sources** none

*no emendations made*

## *Historical collation to 80 But what avails our own Defects to find?*

*none; only one witness exists*

## *Emendations to 81 Whose Meaning still in Riddles*

**main source** *SRO*: SRO 941/47/2, p. 15
**complementary sources** *SRO*: none

| | |
|---|---|
| **81.1** | still] *above deleted* sti *SRO* |
| | is] *above deleted* still *SRO* |

## *Historical collation to 81 Whose Meaning still in Riddles*

*none; only one witness exists*

## *Emendations to 82 In black & white whilst Chloris' Mind you trace*

**main source** John Murray Archive, Letter 4, f. 2r
**complementary source** none

*no emendations made*

## *Historical collation to 82 In black & white whilst Chloris' Mind you trace*

*none; only one witness exists*

## *Emendations to 83 So well the merit of your Words is known*

**main source** John Murray Archive, Letter 4, f. 2r
**complementary source** none

*no emendations made*

## *Historical collation to 83 So well the merit of your Words is known*

*none; only one witness exists*

## *Emendations to 84 As Travellers still think of Day by Night*

**main source** *JMA*: John Murray Archive, Letter 5, f. 1v
**complementary source** *SRO*: SRO 941/47/4, pp. 582–3

**84.2** long in thickest] *above deleted* in the midst of *JMA*
most] *above deleted* long *JMA*

## *Historical collation to 84 As Travellers still think of Day by Night*

**84.1** As Travellers still] *misplaced by amanuensis on line above and added in Hervey's hand above* think of Day by night *SRO*
Day by Night] *followed by* And long in thickest *SRO*

**84.2** And long in thickest] *misplaced by amanuensis on line above and added in Hervey's hand above* Darkness, most *SRO*

## *Emendations to 85 Of all who feel how few so well declare*

**main source** *JMA*: John Murray Archive, Letter 5, f. 1v
**complementary source** *SRO*: SRO 941/47/4, pp. 604–6

*no emendations made*

## *Historical collation to 85 Of all who feel how few so well declare*

**85.7** dispers'd] dispens'd *SRO*
**85.15** Blessings] Joys we *SRO*

## *Emendations to 86 Why doest thou ignorantly mourn his Fate (to Montagu)*

**main source** *SRO*: SRO 941/47/2, pp. 57–8
**complementary sources** none

**86.5** Unwasted] *after deleted* Nor w *SRO*

## *Historical collation to 86 Why doest thou ignorantly mourn his Fate (to Montagu)*

*none; only one witness exists; but compare Poem 89, which reuses some lines*

## *Emendations to 87 Not that in Dogs or Horses I delight*

**main source** BL Add. MS 51345, ff. 77v–78r
**complementary sources** none

*no emendations made*

## *Historical collation to 87 Not that in Dogs or Horses I delight*

*none; only one witness exists*

## *Emendations to 88 In these wise Trifles and important Joys*

**main source** SRO 941/47/4, p. 610
**complementary sources** none

*no emendations made*

## *Historical collation to 88 In these wise Trifles and important Joys*

*none; only one witness exists*

## *Emendations to 89 Why dost thou Ignorantly weep his Fate (to Algarotti)*

**main source** SRO 941/47/4, pp. 612–13
**complementary sources** none

**89.13** to] *inserted in Hervey's hand above the line SRO*

## *Historical collation to 89 Why dost thou Ignorantly weep his Fate (to Algarotti)*

*none; only one witness exists; but compare Poem 86, which shares some lines*

## *Emendations to 90 By an instinctive Folly still we choose*

**main source** *SRO*: SRO 941/47/4, p. 620
**complementary sources** none

**90.1** instinctive] insinctive *SRO*

## *Historical collation to 90 By an instinctive Folly still we choose*

*none; only one witness exists*

## *Emendations to 91 Since all the Pray'rs of weeping Friends were vain*

**main source** *SRO*: SRO 941/47/2, p. 75
**complementary sources** none

**91.12** And all] *after deleted* All that *SRO*
**91.14** ev'ry] *after deleted* all your *SRO*
Hour] *emended from* Hours *SRO*

## *Historical collation to 91 Since all the Pray'rs of weeping Friends were vain*

*none; only one witness exists*

## *Emendations to 92 But whilst in foreign Climes admired you rove*

**main source** SRO 941/47/2, p. 80
**complementary sources** none

*no emendations made*

## *Historical Collation to 92 But whilst in foreign Climes admired you rove*

*none; only one witness exists*

## *Emendations to 93 Too high the Value of such Acts you raise*

**main source** *SRO*: SRO 941/47/2, pp. 86–7
**complementary sources** none

| | |
|---|---|
| **93.9** | Pen] *after deleted* Time *SRO* |
| **93.14** | impelling] *after deleted illegible word SRO* |

## *Historical collation to 93 Too high the Value of such Acts you raise*

*none; only one witness exists*

## *Emendations to 94 Subjects would bless the salutary Sway*

**main source** John Murray Archive, Letter 20, f. 1r
**complementary sources** none

*no emendations made*

## *Historical collation to 94 Subjects would bless the salutary Sway*

*none; only one witness exists*

## *Emendations to 95 When the Philosophers attempt to scan*

**main source** SRO 941/47/2, pp. 86–7
**complementary sources** none

*no emendations made*

## *Historical collation to 95 When the Philosophers attempt to scan*

*none; only one witness exists*

## *Emendations to 96 How must we think the Gods esteem Mankind*

**main source** SRO 941/47/2, p. 114
**complementary sources** none

*no emendations made*

## *Historical collation to 96 How must we think the Gods esteem Mankind*

*none; only one witness exists*

## *Emendations to 97 These kind auxiliary Recruits should bring*

**main source** SRO 941/47/2, p. 115
**complementary sources** none

*no emendations made*

## *Historical collation to 97 These kind auxiliary Recruits should bring*

*none; only one witness exists*

## *Emendations to 98 This world was made for Fools who can compound*

**main source** SRO 941/47/2, p. 121
**complementary sources** none

*no emendations made*

## *Historical collation to 98 This world was made for Fools who can compound*

*none; only one witness exists*

## *Emendations to 99 Did Men (who ne'er act right) inspect with Care*

**main source** *SRO*: SRO 941/47/2, p. 129
**complementary sources** none

| | |
|---|---|
| **99.1** | ne'er act right] *after deleted* neither think *SRO* |
| **99.9** | Pass oer] *above deleted* Except *SRO* |
| **99.17–19** | *no triplet brace SRO* |

## *Historical collation to 99 Did Men (who ne'er act right) inspect with Care*

*none; only one witness exists*

## *Emendations to 100 Ad Regem*

**main source** *Mœstissimæ ac Lætissimæ Academiæ Cantabrigiensis Carmina Funebria et Triumphalia* (Cambridge: s.n., 1714), sig. D1r

**complementary sources** none

*no emendations made*

### *Historical collation to 100 Ad Regem*

*none; only one witness exists*

### *Emendations to 101 Pult'ney soyez en allegresse*

**main source** SRO 941/47/4, pp. 158–9
**complementary sources** none

*no emendations made*

### *Historical collation to 101 Pult'ney soyez en allegresse*

*none; only one witness exists*

### *Emendations to 102 D' Hamton Cour a Milady B*

**main source** BL Add. MS 51441, ff. 24r–v
**complementary sources** none

*no emendations made*

### *Historical collation to 102 D' Hamton Cour a Milady B*

*none; only one witness exists*

### *Emendations to 103 Quand on ne peut pas*

**main source** SRO 941/47/4, p. 213
**complementary sources** none

*no emendations made*

### *Historical collation to 103 Quand on ne peut pas*

*none; only one witness exists*

### *Emendations to 104 rien mieux*

**main source** SRO 941/47/4, p. 194
**complementary sources** none

*no emendations made*

### *Historical collation to 104 rien mieux*

*none; only one witness exists*

### *Emendations to 105 Quant al Padrone, Signor Ste*

**main source** SRO 941/47/4, pp. 268–9
**complementary sources** none

*no emendations made*

### *Historical collation to 105 Quant al Padrone, Signor Ste*

*none; only one witness exists*

### *Emendations to 106 Chanson au Curé de —*

**main source** BL Add. MS 51441, ff. 21r–22r
**complementary sources** none

*no emendations made*

### *Historical collation to 106 Chanson au Curé de —*

*none; only one witness exists*

### *Emendations to 107 Epitaphium Reginae Carolinae*

**main source** *Epitaphium*: *Epitaphium Reginæ Carolinæ. The Second Edition, Corrected. With an English Translation* (London: for T. Cooper, 1738)
**complementary source** *1738a*: *Epitaphium Reginae Carolinae* (London: for T. Cooper, 1738), the 1st edn, without the translation; ESTC T32895

*no emendations made*

### *Historical collation to 107 Epitaphium Reginae Carolinae*

| | |
|---|---|
| **107.51** | Sed Inimicis quidem] *followed by* (Salutem non Ultionem quærens,) *1738a* [seeking well-being not revenge] |
| **107.52** | (Periculi non Injuriæ memor, et] *omitted 1738a* [mindful of dangers not injuries and] |
| **107.81** | apud nos prorsùs ignotâ,] *omitted 1738a* [among us utterly unknown] |

# APPENDIX 1

# Duncombe's translations of Horace's Odes

These translations, included for comparison with Hervey's, are taken from William Duncombe (ed.), *The Works of Horace in English verse. By several hands. Collected and published by Mr. Duncombe. With notes historical and critical*, 2 vols. (London: for R. and J. Dodsley, 1757); ESTC T52759. Horace, Book III, Ode IX (Hervey, Poem 58) is not translated by Duncombe.

## *BOOK I, ODE XI, I, 43–4 (cf. Hervey, Poem 5)*

*To* LEUCONOE

1.

Enquire not thou ('twere all in vain)
My dear *Leuconoë*,
What End the righteous Gods ordain,
Or to thyself or me.

2.

Seek not in Magic or the Stars
To read Events to come;
Nor by imaginary Fears
Anticipate thy Doom.

3.

Whether *Jove* grant one Winter more,
Or this should prove thy last,
Which whitens all the *Tyrrhene* Shore
With many an angry Blast;

4.

Be wisely gay; cut off long Cares
From thy contracted Span,
Nor stretch thy busy Hopes and Fears
Beyond the Life of Man.

5.

Ev'n while we speak, the Stream of Time
Rolls rapidly away;
Then seize the present, use the Prime,
Nor trust another Day.

## *BOOK II, ODE VI, I, 155–6 (cf. Hervey, Poem 6)*

*To* SEPTIMUS

*Septimus!* who with Me to *Spain*
Would'st sail, unpractis'd to sustain
Our Yoke; or *Libya*'s faithless Shore,
Where Sands and Whirlpools guard the *Moor:*

May *Tibur*'s Walls, th'*Argéan* Seat,
Afford my Age a calm Retreat!
There, worn with Journey, Wars, and Seas,
May I enjoy unenvy'd Ease!

But, cross'd by Fate in this Desire,
Let Me contentedly retire
To where *Galesus* glides away,
And Flocks with borrow'd Clothing play.

No Fields, like this, my Fancy please;
Their choicest Sweets here cull the Bees;
The Berry of *Venafran* Soil
Swells not with richer Floods of Oyl.

Long is the Spring, the Winter warm,
Nor blighting Frosts the Meads deform;
Here *Aulon*, friendly to the Vine,
Repines not at *Falernus*' Wine.

That rural Scene, those blissful Towers,
Seem to invite our latest Hours:
Your Bard's warm Ashes there from You
Shall drink the Tear to Friendship due!

## *BOOK III, ODE XXVIII, vol. I, pp. 393–4 (cf. Hervey, Poem 9)*

*To* LYDÉ

1.

What Honours, *Lydé*, shall we pay
To *Neptune* on his Festal Day?
Produce your old *Cæcubian* Wine;
And each grave Thought for frolic Airs resign

2.

You see, from Noon declines the Sun;
And yet, as if he ceas'd to run,
You spare to broach the tardy Jar,
Laid up in Consul *Bibulus*'s Year.

3.

Our Voice, by Turns, to *Neptune*'s Praise,
And to the Sea-green Nymphs, we'll raise;
*Latona*, to the tuneful String,
And quiver'd *Cynthia*, You alone shall sing.

4.

In *Chorus* Her we'll praise, whose Sway
The shining *Cyclades* obey;
Who, drawn by Swans, her *Paphian* Plain
Revives: And favouring *Night* shall close our Strain.

# APPENDIX 2

## Voltaire's 'loose imitation' of an extract from Poem 16

Voltaire's 'loose imitation' of an extract from Poem 16, 'Verse Letter to Lady Hervey from Italy', lines 42–56, in his *Letters Concerning the English Nation* (London: for C. Davis and A. Lyon, 1733), pp. 195–6. Voltaire introduces his translation with an apology.

> He had writ a poetical Description of that Country, which, for Delicacy and Politeness may vie with any Thing we meet with in the Earl of *Rochester*, or in our *Chaulieu*, our *Sarrasin*, or *Chapelle*. The Translation I have given of it is so inexpressive of the Strength and delicate Humour of the Original, that I am oblig'd seriously to ask Pardon of the Author, and of all who understand *English*. However, as this is the only Method I have to make his Lordship's Verses known, I shall here present you with them in our Tongue.

| | |
|---|---|
| Qu'ay je donc vû dans l'Italie? | What then have I seen in Italy? |
| Orgueil, Astuce, & Pauvreté, | Pride, craftiness, and poverty, |
| Grands Complimens, peu de Bonté, | Huge flattery, little goodwill, |
| Et beacoup de Ceremonie. | And a great deal of ceremony. |
| | |
| L'extravagante Comedie, | The absurd Comedy |
| Que souvent L'Inquisition* | That the Inquisition generally |
| Veut qu'on nomme Religion; | Wishes to be called Religion, |
| Mais qu'ici nous nommons Folie | But that here we call Lunacy. |
| | |
| La Nature en vain bienfaisante | Nature, beneficent in vain, |
| Veut enricher les Lieux charmans, | Wants to enrich charming settings; |
| Des Prêtres la main desolante | Priests with hands that distress |
| Etouffe ses plus beaux présens. | Smother its most beautiful endowments. |
| | |
| Les Monsignors, soy disant Grands, | The nobles, supposedly great, |
| Seuls dans leurs Palais magnifiques | Alone in their magnificent palaces, |
| Y sont d'illustres faineants, | Are distinguished do-nothings, |
| Sans argent, & sans domestiques. | Without money, and without servants. |
| | |
| Pour les Petits, sans liberté, | As for the lower orders, without freedom, |
| Martyrs du joug qui les domine, | Martyrs to the yoke that governs them, |
| Ils ont fait vœu de pauvreté, | They have devoted themselves to poverty, |
| Priant Dieu par oisiveté | Praying to God through laziness, |
| Et toûjours jeunant par famine. | And always fasting from scarcity. |

| | |
|---|---|
| Ces beaux lieux du Pape benis | Those fine consecrated seats of the Pope |
| Semblent habitez par les Diables; | Seem inhabited by devils; |
| Et les Habitans miserables | And the miserable inhabitants |
| Sont damnez dans le Paradis. | Are damned in Paradise. |

* His Lordship undoubtedly hints at the Farces which certain Preachers act in the Open Squares.

# INDEX OF TITLES

This list includes titles commonly attributed to poems in complementary sources, even when those are not the title chosen for this edition.

# INDEX OF FIRST LINES

# INDEX (NAMES, PLACES, TITLES AND HISTORICAL EVENTS)

The entry under Hervey has been kept to a minimum. References to his poems are indexed under their titles and relations with other persons come under their names. The events of Hervey's life are most conveniently detailed in the preliminary Chronology, which has not been indexed. The pages presenting Hervey's verse are in bold.